New Trends in Qualitative and Quantitative Methods in Libraries

New Trends in Qualitative and Quantitative Methods in Libraries

Selected Papers Presented at the 2nd Qualitative and
Quantitative Methods in Libraries

Proceedings of the International Conference on QQML2010
Chania, Crete, Greece   25–28 May 2010

Vincennes University
Shake Learning Resources Center
Vincennes, In 47591-9986

Editors

Anthi Katsirikou
University of Piraeus Library, Greece

Christos Skiadas
Technical University of Crete, Greece

World Scientific

NEW JERSEY • LONDON • SINGAPORE • BEIJING • SHANGHAI • HONG KONG • TAIPEI • CHENNAI

020.72
K19n
2012

Published by

World Scientific Publishing Co. Pte. Ltd.

5 Toh Tuck Link, Singapore 596224

USA office: 27 Warren Street, Suite 401-402, Hackensack, NJ 07601

UK office: 57 Shelton Street, Covent Garden, London WC2H 9HE

British Library Cataloguing-in-Publication Data
A catalogue record for this book is available from the British Library.

NEW TRENDS IN QUALITATIVE AND QUANTITATIVE METHODS IN LIBRARIES
Selected Papers Presented at the 2nd Qualitative and Quantitative Methods in Libraries
Proceedings of the International Conference on QQML2010

Copyright © 2012 by World Scientific Publishing Co. Pte. Ltd.

All rights reserved. This book, or parts thereof, may not be reproduced in any form or by any means, electronic or mechanical, including photocopying, recording or any information storage and retrieval system now known or to be invented, without written permission from the Publisher.

For photocopying of material in this volume, please pay a copying fee through the Copyright Clearance Center, Inc., 222 Rosewood Drive, Danvers, MA 01923, USA. In this case permission to photocopy is not required from the publisher.

ISBN-13 978-981-4350-29-7
ISBN-10 981-4350-29-X

Printed in Singapore by World Scientific Printers.

PREFACE

The present volume contains selected papers of the 2nd Qualitative and Quantitative Methods in Libraries International Conference (QQML2010) held in Chania, Crete, Greece, May 25-28, 2010, which was organized under the umbrella of ASMDA International Society.

The conference aims to serve the library community to familiarize Quantitative and Qualitative Methodologies and use them in the everyday management of the library. The conference also aims to serve the research community to present their papers and take the feedback from academia and professionals. As expected, the Conference, consequently its proceedings, is addressed to the library professionals in a more general sense: professors, researchers, students, administrators, librarians, technologists, museum scientists, archivists, decision makers and managers from 50 countries.

Qualitative and Quantitative Methods (QQM) have proved to be increasingly popular tools for library scientists, because of their usefulness to the everyday professional life. QQM are involved in the improvement of the services, the measurement of the functional effectiveness and efficiency, to decision-making and fund allocation.

This unique volume presents the last scientific achievements of library researchers and professionals on the Qualitative and Quantitative Methods of Libraries. Scholars and professionals have now an information resource on methodological tools for library services. Except of the new technologies that facilitate the innovation of libraries, it is the underlying policy and functional changes that have the most lasting effect on the scholarly operation. The book explores items such as library methodologies, marketing and management, statistics and bibliometrics, content and subject analysis, users' behaviours and library policies that play important role at every side of library research in the twenty-first century.

The contents cover issues such as Assessing and Evaluating Reference, Quantitative and Qualitative Methods in Library Marketing and Management, Using Qualitative and Quantitative Methods in Digital Library Education and Research, Library and Information Science and Research, Users and their Behaviours, Applications to Academic Libraries, Applications to Digital Libraries, Data Mining/Content Analysis, Information and Learning.

Once more we would like to acknowledge the support of MAICh in Chania, Greece. Sincere thanks must be accorded to colleagues, friends and partners who have worked hard for the success of the conference and especially the conference committees, speakers and keynote speakers, authors and reviewers. Finally, we would like to heartily thank Aggeliki Oikonomou, Mary Karadima, Iro Tzorbatzaki, Aris Meletiou, Ioannis Dimotikallis and George Matalliotakis for their heartily envaluable support.

Athens, April 29, 2011

Anthi Katsirikou, University of Piraeus Library, Greece

Christos H. Skiadas, Technical University of Crete, Greece

ADVISORY COMMITTEE

Prof. Carla Basili, National Council of Research, Italy

Prof. George Bokos, Ionian University, Greece

Dr. Judith Broady–Preston, Dep. of Information Studies, Aberystwyth University, UK

Dr. Colleen Cook, Texas A&M University Libraries, USA

Prof. Peter Hernon, Simmons College, USA

Dr. Anthi Katsirikou, University of Piraeus Library, Greece

Dr. Martha Kyrillidou, Association of Research Libraries, Senior Director of ARL Statistics and Service Quality Programs, USA

Prof. Maria G. N. Musoke, Makerere University, Uganda

Prof. Lynne M. Rudasill, University of Illinois at Urbana-Champaign, USA

Prof. Christos Skiadas, Technical University of Crete, Greece

Dr. Bruce Thompson, Texas A&M University, USA

Steve Thornton, Editor, Performance Measurement and Metrics, UK

Prof. Sirje Virkus, Tallinn University, Estonia

Prof. Teresa Welsh, The University of Southern Mississippi, USA

INTERNATIONAL SCIENTIFIC COMMITTEE

Svanhild Aabo (Oslo University College, Norway)

Melita Ambrozic (NUK Ljubliana, Slovenia)

Tatjana Aparac (University J.J. Strossmayer in Osijek, Croatia)

Agnes Hajdu Barat (University of Szeged, Association of Hungarian Librarians, Hungary)

Carla Basili (Consiglio Nazionale delle Ricerche, Istituto Ceris, Roma, Italy)

George Bokos (Ionian University, Greece)

Vesna Brujic-Okretic (City University, London, UK)

Stella Chatzemari (Technological Educational Institute, Greece)

Jenny Craven (CERLIM, Joint Editor LWW Conference Series)

Kathy Dempsey (Computers in Libraries, Editor, USA)

Corrado Di Tillio (Comune di Roma, Istituzione Biblioteche, Biblioteca Raffaello, Roma, Italy)

P. Dukic (Belgrade City Library, Serbia)

Blazej Feret (Technical University of Lodz, Library, Poland)

Guisseppi A. Forgionne (University of Maryland, Editor-in-Chief Int. J. Decision Support Systems Technology, USA)

Norbert Fuhr (Dep. of Computational and Cognitive Sciences, University of Duisburg-Essen, Germany)

George Giannakopoulos (Library and Information Systems Dept., TEI of Athens, Greece)

Lindsay Glynn (Evidence Based Library and Information Practice Journal, University of Alberta, Canada)

Gary E. Gorman (Victoria University of Wellington, IFLA Advisory Board, Online Information Review, Editor, New Zealand)

Jillian Griffiths (CERLIM, Manchester Metropolitan University, UK)

Herbert Gruttemeier (INIST-CNRS, President, ICSTI, France)

Dinesh K. Gupta (Dept. of Lib. & Inf. Sc., Vardhaman Mahaveer Open University, India)

Peter Hernon (Graduate School of Library and Information Science, Simmons College, USA, Co-Editor, Library and Information Science Research)

Frank Huysmans (University of Amsterdam, The Netherlands)

Jim Jansen (The Pennsylvania State University, USA)

Ian M. Johnson (Aberdeen Business School, The Robert Gordon University, UK)

Sarantos Kapidakis (Ionian University, Greece)

Sanjay Kataria (Jaypee Institute of Information Technology, India)

Anthi Katsirikou (University of Piraeus, Greece), Co-Chair

Christie Koontz (Florida State University, School of Library and Information, USA)

Marian Koren (Netherlands Public Library Association, Head of RIA, The Netherlands)

Steen Bille Larsen (The Royal Library, Denmark)

Jesus Lau (Universidad Veracruzana, Mexico)

Sue McKnight (Nottingham Trent University, Nottingham, UK)

Sona Makulova (Comenius University, Slovakia)

Paul Nieuwenhuysen (Vrije Universiteit Brussel, Belgium)

Nor Edzan Che Nasir (University of Malaya, Kuala Lumpur, Malaysia)

Steve O'Connor (The Hong Kong Polytechnic University, Editor, Library Management, Library Management, China)

Aldo Pirola (Public Library System in Milan, Italian Librarian Association, EBLIDA, Italy)

Diana Pietruch-Reizes (The Polish Society of Information Science, Jagiellonian University, Poland)

Roswitha Poll (Munster University, Germany)

Niels Ole Pors (Royal School of Library and Information Science, Denmark)

Pirjo Rajakiili (National Library of Health Sciences, Finland)

Blanca Rodriguez Bravo (Universidad de Leon, Spain)

Ronald Rousseau (ISSI, Belgium)

Lynne M. Rudasill (University of Illinois at Urbana-Champaign, USA) Anabela Mesquita Teixeira Sarmento (ISCAP, School of Accountancy and Administration of Porto, Portugal)

Christos H. Skiadas (Technical University of Crete, Greece), Co-Chair Amanda Spink (Queensland University of Technology, Australia)

Gordana Stokic Simoncic (University of Beograd, Serbia)

Ruth Tammeorg (Tartu University Library, Estonia)

Rong Tang (Director, Simmons GSLIS Usability Lab, Graduate School of Library and Information Science, Simmons College, Boston, MA, USA)

Thordis T. Thorarinsdottir (Menntaskolinn vid Sund/University of Iceland)

Steve Thornton (Performance Measurement and Metrics, Editor, UK)

Sirje Virkus (Tallinn University, Estonia)

Sohair Wastawy (Dean of Libraries, Illinois State University, USA)

Sheila Webber (University of Sheffield, UK)

Aleksander Zgrzywa (Wroclaw University of Technology, Poland)

ORGANIZING COMMITTEE

Anthi Katsirikou,
Christos H. Skiadas,
Mary Karadima,
Aggeliki Oikonomou,
Iro Tzorbatzaki,
Aris Meletiou,
Ioannis Dimotikallis,
George Matalliotakis

KEYNOTE TALKS

Prof. Emeritus F. Wilfrid Lancaster: Fifty Years After – Almost.
Graduate School of Library and information Science, University of Illinois at Urbana Champaign, Urbana, Illinois, USA. **Short Biography.** F. Wilfrid Lancaster is Professor Emeritus in the Graduate School of Library and Informotion Science at the University of Illinois where he has taught courses relating to information transfer, bibliometrics, bibliographic organization and the evaluation of library and information services. He served as the editor of Library Trends for a period of 20 years. He was appointed University Scholar for the period 1989-1992. He is the author of twelve books, six of which have received national awards, and has three times received Fulbright fellowships for research and teaching abroad. His books have been translated into Arabic, Russian, Chinese, Japanese, Korean, Spanish and Portuguese. From the American Society for Information Science and Technology he has received both the Award of Merit and the Outstanding Information Science Teacher award. Professor Lancaster has been invoved in a wide range of consulting activities, including service for UNESCO and other agencies of the United Nations.

Dr. Roswitha Poll: Data for New Services: Developments in International Library Statistics.
Former Chief Librarian, Mónster University Library, Germany. **Short Biography.** Dr. Roswitha Poll was chief librarian of Mónster University Library from 1987 to 2004. She is now chairing the committee "Quality-Statistics and Performance Evaluation" and the working groups for "International library statistics", "Performance indicators for national libraries" and "Statistics for library buildings" within ISO (International Organization of Standardization). Since 1989, she has been working in IFLA (International Federation of Library Associations), especially in the section "Statistics and Evaluation". She works in projects dealing with management and evaluation of libraries and information systems. Her present publications deal with measures for the input and output, quality, costs and impact of library services.

Prof. Carla Basili: Information Policies in the Knowledge Economy: A Question of Balance.
National Council of Research, Italy. **Short Biography.** Carla Basili is Promoter and Co-ordinator of the European network on Information Literacy (EnIL) and of the European Observatory on Information Literacy Policies and Research. Her research interests focus on scientific information diffusion and transfer and, since 2001, concentrate on information literacy policies in higher education.

Contents

Chapter 4. Library and Information Science Post-Graduate Student Research

Chapter 5. Users and Their Behaviours

Chapter 6. Academic Libraries

Chapter 7. Digital Libraries

Chapter 8. Library Applications and Methodologies

Chapter 9. Information and Learning

Selected Papers

Fifty Years After – Almost

F. Wilfrid Lancaster

I began my library career in 1949. Being associated with libraries for more than 60 years does give one a somewhat unique perspective on the profession. In this talk, I will look at changes in the way library and information services have been evaluated within the context of changes in the services themselves within the broader context of changes in the environment in which these services have operated.

The library where I began my career was a public library in the north of England. It was a unique experience because it was the last public library in the country to remain a closed-access library. Using this library was rather like using a research library such as the Library of Congress. Users had to find call numbers for books in the public card catalogs or in library book lists and present these at a service desk. A staff member looked for the books and presented them to the user, for borrowing, if they were found. If they were not found, of course, the user had to go through the process again, a very frustrating experience.

Looking at this library service as an evaluation problem, it is clear that one part of the service, the document delivery function, would have been easy to evaluate – a user either left the library with a book, or books, he requested or he did not. The prerequisite evaluation question – was the user able to find what he was looking for in the catalog – would have been almost impossible to deal with.

The library converted to a conventional open-access library a year or so after I began work there. This undoubtedly made users happy. They could browse the shelves and find their own books. Of course, evaluation had become more complicated. There was no easy way of knowing whether a user found what he wanted in the library or not. A book borrowed could be considered a kind of "success" but how many people came to the library and left without finding what they were looking for?

Library and information services have changed very much in the sixty years since I entered the profession. From my perspective, the most fundamental change has been the relentless move by managers of library and information services to make users do things for themselves. As libraries have become increasingly self-service institutions, their activities have become increasingly difficult to evaluate. Moreover, I believe that the managers of these services have, at the same time, become less and less concerned about evaluating them.

Librarians were not much concerned with evaluation back in 1949 either. If you had raised the evaluation issue at a professional meeting back then, the audience would probably have laughed at you. Librarians did not evaluate. They did not need to evaluate. Libraries were universally accepted as "good" for the communities they served, so why did they need evaluating?

Certainly, librarians did quantify. They knew how many books were borrowed, how many reference questions were received and answered, perhaps how many people entered the library. But quantification is not the same as evaluation.

New Trends in Qualitative and Quantitative Methods in Libraries
A. Katsirikou and C. H. Skiadas (eds)
© *World Scientific Publishing Co (pp. 1-7)*

And the statistics collected represented only events presumed to be successes. Nothing was known about possible failures.

Of course, not all librarians of the 1940s, or even earlier, lacked interest in quantification or scientific management. Most obviously, S. C. Bradford, a librarian at the Science Museum in London, had already made a major contribution to the field that we now know as "bibliometrics" with his pioneering paper on the scattering of periodical articles over periodical titles. This was first published in an engineering journal in 1931 but it appeared again in his book <u>Documentation</u> in 1948. Wyndham Hulme, another British librarian, had virtually invented the field of bibliometrics, which he called "statistical bibliography," as early as the 1920s.

Although librarians were not much concerned with evaluation in the 1950s, evaluation criteria did exist. The most obvious were the Five Laws of Library Science, first put forward in 1931 by the Indian librarian Ranganathan. These "laws" were:

1. Books are for use
2. Every reader his book
3. Every book its reader
4. Save the time of the reader
5. The library is a growing organism.

These may seem rather superficial at first but, when you study their implications, they are actually quite profound because they offer essential criteria for the evaluation of library services from the perspective of their cost-effectiveness, as well as their effectiveness, and even point to important cost-benefit considerations.

Ironically, interest in the objective evaluation of library services may well have been stimulated by work on the objective evaluation of information retrieval systems, which began towards the end of the 1950s. The pioneering study was the ASLIB Cranfield Project, with which I was associated for a period of time. This was really a study of indexing systems – i.e., methods of representing the subject content of documents – and was initiated originally to compare the effectiveness of different methods for arranging entries for books in subject catalogs. While this project, which continued over a period of years, yielded many interesting results, it was probably most valuable for highlighting two basic criteria for evaluating the results of a search in any database, recall and precision, the extent to which a search finds the material you were looking for and the extent to which it is able to avoid retrieving a whole lot of material you were not looking for. The ASLIB Cranfield Project had no real information service to evaluate. It was based entirely on simulation. The research questions for which searches were performed were actually based upon documents known to offer good answers to the questions and known to exist in the database.

The Cranfield study occurred at a very opportune time. Computers were just beginning to be used in information retrieval applications and some systems and services of significant size began to emerge. It was natural that the evaluation criteria identified at Cranfield should be applied to these new systems. In the United States, The National Library of Medicine took the lead here. Its Medical Literature Analysis and Retrieval System (MEDLARS) was established in the 1960s and I was fortunate enough to be hired by the Library to undertake an evaluation of its service. Unlike the Cranfield studies, this was not a simulation. It was an evaluation of a real service – computerized searches of a large biomedical database performed to satisfy the information needs of biomedical professionals. The study was unique in its size: the results of 300 searches were evaluated by the biomedical professionals requesting the searches. In those days, computer searches were performed offline. The requesters received printouts of the bibliographic references retrieved by the searches performed for them. The 300 requesters participating in the study evaluated the search results from these printouts and from a random sample of the actual biomedical articles, referred to in the printouts, supplied to them by the library. The results of this evaluation were published in 1968.

At about the same time, the National Library of Medicine also made a major contribution to the development of evaluation methodologies for more conventional library services. The Library was engaged in establishing a Regional Medical Library Program. This involved selecting libraries in different parts of the United States to receive contracts to provide various types of service essentially on behalf of the national library. To help them select these regional representatives, the Library gave a contract to the Institute for the Advancement of Medical Communication to develop criteria and procedures for the evaluation of various basic library services. These investigators came up with a number of valuable evaluation tools. One was a type of inventory which could be used to compare the range and scope of services offered by various medical libraries. The libraries received a numerical point score based on the range and scope of their services, a perfect score being 1000 points. The procedure was quite discriminating. For example, when tested on six academic medical libraries, it produced a high score of 721/1000 and a low score of 533/1000.

An even more important outcome of this contract was the "document delivery test." This simulation tested the ability of academic medical libraries to satisfy the document needs of users. The evaluators enter the library with a sample of 300 bibliographic references for items that library users could reasonably be expected to be looking for at that time. Each item is given a score reflecting immediacy of availability. The best possible score is given if the book or article is immediately available on the shelves; the worst score for the item is given if it is estimated that it could not be available in less than a week (e.g., by borrowing from another library). Based on the sample of 300 items, a capability index for the library could be derived, and this could be used to compare different libraries.

The document delivery test pioneered the objective evaluation of the most basic of library services – its ability to deliver printed items to users at the time these items are needed. The description of this test in the literature, in 1968, inspired a great many related studies in the next two decades. Some of these were very similar simulations, modified for applicability in different types of libraries. Other studies were based on a kind of user survey. Typically, a user entering the library was given a form on which to record details of the items he was looking for on that visit. For each item recorded, he was also asked to indicate success or failure: could he find a call number for it in the catalog and, if he could, was he able to find it on the shelves. Library professionals could later check the failures to determine whether they were catalog use failures or "shelf failures." For items known to be in the collection, a determination could be made of where the item was at the time the user was unable to find it.

The late 1960s and early 1970s also saw the beginning of attempts to evaluate the ability of library reference services to answer factual-type questions completely and correctly. These studies were usually performed by having volunteers pose questions for which the answer was already known and documented. The overwhelming majority of these studies were performed with public libraries and with the questions posed by telephone. Much later, in 1991, I was heavily involved in a study that evaluated the quality of reference service in several departmental libraries in a large academic institution. In this case, we trained students to walk into these libraries with their test questions and to record how the librarians approached the question, what sources they used, what answer they came up with, and the time elapsing.

By the early 1970s, the searching of databases by computer was already beginning to move from an offline to an online mode of operation. The evaluation of online database searches was not significantly different as long as the librarian was still performing the searches on behalf of the user (i. e., they were delegated searches). The nondelegated search, the situation in which a library user performs an online search for himself, is a completely different proposition. The most obvious problem is that of finding out what the user does in the searches and to what extent the user finds the information sought. Even the criteria most often used to evaluate the delegated search, recall and precision, were not really appropriate to the nondelegated situation because these were really secondary measures of success rather than primary measures. The precision ratio was an indirect measure of user effort. In the nondelegated search, the more direct measure was obviously how much time the user spent on the search. The recall ratio was not so relevant either because a user would naturally stop searching when he felt he had found what he was looking for or, alternatively, gave up the search as a lost cause. Nevertheless, the evaluator could not afford to neglect the fact that a search may have missed items that would be much more valuable to the user than those actually found. As online searching developed, it became possible to do some unobtrusive monitoring of use. Online monitoring could be used to discover, for example, what terms, in what combinations, were used in the search, which records were retrieved, and which of these were selected in some way by the user, but such monitoring could not determine the value of the search to the user. This could only be determined by asking him. Even this was not fully satisfactory because the user could only judge success on the basis of what was retrieved, knowing nothing of what was not retrieved. In some cases, the items missed could make those found virtually superfluous. To fully evaluate the success of a nondelegated search really required searches on the same topic to be performed by search specialists with the results compared with the user results and any items not retrieved by the user submitted to him for his evaluation. This was a tedious evaluation process and not completely satisfactory because of a time lapse – an item that might have been highly valuable to a user on January 15 may have no value at all to him on January 20.

The evaluation of library and information services in the 1960s and 1970s was mostly concerned with their effectiveness – the extent to which they were able to satisfy user demands. By the 1980s, however, those responsible for the funding of libraries became increasingly concerned about the costs of these services. This led to new levels of evaluation. Cost-effectiveness evaluations tried to relate the effectiveness of services to their costs. This led to new evaluation criteria such as the cost per item borrowed, the cost per item consulted in the library, and the cost per useful item retrieved in a database search. Some studies began to look at the cost-effectiveness of different methods for the delivery of information services. By the 1990s such studies included comparisons of the cost-effectiveness of providing service from printed versus electronic journal collections.

By this time, too, the very existence of library and information services was threatened, especially in industrial, government and international organizations. Some libraries and librarians found themselves having to justify their existence. Cost-benefit analysis, undertaken to prove the worth of the service to the community, had existed for some time, but studies of this kind became more common in the 1990s, and the approaches used became more sophisticated. The usual approach was to estimate what would happen to the organization if the information service was eliminated – for example, how much it would cost to obtain needed information in other ways. Outstanding cost, cost-effectiveness and cost-benefit analyses were performed by Griffiths and King, mostly in the industrial or government library environments. Their most important analyses looked at the benefits of exposure to information through the library in terms of the impact on the individual of being deprived of this service – loss of productivity, duplication or other waste of effort, and time and costs of obtaining needed information elsewhere. When costs were calculated for such losses, they were able to conclude that potential savings to the organization associated with exposure to library services could exceed the costs of providing these services in ratios ranging from a low of 7.8:1 to a high of 14.2:1.

In the 1990s, library associations in the United States began to concern themselves more actively with the assessment of the quality of the services provided by libraries. One leader was the Association of Research Libraries, which spearheaded the application to libraries of a measure of quality already in existence in the business community. The method, which is now well-known and has been widely applied, involves the measurement of the gap between the service levels expected by library users and the service levels they perceive to exist. Later this methodology was modified to apply more clearly to libraries in digital form,

From the time I first got involved with information service evaluation, in 1962, I have strongly believed that the main purpose of such activities is diagnostic – to identify problems and failures in a particular service and to identify ways to improve the situation. Probably the most important evaluations of this type are those that are able to document information failures and the results of these. Such studies fall into two broad categories: (1) undiscovered public knowledge, and (2) unintentional duplication of research.

Don Swanson used the terms "disconnected" or "noninteractive" to refer to two bodies of literature that are unknown to each other and not linked by conventional bibliographic means (e.g., not indexed in a similar way in databases, not citing each other and not citing a common antecedent literature). Clearly, most disconnected literature pairs are completely unrelated in the sense that the finds of one research area have no possible relevance to the other. In some cases, however, two disconnected literatures may interrelate (i.e., literature A may make a contribution to research area B, B to A, or both). Swanson refers to such literatures as "complementary."

He performed extremely valuable pioneering research on disconnected biomedical literatures for several years. In some cases he was able to discover scientifically significant connections that were previously unknown. For example, one body of literature describes how dietary fish oil may bring about certain changes in properties of the blood while another suggests that changes of this kind could be beneficial in the treatment of Raynaud's disease. Yet, the "fish oil" research (literature) was disconnected from the Raynaud's disease research area. In another example, the literature on magnesium metabolism was shown to have potential relevance to migraine research: magnesium deficiency can bring about neurological changes that may lead to a migraine attack.

There is also much evidence to suggest that the amount of undesirable duplication in science research is not inconsiderable. The best study of its kind was that conducted by John Martyn in 1964 in England. In an investigation of 647 current research projects in government, industry, and academia, Martyn gathered documented evidence of 43 cases of unintentional duplication of research, and 106 cases in which information discovered from the literature, while research was underway, would, if found earlier, have saved time, money, or effort in the research project. Martyn found that, in about 9% of all the projects studied, money could have been saved through an improved awareness of research reported in the literature. An extrapolation to the total expenditure for scientific research in the United Kingdom in 1962 led Martyn to conclude that at least 6 million pounds a year could be saved in U.K. research through more effective use of the literature. This was likely to be a very low estimate, however, because it was based only on cases of duplication or suboptimum approaches to research discovered by the scientists through literature searches that were very probably quite incomplete. Martyn hypothesized that this was only the tip of an iceberg and that much greater waste would be uncovered by more exhaustive searches of the literature. More than 20 years later, Martyn repeated his study, using the same survey methodology. The later investigation revealed that, although literature searching had been greatly facilitated through widespread online access to databases, and researchers were more aware of the importance of such searching activities, the number of cases in which they discovered relevant information too late to be of maximum value to them seemed to be increasing rather than decreasing.

Returning more specifically to the evaluation of library services, I believe that – with the exception of selected work in the areas of cost-effectiveness and cost-benefit evaluation - this field has taken steps that have been mostly backward since the 1980s. Rather than performing diagnostic evaluations of specific services in a single library, the profession preoccupied itself more with comparisons – usually one or more libraries against some norms – and with general subjective surveys of user satisfaction. Using interviews or questionnaires to determine attitudes towards library services in general has much less value than studies that determine the success or failure of the service on a particular incident (the critical incident). Although library user contributions to a general impressionistic survey may give anecdotal information on particular events, this is not a true critical incident study and has little diagnostic value. People best remember the events that are either exceptionally satisfactory or exceptionally unsatisfactory.

To consider what has happened to the evaluation of library and information services in the last decade or so, we need to consider what has happened to library services in this period, and even what has happened to society in general. What has happened in society, of course, is that technology has been used to replace public service. Technology allows us to do things for ourselves that we used to expect others to do for us. The most pernicious aspect of this new self-service society is that technology replaces people. When I make a telephone call to a business or government agency, the chance of actually talking to a human being is decreasing rapidly from year to year. Usually I am subjected to a computerized menu, and cpmputerized voice output, with categories that never seem to match my needs. My satellite television provider even expects a menu of computerized output to diagnose my reception problems. The businesss and other entities that provide such facilities seem to consider that my time is free. My time is not free. If I were not wasting my time on fruitless telephone calls, I could be doing something more productive – like watching soccer on television. The fact that these entities consider my time to be free is all part of a more general malaise, the fact that public service is a thing of the past. Corporations and government agencies no longer care whether the people they supposedly serve are served or not.

Library and information services in general share in this social malaise. In my experience, only public libraries retain any vestige of public service. Libraries in academia, government and industry have increasingly used technology to replace service. There exists a pervasive assumption that using technologies to empower users – to access databases for themselves, to obtain materials from other libraries, to check out books for themselves, and suchlike, means that things are now better for library users than they once were. Moreover, library managers, just like managers of other enterprises, no longer care.

In the library and information service arena, evaluation is no longer a matter of concern or even interest. Take a look, for example, at the <u>Annual Review of Information Science and Technology</u>. Nine of the ten issues from 1966, when it was first published, to 1975 contained chapters dealing in some way with evaluation. In the next decade, 1976-1985, five of the ten issues contained evaluation-related chapters, and the following decade, 1986 to 1995, saw only three. There has not been an evaluation-related chapter since 2001, and now the term "evaluation," or its synonyms or related terms, rarely even appears in the indexes.

But perhaps the compilers of these indexes deserve considerable credit. In actual fact, there have been very many studies in the last decade that claim to be evaluation studies. The indexers just felt that they did not deserve to be given the evaluation label. This is because they usually collect rather gross data through web log analysis or, alternatively, collect general impressionistic data from library users that produce results such as (a real example):

Undergraduates in all ten colleges were reasonably satisfied with the library.

Faculty overall were dissatisfied with information control but reasonably content with service affect and facilities.

Undergraduate students used the physical library facilities much more frequently than did faculty.

Is this evaluation? I don't think so.

In the good old days of evaluation, we first made a list of all the questions we wanted to answer about a service. Then we set about designing a study that would answer these questions. Today, it seems, those claiming to be evaluators have a different approach. The main question of their concern is "What data can we collect in large quantities as automatically and painlessly as possible?" Gross data lead to gross conclusions.

The New Challenges of the Statistics - Case UEF

Markku Laitinen[1] and Aino Taskinen[2]

[1]The National Library of Finland, Finland, Markku.Laitnen@helsinki.fi
[2]The University of Eastern Finland Library, Finland, Aino.Taskinen@uef.fi

Abstract: Traditionally, the statistics of libraries have been based on the classical idea of the library but the structural development of higher education institutions taken place in Finland during the past few years, the changes caused by the new university act and their effects on the financing of the libraries of the higher education, have made it necessary to adopt new ways of measuring the library services and to show the impact of the library. One challenge is the comparability of statistics, key figures and quality measurement before and after the merging of the organisations. We describe the case of the University of Eastern Finland (UEF) Library that was merged by the Joensuu University Library and Kuopio University Library. Even though the UEF was formed so that the frame organisations also were merged, the challenges of the statistics are practically the same.
Keywords: Library statistics, library merger, university libraries, Finland

1. Introduction

The structural development of higher education institutions that was taken place in Finland during the past few years, the changes caused by the new university act and their effects on the financing of the libraries, these institutions have made it necessary to adopt new ways of evaluating the library services and to show the impact of the library.

According to the Ministry of Education, an efficient university network requires more cooperation and the joining of forces *(Ministry of Education, Structural development of higher education project 2009)*. These objectives are supposed to be achieved by forming bigger units that are functionally stronger, and have better preconditions to develop an internationally high level of quality and effectiveness. There are also cost savings associated with such mergers.

Though library statistics still play an important role in the production of information needed as the basis for planning and showing the results, the traditional approach of showing a library's results (the more you have - books, journals, premises, etc. - the better you are) has long ago become obsolete.

This become particularly when library organizations are merged and the new organization is expected to achieve better results.

2. Types of Mergers

The structural development has led to different types of mergers of libraries of the institutions of higher education.

The most complex mergers of libraries take place when the frame organizations of those libraries still carry on as independent organizations. This is the case with the

New Trends in Qualitative and Quantitative Methods in Libraries
A. Katsirikou and C. H. Skiadas (eds)
© *World Scientific Publishing Co (pp. 9-15)*

merging the libraries of consolidated corporations formed by the institutions of higher education of different educational sectors (universities and polytechnic schools). Consortiums of this kind may include the libraries of independent research institutions, too. This is the case in the library consortium of Lapland formed by the University of Lapland, the Kemi-Tornio University of Applied Sciences, the Rovaniemi University of Applied Sciences and the Arctic Centre.

A still more complex form of library merger is encountered when only parts of libraries are merged with the receiving library. This is the case in the Tritonia Library that covers the libraries of University of Vaasa, VAMK University of Applied Sciences and parts of Åbo Akademi University Library, Novia University of Applied Sciences Library and Hanken School of Economics Library.

Creating the library of the University of Eastern Finland (UEF) was considerably simpler, because of the complete merger of the frame organizations, the Universities of Joensuu and Kuopio.

3. The University of Eastern Finland Library

The University of Eastern Finland (UEF) was constituted as a result of merging the Universities of Kuopio and Joensuu at the beginning of 2010. The merger of two middle-sized universities produced one of the biggest universities of Finland, with approximately 13 000 students and 3000 members of staff. There are four faculties in the new multidisciplinary university: the Faculty of Health Sciences, the Faculty of Science and Forestry, the Faculty of Social Sciences and Business Studies, and the Philosophical Faculty.

The University of Eastern Finland Library comprises the campus libraries in Joensuu, Kuopio and Savonlinna, and the Kuopio University Hospital (KUH) Medical Library. The distance between the main campuses is approximately 140 km.The materials acquired for the collections reflect the university's fields of research and education. The contents of the collections in each campus library cater for the needs of teaching and research on that particular campus. The electronic resources are available to all library users in the facilities of the campus libraries. The staff and students of the University of Eastern Finland and staff of Kuopio University Hospital can also access them remotely.

The University of Eastern Finland Library is also one of the six legal deposit libraries in Finland and a European Documentation Centre.

4. The UEF Case

Although both the merged libraries, Joensuu University Library (UJO) and Kuopio University Library (UKU), are university libraries using the same library system, there are differences between their library activities. We gathered statistical data from the Finnish Research Library Statistics Database and benchmarked the activities of these two libraries during 2004 – 2008. The most remarkable differences seem to be library material costs (figure 1), acquisitions and financing, home loans (figure 2), data retrievals in bibliographical databases (figure 3), and use of e-journals (figure 4).

UJO's collections are focused on humanities, education, economics and business administration, agriculture and forest sciences, and psychology. The library has approximately 600 000 printed monographs and it already was a legal deposit library. UKU's collections contain 140 000 monographs and are focused on health sciences, medicine, pharmacy, biosciences, environmental sciences, information technology, business, and social sciences. As a result more printed material is used in UJO, whereas UKU makes more use of electronic material.

Financing and acquisitions

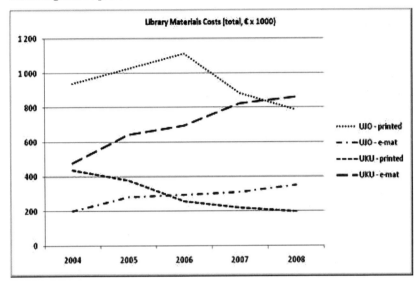

Figure 1. Library material costs in Joensuu University Library (UJO) and Kuopio University Library (UKU) 2004-2008.

The financing for materials acquired was different in UJO and UKU. UJO got mainly indirect financing from the departments of the university, while UKU had direct library budget financing.

In 2008, the direct budget financing was € 1 014 500 in UKU and € 729 900 in UJO and the indirect financing in UKU € 43500 and in UJO € 404 300. The total direct budget financing constituted of total library financing was 69.3 % in UKU and 53.9 % in UJO.

The relative of electronic materials also appears in materials acquisitions costs. In 2008, electronic materials acquisition costs constituted 81.9 % of total library materials costs in UKU compared 37.0 % in UJO.

A collection policy of the University of Eastern Finland Library is being prepared to establish the principles of acquisitions.

Home loans

Hitherto, the merged libraries borrowed each other's items using interlibrary loans, now library users can request and borrow items from another campus library. Course books are located in the library of the campus where the course is taught and the exams take place. The future will show whether the volume of home loans will grow relative to interlibrary loans.

Data retrievals

Comparing data retrievals in bibliographic databases we see that the use of databases has grown faster in UKU (figure 3). However, there are no statistical data on using PubMed, the most important database for medicine and health sciences; PubMed is a freely accessible database on the internet.

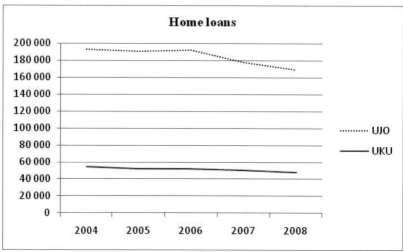

Figure 2. Home loans. Home loans in Joensuu University Library (UJO) and Kuopio University Library (UKU) 2004-2008.

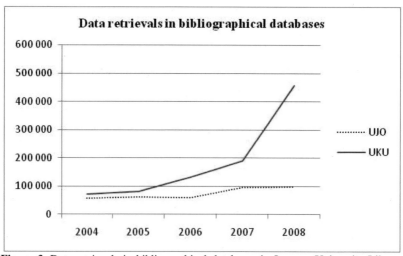

Figure 3. Data retrievals in bibliographical databases in Joensuu University Library (UJO) and Kuopio University Library (UKU) 2004-2008.

Use of e-journals
The number of documents viewed might show that users have found items of interest when searching in databases or electronic journals. Use of e-journals has strongly grown, especially in UKU (figure 4).

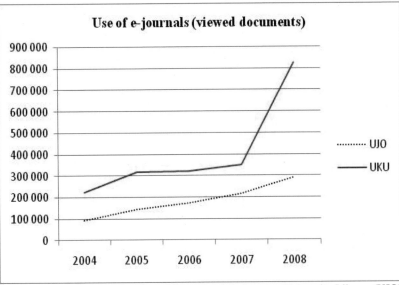

Figure 4. Use of e-journals (viewed documents) in Joensuu University Library (UJO) and Kuopio University Library (UKU) 2004-2008.

The library collections in each campus library are chosen to meet the needs of teaching and research on that particular campus, but the library has now users of all the campuses of the University of Eastern Finland. The collections and the services should be equally available to users on all the campuses. The next few years will show how the merging will change the way the library is used.

5. Challenges and Conclusions

The challenges for the compilation of statistics encountered in the merger of libraries are much the same as the ones that libraries have generally. The uniformity and reliability of the statistical data are important, as are the continuing and the time series, and standardizing the concepts in the library and organizing and systematizing the collection of statistics must be done.

The statistics must be integrated into reporting and result negotiations (budget negotiations) and the quality system, documentation and interfaces between the information processing systems of the administration and the statistics. The set of indicators used in reporting and planning must be suitable for the frame organizations, financiers and stake holders of the library, and support both reliable comparisons and benchmarking. Thus, testing the applicability of the present indicators and developing new ones are of fundamental importance.

How the libraries influence the operation of their frame organizations, the input-output ratio and resources, and the impact and effectiveness of libraries in society define a uniform set of indicators that would be suitable for a tool for management and providing information for the libraries. In doing this we need to consider how libraries could influence the operations.

To assure the economic and administrative position of university libraries and the use of collections, the Ministry of Education will monitor the resource allocation of the library and information services of universities from the year 2012 onwards. The objective is that the university uses at least 5% of its total budget for library and information services *(Ministry of Education, Structural development of higher education project 2009)*.

This target is included in a proposal for a uniform set of ten basic indicators taking into account the needs for reporting, information and benchmarking to be used in Finnish libraries *(Laitinen et al. 2009)*.

We tested whether this objective would have been achieved in the universities of Kuopio (UKU) and Joensuu (UJO) during the five year period 2004-2008. Further, we tested this objective would have been achieved in the University of Eastern Finland if it had then existed. The results of are shown in Figure 5.

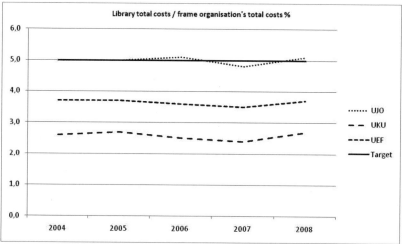

Figure 5. Library total costs in relation to the total costs of the frame organization. (UKU = University of Kuopio, UJO = University of Joensuu, UEF = University of Eastern Finland, Target = Target level of the frame organization's total budget defined by the Ministry of Education.

It would have been achieved on the former University of Joensuu, but in the University of Kuopio, there would have been a gap of more than 2 percentage units to the objective. So, it was not a surprise that merging these two universities produced an organization of intermediate form, and thus the new UEF would not have the target level of 5% (figure 5). However, the curve describing the UEF in the Figure 5 is factitious because it was comprised as a sum of two independent organizations but the entity for budget negotiations from the year 2010 these two organizations were merged is totally different.

The biggest costs of libraries are staff costs, library material costs and space costs. When two organizations operating on different localities are merged, it will be difficult to get cost savings from staff costs and space costs, because a certain basic infrastructure must be retained. It is challenging to reach savings in the material costs also. This holds true especially for printed materials whereas it may be easier to gain the cost efficiency with e-materials because the use of networked materials is not bound to a locality. However, the prices of the licences of e-materials usually depend on the size of the organization. Nevertheless, it is important to inspect the cost efficiency of electronic materials.

Libraries need to find additional qualitative methods in order to understand what is happening and they need new tools to predict future developments (*Saarti et al. 2009*). In addition to the traditional statistical data, Kuopio University Library used different types of methods of evaluating the operations and the results by using the EFQM (European Foundation for Quality Management) model as a tool. Also, the uniform set of indicators for Finnish libraries proposed by Laitinen and colleagues (*Laitinen et al. 2009*) should be tested to find out whether they could be used to show impact and result of the new UEF Library.

Because of the variety of different models of mergers of scientific libraries in Finland, we think it is not useful to give uniform instructions about how the new organization structures of the merged libraries should be presented in the common statistics database *(Finnish Research Library Database)*. It depends on the reporting needs of the new organization. Therefore, the library can choose between two models to start compiling the statistics of the new merged library.

In one model, the new library organization can be presented in the statistics as a union of the former library organizations keeping the old time series of the merging libraries under the new umbrella organization. In the other model the new library organization starts with a clean slate so that the old time series are left in their places, and the new time series start from "zero".

However, in either case, to assure the benchmarking of the libraries and the comparability of the statistics, the uniform principles based on the international standard ISO 2789 of collecting the statistical data must be retained.

Acknowledgements
The authors are grateful to Vivian Michael Paganuzzi for revising the English.

References
Finnish Research Library Statistics Database. Available at
https://yhteistilasto.lib.helsinki.fi/language.do?action=change&choose_language=3 [Last visited 12th March, 2010.]
ISO 2789:2006(E) - Information and documentation - International library statistics. International standard. 4th ed. 2006. ISO. 61 p.
Laitinen, M., Kangas, A. & Saarti, J. (2009): Statistics and surveys as tools for library management in Finland. *Proceedings of 8th Northumbria International Conference on Performance Measurement in Libraries and Information Services. Libraries Plus: Adding Value in the Cultural Community.* Istituto degli Innocenti, Florence, 17-20 August 2009. (In press.)
Ministry of Education, Structural development of higher education project (2009): Opetuksen ja tutkimuksen toimintaympäristö 2020. *Korkeakoulukirjastojen rakenteellinen kehittäminen digitaaliseksi palveluverkoksi. Opetusministeriön työryhmämuistioita ja selvityksiä 2009:26 [Teaching and research environment 2020. University and polytechnic libraries into a digital service network. Reports of the Ministry of Education, Finland 2009:26.]* Available in Finnish at: http://www.minedu.fi/export/sites/default/OPM/Julkaisut/2009/liitteet/tr26.pdf [Last visited 9th March 2010].
Saarti J, Juntunen A, Taskinen A. Multi-faceted measuring of the quality as a tool for quality improvement in the Kuopio University Library, Finland. In: Katsirikou A, Dimotikalis J, eds. QQML 2009. Qualitative and Quantitative Methods in Libraries International Conference, Chania Crete Greece, MAICh Conference Centre, Chania, 26-29 May 2009. ASMDA International, 2009.

Fractal Analysis of Knowledge Organization in Digital Library

Veslava Osinska

Institute of Information Science and Book Studies, Nicoulaus Copernicus University
Toruń, Poland, wieo@umk.pl

Abstract: Visualization of the large-scale collections of information became one of the essential purpose in data analysis. The new methods of visualization are increasingly applied as a significant component in scientific research. Particularly qualitative nature of Infoviz studies (Information visualization) can be combined with quantitative character of digital libraries volumes. This paper describes and demonstrates the case of hierarchical structure visualization i.e. visual representation of both classification adopted by ACM (Association for Computing Machinery) digital library and classification universe. Given maps were processed by nonlinear graphical filters. Finally fractal dimension (FD) and derived techniques have used to analyze the patterns of clusters on the visualization maps. Quantification of output graphical representation by means of fractals makes possible to adjust visualization parameters as well as evaluate initial classification scheme and its dynamical characteristics.
Keywords: Fractal analysis, fractal dimension, visualization, classification scheme, knowledge mapping

1. Introduction to fractal analysis

In analysis of large datasets of digital libraries advanced numerical methods became well-established. It is possible to draw two main approaches in the processing information in library collections. The fist one, so-called conventional is measuring of quantitative characteristics of library database such as number of records, bibliographic data and its dynamical changes. Knowledge of statistical methods in this case is fundamental. Discovered correlations are usually presented in linear way by the tables, diagrams and charts. Another group of techniques lead to find nonlinear dependences between the objects. Non-linearity takes place when we try to describe the unstructured and inhomogeneous data, for example user-based Web 2.0 data. Mapping as common technique in information visualization (Infoviz) provide such complex dataset with nonlinear representation. Infoviz methods can reveal hidden structure of scientific data derived from bibliographic databases (Chen 2006, Börner 2003). By this way constructed visualization maps contribute to a better understanding of the knowledge organization and their dynamics as well as monitoring the scientific output overall. By mapping subject classification in Computer Science domain on a sphere surface it is possible to analyze the development of this dynamic field (Osinska&Bala 2008, 2010). Given visualization maps were processed by selected image processing methods, that is presented in current paper. Inhomogeneous distribution of documents nodes showed some latent structure in a pattern. Describing the data within such complex patterns could be solved by means of fractal analysis. Fractal is was coined by Mandelbrot and defined as "a rough or fragmented geometric shape that can be split into parts, each of which is (at least approximately) a reduced-size copy of the whole" (1982). This is the main feature of fractals and called self-similarity. When we magnify the patterns that are Euclidean, we look more and more details which recur in each level. Objects in nature can be approximated by fractals, for example: clouds, mountain ranges, frost crystals, snow flakes, fern leaves, various vegetables (cauliflower and broccoli).

Practically second significant feature of fractal objects such as fractal dimension is used in fractal analysis. This distinguishes fractals from Euclidean objects, which have integer dimensions. As a simple example, if we magnify a length of a square's side two times its area will increase four-times. The same operation in fractal case causes area changes less than 4 times. Fractal dimension (FD) is non-integer value, usually a smaller than topological dimension of proper primitive figure, thus it determines how fractal differs from Euclidean objects. Fractal dimension measures the degree of fractal boundary fragmentation or irregularity over multiple scales. carries important information about how a fractal fills a space where it is embedded. Another fractal's measure used in current work – lacunarity shows how a fractal fills space and is applied to further classify fractals and textures which, while sharing the same fractal dimension, appear very visually different (Mandelbrot 1982, Plotnick&Gardner 1993).

Fractal dimension of regular figures are the same as topological. For example 1,2,3 for line, square and cube respectively. Some instances of fractal dimension are quoted below[1]. FD for Koch snowflake equals 1.26, cloud – 2.5, Norway coastline – 1.52, cauliflower - 2.66, human brain – 2.79, Tree - 2.7.

For fractal processing of visualization maps fractal analysis toolbox FracLac was used. FracLac is free software with user-friendly and intuitive interface; one can use it directly to perform many tasks in signal and images processing, including estimation, detection, modelling, classification, and so forth.

2. Classification mapping on a sphere

Research work consists of the visualization and analysis of documents classified by ACM Computing System Classification. Collection of abstracts is accessible in ACM Digital Library so own application allowed to gather metadata of articles. Classification tree contains three levels. The upper one consists of 11 main classes coded by 11 capital letters (from A to K). For the more precise categorization every article besides main classification is ascribed (in general by authors and/or editors) to one or more additional. Thus such common for different classes and subclasses documents can be considered as a measure of their thematic similarity. The innovative idea relies on estimation of co-occurrences of classes i.e. counting of common documents for every pair classes and subclasses, that result in construction of classes similarity matrix.

Osinska and Bala (2008, 2010) describe in detail the construction of a new graphical representation of original classification scheme in the 3D space, namely sphere surface. The final number of all possible classes and subclasses in collection was 353. Among all (sub) classes nodes, documents positions on a sphere were calculated from topological relations between main and additional classifications. Three variants of weights: 06:0.4, 0.7:0.3 and 0.5:0.5 were tested. Apparently fractal characteristics are helpful in qualitative comparison of obtained maps as well as selection the proper configuration. Figure 1 represents classes visualization on a sphere using 3 attributes:

colour to indicate main class, intensity – tree level and a size – population of (sub)class. The documents nodes were coloured by their main class color. For convenient analysis cartographic projections of visualization layouts were used.

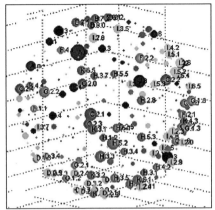

Figure 1. Classes visualization on a sphere.

3. Image set for analysis

By observing natural objects it is easy to notice most fractals have dimensions in the range [1,2], thus these dimensions are bigger than in flat figures case, but less than in solids. Therefore such fractals are some formation between straight lines and flat figures. Natural objects what we see around us (mountains, trees, clouds) are rather three-dimensional and have FD value converged to the value above 2. The object's topology is more complicated, the fractal dimension is closer to number 3.

If a low-resolution image is a small size it perceived by users as one with a good quality and sharp edges because of visual perception feature to focus vision within a limited field of view (Ware 2006). In the case of big size pictures the process undergoes blurring. Webmasters well know this effect and put into web galleries good quality miniatures of images served as links to the larger originals.

Visualization maps as a result of sphere surface projections on a plane were prepared according fractal analysis requirements. They need to be converted to the shades of gray and scaled to one universal size exact to a one pixel. To optimize the computation time three graphic formats TIFF, JPG and BMP were tested. Finally files exported as TIFF type and used for further research.

It is better to compare fractal structures visually if proper illustrations after desaturation[2] are all set into one observation view. This situation is presented on a Figure 2: classification maps for different proportions of the primary and additional classes (a), maps of articles published in different years (b), map for artificially changed original classification (c), control map of random distribution of the same quantity of points (d) and a map of 253 (sub) classes nodes.

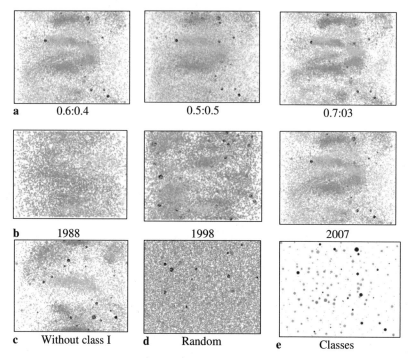

| a | 0.6:0.4 | | 0.5:0.5 | | 0.7:03 |

| b | 1988 | | 1998 | | 2007 |

| c | Without class I | d | Random | e | Classes |

Figure 2. Comparison of given visualization maps after desaturation: a) for different proportions of the primary and additional classes in documents classification; b) for different publishing years; c) for modified classification after removing the class I; d) random distribution's map; e) map of all classes.

4. Results and discussion

Comparing roughly is not sufficient for content-related estimation of visualization maps. Fractal dimension FD provide qualitative evaluation of distributions presented on Figure 2. Calculated values of fractal parameters: self-similarity and lacunarity are attached in Table 1.

Table 1. Fractal characteristics of structures of the visualization maps.

	Map dataset								
	I			II			III		
	0.6: 0.4	0.5: 0.5	0.7: 0.3	1988	1998	2007	W/out class I	Rand	Cla-sses.
Fractal dim. FD	2.761	2.71	2.736	2.86	2.725	2.761	2.731	2.775	2.51
Lacu-narity	0.158	0.179	0.201	0.04	0.113	0.158	0.235	0.13	1,03

For convenience calculation results are grouped in comparative series. First ones consist of three different ratio of main to additional classifications. The higher weight of the main classification (the highest tested is 0.7) the more intensive concentration of documents nodes around their main classes and the more clear division into thematic categories. In the contrary case – main classification weight is comparable with additional (0.5:0.5), the categories more merge with one another. The suitable pattern is to be more blur (Picture 1a) thus any structure is disappeared and as a result fractal dimension is the lowest than in two another cases – 2.71. Output visualization map used in all stages of analysis is characterized by ratio 0.6:0.4. The highest FD value (2.761) confirms the fractal structure is the most distinct on this map. For further tests the classification was modified by eliminating the most spacious class I. Less density and smaller FD value (2.731) identifies this distribution.

Lacunarity is a degree of holes distribution and has the lowest value for indeterminate structure. Interpretation of this is the following: the more even distribution of documents nodes the better space filling and less holes is observed. Therefore the perfectly homogeneous localization of objects must have the smallest lacunarity. To verify this approach random distribution was generated using the same number of nodes (Figure 2d and series III in Table 1). The results prove this assumption is correct.

To interpret a big FD value for random distribution we need to relate to fractal dimension range for organized objects. Trees with linear hierarchy are described by fractal with dimension value above 2 (topological dimension of line is 1, of rectangle is 2). If analyzed visualization map includes some hierarchy structure its fractal dimension must be within a range between 2 and 2.775. The last one is FD value for slight structure i.e. random homogeneous distribution.
In second series fractals parameters of three maps produced for different publishing years are compared (Table 1), called by Garfield longitudinal maps (1994, 1998). In 1988, when ACM classification was in early stage of development, the distribution resembles random sample; FD parameter is very high and equals 2.86. No right structure was found (Figure 2b). The next map shows 10 years later thematic map is more clear. In 2007 the structure of multilevel hierarchy became certainly very definite (last map on Figure 2b); fractal dimension converges to the lower value (2.761).
Original maps are colored by 11 colors. For fractal analysis needs the pictures were desaturated and some information about hierarchy levels was lost. Therefore additionally for longitudinal colored maps spectral analysis steps were performed.

According spectral histograms of visualized collection of scientific articles (Figure 3) it is possible to come to the same conclusion about thematic categorization of ACM classification improved in last decade. Sharp spikes without noise background (which exists on the first two graphs) mean pure colors on visualization maps. Thus the visualization of documents published in 2007 points to a clearly defined organization of thematic categories.

6. Conclusion
Visualization of classification universe depicts scientific knowledge organization in selected domain. Outcome graphic layout facilitates human interaction for exploration and understanding the large amount of data and their correlations. The main problem

of visualization techniques there is still no defined quantitative methods to evaluate their results.

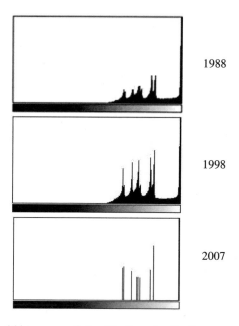

Figure 3. Spectral histograms of classification visualization maps made for different publishing years.

In current paper the advantages of fractal analysis for visualization maps are presented. On the assumption that map structure camouflages some fractal its characteristics like dimension and lacunarity are essential for discovering and further insight the data organization. For example hierarchical trees structures as linear formations have fractal dimension between 1 and 2. The higher FD value the distribution is nearer to even type while the information about hierarchy levels is lost. Knowledge about fractal parameters results in choice of optimal visualization as well as finding the stages of Computer Science domain development.

Some researchers with multidisciplinary background study a potential parallelism between fractal theory and knowledge organization (Barát 2009, Scharnhorst 2003, Crowley 2002), that achieves the interdisciplinary perspective of complex structures research. Physics laws are common and universal in the natural world. There are innumerable examples of natural objects can be approximated to fractals. Representation of different concepts been created in human brain as a result of observing the nature must have fractal structure.

References

Barát Á.H. (2009). The Structures of Concept And its Connection to Sciences. In: *Proceedings of IX ISKO Congres Spain Group, New Perspectives for the organization and dissemination of knowledge.* Valencia: UPV, pp. 372-379;

Börner, K. et al. (2003). Visualizing Knowledge Domains. In Blaise Cronin (Ed.), *Annual Review of Information Science & Technology*, Medford, NJ: Information Today, Inc./American Society for Information Science and Technology 5, pp. 179 255.

Chen Ch. (2006). *Information Visualization: Beyond the Horizon*. London: Springer, 2nd edition, pp. 143-170.

Crowley Ch. (2002). *Overview of Complexity*. Available online at URL: http://wynchar.com/charlie/Complexity/ overviewOfComplexity.html

Garfield, E. (1994). Scientography: Mapping the tracks of science. Current Contents: Social & Behavioural Sciences, 7(45), pp. 5-10.

Garfield, E. *Essays/Papers on "Mapping the World of Science"*. since 1998. Available online at URL: http://garfield.library.upenn.edu/mapping/mapping.html.

List of fractals by Hausdorff dimension. In: *Wikipedia. The Free Encyclopedia* [on-line]. Available online at URL: http://en.wikipedia.org/wiki/List_of_fractals_by_Hausdorff _dimension

Mandelbrot, B.B. (1982). *The Fractal Geometry of Nature*. W.H. Freeman and Company, pp. 6-20.

Osinska, V. & Bala, P. (2008). Classification Visualization across Mapping on a Sphere. In: *New trends of multimedia and Network Information Systems*. Amsterdam: IOS Press, pp. 95-107.

Osinska, V. & Bala, P. (2010). New Methods for Visualization and Improvement of Classification Schemes – the case of Computer Science. *Knowledge Organization*, 37(3).

Plotnick R.E., Gardner R.H. (1993). Lacunarity indices as measures of landscape texture. *Landscape Ecology*, Vol. 8, nr 3, pp. 201-211.

Scharnhorst, A. (2003). Complex Networks and the Web: Insights Nonlinear Physics. *JCMC* 8 (4). Available online at URL: http://jcmc.indiana.edu/vol8/issue4/scharnhorst.html

Sperber D. (2003). Why Rethink Interdisciplinary? *Interdisciplines* Available online at URL: http://www.interdisciplines.org/ interdisciplinarity/papers/1.html

Ware, C. (2004). *Information Visualization: Perception for Design*. San Francisko: Morgan Kaufmann, 2nd edition, pp. 43-80.

---

[1] List of fractals by Hausdorff dimension. In: *Wikipedia. The Free Encyclopedia* [on-line]. Available online at URL: http://en.wikipedia.org/wiki/List_of_fractals_by_ Hausdorff_dimension.

[2] Desaturation is removal from the image the information about colours.

User's Perception and Satisfaction with Reference Services in University Libraries of Punjab: A Survey

Shafiq Ur Rehman[1], Farzana Shafique[2] and Khalid Mahmood[3]

[1]PhD Scholar, Université Charles-de-Gaulle, Lille 3, France, Senior Librarian University of the Punjab, Lahore, Pakistan, s_rehman25@hotmail.com
[2]Lecturer, Department of Library and Information Science, The Islamia University of Bahawalpur, Pakistan
[3]Professor, Department of Library and Information Science University of the Punjab, Lahore, Pakistan

Abstract: User satisfaction and maximum use of library services and resources have become important topic for libraries to maintain awareness of. Many libraries especially the university libraries are focusing on evaluation of the users' needs and their satisfaction with their services. Library user satisfaction surveys can provide better understanding of user's perception and service quality in libraries. Providing high quality reference service is not easy task, and it needs regular feedback and assessment. By knowing of users' perception and satisfaction, libraries can tailor those services according to their needs. Keeping the importance of reference services in view many studies are conducted in the developed world, but in Pakistan the situation is not encouraging. Very few studies are conducted to find out the status of reference services in different libraries of Pakistan but there is no data available on user satisfaction with reference services of university libraries. Keeping the gaps and need of the time in view, the basic purpose of this survey is to get the broad understanding of user's perception with reference services. It also explores their satisfaction with these services. The survey is limited to all public sector university libraries (N = 10) of the Punjab province (Pakistan) having a reasonable collection, staff, and separate reference section, as well as a reference librarian. The data was collected through mail, e-mail and personal visits. Findings of the study can be helpful for the library authorities and professionals for revisiting their reference services and sources.
Keywords: Pakistan, reference and informational services, Punjab, university libraries, user satisfaction.

1. Introduction

Despite the processing and propagation of library resources, a key trait of a university library is the services based around personal interaction between users and the library staff. Libraries should make sure that these services show proper levels of customer care and that the information given to the users is useful and at the right level (Loughborough University Library, 2005). Retting (1993) has pointed out that the distinguishing features of reference include a staff designated to provide the service; a collection of reference works accessible to the public in an area set aside for

New Trends in Qualitative and Quantitative Methods in Libraries
A. Katsirikou and C. H. Skiadas (eds)
© World Scientific Publishing Co (pp. 25-36)

the provision of the service; adequate guides to the library's resources; and a high degree of interaction between the staff and the clientele.

Although in today's world the term reference service encompasses more activities than mentioned by Retting. In this context Mitchell (2008) has rightly said that today's reference librarians are actively engaged with the many emerging new processes by which learning occurs. Further, reference librarians in academic and research libraries are actively engaged with the many emerging new processes not only by which learning occurs, but also by which research is done. To be successful, today's reference librarians need to not only understand but also embrace current and emerging technologies affecting reference functions and the information needs of library users. Indeed, wherever or however we provide reference service, we are all cognizant of the major changes in libraries – changes that stem from countless cultural, economic, legal and social developments that have impacted, and continue to impact, our work. Similarly King (2005) and Hiller (2001) have mentioned that the information needs and expectations are continuously changing in the rapidly changing information scenario. Libraries need to re-orient their collections, services, and facilities to keep pace with these advancements. User feedback is considered as a more reliable factor in measuring the utility and effectiveness of any library. This is the reason that library user surveys have become widespread in academic libraries during the past twenty years. Surveys have often been used as a tool to assess service quality and user satisfaction. By making user surveys a regular part of the library's functions, librarians can provide a comparative 'snapshot' of usage in various temporal contexts.

2. Background of the Study

The provision of reference services has been, and still is, at the heart of all libraries in every sector be it academic, public or special. Until the internet changed forever the way we access information, it was the exclusive preserve of the "Reference librarian" to provide information directly to the client (Weddell, 2008). Evaluation of library reference services began in earnest in the late 1960s and early 1970s when budgetary situations required justification of the existence of all services in the library. A close examination of a reference service provides library administration and involved librarians with a clear understanding of how well the service is meeting its intended goals, objectives, and outcomes, how well the service is helping users fulfill their information needs, and whether the expended resources are producing the desired results (Pomerantz, Luo & McClure, 2006). Evaluation of reference services from different point of view serves different purposes. For example Saxton & Richardson (2002), has pointed out that most reference evaluation studies employ either "the query-oriented approach primarily concerned with testing the accuracy of answers to reference" or "the obtrusive user-oriented approach primarily concerned with testing levels of user satisfaction with the service". Similarly Whitlatch (2000) has mentioned four primary features of reference services for evaluation such as "economic feature", e.g. cost effectiveness, productivity measure; "service process", e.g. measures of satisfaction with the service provided; "resources", e.g. measures of quantity and quality of materials, staffing, equipment, and facilities supporting the service; and "service outcomes or products", e.g. measures related to the quality of answers or information delivered. Grossa & Saxton (2002) reported a secondary analysis of a user survey administered in 13 public libraries and examined user ratings of reference services by transaction type. Transaction type is defined dichotomously as self-generated (users transacting questions they have determined for themselves) or imposed (agent users in the library seeking information on behalf of someone else).

Users with self-generated questions rated library services lower than did users with imposed questions. Both groups rated the library experience lower than their reference desk experience, and imposed queries were responsible for proportionately higher "first time" use of the reference desk. No significant difference existed between groups for ratings of finding useful information in the library, finding everything wanted in the library visit, frequency of library use, or levels of attained formal education. There were significant differences found for ratings of the reference librarian's service behaviors, user satisfaction with reference service, and frequency of reference desk use.

User satisfaction and optimization of resources have become important areas for libraries to maintain awareness of. Many libraries esp. the university libraries are focusing on evaluation of the users' needs and their satisfaction with their services. User surveys can provide useful perceptions of service quality in libraries. For example Texas A&M University libraries conducted focus group studies in 2001 with graduate and undergraduate studies in order to gather specific information related to their satisfaction with and confidence in the assistance provided at library service points. The sessions revealed that users were generally pleased with the assistance provided them by professional staff at reference desks and that they found librarians to be usually patient and helpful although there were some elements of dissatisfaction identified by the respondents. The findings of such studies are being used to improve library directional tools and to improve staff training for public service staff (Crowley & Gilreath, 2002).

Similarly, Loughborough University Library decided the annual user survey for 2004/ 2005 academic year. The purpose of the survey was to gather a broad understanding of how users perceive the service they receive at the various desks. The focus specifically was on perceptions of the customer care they receive and the level of information provided (Loughborough University Library, 2005). Loorits & Dubjeva (1997) have reported the satisfaction of the users with reference services at Tartu University Library. The results of a user survey carried out in the framework of a Baltic-Swedish joint project at the library in spring 1995, and the statistical data gathered at the same time were analyzed by them. According to them the same autumn another survey was organized to gather statistical data to follow the dynamics of reference services. Similarly Novotny & Rimland (2007) have discussed a service quality study conducted in the Pennsylvania State University Libraries. The Wisconsin–Ohio Reference Evaluation Program survey was selected as a valid, standardized instrument. They presented their results, highlighting the impact on reference training. According to them a second survey a year later demonstrated that focusing on behavioral aspects of reference can improve service quality ratings. Providing quality reference service is not easy, and any approach needs constant evaluation. Close attention to user needs can guide the reference staff about future changes. For example, Fitzpatrick, Moore & Lang (2008) have predicted the future directions of reference service based on the findings of a study such as programmatic information literacy instruction, integration of library resources into the curriculum, and librarians spending more time in academic buildings outside of the library in high-activity locations. Reference service is most effective and efficient when the librarian has a presence at the point of need. In the changing scenario many reference departments have reduced librarian time at the Reference desk. Instead, they are creatively seeking users' multiple points of need online via instant messenger, chat, phone, email, and face-to-face outside the library in classrooms, labs, and cafés. According to Dent (2000) the Interactive Reference Assistance (IRA) project is an example of one such service innovation at the University of Michigan. Keeping the importance of reference services in view many studies are conducted in the developed world, but in Pakistan the situation is not encouraging. Very few studies are conducted to find out the status of reference service in different libraries of Pakistan. For example, Raziuddin (1998) studied different aspects of reference services like reference questions, reference interview, and reference librarians' competencies, kinds of reference sources and impact of computer on reference services. She pointed out that reference services are almost out of practice in Pakistan and very few libraries provide reference services and have reference librarian. Bashir (1977) discussed the reference services in college libraries, while Haq (1993) investigated the reference services in the Quaid-e-Azam Library and emphasized on the improvement of not only reference services but the skills of librarians as well. He mentioned that active and knowledgeable reference librarians along with adequate reference tools are more helpful for library users and suggested the frequent performance evaluation of libraries. Khan (1979), Mirza (1981) and Khan (2006a) described the impact of electronic data processing on reference services and highlighted various computer based reference services in Pakistan. Khan (2006b) probed the 153 students' perception of the reference librarian and how do they approach them for services at Peshawar University Library. Majeed (1998) investigated the public services of Punjab University Library and she presented the status of reference services in the Library. Rafi (2006) conducted an appraisal of reference services offered by Quaid-e-Azam Reference Library. She mentioned that majority of users were satisfied with reference services but there is a need to update the printed reference sources. She furnished various recommendations for further improvement. Similarly, Saddique (2006) surveyed the reference services offered by the IRC (previously known as Reference Section) of the University of Punjab, Lahore. He investigated the user's perception about IRC. He found that during last few years IRC services have improved but there is a need for more training of staff and the users as well. Extensive information literacy program should be developed for users. Keeping the problems of developing countries like Pakistan in view, Lopes (1992) has rightly pointed out that the setting up reference services and referral centers in libraries in developing countries must be considered as an increasingly important factor in the development of effective libraries and information systems in developing countries.

3. Problem Statement, Objectives and Methodology of the Study

Review of the above literature reveals a wide gap in the provision of reference services. As the situation of university libraries in Punjab is better than other provinces, so to take a broader understanding of reference services in university libraries of Punjab, a reasonable sample of well established general universities of Punjab was selected for this study. The basic objective of this study was to gather a broad understanding of how users perceive the reference services they receive at their university libraries and their satisfaction with these services.

3.1. Methodology

The survey is limited to all public sector general university libraries (central library/main library) (N=10) of the Punjab province (Pakistan) having a reasonable collection, staff, and separate reference section, as well as a reference librarian. One hundred questionnaires were distributed in each university library selected for the study. The sample from all public sector universities was purposefully selected from library users. To be included in the selection, a library user had to be full time student or faculty/staff member. Additionally, he also has some experience of using library reference services. The questionnaire was distributed to the users during their physical visits to the concerned library.A questionnaire-based cross-sectional survey research design was employed. It was a cross-sectional survey because the data were collected from the subjects at one point in time. This was done keeping in view the time constraints. Out of 1000 questionnaires distributed, 507 filled in questionnaires were returned to the researchers in the usable form. The rate of response was, therefore, 50.7% in our case which was sufficiently high with regard to a survey research design. All areas of reference services to measure different constructs were combined in the form of a questionnaire (containing 24 questionnaire items/statements). It used a five-point Likert scale. The scale used for each item was from 1 (strongly disagree) to 5 (strongly agree). To assess the reliability and validity of the scale, Cronbach's alpha (α) was executed on the scale. The Cronbach alpha value is 0.911, which is higher than the general standard of 0.80, items suggesting a good reliability of overall questionnaire. The first part also contained demographic questions i,e. status, sex, frequency of library visit, frequency of reference section visit, name of the organization etc. and an open-ended question for gathering further opinion. The questionnaires were received by the authors through mail, email (scanned copy of the filled questionnaires) and personal visits. The data were analyzed both qualitatively and quantitatively to reach at conclusions. Quantitative analysis was done with the help of Statistical Package for Social Sciences (SPSS-version 16).

4. Data Analysis and Related Discussion
4.1. Personal profile of the respondents
Acquired responses reveal that in total 507 i.e., 277 (55%) male and 230 (45%) female users from different university libraries responded against the questionnaire (Table 1). Table 2 presents the frequency distribution of responses acquired from each university. Most of the responses were received from the Islamia University of Bahawalpur (94, 19%) and then from University of the Punjab, Lahore (89, 18%) due to personal visits by the authors. Of the 507 respondents, 460 (91%) were students, 22 (4%), faculty members and 13 (3%) different staff members of the relevant universities (Table 3). Most of the students were studying in MA/MSc programs (321, 63%), while 125 (25%) did not mention their level of studies (Table 4).

Table 1: Frequency Distribution of Respondents' Gender

Gender	Frequency	Percent
Male	277	55
Female	230	45
Total	507	100

Table 2: Frequency Distribution of the Responses Acquired from Each University

Rank	Names of Responded University Libraries	Frequency	Percent
1.	Islamia University of Bahawalpur	94	19
2.	University of the Punjab- Lahore	89	18
3.	Government College University-Lahore	60	12
4.	University of Engineering and Technology-Lahore	50	10
5.	University of Gujrat	46	9
6.	Allama Iqbal Open University- Islamabad	43	9
7.	Bahaudin Zakria University-Multan	40	8
8.	International Islamic University- Islamabad	34	7
9.	UVAS- Lahore	26	5
10.	Government College University-Faisalabad	25	5

Table 3: Frequency distribution of Respondents' Status

Respondents	Frequency	Percent
Student	460	91
Faculty	22	4
Staff	13	3
Missing	12	2
Total	507	100

Table 4: Frequency Distribution of Respondents' Level of Studies

Level of Study	Frequency	Percent
MA/MSc	321	63
Missing	125	25
M. Phil	29	6
PhD	18	4
BA-honors/BSc	14	3

4.2. Frequency of library and reference section visits

Table 5 shows the frequency with which the respondents were visiting the library. The response shows a good trend of library visits because most of them were daily (219, 43%) and twice a week (198, 39%) visitors of the library. On the other hand the results show that 172 (34%) respondents were visiting the Reference section of their respective library twice a week and 110 (22%) were visiting it daily. A great number of respondents (106, 21%) were visiting it rarely (Table 6).

Table 5: Frequency of Library Visits

Library Visits	Frequency	Percent
Daily	219	43
Twice a week	198	39
Monthly	31	6
Fortnightly	21	4
Missing	15	3

Table 6: Frequency of Reference Section Visits

Reference Section Visits	Frequency	Percent
Twice a week	172	34
Daily	110	22
Rarely	106	21
Fortnightly	42	8
Missing	40	8
Monthly	37	7

4.3. Respondents' perception and satisfaction with the reference section and its services

Table 7 shows the descriptive statistics of respondents' perception and satisfaction with the Reference section of their respective university library. They were asked to rate different statements against a five point Likert scale. Some statements were asked repetitively from different angles in order to get the clear feedback. To interpret the results of the study the researchers considered satisfied services those have mean score of 3.5 or above. These statements are categorized and ranked for the purpose of data analysis. The categories and acquired responses are as followed:

4.3.1. Reference collection

Respondents were agree with the statement that Reference collection is adequate for their information needs (mean=3.67), well-organized and easy to use (mean= 3.57) and appropriate material is available for answering the reference questions (mean= 3.56). On the other hand most of the respondents gave no opinion about the adequacy of print (mean= 3.44) and electronic (mean= 3.17) reference collection.

4.3.2. Reference staff

They agreed that the reference staff is competent and helpful (mean= 3.84) and demonstrates good communication skills (mean= 3.58), but most of them did not give any opinion about the statement that the reference staff immediately answers their ready reference questions (mean= 3.44). It seems that they have shown their perception and satisfaction with all the library staff rather than only about reference staff.

4.3.3. Reference services

The results show that most of the respondents showed no opinion about the reference services of the library.

4.3.4. E-Reference services

Respondents were also asked about the electronic reference services provided by their libraries. They mentioned that they are strongly agree with the statement that library Web pages are informative, helpful, and easy-to-use and a good source for e-reference services (mean= 4.53). On the other hand they gave no opinion about other statements probing their perception and satisfaction about the E-reference services.

4.3.5. Facilities

The respondents agreed that Reference section's environment (noise level, heating / cooling, lights, furniture, cleanliness, etc.) is conducive to study and convenient to use (mean= 3.88), and approach (mean= 3.86), its opening and closing hours meet their needs (mean= 3.78) and it is easy to borrow reference material for photocopy (mean= 3.71). On the other hand they expressed no opinion regarding the provision of access to adequate electronic reference sources (mean= 3.28), good Internet facility for searching online reference sources (mean= 3.21) and availability of adequate computers for use of electronic reference sources (mean= 3.06).

4.3.6. Overall satisfaction

It is revealed from the acquired results that the respondents were agreed that they were satisfied with the overall quality of reference services (mean= 3.6).

Table 7: Descriptive Statistics of Respondents Perception and Satisfaction with the Reference Section and its Services

Statements	Mean	Std. Deviation
Reference Collection:		
Reference collection is adequate for my needs	3.67	1.104
Library's reference collection is well-organized and easy to find	3.57	1.178
Library has appropriate reference material for answering reference questions	3.56	1.082
Print reference collection is adequate	3.44	1.058
Electronic reference collection is adequate	3.17	1.140
Reference Staff: Reference staff is competent and helpful	3.84	1.125
Reference Staff demonstrates good communication skill	3.58	2.123
Reference staff immediately answers my ready reference questions	3.44	1.236
Catalog of reference material is easy to use	3.42	1.723
Reference Services:		
Current Awareness Service (CAS) is helpful	3.33	1.417
Library provides adequate training on the use of reference services and resources	3.13	1.225
Library provides good Interlibrary loan and document delivery services	3.10	1.093
E-Reference Services:		
Library Web pages are informative, helpful, and easy-to-use and a good source for e-reference services	4.53	24.767
Digital (E-mail & chat) reference services satisfy my need	3.10	2.075
Library answers the digital/electronic reference queries	3.10	1.054
Facilities:		
Reference section's environment (noise level, heating / cooling, lights, furniture, cleanliness, etc.) is conducive to study	3.88	2.09
Use of Reference section procedure is convenient	3.88	1.019
Reference section is convenient for visitors to approach	3.86	.936
Opening/closing hours of reference section meet my needs	3.78	1.059
Borrowing reference books for photocopying from the library is easy	3.71	1.076
Library provides access to adequate electronic reference sources for research and information	3.28	1.921

Reference section provides good Internet facility for searching online reference sources	3.21	1.344
Adequate computers are available for use of electronic reference sources	3.06	1.341
Over all Satisfaction:		
I am satisfied with the overall quality of reference services	3.6	2.038

Scale: 5= strongly agree, 4=Agree, 3=No opinion, 2=Disagree, 1=strongly disagree

Table 8: Difference on the Basis of Universities

Overall Satisfaction	Sum of Squares	df	Mean Square	F	Sig.
Between Groups	7047.797	9	783.089	3.636	.000
Within Groups	106837.049	496	215.397		
Total	113884.846	505			

4.4. Comparison of user satisfaction with the reference services among the university libraries

Opinions of the users about their satisfaction with reference services among different libraries were compared on a a five-point scale. Mean scores of their satisfaction level of reference services about different libraries are given in Table 8. To see the significance of difference between means of satisfaction, analysis of variance (ANOVA) was used. It is a technique that partitions the total variation – a term distinct from variance and measured by the sum of squares of deviations from the mean – into components, each of which may be attributed to a definite source of variation (Shafique & Mahmood, 2007). The results of ANOVA show that there is significant difference (at the 0.05 alpha levels) among the means of different universities. The results show that satisfactions of the respondents about different services in universities are different (See Table 8).

4.5. Suggestions provided by the respondents

The analysis of the free-text comments also provides more qualitative information from the users' perspective. Of the 507 respondents, 274 (54%) provided their suggestions for the improvement of reference and other library services. Most of them recommended for the provision of more facilities and reference services (n= 99), acquisition of new and updated reference material for all subjects (n= 84) and provision of more reference services as mentioned in the questionnaire. Other important suggestions were that the reference librarian and other reference staff should be competent, well trained and should be able to answer all the queries of the users. They recommended the provision of good ICT facilities and online reference services as well (See Table 9).

Table 9: Frequency Distribution of Suggestions Provided by the Respondents

Rank	Suggestions	Frequency
1.	Library should provide more facilities and reference services	99
2.	New and updated reference material should be acquired by the library in all subjects	84

3.	More reference services should be started as mentioned in the questionnaire	83
4.	Reference librarian should be competent	71
5.	Reference staff should be well trained and answer all the queries of the users	61
6.	Internet and other ICT facilities/need good Internet speed	58
7.	Online reference service should be started	57
8.	Environment of the section should be conducive for research and study	33
9.	Proper reference services should be started. Our library has no proper concept of reference services	27
10.	Reference material should be processed and arranged properly	26
11.	More print/e-journals should be subscribed by the section	23
12.	OPAC should be provided in the reference section as well	13
13.	Reference material should also be issued to the users	11
14.	Reference services should be of international standard	11
15.	More trained reference staff should be appointed	9
16.	User education programs should be started	8
17.	Departmental libraries should also provide reference services	6

5. Findings
The study reveals that although respondents have shown their overall satisfaction with the reference collection, staff, facilities and services provided by their libraries but they did not rank highly satisfied to any category of reference service. Out of 24 statements 14 falls in the category of satisfaction level, but a review of responses against other similar statements and provided suggestions/comments indicate that in some cases they gave their opinion about the overall library collection, staff and services etc. rather than about reference section in particular. Although most users do not have clear understanding of the complexities of library systems, in order to implement customer-based changes, library administration must accept user perceptions as valid statements of how patrons feel. Some suggestions provided by the users were interesting such as regarding the provision of reference services mentioned in the questionnaire i.e., chat reference etc. Any how this is a significant finding that the respondents have valued the investment in reference services by their university libraries. The level of user satisfaction with these investments is also satisfactory.

6. Conclusion and Recommendations
We are living in the information age, where information explosion and customer care are one of the major challenges. In this context, it is inevitable for a library to provide richer information diets to their customers for fulfilling their information needs. This reality is very well felt by the developed world and in those countries reference and information services have seen revolutionary changes to meet the new challenges of information age. This study investigated the overall user's perception and satisfaction with reference services in public sector university library of largest province of Pakistan. This is first effort to investigate the user's satisfaction with reference services in Pakistan. The researchers hope that this study will further motivate the future research on the topic in Pakistan. The Reference services are often criticized due to lack of customer focus and input. This study result suggests that concerned

authorities should pay attention for the improvement of present level of user satisfaction. Keeping this reality in view the survey was an initial step for finding the status of such activities in the largest Province of Pakistan. On the basis of findings of the study some recommendations are made, which are as followed:

1. Libraries should pay special attention on the provision of good collection, staff and services in their reference sections.
2. New ICT based services i.e., Electronic or virtual reference services should be introduced by the libraries.
3. Consideration should be given on future service development. The reference staff should be trained in maintaining high level of customer satisfaction in face to face services.
4. University libraries should consider the features of "user friendliness and helpfulness" while designing online or electronic services for their users.
5. The concept of customer care training should be introduced at the library schools and libraries as well.
6. Library instruction program should target undergraduate students who are most in need of assistance in the use of different library resources and services.
7. Such studies should be conducted more frequently. Other provinces of the country are also needed to be studied.
8. User satisfaction survey research should be conducted in Pakistan at the macro and micro levels on different aspects of reference services.
9. Library schools should pay special attention on training the future reference librarians by giving them the assignments of long and short range questions and electronic reference services.
10. Findings of the study should be considered by the relevant individual university libraries in particular and other libraries in general for improvement of their reference services.

References

Bashir A., (1977). College Libraries and Reference Services. *Pakistan Library Bulletin*, Vol.8, No. 3/4, 68-74.

Crowley, G. H. and Gilreath, C. L., (2002). Probing user perceptions of service quality: Using focus groups to enhance Quantitative surveys. *Performance Measurement and Metrics,* Vol.3, No.2, 78-84.

Dent, V. F., (2000). Technology provides innovative reference services at University of Michigan libraries. *Research Strategies,* Vol.17, No.2/3, 187-193.

Fitzpatrick, E. B., Moore, A. C. and Lang, B. W., (2008). Reference Librarians at the Reference Desk in a Learning Commons: A Mixed Methods Evaluation. *The Journal of Academic Librarianship,* Vol.34, No.3, 231–238.

Grossa, L. and Saxton, M. L., (2002). Integrating the imposed query into the evaluation of reference service: A dichotomous analysis of user ratings. *Library & Information Science Research,* Vol.24, No.3, 251–263.

Haq, I., (1993). Reference Services in Quaid i Azam Library. In Asghar, M., et al. (Eds.).*Hallmarks of Library and Information Services in Pakistan* (pp. 79-90). Lahore: PULSAA.

Hiller, S., (2001). Assessing user needs, satisfaction and library performance at the University of Washington Library. *Library Trends,* Vol.49, No.4, 605-625.

Khan, A., (2006a). Digital/Virtual Reference Services in Libraries: An integrated-based reference service. *Pakistan Library & Information Science Journal,* Vol. 37, No.1, 13-19.

Khan, A., (2006b). Reference librarians' service and customers satisfaction. *Pakistan Library & Information Science Journal,* Vol.37, No.2, 30-37.

Khan, M. A., (1979). Impact of electronic data processing on reference service. *Pakistan Library Bulletin,* Vol.10,No.1/2, 1-8.

King, Dwight B., (2005). User surveys: Libraries ask, 'Hey, how am I doing?' *Law Library Journal,* Vol.97, No.1, 103–115.

Loorits, E. and Dubjeva, L., (1997). *Reference services at Tartu University Library.* Retr. 24.7.2008, http://www.utlib.ee/ee/publikatsioonid/1997/ryt/elsa_resume.html

Lopes, R. R. V., (1992). Reference services in developing countries. *Information Development,* Vol.8, No.1, 35-40.

Loughborough University Library. (2005). *Survey of Loughborough University Library users' perceptions of levels ofquality and customer care from Circulation Desk, Support Services desk and Levels 1, 2 and 3 enquiry desks.* Retrieved July 27, 2008, from: //www.lboro.ac.uk/library/about/PDFs/custcare05.pdf.

Majeed, S. (1998). *Evaluation of reader's services of the Punjab University Library.* Unpublished masters thesis, Department of Library and Information Science, University of the Punjab, Lahore.

Mirza, B. H., (1981). Computer Based Reference Services in Pakistan. *Pakistan Library Bulletin,* Vol.12, No.1, 17-22.

Mitchell, E., (2008). Thumbs up: A new definition of reference-Editorial. *Reference Services Review,* Vol.36, No.1, 5-6.

Novotny, E. and Rimland, E., (2007). Using the Wisconsin–Ohio Reference Evaluation Program (WOREP) to improve training and reference services. *The Journal of Academic Librarianship,* Vol.33, No.3, 382–392.

Pomerantz, J., Luo, L. and McClure, C.R., (2006). Peer review of chat reference transcripts: Approaches and strategies. *Library & Information Science Research,* Vol.28, No.1, 24-48.

Rafi, S. (2006). *Status of R&I (Reference and Information) Services of Quaid-e-Azam Library, Lahore: A case study.* Unpublished masters thesis, Department of Library and Information Science, University of the Punjab, Lahore.

Raziuddin, M. S. (1998). Reference Services in Libraries. *Pakistan Library Bulletin,* Vol. 29, No.1/2, 35-41.

Retting, J. R. (1993). Reference and information service. In R. Wedgeworth (Ed.), *World encyclopedia of library and information services* (3rd ed.) (pp. 703–708). Chicago: American Library Association.

Saddique, A. (2006).). *Status of the services of IRC (Information Resource Centre), University of the Punjab: A case study.* Unpublished masters thesis, Department of Library and Information Science, University of the Punjab, Lahore.

Shafique, F., & Mahmood, K. (2007). Librarians' opinions about library software: a survey of libraries in Lahore. *The Electronic Library,* 25(6), 766-777.

Weddell, S. (2008). Transforming reference into a proactive knowledge advisory service: A case study. *Reference Services Review,* Vol. 36, No.2, 147-155.

Whitlatch, J. B. (2000). *Evaluating reference services: A practical guide.* American Library Association: Chicago, IL.

User Centred Libraries and Brand Name: The Case of Greek Public Libraries

Anthi Katsirikou and Ageliki Oikonomou

University of Piraeus Library, Greece, anthi@asmda.com, oikoang@yahoo.gr

Abstract: The paper seeks the attitudes of the Greek public libraries about the case of brand name and if they undertake the responsibility and their efforts to obtain one. Generally speaking, the paper insists that is a matter of libraries to engage people to the library and persuade them that they need it. But that is a communication matter, a matter beyond marketing. Also, the paper examines if libraries measure their users' response to their efforts to promote their services and events. Relevant to that is whether libraries have a promotion program and also a communication strategy based on the statistical data which (or not) they collect (or not) from their users and non-users. Research and study of users' attitudes is one more of the paper questions which are considered important in libraries' decision making processes and in finding optimized solutions.
Finally, some best practices and lessons learned, proper for Greek reality will be proposed.
Keywords: Marketing plan, library marketing, public libraries, brand name, library communications, Greek libraries

Introduction

The goal of the paper is to seek whether public libraries have a strategic planning to communicate their users and potential users. It also seeks the public response to the services provided by libraries as well as libraries' beliefs about abstention of the general public and pointing out the causes and potential solutions. The issue is important and closely related to that of brand name, because both demonstrate the openness of the library, both demonstrate the library's decision to appeal to those who do not know.

The paper's methodological approach is a research survey via questionnaires. The questionnaires were disseminated to libraries and were filled in by the director or the information policy responsible person. The questionnaires will seek definite services and if necessary some interviews will add the survey.

Public libraries face a decreasing use

It is supposed that the circumstances of everyday life should increase the members of the libraries and not the opposite. It is researchable if libraries seek practical ways to attract the potential users, marketing and communicating methods.

The libraries are supposed to be non-profit organizations; however the operations and the services of the libraries involve an enterprise-profit dimension: the pursuit of the best, if possible, utilization and exploitation of the available resources. This has to do with the communication capacity and capability of the library in order to identify and attract its potential audience. The composition of this audience is a variable factor, because the audience is continuously enriched by new groups of patrons, more and

New Trends in Qualitative and Quantitative Methods in Libraries
A. Katsirikou and C. H. Skiadas (eds)
© *World Scientific Publishing Co (pp. 37-42)*

more new users are attracted. Generally speaking, there is a mobility in the composition of library's population.

The process of identifying the audience is a standing procedure for every library, according to the continuing change that happens in three dimensions:

- The users themselves are changing,
- They are changing needs and/or expectations from libraries,
- They are changing attitudes and requirements.

The identification of the audience is part of the marketing program that public libraries have to develop; however,

- 49% of public libraries declare that they do not specialize a marketing plan,
- 31% of them simply distinguish the image of the library.

Nevertheless, users' responsiveness is high, as indicated by the following questions:

Figure 1. Responsiveness of the public. Cartoon by Peter Lewis http://www.bibl.u-szeged.hu/ejszaka_2005/field_guide_eng.htm

Do all the participants in the library events become its members?

- 43% yes
- 27% no
- 30% there no recorded data

Do the library members attend to its events?

- 86% yes
- 7% I don't know
- 7% no.

A percentage 71,1% of the libraries answers that has established procedures for informing the public about their services and a percentage of 55,6% organizes events and happenings for her public. Both the communication and the events are tools for attracting potential users. The content and the kind of communication disclose if they are random happenings or targeted to special population groups campaigns.

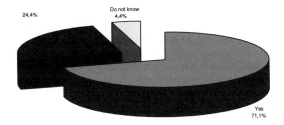

The conclusion about libraries' prestige is that it turns positive in those using it, though half of the libraries reported that they did not have recorded data on users satisfaction, but the problem of those who do not use it remains. How does the library increase the percentage of users of the entire population? What policy and communication strategy does the library imply to approach new group of population? The problem would be partially solved if libraries have adopted the Brand name practice. What brand name is about?

Brand name

A brand is an idea; it is a non tangible assets of an organization. Brand is the opinion that consumers have about one organization's products or services. This would entail that the brand name is the power of the organization that consumers create in their minds, because of the quality of the service or of product.

In what brand is interpreted in library procedures?

What brand means to libraries? Organizations exist to provide value. If that value is no longer perceived to be in sync with the consumers' needs, the perceived value of the organization, and its brand, wil be minimized.

Is it time to revitalize the library brand? Your library brand is your reputation. You build it by giving your patrons a desirable experience they can't get elsewhere. In your neighborhood, desirable might be free computer access, kids' reading programs, book clubs, small business resources of "meet the author" events. (Stacey, 2006).

Changing the library's image in the marketplace, however, must start with changing librarians' perceptions. That means adjustments the librarianship culture and operations before persuading consumers that libraries have been reborn.

All experienced librarians know very well that each new member will develop a perception about the organization, about the services and policies of the library, through which perception does not change; only with great difficulty.

Brand names are not empty of meaning for libraries, contrary it provides significant benefits to the consumer:

1. Brands reduce the level of effort a consumer must put into assuring a specific, desired level of quality. A researcher or student must use his or her time and financial resources with care, and in choosing the library in which to conduct research, a "name brand" library is most likely to give a reasonable return on that investment.

2.   Brands reduce the perceived risk of making a costly mistake. Colleagues and advisors are less likely to criticize, and researchers are less likely to return empty handed from a research trip to a brand name library.

3.   Brands provide certain psychological rewards to the consumer such as prestige or status. Researchers can brag about spending a sabbatical at a prestigious, name-brand library. Compare this prestige and stature to the reaction of professional colleagues if a sabbatical were spent surfing the Web in search of scholarly materials. (Wolpert (1999)

Few libraries neglect the importance of quality when deciding on their collection, but often neglect the quality of the equipment, the service and support. The image of the library, as a trademark, is also strong factor. The positive attitude towards libraries depends on the personal contact that is based on simple communicative techniques and creates positive thoughts. Such techniques are the trademarks, the emblems and the slogans, related to the services. Under this philosophy IFLA and ALA created the slogan "@ your library", declared it as a trademark and proposed a wide range of activities to the libraries all over the world. In every case, librarians are responsible for the relations between the library and its users; they have to have it in mind especially in the cases of changes.

Potential users and brand name

Is the brand name adequate to concentrate users, stakeholders and associates? It depends on the library staff attitude on branding:

*   27% of public libraries refers that their staff understand the real meaning of a brand name,
*   42% has not recorded the opinion of public on their image.

The policy and strategy of the libraries to attract new members or groups is obvious to the question if they target to the population categories:

*   56% of the libraries answered that they don't rank the attractiveness of the library to different target groups, while,
*   17% of the libraries chooses the most populous target groups to cooperate.

What is the reason of non-participating in the library's events? The percentage of the choices is referred to the next figure:

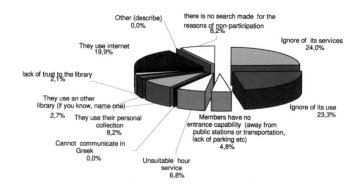

What are the most common reasons people argue that they don't use the public library?

- 19% ignorance of its services,
- 26% ignorance of its usefulness,
- 19% they are served by the Internet,
- 11% they use their personal collections,
- 7% inadequate schedules,
- 5% inability of access,
- 4% use another library,
- Unable to contact the library.

Only a percentage of 4% of the people declare a positive attitude towards libraries, in general, as they use another library. All other answers indicate the unfamiliarity of the public about the library, namely indicate the introversion of libraries. The factors that prevent library to address new members/ target groups are ranked as follows:

The attitude of the staff and administration in the regular partnerships and alliances	289
Training and skills of the personnel	279
The decisions of the administration of the organization	277
Organizational and staff working culture	271
The priorities of the library's administration	259
Library's opening hours	231
Sufficient number of staff	208
Space	205
Budget adequacy	193
Infrastructures	188

The reality is somewhere in the middle: Libraries stated that they open to innovative procedures. In the question if libraries accept new ideas about services and strategic alliances to attract new users, they answered as follows:

- 52% they do not have determined process for new ideas,
- 16% they do not make systematic research for new determined process for new ideas among users, public institutions etc,
- 26% they recognize the necessity of the procedure,
- 52% they would evaluate by any chance proposals of public institutions collaborations,
- 22% they have negative attitude in the strategic collaborations, and
- 26% they have applied strategic alliances for approaching new target groups.

In this case, what are the factors affecting the library to fail attracting new members? The lack of a single strategy (e.g. cooperation of educational and library community) about the importance of libraries in the educational process (especially in a small community) leads to the ignorance of their usefulness, especially to students who are then the potentially permanent users.

Similarly, the use of the Internet, gives the opportunity to the citizens to be served from their homes or elsewhere (e.g. Internet cafe).

The picture is also confirmed by the recording of their services, as circle of life product:

- This questions record how the Greek public libraries perceive themselves, their roles and their place in the society.
- From the answers result that their any modernisation keeps pace with the development of technology, but it is limited to its use.
- The goal of technology transfer is the innovative processes and the organisational changes.
- Otherwise, it does not turn out efficient and effective and does not develop the available resources, human and economic, at the most excellent way.

Conclusions

What are the elements of libraries self-knowledge and self-estimation is low and needs serious efforts for improvement. It is a positive issue that when libraries critique their behaviour and choices don't use alibis for their weaknesses. The image that libraries present is that they are good organised and well informed units and wait for their readers.

These days, however, the socio-economic conditions and problems of people require a different approach and policy. The Brand name of services in the public libraries brings awareness and loyalty. Branding is an opportunity to reexamine a service or a procedure, involves staff as creative and innovative and gives a portion of "Excellency" to the library users. The key of the library decision is to come out from its space in order to seek the target groups and their special problems to be solved.

Finally, the extroversion of the library will be:

- the confrontation of social exclusion,
- the financial and the cultural growth of regions and districts.

In this entire context, Branding is both a goal and a way of thinking and working.

Bibliography

Storey, Tom (2006): How legacy brands are reenergized, and what libraries can learn from them. Next Space. The OCLC Newsletter, 1. Available at http://www.oclc.org/nextspace/001/1.htm. Last visit: 30.3.2011.

Wolpert, Ann (1999): Commercial Brand *Management. Proceedings of 20th IATUL Conference,* Chania, 17-21 May 1999. Available at: http://www.iatul.org/conferences/pastconferences/1999proceedings.asp. Last visit: 30.3.2011.

Chapter 1: Assessing and Evaluating Reference: Views from the Academic Library Reference Desk

View from a Virtual Reference Desk

Lynne Rudasill

University of Illinois at Urbana, Champaign, USA

Abstract: A number of articles have been published in recent years relating to the field or embedded librarian. In addition to this changing model of librarianship, many more librarians are working a virtual world with users approaching them through chat or IM reference sites and e-mail. What are the other ways in which reference is provided in the virtual world, and more importantly, how do we assess these avenues? This paper will discuss the variety of tools that are available to the embedded librarian who works without a physical library and will also explore efficient and effective ways to assess of virtual reference that are both quantitative and qualitative.

Keywords: Reference, virtual, digital, assessment, new models, field librarian, embedded librarian

1. Introduction

The myriad ways in which libraries and librarianship have changed in the last ten to fifteen years almost defies description. Card catalogs to metadata, quiet study to texting call numbers, physical reference desks prominently placed at entrances to virtual reference available through chat, IM, SKYPE, and QuestionPoint software, the changing technology seems to be making the reference librarian's job more physically remote from the user, while at the same time creating new relationships. Larger academic libraries, where subject specialists have been more commonly found, are now moving in some cases to the model of embedded librarianship.

The Special Libraries Association commissioned a study of embedded librarianship that showed, by the authors' definition, the number of field or embedded librarians is growing. The research also discovered that the trend is not entirely new, with many indicating they had enjoyed this status for a decade or more. (Shumaker and Tally, 2010) Viewed in combination with the technology that allows the embedded librarian to "be" in several places at once, a new model is clearly emerging. But, is a new model of *assessing* reference activities emerging and, if so, what does this assessment look like?

2. Counting the hits

In 2004 the Center for Global Studies and the University Library at the University of Illinois at Urbana-Champaign created the post of Global Studies Librarian. This individual was to create a collection and suite of services in a digital environment as a

New Trends in Qualitative and Quantitative Methods in Libraries
A. Katsirikou and C. H. Skiadas (eds)
© *World Scientific Publishing Co (pp. 43-48)*

librarian embedded in the research center. There would be no physical collection of materials at the Center. Instead, resources would be distributed either among the other library units with physical collections or deposited in the central storage area known as Main Stacks.

Beyond collection responsibilities, this post came with innovative and interesting service responsibilities. The individual was hired to provide reference and research support while embedded in the Center, and also support the outreach mission of the Center. The question always at the heart of the research being done is "How can over 6 billion human beings learn to live with each other?" The research staff worked initially to identify "Clusters of Excellence" on the campus that would qualify for additional financial and curricular support from the Center. The areas would support research into the primary question in a significant way. Those identified included Global Studies Education; Language and Culture; Sustainable Development; International Security; Social and Policy Sciences; and Information, Communications, and the Media. There are almost three hundred faculty members affiliated with the Center, but most, if not all, belong to departments already served by subject specialists in the University Library. The Center was a research unit, not a teaching unit at the outset and remains so today.

The library unit attempts to answer traditional reference questions via email, chat/IM, and telephone. Individual consultations are also provided, and the librarian observes regular office hours for walk-in students. The unit also works cooperatively with the Slavic Reference Service in the Main Library to support a program called GIVES (Global Interlending Verification Enquiry Service) that can assist scholars from around the world to verify citations and locate materials in Slavic, Eurasian, East European, Turkish, and Persian languages. The reference service of the unit exists in a digital world. How does one provide meaningful data regarding the work of reference in such a unit?

Initially, of course, traditional hard numbers were looked at to determine the amount of reference events. Since there is no real physical reference desk, statistics from the DeskTracker program showed few events, but more complexity. However, assuming that users come to a digital library from a digital world, it has been argued that entry to the site also be considered as a basis for quantitative assessment. The University Library has a tool to track weblog statistics that requires the user to specify several parameters – time period and specific URL – and provides a report on the base number of hits for each page. At a minimum, this might equate to keeping track of the number of print resource guides distributed during a given time period if one looks only at the numbers generated by those pages.

The Center for Global Studies is set up to work with two log analysis programs. The legacy system used is AWStats which provides a little richer content as seen in Figure 1. below.

These statistics are little more robust showing us not just raw numbers, but also the types of search engines that were used to find us. The specific links related to the library can easily be accessed and the number of unique visitors, number of visits, number of pages crawled, number of page hits, and bandwidth required are all accessible for analysis.

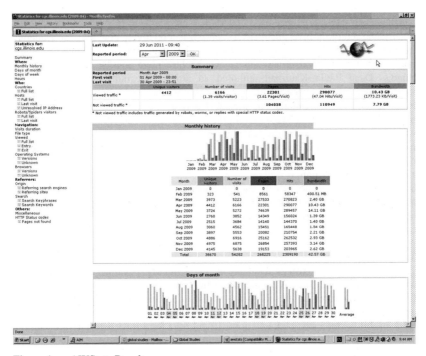

Figure 1. – AWStats Results

More recently the Center for Global Studies has also begun to use Google Analytics to track web use. This provides an even greater amount of information regarding web use, including bounce rates and time on site. Events from both tools were used to determine the number of times the virtual user "entered" the library. This also provide some challenges. The Global Studies Library stands in two worlds with a more traditional library portal from the Library site and the virtual new books shelf and other resources sitting on the Center for Global Studies website. A combination of statistics from both of these sources is necessary to fully round out the usage of the web site.

However, the number of hits on the webpage and the numbers of recorded reference events do not paint an entirely accurate picture of the reference that is provided. Just as a user simply looking at the reference desk as he or she passes by does not count as a reference event, passing through a web page does not either. Reference events might be more closely related to clickthroughs on web pages, highlighting user behavior, and perhaps giving the librarian a better idea of what is being used. Perhaps, too, time on task within each page might provide a closer quantitative evaluation of the use of any given website. Mat-Hassen and Levin explore the relationship of clickthroughs and user behavior and their work may provide a baseline for understanding how log analysis can really be used to focus on searching behavior.(2005) Perhaps at some point this could also be applied to "finding" behavior. Combining log statistics from the library page with numbers on indexing and abstracting databases, as well as journal use statistics, may also provide a way in which we can assess reference use in the digital environment.

Finally, the return on investment (ROI) concept is a relatively new idea for academic libraries. Perhaps because of the business models that have been adopted by some universities, this method of assessment may become more popular in the future. At Illinois, Dean Paula Kaufman authored an article that indicated the return on investment for the University Library as a whole was $4.38 for every dollar invested in the Library. If the calculations pertained only to the expenditures on collections, the total came closer to a $12.00 return on investment for each dollar spent. Figures were largely based upon the amount of grant monies that were received by investigators using citations in their grant applications. Kaufman (2008) The general numbers involved in a study of this sort might be teased down a level to the ROI for an embedded library unit as well.

Simple arithmetic cannot tell us enough about how pages are being used, and raw numbers do not represent either person-to-person reference in the traditional library or library to user reference in the virtual library. Sometimes, numbers simply are not enough.

3. Beyond quantity

The majority of the writings available in the scholarly literature regarding library website quality tend to refer to the interaction between the user and the site itself. Less has been written about the quality of the information that is available. A good deal of relevant material relates to those aspects of a page that appeal to the user. Basic usability studies let us know how difficult it is for our users to interact with the tools we develop in the digital environment. Other studies have revealed specific values users have articulated for reliable, useful websites, with most of these studies originating in the world of commerce. (Kastania and Zimeras, 2010; Bressales and Nantel, 2008; and McCarthy, Riegelsberger and Sasse, 2005)

SERVQUAL, WEBQUAL, and LIBQUAL are all instruments developed in the non-digital world to measure service quality. (Furneaux, 2006; Loiacono, Watson and Goodhue, 2007; ARL, 2010) The last in the list is familiar to many in the U.S. library world and elsewhere, having been developed by the Association of Research Libraries with assistance from Texas A & M University. The attempt has been made to apply the concepts underlying these assessment tools to the electronic world as well. The E-S-QUAL scale provides an assessment tool for measuring electronic service quality by looking at concepts such as efficiency, system availability, fulfillment, and privacy. The E-RecS-Qual assessment includes factors such as responsiveness, compensation, and contact. (Parasuramam, et al., 2005) Hernon and Calvert have explored "Library e-SERVQUAL" as a means to assess and improve service activities. (2005) These instruments provide lists of variables for the user to rank and/or rate. The results of these rankings can be used for benchmarking to see where improvements need to be made in the way the user is interacting with the website or the information that is presented on the site. All of these instruments can be helpful to the digital, embedded librarian given enough time and resources.

As important as human-computer interactions are in delivering services, they do not tell the whole story. In the area specific to reference interactions, many people are using instruments that provide an idea of the degree of satisfaction in reference service delivery. The Wisconsin Ohio Reference Evaluation Program (WOREP) is one of the more recently developed tools to determine effectiveness of reference interactions. (Kent State Univ., 2009) In this instrument both the patron and the staff member are asked a set of questions after the completion of a reference transaction.

The results are meant to provide a way to benchmark this service and help improve interactions. At this time, the test instrument is print based, but no doubt an electronic version of the test, or a variant thereof will be produced. This would greatly facilitate the delivery of the questionnaire for the digital reference desk.

Another, perhaps less elegant but useful tool for assessing reference transactions is the Reference Effort Assessment Data (READ) scale. This requires the person providing reference to indicate the depth of a particular reference question or event on a six-point scale. The scale "places an emphasis on recording the skills, knowledge, techniques, and tools used by the librarian during a reference transaction." (Gerlich and Berard, 2010) The instrument is helpful in determining differences between various reference desks in the library as well.

The previously mentioned study supported by the Special Libraries Association identified several indicators of success for embedded librarians whether they were strictly virtual or not. These indicators include growth in the number of embedded librarians working in a given "customer group," an increased demand for these services from the group, and the development and delivery of new services to the group over time. Various other aspects were seen as important to the success of the embedded librarian in the including marketing. It was also mentioned that the most successful embedded librarians could prove a return on investment in their services. (Shumaker and Tully, 2009)

4. Conclusion

Ultimately, the changing delivery systems for reference service will have a telling effect on the types of assessment that are done. It is necessary for many of us to combine possible approaches to this assessment.

For the GIVES project, we are proposing several means of measurement of service delivery. The staff of the project recently began embedding links to the pages of Wikipedia and WorldCat in relevant areas in order to lead scholars from all over the world to their resources. They will continue to keep the reference statistics that are required by the Department of State since most of their funding comes as a grant from this federal agency of the United States. These statistics require notation of how the question was received (chat, email, etc,) as well as the time it took to answer the query, and some indication of the resources that were necessary to answer the question. Implementing the Google analytics software will provide more of a feel for how individuals who do not directly contact the unit might behave in the online environment. In addition, we feel it is very important to get textual feedback on the project. This might include something akin to the WOREP survey, or at the very least, a "contact us" page that is prominently displayed to provide synchronous reference assistance if desired. It would be very interesting as well to discover if individuals are coming back to our site and, if so, what kinds of questions are bringing them back. Finally, we would like to run a longitudinal study that compares the number of hits on the site with time spent on each page and the number of reference events that occur to discover if there are any correlations there.

By comparison, the assessment of reference service by the actual Global Studies Library needs to be greatly improved, using many of the same tools and techniques that have been implemented by GIVES. The audience for the Global Studies Portal also goes beyond our campus. The nature of the grant that supports the Center for Global Studies is somewhat different. As part of the Title VI Department of Education network, in addition to an emphasis on research over teaching, it is extremely important for resources to be provided to the K-12 (primary, elementary and secondary) school systems in the United States. Marketing these tools is every bit as important as providing them to users.

In any case, it is necessary to articulate a framework for the virtual library that allows assessment at many levels. Perhaps the guidelines promulgated by IFLA or the RUSA division of the American Library Association can provide a starting place. Or perhaps it is time to start over and develop new methodologies to explore the results of reference activity both in-person and virtual, synchronous and asynchronous, dynamic and static. Our users certainly explore a number of ways to get answers for their questions, and they no longer need to walk up to the traditional reference desk to find information, for better or worse. We need fresh, inventive ideas to move assessment into a shared future with reference.

References

Association of Research Libraries. 2010. LIBQUAL+ Charting Library Service Quality. Available from http://www.libqual.org/home (accessed 3/31/3010).

Bressolles, G., and J. Nantel. 2008. The Measurement of Electronic Service Quality: Improvements and Application. *International Journal of e-Business Research* 4, (3): 1 - 19.

Furneaux, Brent. (2006) Theories Used in IS Research – SERVQUAL, Appalachian State University. Available from http://www.istheory.yorku.ca/SERVQUAL.htm (accessed 3/31/2010).

Gerlich, Bella Karr, and G. Lynn Berard. 2007. Introducing the READ Scale: Qualitative Statistics for Academic Reference Services. *Georgia Library Quarterly* 43, (4) (Winter): 7 - 13.

Kastania, Anastasia N. and Stelios Zimeras. 2010. Evaluation for Web-Based Applications. In *Annals of Information Systems, Web-Based Applications in Healthcare and Biomedicine,* ed. A. Lazakidou. Springer Science+Business Media. 157 - 166.

Kaufman, Paula T. 2008. The Library as Strategic Investment: Results of the Illinois Return on Investment Study. *Liber Quarterly* 18, (3/4): 424 - 436.

Kent State University. 2009. WOREP - Wisconsin Ohio Reference Evaluation Program. Available from https://worep.library.kent.edu/index.php?page=home (accessed 3/31/2010).

Loiacono, E. T., R. T. Watson, and D. L. Goodhue. 2007. WebQual: An Instrument for Consumer Evaluation of Web Sites. *International Journal of Electronic Commerce* 11, (3): 51 - 87.

Mat-Hassan, Mazlita, and Mark Levene. 2005. Associating Search and Navigation Behavior through Log Analysis. *Journal of the American Society for Information Science and Technology* 56, (9) (Jul): 913 - 934.

McCarthy, John D., Jens Riegelsberger, and M. Angela Sasse. 2005. The Mechanics of Trust: A Framework for Research and Design. *International Journal of Human-Computer Studies* 62, (3) (Mar): 381 - 422.

Parasuraman, A., V. A. Zeithaml, and A. Malhotra. 2005. E-S-QUAL a Multiple-Item Scale for Assessing Electronic Service Quality. *Journal of Service Research* 7, (3): 213 - 33.

Shumaker, D., & Talley, M. (2010). Models of Embedded Librarian: A Research Summary. *Information Outlook, 14*(1), 26-35.

Using Data to Make Quick Decisions about a New Merged Service Desk: A Case Study

Elizabeth Cooper

Reference Services Team Leader, Robert W. Woodruff Library, Emory University, Atlanta, Georgia, USA

Abstract: The Robert W. Woodruff Library at Emory University is working on a project to merge its reference, circulation and technology help desks into one service point. The timeframe to implement this project is very short. Therefore, reference staff, working with circulation staff, have developed quick methods to analyze existing data and quickly gather new data to help inform decision-making about staffing levels, training, and a location for the new service point. This paper is a case study detailing some of the methods and processes used by staff to make decisions.
Keywords: Simulations, reference desk, merged service desk, data collection, Wordle, service desk location

1. Introduction

Emory University, located in Atlanta, Georgia, is a private research university known for its liberal arts college, professional schools and healthcare system. It ranks among the top 20 national universities in U.S. News & World Report's *America's Best Colleges* and serves a population of 12,256 students (6,927 undergraduates; 3,949 graduate students; 1,650 professional school students). The Robert W. Woodruff Library is the largest of the university's nine libraries and is the primary library supporting undergraduates and graduate students in the arts and sciences. Its collections include approximately 2.5 million volumes.

The administration of the Robert W. Woodruff Library recently determined it would be more cost effective and more convenient for patrons to combine its circulation, reference and technology help desks into one service point on the main entrance level of the library building. This decision, following a reduction in force in fall 2009 and a sustained period of unfilled vacancies in the Services Division (which includes circulation and reference), also attempted to mitigate the staffing shortages each department was facing. Additionally, Library staff have long wanted to move the circulation desk from its level 3 location (which often confused users) to a more intuitive location on the main entrance level. The reference and technology help desk, located on the main entrance level (level 2) of the library building, is often heavily burdened by directional questions and is open fewer hours than the circulation desk. We hoped that a combined service desk would be less confusing to patrons and provide better and longer service on the main entrance level.

Once the decision was made in fall 2009 to merge service points, staff had to work quickly to develop an implementation plan for a merged service desk that would be

New Trends in Qualitative and Quantitative Methods in Libraries
A. Katsirikou and C. H. Skiadas (eds)
© *World Scientific Publishing Co (pp. 49-54)*

operational in summer 2010. Some of the questions that immediately arose included: how similar are the types of questions received at each service desk? How valuable is walk-up reference service? Do we really need professional librarians at the reference desk? And, where should this new service point be located? As we did not have time to gather much new data, we began by looking at data we had already collected and thinking about how we could use it to inform our decision-making about our new service point.

2. What data did we already have? What could this existing data tell us?
When we examined our existing data we realized that we had more than we initially thought. However, much of it had never been analyzed in a comprehensive way -- it had been used to drive daily decision-making (hours, staffing patterns, etc.) but had been waiting for someone to have time to spend manipulating and analyzing it. The data we had included:
- reference desk transaction statistics for multiple years
- text of all questions asked at the reference desk fall 2008
- text of all questions asked at the circulation and reference desks for three weeks in 2007
- reference desk comment cards fall 2009
- Library survey questions about reference service 2008
- comments from faculty focus group spring 2010

How similar are the types of questions asked at the service desks?
We hoped this existing data could help us learn about the types of questions asked at each service desk. We had always intended to code the list all of the reference questions collected in fall 2008 and put them through qualitative analysis software to get a better understanding of the types of questions asked at the desk and the frequencies with which they were asked. However, when it was time to merge the service desks, we had still not done the analysis and did not have access to qualitative data software. After thinking about the data (3000 recorded questions), the limitations on time and technology, and the questions we hoped the data could help us answer, we determined that it might be useful to put all of the questions into Wordle (http://www.wordle.net/). We hoped that Wordle, a free online tool that creates word clouds that give greater prominence to words that appear more frequently in a text, might foreground some patterns in our questions.

To use Wordle, we first extracted all of the directional questions and then all the reference/consultation questions from a spreadsheet of fall 2008 reference desk transaction data. We put each, as a separate group, into MS Word text files that we then put into Wordle. After our first try with Wordle we realized we would need to spend a bit of time cleaning up the data -- at a minimum, standardizing spellings and capitalizations, linking multi-word phrases, and removing words such as "library" from the texts, to make the Wordle diagrams generated more useful. Cleaning up 3000+ questions took a couple of hours, but generated diagrams that when we compared them, helped us to see several things, including:
- there was not as much difference as we expected between the directional questions Wordle and the reference/consultation questions Wordle;
- answering questions about/related to books was the primary focus of both reference and directional questions.

The lack of difference between the directional and reference/consultation Wordles made us go back and scan through the questions looking for why this might be.

Examining these questions we realized that we had a problem in the way reference librarians defined directional versus reference/consultation questions. We noticed that there were types of questions, especially related to finding books and call numbers, that different librarians had categorized differently. This meant that data we had used in the past, of the number of directional questions versus the number of reference/consultation questions, was inaccurate because of categorization errors by librarians. We had believed that one-third of our questions were directional and two-thirds were reference/consultation, however, with the new information provided by our Wordle analysis, we were able to quickly re-examine the questions and realize that approximately half our questions were directional and half were reference/consultations. This new information brought to light that the reference desk and circulation desk had more similarities in question type (i.e. both had high levels of directional questions) than we originally thought. This was useful in helping us develop a training program as well as demonstrate to staff that there would not be as many changes at the combined service desk as some feared as we shared much work in common.

The Wordles also demonstrated that for both directional questions and reference questions the most common word in all our questions was "book". Although we had always known questions related to identifying and locating books were common, we had not realized this was the primary reason people stopped for help at the reference desk. This knowledge was very useful to help us develop our training program for the new service desk. As an aside, this information was also useful to demonstrate to library administration that though e-resources are growing in use, books are still a key resource for researchers. It also reinforced our belief that our tools for finding and locating books are not intuitive to users.

When we compared the information we gleaned from our Wordles with the data we had gathered from our three week project in 2007 to compare reference and circulation questions, we discovered that the 2007 data confirmed our Wordle findings. Like the Wordles, which dealt with reference desk transactions, the 2007 data showed very high levels of directional questions at the circulation desk, similarities between questions asked at the reference and circulation desks related to basic research, and a focus on the book at both desks (even more so at Circulation, which was expected).

Similarly, our reference desk statistics also corroborated our findings. These statistics showed, for example, that 73% of what were coded as reference/consultation questions took under 5 minutes to answer. Therefore the majority of our reference/consultation questions were not in-depth questions (and many of these may actually have been miscoded directional questions – as our Wordles had shown).

Examined together, this data quickly helped to create a picture of the types of questions asked at both the reference and circulation desks. It helped us to see that we had more similarities than differences in the types of questions asked and that the majority of questions asked at our desks were quick or directional. It also led us to believe that with good training and a good referral system, we could staff the new desk with a variety of staff and not just professional librarians.

How valuable is walk-up reference service? Do we need professional librarians at the reference desk?

The Woodruff Library at Emory currently offers both walk-up reference service as well as appointment-based consultations. Recognizing the trend in libraries of decreasing reference desk activity, library administrators have been questioning whether the library needs to offer walk-up reference service, especially provided by professional librarians, or whether it could move to a system of referrals and appointment-only research consultation services.

Our annual library survey data has shown that walk-up reference service is valued. For example, according to our 2009 library survey, 84% of respondents believed the reference desk to be either "important/essential" or "somewhat important" and were "very satisfied" or "somewhat satisfied" with the service.   Additionally, comment cards that were distributed in fall 2009 to patrons who had completed a reference transaction at the reference desk showed that patrons were exceedingly satisfied with the service (100% ranked their satisfaction, on a 5 point scale, as "very high" or "high") and 94% marked that they had learned something new they could apply in their future research. Additionally, in spring 2010 the library conducted faculty focus groups. The focus groups were directed at issues relating to faculty research and collaboration, and in these discussions faculty frequently mentioned the constraints they have on their time and their reliance on the library to help them save time. Faculty stated that the librarians at the reference desk were an essential resource they relied upon on to help save them time by teaching their students essential research skills.

Additionally, when we analyzed our reference desk statistics we found that the largest category of reference users was undergraduates (63%) and the next largest category of users was visitors (17%).   Therefore 80% of our users were undergraduates and visitors – groups that are often new to research and to our facility and are more likely to need walk-up on demand service.

Together, these pieces of data -- the library survey, reference desk comment cards, faculty focus group comments, and user data -- present a picture of a need for and support for walk-up reference desk services.

3. What new data could we gather quickly?
Where should the new service desk be located?
One of the first questions to arise around the new service desk was where it should be located. Although everyone agreed the desk should be on the main entrance level of the building, there were many potential locations on that floor. The reference desk's existing location on the main entrance level did not have adequate space to accommodate adding the circulation department.   So in fall 2009, a team of stakeholders and facilities planners decided to test a new location as soon as possible. After many discussions, in January 2010 we decided to reconfigure and move the existing reference desk to a potential location for the merged service point (which we hoped to have in place by August 2010). This first test location did not work -- sight lines were bad for staff and patrons could not easily see the desk in its new location. Reference staff recorded all issues with the new location and shared this data with facilities planners. We knew we needed a different location and time was running out: we did not have the time or money to move the existing reference desk again to test a new location. We needed to be sure that wherever we established the new merged service desk that the location would work. As many of us had recently attended a workshop on measuring and analyzing process performance – learning to simulate processes and measure them before making changes – we decided it might be helpful to apply what we had learned to solve this problem.

We began by forming a group of key staff from reference and circulation to organize simulations to test six potential desk locations. We envisioned setting up a mock desk and having staff/students pretend to be patrons as well as desk staff and then solicit feedback on how each location worked as a service point, paying particular attention to problems that had been identified in our first test location.   In planning the simulations, we first ordered cheap tables from Ikea that we could easily move around to stand-in for our new merged service desk (we did not own any moveable counter height tables we could use for the test and planned to use these later for other purposes in the Library). Then, we determined what we wanted to test in each location, made lists of the types of questions most frequently asked at each service point, and determined the various tools and equipment we would need at the service desk and found stand-ins for those items. We scheduled the simulations, recruited students and staff to participate, created scripts and feedback forms for participants, organized videotaping/photographing of the simulations, and informed library staff of our plans. Although we had six potential locations, we did not feel that we had the time to test each of these locations in a full simulation, so a core group of reference and circulation staff did a quick test of each location. In these pre-simulations, we had staff approach the desk and act as patrons as well as stand behind the desk, acting as staff, and we recorded and compiled participants' comments. These pre-simulations helped us to quickly determine that four of the locations would not work well. For example, there had been energy around locating the desk in the middle of the entrance walkway, and we had looked at several architectural drawings related to this location, but once we tested it, we realized immediately that there was not enough room to establish a service desk in this location. In fact, we realized that if we had done these tests earlier the previous semester we could have removed several locations from our discussions before we wasted time and energy on them.

Our pre-simulations helped us choose three locations to test in full simulations. These full simulations took approximately 30 minutes each, plus approximately 10-15 minutes of set up time, and approximately 30+ minutes of debriefing (in which participants filled out feedback forms and had brief discussions about what they liked/did not like about each location). During the simulations, our "patrons", approximately five students we recruited to participate, were each given a list of tasks/questions to do/ask at the service desk. We decided to use undergraduate students as our test "patrons" as they are the primary customers at our service desks and we wanted to know their thoughts about the various locations. The compiled feedback we collected from students and staff was invaluable and helped us to make a decision about where to locate the desk.

4. Conclusions

The data about the types of questions asked at the service desks that we had from our statistics and Wordle analyses, balanced against the data that we had about the value of walk-up reference desk research service (especially as staffed by professional librarians) from surveys and focus groups, led to important, fact-based discussions about staffing levels and training for our new merged service desk. Theses discussions ultimately led to more effective decision-making and hopefully better service for our patrons. Although none of this data was originally gathered to answer specific questions related to a merged service desk, the fact that we had consistently been gathering data on satisfaction, use, and importance of reference desk services, via several methods of data collection, was extremely useful to us when it was time to make decisions about the new service desk.

The simulations we conducted to help us choose a desk location were also extremely useful and successful. First, they were quick. With a few days worth of work, we were able to gather information and make decisions that the previous semester had taken us many hours of meetings and had still ended in unsuccessful decision-making. The simulations helped us to see, experience and learn things about each location that were impossible to learn any other way. At the end of the simulations we had a very good understanding of the pros and cons of each location. Additionally, the simulations allowed us to include many people in the information-gathering and decision-making process. Students and staff were invited to participate and/or observe (and we had video of the event for anyone who was unable to attend) and their feedback was invaluable. It was also very useful to have staff see for themselves why one location worked better than another. Many people approached the simulations with an idea of what they thought the best location might be, and allowing them to participate in the simulations helped to build consensus and buy-in around the location that was ultimately selected. Staff could see in real-time how or why their originally favored location may or may not work as compared to other locations. In addition, we believe that the compiled comments and feedback collected from the simulations will be useful as we continue to make decisions related to the new service desk.

Moving Out from Behind the Desk and into the Flow:
Assessing the Impact of Research Support Activities

JoAnn Jacoby

University of Illinois Library, Coordinator, New Service Model Programs, USA

Abstract: In recent years, the University of Illinois Library has developed a range of service programs that provide research support that is closely integrated into scholarly practice. These initiatives include librarians that are embedded, physically and virtually, in campus departments and programs, as well as more broadly-focused efforts such as the Scholarly Commons (which will provide coordinated support for data services, digitization, and scholarly communications) and the development of mobile and digital library services. This paper considers how these new initiatives have complicated traditional definitions of reference and provided the opportunity to rethink how we assess the impact of library support for research, teaching and learning.
Keywords: Reference, research support services, assessment, new service models

1. Introduction

In Support for The Research Process: An Academic Library Manifesto (Bourg et al. 2009) call on academic & research libraries to reexamine their basic assumptions about libraries and their role in the academy. The group began with an assessment of challenges and opportunities in the current scholarly environment:

> ...enticing opportunities in digital research and scholarship are coupled with new challenges for the research community. Researchers are drowning in a deluge of raw data and published information and face a bewildering array of options for disseminating and sharing their work...budgets across higher education are shrinking [and] some in the academy are questioning the continued value of large academic libraries. At the same time, many academic libraries are providing vital and innovative services and resources in support of emerging forms of research, publishing, and information management. While some would argue that academic libraries are playing an increasingly important role in scholarly research, others fear that they are on the brink of extinction and must change radically to survive. It's time to rise above the debate, and take a fresh look at the role of academic libraries in supporting research.

Based on this assessment of the current scholarly environment, the *Manifesto* identifies specific actions for libraries to pursue in order to remain vital, including:

- Embed library content, services, and staff within researchers' regular workflows; integrating with services others provide on campus, at other universities, or by commercial entities.

New Trends in Qualitative and Quantitative Methods in Libraries
A. Katsirikou and C. H. Skiadas (eds)
© World Scientific Publishing Co (pp. 55-62)

- Embrace the role of expert information navigators and redefine reference as research consultation.

This paper reviews new service programs at the University of Illinois Library that provide research support embedded in scholarly practice. The paper concludes with some thoughts on implications these new approaches have for measuring and assessing the impact ofacademic libraries on research, teaching and learning.

2. Why rethink library service models?

The local situation at Illinois provides a window into the global issues shaping the evolution of academic and research libraries. As one of the largest publicly-funded research libraries in the United States, the University of Illinois Library has long been distinguished by the size of its collections. The Main Stacks at Illinois, with 6 million volumes in browsable, open shelves, has been a treasure trove for scholars for more than 100 years. The Main Stacks are supplemented by over 30 departmental libraries, many with their own extensive collections, some of which have cumulated with little or no weeding of supercedes to the nearby offsite storage facility.

But despite these riches, fewer and fewer people are going directly to the shelves, either in the Main Stacks or departmental libraries. Why have students and faculty coming in to the Library to do research as often as they used to? Quite simply, the game has changed. In the digital age, many scholarly works are available not just on the shelves of the great research libraries, but via any device with a network connections and a document reader. The way people access the research literature is changing (Figure 1).

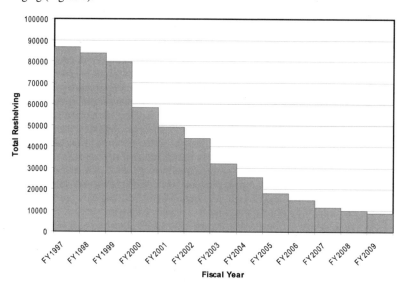

Figure 1: Biology Library reshelving statistics for all items, 1997-2009.

With a network connection and computer or smartphone, most of the resources the Library provides are available wherever students and faculty choose to work -- in a coffee shop, a lab, or an airport enroute to a conference. As the site for bibliographic research shifts from a centralized repository around which scholars gather to a more diffuse and integrated movable feast, more and more people opt not to come in to browse the shelves at Illinois. Even when they need print materials, they are increasingly more likely to do an online search and request books they need for delivery to their campus mailbox (a highly valued service at Illinois) or for pickup at the nearest campus library.

It's not just the sciences who have found new ways of working. A fall 2009 survey of faculty and students studying literature, linguistics, and related fields suggest that humanists are starting to develop new research habits. Almost 80% of respondents prefer to access the back issues of journals online. Open ended responses to a question about how digital texts have changed research, teaching and learning suggests that the affordances offered by online texts (searching across corpora, development of thesauri and concordances) are changing not just the way they work, but the questions they can ask (Figure 2).

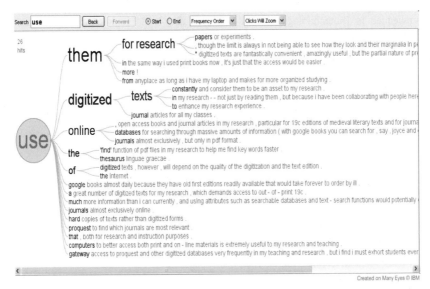

Figure 2: Responses from faculty and students in the humanities to the question: "Please describe how you might use digitized texts, or why they aren't relevant to your research and teaching." See http://www.library.illinois.edu/nsm/lit/planning_team/litsurvey.html for full survey results.

So to answer the original question, why should we rethink library services models? For many of the same reasons articulated in the *Academic Library Manifesto*. What made us great in the 20th century (vast print collections, located near scholars at the heart of campus or in departmental libraries) is not what is needed by 21st century scholars and students. It no longer makes sense to disperse collections across silos and devote staff to serving a model that scholars are finding less and less useful in supporting the ways they are doing research. Instead need to find ways to be relevant and engaged in the new scholarly environment, an environment where scholars don't necessarily have to come into the library to do research and are using of new tools (vast online corpora, geo-referenced data, multimedia, Web 2.0 technologies) to facilitate the creation and dissemination of scholarly knowledge.

3. Research support services at Illinois
The University of Illinois Library is moving from a model centered on departmental libraries to one that involves two main directions: 1) embedded librarians, and; 2) cross-cutting service programs that directly engage scholarlywork, how and where it happens in the current environment.

Example 1: Embedded Librarians
Some definitions of "embedded librarians" refer specifically to librarians involved in online course management software and/or virtual environments (Ramsay & Kinnie 2006). At Illinois, we use the term in its broader sense (as per Kesselman & Watstein 2009) to indicate a librarian who is highly integrated, physically and/or virtually, in the scholarly activities and intellectual life of targeted academic departments or programs (Figure 3). Illinois has a number of librarians embedded to varying degrees, so it is impossible to draw a hard and fast line, but some examples include librarians embedded in Biotechnology, Global Studies, Labor and Employee Relations, and Library and Information Science. In some cases these services evolved from a departmental library that is now closed (Laborand Emplee Realtions, Library and Information Science) while the other examples are new positions created in conversation with the programs served. Also on the continuum of embedded services are walk-up services in a few strategic locations outside the Library (e.g., the LGBT Center and Foreign Language Building) as well as a multi-faceted multicultural outreach program http://www.library.illinois.edu/ugl/diversity/outreach.html.

WAYS OF BEING EMBEDDED
- Librarian provides some office hours, consultations by appointment or other services in department
- Designated office space in department
- Joint appointment or partial funding from the department
- Attend faculty meetings/on faculty listserv
- Serve on committees or advisory/governing boards
- Attend lectures, roundtables, brownbags, etc.
- Guest lecture in classes or teach credit courses
- Socially embedded (Facebook, parties, social activities)
- Robust virtual services and web portals, integrated into online courses
- Involved in collaborative projects, research teams, grants
- Focus effort toward outcomes aligned with goals of the department

Figure 3: Some characteristics of embedded librarian services

The librarians who have transitioned from providing services in a departmental library to an embedded model report that an increasing proportion of the reference questions coming to them are longer and more in-depth and that they are having more frequent interactions with faculty. The proportion of reference questions coming from faculty growing and a higher proportion of their reference questions take form of extended research consultations that continue throughout the year. Embedded librarians report that a new sort of relationship is fostered by virtue of their being in (and of) the department. These relationships are both intentional and informal. They are intentional because the embedded librarian is focused on being engaged in a meaningful way in research, teaching and learning activities, The relationships are informal because the very fact of being present, physically or virtually, increases the opportunities for casual interactions. The significance of these informal interactions should not be underestimated, as these sort of hallway encounters can be the building blocks of strong professional relationships.

The range of interactions with students and faculty as not adequately captured by the existing form used to track reference transactions across the Library. To fill the gap, the Library and Information Science Librarian (Sue Searing) created a homegrown form to track these "non-reference" interactions. With input from the other embedded librarians and the Library Assessment Working Group, this form was refined and made available through DeskTracker, the software used to record reference activity library-wide (Figure 4). This form helps to foreground the importance of many activities that are an integral part of the traditional role of subject or departmental librarians and can be used by any liaison librarian, not just those who are officially

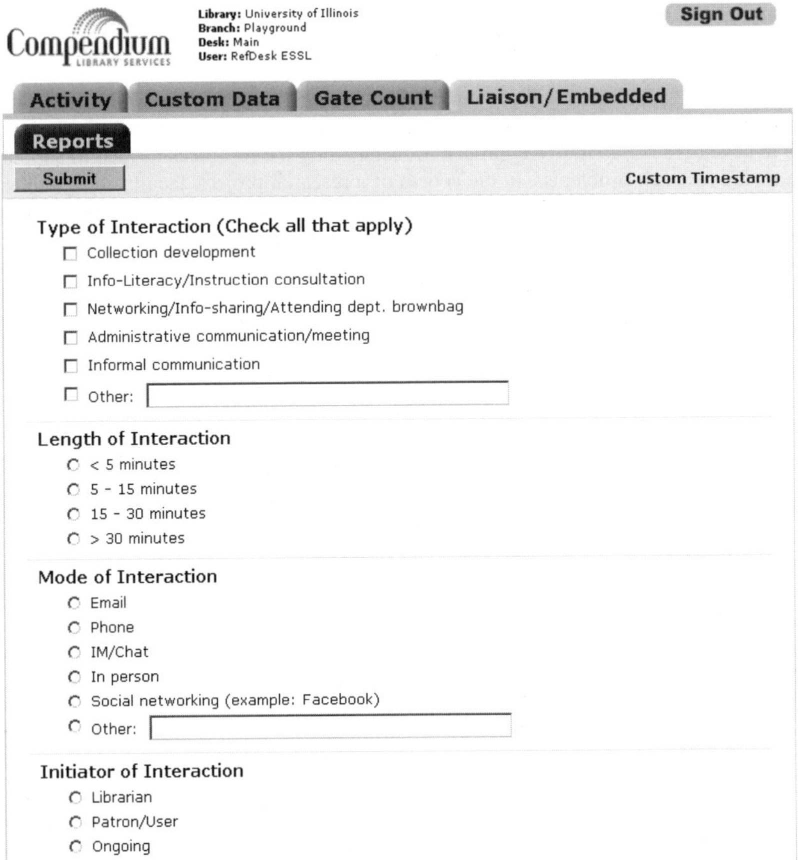

Figure 4: Form for tracking non-reference interactions

"embedded." The emphasis is on interactions that may have an impact on research, teaching or learning and those casual encounters that build relationships (i.e. "informal communication," "networking/info-sharing"). That said, the data gathered also provide an indication of the level of activity, over time and in different locations.

Example 2: Scholarly Commons

Embedded librarians provide services that are finely tuned to the needs of a particular department or programmatic area. As a complement to this approach, the University of Illinois Library is also developing new research support services that cut across—and hopefully, create connections between—pockets of domain and technical expertise inside the Library and elsewhere on campus. These include development of mobile library services and other digital library services focused on user-centered search and discovery tools. This paper focus on just one example of these cross-cutting services, the Scholarly Commons, which will open at this fall. Collaborating with partners inside and outside the library, the Scholarly Commons will provide expert, interdisciplinary research support services and open workshops for faculty and grad students to develop skills in: digital content creation and manipulation, e-learning and teaching, working with digital repositories, curation of research data, understanding copyright issues and author rights, working with geospatial and numeric data.

The Scholarly Commons will provide a technology rich environment with specialized software and tools in the areas of focus listed above, but more fundamentally the goal is to develop a collaborative approach to marshalling the resources needed to support complex research problems. In the course of a research project, faculty and graduate students may grapple with discovering and getting access to hard-to-find publications or data, analyzing the sources found statistically, visually or spatially, or through text-analysis, disseminating the results in the most appropriate formats (as a peer-reviewed publication, a podcast or a dynamic web page) and ensuring that the final products are stewarded in such a way that they continue to be available to scholars of the future.

Currently, we hear from faculty that the onus is on them to discover who in our large university has the technology or domain expertise needed, but a more coordinated approach would allow faculty and graduate students to work more productively and not divert energy to figuring out how to do something or where the resources needed are located. The Scholarly Commons seek to address this need so that a researcher can come in with a project or a problem and a team of content and services specialists, information technologists and tools, will assemble around their research support needs. The team's role will be to collaborate with the researcher to find ways to address their unique challenges related to discovering, analyzing and sharing information. The team will draw on the partners participating in the Scholarly Commons which includes librarians with domain and technology expertise, as well as partners from other information technology support center on campus. These partners, in turn, may draw on a broader network of colleagues and contacts.

The example I like to use to explain the power of assembling a consultation team around a particular research project is the seemingly counterintuitive relationship between health care costs and outcomes described by Atul Gawande (2009). He found that some of the worst healthcare outcomes were in hospitals with the highest costs, while some of the most effective providers (such as Mayo Clinic) had some of the lowest costs. How do they do it? By focusing on outcomes and putting the needs of the patient first. This often involves things that may seem expensive, at first glance, in terms of staff time or money. Gawande describes his impressions of the Mayo system formed during as brief stay as a visiting surgeon:

Among the things that stand out from that visit was how much time the doctors spent with patients. There was no churn—no shuttling patients in and out of rooms while the doctor bounces from one to the other. I accompanied a colleague while he saw patients. Most of the patients, like those in my clinic, required about twenty minutes. But one patient had colon cancer and a number of other complex issues, including heart disease. The physician spent an hour with her, sorting things out. He phoned a cardiologist with a question.

"I'll be there," the cardiologist said.

Fifteen minutes later, he was. They mulled over everything together. The cardiologist adjusted a medication, and said that no further testing was needed. He cleared the patient for surgery, and the operating room gave her a slot the next day.

The whole interaction was astonishing to me. Just having the cardiologist pop down to see the patient with the surgeon would be unimaginable at my hospital. The time required wouldn't pay. The time required just to organize the system wouldn't pay.

Although the idea of pulling together experts on the spot seems costly, cumbersome, and inefficient, the data suggest otherwise. In the long run, bringing together a few good minds costs less than running a series of expensive tests and sending the patient from silo to silo. Not only does it reduce costs, but it improves the outcomes and saves the patient's time (think Ranganathan's "Save the Time of the User"). Libraries might do well to consider the benefits of the "patient" centered team approach. Is a series of referrals really the best way to handle a complex research question?

4. What will success look like?

How will know if the shift from reference transactions to research support services has been effective and is worth continuing? As Gawande's analysis of the healthcare industry suggests, focusing on outcomes rather than narrowly focused measure of efficiency is key to creating real value. Some processes that a superficial analysis might suggest are costly or inefficient can deliver the desired outcomes at a lower cost.

For Illinois, shifting the value equation to one that is focused on the needs of the scholar has included focusing not just on counting reference transactions to looking more broadly at the building blocks of relationships that can form the basis of meaningful contributions to research, teaching and learning. We have also shifted our attention from volume count to usability and use value. It is one thing to have lots of books, but another for people to be able to find what they need, when they need it. The right book at the right time is more important than lots of books that nobody uses. In terms of both collections and services, moving from a just in case to a just in time model involves new metrics. The best measure of the value licensed resource may not be the number of downloads, but the fact that this supported a particular research project that would not have been possible otherwise (Figure 5). It not how many but how much impact did this have – not as easy to quantify, perhaps, but quite tangible.

UNIVERSITY LIBRARY DATA GRANT
- Competitive grants to faculty & grad students that support research projects requiring access to numeric or spatial datasets
- Library only commits to supporting licensed data sets for a period of one year

Usage/Downloads are **not** *the most useful measure:*
- Only helpful in deciding whether to continue licensing (that is, did we find a larger audience?)

Better measures of success:
- Citations in thesis/publications (with credit to the Library as a research sponsor!)
- People hear about the Library through the grant announcements, word of mouth
- Library/librarians are active partners in the research process
- New relationships established
- Opportunities to partner around issues of scholarly communication, data curation, etc are created

Outcomes: facilitate research, forge relationships

Figure 5: Data Grant: What will success look like?

References

Bourg, Chris; Coleman, Ross and Erway Ricky (2009), Support for the Research Process: An Academic Library Manifesto (Dublin, OH: OCLC), www.oclc.org/research/publications/library/2009/2009-07.pdf.

Gawande, Atul (2009) The Cost Conundrum: What a Texas town can teach us about health care. The New Yorker, June 1, 2009 < http://www.newyorker.com/reporting/2009/06/01/090601fa_fact_gawande>

Kesselman, Martin A. and Watstein, Sarah Barbara (2009) 'Creating Opportunities: Embedded

Librarians', Journal of Library Administration, 49: 4, 383 – 400.

Ramsay, Karen M. and Kinnie, Jim (2006),"The Embedded Librarian: Getting Out There via Technology to Help Students Where They Learn," Library Journal (April): 34–35.

One Librarian at a Time: Group Assessment via Self-Assessment

Cynthia Johnson[1] and Carol Ann Hughes[2]

[1] Head, Reference, University of California, Irvine, USA
[2] Associate University Librarian for Public Services, University of California, Irvine, USA

Abstract: This paper looks at two modes of assessment to improve reference customer service. The first mode is self-assessment: librarians choose a specific skill from the RUSA Guidelines for Behavioral Performance of Reference and Information Service Providers and focus on improving that one skill. Librarians and other service providers then engage in regular self-reflection on his or her reference skills and practice the behavior, regularly articulating their self-assessments in writing. The second mode of assessment uses digital reference transcripts as a learning opportunity. Individual librarians review reference transcripts for behavioral positives and negatives, discovering behaviors to emulate and behaviors to avoid.
Keywords: Reference, assessment, customer service, train

In 2005 the University of California, Irvine Libraries' adopted the RUSA Guidelines for Behavioral Performance of Reference and Information Service Providers as our customer service philosophy and values. RUSA (2004)   This was symbolically important because the Libraries have mainstreamed a wide variety of reference services (in-person, email, and chat) and adoption of the Guidelines emphasized for us that patrons using any of these modes deserve excellent service. As the department grew, the Head of Reference and a senior reference librarian reviewed the RUSA Guidelines with each new hire. This was significant to us because we hired ten new librarians within three years and they were all providing reference service as part of their regular responsibilities.

In 2008, having reviewed the Guidelines with all new reference librarians, we asked ourselves if the Guidelines are being truly embraced by both our junior colleagues and our more experienced librarians and staff (a total of twenty-nine librarians and career staff provide in-person and digital reference service). Therefore, a small group (the Head of Reference, the Research Librarian for Biology, and the Research Librarian for Anthropology and Sociology) brainstormed to develop a process that would emphasize behavior as an important aspect of reference service. Our goals were to:

1. Create an easy assessment process which encourages open dialogue among the librarians about their reference experiences.
2. Avoid exercises where reference providers felt they were being watched and judged.
3. Find a way to measure both patron satisfaction and librarian satisfaction with the interaction.
4. Train librarians to reflect on the signs of satisfaction in the patron's behavior.
5. Develop a method that would provide us with information about where training in customer service and behavior skills would be most beneficial,

New Trends in Qualitative and Quantitative Methods in Libraries
A. Katsirikou and C. H. Skiadas (eds)
© *World Scientific Publishing Co (pp. 63-66)*

and communicate that information to a committee charged with developing training (Reference Customer Service Training Team, RCSTT).

The process we developed has multiple parts. In 2009, sponsored by the RCSTT, we reviewed the RUSA Guidelines with all reference providers. We then asked each librarian to choose a minimum of one area, based on the Guidelines, that s/he would focus on during the year. By asking each person to write down a goal we could immediately tally the results and see the areas of greatest interest. We found that over 50% planned to focus on open-ended and closed/neutral questions. We informed the RCSTT that this is where they should focus their initial training efforts. Other areas of interest expressed by the librarians included: slowing down while speaking; rephrasing questions; trying to be approachable, either in-person or online.

The process of writing a goal is a key element of the project. Writing about a reference interaction encourages people to reflect on what worked well and didn't work well in their reference work. In addition, we hope that by creating a situation requiring self-reflection about customer service, librarians will become accustomed to thinking at a higher level about their own behavior when providing reference. "High level thinking involves thoughts that are self reflective, demonstrate awareness of emotion, and incorporate a broad perspective." Pennebaker, et al. (1990) Ultimately, we hope that a year of focusing on one behavior, and reflecting regularly on that behavior while providing reference, will motivate individuals to improve their customer service skills.

After each librarian decides on the specific behavior he or she will focus on, we asked for one written self-assessment each quarter. The librarian controls what she writes about, because she chooses the transaction to assess. The transaction could be from a drop-in at the reference desk, a scheduled consultation, or a digital reference interaction. The self-assessment is mailed only to the Head of Reference and is kept confidential.

The questions we asked each person to reflect upon are:

What technique, behavior or tool were you trying during this session? Be specific (example: I want to improve my use of open ended questions by asking "Can you tell me more about your topic?")

Was the patron satisfied? Why do you think the patron was satisfied?

Were you satisfied? What would you do differently, or keep the same, next time?

The result of our first foray into self-assessment allowed us to see what our colleagues used for open-ended questions. Surprisingly, some librarians, while stating that they were focusing on open-ended questions, actually asked the patron neutral or closed questions. Devin and Dewdney (1986) The RCSTT took this information and developed a 30 minute training session that included a skit demonstrating the importance of recognizing when to ask open-ended questions and when to ask closed-questions. The skit was followed by small group discussions and review of possible open-ended questions to use, as well as a broader discussion among the entire reference staff about when to use open-ended questions versus closed questions. Leita and Pine (2004)

Overall, results were mixed the first time we asked for a self-reflective analysis. Some librarians wrote detailed descriptions of the interaction, including critical analysis of the behavior they were seeing in response to their own behavior. For example, one person deduced a high degree of patron satisfaction with the reference transaction merely because the patron continued perusing a bibliography while the librarian helped another patron, and the first patron was not impatient or demanding.

Many librarians reflected on what they might do differently the next time in order to improve their reference service. We also found, however, that some librarians did not provide much analysis but only a basic description of what occurred. They also did not answer why they thought a patron was satisfied, or what they might do differently next time. For our second round of self-assessments, because we wanted to elicit more analysis, we altered the final question about satisfaction and what the librarian might do differently. We added the following to the question:

> Please restate the technique you are working on and what you are trying to change or improve. Be specific about the actions you took in trying to make a change, and in what you might do differently or keep the same.

In the second round of self-assessments we have seen improvement in the amount of analysis each person brings to bear upon their individual transaction. We also have concrete information now about which behaviors are the most difficult to self-assess, such as approachability. Approachability, in-person and through digital reference, will be the next major training session developed by the RCSTT.

In addition to providing ideas for directly applicable training to be provided by the RCSTT, gathering people's descriptions and analyses of reference transactions has provided specific examples that we all share over email, pointing out what is interesting in an individual's description. These examples are sent out anonymously (the librarian's name is deleted from the transcription), and are only sent out if the librarian agrees in advance that his self-assessment can be shared. A self-assessment is sent out only if it answered the questions fully and shows critical thinking and an ability to be self-critical. These are then discussed in reference meetings to encourage continued self-reflection and self-motivation to improve reference behaviors. These department discussions may also lead to more ideas about programmatic training to improve service.

Another project at the UC Irvine Libraries which depends on individuals assessing behavior and then focusing on self-improvement is taking place within our digital reference services. Transcripts from our QuestionPoint virtual reference service provide a wealth of information, not just about whether a librarian knows the best place to find an answer, but also about what behaviors can be improved in order to create a welcoming virtual environment for our patrons. We did a pilot to review the transcripts of non-UC Irvine librarians' answers to UC Irvine patrons' questions and compared the librarian's behavior to the QuestionPoint 24/7 Best Practices. QuestionPoint (2009) We wanted our UC Irvine librarians to identify positive and negative behaviors in the virtual environment, and then apply that information to their own virtual reference transactions by becoming more aware of their own behavior. The QuestionPoint 24/7 Best Practices includes behavioral practices, such as how the librarian greets the patron; chatting frequently so that the patron knows the librarian is still there; including positive phrasing when answering questions; asking if the patron's question has been answered.

The pilot group consisted of four librarians who examined 50 transcripts each. They compared customer service elements in each transcript to the Best Practices document, and then discussed what they observed. The outcome of the pilot was a recommendation that the process of comparing transcripts to Best Practices be mainstreamed because it would encourage high standards for our own responses. The Team wrote "This process facilitated an increased focus on the best practices and afforded us time to reflect on how we provide services through QP." Regular training about the Best Practices, as well as regular training to analyze transcripts, will be the next steps towards mainstreaming transcript assessment, looking specifically at behavioral cues. If this assessment model is successful at UC Irvine, we believe that other University of California libraries may begin to do similar analyses, in order to encourage high quality reference service among all the UC reference providers participating in the UC digital reference collaborative.

Both assessment projects described above involve individuals' honest critiques of their customer service skills instead of focusing on subject expertise and knowledge of complex databases. The customer service self-assessments have provided a springboard for discussions among reference librarians about the different approaches people take in eliciting information from patrons, without immediately devolving to a discussion of the best resources to show a patron. The self-assessment goals also provide the opportunity for the Head of Reference to discuss with a librarian a concrete goal that the librarian is trying to achieve, and how well the librarian feels he or she is making to improve a specific behavior. She can also provide guidance about where librarians see a need for training. These discussions, the actual self-assessments, and general group discussions around the self-assessments, provide data about areas for training that are focused on behavior, not on learning new resources.

The articulation of a self-determined goal, and the regular discussions with the Head of Reference about that specific goal, provides information for the Head of Reference about the individual's commitment to excellence in reference services which can be included in the librarian's performance review. We hope that by comparing digital reference transcripts to Best Practices, and encouraging librarians to reflect on others' behavior when providing digital reference, a similar reinforcement of behavioral excellence will appear. Both of these assessment techniques are intended to move from individuals' evaluation about what they personally find difficult to an observable improvement in each individual's performance that can be commented upon in performance evaluations and reviews.

Note: Throughout this paper, the term "librarian" applies to all who provide reference and informational services directly to library users.

References

Reference and User Services Section/American Library Association, (2004). *Guidelines for Behavioral Performance of Reference and Information Service Providers.*
    http://www.ala.org/ala/mgrps/divs/rusa/resources/guidelines/guidelinesbehavioral.cfm

Pennebaker, J. W., Czajka, J. A., Cropanzano, R., & Richards, B. C. (1990). Levels of thinking. *Personality and Social Psychology Bulletin.Special Issue: Centennial Celebration of The Principles of Psychology, 16*(4), 743-757. doi:10.1177/0146167290164014 page 743.

Dervin, B., & Dewdney, P. (1986). Neutral questioning: A new approach to the reference interview. *Research Quarterly*, 25 (4), 506-513.

Leita, C. & Pine, S (2004) "Open-Ended Questions for Reference Interviews" *Reference Interview Skills 2004: Looking for Questions in all the Right Places Spring 2004 -* (This material has been created by Carole Leita and Sallie Pine and provided through the Infopeople Project [infopeople.org], supported by the U.S. Institute of Museum and Library Services under the provisions of the Library Services and Technology Act, administered in California by the State Librarian. Any use of this material should credit the author and funding source. http://infopeople.org/training/past/2004/reference/open-ended_questions.pdf

QuestionPoint Reference Services (2009) *Best Practices for 24/7 Reference Cooperative Sessions.* http://wiki.questionpoint.org/247-Best-Practices

Access and Use of European Information: A Comparative Analysis

Ana Lúcia Terra

Superior School of Industrial Studies and Management, Oporto Polytechnic Institute, Portugal

Abstract: This paper presents some results of a survey on access to European information among a group of 234 users of 55 European Documentation Centres (EDCs), from 21 European Union (EU) Member-States. The findings of the questionnaire made to 88 EDCs' managers, from 26 EU Member-States, will also be analyse. Two different points of view regarding issues related to reasons to access European information, the valued aspects during that access and the use of European databases will be compare.
Keywords: Information behaviour, information access, European information

1. Introduction
The statement expressed by the French Foreign Minister, Robert Schuman, on the 9th of May 1950, launched Europe in an innovative project, turning torn countries by World War II into partners. The proposal was to place the Franco-German production of coal and steel under the tutelage of a High Authority promoting joint participation of other European countries. Thus, the European Coal and Steel Community (ECSC) was created, with six countries, progressing gradually to the current European Union (EU) with 27 countries (Austria, Belgium, Bulgaria, Cyprus, Czech Republic, Denmark, Estonia, Finland, France, Germany, Greece, Hungary, Ireland, Italy, Latvia, Lithuania, Luxembourg, Malta, Netherlands, Poland, Portugal, Romania, Slovakia, Slovenia, Spain, Sweden, United Kingdom).
Due to its innovative character, the European integration raised, from its outset, interest of the academic community, becoming a study and research subject in several scientific fields including law, economics and history. In order to satisfy this demand for information in Universities, the European Commission, still during the 60s, began to send, free of charge, documentation produced by European institutions. This set of documents contained reports, technical recommendations, legislation, statistics and dissemination papers of the activities of the European Parliament, the Council and the Commission. Thus, several universities' specialized libraries in European affairs have emerged. The origin of European Documentation Centres (EDCs) can be find here. It is, therefore, the first European information network created in partnership between European Commission and host institutions, usually universities. The community institutions' publications service, based in Luxembourg, now the Publications Office of the European Union, was charged of sending documents while each host institution was responsible to organize this collection and to provide a space to make it accessible to the academic audience.
Increasingly, these special libraries multiplied, both in Member States of the European project and in other countries. Consequently one of the most important European information networks emerged (Parker, 2004, 94-102). In fact, the EDCs

network stands out by the number of units involved, since at present there are nearly 350 across the EU. However, its importance also stems from the fact that they approach a group able to multiply European information through teaching, conferences or publications, spreading the analysis of the European phenomenon to quite a diverse audience.

Country	Officially existing EDCs in EU (May 2007)	EDCs' managers that answered the survey	EDCs' users that answered the survey
Austria	10	2	10
Belgium	9	2	7
Bulgaria	9	2	9
Cyprus	1	1	5
Czech Republic	7	2	6
Denmark	8	2	0
Estonia	2	2	3
Finland	10	10	16
France	48	2	0
Germany	51	2	8
Greece	11	2	6
Hungary	13	11	28
Ireland	5	5	15
Italy	45	2	9
Latvia	1	1	4
Lithuania	2	2	9
Luxembourg	0	--	--
Malta	1	1	0
Netherlands	14	3	1
Poland	16	2	10
Portugal	19	19	64
Romania	0	1	0
Slovakia	4	2	0
Slovenia	2	2	10
Spain	37	2	6
Sweden	11	3	4
United Kingdom	42	3	4
Total	**378**	**88**	**234**

Table 1. EDCs that comprised the sample

Despite the relevance of EDCs on European information, its analysis, in an academic area and in a comparative perspective at a European level, still represents a largely unexplored field. This finding represented the starting point of a PhD research in Information Science (Terra, 2008). In this study, the evolution of information policy of the European institutions since the 1950s, and the role of EDCs was analyzed. In addition to this diachronic and macro-level approach, made from the analysis of official documents on this matter produced by the European Parliament, the Council and the Commission; some issues related to access to information on a sample of EDCs were studied on a micro level and synchronous analysis. In this paper, some of the data collected in this second phase of the research are presented, deriving from the two questionnaires applied to managers and users of a sample of EDCs.

To create the sample of EDCs [Table 1] two units in 26 Member-States of the EU were selected. In Luxembourg there was no EDC and in Romania this information network was not identified at the official EUROPA gateway, although it was possible to identify one EDC in this country. However, in order to facilitate a comparative view of countries which joined the European project at different times, as for instance Finland (1995), Ireland (1973), Hungary (2004) and Portugal (1986), it was decided that all EDCs in these countries would comprise the sample. This has enabled a monographic study of EDCs in each of these countries, and a comparison between them and the EU average.

The first questionnaire, addressed to the managers, was sent to 90 EDCs. 88 participants composed this set, five of whom left the questionnaire incomplete. The response rate to the survey was of 98%, while the completion rate was of 92%. This sample covered a quarter of the total EDCs existing at that time.

The questionnaire to the EDCs' managers was distributed via the Internet between August and November 2007.

As for the questionnaire for EDCs' users that had answered the first survey, and considering that 88 responses were obtained and five questionnaires to each of the EDCS were intended, the total sample should consist of 440 questionnaires. In this case the response rate was significantly lower, as 234 questionnaires were obtained, which equates to a response rate of 53%. The five copies of the questionnaire were sent by post, at the care of the EDCs' manager. The responses acceptance period lasted from November 2007 to March 2008.

These two surveys had some similar questions in order to enable comparison between both responses. The survey to the EDCs managers had a set of questions that can be divided into two main groups: characterization of the EDC and opinions of their managers regarding aspects of users' information behaviour. As for the EDCs users' questionnaire it considered the general identification of respondents; their contact with information services, especially those of European nature; and aspects of their information behaviour, mainly aspects of access to information.

Following, some of the obtained results will be presented and analyzed.

2. Circumstances of the access to European information

Based on their everyday experience, EDCs managers were asked to express their opinion about certain matters relating to access to European information by EDCs' users.

They were questioned about the three main reasons that motivate the search for European information. In their opinion, the EDCs' users seek this information primarily to conduct academic work and do research on the EU [Table 2].

In fact, these two options are at the first and second place respectively in the European average (28% and 25%) and in Portugal (32% and 25%). In Finland (30%) and in Ireland (27%) both options have equal proportions. Only in Hungary, after the first place, occupied by the choice to carry out academic work, comes the option to produce school assignments and to solve professional matters

	EU Average	FI	HU	IR	PT
Produce school assignments	10%	0%	21%	0%	23%
Produce academic assignments	28%	30%	24%	27%	32%
Research on the EU	25%	30%	15%	27%	25%
Gather general information on the EU	10%	3%	15%	7%	11%
Resolve professional matters	17%	20%	21%	20%	11%
Know the rights of European citizenship	3%	3%	3%	0%	0%
Cultural or leisure motive	1%	3%	0%	0%	0%
Without answer	6%	10%	0%	20%	0%

Table 2. The three primary reasons for EDCs' users to search information on the EU, according to managers' opinion

Overall, the third place is filled by the option to resolve professional matters, with percentages ranging from 11% in Portugal, on par with the option to gather general information on the EU, and the 20% in Finland and in Ireland, which is above the EU average of 17%. Also here, Hungary adopts a different position, because the third position is filled *ex aequo* by the options to develop research on the EU and to gather general information on the EU (15%).

	EU Average	FI	HU	IR	PT
Produce school assignments	28%	6%	36%	13%	36%
Produce academic assignments	65%	69%	57%	80%	70%
Research on the EU	55%	75%	64%	80%	33%
Gather general information on the EU	44%	50%	39%	73%	42%
Resolve professional matters	46%	69%	46%	20%	36%
Know the rights of European citizenship	24%	6%	14%	7%	31%
Cultural or leisure motive	22%	13%	36%	13%	19%

Table 3. Situations that conduct EDCs' users to search for information on the EU

In the survey given to the EDCs' users, they were asked to indicate the situations that had led them to search information about the EU. There were eight possible responses and, in theory, all could be selected simultaneously. However, the option "others" was not selected by any of the respondents.

In accordance with the opinion of the EDCs' managers, in the EU average, the production of academic assignments (65%) and research on the EU (55%) are respectively the first and the second reason for this search. In Finland (75% and 69%) and Hungary (64% and 57%), the situation is reversed since the research outweighs the production of academic assignments. In Ireland, these two options have the same percentage of 80%.

In third place is the need to gather general information about the EU with 44% in the European average, 50% in Finland, 73% in Ireland and 42% in Portugal.

Since the EDCs' users belong mainly to the academic world (cf. other studies on the subject, namely Sargent, Parker, Marcella, 2000, 169-170; Alleweldt, 2007, 37) where these specialized libraries exist, it is natural that their search for European information is oriented towards a subject analysis, either for the purpose of obtaining a degree or to develop research that will be disseminated at conferences, in classes or in academic publications. Still, it is nonetheless remarkable that this audience of professors, researchers and graduate or post-graduate students also acknowledges searching general information about the EU. However, it seems clear that this specific public accesses European information primarily for professional and study reasons. The cultural and leisure motives achieve a 36% rate in Hungary, but the other countries monographically surveyed and in the European average this option has lower levels.

This represents an important element to take into account when defining the services provided by the EDCs to its users and the strategies to capture new audiences. Thus, it seems natural that EDCs should focus on disclosure the main information resources on the topic Europe in order to train the beginners, namely graduate students, without forgetting experienced users such as professors and researchers seeking information constantly updated.

3. European databases use

Nowadays, in order to access updated and quality information on European matters, it is essential to know and use specialized databases, produced and maintained by the European institutions (Martín González, 2007, 155-191). In fact, the general search engines or even the simple or advanced search on EUROPA gateway are insufficient to find the appropriate information. Therefore, the question arises to what extent the EDCs' managers and its users are familiar, use and know how to take advantage of European databases.

In the 1980s, European institutions started to strongly invest in databases in order to manage the increasing amount of information produced by its administrative and legislative activities. This access was very restrictive but from the 1990s it became available from the Intranet information networks sponsored by the EU Commission. By 2000, its access was free of charge through the EUROPA gateway. With this wide and free accessibility, the EDCs' librarians were no longer the privileged brokers between users and European databases. Anyway, actually, the EDCs' librarians continue to use databases to provide answers to users who seek them. It is therefore important to know which databases are most used and compare these data with the responses provided by EDCs' users [Table 4].

The database more commonly used is indisputably Eur-Lex, as the percentages are always above 80%, even reaching 100% in Hungary and Portugal. This is a key resource on the legislation produced by the European institutions, offering the consultation of the *Official Journal of the European Union*, from treaties to the jurisprudence as well as legislative proposals. This predominance of law in the search for information is stressed by the fact that the database CURIA represents the second most widely used in Finland and Ireland, and is the third in the EU average and in Portugal. In this database one can find the full text of judgments, opinions, notices and orders of the Community Courts and the summaries of its judgments and orders.

The database ECLAS, the catalog of the Commission's central library, enabling the consultation of bibliographic data, represents the second choice in Portugal and the EU average. While in the other three countries is presented as the third option selected.

	EU Average		FI		HU		IR		PT	
	M %	U %	M %	U %	M %	U %	M %	U %	M %	U %
ARCHIplus	6	6	0	0	0	4	0	0	0	2
CURIA	42	25	70	31	36	18	40	27	32	14
ECLAS	49	21	40	13	45	18	80	13	68	22
EurLex	94	60	90	75	100	57	80	73	100	53
EU Whoiswho	9	17	0	25	27	21	0	0	0	13
PreLex	42	23	30	44	55	14	20	13	32	19
RAPID	28	15	40	31	27	18	20	0	42	14
REGISTER	2	6	0	13	0	7	0	7	5	3
Others	9	3	0	19	9	7	0	0	21	3

Table 4. Databases more commonly used by the EDCs' managers (M) and users (U) to satisfy European information needs

Also for EDCs' users the use of Eur-Lex database is prevailing in all countries, but with percentages less emphatic in relation to EDCs' managers. In fact, the lowest percentage corresponds to Portugal, with 53%, and the highest in Finland with 75%. The CURIA database ranks second among EDCs' users in Ireland (27%) and in the EU average (25%), while in Finland it is the selected third option (31%). Note that this database should be complemented with Eur-Lex database, for documents prior to 1997.

From the PreLex all proposals (legislative and budgetary, international agreements) and communications from the Commission can be tracked, since the time of its transmission to the Council or Parliament. It also has links to access directly the available electronic texts (COM documents, *Official Journal*, the European Parliament documents or the Council's press releases, among others). In the studied sample, it represents the second choice for Finnish users (44%) and third in the European average (23%).

In Hungary, the European database Whoiswho ranks second, with 21%. It distinguishes from previous databases, which are related to European law and institutional procedures, because it is an electronic directory where one can consult the flowchart of European institutions, bodies and agencies.

Based on this analysis of the databases used, the EDCs' managers can develop training and educational resources such as online tutorials, to familiarize students with these sources of information or manuals to improve the usage of professors and researchers.

4. Valued aspects to access European information

The surveys distributed also included a question about the most valued aspects by users when accessing European information.

The question asked to choose three aspects among the options. With regard to this set of choices, we can distinguish those that are more related to aspects of physical access to information from those which relate to the inherent characteristics of information as a specific content. The first group included information easy to access and the availability of information in electronic form. In the second set the remaining options are included, namely updated, unbiased and intelligible information. The option regarding information in the mother tongue is related to translation issues and can also be included in this last group.

	EU Average	FI	HU	IR	PT
Information easy to access	64%	44%	64%	80%	69%
Information available in mother tongue	47%	38%	21%	33%	61%
Information available in electronic form	68%	75%	71%	53%	63%
Updated information	69%	81%	86%	80%	66%
Unbiased information	17%	25%	11%	20%	16%
Intelligible information	26%	31%	32%	33%	22%
Without answer	8%	0%	14%	0%	5%

Table 5. Valued aspects by EDCs users when accessing information

In the survey of EDCs' users [Table 5], it appears that the most valued options are information available in electronic form and updated information. In fact, these two options record the highest percentages in the European average, with 68% and 69%, respectively. Finland also follows this trend (75% and 81%). In Portugal, although these two options register a large percentage the first place belongs to information easy to access (69%). For Ireland, the first option chosen is also the information easy to access (80%), on par with updated information.

It should also be noted that information available in mother tongue is an important factor in the EDCs user's opinion for it reaches 61% in Portugal and 47% in the EU average. By contrast, in Hungary it reached only 21%; in Ireland 33% and in Finland 38%. These variations demonstrate the differences between users of different countries regarding the domain of other languages. Notwithstanding, in Ireland, and since English is an official language, the difficulties in finding information available in this language should be relatively small.

Regarding the survey results of the EDCs' managers [Table 6], one can highlight that in the European average, the highest percentage was reached by the option information available in electronic form with 68%. This figure is closely followed by two options with 64%: information easy to access and updated information. In Portugal, these three options record similarly the highest percentage (74%). As for Finland, the two options related to the physical access to information get the highest rate, with 90%; while the category on the updated information has a value of almost half (50%) still holding second place.

On the contrary, in Hungary, this choice of updated information has the highest value with 82%, followed by information accessible in electronic form (64%) and then the information easy to access (55%), third place *ex aequo* with those who choose not to respond.

Finally, in Ireland, the most valued aspect of accessing information is related to its availability in electronic form (80%), followed, in parity, by the options information easy to access and updated information with 40%.

	EU Average	FI	HU	IR	PT
Information easy to access	64%	90%	55%	40%	74%
Information available in mother tongue	45%	30%	36%	20%	47%
Information available in electronic form	68%	90%	64%	80%	74%
Updated information	64%	50%	82%	40%	74%
Unbiased information	3%	0%	0%	0%	16%
Intelligible information	2%	0%	9%	0%	5%
Without answer	52%	40%	55%	20%	5%
Others	1%	0%	0%	0%	5%

Table 6. Valued aspects by users when accessing information, according to the EDCs' managers opinion

We should also stress that the aspects related to the physical conditions of accessing information (information easy to access and information available in electronic form) have, jointly, very significant percentages. Whereas adding the percentage values of the options related to the characteristics inherent to information (information in their mother tongue, up to date, unbiased and intelligible), the average is significantly lower.

Moreover, the options for unbiased and intelligible information feature very low percentages, never exceeding 16%, and in many cases null percentages. In this sense, it seems that the EDCs' managers believe that users do not impute great importance to these features of information; which one can consider very peculiar given the fact that it is a specialized public, research or teaching oriented to the subject Europe and therefore should enhance both aspects but especially the impartiality and objectivity of information. However, it is also true that even the EDCs' users chose these options with very low percentages, ranging from 11% to 33% that is the lowest values of the entire (Table 5).

The focus on electronic information tends to confirm the increasing preference of both students and professors, to access information on the Internet, permanently available and easily changeable (Frand, 2000; OCLC, 2006). In this sense, these users are not agnostic about the format of information, preferring the digital media at the expense of traditional paper documents. However, the EDCs' managers should work to promote printed materials available in the collection, especially for diachronic studies in which older sources are essential. Not everything is on the Internet and users should be aware of this fact, especially in the case of individuals with very specific needs of information.

Moreover, even regarding the use of available resources on the Internet EDCs', librarians should invest in training materials for research, use and evaluation of information; because its users demonstrate some gaps in the information literacy skills (Terra, 2009).

5. Conclusions
One of the aims of this research was to compare the perspectives of EDCs users and managers regarding issues related to reasons to access European information, the valued aspects during the access and the use of European databases. Thus, it became

possible to ascertain to what extent the vision of librarians was coincident with the views expressed by EDCs' users. Moreover, with these results in mind, it is possible to define strategies to improve the search capabilities of information users and also to create librarians services that meet the expectations of their audience. Only then, it will be possible to meet the needs of future researchers (Rowlands, Ian, et al., 2008). In parallel, the European issues professors can collect data that allow them a better understanding of the information search processes of a new generation of students strongly influenced, or even determined, by the promptness of Google and the ubiquity of information on the Internet.

References

Alleweldt, F. (2007) *Evaluation of the EUROPE DIRECT European Documentation Centres.* Berlin: CIVIC Consulting.

Frand, J. L. (2000) The information-age mindset: changes in students and implications for higher education. *EDUCAUSE Review Magazine*, Vol.35,N.º5, 14-22.

Martín González, Y. (2007) *Manual de documentación de la Unión Europea: análisis y recuperación de la información eurocomunitaria.* Gijón: Ediciones Trea.

OCLC (2006) *College students' perceptions of the libraries and information resources: a report to the OCLC membership.* Dublin, OH: OCLC.

Parker, S. (2004) *Provision of European information: Commission policy and its implementation in libraries and information services in the United Kingdom.* Aberdeen: Robert Gordon University.

Rowlands, I. [et al.] (2008) The google generation: the information behaviour of the researcher of the future. *Aslib proceedings:* Vol.60,N.º4, 290-310.

Sargent, C.; Parker, S.; Marcella, R. (2000) The provision of European information to the academic community in university libraries: a case study of a European Documentation Centre. *New Library World.* Vol.101,N.º1156, 161-174.

Terra, A. L. (2009) The need for information literacy skills among users of European Union information. *Proceedings of BOBCATSSS' 09: Challenges for the new information.* Porto: Universidade do Porto;

Terra, A. L. (2008) *As políticas de informação e comunicação da União Europeia. Uma leitura diacrónica e exploratória no âmbito da Ciência da Informação.* Coimbra: Universidade de Coimbra.

Evaluation of Information Services in the Library: Areas Identified by Graduate Students

Naresh Kumar Agarwal

Graduate School of Library and Information Science, Simmons College, 300 The Fenway, Boston 02115, USA, agarwal@simmons.edu

Abstract: Evaluation is the systematic assessment of the operation and/or the outcomes of a program or policy, compared to a set of explicit or implicit standards, as a means of contributing to the improvement of the program or policy (Weiss, 1998). Neal (2006), in the context of academic libraries, says that "decisions are routinely not supported by the evidence of well-designed investigations" and that "research in the field is poorly communicated, understood and applied" (quoted by Peter Hernon, in the forward to Matthews, 2007). In addition, more and more libraries are either closing down or being forced to cut down on services due to recession (Powell, 2009; Applegate, 2009). Thus, identification of different areas of library services for systematic evaluation becomes extremely imperative in the current economic scenario. In an assignment to graduate students in a Master of Science in Library and Information Science program (with most students currently working in library or archive settings), the students were asked to describe an evaluation research scenario and a problem statement based on the scenario. An important criterion for grading was the significance of the scenario proposed. Using the areas of library (and archive) evaluation identified by the students as a case study, this study seeks to propose research questions and current areas of interest in the evaluation of library services. The study should shed light on the evaluation areas of importance in the current economic scenario and also help drive future research in this area.

Keywords: Evaluation of library services, evaluation research scenario, graduate students, assignment, research questions, problem statement

1. Introduction

Evaluation is the systematic assessment of the operation and/or the outcomes of a program or policy, compared to a set of explicit or implicit standards, as a means of contributing to the improvement of the program or policy (Weiss, 1998).

Neal (2006), in the context of academic libraries, says that "decisions are routinely not supported by the evidence of well-designed investigations" and that "research in the field is poorly communicated, understood and applied" (quoted by Peter Hernon, in the forward to Matthews, 2007). In addition, more and more libraries are either closing down or being forced to cut down on services due to recession (Powell, 2009; Applegate, 2009). Thus, identification of different areas of library services for systematic evaluation becomes extremely imperative in the current economic scenario.

New Trends in Qualitative and Quantitative Methods in Libraries
A. Katsirikou and C. H. Skiadas (eds)
© *World Scientific Publishing Co (pp. 77-88)*

This study lists 28 problem statements adapted from an assignment submitted by students in a graduate class. These also serve as 28 examples on how to effectively write problem statements for any research study.

Using the areas of library (and archive) evaluation identified by the students as a case study, this study seeks to propose research questions and current areas of interest in the evaluation of library services. The study should shed light on the evaluation areas of importance in the current economic scenario and also help drive future research in this area. The 28 examples of problem statements would be useful to researchers preparing to write studies, librarians, as well as graduate LIS students learning to write problem statements for an evaluation research study.

2. Methodology
In an assignment in Fall 2009 to 28 graduate students in a Master of Science in Library and Information Science program (with most students currently working in library or archive settings), the students were asked to explore and describe an evaluation research scenario in the Library and Information Science field for a specific research topic; and to write a problem statement derived from the research scenario. An important criterion for grading was the significance of the scenario proposed[1]. The students were given 2 weeks to complete the assignment (distributed during Week 2 in a 12 week semester; due on Week 4).

In the scenario, the students were tasked to include the following in their narrative: 1) the specific library, archives or museum *setting* (either hypothetical setting or modeled on a real one) where the evaluation study is conducted (e.g. medium-sized academic library, large public library, small music library, university archives, historical society, etc.); 2) the *evaluand* (any product, service or policy which is to be evaluated) of the evaluation study, which could be any component of information services, such as a newly launched information system or a specialized information service; 3) the position/role of the student in the organization/setting as the *evaluator* in the study; 4) *stakeholders* concerned with the evaluation results; 5) *participants*, if any, in the evaluation study; 6) specific range of *data* that the student (as the evaluator) planned to collect for the study; and finally, 7) the likely impact and *significance* of the evaluation study.

Based on their scenario, the students were also required to come up with a problem statement. Hernon and Schwartz (2007) mention 4 components of any problem statement in the social sciences (which would apply to library and information science) as stressed by Dr. David Clark: 1) lead-in; 2) declaration of originality (e.g., mentioning a knowledge void, which would be supported by the literature review); 3) indication of the central focus of the study; and 4) explanation of study significance or the benefits to be derived from an investigation of the problem.

For the purposes of this paper, each 2-4 page assignment was adapted into a problem statement format recommended by Hernon and Schwartz (2007).

3. Findings and Discussion
Given below are 28 problem statements based on the scenarios that the students came up with. Keywords in the setting and evaluand for each problem statement have been highlighted in **bold**. These help shed light on the current areas of research interest as identified by graduate students, most of who work in library or archive settings. Read each case from left to right. Column 3 on what each study does provides examples of research questions in the library and archive settings.

---

[1] The assignment was adapted from one used by Associate Professor Rong Tang in her class.

	Lead-in (setting)	Knowledge gap	What this study will do? (evaluand)	Significance
1	The database in the **Suffolk County Historical Documents Library** is managed by both professional and part-time staff.	However, no study has compared the accuracy of databases set up by part-time staff to the accuracy of those set up by professionals.	This study will compare the **efficiency and accuracy of database set up by part time staff to those by their professional peers**.	This will help libraries make better informed, cost-productive decisions when assigning database creation/managemen t tasks to staff.
2	As the digital age is now upon us, many researchers enjoy being able to search archival finding aids online and browsing digital collections from the comfort of their own home.	However, many **archives** often have lone arrangers or a small staff and it is often difficult to find time for digitization projects.	This study will investigate **whether providing online finding aids** and **partially digitizing collections will** help draw in **more researchers**.	The study will help archives decide whether or not to digitize collections and post finding aids online, and which collections they should digitize because of the cost and time involved in the process
3	**Project SAVE Armenian Photograph Archives** in Watertown, MA has over 30,000 images in its collection and is the premier archive of Armenian photos.	However, no study has been performed to determine the needs of image-seeking users of the archives.	This study will evaluate the **user needs with regards to digitization of collection**, to determine if digitization is necessary and to what extent.	The knowledge gained from such a study would aid in procuring the funds necessary to digitize the large collection so that the information within the archive could reach a larger audience.
4	The **local history room of the Somerville Public Library** is a **collection** that has grown organically over the years.	However, local history collections have constituted very little of the discussion of archival practices,	This study will help evaluate **if the local history collection is meeting the needs of the patron**, and help	This will help libraries better position their legacy collection, or create a new collection for educational purposes.

		although many local libraries in New England maintain a collection.	determine what patrons need from history resources in the public library setting.	
5	The **Farr Regional Library,** the main branch of the High Plains Library District, has implemented a **self-checkout program**.	However, it is not clear how effective the program has been in providing patrons with faster service, giving more control over their library experience and in allowing circulation staff to spend more time on other tasks.	Before the library board decides to implement self-checkout systems on its other branches, this study will evaluate the **effectiveness of the system** at the Farr Regional Library.	The evaluation will help determine patrons' level of satisfaction with the system, potentially save the library money over time, and provide for better overall customer service for library patrons.
6	A new service is being offered by the medical school reference librarians to encourage use of their expert abilities and the library, whereby the **reference librarians set up a portable station in the cafeteria** during peak dining hours.	Since this is a relatively new service, it is unknown if the users are actually finding this portable reference service useful and if anything could be done to make it better.	This study will investigate **if users find this new service useful**, and if they are willing to return or are returning.	More information on the efficacy of this service should help the library better serve the needs of and be a useful part of the medical school community.
7	A new digital circulation system has just been implemented in a **small library for a private**	However, it is not clear how the new system will impact patrons used to an older system.	This study will evaluate **whether the process of implementin g the digital circulation**	The evaluation will help shed light on aspects of the new system which patrons find frustrating and those they find useful, and

	educational institute in Boston, MA that was used to a rolodex of old book inserts ranging in dates from ten years ago to the present.		system adequately takes into account the concerns of users who are used to the older system.	allow the library staff to adjust operations based on those issues.
8	A new lecture series at the Boston Public Library offers free admission to all Bostonians, caters to people from a wide variety of academic programs and schools in a city with many universities.	However, it is not apparent how useful do scholars of different sorts find these series – academic researchers, librarians and curious Bostonians in search of an afternoon of enlightenment.	This study will evaluate the effect of the new literary lecture series at the library on all those who benefit scholastically from the resources of the Boston Public Library.	An evaluation of this particular lecture series could shed light not only on its effectiveness for the Boston Public Library, but on the way literature lecture series affect urban and/or academic communities in general.
9	Marketing serves a valuable role in promoting library services to known and unknown users.	Yet, no study has been commissioned by the Cambridge Public Library to observe how patrons of the Central Square branch found out about the services offered here.	The library will conduct a study of new patrons registering for library cards focusing on their method of acquaintance with the library.	Through the study, the library can determine how effective its current marketing is and what can it do to improve.
10	Overdrive Media currently supplies online downloadable media (audio and e-books) for more than 8,500 libraries	While much research has been devoted to the study of user characteristics and the use of e-book and e-journals in a	This study will evaluate the selection criteria for audio books in a shared virtual branch called CW/Mars.	Understanding the use and demand for this type of service and the effect it has in the library marketplace is essential to establishing a development plan

	across the U.S.	research setting, audio books have not been studied all that much.		for online downloadable media collection that will be sustainable and effectively meets patron needs.
11	A **university archives** with a medium-sized repository has just implemented a new website.	However, it is not clear if the website is effective in helping visitors decide what they want before they come to the physical building.	This study will evaluate the **effectiveness of the website** in disseminating information about the materials stored in the archives.	The evaluation will help the stakeholders ascertain if the website is effective in meeting user needs and what, if any, changes are required.
12	The **State Library of Massachusetts** is an important resource for state employees.	However, there is no data suggesting that there is currently a working marketing plan.	This study will evaluate the **marketing practices of the library and** determine **its efficacy**.	The study will help the library understand the efficacy of its marketing practices and to modify the practices to increase the number of patrons.
13	**Facility design** is a high priority for librarians who want to effectively attract users to their space.	Yet, no assessment has been made to address the lack of successful facility design in regard to teen space at the **Honan-Allston Library**.	This study will evaluate **the young adult's facility** to ascertain whether the space is **effective** in encouraging positive teen experiences in the library.	Such a study will result in the redevelopment of a space that is inviting and meets the needs of young adults, leading to higher young adult library patronage in the Allston community.
14	Any training provided to implement a **disaster recovery plan in a university archive** must focus not just on the preservation of	Despite the importance placed on the competency of staff members during a disaster, very little data is available on how feedback	This study will determine **how comfortable and confident staff feels when performing their role**	The study will allow the institution to modify and perfect their plans so that the staff feel involved in the process, and may lead to an increased likelihood of successfully

	the collection, but also on the way staff should handle their individual responsibilities.	from staff about their training can assist in effectively executing the disaster plan.	**within the disaster plan**.	preserving the collection in the unfortunate event of a disaster.
15	The **Thomas Crane Public Library's music CD collection** constitutes a significant portion of the library budget, and the items that comprise it are consistently sought after.	Yet, no studies have been performed measuring the collection's usability or physical accessibility, and patrons and staff have called these aspects of the CD collection into question.	An evaluation using a questionnaire will gather data on the **collection's usability and physical accessibility**.	The study will benefit the patrons by making a more accessible music collection. The library staff will likely get fewer questions about the collection and be more comfortable explaining the simpler classification scheme and physical layout.
16	**Collins, the smallest branch of the Cambridge Public Library** is **adding several computer terminals** to help make it more child-friendly.	However, in order to justify the computer purchases to the stakeholders, it is necessary to evaluate how much use the services receive, and whether patrons are actually valuing the services being offered.	This study will help determine **how much use the computers receive**, and **whether their placement** in the children's area **results in greater use of the online catalog**, which has previously received very little use.	If the evaluation shows increased computer use and overall increase in online catalog use, the library will be able to claim that the service fulfills patron need and possibly recommend further computer services for youth patrons. A negative outcome will demonstrate that the computers might be better served elsewhere.
17	A grant-funded feasibility study suggested **modifying and expanding the Bancroft Memorial Library**, a small public library with a	Unfortunately, residents did not want to change the historic library leading to continued challenges in effective utilization of	The library staff and trustees would like to see **if relocating the large print collection will increase circulation**	Getting patron perceptions before and after the collection is moved will help determine if patrons have a safe and convenient access to browsing and selecting books, and may also prepare

	rich history and exquisite architecture, that is **suffering with outdated and insufficient building features**.	the limited space in which to store/display materials for patrons.	**and alter patron attitudes** toward building improvements in the library.	them to consider modifications to the building recommended by the feasibility study.
18	**Online book-marking tools such as 'Delicious'** make finding hard-to-remember websites with obscure domain names and relevant information easier.	Yet, no study has sought to discover if these can be successfully used by young children from Kindergarten to Second grade, some non-readers, to navigate the often dangerous world of the Internet.	This study will record the **frequency of young student use of 'Delicious'**, the **time it takes them to find the required website**, and whether they would use it for personal use.	The study would be useful to elementary schoolteachers and librarians who use the Internet as a vital teaching tool and information source but lack the time and ability to type in domain names for each child's computer.
19	Since the release of the first **Amazon Kindle** in November 2007, interest in e-book readers such as Kindle or **Sony e-reader** has quickly increased.	To date, there is little information available about the issues faced by libraries choosing to lend e-readers to patrons.	This study will gather **patron input to determine current and future e-reader circulation procedures** and ways in which the service could be improved.	The study could serve as a road map of sorts for libraries wishing to purchase e-readers and to implement this type of service.
20	The **Portsmouth Public Library provides access to 166 licensed electronic databases**, a service offered at substantial cost.	However, the extent to which library patrons avail themselves of this resource is unknown.	The study will help determine **if the databases are those that the patrons want** or if the library should subscribe to others.	The results of this study will help the Portsmouth Public Library allocate its limited funds in a manner consistent with the needs of its patrons.
21	The **Waltham Public**	Unfortunately, as most of the	This evaluation	Results of the evaluation will be

		information from the archives is not catalogued or bar-coded, there is no consistent way to track the value of the archives.	will determine the **satisfaction of archival users, and the frequency** with which they **avail** themselves of the **services offered by the archivist.**	used by the library to strengthen outreach programming, reconsider staffing and hours, and include information in annual budget reports– an important issue for the library as it has faced a $75,000 budget cut.
	Library's **archives** contain personal historical information like high school yearbooks, marriage notices, and other materials of local and personal importance.			
22	The **Luther W. Brady Art Gallery** is the professional showcase for art at George Washington University, Washington D.C.	There isn't an information system for the gallery that would organize the various holdings in the Permanent Collection, and would also make them accessible to those unfamiliar with cataloging rules.	This evaluation seeks to **determine the language preferred by patrons to describe the artworks** – cataloging methods such as AACR2 or MARC, or a proprietary language of descriptions for the repository.	Insight gained from this study would assist Art Librarians in describing art in a way that is accessible and helpful to patrons from all backgrounds.
23	The **"One Card...Endless Possibilities!" program encourages** Manchester City **Library patrons to visit local businesses in the city to obtain discount**s/freeb ies by showing their library card.	Since the inception of the program 3 years ago, a formal evaluation has never been conducted regarding the **community response or effectiveness of partnering with businesses**.	This study will seek to understand the unique experience of each business and patron through the program.	The results of the study will help determine the connection between library patrons and local businesses, reveal areas where the program is lacking, establish if the program was responsible for new library cardholders, and ultimately decide if the program will continue in the future.

24	**Historical societies** offer a wealth of research material, trained staff eager to assist with queries, and an array of exhibitions and lectures, yet their attendance levels are modest compared to those of libraries, museums and universities.	No study has previously been conducted to **analyze the way in which moderately-sized historical societies approach user programs and outreach,** and their **effectiveness.**	This study will help a historical society similar to the New England Historic Genealogical Society evaluate its user programs and outreach and compare these with those offered by peers.	Insight gained from this study will illustrate whether or not there is a need for the historical society to implement a more aggressive outreach program and offer a larger selection of user programs.
25	A small-to-medium-sized **corporate library of the law firm,** Greeley and Cour has **purchased a new Online Public Access Catalog** (OPAC) to replace their ugly and underused 10-year old system.	There is much literature about evaluation of launching technology and even OPACs, but not many in small, insular settings like this one.	This study will evaluate the **usability of the new OPAC** with respect to ease of use, intuitiveness, expected future use, attractiveness of interface, and search precision.	The evaluation will help the library improve the interface and contents of the OPAC. With better access to information, the firm can make better legal representations and the library could become the place where patrons go for top quality legal information.
26	**Small Liberal Art College's library** has **always offered introductory workshops** covering library **resources and** basic **research methods** during the first few weeks of the semester.	However, an increasing number of professors, students and library staff members are questioning the effectiveness of these.	This study will evaluate the **effectiveness of these workshops and the usability of the library website.**	The study will help determine the usefulness of these resources to students in meeting the stated learning outcomes of the college, of which research skills are a major component.

27	**The Night Owl Program is an innovative new method of the Annenberg Library collaborating with professors** of the Pine Manor College, Chestnut Hill, MA and incentivizing students to use the library.	The course integrated approach used by the program is recommended in LIS literature but few studies have been done to compare its effectiveness with other methods.	This study will determine **if a curriculum integrated user instruction method is more effective for first year students** at a small/diverse liberal arts school than the traditional method.	The outcome of this study is crucial in gaining a better understanding of the most effective way to provide user instruction to first year students at Pine Manor College, and helping create information literate students.
28	Libraries' role in helping new college students succeed is often assumed, and certainly one can see many first-year students in libraries, or connecting to their school libraries online in the beginning of their college education.	However, it is not clear if the **reference interview** contribute to the students' first year academic success and eventual information literacy.	This study will evaluate **how students' visits to the reference desk affect those students' first year grades.**	This study will help reference librarians justify their salaries with the library's budget and bring forth their crucial role in helping promote information literacy.

The problem statements above provide different examples of areas of current interest in the library/archives/information settings. As seen in the cases above, many students choose to study the efficacy of services provided (an area of primary concern to a service-oriented field such as Library and Information Science). Many students have mentioned limited budgets/funding and the need to streamline services to best meets patron needs.

4. Implications and Limitations
The examples above would be useful to researchers preparing to write studies, librarians, as well as graduate LIS students trying to look for questions to evaluate, as well as learning to write problem statements for an evaluation research study.

Limitations of this paper are also to be noted. The scenarios/problem statements could be based on either hypothetical or real-life settings. Also, at the time of doing this assignment, most students were not trained researchers or evaluators, but training to be one (though most of them did work in real-life library/information settings). Due to lack of space, the individual components of the scenarios, such as stakeholders, participants in the study and specific range of data to be collected (as identified by the students) were not included in this paper. While the scenarios above serve as good examples, they hardly touch the surface of the countless possibilities for evaluation that could take place within a library and information setting (see Matthews 2007 for a detailed treatment on the evaluation of various information services in a library).

5. Conclusion and Future Work

This study has highlighted 28 problem statements identified by graduate students in a class assignment. Using these areas of library/archive/information services evaluation identified by the students as a case study, this paper provides examples of current areas of research interest in the evaluation of library services. The paper also builds on Hernon and Schwartz (2007)'s editorial on problem statement by providing various examples on writing problem statements.

Future work will involve expanding upon each case by identifying the participants in each study and the specific range of data to be collected. Scenarios and problem statements identified by future batches of students will also be incorporated. There might also be a need to group scenarios based on specific themes and specific types of questions.

Acknowledgements

The author is grateful to all his students who helped identify these areas of evaluation research interest as part of their class assignment.

References

Applegate, L. (2009). Libraries hit hard by recession. *Chicago Parent*, October 26, 2009. Retrieved January 30, 2010, from http://www.chicagoparent.com/magazines/chicago-parent/2009-november/libraries-hit-hard-by-recession

Hernon, P. and Schwartz, C. (2007). What is a problem statement? *Library and Information Science Research*, 29(3), 207-309.

Matthews, J.R. (2007). *The evaluation and measurement of library services.* Westport, CT: Libraries Unlimited.

Neal, J.G. (2006). The Research and Development Imperative in the Academic Library: Path to the Future. *Portal: Libraries and the Academy*, 6(1), 2006, 1.

Powell, K. (2009). Libraries Closing Due to Budget Cuts. *About.com: Genealogy*, September 15, 2009. Retrieved January 30, 2010, from http://genealogy.about.com/b/2009/09/15/libraries-closing-due-to-budget-cuts.htm

Weiss, C.H. (1998). *Evaluation* (Second Edition). Upper Saddle River, NJ: Prentice Hall.

Chapter 2. Quantitative and Qualitative Methods in Library Management: A Practical Approach

How to Teach Library Management

Angela Repanovici

Transilvania University of Brasov, Romania

Abstract: Quality of library services is in fact the goal of a good library management. We present the method of teaching and how to do library management and practical approach using some strategical models for Information Science students in Library management course at Transilvania University of Brasov, Romania. In this paper we try to present Deming Weel scheme in libraries - PDCA (plan- do-check-act) like methods to approach strategic plans to improve different services in the library. After theoretical presentation the students do strategic plans working in teams. They are in double perspective: as users and as managers wanted to improve library services. The students are taught to use statistical methods to interpretate data. We will present the pedagogical method and the students conclusion, the very inventive strategic plans proposed by Transilvania university of Brasov, Romania students in Information Science field.
Keywords: Library management, pedagogical aspects, strategic plans, statistical methods

Introduction
The course Library management aims in the sphere of concrete knowledge management disciplines for students in library and information science education. To the end of this course, students will be able to:

- operate with such notions as: the concept of quality and evaluation of library services quality performance indicators;
- identify performance indicators;
- identify the factors wich influencee user satisfaction
- to develop models and strategic plans of development of library services;
- to develop marketing research using the survey instruments.

We present Deming Weel scheme in libraries- PDCA (plan- do-check-act) like methods to approach strategic plans to improve different services in the library.[6]

Quality in library
Interest in assessing and improving quality of service has become one of the main objectives of the library. Providing a quality service means to adapt to user expectations. These expectations are outlined following an assessment of user satisfaction. When speaking of quality one often refers particularly to user satisfaction.[3]

New Trends in Qualitative and Quantitative Methods in Libraries
A. Katsirikou and C. H. Skiadas (eds)
© *World Scientific Publishing Co (pp. 89-95)*

In this context one can start by considering the five laws of librarianship, compiled in 1931 by Shiyali Ramamrita Ranganathan (1892-1972):

1. Books are for use
2. Every reader his book
3. Every book its reader
4. Save the time of reader
5. The library is a growing body

Library service quality criteria by Peter Brophy

Philip Bayard Crospby[2], businessman and author who contributed to management theory, says that there is never a problem in terms of quality. Quality problems are not independent. They are always caused by bad management and may also be directed

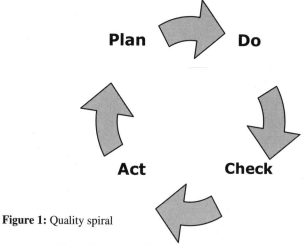

Figure 1: Quality spiral

by management. Just take note of the wishes and needs of consumers of information (in an organization such as the library) and do everything possible for them to reach fulfilment.

Peter Brophy, taking as its starting point the general management literature has adapted a set of quality attributes for libraries. Later, in 1984, Garvin recognized and defined the time complexity of at least five perspectives of the quality concept can be regarded as:

- transcendental view: quality can be recognized, but can not be defined;
- consumer view: quality as its requirements;
- manufacturer view: quality that meet specifications;
- product view: quality is related to inherent characteristics of the product;
- view based on value: the quality depends on the amount that the client is willing to pay;

Deming's wheel

A different method of continuous quality improvement was designed and plotted by WE Deming as "PDCA cycle (Plan-Do-Check-Act), also known as Deming's cycle. It consists of four phases: Plan (planning, designing, preparing), DO (running), check (verify) and ACT (act)..(figure 1).

In the process of defining and establishing the level of quality, the first issue of great importance to the development of organizational quality is, **user needs is a transcript** measurable characteristics. **With these features can already crystallized.**

With these features already crystallized design and development services to meet the needs and expectations can be done, using stages set out below. Here's **what the each of the four phases**.[4]

1. Planning Phase (PLAN). This phase consists of recognizing and defining the need to improve. As satisfying customers / users is the focus; assess the differences between the needs of customers (from market research) and performance processes (from the information feedback). In this phase decisions must be taken to achieve the objectives, types of performance measurement to be used and who will be responsible for what. To observe and analyze the main causes of quality problems in order to develop the improvement plan, one may apply statistical tools and techniques.

2. Execution Phase (DO). involving all employees, applying scales, discussing the purpose of testing, and the improvement plan, developed during the planning phase,. This will include training in scientific methods, examination of the information obtained as feedback from customers about their expectations, collecting statistical information of processes, understanding and control process changes, training for project teams working to improve communication and success results. In this phase small-scale implementation of **any** changes will take place and **any** planned test and results data will be collected.

3. Verification Phase (CHECK). In the verification phase the results of implementation on a small scale improvement plan are investigated. This check involves measuring and observing the effects of any change or any test, carried out in the enforcement phase, analyse results and the analysis of the extent to which differences in customer needs and performance processes were further reduced by adopting the plan. The analysis results will be useful statistical methods. The verification results can confirm or not whether the proposed improvement is correct.

4. Action Phase (ACT). At this stage a decision is made on the implementation plan: change will be adopted or discarded according to the results of the previous phase. One will get feedback from customers and processes following the large-scale implementation plan. Such information will provide a real assessment of the success of the plan, if they do not come to light in the verification phase.

Operational process of PDCA method is based on three subcicluri:

- Subciclul maintenance;
- Subciclul corrective action (or prevent recurrent);
- Subciclul improvement.

Subciclul maintenance. [5] In this subciclu must take place as planned and put into action, at the final there should be a check (check), if the check is positive, the status quo will be maintained as at present. The process and should be continuously monitored to make sure it takes place in a safe manner. If the check shows something that does not work, they must have enabled **subciclul** corrective action. **When the CHECK phase confirms the effectiveness of the plan (measure) to improve, apply corrective action.** This action will be a remedy to eliminate the negative things found, and for maintenance, such activities must be eliminated through regular preventive actions, causes of defects or errors in processes.

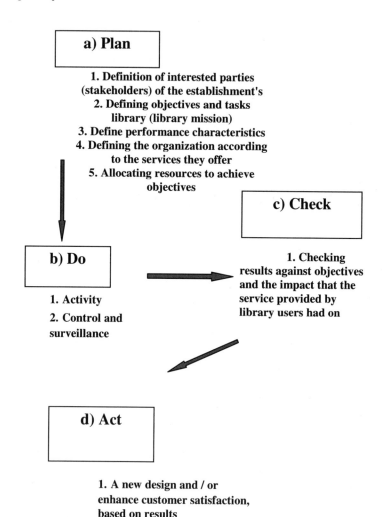

Figure 2: Deming's wheel scheme in the library

Subciclul improvement should be based on the first two subcicluri. When the work of maintaining the state of affairs is well done, with positive results, at some point one must act to improve it, things should be made simpler, lower cost, better, faster, safer, therefore,one must resume phases PLAN - DO. If, when starting from the new plan, CHECK phase gives positive results, continue with subciclul maintenance.

Continuous quality improvement process can be considered as a series of rotations of PDCA, made as of all persons working in the enterprise. Continuous quality improvement process can be considered as a series of rotations of PDCA, made as of all persons working in the enterprise. The whole strategy is based on continuous management PDCA method for any process of undertaking.

Deming's wheel in the library (figure 2)
A: Plan (Plan)
1. Definition of interested parties (stakeholders) in the functioning of the institution
If a library they are:
- Users (actual and potential) [1]
- financial institutions (the university, the community, a commercial firm, etc.).
- Library staff
- Library managers
- Other groups: representatives of employees, and control of the library committee

2. Defining objectives and tasks of the library (library mission)
Library mission could be summarized as follows: to select, organize and provide access to information of users, primarily the primary users, and expand information literacy with help and training services. The mission of libraries must be built on the following questions:
- Why is the library?
- Who is the customer / user?
- What has value for the customer / user?

3. Defining characteristics of performance
According to the strategic model for libraries, proposed by Christine Abbot, the following characteristics are relevant in the assessment process for all types of libraries:
- Customer Satisfaction;
- Economic efficiency;
- market penetration;
- The number of real customers in relation to the number of potential;
- Acceptance of services;
- Speed in the provision of products and services to customers;
- Turnover (loans, information);
- Release of documents or information in a timely manner;
- Productivity.
- Accuracy of products and services;
- Reliability (relevance);
- Costs;

4. Defining the organization according to the services they offer:
Libraries are public, service organizations (information, culture and education) with specific characteristics, customize them in relation to other social and cultural institutions, such as:
- libraries are agents or institutions that are not oriented towards profit;
- libraries provide information and invoice services or products; not material products;
- libraries react both to resources and to customers in a dualistic way, sometimes even contradictory, with some staff characterized by a predominant orientation towards books, and some being more oriented to users, seen as beneficiaries.

5. The allocation of resources for achieving
When it comes to organization, resources are divided into three categories:
- financial and economic
- Human Resources
- logistics resources and infrastructure [5]

B: Do (Execute)
1. Logs
In this phase, the library will implement, scale, objectives which they set in the first round. The work will involve all library staff. To fulfil the mission, the library staff will be trained on the scientific methods used and consider the continuous feedback information obtained from customers about their expectations.
2. Control and continuous surveillance

C: Check (Check)
1. Checking the results achieved against objectives and the impact that the service provided by the library had on users.
The verification phase are investigated results of the implementation of small-scale improvement plan, the effect that the plan had for each sector of the library and the degree of achievement of the objectives of the institution. Verification will have two dimensions: one internal order - the systematic research of organizational climate (which shows the harmony of relations between individuals of an organization and between individuals and technology resources available at work), and one external nature - a systematic research library customer satisfaction. Constant operation of library services, and systematic research regarding user satisfaction is the key to continually improving the service organization.

D: Act (Act)
1. A new design and / or enhance customer satisfaction, based on results obtained
In this phase one will compare the results from implementing small scale improvement plan with the objectives in the planning stages. Check also if the resources were used properly. Depending on the results, one can propose revision of objectives and make redistribution of resources, whether human, financial or material, or maintaining and strengthening the objectives which gave positive results and were appreciated by library users. For each PDCA cycle, a library manager learns something. Decisions taken at this stage are channelled towards improving the service. So, the cycle is repeated.
Deming's PDCA cycle or wheel is available anywhere where the ultimate goal is to improve performance. It provides a method for improving any process systematically and only if used consistently can provide significant improvements. The central goal of the library is to provide quality services to its users, therefore Deming's wheel must rotate continuously for continuous improvement of quality arrogate.
Course objectives
At the end of this module students will be able to:
* make a strategic plan to develop a library service.
* to identify performance indicators that can and measured and calculated.
* to guide development activities to the users satisfaction.
* be aware for measuring the activities

Control themes
Choose a service of university library and develop a strategic plan for improving the services having regard to the following:
a) Description of products and services.
b) Which users is addressed or offer the service?
c) Rating of quality indicators key

d) Presentation of some method of verifying the effectiveness of the proposed strategic plan.

Student's conclusion
• Quality assessment of library services - deals, at a theoretical level, the concept of evaluation and quality at the library.
• To emphasize the importance of performance evaluation of a library, I presented "PDCA cycle (Plan-Do-Check-Act), also known as Deming's wheel - a model for continuous improvement of services offered by an organization. We showed how this model can be applied in an organization as the library and how important phase of testing (Check) in this process.
• The library will check two dimensions: an internal order - the internal processes of the library - and one external nature - a systematic research on library customer satisfaction.
• These two types of evaluation are not mutually exclusive but complement each other, the evaluation process is not fully realized only when one of these perspectives.

Let us remember
Library is a public competing for a place on the information market. To win, it must be based on a culture of management to take center library user – the ultimate goal of all activities that happen inside a library. Therefore, it is important that the library should have available forms of measurement that reflects how users of the services it offered. Therefore, assessment is an essential point in the growth of any library.

References
[1]   **BELLINI, Paolo, RIZZI, Ivana.** ISO 11630. "Stima della target populazione. Indicatore B1.1.1 user satisfaction", în *Biblioteche oggi*, 19 (2001), p.*53-68*
[2]   **BROPHY, Peter.** "The quality of libraries". In K. Hilgermann and P. te Boekhorst, eds. *The effective library.* München: K. G. Saur. 3003, p. 30-46
[3]   *Biblioteconomia. Principi e questioni.* Coord: Giovanni Solimine şi Paul G. Weston. Roma: Carocci, 3007, p. 488 Cap. 5 "Le culture e le pratiche della qualità in biblioteca" / Giovanni Di Domenico. Cap. 6 "La valutazione dei servizi" / Anna Galluzzi. Cap. 7 "La soddisfazione degli utenti in biblioteca: obiettivi e metodologie di valutazione" / Giovanni Di Domenico
[4]   **POLL, di Roswitha, BOEKHORST, te Peter.** *Measuring Quality: Performance Measurement in Libraries.* Walter de Gruyter: Berlin – New York, 3007, p.369
[5]   **REPANOVICI, A.** and **LANDOY, A.** (2009): "Knowing the needs. A system for evaluating the university library." *Conference paper from QQML2009 (Qualitative and Quantitative Methods in Libraries), 26.-29.* May 2009. http://hdl.handle.net/1956/3705
[6]   **SUMSION, John.** "Library statistics to enjoy – Measuring success" în *IFLA Journal 37 (3001) 4* , p. 311-314 [online] document disponubil la adresa: http://ifla.queenslibrary.org/V/iflaj/art3704.pdf [cited în 10 ianuarie 3009]

Using Statistics for Quality Management in the Library

Ane Landøy

University of Bergen Library, Norway

Abstract: In the light of the ever changing and developing technology in the libraries, library managers across the sector and all over the world need to utilize all possible means of ensuring that the quality of services remains optimal. This paper shows some of the uses of different evaluation tools in an academic library. The paper will describe the practical use of surveys, larger and smaller, questionnaires, focus groups and stake holder meetings, all of which will yield different kinds of data. As part of quality management, the practical uses of this data will be explored.
Keywords: Quality in libraries, leadership, statistics, focus groups, surveys

1. Introduction

Library managers all over the world need to utilize all possible means to ensure that service quality always is the best it can be. In this paper I will, very concretely and very practical, show some of my own experiences with different kinds of statistics, surveys and other kinds of systematic feed back from the library users, and how I have utilized this for a better library.

Let me first say a few words about my library. I work at the University of Bergen Library, on the Western coast of Norway. Here, I am leader of the Social Science, Arts and Humanities Library, which is located in two different newly refurbished Library buildings at the campus. We serve somewhere around 6.000 students and 1.000 academic staff from the faculty of humanities and faculty of social sciences. 40staff are working in this part of the library.

2. Theories on quality

As a theoretical background, I would like to start with K.A. Røvik, and his important work on how different organizations employ adaptations of different programs for ensuring quality in their organizations. In his research Røvik finds that different waves or tides of reform also highlight different aspects or tools at different times. Reform tools tend to follow a cyclical pattern, coming into and going out of fashion. A management concept is not only a toolkit for identifying and correcting organizational failures and improving organisational efficiency, but it is also a symbol that can give legitimacy and credibility to organisations (Røvik 1998, Pors 2008)

In fact, several of these ideas have become so popular that they can be found nearly everywhere and in all kinds of organizations. Røvik (2002) labels such ideas organizational super-standards, of which Management by Objectives and Total Quality Management are currently two of the most popular. Quality management reforms involve a shift in focus away from procedures and input and towards products, performance, and quality of output, customer satisfaction, and employee empowerment.

New Trends in Qualitative and Quantitative Methods in Libraries
A. Katsirikou and C. H. Skiadas (eds)
© *World Scientific Publishing Co (pp. 97-102)*

Røvik works especially with organizations within the public sector of Norway and Scandinavia. From the library point of view we must look to professor Niels Ole Pors and his ground breaking work, with professor Carl Gustav Johannsen, on Danish libraries and managers. We can see that this is the same in libraries. Pors finds that there appears to be two main reasons for introducing management tools. One is to meet external requirements, the other is symbolic, to market the library as modern and in the forefront. (Pors 2008)

LIS researchers have looked to marketing and other research to focus attention on expectations and an alternative view of quality, one representing the user's or customer's perspective on the services used. Those researchers who have examined quality from that perspective concur with their peers in marketing that "only customers judge quality; all other judgments are essentially irrelevant."(Zeithaml et al 1990) They emphasized, "service-quality perceptions stem from how well a provider performs vis-a`-vis customers' expectations about how the provider should perform." (ibid) As a result, the research has tended to define service quality in terms of meeting or exceeding customer expectations, (Reeves & Bednar 1994) or, more precisely, as the difference- or gap-between customer perceptions and expectations of service.

Within the LIS-field Peter Hernon and John R. Whitman has argued that it is possible to examine expectations from two coequal and probably interrelated concepts, service quality and satisfaction. Service quality deals with those expectations that the library chooses to meet, and satisfaction is more of an emotional and subjective reaction to a time-limited event or the cumulative experiences that a customer has with a service provider. (Hernon and Whitman 2000)

3. Different perspectives on quality

Many of the problems of defining and recognising quality arise because the concept can be approached from many different perspectives. Already in 1984, Gavin suggested that at least five views can be identified in the literature and in practice:

• the transcendental view: quality can be recognised, but cannot be defined;
• the customer view: quality as fitness for the customer's purposes or conformance to the customer's requirements;
• the manufacturer view: quality as conformance to specification;
• the product view: quality is related to inherent characteristics of the product;
• the value-based view: quality is dependent on what a customer is willing to pay for it. (Garvin, 1984 in Griffiths 2008)

In the early 2000s, Griffiths and Brophy adapted Gavin's "Quality Attributes" further and produced a set of ten attributes that they find useful for assessing the quality, usability and impact of services and resources. These attributes are: Performance, Conformance, Features, Reliability, Durability, Currency, Serviceability, Aesthetics, Perceived Quality, and Usability. (Griffiths 2008)

These are some examples, and more can be found in the literature. The different questions and perspectives will require different approaches, maybe to be asked from different people, who will give different weight to the questions and to the library. And we, the practitioners and leaders, will also have different wishes, and different needs.

In my work, as a library leader, I want to a use a select number of methods in order to get specific feed back from the users of the library.

4. Statistics

First, I will keep an eye on the main statistics: The number of visitors, the number of loans in total, the number of loans from our primary groups, downloads of central electronic journals and databases. As long as they are stable or even rising (at least not falling dramatically and unexplainable) I will be content and not worry. If they start falling, I will have to investigate quickly what is happening. What are the factors that can explain this decline? Another new library for some of our users? Reduced opening times? More electronic books? Reduced acquisitions?

5. Questionnaires

For times of change I have found that questionnaires asking about the service to the patrons will be useful. The questionnaire should not be too large and not have too many questions. At the same time, some few openings for open answers are always valuable. It should contain enough of the relevant background questions to be valid, but not so many that the patrons find themselves un-anonymous. And the total number of questions and questionnaires ought to be low enough for you to be able to handle inside the library.

6. Example: A small survey

When we opened our new Arts and humanities library in August 2005, we went from a 1961 type of very closed library to an open and modern 2005 library, complete with RFID and self service machines for loan and return. We were very proud (we still are, in fact). Still, we were not certain that this was as good as it could be, so in the fall of 2005 and early spring of 2006 we did a small user survey for the people coming into the library. We asked about what they had been doing in the library, what they wanted us to prioritize in the near future, and how satisfied they were. We also had some questions with possibility for open answers (What are you satisfied with, what can we do better, and how, etc) that also gave us some very important feed back.

I will just give you a few examples of the comments we got, and what we did with those comments:

- The students all loved the new, roomy and airy library. Their major suggestion for improvement was that we must make more working/reading places for the students. The professors all loved the new, airy and roomy library. Their major suggestion for improvement was more books, especially from the closed stacks. So what did we do? Of course if we were to fill the library with new study places and more shelves with books on them, we might as well forget about the nice, roomy and airy library. So we put up a few more shelves and we made an effort to take the most asked-for books out of the closed stacks, while at the same time putting some of our less used books from open into closed stacks. We put up some more proper working tables for students instead of the "relaxing" low tables we earlier had had in an area, and also along some walls where there had not been study places before.
- We got comments that it was noisy in the library from about 5% of the questionnaires. We also got comments that it was nice to be able to talk in the library from 5%. So what did we do? We made smaller signs saying "please be considerate, people are trying to concentrate", we made special zones where patrons could use their mobiles, and we trained the librarians to talk more quietly. At the same time, we told patrons that "this is not a reading room; this is not a quiet library".

A final comment: This survey was done within the library, on paper, by handing out questionnaires to patrons, and the librarians coming back to pick them up after a little while. It was supposed to tell the library about how to improve the quality of the services, by asking for comments from the patrons already in the library; and it did.

7. Example: A large survey

In the spring of 2009, University of Bergen Library along with several other institutions of Higher Education joined in a LibQual survey. This is a totally different kind of survey, a web-survey where the questions are already set, and where all in the university, not only library patrons, were asked about service and satisfaction with the library. I will not go into the technicalities and details of this survey, but only about some of the results and our subsequent actions.

The Social Science and Arts and Humanities library both got very high marks for personal service from the librarians, actually, one could almost say "too high", going above and beyond all that can be expected of us. The area most clearly marked out for improvement was the web based resources, which were considered difficult to find and use. So since then, we have made a special project to make better web pages for patrons (I am glossing over a lot of hard work and fights with other University departments here) and also to be especially pedagogic when it comes to showing new students about our electronic resources. We have made a point of going to the departments and showing them subject specific electronic resources.

A final comment: The data from LibQual is handled in the US, and we lost the feeling of ownership to the data and the process.

8. Example: Focus groups

So when the results from the questionnaires are in, and you still need more information on one special point, it can be very useful to have set discussions with a certain focus group.

One focus group that we use a lot is the seminar leaders for the first-term students. They are important for us when it comes to the content of our teaching for this group of student. So late in every spring term we have a meeting with the seminar leaders that are going to work the following fall term. We show them what we are planning to teach the new students, tell them what the last batch of students told us in their feed back to the teaching, and get suggestions and comments.

In the course for the first-term students we teach about library resources that will be of importance for their first essay-exam, and about ethical and correct use of information in academic life. One improvement that grew out of the seminar leaders' focus group was that they now, for some of the teaching, will do an exercise first, and we will explain the theory afterwards. We will ask them to evaluate some web pages in groups of two or three, and then after show them the list of criteria for evaluating web pages as sources of scholarly information. Together we will then discuss what are good and not so good criteria to use, and give examples.

In addition to improving the library's teaching, the focus group with seminar leaders also provides us with a forum for aligning our teaching and the seminar leaders teaching for the same group of students. This is important to ensure we only "double" the teaching we want to "double".

9. Example: Stake holders meetings

Our most loved users and patrons in a university library are of course students and academic staff. Once we have identified what group of patrons are the most important and most highly prioritized, we must try to get in touch with them to ask for their comments and suggestions regarding better quality. It is nice if those meetings can be with a representative body, or in a larger setting, and also if one can manage to have them regularly.

We started with meeting the deans and faculty administrative leadership for both the faculties. Then we invited ourselves to the Departments, at times when they had already gathered most of the scholars. As for the students, we invite the Student Union Representative to the two faculties regularly for a chat.

From these contacts we pick up some points to do with the quality. One is a suggestion that we enable scholars to have books sent between the branch libraries, also the ones that are very to each other. We are currently looking into that. Another, from the students, concern the way some students will occupy the working places with stuff even when they are at lectures.

We have good relations with our major stakeholders and are eager to listen to their suggestions for better quality in the library

10. Conclusions

The usefulness of a large and differentiated tool-box for finding the views of important stakeholders and patrons can not be underestimated. Most of us, as library leaders, know very well how to deliver a good quality service, but by engaging even closer with the patrons, we may be able to gain those insights and little new ideas that lift our library services from good to great.

References

Ellis, D. (1984). "The effectiveness of information retrieval systems: the need for improved explanatory frameworks". *Social Science Information Studies*, **4**, 261-272.

Griffiths, J.R. and Brophy, P. (2002) "Student searching behaviour in the JISC Information Environment." *Ariadne*, 33, [Online] http://www.ariadne.ac.uk/issue33/edner/intro.html

Griffiths, J.R. (2008) "Measuring the quality of academic library electronic services and resources" in http://17conf.lib.uoi.gr/index.php/en/programma.html

Hernon, P and N. Rossiter, (eds) (2007) Making a difference: leadership and academic libraries,

Hernon, P & J. R. Whitman, (2000) Delivering Satisfaction and Service Quality: A Customer-Based Approach for Libraries (Chicago, IL: American Library Association).

Landøy, A & A Repanovici (2009): "Marketing research using online surveys" in *Bulletin of the Transilvania University of Brasov* • Vol. 2 (51) – 2009, Series V: Economic Sciences, p 37 - 40

Lægreid, P, P. G. Roness, and K. Rubecksen, (2007) "Modern Management Tools in State Agencies: The Case of Norway", *International Public Management Journal*, 10: 4, 387 — 413

Nitecki, D A,and P. Hernon (2000) "Measuring service quality at Yale university's libraries" in *The Journal of Academic Librarianship* Volume 26, Issue 4, July 2000, Pages 259-273

Pors, N. O. 2008: "Management tools, organisational culture and leadership: an explorative study" in *Performance Measurement and Metrics*, Vol 9 No 2, 2008, pp 138-152

Reeves C. A & Bednar, D. (1994) "Defining Quality: Alternatives and Implications," *Academy of Management Review* 19 (July 1994): 437.

Repanovici, A, Alexandrescu B and Enoiu R: (2009) "Statistical methods and applied computing in academic educational marketing" *in WSEAS transactions on computers* 2009

Repanovici, A and A. Landoy, (2009): "Knowing the needs. A system for evaluating the university library." *Conference paper from QQML2009 (Qualitative and Quantitative Methods in Libraries),* 26.-29. May 2009. http://hdl.handle.net/1956/3705

Røvik, K. A. (1998). Moderne organisasjoner. Bergen: Fagbokforlaget.

Røvik, K. A. (2002). ''The Secrets of the Winners: Management Ideas That Flow.'' Pp. 69–92 in K. Sahlin-Andersson and L. Engwall, eds., *The Expansion of Management Knowledge.* Stanford: Stanford University Press.

Zeithaml, V, A. Parasuraman, & L. L. Berry, (1990) Delivering Quality Service: Balancing Customer Perceptions and Expectations (New York:The Free Press), p. 16.

Greek Academic Repositories: Policies for Making Available Scientific and Cultural Content

Manolis Koukourakis

University of Crete Library, Greece

Abstract: Most Greek academic institutions have in our days implemented and put into productive operation depositories for the registration, promotion and preservation of scientific / intellectual work produced in them. Many of them also operate digital repositories that contain various cultural material. The vast majority of them make use of open source repository systems, and have adopted open access policies for the disposal of the contained material to the global public through the Internet. This paper surveys the current situation with respect to systems used, interoperability standards and policies adapted, with a view to the visibility of the contained material, examining if and how the need for making available Greek material to the general public is served by recent developments regarding IRs and open access in Greece.
Keywords: Digital libraries, institutional repositories, open access, national policy, interoperability standards, metadata harvesters

Introduction

Although it is only a dozen of years, a long time has gone -and much progress on the field has been made- since University of Crete Library created the first digital library in a Greek academic institution in 1997 (Tzanodaskalakis 1998, Kapidakis 1999). This early attempt was meant as a pilot step to implement both what is now formally called an institutional repository and a digital library for various forms of cultural content. It included mainly the University's grey literature (electronic Masters Theses and Dissertations), and a few more experimental collections of digitized images, university guides, journal pamphlets and technical reports. It was based on the Dienst system, it included some basic bibliographic metadata (basic Dublin Core elements, but not in Dublin Core format) and provided access to the full-text (acceptable document formats were MS-Word, PDF, PS for document files, and JPEG, TIFF and GIF for images). Since then various attempts have been made at both departmental and institutional, as well as interuniversity or disciplinary level, to create similar digital libraries. In our days Most Greek academic institutions have implemented and put into productive operation depositories that host not only an institution's scientific production, but also various kinds of cultural content. Of course, unlike the late nineties, in our days those two kinds of digital depositories, the institutional repositories and the digital libraries that host cultural material are separated in their field and scope, being considered two distinct things. However, for the purposes of the present paper, we will not remain in their distinct content, but rather focus on their common elements, as digital archives freely accessible online, with a view to the visibility of the contained material. We will try to examine if and how the need for making available Greek research or cultural material to the global internet community is properly served by recent developments regarding IRs and open access in Greece[1].

New Trends in Qualitative and Quantitative Methods in Libraries
A. Katsirikou and C. H. Skiadas (eds)
© *World Scientific Publishing Co (pp. 103-120)*

Greek academic institutions and their libraries are are not the only relevant bodies, but they are preemptive agencies in the field, not only because they are by definition interested in the communication and promotion of their work, but also because they have a leading role in relevant activities, having already established operational repositories that host both scientific and cultural material. IR software platforms (Dspace, Eprints, Fedora, Invenio etc) can in fact be used to host and handle various, multiple types of content, and this is also the case with Greek institutions. Most of them use their repository systems to host various different types of digital collections[2].

1. Major initiatives related to OA the last decade
Over the past decade, Greek academic institutions, and more specifically academic libraries, apart from the worldwide progress in the field, as regards systems infrastructure, functionality, metadata and interoperability standards, have greatly benefited from two major national funding opportunities for implementing such systems, namely the two phases of "Operational Programme for Education and Initial Vocational Training" (EPEAEK I & II, 2nd & 3rd CSF) and "Operational Programme 'Information Society'" (3rd CSF).

1.1. "Operational programme for education and initial vocational training"
The "Operational Programme for Education and Initial Vocational Training", whose managing authority was the Hellenic Ministry of National Education and Religious Affairs, was a national program to reform the educational system at all levels of education, aiming at developing a modern education system capable of responding effectively to modern requirements. It was designed to aid meeting the challenges arising internationally due to the development of innovative technologies and turning these challenges into opportunities for development and improvement of the quality of life. During EPEAEK I & II academic libraries, both through vertical actions and through the horizontal action had the opportunity to develop or to get equipped with various library systems for all their functional needs, among them also with Digital Library Systems for the management of various digital collections, institutional repositories, electronic journals, etc. By the end of the Programme, most higher education institutions had implemented their institutional repositories. In many cases they also implemented digital library systems to host various cultural material that academic institutions or their libraries had at their possession and were able to digitize, or got permission to digitize/host, utilizing EPEAEK funding[3].

1.2. "Operational programme 'information society' 2000-2006"
Almost in parallel with EPEAEK II, another major program also under the Third Community Support Framework, the "Operational Programme 'Information Society' 2000-2006", with its renowned Call Nr. 65 of the Priority Axis 1 - Education and Culture, Measure 1.3: Documentation, Utilization and Promotion of the Greek Culture, marked the first national systematic attempt for the digitization and promotion of the Greek cultural heritage. The three main objectives of the Call 65 were saving the country's cultural material through high quality digitization, easy access to such material through documentation and storage in information systems, and its projection and promotion, at a lower resolution, through Internet and electronic publishing.
The call was not specifically addressed to the academic institutions, but it was rather originally conceived as having as ultimate beneficiaries the various cultural organizations supervised by, or affiliated with, the Ministry of Culture. Yet it was eventually opened to the broader community of all organizations related to Greek culture, mainly when it was realized, from the number of proposals originally

submitted, that the bodies directly affiliated to the Ministry of Culture were not ready or mature enough to undertake and successfully implement such kind of projects. This allowed various holders of historical or cultural material, such as Museums, Archaeological Sites, Libraries, Archives, Cultural Organizations, Clubs / Associations, Metropolises, Monasteries, Public Sector Bodies, Private not for profit Organizations and various other cultural institutions to submit proposals and implement projects. This broader opening of the Call 65 really came at a very happy moment for the academic institutions, when most of them had already been actively involved in the creation of digital depositories, thus having had already acquired some specialized experience and know-how both on the digitization of cultural material, and on implementing digital library systems[4].

The complementary Call 172: "Creation of digital cultural reserve, highlight, promotion and communication of Greek Culture in the Information Society", was announced in 2006 as a call of excellence, meant both as a reward to those institutions who were effectively implementing successful projects within Call 65[5], and at the same time as an effort to introduce and establish an Institution of Excellence and promote good practice[6]. Call 172 thus rewarded the successful implementers with the possibility of a new, additional project for the documentation, digitization, and promotion of cultural and historical content, but also gave them the opportunity to further enhance the visibility of the cultural reserve of the country with new, more innovative applications[7].

1.2.1. Accomplishments of the OP IS
1.2.1.1. Digital reserve

These projects resulted at the digitization, promotion and enhancement of cultural reserves held and managed by the cultural institutions of the country but also at the development of the most innovative applications, such as educational software applications based on the cultural heritage or multilingual electronic publishing with cultural content. The successful completion of these projects thus created in a rather short time (roughly, in less than three years, in most cases), a major digital cultural reserve[8] in the Greek territory. This was an exceptional case not only in Greece, but even within European Community, as officially acknowledged by European Commission itself. Describing the evolution of the "Digital Libraries" initiative from 2005 to 2008, the European Commission made a special reference on Greece, presenting the country as an example Member State that actively promotes and finances the digitization and enhancement of the historical and cultural reserve, within the framework of the followed Digital Strategy:

> *Between 2003 and 2007, Greece supported 180 different digitisation projects from museums, libraries and archives with total funding of €100 million. Under the Greek national digital strategy for 2008-2013 a similar amount is earmarked for digitisation*[9]

1.2.1.2. Provision for standards and OA mandate

What was also exceptional about invitation 65 and marked a major difference with regard to previous digitization efforts, as those included in EPEAEK I & II was the fact that it made two very important provisions. First, it established as a compulsory, legally binding requirement that all material digitized by invitation 65 funding should be made openly available to the general public through Internet. This open access mandate was by itself a very important step, officially supporting open access for the first time in Greece. Second, it provided for the adoption of standards and best practices to be followed for the implementation of the awarded projects. Within the framework of the invitation 65 six studies[10] were carried out by major universities and institutes in the country[11], with the very specific goal to clearly designate and establish standards and best practices for the digitization, documentation, management, protection and promotion of cultural content, to be followed by projects funded out of the OP IS and the Ministry of Culture. Performed by specialized research centres with specific expertise at the respective fields, those studies worked towards the evaluation of research and experimental results and practices, the highlighting of best practices and methodologies, following an analysis of internationally recognized technical standards and guidelines, and the harmonization of the methodologies and standards with the guidelines set at EU level. Each of those projects concluded at respective full-text studies and both short and detailed guides, which were altogether gathered in the comprehensive guide "Techniques and standards for the digitization and utilization of the country's digital cultural content"[12], with the aim to be used for planning and implementing projects to Call 65.

1.2.1.3. Institution of Excellence

An additional exceptional move of the complementary call 172 was that the Managing Authority, for the purpose of rewarding the encompassed projects with an Award of Excellence[13], commissioned an external scientific body, having the adequate group of experts, to study the physical object and results of the projects and establish procedures and criteria for their evaluation. In the study, the experts worked on the methodology and developed specific criteria for the identification of best practices in the context of excellence in the fields of documentation, digitization and enhancement via the Internet, of cultural heritage at national and European level. These criteria formed then the basis on which the group of experts evaluated and rated the projects and by extension their implementing agencies[14].

Altogether those three lines of action related with Call 65 of the OP IS, the open access mandate, the provision for guidelines and standards regarding the implementation of the physical object of projects, and the introduction of the Institution of Excellence, provide clear evidence for the careful and systematic conception and design of the OP IS as a major national initiative in the field of cultural heritage, based on a comprehensive, both detailed but also integrated strategy[15], covering all aspects of the work undertaken[16].

1.2.1.4. Greek version of the Creative Commons licenses

Another important recent step in the promotion of the open access movement in Greece was the launch (13 October 2007)[17] of the Greek version of the Creative Commons licenses (www.creativecommons.gr), a task also taken under the OP IS[18]. Now Greek authors also have at their disposal a more flexible than the "all rights reserved" copyright model, to take control of the way they choose to share their intellectual property, and clearly communicate which rights they reserve, and which they waive for the benefit of recipients or other creators. The porting of the Creative Commons to the Greek jurisdiction, by enabling Greek authors to use these licenses in the Greek territory, promotes sharing of scientific and academic knowledge, encouraging and further enhancing the open access publishing and archiving.

1.3. Additional projects within 3rd CSF

Some major additional related digitization steps within 3rd CSF were the projects "Digitization of Public Libraries material", one of the largest digitization projects in our country, involving the digitization of material held at 46 Public Libraries supervised by the Ministry of Education and located throughout the Greek territory, which resulted in 16.2 million digitized pages, representing 41,444 titles of books, newspapers, magazines, maps, documents and manuscripts[19], the project "General State Archives's Digitization of Cultural Collections", involving the digitization of material held at thirty seven State Archives, which produced 7,360,000 digitized pages of various archival material dating from the 17th to the 20th century,[20] and the project "Documentation, Utilization and Promotion of the collections of the Library of Parliament", which digitized more than 15,000 microfilms of newspapers and journals volumes (9,000,000 shots), representing 8,000,000 digital items, and more than 3,000 rare manuscripts and printed material[21].

The completion of the two Operational Programmes, "Information Society" and "Education and Initial Vocational Training" under the Third Community Support Framework, by the end of the 2000 decade, thus marked a major advancement for Greece in the fields of open access, institutional repositories and cultural reserve. Most academic institutions now have their own IRs, containing both scientific and cultural material, while a variety of cultural institutions have also created numerous digital collections that are openly available on the Internet.

2. Comprehensive visibility of the national digital reserve?

The remaining question is if and how the overall Greek scientific and cultural production, is properly represented on a comprehensive national level: if the work done and the resources now available have the adequate impact regarding the visibility and promotion of this major national scientific and cultural reserve, at a national and international level. The current situation reveals that no serious effort is made from a national perspective: Neither of the aforementioned major operational programmes provided for the implementation of a general, centralized or distributed, search or aggregation system which could provide comprehensive access to the digital or digitized material that was made available within their frameworks. Although all the material is in fact there, in most cases openly available to the internet community, having no single point of access to it, it remains scattered and dispersed. Thus the overall Greek production, scientific research or cultural material, remains practically difficult to exploit from a comprehensive point of view, therefore not properly represented.

Although special emphasis and considerable proportion of funding was given to a wide awareness and information action in order to disseminate the potential of IS applications and services amongst the population, no serious efforts have been made for the practical and effective utilization of the projects outcomes from a national point of view. The active promotion of the projects and their results, through various events, information leaflets and even the creation and distribution of multimedia products serve the publicity and dissemination goal, however all the aforementioned actions can not have the desired effect without providing points of comprehensive access to the available material on a larger, national scale.

It is true that a few efforts have indeed been made, in existing sub-fields, but not in a comprehensive way, from the perspective of a national strategy for the interconnection and enhanced visibility of all the available material. Thus, although some important steps are actually done, however those actions also remain dispersed themselves, not leading to effective and practical, comprehensive access to the available scientific and cultural reserve[22].

EPEAEK gave academic libraries a great opportunity to make remarkable improvements in all fields. However, although it was a centrally managed project, it rather followed a bottom-up approach as regards its priorities and goals, and the ways of implementations by the individual institutions. This allowed the majority of academic libraries to make a major progress towards their modernization, but also marked a considerable gap in the co-ordination of the overall project and its implementation by the academic institutions: apart from the Legal Framework that provided the managerial and administrative structure, the regulations to be applied for the implementation of operations, no central, clearly defined methodology was provided regarding the implementation of the physical object of the projects, to form the main framework within which all library development teams should work. The lack of joint coordination or provision for implementation guidelines regarding the physical object of the projects -e.g., suggestions for applying specific standards, following appropriate routines, proposed scenarios and guidelines of good practice- from the part of the central authority, resulted in each institution finding its own way in implementing various systems that addressed the same needs, and in frequent overlapping, leading to considerable loss of valuable resources. The majority of institutions gained valuable experience and considerable expertise which could, through proper coordination, act multiplier, yielding significant savings in view of the overall project, regarding both the various implementations and their interoperability, as well as the visibility of their results. This, however, was an essential step not taken.

Cooperation and coordination efforts within EPEAEK

Greek academic libraries themselves made within EPEAEK major moves towards their cooperation and mutual coordination. The most important action from this respect was the conception and implementation of the Libraries Horizontal Action, which resulted in the establishment of the consortium of the Greek academic libraries, the Hellenic Academic Libraries Link (HEAL-Link).

Two of the actions carried out within the Horizontal Action for the Networking of the Libraries of Higher Education Institutions were related to the creation of:

- a union bibliographic catalogue of Greek academic Libraries
- an interuniversity digital library system for the electronic documentation of modern Greek grey literature.

However, although in the direction of the creation of the union bibliographic catalogue there was provision for the parallel development of two different systems, one centralized and one decentralized[23], no similar provision was made for the institutional repositories and other digital library systems. The single system chosen was designed as a comprehensive, distributed online documentation unit, but the specific approach, model and platform adopted did not achieve the expected results.

Artemis "Interuniversity digital library system for the electronic documentation of modern Greek grey literature" (http://artemis.cslab.ntua.gr/), based on Dienst, aimed to systematically document and disseminate the intellectual production of the country's higher education institutions by using digital libraries technology[24]. However, although it was conceived as part of the horizontal action of Greek academic libraries, Artemis did not receive the expected acceptance, and was finally supported by only a very few academic institutions. Two possible reasons for the low acceptance maybe were the facts that it was not directly attached to the library community, thus did not address a variety of policy issues pertaining to library material, and that the Dienst system, although distributed, was a bit restrictive, at a time when major academic libraries were each trying to find its way in the digital libraries field.

Thus current situation as regards academic institutional repositories is that most institutions have developed such systems, which are in their vast majority open and interoperable, but no provision has been made for their interconnection in a comprehensive aggregating system.

On the other hand, apart from an aggregating service, no provision has either been made for even the searching of the IRs contents from a modern meta-search engine. Horizontal Action has implemented a very advanced federated metasearch platform (based on MuseGlobal "the most full-featured broadcast search technology available") for the comprehensive searching to all available e-resources, which also provides access to institutional repositories. However, from the total thirteen repositories available through Heal-Link MuseSearch engine (http://muse.heal-link.gr), only four refer to Greek institutions[25].

It is understandable that Greek academic libraries had to address the most pressing need of providing common access to all their OPACs and the e-journals and databases, as well as to establish and interlibrary loan network, so that interconnecting IRs were not such an ultimate priority. It is also understandable that the various institutions did not move that quickly on this direction, because they were first and foremost caring about establishing and operating their own systems. Yet, interconnecting the individual IRs seems an obvious step, given the progress libraries have done in the field, establishing and operating open access repository systems. Since it is the very idea of IRs to promote coherent handling strategies and interoperability procedures in order to allow the different systems used by the repositories to communicate and exchange data, the absence of any effort to provide comprehensive access to all Greek IRs is a considerable gap. The case is even more striking, when Greek academic IRs are implemented on a very limited number of open platform repository systems that use DC and are OAI compatible (CDS Ingenio, DSpace, Eprints, Fedora, Keystone -of which DSpace implementations prevail, with a percentage of more than 60%). However, the existence of non-communicating instances even within the same institution shows that there is some way for Greek institutions to go in this direction.

Directory of Greek Digital Resources

Another important step taken also within EPEAEK II but not within horizontal action is the Directory of Greek Digital Resources[26], an initiative of the Library & Information Center of the University of Patras, aiming to become the unique access point of useful information to all scholarly and related Greek digital resources available on the web. The Directory has been developed and operates in a pilot version since 2008, providing the only comprehensive inventory of existing Greek digital collections so far. As the developers and maintainers of the Directory report, «according to current data [April 2010] of the Directory of Greek Digital Resources there are more than 200 active resources, including e-journals, journals archives and IRs" (Georgiou & Papadatou 2010, p.18). Of them 22 are formal academic IRs (among all 33 Academic Institutions, 17 run their own OAI IRs while 2 more run a non OAI-PMH compliant IR, based on custom/commercial applications and 2 more keep operating an IR on an obsolete Dienst platform)[27], 22 are OAI compliant digital collections, and 65 are non OAI-PMH compliant Digital Collections.

Cooperation and coordination efforts within the OP IS

The implementation of the projects in the OP IS was the largest ever intervention in the area of attempting to combine new technologies with the cultural and historical heritage[28]. The digital collections created contain hundreds of thousands of documents, covering all aspects of cultural and historical heritage, such as literature, theatre, music, dance, cinema, audio-visual arts, architecture, archaeology, Greek tradition and folklore, anthropology, social and political history, geology, natural history, etc. Although, however, a lot of emphasis has been given in the adoption of metadata and interoperability standards, no effective provision has been made for the implementation of a comprehensive service that would build on this interoperability to establish a point of unified, common access to all the digitized material, conveying to the user the original and multifaceted experience of all the Greek cultural heritage. What would also have been of great help, especially to small institutions or institutions with no previous experience in digitization and digital library systems, would have been to have provided for a set of relevant tools and repository systems, customized for the needs of Greek material, to be readily available for the institutions wishing to implement such systems[29]. The provision for the creation of national aggregating services would at the same time act as a real-time test-bed for the various individual infrastructures created and their compliance to the standards adopted.

It is true that some steps are undertaken in order to participate in the European effort to develop the field of digital cultural content and key management services, so as to achieve interoperable connection of online cultural content. For example, in the field of culture, the Ministry of Culture, together with the National Technical University of Athens, have active participation in very important European Projects aiming to create common platforms for the digitization and management of cultural reserve in a pan-European level, such as the MINERVA-EC and MICHAEL, and their successors ATHENA and MICHAEL Plus. The website www.michael-culture.gr has been registered for the Greek national MICHAEL instance. The Ministry of Culture also cooperates with the Council of National Representatives of European countries (National Representatives Group) on the aim to ensure synergy and interoperability between all the technological applications for the promotion of cultural reserve across Europe. A recent effort for harvesting metadata of Greek institutional repositories in the context of EuropeanaLocal is also under development[30]. However, those efforts do not have the expected results and impact as regards the promotion of the overall Greek cultural reserve across Europe, mostly because they remain constrained within their own specific limits, not functioning within a certain, coherent national strategy. Taking into account the tremendous mass of digital reserve created under calls 65 and 172, the amount of material being accessible through the local MICHEL instance or the Europeana portal is rather not very encouraging.

The lack of a national policy for the effective communication of the accomplished work is also evident in the operational programme's websites, that are supposed to be specifically designed to communicate the OP IS activities: the Information Society website is mainly designed to incorporate informative data of the various projects from the administrative point of view (e.g., announcements of calls and tenders), but not with a view to promote the work accomplished in an expressive way, so that to be of real benefit for the end user. E.g., there is no single webpage to contain a full list of the projects funded and the websites created. The only comprehensive list published is a table that includes those 59 agencies and websites of the projects that were awarded with the Award of Excellence[31].

Existing comprehensive efforts at the national level

Thus, despite the major progress done in the field, the only national-level service providing comprehensive access to Greek scientific content is the National Archive of PhD Theses developed and maintained by the Greek National Documentation Centre (EKT), from as early as 1985. It is so far the only example of a successful national initiative to gather all research material, although it was not directly related to the institutional repositories efforts of the academic institutions. It was a separate initiative, mandated by law, entailed in a comprehensive policy covering all aspects of relevant procedures[32]. The National Archive of PhD Theses went under various stages as regards its infrastructure, but was very recently migrated to an open source repository platform[33], also providing open access "to anyone in the world for searching and browsing" (http://phdtheses.ekt.gr): "As of April 2010, the archive contains more than 24.500 dissertation theses, the majority is completed at Greek Universities since 1985 and nearly 10% of them are from Universities outside Greece. The archive also includes some Dissertations dating as far back as the mid 1930's. The full-text of more than 13.680 theses is available for browsing and printing one-page-at-a-time. The PDF is made available for download only to registered users that have accepted the pertinent terms and conditions." NDC is also the national representative, contributing with the National Archive of PhD Theses, to DART-Europe (www.dart-europe.eu), the European partnership of research libraries and library consortia who are working together to improve global access to European research theses.

NDC has recently undertaken an active role in the support and promotion of Open Access movement and has created the portal www.openaccess.gr as the Greek website for open access, to actively promote Open Access issues in Greece[34].

This striking lack of a national policy to provide a single point of access to the Greek research and cultural reserve has been partially but effectively covered by a private initiative. Openarchives.gr (www.openarchives.gr) is the outcome of a personal effort to take advantage of the OAI-PMH protocol functionality of the existing Greek IRs and digital libraries to implement a harvesting service and federated search engine that can search simultaneously across them via a common interface. Openarchives.gr currently harvests and provides simultaneous access to a collection of 41 Greek digital libraries and institutional repositories, summing up to a total of nearly 357.000 documents (11-5-2010), while its index is updated on a daily basis.

3. Required initiative: A comprehensive, coherent national policy

What is therefore of ultimate and urging importance from a national perspective, given the advances accomplished in the field of open access, institutional repositories and digital collections, is the provision of a comprehensive national policy on open access and interoperability issues. This national policy should address the remaining challenges regarding further enrichment and conservation of the existing digital reserve, enhancement of its online accessibility and interoperability and development of new services based on existing content. It should conclude in the creation of an authoritative National Registry and Directory of Greek digital sources, an OAI harvester to aggregate all those collections and a modern meta-search portal that would allow more sophisticated access to all the various types of material available online. This national policy would elaborate on the various aspects and relevant procedures and issue recommendations and guidelines for which the above mentioned services would also provide real-world test-beds.

The vast majority of existing academic repositories are open and interoperable, as proved by both openarchives.gr and the most important international OAI registries and harvesters to which they are included (see, for example, Georgiou & Papadatou 2009, p.23). However, even a cursory comparative glance at the data provided by those registries also reveals a great variety regarding the representation of the Greek digital reserve to the global community, proving both a general neglect or indifference on behalf of the Greek institutions and a great formal diversity of the existing collections: of the overall 22 Greek OAI-PMH Digital Collections registered in major International Harvesters & Registries, 10 are included at OAIster, 13 at BASE, 7 at Scientific Commons, 16 at ROAR, 12 at Open DOAR, 1 at Europeana and 3 at DRIVER (Georgiou & Papadatou 2010, Table 14)[35]. Recent studies have shown that there is also a considerable variety as regards the levels of implementation of metadata schemas and interoperability protocols (Peponakis & Sfakakis, 2008).

The requested national policy would thus first have to clearly designate the conceptual framework for all the stages of the creation and effective operation of a repository, by providing guidelines and minimum implementation requirements at all levels, and also contribute to a practical understanding and solution of interoperability issues across all scientific and cultural capital domains, taking account of the particular needs of all individual agencies.

3.1. Actions to encourage open access archiving of scientific research

ithin the general conceptual framework, a major issue in the field of scientific research is to provide for procedures that would encourage the open access archiving of the work done. This line of action should make provisions for all legal rights and intellectual property aspects involved in registering scientific research material to open access systems, and also mechanisms for self-deposit. Many academic institutions have developed policies -by University Senate decision, responding to library initiative- to mandate the deposit of MA and PhD theses to the Library, and have also undertaken actions in support of the open access movement (Chantavaridou 2009). However, apart from the 1985 law that provided for the creation of the National Archive of PhD Theses, no further legal framework has since then been adapted on the matter of IRs at the national level, a lack that leaves existing IR mandates with no officially legal base. Another relevant significant issue is the absence for any national open access policy for publicly-funded research, in the model of similar mandates existing in many countries[36]. Although Greece was one of the 34 countries that signed the OECD "Declaration on Access to Research Data From Public Funding" (January 30, 2004)[37], only the National Hellenic Research Foundation out of the total 14 national Research Centres, has developed a repository for the registration, management and preservation of its research output (Georgiou & Papadatou 2010, p.15)[38].

3.1.1. Mandating

Yet, as regard mandating, we have to note that to our view, making deposit compulsory and putting no or low barrier to open access should not be considered an uncomplicated, straight-forward issue. A strategy set up at the national level should provide for flexible policies and different levels of access barriers in respect to the authors or other content providers. Apart from the fact that "a variety of legitimate circumstances might require an institution to limit access to particular content to a specific set of users"[39], the various wishes of the authors should also be respected. Mandating is not the solution, if researchers do not realize the need for open access. The real issue is not to mandate, but facilitate the adoption of specific standards and software solutions within a policy-setting that promotes and encourages deposit, and also to have a way to incorporate and present the country's scientific production at a national level. Acknowledging and respecting the authors' sensitivities about their work and providing policy framework and mechanisms to address such concerns is also crucial for the promotion of open access. To our view, allowing for various levels of access to the full text is not a real problem either. Even if there is only access to bibliographic data, the academic and research community would benefit a lot, and this for sure would advance things as regards the open access movement. The most important thing is that the research done is communicated in a comprehensive way, so that there can be an overview of the research taking place. The fact that the vast majority of Greek academic IRs contain mostly Master theses and Doctoral dissertations, but only very few, and in a low level, also incorporate current scientific production of the faculty members, is indicative of the work that remains to be done in this direction[40].

3.2. Repository systems infrastructures

As regards the repository system infrastructure, a major step in the field would be to provide a set of guidelines and technical requirements that digital library systems must meet to be compatible with the specific needs of the various Greek institutions. What is of great importance is that this effort should not be constrained in the field of recommendations, but also be coupled with a set of relevant tools and software, fully documented as to their installation, parameterization, development and use, to be available for those interested to implement digital library systems. The main issue here is of course not to 'reinvent the wheel' by adding yet another set of guidelines for institutions to look at -since there are already available existing sets of guidelines that do a very good job at meeting the various needs of institutions, many of which have already been implemented by academic repositories- but to come up with a coherent national policy which would also provide practical and effective help for the establishment and maintenance of repository infrastructure. For example, OP Information Society has significantly contributed in the direction of guidelines and recommendations for the Greek cultural reserve, with its support and introduction of both the best practices and the criteria for the awards of excellence among the projects funded. The Central Library of Alexander Technological Educational Institution of Thessaloniki has also made an important contribution for the preparation of a national certification policy for IRs, determining -through a comparative examination of major relevant policy schemes (DINI, NESTOR, RLG-NARA and DRIVER Project)- the main control sections and minimum desirable characteristics of the total quality of institutional repositories on the national level[41].

What would be of additional great, effective and practical usefulness would be the provision for a set of readily installable repository tools and platforms properly customized for the Greek institutions. Many Greek institutions have already made significant progress in the field, adopting major existing open source systems (CDS Invenio, Dspace, Eprints, Fedora, Keystone) for the purpose of implementing their own repositories, from which such an effort should greatly benefit. For example -to mention only the IR platform that seems to be the most preferred- a lot of work has already been done by Greek institutions for the adoption of MIT's DSpace repository system into Greek. University of Patras Library has already proceeded in translating DSpace into Greek and also created the Greek DSpace wiki[42], while both the Central Library of Alexander Technological Educational Institution of Thessaloniki (ATEI-The) and National Documentation Centre (EKT) have also proceeded with significant parameterizations, changes, extensions and additions[43].

3.3. National Registry and Directory of Greek digital sources

The creation of a National Registry and Directory of Greek digital sources would also be a crucial development for the overall representation and promotion of the Greek scientific and cultural capital. Providing a single point of reference for the comprehensive gathering and presentation of the scientific and cultural digital map of Greece would significantly update the academic community and the general public about all available sources of information, display existing material and improve the coordination of relevant activities at national level. Such an effort should start by defining common national procedures, methods and tools appropriate for the description, recording and presentation of research or digitization projects that are implemented by various institutions within the Greek territory and the content produced by them. The provision of an appropriate description scheme -or possibly individual compatible sub-schemes- for the adequate recording of the various sources (which is the necessary information, and how it should be recorded) is of great importance. Another important part of the whole procedure is also the development of a clear set of compliance instructions to be available for the various individual institutions. The designation of necessary technical specifications and standards to implement such a registry service would be of additional help in the direction of its communication with similar services existing outside Greece.

3.4. National OAI harvester

The development of the National Registry and Directory of Greek digital sources should also be coupled by the creation of a National OAI harvesting service that would be able to aggregate all Greek collections available and provide for a single point of simple access to their material via a common search interface. This national level service could start by retrieving information from existing academic repositories, since they are already OAI compatible. It should be noted, however, that the absence of a formal repository infrastructure in some institutions is not a real issue for the harvesting of their data, since the intended simplicity of the OAI technical framework, created with the aim of providing low barrier interoperability, places no limitations on the nature of metadata format. Although OAI protocol mandates the Dublin Core elements set, as a de facto standard for simple and common, cross-discipline metadata format, it also supports the notion of multiple metadata sets. The only limitations OAI architecture places on the nature of other parallel sets is that the metadata records should be structured as XML data, and a corresponding XML schema for validation should also be provided[44]. Therefore, even if some institutions have chosen, for various reasons, to not implement a formal repository infrastructure but only use a web platform, such as Joomla, to host and promote their cultural reserve, their material can be harvested by OAI compatible aggregators, and thus widely represented.

The national OAI harvester would also make up the basis for the implementation of an integrated platform for the long-term preservation of the digital material at the national level. This platform should provide a comprehensive conservation plan for all digital evidence through a digital curation solution (in platform and application independent formats and schemas, such as XML) which will, in an ongoing process, ingest, store and maintain not only the digital objects and semantic data, but also the workflows and customizations of various digital libraries.

3.5. A comprehensive meta-search platform

Apart from the simple search functionality to the content of the repositories enabled via the implementation of a National OAI Harvester, a national policy should also provide for the implementation of a modern comprehensive meta-search platform which would allow more advanced, federated access to a variety of information resources, combining the repository systems with various other relevant information sources. Such a service would consist of a virtual platform for searching and retrieval of all documents contained in Greek IRs by either utilizing the automated collection and storage of metadata achieved by the national harvester, or by directly searching each individual institutional repository, through appropriate communication protocols. At the same time it could virtually unite in a common interface the repository systems with various other library catalogues and information sources available to Greek institutions, supporting a collaborative mix that would create a significant added value in support of the end user needs. Such a service would be of great benefit specifically to academic institutions, which are already offering various information sources to their members, having individual or consortium access to a bit variety of scholarly resources.

In our days federated and faceted search and web 2.0 navigation tools provide the ability to develop services that increase the degree of interoperability offered by the various catalogues of institutions, offering enhanced access to them, enriching them with additional features and optimizing performance. Search results can be presented from various different angles, allowing the user to quickly filter and identify the information he wants. A modern search tool tailored to the requirements imposed by diverse and heterogeneous sources can virtually incorporate digital collections with various other information sources of interest to members of the academic community but also to the general public. Such a tool can perform distributed searches in a federated search environment, allowing faceted searching that could incorporate, e.g., the individual digital library systems of all academic libraries with their OPACs, electronic journals systems, e-learning catalogues and various other possible sources of interest which provide interoperability functionality such as Z39.50, SRW/SRU, OpenURL or OAI-PMH. This could also be the first step towards exploring ways to utilize semantic web technologies which would go much further from syntactic interoperability in making available a great variety of information otherwise inaccessible to the end user (deep web, hidden web).

Many academic libraries have already implemented, mainly by adopting existing relevant software, their own meta-search portals that provide comprehensive access to all the material they own or have access to[45].

4. Concluding remarks

It goes without saying that making the case for such inclusive nation-wide infrastructures is not an easy task, mostly because it requires effective and sustainable links between organisational and technical concepts and practices, within a coherent national policy that needs constant support from the state. As we have seen Greek institutions have already done great progress both in the field of IRs and digitization of various types of cultural material. The joint co-ordination of those activities will significantly contribute to the national information network, facilitate updating on available material, highlight research being done in Greek academic institutions and enrich the Internet with research results in Greek. Such an inclusive national infrastructure, by responding to the need of a practical mechanism for gathering together digital content, would develop and broaden the integration of all kinds of resources used by individual institutions, and thus help in the direction of adequate representation of the broad diversity of cultural and scientific reserve. Apart from making the country's cultural and scientific resources accessible for all, establishing simple, efficient and sustainable processes through which the involved institutions can easily make their content available, would put in place an infrastructure that will also facilitate continuous increasing of content. One of the most important points, however, is that this would by itself be an establishment of a cooperation structure for managing the relationship among the involved institutions, which will benefit scientific and cultural bodies of all types and levels, while at the same time will also promote effectively the creation of new patterns of cooperation at national and international level.

It should be noted that an important aspect of the required initiatives is that all tools and services to be developed should be based on open source software to ensure the sustainability of outputs in the long term, beyond their initial implementation. It is also very important that the institutions or group of institutions chosen to develop and implement such national level services should be relevant to content providers and to major institutions which have already established repositories and work in close co-operation with them. Technical expertise is a key issue, but it should also be coupled with the knowledge and experience of institutions which have learned from creating repository services, to conclude to practically effective and realistic solutions[46].

It is understandable that such large-scale initiatives are indeed not among the easiest tasks to undertake in the current environment of economic crisis. However, they seem -if not the only- the preferable way to go, since they also create economies of scale, helping for further exploiting the national scientific and cultural capital.

References

Chantavaridou, Elisavet (2009a), "Open access and institutional repositories in Greece: progress so far", *OCLC Systems & Services: International digital library perspectives*, v. 25, n.1, pp. 47-59.

Chantavaridou Elisavet (2009b), "Contributions of open access to higher education in Europe and vice versa", *OCLC Systems & Services: International digital library perspectives*, v. 25, n. 3, pp. 167-174.

Georgiou, P., Papadatou, F. (2007), "Digital Greek content and open access", *Proceedings of 16th Annual Greek Academic Libraries Conference, Piraeus, September*, pp. 224-41.

Georgiou Panos, Papadatou Fiori (2009), *Scholarly Publishing & Open Access in Greece: 2009 Report* -version 01/2009, [Southern Europe Open Access National reports], Hellenic Academic Libraries Link HEAL-Link, Patras, 23/10/2009. http://oaseminar.fecyt.es/Resources/Documentos/Greece2009.pdf

Georgiou Panos, Papadatou Fiori (2010), *Scholarly Publishing & Open Access in Greece: 2009 Report* – v.2, May 2010, [Southern Europe Open Access National reports], Hellenic Academic Libraries Link HEAL-Link, Patras, 03/05/2010, http://www.heal-link.gr/SELL/OA_reports/Greece2009.pdf

English, R. (2006), "Open access to federally funded research – the time is now", *Portal: Libraries and the Academy*, Vol. 6 No.3, pp.249-52.

Hayes Helen (2005), *Digital Repositories: Helping universities and colleges*, JISC Briefing Paper – Higher Education Sector, August.

Kapidakis, Sarantos (1999), "Issues in the Development and Operation of a Digital Library", Lecture Notes in Computer Science, vol. 1696 (Research and Advanced Technology for Digital Libraries), Springer-Verlag, pp. 363 - 382.

Katsiadakis Helen & Kouriati Katerina (2009), *Current Status Survey on Greece*, DARIAH - Digital Research Infrastructure for the Arts and Humanities, December 2009. http://dariah.eu/documents/DARIAH_Current_Status_Survey_Greece.pdf

Moreleli-Cacouris, Mersini ; Makridou, Elisa; Asmanidis, Ypatios (2007), "Institutional Repositories: A Proposal for a national policy based upon a Greek case", 16th Conference of Hellenic Academic Libraries, "The human factor in the configuration of the current and future library", University of Piraeus Library, 1-3/10/2007, http://hdl.handle.net/10184/657.

Peponakis Manolis & Sfakakis Michalis (2008), "Evaluation of metadata interoperability between institutional repositories and catalogs (OPACs) of Greek academic libraries", 17th Greek Academic Libraries Conference, "Evaluation of Libraries as a Quality of Academic Institutions", Ioannina, 26-28 September 2008. http://17conf.lib.uoi.gr/files/b11.2.Peponakis.pdf

Theodorou, R. (2007), "Viability of open access academic publishing", *Proceedings of 16th Annual Greek Academic Libraries Conference,* Piraeus, September 2007, pp. 281-92.

Tzanodaskalakis, Grigoris (1998), "The Digital Library of the University of Crete", Proceedings of the 7th Conference of Hellenic Academic Libraries, University of Thessaly Library, Volos 1998, pp. 383-396. http://eprints.rclis.org/archive/00010357.

Footnotes

1. In recent years there has been a number of studies that record and analyse open access development and current situation in Greece. See for example Chantavaridou 2009a, Georgiou & Papadatou 2007, Peponakis & Sfakakis 2008 and most comprehensively Georgiou & Papadatou 2009 & 2010, the national report on open access prepared within the framework of Southern Europe Open Access National reports of the SELL (Southern European Libraries Link) Consortia. The reader can find in them detailed recordings of the current situation. Our main concern in this paper is not to provide one more survey, but to reflect on the situation from a national policy perspective.

2. This is not a case pertaining to the Greek paradigm, the situation is the same all over the world. Apart from having a special interest in maintaining repositories for storing, communicating and promoting their work, universities also play a key role in the development of repository software. To name the most common, arXiv was

developed by Cornell University, DSpace was jointly developed by the MIT Libraries and Hewlett-Packard, EPrints was developed the University of Southampton, Fedora open source software for digital object repository systems was developed by Cornell University together with the University of Virginia, while Greenstone, which is developed and distributed in cooperation with UNESCO and the Human Info NGO, is produced by the New Zealand Digital Library Project at the University of Waikato.

3. The Operational Programme for Education and Initial Vocational Training was co-financed by the European Social Fund, the European Regional Development Fund and national resources. EPEAEK phase I (1994-1999) was implemented under the Second Community Support Framework, while EPEAEK II (2000-2006[**30/5/2009**]) under the Third Community Support Framework. For the period 2000-2006 the Programme's co-financed budget amounted to 2.484,6 million euro, with 75% of the funding coming from the European Social Fund (ESF) and the European Regional Development Fund (ERDF) and 25% from national resources.

4. This was originally proved by the fact that many academic institutions were able to prepare and submit relevant and mature project proposals at the very limited submission time provided for the wider opening of the call to all culture-related bodies. Additionally, it was also verified by the fact that they were able to successfully carry out the awarded projects and be among the first beneficiaries that came to project completion.

5. Call 172 was solely aimed at institutions which, as final beneficiaries in the Invitation 65, had implemented or continued to implement projects in the OP IS and covered specific conditions at the time of the submission of the proposal. The two specific criteria set by the Call 172 were that call 65 projects should have advanced to having contracted 80% of the total project budget, and have submitted to the managing authority eligible costs up to 50% of the contracted value of work. An additional prerequisite, however, for the final inclusion of a project to the OP IS, was the verification of the proper management and certification of both the physical and financial object, through site inspections by a Managing Authority team.

6. http://www.infosoc.gr/infosoc/el-GR/specialreports/digital_culture. See also "The establishment of the Institution of Excellence in the OP "IS"", http://www.infosoc.gr/NR/rdonlyres/D5C2CCB5-41E8-4473-A82C-6BEF20C55E89/6007/ΚαθιέρωσηΑριστείας1.doc (in Greek).

7. From 71 proposals submitted, 61 were evaluated positively and finally 59 projects were implemented.

8. Despite the different thematic content, the types of cultural material are common in most cases, such as texts, documents, books, magazines, newspapers, journals, photographs, slides, paintings, posters, maps, drawings, sketches, paintings, engravings, sculpture works, porcelain works, silk screens, clothing -textiles, suits-costumes, sets, scores, audio tapes, videotapes, films, glass plates, museum objects, religious objects, monuments, three-dimensional representations of memorials and buildings.

9. Commission of the European Communities, *Europe's cultural heritage at the click of a mouse: Progress on the digitisation and online accessibility of cultural material and digital preservation across the EU*, [Communication from the Commission to the Council, the European Parliament, the European Economic and Social Committee and the Committee of the Regions], Brussels, 11.8.2008, p. 5. http://ec.europa.eu/information_society/activities/digital_libraries/doc/communicatio ns/progress/communication_en.pdf. This Communication (COM (2008) 513), together with other information materials, was distributed by the European Commission on the occasion of the 20.11.2008 presentation of the "Digital Libraries" initiative and the presentation of the European digital library "Europeana" by European Commission President José Manuel Barroso and the Commissioner for Information Society and Media Mrs Viviane Reding.

10. The specific objects of those studies were: "digitization of two-dimensional images and best practices for digitization and documentation", "digitization of three-dimensional objects", "digitization of video and audio", "development of cultural

documentation systems and interconnection of digital cultural reserve", "protection & management of intellectual property rights of digital content", "design and development of cultural institutions websites".

11. It is very important that those study-projects were awarded to specialized research centres with specific expertise at the respective fields, such as, for example, the High Performance Information Systems Laboratory of the University of Patras (www.hpclab.ceid.upatras.gr), and the Centre for Cultural Informatics of the Information Systems Laboratory of the Institute of Computer Science, Foundation for Research and Technology - Hellas (www.ics.forth.gr/isl/cci.html).

12. http://www.infosoc.gr/infosoc/el-GR/services/elibrary/reports_list/psifiopiisi.

13. The action of excellence was part of the Publicity and Promotion work plan of the OP "Information Society", co-financed by 80% from the European Social Fund and 20% by National Resources.

14. All 59 projects implemented under the Call 172 got rewarded with the title of Excellence. Those whose performances were evaluated and rated over 65 points on a scale 1-100, were in addition rewarded with the award of good practice.

15. George Papaconstantinou, "EU Structural Funds and the Development of the Information Society in Greece", *Journal of Information Technology Impact*, Vol. 2, No. 2, pp. 39-42, 2001. www.jiti.net/v02/v2n2.039-042.pdf

16. The credits for the overall conception and implementation of the OP IS have to be awarded to the "Special Secretariat for the Information Society" (later renamed to "Special Secretariat for Digital Planning") of the Ministry of Economy and Finance, which had as its basic mission the planning, monitoring and supervision of "Information Society", while the "Special Managing Service" had the responsibility for the management and implementation of the OP IS (the two authorities are now responsible for both OP "Digital Convergence" and "Information Society").

17. The launch was celebrated as a major event: was held in the Ceremonies Hall of Athens University, invited Speaker was law professor Lawrence Lessig himself, one of the founders of Creative Commons at 2001. http://www.creativecommons.gr/?p=24.

18. It was the outcome of the "Task I3: Comparative study of the application of the Creative Commons licenses and GPL & LGPL to EU countries and Greece" of "e-business forum" (www.ebusinessforum.gr), a project also encompassed in the OP IS (Measure 3.1), undertaken by The Greek Research and Technology Network (www.grnet.gr).

19. http://diglib.ypepth.gr/awweb/main.jsp?

20. http://www.gak.gr/frontoffice/portal.asp?cpage=NODE&cnode=39&clang=1, http://arxeiomnimon.gak.gr/about/index.html

21. http://catalog.parliament.gr, http://voulibeu.parliament.gr.

22. The lack of a coherent national policy for the establishment of a comprehensive digital infrastructure was also pointed out by the recent DARIAH (Digital Research Infrastructure for the Arts and Humanities) Current Status Survey of Digital Humanities in Greece: "The lack of major data repositories and a national depository is a significant gap that is attributed to the lack of a national strategy to establish a digital infrastructure." "However, initiatives by institutions need government backing. A comprehensive national digitisation strategy formulated by the government at a national level is essential. The work is being done on the ground; it now requires the input of government to bring it together into a national policy and a trusted digital repository." (Katsiadakis and Kouriati, 2009).

23. Zephyr (http://zephyr.lib.uoc.gr) applied a decentralized approach to implement a virtual union catalog and search portal, providing real-time access to the contents of the academic library OPACs based on the Z39.50 protocol. Union catalog (www.unioncatalog.gr) followed a centralized, collective model that gathers and hosts all the bibliographic records of the individual library systems in one main physical system.

24. Artemis system, designed as a comprehensive, distributed online documentation unit, was developed and supported by the Parallel and Distributed Systems Group of the Computing Systems Laboratory of the National Technical University of Athens.
25. Two repositories containing PHD theses: "AUTH -Digitized Doctoral Theses" and "National Archives Doctoral Theses", and two other material: "AUTH - Digitized Articles & Journals" and "ATHENS -Athens Academy".
26. www.lis.upatras.gr/Libworld/gr_resources_EL.php
27. "Concerning the rest of the Academic Institutions, some are already in a transition phase to a new OAI IR, some are rather newly established institutions and they hardly have any data/content at all, and some are very small ones with limited resources to develop and maintain such a service". (Georgiou & Papadatou 2010, p.16).
28. By the time the Awards of Excellence were given (31 March 2009), about 390 projects were implemented under the OP IS, with a total budget of nearly 150 million euro.
29. The absence of any such provision may explain why many institutions did not use for hosting their digitized material "proper" repository software system platforms that are widely used for these purposes (such as, Dspace, Invenio, Fedora, etc).The majority of those institutions did not have previous experience in implementing such projects, or were rather small implement from the scratch and support such infrastructure. The last may also explain why in many cases the standards and recommendations promoted by the OP IS were not adequately followed. On the other hand, some of the major projects had already started their procedures when the InfoSoc recommendations were officially issued.
30. Trohopoulos, I., Koulouris, A., Garoufallou, E., Siatri, R. (2009). "Harvesting metadata of Greek institutional repositories in the context of EuropeanaLocal". Workshop on harvesting metadata: practices and challenges, 13th European Conference on Digital Libraries (ECDL 2009), Corfu, Greece, September 29-October 2, 2009. http://www.ionio.gr/conferences/ecdl2009/ws_europeannalocal.php
31. http://www.infosoc.gr/infosoc/el-GR/specialreports/digital_culture. See also "The establishment of the Institution of Excellence in the OP "IS"", http://www.infosoc.gr/NR/rdonlyres/D5C2CCB5-41E8-4473-A82C-6BEF20C55E89/6007/ΚαθιέρωσηΑριστείας1.doc (in Greek), and ΚΑΙΝΟΤΟΜΙΑ ΕΡΕΥΝΑ & ΤΕΧΝΟΛΟΓΙΑ, 03-04 / 2009, pp.18-23 http://www.ekt.gr/content/img/product/77479/18-23.pdf.
32. Law 1566/1985 (article 70, paragraph 15) designated the National Documentation Centre as the institution responsible for the systematic collection, development and maintenance of the National Archive of PhD Theses.
33. As stated at its website, "The open source repository platform DSpace has been adopted as the best solution, due to its user-friendly, highly configurable services, easier interoperability with other systems and high compatibility with major search engines and international repositories". http://phdtheses.ekt.gr/eadd/aboutEADD.jsp
34. "The Greek website for open access is part of the project "National Information System for Research and Technology, Phase III – Open Access Electronic Repositories and Journals" which is being implemented by the National Documentation Centre under the framework of "Digital Greece" (www.psifiakiellada.gr) and is co-funded by the European Union - European Regional Development Fund (80%) and by the Hellenic State (20%) through the Operational Programme Information Society (3rd CSF 2000-2006)". www.openaccess.gr
35. Such is also the case in the field of cultural reserve: from all 116 collections included at the local MICHAEL instance, only 18 are presented by the MICHAEL European service (http://www.michael-culture.org/en/search/results_org.html?q=fadrcountry:lgrl&base=institution&from1=b rowseOrgPlace&val1=GREECE&sf=ftitle).
36. Like for example the open access mandates already in place or planned for all seven of the UK's Research Councils. SPARC Europe's summary of the policies is available at http://www.sparceurope.org/resources/hot-topics/institutional-repositories/policies-

and-statements. See also ROARMAP (Registry of Open Access Repository Material Archiving Policies) as recommended by the Berlin Declaration (www.eprints.org/openaccess/policysignup/).

37. www.oecd.org/document/0,2340,en_2649_34487_25998799_1_1_1_1,00.html
38. Helios repository of the NHRF is available at http://helios-eie.ekt.gr.
39. R. Crow, "The case for institutional repositories: a SPARC position paper", *ARL Bimonthly Report*, 2002 -
    http://ignucius.bd.ub.es:8180/dspace/bitstream/123456789/315/1/Crow_02.pdf
40. According to Web of Science and Scopus data the total number of articles published in international peer review journals by authors affiliated with Greek institutions for the period 2000-2009 is 105.716 (Georgiou & Papadatou 2010, Table 5). According to the SCImago Journal & Country Rank portal the total number of documents by authors affiliated with Greece contained in the Scopus database for the period 1996-2008 is 109.208, which makes Greece 26th country internationally, with an H-index of 179 (http://www.scimagojr.com/countryrank.php).
41. Moreleli-Cacouris et others, 2007.
42. http://nemertes.lis.upatras.gr/wiki/
43. http://phdtheses.ekt.gr/eadd/aboutEADD.jsp : "The IT Department of EKT proceeded with important parameterizations of DSpace in order to achieve the improvement of searching and browsing operations for the Greek language, the interconnection of material, the presentation of the content, the automatic qualitative control and the manipulation of data. All efforts where targeted to ensure maximum future maintainability, flexibility, sustainability of the system and high interoperability among systems". http://www.openaccess.gr/ekt_oa/repos/infrastructure.dot : "EKT has developed significant extensions in DSpace mostly in issues that pertain to improvement in search functions, indexing in the Greek language, record interconnectedness, customized record presentation, automated quality-control and data processing. In this way the best possible functionalities for were developed for the repositories, and the long term preservation and accessibility to the records, as well as interoperability issues with other repositories were ensured". ATEI-The has also implemented changes and additions into the repository system, in order to "make it more functional and flexible, while at the same time improve the interaction with users, adding value to its services": http://hdl.handle.net/10184/657.
44. http://www.openarchives.org/documents/FAQ.html
45. Such as Ichnae of the University of Patras Library (http://ihnaee.lis.upatras.gr), Ichnilatis of the Aristotle University of Thessaloniki Library (http://www.lib.auth.gr/site/en), Livesearch of the University of Crete Library (http://livesearch.lib.uoc.g) and WebFeat of the Athens University of Economics and Business Library (http://wfxsearch.webfeat.org/wfsearch/search?cid=11683).
46. This does not seem to be the case with similar national efforts so far. For example, none of the major academic libraries providing content has been chosen for participating at EuropeanaLocal and Athena projects.

Library Network Support Services: Quantitative and Qualitative Measures for Assessing the Impact of Information Literacy Initiatives on Learners

Jerald Cavanagh and Padraig Kirby

Limerick Institute of Technology, Republic of Ireland, Ireland

Abstract: Recent developments have seen an interest in quantitative and qualitative measures in the field of information literacy now widely considered the trademark pedagogy of librarians (Kapitzke 2003 cited in Montiel-Overall 2007). International frameworks for assessing information literacy through which positive developments at both international and national levels can be demonstrated and future efforts can be better focused are being identified. This article reports on the Library Network Support Services (LNSS) project - a collaboration to implement and champion online information literacy initiatives across a consortium consisting of a university, a teacher education institution and two Institutes of Technology in the Republic of Ireland. The paper describes the origin and development of the LNSS, deals with the growing importance of information literacy - in the Republic of Ireland and internationally. We will describe the process and methodology for implementing online information literacy initiatives including information literacy teaching across the consortium and also suggest possibilities for measuring the impact of information literacy initiatives on learners for the development of knowledge societies.
Keywords: Information literacy, knowledge societies

1. Introduction

Researchers in library and information science have examined information needs, user wants and user perceptions about the value of library services for many years. The subject of *quality*- that elusive concept in terms of collections e.g. size, titles held, breath of subject coverage and *effectiveness*- the extent to which goals and objectives are set and met has also been widely examined (Nitecki and Harmon 2000). Recent years have seen important studies on the topic of e service quality in libraries and instruments for measuring e services have been developed (Harmon and Calvert). Only in very recent times has the topic of measuring the effectiveness of information literacy come to the fore largely driven by organisations such as UNESCO and by various scholars. The importance of international frameworks for measuring information literacy through which achievements at both international and national levels can be demonstrated and future efforts can be better focused has been stressed (UNESCO 2008). There is a realisation that information literacy has been a neglected aspect of knowledge societies and that it underpins many of the Millennium Development Goals (MGD's) and hence the development of indicators is vital (Catts and Lau 2008). In our mission to develop and champion information literacy initiatives in the Shannon Consortium LNSS have been mindful of qualitative and

New Trends in Qualitative and Quantitative Methods in Libraries
A. Katsirikou and C. H. Skiadas (eds)
© *World Scientific Publishing Co (pp. 121-132)*

quantitative techniques and its strategy has been informed by this. We will now depict the development of the LNSS project and display how its development has been aided by a commitment to identifying quality information literacy products and services for implementation across Shannon Consortium and the use of qualitative techniques to justify decisions.

2. Library Network Support Services

Library Network Support Services (LNSS) is deeply committed to collaboration and capacity building and exploring reusability, sharing, repurposing and reusing existing and innovative IL content, services and initiatives. Consisting of Shannon Consortium partners Limerick Institute of Technology, Institute of Technology Tralee Co. Kerry, Mary Immaculate College Limerick and the University of Limerick the partnership is committed to a bold vision to transform the higher education landscape in the region in a unique integrated approach across a university, a teacher education institution, and two Institutes of Technology. Its mission is to enhance and champion IL initiatives across the Shannon Consortium through the introduction of innovative web based support services and supporting information literacy teaching and training responding to the changing expectation of library users. The aim is to select, develop, implement and evaluate a suite of IL initiatives to International IL standards for the partner's libraries as a framework of support for learners over 2008 for rollout in 2009/2010 consisting of web based interactive IL modules. The LNSS project has a lifespan of 2.5 years lasting from 2008-2011 and is funded by the Strategic Innovation Fund (SIF) which encouraged colleges to collaborate and compete for finance to meet wider economic and social targets.

As the project progresses steadily through 2010 and nearly all of its goals have been or are in the process of being achieved such as rollout of online modular IL suites LNSS are now exploring new territory such as the development of Student Study Skills Online- a collaboration with 15 leading universities form around the world and Epigeum Ltd. - a spinoff company of Imperial College.

LNSS realise that international collaboration is vital for the development of IL and have formed RINGIDEA – a European collaboration involving Ireland (LNSS), Romania, Greece and Norway to develop cutting edge IL initiatives and products through organisation of workshops, conferences and the identification and exploitation of suitable EU funding mechanisms such as Tempus IV all for the development of IL services and initiatives for education.

Not just content with developing standard IL content such as referencing, citation and plagiarism, internet searching and evaluation, the research question etc. LNSS have chartered new territory as it drives information literacy in the Shannon Consortium and the "phenomenal push toward librarians demonstrating their pedagogical skills (Bloom and Deyrup 2003). Stand alone IL Modules dealing with areas such as research ethics, intellectual property, research methods, dealing with your research supervisor, the literature review have been developed incorporating innovative multimedia and active learning. The limitations of overly text based IL modules as emphasised by Xiao e al (2004) have meant that LNSS were careful to ensure that the IL modules selected for development incorporated use multimedia and active learning exercises and particularly online video.

3. Information Literacy: Growing in Importance Day by Day

Especially in the last 20 years library scientists have advocated the importance of information literacy (Kuhlthau 1987; Bruce 1997). Recent years have indicated a phenomenal push toward librarians demonstrating their pedagogical skills (Bloom and

Deyrup 2003). In today's turbulent economic environment Information Literacy is a critical transferrable skill which can empower and help our students to achieve their goals:

Information literacy is about people's ability to operate effectively in an information society. This involves critical thinking, an awareness of personal and professional ethics, information evaluation, conceptualizing information needs, organizing information, interacting with information professionals and making use of information in problem-solving, decision-making and research. It is these information based processes which are crucial to the character of learning organizations (Bruce 1999).

The rise of information literacy has been supported and inspired by the development of numerous standards, guidelines and reports particularly United States, United Kingdom and Australia/New Zealand. The publication of standards such as the *American Library Association Presidential Committee on Information Literacy*, the *Australian and New Zealand Information Literacy Framework: principles, standards and practice* and *Information skills in higher education- Standing Conference of National and University Librarians* "seven pillars" model (SCONUL 1999) have been seminal moments for information literacy and have guided and inspired many by providing frameworks for the development of information literacy initiatives globally.

4. Information Literacy and Ireland

If we define information literacy as the fusion of different concepts, the integration of library literacy, computer literacy, media literacy, information ethics, critical thinking and communication skills (Parang et al., 2000 cited in Bloom and Deyrup 2003) the focus in Ireland has tended to be on information technology and not information literacy (Webber and McGuinness 2007). However the Consortium of National and Research Libraries (CONUL) Working Group on Information Skills Training have taken information literacy on board and are concerned with establishing best practice in information literacy skills training (IST), investigation of current Information literacy practice in CONUL and other relevant libraries, the integration of information literacy into institutional teaching and learning programmes, with regard to teaching and learning developments, and virtual learning environments /managed learning environments. CONUL also suggest areas of development opportunity, promotional material and guidelines for information literacy in CONUL libraries (CONUL 2004). While some academic libraries are developing institutional literacy frameworks (Breen and Fallon 2005) there is no coherent approach to developing information literacy skills in Ireland and no cohesive national strategy (Russell 2008). Information literacy development in recent years has seen Irish Universities and Institutes design and develops online information literacy suites. Some attempts at creating these resources have suffered from being overly text based and lacking engaging active learning exercise however a very recent and significant development has been the SIF funded collaboration between the National University of Ireland, Galway, University College Cork and Trinity College Dublin and their design and development of an innovative and engaging information literacy tutorial at a cost of €100,000 with €600,000 provided for Generic Skills Project and available at http://sifinfolit.nuigalway.ie/ (McSweeney and Conrick 2009). This resource features good use of online video and the provision of self reflective activities to help ensure student engagement.

A recent and significant development saw LNSS team up with the UK based CSG Information Literacy Group (CILIP) to host what is arguably the most important international conference dedicated to Information Literacy. March 29th-31st 2010 saw

LNSS host the LILAC Librarian's Information Literacy Conference in Limerick city which was attended by over 300 delegates. Prior to this LNSS hosted the LNSS Information Literacy Implementation Seminar and workshops which was attended by universities and Institutes of Technology in Ireland and from the UK which focussed on best practice for implementation of information literacy using Resusable Learning Objects and training programmes.

5. Information Literacy in the Shannon Consortium

The LNSS project commenced in August 2008 with an in depth project scoping coordinated by the LNSS Librarian Project Coordinator consisting of extensive international research into Information Literacy suites and learning outcomes, learning design and multimedia as well as analysis of the needs of learners and existing IL initiatives across the Consortium. It quickly became apparent of the need to aim the IL suite at undergraduates and postgraduates audiences. Following extensive consultation with stakeholders using workshop, meeting and interview techniques and research into IL tutorials it soon became clear that the LNSS would need to develop initiatives which would disseminate both lower and higher order IL skills. The learning design would need to include lower order IL skills such as searching, using and evaluating information as well as higher order skills such as research management and good practice, getting published and writing skills as well as career planning.

Through careful research, assessment and selection of appropriate web based information literacy modules incorporating implementation of appropriate teaching and training programmes via the Regional Network for Staff Development strand of the LNSS the project would need to address the two-fold challenge which is facing all libraries: How to facilitate online support on a 24/7 basis? How to communicate effectively to address queries covering a wide range of topics from users differing in skills and learning styles? (Xiao et al. 2004).

The LNSS Stakeholder Workshop October 6th 2008 Information Literacy component was attended by staff at Director of Library Service level as well as other senior level staff from Shannon Consortium libraries. The purpose of the workshop was twofold: to identify the current level of information literacy practice in the Consortium and secondly to identify suitable online modular information literacy for selection and rollout by the Consortium. In order to identify the current level of information literacy practice in the Consortium groups from each partner institution were asked to reflect on a number of questions that they were required to answer to ascertain the position in their own institution. The purpose of this session was to ensure that when the group were reviewing the possible IL suites that could be used, that they would use the information gathered in this session to ensure that the needs of their own institutions would be met within whatever suite was chosen. The questions that each group considered were as follows: Current IL approach used in their institution? Key challenges the institution faces in IL? How the institution is marketing/ensuring a presence of the current IL offering? IL needs in institution? (Any unique issues to be considered?) Preferred direction of IL project for each institution? Any specific requirements that the institution would like the model to include?

The conclusions were: IL was being provided across the Consortium in the following ways: provision of study guides online and paper, information literacy guides/tutorials on the Library Website e.g. on plagiarism, referencing, use of VLE's such as Moodle/Blackboard for online delivery, subject specific tutorials- presentations delivered by subject librarians in Library Training Rooms, general orientation for 1st years- e.g. library tours, support provided by the Learning Support Unit., "drop in" information literacy sessions for students.

The challenges facing Shannon Consortium libraries regarding information literacy were identified as follows: for some libraries it emerged that there was a perceived lack of coordination with regard to information literacy efforts and an overreliance on subject librarians as well as a need for a 24/7 access online information literacy resource. The need for increased marketing of current information literacy initiatives to students and staff was raised as well as a lack of confidence of library staff regarding information literacy teaching and training. Convincing academic staff of the importance of information literacy was also stressed at the workshop. Other problems identified were a shortage of staff to deliver information literacy initiatives particularly hands on tutorial based information literacy provision; lack of facilities for IL training; the need for Library involvement in the institutional marketing strategy in order to promote information literacy initiatives and the need to better cater for distance learners and international students.

The decision to select information literacy content from suitable providers rather than design in-house was guided by research into the cost of designing e learning /information literacy. Research into the cost of designing content in- house had shown that the LNSS could achieve better value by assessing, selecting and modifying content from suitable

vendors. Rumble (2001) estimated the cost of developing an e learning resource as between $6000 and $1,000,000. In a more recent study an e learning resource for 23, 000 students was launched at a cost of $1.1 million (Lee et al 2004). While e learning must be successful in reaching learning objectives, have easy accessibility, have a consistent and accurate message, be easy to use, entertaining, memorable, relevant, and if possible result in reduced training costs (Angeliki et al 2005 cited in Steen 2008) it need not be developed from scratch and existing best models may be adapted and utilized thereby avoiding duplication, repetition and ensuring cost efficiencies.

6. Methodology for Selecting Online, Modular Information Literacy Initiatives

Prior to the LNSS Stakeholder Workshop research was conducted across the Consortium coordinated by the LNSS Librarian Project Coordinator into online information literacy suites available worldwide. Using criteria influenced by research into current practice in Reusable Learning Objects (University of Cambridge 2003) and instructional design 20 potential suites were identified which were subsequently reduced down to 8 using interview email and survey techniques. These 8 tutorials were subsequently reduced down to 2 at the LNSS Stakeholder Workshop which stakeholders selected for implementation across the Consortium.

The criteria agreed by stakeholders with which to evaluate the online information literacy suites was influenced by research into reusable learning object specification (University of Cambridge 2003) and instructional design. The criteria were: Does it meet a variety of learning styles? What is the degree of interactivity? Does it promote active learning and hence is the pedagogy sound? Can the resource stand alone or is substantial customisation required? Can the resource be customised if required? Does the resource cater for different levels of IL needs of students? What is the level of ongoing maintenance? How does the resource look? Will students find it appealing? Has the resource been created using learning outcomes based on information literacy standards? Is the duration a good estimate of the time it will take to work through? Is content factually accurate?

At the workshop stakeholders were given a short presentation for each of the 9 suites which were in contention. Prior to these presentations stakeholders agreed on the following criteria with which to assess and score each resource: meets a variety of learning styles; degree of interactivity; ability to stand alone (with no need to customise); ability to customise if desired; caters for different levels of IL needs of students; level of ongoing maintenance required (from a systems point of view); student appeal but professional looking.

Each suite was scored out of 5 taking into account the criteria. To arrive at each score the total score for the suite was divided by the number of people who actually scored the suite. Where a member did not score against certain criteria in a suite, a score of zero was allocated. The results were as follows:

Suite title	Average score	Order of preference
Epigeum	16.1	1
Cranfield	15.7	2
Quickstart	11.6	3
Texas	10.8	4
Queensland University	10.4	5
Info Skills	9.3	6
Pilot	8.9	7
Oasis	8.9	7
FIRST	8.9	7

Epigeum *Research Skills Online*, an online research and information literacy skills resource aimed at postgraduates and researchers and the *Cranfield Online Information Literacy Tutorial* largely geared towards undergraduates with a score of 16.1 and 15.7 were selected for implementation and rollout by the LNSS. Both these resources met the criteria. With regard to the Cranfield product it catered effectively for varying learning styles, featured active learning activities in each module, was customisable to some extent and needed not be customised if required. It catered for lower order information literacy skills, pillars one to four of the Sconul Seven Pillars Advisory Committee on Information Literacy, 1999 as well as higher order IL skills, SCONUL's pillars five to seven. (Hunn and Rossiter 2007). Learning outcomes for each tutorial were written and reviewed by library professionals and then mapped against each of the SCONUL Seven Pillars of Information Literacy. The resource also had high student appeal due to its effective navigation and use of engaging active learning activities and tests. Epigeum *Research Skills Online* also met the criteria. It met a variety of learning styles and provided active learning activities in each module. Unlike many online information literacy modules which are essentially static or cumbersome to modify at best, the resource is updated regularly with regular Update Workshops run by the supplier and modification can also be made within the organisation at any time and so the resource is essentially a living thing which can change, adapt and be repurposed to meet the needs of students. The interface is highly sophisticated and attractive to the user. Similar to the Cranfield product it is always clear to the user where they are in the tutorial and has impressive innovative use of online video, metaphor and engaging learning activities.

Perhaps the main reason why these were selected was due the fact that stakeholders were particularly interested in IL suites that used tools such as online video where experts speak about such topics as plagiarism, research methods, career planning or getting published as opposed to tutorials which were overly text based. Epigeum

Research Skills Online was particularly innovative and engaging in its use of online video. The limitations of text based tutorials has been emphasised:

Text based tutorials offer little help when dealing with complex concepts or processes. Direct assistance from library personnel is only available when the libraries are open. In today's web environment, a more effective learning tool [online video] is required to facilitate the support and instruction of electronic resources in a manner that appeals to the user. (Xiao et al. 2004)

7. Information Literacy and Staff Development Initiatives

Delivering information literacy skills training has particularly over the last decade become a core function of academic libraries and librarians throughout the world (Brown 2007). Stakeholders and particularly the LNSS Steering Group were concerned that it was not enough just to upload information literacy suites to our servers in the hope that students would locate and use them. Library staff would require training in information concepts and practice as well as teaching skills in order to deliver effective information skills training. The importance of having experts in information literacy skills training and use of a *train the trainer's* approach to instil a comprehensive knowledge of information literacy in persons who can return to their organisations and training and inspire others was realised (Horton 2008).

Project scoping conducted at the LNSS Stakeholder Workshop identified Web 2.0, teaching and information literacy skills as major staff development needs for Shannon Consortium institutions and to address this need the LNSS have organised and championed a new hands-on immersive Web 2.0 online learning course giving staff an opportunity to open "a whole new bag of tricks to use and connect with our users" (Godwin 2007), to explore tools such as Blogger, Flikr, YouTube and del.icio.us and the impact these tools are having on libraries and library services. Participants use freely available online tools to complete a number of active learning activities over a 12 week period leading to empowerment and greater participation in this *transparent library* of the 21st century (Casey and Stephens 2008).

8. LNSS: Mainstreaming, Embedding, Collaboration

Although LNSS has in theory a definite lifespan, an important requirement is a strong and consistent commitment to mainstreaming and sustainability activities. LNSS must not just deliver its immediate goals, it must also look to the future and seek out new products, services and initiatives to keep information literacy, library staff development and perhaps most importantly the impressive collaboration that has been achieved through the running of IL workshops, seminars and Library Staff development courses alive into the future.

The participation of library professionals in information literacy takes many different forms. The ideal one is to have a program that is part of the curricula because information literacy requires sustained development throughout all formal educational levels, primary, secondary, and tertiary. The level and quality of IL provision in educational institutions worldwide differs greatly. In some institutions and with reference to the work of Peacock (2007) *extra-curricula* information literacy learning through information literacy learning activities which develop generic enabling skills and are supplemental to the core curriculum of students are being implemented. At another level *inter curricula* information literacy activities in the form of tutorials, workshops and/or short training and information sessions on basic information skills in consultation with, or at the request of, the individual teaching academic and or Department are being followed in a more integrated and embedded approach. *Intra-*

curricula where information literacy is fully embedded in student life and courses facilitating deep, durable learning and transferable understanding and application of information literacy and skills is the difficult goal which most libraries are attempting to achieve. Within LNSS partner libraries elements of all 3 types are visible although full Intra curricular IL will take much time and effort.

LNSS strategy for embedding IL has involved providing IL services/forging string links with Academic Departments, providing information skills services both in class as requested by lectures and through training arranged in the Library, providing services/forging strong links with Research Departments e.g. training in referencing and citation,

research methods, research ethics, conferencing skills, the literature review, intellectual property, dealing with your research supervisor, Endnote; providing services/forging strong links with Learning Support Units e.g. Dissertation Workshops for final year students, Mature Student Workshops; workshops for: Learning Support Unit Tutors. A certain amount of embedding of IL online modules into courses has occurred and lecturers use modules themselves for assignment purposes e.g. to test the level of referencing and citation skills.

Vital for mainstreaming and sustainability is the continuous scanning for new IL products and initiatives and also the promotion and fostering of international cooperation for the development of IL services. Having rolled out new products Epigeum Research Skills Online and Cranfield Information Literacy Tutorial across Shannon Consortium libraries LNSS are not standing still but are moving forward into new territory are developing Student Study Skills Online with Epigeum Ltd.- a spin off company of Imperial College London and 15 leading universities. Student Study Skills Online will see LNSS develop 15 online modules covering course topics and diagnostic tests aimed at all learner types incorporating extensive and innovative use of multimedia; e.g. online video, quizzes, simulation- active learning with modules such as academic writing, reading skills, information literacy and working in groups, transition points (school or work to university), getting the most from your time at university , knowing yourself as a learner , working at a distance / part-time study ,working in groups, information literacy , reading skills, academic writing – argument based-essays, academic writing – projects and lab reports , academic writing – reflective writing, avoiding plagiarism, managing your time, presenting your work and managing budgets.

For LNSS collaboration and capacity building across the Shannon Consortium is vital but the international dimension is important. With this in mind in 2008 LNSS formed the RINGIDEA network involving educational institutions in Ireland (LNSS), Romania, Greece and Norway with the aim of identifying new IL initiatives, products and services and their development for the benefit of EU countries.

9. Measuring Information Literacy

Various options have been considered for the development of IL indicators (Catts and Lau 2008). They include the setting up of indirect indicators of IL encompassing products of IL such as numbers of books published, numbers of patents registered and volume of internet usage- an approach considered flawed due to the influence of economic conditions and are more considered outcomes of IL practice rather than indicators of IL. Another option which has been considered is the design of a new international survey of IL skills which would have the benefit of being a full and comprehensive survey of IL but this approach is considered costly in terms of development and implementation (Catts and Lau 2008). The most appealing option seems to be to develop a set of indicators of IL from items in an existing survey such as the LAMP survey being developed by UIS which contains sufficient items to provide adequate coverage of information literacy with the exception of the ethical use of information component.

However theorists and experts in many countries are still searching for answers to two vital questions: How to measure information literacy? How to ascertain the effectiveness of information literacy training? (Gendina 2008) Perhaps when answering these questions we assume that we know exactly the parameters that are subject to measurement and that we have the tools for such measurement when really the essence of the problem lies in the search for adequate measurement tools. Although many researchers have developed tools for measuring students' knowledge of a specific library system or database, and for determining affective responses to library instruction (e.g., degree of confidence felt by students), there is not yet a standardized method for measuring information literacy that is easily administered and applied across institutions and this problem has been tackled by some. An example can be found in O Connor et al (2001) and their development of a *Standardized instrument for institutional and longitudinal Measurement* involving assessment at the institutional level, not the instructor level, for longitudinal data gathering. Pre- and post-testing is combined with experimental and control conditions to answer such questions as, "Does library instruction make a difference on campus? Teaching of information literacy skills are assessed through session-specific evaluation facilitating evaluation of alternative methods and approaches to library instruction and information is gathered from both students and instructors and geared national information literacy standards.

Other studies include those of Streatfield and Markless (2008) and the use of Facilitated Action Research process to support a total of 22 university teams drawn from across England and Scotland in two annual cycles, working through a series of three linked workshops to equip them to conduct their own evaluations of interventions. This study produced some interesting results- each of the library teams at the end of their involvement with the project showed that participants had opted for a wide variety of evidence collection methods, such as development of diagnostic tests. The study found that collaboration between academic and library staff is vital, and that networking throughout the university and within the LIS team is critical to find support and to "keep people informed and in the picture".

Conclusion

This paper has attempted to depict the LNSS project and quantitative and qualitative techniques utilised to enhance project deliverables employing the use of devices such as workshops and surveys. We have also briefly examined various tools and initiatives which have been developed to attempt to assess the effectiveness of information literacy initiatives and have found that such engaging with students and academic staff is vital for the success of information literacy programs

For all who are engaged in learning in this information rich society the challenge to achieve information literacy is vital in capitalising on the diverse and often overwhelming range of information choices with which we are continually faced. These challenges are compounded further by the internet- a gift which has presented us with near instantaneous access to the World's information but which has also forced us to develop strategies for confronting issues concerning accessibility, reliability, authenticity and validity as well as information overload. Such challenges require a united and collaborative approach, a commitment to resource sharing and the courage to repurpose, reuse, adapt and improve and resist unwittingly and in isolation reinventing the wheel.

The LNSS in fulfilling its mission to champion innovative web based support services and supporting information literacy teaching and training responding to the changing expectation of library users must also consider its legacy and ensure that information literacy is firmly embedded across the Shannon Consortium. It must go beyond mere implementation and bequest a model of resource sharing and a foundation which will strengthen the future potential of the region, increased opportunities for blended, active and online learning opportunities, highly skills staff who are aware of the most up to date IL practice, increased collaboration and capacity building and most importantly students who "recognise when information is needed and have the ability to locate, evaluate, and use effectively the information needed".

Focussed on reusability and repurposing rather than reinvention and duplication of resources; on collaboration and resource sharing rather than isolation and unwitting repetition; on capacity building and integration the LNSS continue to deliver information literacy across the Shannon Consortium and furthering lifelong learning always mindful of the importance of quantitative and qualitative techniques to enable high quality library services.

References

Bloom, B. and Deyrup, M. (2003). *Information literacy across the wired university.* Reference services review **31**(3): pp. 237-247.

Breen, E. and Fallon, H, Eds. (2007). *Developing Student Information Literacy Skills to Support Project and Problem-based learning;* in Handbook of Enquiry and Problem-based Learning, CELT. NUI Galway. Available at http://eprints.nuim.ie/539/1/chapter17.pdf

Brown, L. and Mokgele, M. (2007). *Information literacy skills training of staff and students in the Unisa Library: challenges and opportunities.* World Library and Information Congress: 73rd IFLA General Conference and Council 19th-23 August 2007, Durban South Africa, IFLA.. Available at http://www.ifla.org/IV/ifla73/papers/151-Brown_Mokgele-en.pdf.

Bruce, C.S. (1997) *The relational approach: a new model for information literacy.* The New Review of Information and Library Research **3** pp 1-22

Bruce, C. S. (1999). *Workplace experiences of information literacy.* International journal of information management **19**: pp.33-37.

Bruce, C.S. (2002). Information Literacy as a Catalyst for Educational Change: A Background Paper. In *Proceedings Information Literacy Meeting of Experts*, Prague, The Czech Republic. Available at http://dlist.sir.arizona.edu/300/01/bruce-fullpaper.pdf

Carver, B. (2008). *Creating an institutional repository: a role for libraries.* Ex-Libris: a weekly E-Zine for librarians and information junkies. June 27th 2003. Available at http://marylaine.com/exlibris/xlib181.html

Casey, M. and Stephens, M. (2008). *The transparent library: insights from the front line.* Library Journal. February 15 2008.

Catts, R and Lau, J (2008). Towards Information Literacy Indicators. UNESCO; Paris. Available at http://unesdoc.unesco.org/images/0015/001587/158723e.pdf (accessed 12-12-2009

CONUL Working Group on Information Skills Training. (2004). *Report of the CONUL working group on information skills training. Dublin:* Consortium of National and University Libraries. Available at: http://www.conul.ie/committees/activities.shtml

FORFAS (2007). *The role of Institutes of Technology in enterprise development: profiles and emerging findings.* Dublin, FORFAS. Available at http://www.hea.ie/files/files/file/archive/policy/2007/forfas-role-IOT-enterprise-development.pdf [accessed 2nd February-2009]

Gendina, N. (2008). Could learners outcomes in information literacy be measured: pluses and minuses of testing?. World Library and Information Congress: 74th IFLA General Conference and Council 10-14 August 2008, Quebec, Canada. Available at http://www.ifla.org/iv/ifla74/index.htm

Godwin, P. (2007). *The web 2.0 challenge to information literacy.* INFORUM 2007: 13th Conference on professional Information Resources Prague, May 22-24. Prague. Available at http://www.inforum.cz/pdf/2007/godwin-peter.pdf

Hernon, P and Calvert P. (2005). *E-service quality in libraries: exploring its features and dimensions.* Library and information science research. 27(3) pp. 377-40

Horton, F. W. (2008). *Encouraging global information literacy.* Computers in libraries November/December: pp. 6-33.

Hunn, R. A. and Rossiter, D (2006?) *Design and development of an online information literacy tutorial: evaluation and lessons learnt (so far).* Available at http://www.ics.heacademy.ac.uk/italics/vol5iss4/hunn-rossiter.pdf

Ireland, Department of Education and Science. (2006) *Hannafin approves over €42 million for higher education reforms,* 20th Feb. Available at http://www.education.ie/home/home.jsp?maincat=10861&pcategory=10861&ec ategory=10876&sectionpage=13637&language=EN&link=link001&page=1&d oc=33111

Kuhlthau, C. (1987) *Information skills for and Information Society: a review of the research.* Syracuse, N.Y. ERIC Clearinghouse on Information Resources.

Lee, S.C, Tan, D.T.H. and Goh, W.S. (2004). *The Next Generation of E-Learning: Strategies for Media Rich Online Teaching and Engaged Learning.* Journal of distance education technologies. **2** (4). pp. 1-17. Available at http://www.infosci-journals.com/downloadPDF/pdf/ITJ2614_I17LU7hMOc.pdf

McSweeney, N and Conrick, M (2009**).** *Graduate Information Literacy Skills: A collaborative SIF funded approach.* Available at http://www.lilacconference.com/dw/2009/Programme/tuesday_pm_abstracts.ht ml#niall

Montiel-Overall, P. (2007). *Information literacy: toward a cultural model.* Canadian Journal of Information and Library Science **31**(1): pp. 43-68.

Nitecki, D.A. and Harmon, P. (2000). Measuring service quality at Yale university's libraries. The Journal of Academic Librarianship. 26(4) pp.259-273

O'Connor, G, Radcliff, C.J and Gedeon, J.A. (2001). *Assessing Information Literacy Skills:*
Developing a standardized instrument for institutional and longitudinal measurement. ACRL Tenth National Conference March 15–18, 2001, Denver, Colorado. Available at http://66.158.92.116/ala/mgrps/divs/acrl/events/pdf/oconnor.pdf

Parker, J. (2003). *Putting the pieces together: information literacy at the Open University.* Library Management, **24**(4/5) pp. 223-228

Rumble, G (2001). *The costs and costing of networked learning.* Journal of Asynchronous Learning Networks **5** (2) pp. 75-96. Available at http://www.aln.org/publications/jaln/v5n2/pdf/v5n2_rumble.pdf

Russell, P. (2008*). Information literacy support for off campus students by academic libraries in the Republic of Ireland.* Journal of information literacy **2**(2) pp. 46-62.

SCONUL Advisory Committee on Information Literacy. (1999). *Information Skills in Higher Education: Briefing Paper.* London, SCONUL. Available at:

http://www.sconul.ac.uk/groups/information_literacy/papers/Seven_pillars2.pdf [Accessed 11th December 2009]

Steen, H. (2008). *Effective eLearning design*. MERLOT Journal of Online Learning and Teaching. **4** (4) 2008. Available at http://jolt.merlot.org/vol4no4/steen_1208.pdf

Streatfield, D and Markless, S (2008). *Evaluating the Impact of Information Literacy in Higher Education: Progress and Prospects*. Libri, 2008, vol. 58, pp. 102–109

Sundin, O. (2005). *Negotiations on information-seeking expertise: a study of web-based tutorials for information literacy*. Journal of documentation **64**(1): pp. 24-43

UIS (2007). A statistical framework for information literacy. Working Group on Measurement, April 3.

University of Cambridge (2004). *Universities collaborating in eLearning: production pack for RLO's* . available at http://www.ucel.ac.uk/resources/dev_pack.html.

Webber, S. (2008). *Information literacy: an international concept*. Available at http://www.slideshare.net/sheilawebber/information-literacy-an-international-concept-presentation

Webber, S. and McGuinness, C. Eds. (2007). *Information literacy: an international state of the art report*, IFLA; UNESCO p. 113-122. Available at http://www.infolitglobal.info/docs/UNESCO_IL_state_of_the_art_report_-_Draft070803.doc

Xiao, D. Y., Pietraszewski., B.A. and Goodwin, S.P. (2004). *Full stream ahead: database instruction through online videos*. Library Hi Tech **22**(4): pp. 366-374.

Electronic Academic Libraries Services Valuation: A Case Study of the Portuguese Electronic Scientific Information Consortium b-on

Luiza Baptista Melo[1] and Cesaltina Pires[2]

[1]CIDEHUS-UE, University of Évora, Portugal, lbmelo@fc.up.pt
[2]CEFAGE-UE and Management Department, University of Évora, Portugal, cpires@uevora.pt

Abstract: This paper investigates the factors that influence the value for the users of the Portuguese electronic scientific information consortium b-on (Biblioteca do Conhecimento Online). In order to be able to estimate this value in monetary terms we used the contingent valuation method based on a willingness to pay scenario. Data was collected through an e-survey sent to the whole Portuguese academic users. The main aims of this study are: (i) to investigate how the Portuguese academic community values b-on; (ii) to investigate the set of factors that determine whether the user is willing to pay the b-on services which allows us to estimate the demand function of b-on services. In order to achieve these objectives we use several regression analysis techniques – linear probability model (LPM), Logit and Probit models. The results show that the demand for b-on services is quite sensitive to the «price», frequency of use, whether the user knew previously b-on or not, the type of the user and the scientific area of the user.
Keywords: Academic libraries, electronic sources, impact evaluation, logit, probit

1. Introduction

At present, the world is in a global economic crisis, in all developed countries there are several kinds of economic problems. Most public institutions are under increasing pressure on your own budgets. Portuguese researcher and academic institutions are no exception and it is urgent to study the problem of the academic libraries, the cost and the benefits of its services. Nowadays the Portuguese electronic scientific information consortium b-on – Biblioteca do Conhecimento Online provides unlimited access to research and academic institutions to the full texts of more than 16,750 scientific publications, via Internet, at the national level (FCCN, 2009). The Portuguese Government has been investing to improve the access to the production of knowledge so as to develop the country. It is important to know the return on the investments in university libraries. The purpose of this study is to identify the impact of the electronic sources in the Portuguese academic libraries.

This paper explores some issues, they are the following: (i) to investigate how the Portuguese academic community values b-on; (ii) to investigate the set of factors that determine whether the user is willing to pay the b-on services which allows us to estimate the demand function of b-on services. We consider the following factors: the price, the frequency of use, whether the user knew previously b-on or not, the type of the user, the scientific area of the user, and the institution of the use. In order to investigate these problems we use regression analysis techniques - Linear probability

New Trends in Qualitative and Quantitative Methods in Libraries
A. Katsirikou and C. H. Skiadas (eds)
© *World Scientific Publishing Co (pp. 133-145)*

model (LPM), Logit and Probit models. The remainder of this paper is organized as follows: in Section 2 we present the methodology used. Section 3 presents and discusses the results. The final section concludes the paper.

2. Methodology

Murgai and Ahmadi (2007) refer the studies of Tenopir, from 1991 to 2000, and argue that "her findings indicate that libraries have adopted digital information sources and services at an accelerated rate due to availability of internet, in particular the World Wide Web." The digital resources have changed the services of the academic libraries. These authors emphasise the need to keep and report statistics for accreditation and comparison purpose still remains.

According to Noonan (2003) "contingent valuation methodology (CVM) has been increasingly applied to cultural resources" and thus it is a natural candidate to estimate the monetary value of library services. In fact, in the last decade, some authors have used the contingent valuation method for monetary valuations of libraries' services (Holt, G.E.; Elliott, D. and Moore, A., 1999; McDermott Miller, 2002; Morris, A.; Sumsion, J. and Hawkins, M., 2002; Holt, G.E. and Elliott, D.S., 2003; British Library, 2004; Barron et al., 2005; Aabø, 2005a; Morris; Ayre and Jones, 2006; Elliott, D. S. et al., 2007: Hider, 2008) e.g. of public libraries, (Harless and Frank, 1999) academic libraries, (Chung, 2007) and special libraries.

In the last decade, some of the libraries evaluation has applied regression models for demonstrating the impact of the academic libraries services. Logistic regression analysis has been used to study some libraries issues, for instances: to predict the relevance of a library catalogue search in University of Californias' Melvyl online catalogue (Cooper and Chen, 2001); to reflect the relationship between library collections and the prestige of universities (Liu, 2003); to study users' emotional and material satisfaction at micro/macro levels in an academic library (Yu, 2006); to predict the number of patrons that seek assistance at the reference desk of a library from the University of Tennessee (Murgai, Ahmadi, 2007) and to study the use and non-use of public libraries in the information age (Sin and Kim, 2008). We emphasise the studies of Aabø (2005b) in a research of valuing the benefits of the Norway public libraries, based in a contingent valuation, studied how citizens value these services and presented several measures of average valuation including estimations with the standard logistic distribution function.

In a previous research (Melo and Pires, 2009) we estimated the economic value in monetary terms for end-users of the services provided by the electronic scientific information consortium b-on. In order to estimate the monetary value for the end-users of the services provided by b-on we use two alternative valuation methods. On the one hand we estimate the value of the time saved by using this resource. On the other hand, we use the contingent valuation method (CVM) to estimate how much the user is willing to pay for the service. The data was collected through study an e-survey of Portuguese academic community. In this study we are going on our investigation with the same data.

In our study we would like to explain patterns behaviours based on regression models. We want to study the willingness to pay (WTP) of the b-on users as a function of the frequency of use, whether the user knew previously b-on or not, the type of the user, the scientific area of the user, and the institution of the user. Hence, the dependent variable, the willingness to pay, can take only two values: 1 if the user wants to pay some per month to continue having access to the services of b-on and 0 if the user does not want to pay to continue having access to the services of b-on. A feature of this dependent variable is the type that elicits a "yes" or "no" response. In this case the dependent variable is dichotomous. There are three most commonly used approaches to involve dichotomous response variables: Linear probability model (LPM); Logit model and Probit model.

2.1. Regression models for the probability of paying to access the services of b-on

$$P(y = 1 \mid x) = G(\beta_0 + \beta_1 x_1 + \ldots + \beta_k x_k) = G(\beta_0 + \mathbf{x\beta}). \qquad (1)$$

Linear Probability Model (LPM)
We can equate Linear probability model (LPM) considering the following (Wooldridge, 518:2007):

Where:
The dependent variable y is dichotomous ($y = 1$ if the user want to pay something to access to the b-on service and $y = 0$ if the user does not want to pay to access to the b-on service);

The independent variables are x_k, such as; the frequency of use, whether the user knew previously b-on or not, the type of the user, the scientific area of the user, and the institution of the user; and,
The function G must lie between 0 and 1, i.e. $0 < G(z) < 1$ and $\mathbf{x\beta} = \beta_1 x_1 + \ldots + \beta_k x_k$.

Gujarati (576:1995) affirms that Linear probability model (LPM) is simple and it has several limitations, for instances, this model assumes that the conditional probabilities increase linearly with the values of the explanatory variables, for instances, the probabilities will tend to tapper off as the values of the explanatory variables increase or decrease indefinitely. This author says that "in group data, Logit and Probit estimates are fairly straightforward."

Logit model
Wooldridge (518:2007) explains that the standard logistic distribution function G is the following:

$$G(z) = \frac{e^{(\beta_0 + \beta_1 x_1 + \ldots + \beta_k x_k)}}{1 + e^{(\beta_0 + \beta_1 x_1 + \ldots + \beta_k x_k)}}. \qquad (2)$$

Where G is distribution function, when y is, for example, the value that x_k a person places on b-on (Portuguese electronic scientific information consortium), might contain various individual characteristics, such as, frequency of use, whether the user knew previously b-on or not, the type of the user, the scientific area of the user, and the institution of the user, β_k are parameter estimates to be calculated. The logistic regression is a useful way of describing the relationship between one or more outcomes expressed as a probability, that has only two possible values such as (yes=1 and no=0).

In the Logit model the magnitudes of the regressors on the dependent variable are difficulty interpretations and they are not useful (comparing to the linear probability model). Many researchers prefer to estimate the effect of x_j on the probability of success of $P(y = 1 | x)$. To compute this effect we must obtain the partial derivate (Wooldridge, 2003).

Li and Mahendra (2009) explain that the "marginal effects measure the expected instantaneous change in the dependent variable as a function of a change in a certain explanatory variable while keeping all the other covariates constant."

To find the marginal effects of roughly variables on the response probability we must calculate the partial derivate (for more details see Wooldridge (556:2003)), for instance:

$$\frac{\partial p}{\partial x_j} = g(\beta_0 + \mathbf{x}\boldsymbol{\beta})\,\beta_j. \tag{3}$$

Probit model

Wooldridge (519:2007) refers that in the Probit model the standard normal cumulative distribution function G is:

$$G(z) = \boldsymbol{\Phi}(z) \equiv \int_{-\infty}^{z} \varphi(v)dv. \tag{4}$$

Where ϕ *(z)* is the standard normal density:

$$\varphi(z) = (2\pi)^{\frac{1}{2}} \exp(-z^2 / 2). \tag{5}$$

And *0< G(z)<1*, when $G(z) \rightarrow 0$ as $z \rightarrow -\infty$ and $G(z) \rightarrow 1$ as $z \rightarrow \infty$.

As we mentioned above, for the Logit model, it is similar for this model - the magnitudes of the regressors on the dependent variable are difficulty interpretations. The marginal effects of roughly variables on the response probability is the partial derivate:

$$\frac{dP_i}{dx_i} = \varphi(\beta_0 + \beta_1 x_1 + ... + \beta_k x_k)\beta_i. \tag{6}$$

For large samples the β coefficients are similar when we use models Logit and Probit to estimate them. The Probit model is specific for a binary response, for example problems that have only two possible outcomes which we will denote as yes=1 and no=0.

2.2. Data collection

The data was collected through an electronic questionnaire. The questionnaire was based on the International Standard performance indicators and the contingent valuation method (CVM) to assess academic library electronic services. The questions were based on the International Standards ISO 11620:1998, 1:2003 Amendment, ISO 2789:2006 performance indicators: percentage of the target population using traditional library, percentage of the target population using digital library, percentage of the target population using both libraries, preferred location of use of the electronic services, service used (data bases, electronic collections, pay e-journals or Open Access journals). The scenario designed in this research to valuate electronic services of the Portuguese academic libraries is based on a hypothetical idea. The

WTP scenario describes an economic situation which forces the Portuguese electronic scientific information consortium, b-on, to stop. It is suggested that the consortium b-on will continue if the users maintain the cost of these services paying a monthly tax with values between 5 to 50 Euros (Melo and Pires, 2009).

This questionnaire (paper version) was piloted with fifty academic library users. Then it was send by e-mail to thirty three Public Portuguese Universities (professors, researchers, students, administrative staff and everyone who usually uses academic services). The answers were received from 15th January to 15th May 2009. During these four months we received 1930 answers. The composition of the respondents sample is the following: professors 28.0%, PhD students/researchers 13.9%, master students 19.3%, undergraduate students 31.1% and others 7.7% (administrative and library staff). We can verify that the professors and the PhD students/researchers are overrepresented in the sample whereas the undergraduate students are underrepresented. This is an expected result. These two groups of users are the ones who are more directly involved in research and who are more aware about the scientific information consortium b-on and thus it is likely that they were more interested in answering.

2.3. Data analysis
The first step of the analysis was to summarize the data collected. The next step involved the comparison between different types of users and between various scientific disciplines. We considered five groups of users: Professor, PhD Student/ Researcher, Master Students, Undergraduate Students and Others. The scientific disciplines were aggregated in the following six groups: Physiques and Chemistry Sciences; Humanities and Social Sciences; Earth and Planetary Sciences; Life and Health Sciences, Engineering; Mathematics and Computer Sciences.

As we referred above in order to estimate same coefficients to describe several user behaviours we use statistic and probabilistic data analysis - Linear probability model (LPM), Logit and Probit models for binary response. Our statistical and probability analysis was performed with the STATA – Data Analysis Statistic Software.

3. Analysis of the Results
We start by analyzing the results of user e-surveys. The user e-surveys involved 1930 answers. Table 1 presents the frequency of maximum willingness to pay (WTP) to continue to access Portuguese electronic scientific information consortium b-on (Melo and Pires, 2009). The two F statistics and the corresponding p-values, lead us to conclude that there exist statistically significant differences across groups. An overview shows us that the professors and the PhD students/researchers on average are willing to pay much higher amounts than the master and undergraduate students.

Table 1: Frequency of maximum willingness to pay (WTP) to continue to access Portuguese electronic scientific information consortium b-on (Melo and Pires, 2009).

User	How maximum willingness to pay (WTP) to continue access scientific e-resources (Euros for month)?																
	Accepting null value									Not accepting null value							
	0	5	10	15	20	30	40	50	Average	5	10	15	20	30	40	50	Average
Professor (%)	29.6	22.4	21.3	6.3	9.8	4.3	0.9	5.4	10.5	31.8	30.3	8.9	13.9	6.1	1.3	7.6	14.9
PhD Student /Researcher(%	43.3	22.8	13.8	5.2	7.8	3.0	0.7	3.4	7.8	40.1	24.3	9.2	13.8	5.3	1.3	5.9	13.7
Master Student (%)	45.7	30.9	14.5	3.5	4.0	1.1	0.0	0.3	4.8	56.9	26.7	6.4	7.4	2.0	0.0	0.5	8.8
Undergraduate Student (%)	43.7	32.5	15.3	4.0	3.5	0.5	0.2	0.3	4.9	57.7	27.2	7.1	6.2	0.9	0.3	0.6	8.6
Other (%)	43.3	20.0	12.3	4.0	6.7	5.3	0.7	6.7	9.5	35.3	23.5	7.1	11.8	9.4	1.2	11.8	16.3
ANOVA analysis	F=31.72 and p-value=0.000									F=27.68 and p-value=0.000							

Table 2 summarizes the data to estimate, by regression analysis, the probability of being willing to pay to continue to access the Portuguese electronic scientific information consortium, b-on. We estimated the β coefficients and their p-values, in parenthesis, for Linear probability, Logit and Probit models. We decided to use these three models because they give us a more consistent analyses data. We ran regressions including the observations with null values (1930 observations) and regressions not including those observations (1157 observations).The signs of the coefficients are the same across the models and the same independent variables are statistically significant in each model.

Linear probability model

Table 2 first item presents the data accepting null values. The bottom of the column shows the value of F statistics that tests the null hypothesis that all explanatory variables coefficients are equal to zero. The F-statistics is equal to 21.67, with a p-value of 0.000. This means that the null hypothesis should be rejected, telling us that our model as a whole is statistically significant. The R-squared is equal to 0.19 which means than 19% of the total variation is explained by the model. This value seems low, however it is quite normal in regressions using cross-sectional data and in earlier studies in the library and information literature (see Aabø (2005) and references therein).

Let us now interpret each one of the coefficients in the regressions. The coefficient associated with a given explanatory variable "gives the change in the conditional probability of the event occurring for a given change in the value of the explanatory variable" (Gujarati, 550:1995). In what follows we only interpret the coefficients which are statistically significant (meaning that we can reject the hypothesis that they are equal to zero).

The coefficient -0.0098 attached to the variable "Bid" means that, holding all the other factors constant, the probability of being willing to pay to access b-on decreases by a factor of 0.0098 or 0.98 percent. Thus the higher the «price» of the b-on service, the lower the probability of a given user «buying» the service. In other words, the demand for the service is negatively related to its price.

The coefficient 0.0051 attached to the variable "Frequency digital library use" means that, assuming all other factors constant, the probability of being willing to pay the service of b-on increases 0.0051 or 0.5 percent for each additional day of digital libraries use. The coefficients of 0.1032 and 0.1061 attached, respectively, to the variables "Professor" and "Other" (mainly library staff) mean that, assuming all other factors constant, the probability of being willing to pay to access b-on by the "Professor" and "Other" categories are higher about 10 percent and 11 percent as compared with the base category of the "Master student".

Similarly, the coefficients of 0.0403 and 0.0512 linked, respectively, to the variables "Life and Health Sciences" and "Humanities and Social Science" mean that, assuming all other factors constant, the probability of being willing to pay to access b-on by the users of these two scientific areas are higher about, respectively, 4 and 5 percent as compared with the base scientific area of "Engineering".

We also can look to the coefficient 0.0588 linked to the institution "Universidade Nova de Lisboa" and say that the probability of being willing to pay to access b-on by the users of this university are higher about, 0.6 percent as compared with the base category "Polytechnic Institutes".

The fifth column in Table 2 shows the results of the linear probability model without including the observations with null values (1157 observations). Considering the F-statistics we can conclude that the model as whole is statistically significant. In this regression, the explained variance (R-squared) is 35.5%.

The variables that are statistically significant and the signs of the coefficients are the same than in the regression including all the observations, except for the institution "Universidade Nova de Lisboa" and the area of "Humanities and Social Sciences". The magnitude of the coefficients is similar in the two regressions but with some interesting differences. For instance, in this regression demand is more sensitive to the price and there is a larger difference between users from "Life and Health Sciences" and "Engineering".

Table 2: Determinants of the probability of being willing to pay to access b-on, with all observations (columns 2, 3 and 4) and excluding null values (columns 5, 6 and 7).

Independent variables	Regression analysis of WTP to continue access scientific e-resources b-on					
	Accepting null values			Not accepting null values		
	LPM (OLS) z-coefficient	Logit (MLE) B-coefficient	Probit (MLE) B-coefficient	LPM (OLS) z-coefficient	Logit (MLE) B-coefficient	Probit (MLE) B-coefficient
Bid	-0.0098(0.000)***	-0.1199(0.000)***	-0.0612(0.000)***	-0.0166(0.000)***	-0.1599(0.000)***	-0.0829(0.000)***
Frequency digital library use (0=No, 1=Yes)	0.0051(0.000)***	0.0039(0.000)***	0.0025(0.000)***	0.0007(0.000)***	0.0054(0.000)***	0.0033(0.000)***
Knowledge of b-on (0=No, 1=Yes)	0.0231(0.259)	0.2073(0.284)	0.1142(0.297)	0.0359(0.219)	0.2123(0.354)	0.1201(0.374)
Professor	0.1032(0.000)***	0.9237(0.000)***	0.5485(0.000)***	0.1048(0.006)***	0.9000(0.003)***	0.5469(0.002)***
PhD Student /Researcher	0.0453(0.133)	0.4060(0.138)	0.2112(0.177)	0.0577(0.181)	0.3851(0.253)	0.2178(0.266)
Undergraduate student	0.0309(0.206)	0.2854(0.224)	0.1661(0.208)	0.0344(0.325)	0.1957(0.478)	0.1409(0.387)
Other	0.1061(0.005)***	0.9244(0.003)***	0.5454(0.003)***	0.1904(0.000)***	1.6064(0.000)***	0.8693(0.000)***
Life and Health Sciences	0.0403(0.089)*	0.3500(0.100)*	0.2108(0.082)*	0.0474(0.153)	0.3126(0.233)	0.2134(0.157)
Physiques and Chemistry Sciences	0.0354(0.212)	0.3635(0.135)	0.2026(0.144)	0.0475(0.243)	0.3626(0.233)	0.2149(0.218)
Humanities and Social Science	0.0512(0.046)*	0.4496(0.052)*	0.2776(0.034)**	0.0577(0.104)	0.3355(0.228)	0.2449(0.124)
Earth and Planetary Science	-0.0135(0.720)	-0.0067(0.985)	-0.0293(0.885)	-0.0418(0.424)	-0.4012(0.347)	-0.2142(0.388)
Mathematics and Computer Sciences	-0.0315(0.330)	-0.3857(0.214)	-0.2300(0.192)	-0.0408(0.385)	-0.4537(0.231)	-0.2657(0.231)
University of Algarve	-0.0029(0.934)	-0.0336(0.914)	-0.0200(0.910)	0.0137(0.777)	0.1656(0.666)	0.0813(0.715)
University of Aveiro	-0.0049(0.911)	-0.0723(0.844)	-0.0600(0.777)	-0.0114(0.845)	-0.0799(0.859)	-0.0987(0.700)
University of Évora	0.0140(0.754)	0.7576(0.851)	0.0429(0.853)	0.0201(0.742)	0.1004(0.840)	0.0381(0.896)
University of Lisboa	-0.0230(0.551)	-0.2599(0.433)	-0.1075(0.560)	-0.0191(0.720)	-0.1859(0.652)	-0.0405(0.861)
University Nova de Lisboa	0.0588(0.094)*	0.4772(0.118)	0.2760(0.112)	0.0550(0.245)	0.5028(0.178)	0.2743(0.197)
University of Porto	0.0252(0.394)	0.2017(0.418)	0.1346(0.336)	0.0433(0.277)	0.3951(0.198)	0.2352(0.172)
University Técnica de Lisboa	0.0227(0.616)	0.1664(0.655)	0.0991(0.643)	0.0819(0.197)	0.7598(0.126)	0.4130(0.142)
University of Coimbra	-0.0478(0.232)	-0.6420(0.078)*	-0.3300(0.100)*	-0.0512(0.361)	-0.4888(0.269)	-0.2695(0.283)
Other Universities	0.0301(0.419)	0.2592(0.391)	0.1407(0.417)	0.0160(0.746)	0.1570(0.673)	0.0586(0.782)
Constant	0.2822(0.000)***	-0.6481(0.049)**	-0.5175(0.004)***	0.5239(0.000)***	0.7011(0.079)*	0.2459(0.269)
Number of observations	1930	1930	1930	1157	1157	1157
Statistic F	21.67(0.000)***			29.76(0.000)***		
R-squared	0.1926			0.3551		
Pseudo R2		0.2631	0.2600		0.3942	0.3839
LR chi2(21)		471.10(0.000)***	465.56(0.000)***		551.03(0.000)***	536.64(0.000)***
Log likelihood		-659.8280	-662.5982		-423.3755	-430.5673

The p-values are indicated in parentheses.

*** variable is significant at 1% significance level, ** variable is significant at 5% significance level and * variable is significant at 10% significance level.

Logit and probit models
As previously mentioned our main aim is to study the set of factors that influence the probability of an academic user being willing to pay the b-on services. Ordinary least square regression (OLS) is a very common estimator, but presents some problems when using a binary response variable. The adequate models for binary dependent variables are Logit and Probit models.

The bottom of Table 2 shows the likelihood ratio chi-squared (LRchi2(21)) of the Logit an Probit models with the p-values, respectively, 471.10 (0.000), 465.56 (0.000), 551.03 (0.000) and 536.64 (0.000), tell us that the models as a whole fit significantly well. The pseudo-R-squared is also given. It is a pseudo-R-squared because there is no direct equivalent of an R-squared (from OLS) in non-linear models. The explained variance in the three models are about 19-26 percent (0.1926, 0.2631), for the data accepting null values and 36-39 percent (0.3551, 0.3942) to data not accepting null values. These values are low and higher values indicating better model fit. However they cannot be interpreted as one would interpret an OLS R-squared. Aabø (2005b) explains that more important than the high of the pseudo R2 are the signs of the significant explanatory factors.

The values of log likelihood can be used in comparisons of the Logit and Probit models. The higher values, -659.8280 and -423.3755, mean the Logit model is the best one to explain the impact of the different variables.

In the Table 2 we see the β coefficients and the associated p-values. This table shows that these two models, which consider the maximum likelihood estimation (MLE), produce similar results. We obtained statistically significant values for the independent variables "Bid", "Frequency digital library use", "Professor", "Other" and "University of Coimbra" (this last variable is not significant when null values are excluded). We emphasise that the signs of the coefficients are the same in the Logit and the Probit regressions.

The interpretation of the β coefficients in the Logit and Probit models can be difficulty. For this reason, as many other researchers, we prefer to compute the more intuitive "marginal effects" of the independent variables on the probability. For continuous independent variables, to find the marginal effects on the probability we must calculate the partial derivate. Equations (3 and 6) give us these values. We computed these data with STATA.
Let us interpret marginal effects for Logit and Probit models show in Table 3 second ant third columns.

We obtained statistically significant values for the independent variables "Bid", "Frequency digital library use", "Professor", "Other" for observations accepting null values and observations not accepting null value. The signs of the coefficients are the same and the magnitudes are similar, exception for "Other". Now we can say for the results, of the Table 3 third item, that when "Bid" increases by one euro, the probability of buying the b-on services decreases by a factor 0.0086 or 0.9 percent in the academic population. On the other hand, the probability of being willing to pay to access b-on increases by a factor of 0.0003 or 0.03 percent for each additional day of digital library use. We can also tell that the probability of a Professor buying the b-on services is 8 percent higher than the probability of a master student doing so.

For Probit models, we say that the probability of a user, from area of "Humanities and Social Science", paying the b-on services increase by a factor 0.0495 or 0.5 percent comparing user from the "Engineering" area.

Table 3: Marginal effects of LPM, Logit and Probit models explaining the probability of being willing to pay to access the b-on services, with all observations (columns 2,3 and 4) and excluding null values observations (columns 5,6 and 7)

Independent variables	Accepting null values			Not accepting null values		
		Marginal Effects			Marginal Effects	
	LPM (OLS) z-coefficient	Logit dy/dx	Probit dy/dx	LPM (OLS) z-coefficient	Logit dy/dx	Probit dy/dx
Bid	-0.0098(0.000)***	-0.0086(0.000)***	-0.0098(0.000)***	-0.0166(0.000)***	-0.0177(0.000)***	-0.0201(0.000)
Frequency digital library use (0=No, 1=Yes)	0.0051(0.000)***	0.0003(0.000)***	0.0004(0.000)***	0.0007(0.000)***	0.0006(0.000)***	0.0008(0.000)
Knowledge of b-on (0=No, 1=Yes)	0.0231(0.259)	0.0145(0.272)	0.0178(0.285)	0.0359(0.219)	0.0228(0.341)	0.0284(0.363)
Professor	0.1032(0.000)***	0.0800(0.002)***	0.1034(0.001)***	0.1048(0.006)***	0.1127(0.008)***	0.1446(0.003)***
PhD Student /Researcher	0.0453(0.133)	0.0331(0.190)	0.0375(0.220)	0.0577(0.181)	0.0475(0.302)	0.0570(0.301)
Undergraduate student	0.0309(0.206)	0.0215(0.248)	0.0278(0.227)	0.0344(0.325)	0.0224(0.492)	0.0352(0.4000)
Other	0.1061(0.005)***	0.0926(0.027)	0.1165(0.016)**	0.1904(0.000)***	0.2776(0.004)***	0.2795(0.002)***
Life and Health Sciences	0.0403(0.089)*	0.0271(0.128)	0.0362(0.104)	0.0474(0.153)	0.0366(0.259)	0542(0.176)
Physiques and Chemistry Sciences	0.0354(0.212)	0.0294(0.181)	0.0359(0.183)	0.0475(0.243)	0.0445(0.278)	0.0562(0.251)
Humanities and Social Science	0.0512(0.046)*	0.0362(0.083)	0.0495(0.055)*	0.0577(0.104)	0.0399(0.260)	0.0633(0.147)
Earth and Planetary Science	-0.0135(0.720)	-0.0005(0.985)	-0.0046(0.882)	-0.0418(0.424)	-0.0390(0.279)	-0.0470(0.336)
Mathematics and Computer Sciences	-0.0315(0.330)	-0.0243(0.153)	-0.0323(0.132)	-0.0408(0.385)	-0.0436(0.163)	-0.0572(0.171)
University of Algarve	-0.0029(0.934)	-0.0024(0.913)	-0.0032(0.909)	0.0137(0.777)	0.0192(0.680)	0.0203(0.723)
University of Aveiro	-0.0049(0.911)	-0.0051(0.839)	-0.0092(0.768)	-0.0114(0.845)	-0.0086(0.855)	-0.0229(0.686)
University of Évora	0.0140(0.754)	0.0056(0.855)	0.0071(0.857)	0.0201(0.742)	0.0115(0.845)	0.0094(0.897)
University of Lisboa	-0.0230(0.551)	-0.0170(0.387)	-0.0162(0.534)	-0.0191(0.720)	-0.0194(0.631)	-0.0096(0.858)
University Nova de Lisboa	0.0588(0.094)*	0.0401(0.179)	0.0508(0.161)	0.0550(0.245)	0.0641(0.236)	0.0733(0.237)
University of Porto	0.0252(0.394)	0.0151(0.437)	0.0225(0.355)	0.0433(0.277)	0.0471(0.231)	0.0602(0.194)
University Técnica de Lisboa	0.0227(0.616)	0.0128(0.675)	0.0169(0.662)	0.0819(0.197)	0.1083(0.215)	0.1186(0.200)
University of Coimbra	-0.0478(0.232)	-0.0366(0.024)	-0.0433(0.041)	-0.0512(0.361)	-0.0461(0.188)	-0.0576(0.217)
Other Universities	0.0301(0.419)	0.0205(0.433)	0.0244(0.452)	0.0160(0.746)	0.0183(0.687)	0.0145(0.787)
Constant	0.2822(0.000)***	--	--	0.5239(0.000)***	--	--

The p-values are indicated in parentheses.
*** variable is significant at 1% significance level, ** variable is significant at 5% significance level and * variable is significant at 10% significance level.

We can make the other comparisons very easily with all data reported in Table 3 with statistically significant. For instance, looking the data of Logit model and not accepting null values, we can say the probability of a Professor paying the b-on services increase by a factor 0.1127 or 11 percent comparing with the category of Master student, and so on.

4. Demand Curve of the b-on Services

The demand curve is defined as the relationship between the price of the good and the amount or quantity the consumer is willing to purchase in a specified time period, maintaining constant the other determinants of demand (frequency of use, the type of the user, the scientific area and the institution of the user, in our case).

We analyse demand curve of the Portuguese electronic scientific information consortium b-on – Biblioteca do Conhecimento Online. Figure 1 shows the demand curves, respectively, to Professors and Master students, of the area of Humanities and Social Sciences, from University Nova de Lisboa, with an average frequency digital library use of about 53 days per year. The demand curves shows how the probability of being willing to pay to access b-on varies with the price. The curves were drawn considering the results of the Logit model as it describes better the behaviour of the academic Portuguese users. In our computations we took into account only the statistically significant variables, since for the remaining variables we cannot reject the null hypothesis of β being equal to zero.

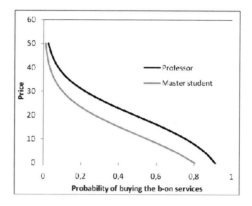

Figure 1: Demand curves for the Portuguese electronic scientific information consortium b-on – Biblioteca do Conhecimento Online, respectively, to Professors and Master students of the area of Humanities and Social Sciences, from University Nova de Lisboa, with an average frequency digital library use of about 53 days per year

The demand curves show that, for a given price, the probability of a Professor buying the b-on services is higher than the corresponding probability for a Master student. For instance, if the price is 15 Euros per month, the probability of being willing to buy is 63% for a Professor and 41% for a Master student.

5. Conclusions

The levels of importance of access and cost of e-resources in academic environment have quickly increased; WWW, e-books, e-journals and other e-resources have become important sources in libraries. However, there are not enough studies of the impact of the e-resources in the Portuguese academic libraries. This study aimed to improve the knowledge of the value in monetary terms of the scientific e-resources. In order to conduct an accurate assessment we used the contingent valuation method (CVM) to estimate the maximum willingness to pay (WTP) and regression analysis techniques - Linear probability model (LPM), Logit and Probit models – to identify the factors that influence the probability of an user being willing to pay to access the b-on services. The Logit and Probit models are used when the dependent variable is a dichotomous qualitative variable (in our case the categories are: willing to buy, not willing to buy). A qualitative variable can be transformed into a binary variable that takes the value 1 if the respondent answers «yes» and takes the value 0 if he answers «no».

In this paper we studied the factors that influence the probability of a user being willing to pay to access the b-on services. The results show that the probability of buying the b-on services is decreasing with the price charged for the service, showing that the demand for b-on services is quite sensitive to the «price». On the other hand, the users who use more frequently the digital library services present a higher probability of paying to access b-on. Among the various types of users, the Professor category is the one that shows higher probability of buying the services of b-on.

References

Aabø S., (2005b). Valuing the benefits of public libraries, *Information Economics and Policy,* Vol.17, No.2, 175-198.

Barron, D., Williams, R.V., Bajjaly, S., Arns, J. and Wilson, S., (2005). *The economic impact of public libraries on South Carolina.* University of South Carolina, Columbia. Retrieved, June, 3, 2009. Available at: http://www.libsci.sc.edu/SCEIS/home.htm

British Library, (2004). *Measuring Our Values.* British Library, London. Retrieved January, 4, 2007. Available at: http://www.bl.uk/pdf/measuring.pdf

Brown, B., Found, C. and McConnell, M., (2007). Federal Science eLibrary Pilot: Seamless, equitable desktop access for Canadian government researchers, *The Electronic Library,* Vol.25, No.1, 8-17.

Chung, H.-K., (2007). Measuring the economic value of special libraries. *The Bottom Line: Managing Library Finances,* Vol.20, No.1, 30-44.

Cooper, M. D. and Chen, H.-M. (2001). Predicting the relevance of library catalog search, *Journal of the American Society for Information Science and Technology,* Vol.52, No.10, 813-827.

Elliott, D.S.; Holt, G.E.; Hayden, S.W. and Holt, L.E., (2007). *Measuring your library's value: how to do a cost-benefit analysis for public library.* ALA, Chicago.

Harless, D. W. and Allen, F. R., (1999), Using the Contingent Valuation Method to Measure Patron Benefits of Reference Desk Service in an Academic Library, *College & Research Libraries,* Vol.60, No.1, 56-69.

FCCN – Fundação para a Computação Científica Nacional, (2009). *b-on Biblioteca do Conhecimento Online.* Retrieved December, 10, 2009. Available at: http://www.b-on.pt/index.php?option=com_content&view=article&id=116& Itemid=34&lang=

Gujarati, D.N., (1995). *Basic Econometrics,* 3rd ed. McGraw-Hill, New York.

Hider, P., (2008). Using the contingent valuation method for dollar valuations of library services, *Library Quarterly,* Vol.78, No.4, 137-158.

Holt, G.E., Elliott, D. and Moore, A., (1999). Placing a value on public library services, *Public Libraries,* Vol.38, No.2, 98-108.

Holt, G.E. and Elliott, D., (2003). Measuring outcomes: Applying cost-benefit analysis to middle-sized and smaller public libraries, *Library Trends,* Vol.51, No. 3, 424-440.

Kerins, G., Madden, R. and Fulton, C., (2004). Information seeking and students studying for professional careers: the cases of engineering and law students in Ireland, *Information Research,* Vol.10, No.1, paper 208. Retrieved November , 20, 2009. Available at: http://InformationR.net/ir/10-1/paper208.html

Koenig, M.E.D., (1992). The importance of services for productivity: under-recognized and under-invested. *Special Libraries,* Vol. 83, No. 4, 199-210.

Li, Z. and Mahendra, G., (2009). *Using "Recycled Predictions" for Computing Marginal effects s.* Retrieved January, 20, 2010. Available at: http://www.lexjansen.com/wuss/2009/hor/HOR-Li.pdf

Liu, L. G., (2003). The economic behaviour of academic research libraries: toward a theory, *Library Trends*, Vol.51, No.3, 277-292.

Manduca, C.A., Fox, S., et al., (2006). Digital library as network and community center, *D-Lib*, Vol.12, No.12. Retrieved May, 16, 2009. Available at: http://www.dlib.org/dlib/december06/manduca/12manduca.html

McDermott, M., (2002). National Bibliographic Database and National Union Catalogue: Economic Evaluation for the National Library of New Zealand. National Library of New Zealand. Wellington. Retrieved December, 3 2006. Available at: http://www.natlib.gov.nz/catalogues/library-documents/economic-valuation-nbd-nuc.pdf

McMartin, F., Iverson E., Wolf, A., Morrill, J., Morgan, G. and Manduca, C., (2008). The use of online digital resources and educational digital libraries in higher education, *International Journal of Digital Libraries*, Vol.9, 65-79.

Melo, L.B., Pires. C., (2009). Measuring the economic value of the electronic scientific information services in Portuguese academic libraries. *Journal of Librarianship and Information Science*, [accept to publication December 2009].

Missingham, R., (2005). Libraries and economic value: a review of recent studies, *Performance Measurement and Metrics*, Vol.6, No.3, 142-158.

Morris, A., Ayres C. and Jones A., (2006). Audiovisual materials in UK public libraries: economic sense?, *Journal of Documentation*, Vol.62, No.5, 555-569.

Morris, A., Sumsion, J. and Hawkins, M., (2002). Economic value of public libraries in the UK, *Libri*, Vol.52, 78-87.

Murgai, S. R. and Ahmadi, M., (2007). A multiple regression model for predicting reference desk staffing requirements. *The Bottom Line: Managing Library Finances*, Vol.20, N°2, 69-76.

Noonan, D. S., (2003). Contingent Valuation and Cultural Resources: A Meta-analytic Review of Literature, *Journal of Cultural Economics*, Vol.27, 159-176.

Plott, C. R.; Zeiler, K., (2005). The willingness to pay-willingness to accept gap, the "endowment effect", subject misconceptions, and experimental procedures for eliciting valuations, *American Economics Review*, Vol.95, No.3, 530-545.

Sin, J. S.-C. and Kim, K.-S., (2008). Use and non-use of public libraries in the information age: a logistic regression analysis of household characteristics and library services variables, *Library & Information Science Research*, Vol.30, No.3, 207-215.

Tenopir, C.; Read, E., (2000). Patterns of database use in academic libraries. *College & Research Libraries*, Vol.61, No.May, 234-246.

Tenopir, C., (2003). *Use and users of electronic library resources: an overview and analysis of recent research studies.* Council on Library and Information Resources, Washington, D.C. Retrieved November, 6, 2009. Available at: http://www.clir.org/pubs/reports/pub120/pub120.pdf

Troll, D.A., (2001). How and why are libraries changing?, *Digital Library Federation*. Retrieved November, 5, 2009. Available at: http://www.diglib.org/use/whitepaper.htm

Wooldridge, J., (2003). *Introductory econometrics: a modern approach*. Thomson, South-Western.

Wooldridge, J., (2007). *Introdução à Econometria: uma abordagem moderna*. Thomson Learning, São Paulo.

Yu, F., (2006). Users' Emotional and Material Satisfaction at the Micro/Macro Levels in na Academic Library. Thesis submitted for to the Graduate Faculty of School of Information Science for the degree of Doctor of Philosophy, University of Pittsburgh, Pittsburgh. Retrieved December, 6, 2009. Available at: http://etd.library.pitt.edu/ETD/available/etd-07242006160531/unrestricted/FEIYU_ETDDISSERTATION.pdf

The Use of Marketing Research Methods for the Evaluation of Information Literacy Services

Dionysis Kokkinos, Eleni Papadatou and Nina Sisamaki

Central Library, National Technical University of Athens, Greece,
dennis@central.ntua.gr

Abstract: In recent years, services provided from any organization are being evaluated in terms of their necessity for the aims of the organization and libraries can be no exception. Many library researchers have used marketing methods, such as quantitative and qualitative research.
The Central Library of the National Technical University of Athens conducted a quantitative research in order to evaluate the services provided within the concept of Information Literacy.
However, both qualitative and quantitative methods are necessary. In the case of the Central Library of the National Technical University of Athens, the need for evolvement in the existing Information Literacy services requires the use of a qualitative research method, using focus groups, in order to identify unexplored user needs and library shortcomings through the suggestions of the members of the institution.
Keywords: Quantitative research, qualitative research, information literacy, evaluation, marketing research methods

1. Introduction

Marketing, as a managerial process, appears more often in profit organizations. In business, for example, the role of the marketing is to promote specific services and products as well as to attract more customers. In non-profit organizations such as libraries the role of the marketing is just to attract more 'customers' that in the particular situation are 'users', without making any profit. The Chartered Institute of Marketing stresses that "*marketing is the management process responsible for identifying, anticipating and satisfying customer requirements profitably*" (Chartered Institute of Marketing, 2005). Moreover as Coote and Batchelor claim marketing is a mixture of planning, analysis, on going action as well as a management process (Coote and Batchelor, 1997). All the organizations focus on their customers, try to identify their needs and satisfy their requirements. Gambles and Schuster add that marketing role is to predict the current and future needs of the organization so as to improve the existing services and create new services and facilities (Gambles and Schuster, 2003).

There is a debate about the utility of marketing in libraries. From one part, it is believed that marketing and promotion of services is only useful in profit organizations, so libraries that are non-profit organizations do not need it. Marshall claims that many directors of academic libraries are still uncomfortable with the public relations of their job (Marshall, 2001). On the other hand, it is believed that the appropriate marketing could not only improve library services but also could attract more people to use these facilities. Drucker asserts that the marketing in a non-profit

New Trends in Qualitative and Quantitative Methods in Libraries
A. Katsirikou and C. H. Skiadas (eds)
© *World Scientific Publishing Co (pp. 147-151)*

organization is very important, and that nobody trusts something that is completely free, even if it is a beneficial service (Drucker, 1998).

In recent years, services provided from any organization are being evaluated in terms of their necessity for the aims of the organization and libraries can be no exception (Wilson, 1985). The focus of the library should be on its users and the quality of services that they receive (Matthews, 2005). Academic libraries in order to achieve this goal should follow marketing research strategies and techniques. "*In a world that is forever changing, the only certainty is change. Therefore, strategies for building the 21st century libraries and librarians must focus on the ability of librarian and libraries to not just adapt to change, but to prepare for it, facilitate it, and shape it*". Rot Tennant (Matthews, 2005, p. 43). Moreover, Dodsworth claims that "*a marketing plan should be an integral part of libraries strategic plan*" (Dodsworth, 1998, p. 320). Many library researchers have used marketing research methods, such as quantitative and qualitative research, in order to focus attention on expectations and quality, capturing the user's perspective on services used (Cook and Thomson, 2001). Quantitative research is a method where the data are in form of numbers and can be counted or measured. In this case the researcher organizes the data in order to produce numerical information (Preece, 1994). The main problem of the quantitative analysis is that the quality of the results depends on the quality of the original data. If the data are not accurate, the results will also be improper. On the other hand, qualitative research, that is the opposite of quantitative, involves in-depth investigation. Moreover, it is a way of recording people's attitudes, feelings and behaviours in greater depth. It pays more attention to individual cases and looks further than precise numerical evidence. One of the most important disadvantage of qualitative analysis is that usually analyzes few people and so it is difficult to generalize and make systematic comparison (Blaxter et al, 2001).

However, both qualitative and quantitative methods are necessary because qualitative data typically involves words and quantitative data involves numbers. There are various ways to combine these different research methods. User data gathered via various means can reveal information on services needing improvement, which can help in anticipating future user needs, becoming a measure to judge the library's effectiveness (Wood, 2007).

2. Quantitative approach

The Central Library of National Technical University of Athens (NTUA) has been providing for several years certain services within the concept of Information Literacy. These services include seminars addressed to the first year students, aiming to establish an understanding on how to search in the library's Online Public Access Catalogue (OPAC), e-journals, databases and also in the e-books, encyclopedias and dictionaries. Due to the fact that these seminars address the first year students, thus are an introduction to the library's services, the focus is mostly on the basic search through the library's OPAC.

The Information Literacy services of the Central Library of NTUA also includes tutorials for specialized databases, as well as print and electronic guides with information on loan regulations, renewal procedures and information on hold requests. Finally, there is the help-desk service which gives the opportunity to the users to state their questions concerning all services offered by the library.

However, in order to be better, it is necessary to focus on an existing service and try to improve it (Matthews, 2005). Aiming to such an improvement the Central Library of the National Technical University of Athens conducted a quantitative research in order to evaluate the services provided within the concept of Information Literacy. A questionnaire of eleven closed ended questions was uploaded in the library's website.

The number of the questions was limited because the nature of this research required relatively high numbers of respondents. Questions were structured in a closed ended format in order to assist data entry and statistical analysis (U.S. Department of Health and Human Services (HHS), 2010). The research sample consisted of 272 of the library's users, from which 41% was undergraduate students, 4.8% postgraduates, 26.2% PhD students, 18.5% teaching staff and 9.6% employees of the National Technical University of Athens (Kokkinos, Papadatou, Sisamaki, 2008).

The choice of quantitative research depended on the research aim (Hara, 2005), objectives (DJS Research Ltd, 2009) and the researcher's belief that the quantitative approach was most suitable for the topic under consideration. This was the appropriate way to state the research problem in very specific terms making possible to evaluate predetermined services provided. It was considered to be very reliable due to mass surveys (Matveev, 2002), allowing for a broader study and enhancing the generalization of the results for the larger population of interest (U.S. Department of Health and Human Services (HHS), 2010). Finally, it is a method that enabled comparisons across categories, which was essential in this situation.

The findings of this research project indicated the need for further training on the search techniques for the electronic resources of the library. Therefore there was an development of the educational seminars addressing students who needed more analytical information on such search techniques. Similar seminars are planned to take place in the near future addressing postgraduate and PhD students as well as the teaching staff (Kokkinos, Papadatou, Sisamaki, 2008).

The research also revealed the need for subject indexing of the databases as well as the need for a search option using key-words. These services will be provided to the library's users through a meta-search tool called Metalib, which will establish an easy and quick way to search among all the library's resources, making scientific research more efficient. Finally, as an attempt to update the library's users and staff regarding its e-resources, presentations from the publishers of these resources will be scheduled.

3. Qualitative approach

Quantitative researchers in some cases have met difficulties in expressing their data when using only the quantitative way. Therefore, they have attempted to incorporate a qualitative approach into the research (Hara, 1995). Both qualitative and quantitative methods are necessary. Both methods are used to combine a general picture of the study by complementing each other (Shuttleworth, 2008).

In the case of the Central Library of the National Technical University of Athens, the need for evolvement in the existing Information Literacy services requires the use of qualitative research methods, since the quantitative research approach had difficulties in expressing the problem further (Hara, 2005). When the topic of the research is not predetermined and well established, then qualitative research is the appropriate choice, because it provides an initial understanding for further decision making and enables to generate hypotheses or research questions for further investigation (Barbour, 1999).

Library's goal at this point is beyond the improvement of existing services. The goal is the achievement of innovation. Innovation requires identifying new user needs, and new ways of providing services (Matthews, 2005). As a result, the Central Library of the National Technical University of Athens aims to conduct a qualitative research, using focus groups, in order to identify unexplored user needs and library shortcomings through the suggestions of the members of the institution. Focus groups will be used to help shape the future needs of the library as part of a strategic planning process (Moore, 2001), and hopefully will lead to operational excellence (Matthews, 2005).

4. Conclusions

In this paper arguments have been used to prove that a quantitative research method is most appropriate when the aim and the objectives of a research are well stated. Therefore, in the early stages of the evaluation process of Information Literacy services in the Central Library of NTUA a survey was appropriate.

According to Matthews (2005), the information that results from a survey must be discussed with various groups of users in focus groups. This will be the next step in the case of the Central Library of NTUA. Listening hard and asking users to share their opinion will help view the library services from the perspective of the user. This will ensure that the library understands the perceptions of its users and the services the library provides, rather than drawing conclusions using the library's assumptions. Employing both macro-view satisfaction surveys as well as micro-view discussions with groups of users will provide a more complete picture (Matthews, 2005), resulting to a more targeted planning for future services.

References

BARBOUR, R.S., 1999. The case for combining qualitative and quantitative approaches in health services research. *Journal of Health Services Research & Policy.* **4** (1), pp. 39-43. http://www.ncbi.nlm.nih.gov/pubmed/10345565

BLAXTER, L. et al., 2001. *How to research.* 2nd edition. Buckingham: Open University Press.

CHARTERED INSTITUTE OF MARKETING [online] [Accessed 10 March 2010] http://www.cim.co.uk/cim/index.cfm

COOK, C. and THOMSON, B., 2001. Psychometric properties of scores from the web-based LibQUAL+ study of perceptions of library service quality. *Library Trends* **49**, pp. 585-604.

COOTE, H. and BATCHELOR, B., 1997. *How to market your library service effectively.* 2nd edition. London: Aslib.

DJS RESEARCH Ltd. *Definition of Market Research,* 2009. [online] [Accessed 19 March 2010] http://www.marketresearchworld.net/index.php?Itemid=38&id=14&option=com_content&task=view

DODSWORTH, E., 1998. Information policy: Marketing academic libraries: A necessary plan. *The Journal of Academic Librarianship* [online] 24 (4) July, pp. 320-322. [Accessed 10 March 2010] http://www.sciencedirect.com

DRUCKER, P., 1998. *Managing the non-profit organisation: practices and principles.* Oxford: Butterworth-Heinemann.

EXPERIMENT RESOURCES (2009) *Quantitative Research Design.* [Accessed 15 March 2010] http://www.experiment-resources.com/quantitative-and-qualitative-research.html

GAMBLES, B. and SCHUSTER, H., 2003. The changing image of Birmingham libraries: marketing strategy into action. *New library world* [online] **104** (9), pp. 361-371. [Accessed 12 February 2010] http://www.emeraldinsight.com

HARA, K., 1995. Quantitative and Qualitative Research Approaches in Education. *Education,* Vol. 115.

HIGA-MOORE. M.L. et.al., 2002, Use of focus groups in a library's strategic planning process. *Bulletin of the Medical Library Association.* 90 [1], pp. 86-92. [Accessed 20 March 2010] http://www.ncbi.nlm.nih.gov/pmc/articles/PMC64762/

MARSHALL, N.J., 2001. Public relations in academic libraries: a descriptive analysis. *The Journal of Academic Librarianship* [online] **27** (2), pp. 116-121. [Accessed 10 March 2010] http://www.sciencedirect.com

MATTHEWS, J., 2005. *Strategic Planning and Management for Library Managers.* London: Unlimited Libraries.

MATVEEV, A.V., 2002. *The advantages of employing quantitative and qualitative methods in intercultural research: practical implications from the study of the perceptions of intercultural communication competence by American and Russian managers.* Collected research articles, Bulletin of Russian Communication Association *"Theory of communication and applied communication,* Edited by I.N. Rozina, Issue 1, pp. 59-67.

PREECE, R., 1994. *Starting research: an introduction to academic research and dissertation writing.* London: Continuum.

SHUTTLEWORTH, M., 2008. Quantitative Research Design. [Accessed 15 March 2010] http://www.experiment-resources.com/quantitative-research-design.html

U.S. Department of Health and Human Services (HHS), 2010. *Audience Research Basics* [online] http://www.health.gov/communication/primer/ aud_res_prim.asp#overview

WOOD, E., RUSH, M., KNAPP, A., 2007. *Beyond survival, managing academic libraries in transition.* London: Unlimited Libraries.

WILSON, T., 1985. *Evaluation strategies for library/information systems.* University of Sheffield, http://informationr.net/tdw/publ/papers/evaluation85

KOKKINOS, D., PAPADATOU, E., SISAMAKI, N., 2008. Information Literacy and user education in NTUA Central Library. *1st Scientific Symposium Information Literacy and Greek Higher Education: the contribution of EPEAEK II in Academic Library Project,* University of Thessaly, Volos, 11-12 December 2008 (In Greek).

Development of Management Methods in Polish Libraries and Information Centers. Hitherto Existing Solutions, New Trends and Directions of Research

Maja Wojciechowska

Library of Ateneum University in Gdańsk, University of Gdańsk, Poland

Abstract: The paper presents a recent transformations of management methods in libraries and information centers. There is discussed an influence of management techniques on the effectiveness of library services. The variety of methods which can be useful for libraries are presented as well as criteria that management staff should use during the selection phase. The paper also contains a summary results of recent years, poll-based research on the use of management methods in Polish libraries, including comparison of the state from 2003 with the present state in 2010. There are also discussed a nowadays research trends in the library management.
Keywords: Methods of management, efficiency of management library, changes management

1. Introduction

Among the chief factors that determine the effectiveness of a library are: the quality of management and the methods, techniques and tools of management selected by its directors and managerial Staff. By applying all of these correctly, a library can achieve its strategic goals more efficiently.

Making the right decisions is a precondition for effectively using the methods and instruments of management in a library setting. Before applying any method, a detailed assessment has to be carried out as to its aims and scope. Next, one must identify the criteria that a library has to fulfill prior to implementation, not to mention possible obstacles and practical benefits. Management methods should not be seen as a trend that has to be followed, nor should applying them ever become an aim in itself. Like any other tool, management methods serve a purpose, i.e. enabling a library to function more efficiently. For this reason, the objectives that are to be realized using these methods have to be well defined prior to embarking on the implementation phase. In a library, well-considered strategic decisions can be made only after reviewing all the options presented by various methods, techniques and management tools on offer. Methods such as TQM, Library Benchmarking or Just in Time are useful instruments by means of which a library may enhance its work effectiveness, but they will never replace wise and thoughtful management.

2. Management methods

Methods of management can be subdivided into two categories. **Soft methods**, i.e. TQM and Library Benchmarking, call for gradual evolutionary changes that are to be carried out by consistently raising the quality of service. **Hard methods** like reengineering, by contrast, bring about revolutionary changes. Not every method may be used in all fields of library activity. Most methods, however, are complementary to each other and can be used simultaneously.

New Trends in Qualitative and Quantitative Methods in Libraries
A. Katsirikou and C. H. Skiadas (eds)
© *World Scientific Publishing Co (pp. 153-160)*

Among some of the most commonly used terms from the field of organization and management there are management instruments, management techniques, management methods, approaches, methodics, methodologies, and the methods and techniques of organization. Many of these terms overlap; they are sometimes used indiscriminately or interchangeably, resulting in unnecessary confusion. For this reason, in the remaining sections of this article, we will use terms found in source literature from the area of management and organization, as listed by J. Antoszkiewicz (from the general to the specific).

By **management methods** we understand "a combination of means and activities recommended by science and applied by managers with the aim of enhancing the effectiveness of management, while taking into account its goals and functions. Management methods are created by selecting the proper methods for planning, organizing, motivating and exercising control in such a way as to ensure that they constitute a complementary whole" (Penc 1997). **Management techniques** are "the procedures and instruments used to solve specific problems in the area of management" (Penc 1997). **Organizational methods** are "purpose-built sets of recommendations relating to the mode of conduct in solving organizational problems; they are based on research and adapted to multiple use" (Penc 1997). **Organizational techniques** comprise "the entirety of systematic modes of conduct based on methods of scientific research, applied in order to solve organizational problems. These techniques are essential components of all methods and techniques of management" (Penc 1997).

Many organizational and managerial methods and techniques, which until now have been used primarily in the corporate world, can also be used in libraries in order to raise effectiveness and affect the process of change. These methods include: strategic management, marketing management, quality management, knowledge management, lean management, library benchmarking, reengineering, Just in Time, teamwork, project management, outsourcing, controlling, Delphi Method, staff assessment system, competency management, participation management, and the card technique.

Strategic management can be defined as method of guiding the long-term development of a library by means of a decision-making process, planning, task realization and control. It means that a library co-participates in shaping its own future, as opposed to passively submitting to change. Strategic management is related to the need to monitor the library's environment, the risks and opportunities that these surroundings generate, the trends and changes occurring in them, and finally the library itself – its resources, capabilities, etc. Strategic management is concomitant to formulating the mission and vision of the library, its strategic goals, strategic plan, and analyzing the internal and external environment.

The aim of **quality management** is to create in the library a quality-oriented work culture. This entails openness in relation to the demands of its users, a friendly and competent service, and ensuring that its book collections are comprehensive and in line with the interests and needs of its patrons. The criteria of quality management can be implemented using any of the following selected qualitative approaches: Total Quality Management, Quality Assurance, Servqual, Quality Function Deployment, Strategic Quality Management and ISO standards.

Knowledge management is a systematic, coordinated process of gathering, verifying, processing, storing and providing access to knowledge, which – in conjunction with other knowledge-related processes – can increase a library's effectiveness. Knowledge management entails organizing a library in such a way as to bring together all available knowledge resources in a single shared fund of knowledge. These resources comprise both the expertise of individual librarians and the knowledge of the institution as a whole, understood as skills, experience, instruments and procedures, methodologies, relations with the environment and interpersonal relations between library staff.

Lean management is a management method in which, by optimizing, rationalizing and increasing the quality and effectiveness of work, a library can limit the use of resources that it requires to function effectively and realize its statutory goals. In the more specific definition proposed by Jan Sójka, "lean management means that a library comes up with an array of products which correspond to the demands of its users, and that it offers a particular service only when the need occurs" (Sójka 1998). Lean management is based on a sense of economy and on a rational use of library resources, i.e. library staff (basic-level employees as well as office-administration, maintenance and support personnel), materials, buildings and office space, equipment, time and funding.

Benchmarking can be defined as a method of promoting a library's development and increasing its effectiveness by comparing it to the best libraries or to other institutions that can serve as standards of excellence within the relevant group, and transferring their most effective solutions to one's own organization.

Reengineering is a method of rapidly and radically redesigning both strategic processes (with added value for users) and the organizational structure and procedures – with the aim of raising the library's efficiency and effectiveness.

Just in time is a method that enables a library to operate more flexibly by eliminating bottlenecks that might occur when information is delivered to clients. By preventing bottlenecks from forming during gathering and distribution, information reaches the client without losing its relevance. This method enforces a focus on the recipients of information, as all the library's operations are tailored to their needs. Users determine the profile of services and collections offered by the library, helping to eliminate wastefulness. Just in time means that instead of building extensive collections, a library focuses on acquiring only the information that is sought after by its patrons, e.g. by increasing the share allotted in its collections to digital information carriers, using databanks, databases and digital information networks, etc. The just in time method is a rational choice whenever an organization faces the risk that the information that it provides may quickly become outdated, as in the case of institutions serving legal or corporate clients.

Teamwork entails cooperation between library staff from different departments, who work together on specific tasks. Teamwork is most effective when responding to inadequacies in a library's organizational structure and division of responsibilities. It is a method that enables team members to focus on carrying out a single task or project assigned to them. By concentrating in one place the skills and knowledge of staff during group problem-solving sessions, it allows the library to make better use of their potential.

Project management is the method which is focused on a particular targets fulfilled by a team, e.g. computerization of library, digitization of museum collections or organizing readers meeting on specific schedule. Project management becomes widely used by librarians, because it provides clearly noticeable effects of team cooperation.

Participation management is the type of management, which allows librarians to fulfill a part of management tasks and entitlement, and to cooperate in decisive process and realization of objectives, but also to take a responsibility for their activities. This methods broaden the involvement of library staff.

The Delphi Method is an expert method that can be used to create long-term forecats related to a chosen problem or issue that might potentially impact on the functioning of the library in the future. The Delphi Method is one of a group of methods used for opinion polls. A questionnaire is sent to a group of experts, who are asked to give their opinion on what they expect to be the course of events. The identity of other participants is withheld from each of the experts, and as the participants of the survey cannot communicate with each other, partiality or susceptibility to outside influence can be largely ruled out. Extreme views are filtered out to ensure greater objectivity. Instead of random selection, experts are chosen in terms of their experience and expertise in a given field. The final result is a scenario of future events created on the basis of their opinions.

The aim of **assessment systems** and **staff self-assessment** is to help employees become more aware of their skills, competence and performance, and of their role within the organization. Staff self-assessment has a positive impact on many librarians by stimulating self-analysis, self-development and self-accomplishment. It gives employees a better picture of the aim of their work, and helps them to structure their tasks. It helps library managers to make the most of the available human resources by better mining the potential of staff and cooperating with them in planning careers, professional development and training. Assessment system is a powerful instrument for improving quality.

The card technique, also known as organizational stenography, is a method in which predetermined signs (graphic symbols) replace lengthy and complex verbal descriptions as a means of keeping a record of activities. A graphic symbol is assigned to each activity or event, and the time needed to perform each activity is recorded alongside it. The order in which the symbols are written down corresponds to the chronology of events. Additional information includes the name of the event, the distance of dislocation, and (optionally) a concise explanatory description. The card technique can be used for registering the actual state and finding new ways of streamlining the work cycle. It works well as part of the work method measurement cycle. This cycle, as described by Z. Martyniak (Martyniak 2001), consists of the following phases: (1) selecting the goal and item to be analyzed, (2) recording the actual situation, (3) carrying out a critical assessment and analysis of the situation, (4) designing improvements, (5) implementing the designed improvements. The card technique proves its usefulness most of all in recording the actual situation (2) and designing improvement solutions (4). The card technique can be used to create Document Circulation Cards, Process Cards, Activity Cards (also called Team Activity Cards) and Library Material Circulation Cards, otherwise known as Book Circulation Cards – an equivalent of the Material Circulation Card used in industry.

The methods and techniques of management presented here differ in object, range, complexity and character. They harness the results of various disciplines (psychology, sociology, praxeology, ergonomics, system theory, mathematics, organization and management science, etc.). They can be grouped together in clusters of: heuristic methods based on inventiveness and processes of discovery; rationalized methods, operating with control and verification procedures; and classical (empirical) solutions backed up by experience. They can be used to reach a variety of objectives, e.g. optimizing decision-making, enhancing the quality of service, improving interpersonal relations, achieving a more efficient use of resources, strengthening the library's cooperation with its environment, or raising the effectiveness and efficiency of the institution as a whole. All of these methods, however, have one overarching goal, and that is to supply libraries with the conceptual instruments that can help them to better organize work processes by improving the use of human, material, informational and financial resources at their disposal. In addition to his, management methods can provide an answer to such questions as:

- How can a library achieve greater efficiency in managing its human resources?
- How can it organize work more effectively?
- How to minimize the labor-intensity of selected tasks?
- How to minimize the use of materials?
- How to make sure that equipment is used to greater capacity?
- How to choose a management style?
- How to motivate library staff?
- How to improve their working conditions?
- How to control the realization of tasks?
- What criteria should be chosen to evaluate the work that is carried out?
- How to achieve better cooperation with the external environment?
- How to improve the quality of services?
- How to make the work of the library more efficient and how to raise its effectiveness?

Libraries that wish to improve their effectiveness can apply a range of other methods and techniques of management. The include crisis management, management by objective, management by decentralization, management by innovation, management by motivation, management by values, and others. The choice depends on many individual factors, such as the available expertise related to applying management methods, an understanding of the library's environment, awareness of its organizational potential and the ability of library staff to effectively engage in the cooperation.

The methods of library management evolve constantly in response to the demands of a changing environment while new solutions replace outdated ones. It is essential, therefore, that managerial staff and library directors track these changes and adapt the rules of management to the demands of the situation. By doing so, they will improve the library's relationship with its environment and raise the patrons' level of satisfaction with regard to the services on offer. This, in turn, will create a positive image of the library as a modern service-providing institution.

Most of the methods and management tools reviewed here were first developed in the business world by global production companies such as Toyota, IBM or Xerox. It was only later that they reached commercial and, as time went by, non-profit service-providing institutions. Libraries – belonging to the latter group – have used scientific methods of management rather infrequently and inconsistently. Where these methods have been implemented, it has mostly been at the instigation of library Chief Executive Officers. Consequently, wide-scale research describing the process of implementation and evaluating the results is virtually non-existent, and literature on the subject is limited to a handful of articles.

Even though the methods surveyed here – both those adapted to a commercial and a non-commercial (library) setting – were developed over a period of time, the ones that were created later have not supplanted the older ones but – instead – act as a complement to them. Apart from a common goal – effectively managing the process of introducing changes and raising the work-quality and efficiency of the library – each of the methods presented here reflects the typical trends of the second half of the 20th and the beginning of the 21st century. These tendencies include: a flattening of the organizational structure, limiting the role of intermediate-level management, training and educating personnel, raising their level of involvement, teamwork and delegating competence and responsibilities.

3. Research

Despite the dearth of research on this topic, in the years 2003-2010 a research initiative was carried out aimed at examining the level of interest among Polish libraries in implementing management methods. Over 1,000 libraries nationwide were asked to complete a brief survey on the use of such methods and on the plans for implementing them. The questionnaire was addressed to a wide variety of institutions, ranging from the smallest ones (staffed by one employee) to the country's largest research libraries. The poll was carried out on a sample of libraries from each voivodship in Poland, i.e., public libraries, libraries of institutions of higher education, pedagogical libraries, technical libraries, professional libraries, medical libraries, museum libraries, church libraries, scientific institutes' libraries, agricultural libraries, libraries of the Polish Academy of Sciences (PAN), libraries run by associations, archives, economic libraries and military libraries. Its size and diversity allowed the researchers to come up with a general hypothesis as to the growth tendencies related to the use of management methods in libraries nationwide.

Nearly 300 libraries responded to the poll. The size of this sample, while constituting approximately 30% of the overall target group, is still large enough for statistical purposes, and gives a clear indication of the use of management methods by libraries in Poland. Most of the responding libraries do not use methods of management, nor are they planning to introduce methods of this type n the near future. Many of them do not have even the most basic knowledge in this respect. Other libraries are planning to introduce a chosen range of methods, or are studying them with a view to implementing them at a later date.

Out of the libraries examined, 45 institutions, i.e. 15.9% of the sample, are using one or more methods. The remaining 84.1% of libraries do not use any method, although some of them have been making plans to start the implementation process. Libraries typically employ one or two methods linked together, with a small percentage of libraries using up to four methods. The biggest users of these methods are academic libraries, pedagogical libraries and public libraries located in large cities. Incidental users include school libraries, technical libraries, medical libraries, economical libraries and military libraries. Most of the libraries that do not use such methods include museum libraries, church libraries and scientific institute libraries, libraries run by associations, archives, and the libraries of the Polish Academy of Sciences (PAN). This might be linked to the character of these libraries (except for the larger PAN libraries), as most of them are staffed by a small number of employees, local in nature, and vested in history and tradition.

The methods most frequently used by Polish libraries include strategic management (implemented by 31% of the libraries declaring the use of any method management), a range of qualitative approaches (24%), and staff assessment (20.3%). Among the methods used less often are task-oriented teamwork (11.1%), the card technique (9.2%), benchmarking (9.2%), reengineering (5.5%), knowledge management (3.7%)

and just in time (3.7%). None of the libraries participating in the poll declared the use of lean management or the Delphi method.

Even though several dozen libraries admitted to using selected methods of management, many institutions made the point that these techniques were being implemented as part of a pilot-project, and that this was not being carried out to strict professional standards. The managers of these libraries emphasized a lack of skills needed to use these methods and referred to restricted options with respect to training, courses, seminars and professional literature (primarily textbooks and applications). In spite of this, many librarians are working to extend their knowledge and experience in the field of modern forms of managing non-profit institutions. Many see this as a chance to further their own development. On the other hand, many library employees oppose the introduction of management methods, believing that they would form a threat to the character of their libraries, their work culture and traditions. These employees see management methods as an artificial and unnatural attempt at placing libraries on the same level as commercial institutions.

From 2009 to 2010 the similar research was done to indicate changes in library management and organization. The poll was responded by 92 libraries (public, school, pedagogical, academic, and scientific). The 52 of them, which is equal to 56,6%, do not apply any of management method. The remaining libraries utilize one or several methods among these listed in the table.

METHODS	NUMBER OF LIBRARIES USING THESE METHODS
Teamwork	27
Staff assessment	15
Knowledge management	10
Strategic management	9
Competence management	9
Participation management	7
Project management	7
Benchmarking	5
Marketing management	4
Controlling	3
Quality management, including: TQM ISO standards	 3 3
Outsourcing	2
Just in time	1
Lean management	1
Delphi Method	1

Tab.1. Information on the types of methods used by Polish libraries can be fund in 2010

Among the most important changes (in respect to results from 2003) are a significant increase of interest of work organization and staff evaluation systems.

4. Conclusion

Even though several dozen libraries admitted to using selected methods of management, many institutions made the point that these techniques were being implemented as part of a pilot-project, and that this was not being carried out to strict professional standards. The managers of these libraries emphasized a lack of skills needed to use these methods and referred to restricted options with respect to training, courses, seminars and professional literature (primarily textbooks and applications). In spite of this, many librarians are working to extend their knowledge and experience in the field of modern forms of managing non-profit institutions. Many see this as a chance to further their own development. On the other hand, many library employees oppose the introduction of management methods, believing that they would form a threat to the character of their libraries, their work culture and traditions. These employees see management methods as an artificial and unnatural attempt at placing libraries on the same level as commercial institutions.

In the context of this debate and the research results quoted above, the following questions appear to be relevant:

1. To what degree does the use of management methods in libraries reflect the current needs of these institutions based on rational considerations?

2. How high is the risk that using management methods in libraries might result in depriving them of their character as non-profit institutions?

3. Should the use of management methods remain limited to large library institutions or research libraries staffed by employees with well prepared academic background?

References

Martyniak, Z. (2001). *Organizacja i zarządzanie.* Antykwa, Kraków, Kluczbork.

Penc, J. (1997). *Leksykon biznesu.* Placet, Warszawa.

Sójka, J. (1998). Szczupłe zarządzanie (Lean Management – LM) dla bibliotek. *Acta Universitatis Nicolai Copernici, Bibliologia,* 328, 553-570

Chapter 3. Using Qualitative and Quantitative Methods in Digital Library Education and Research

The Use of Phenomenographic Approach to Investigate Students' Conceptions of the Use of Web 2.0 Tools

Alice Adejoke Bamigbola

Institute of Information Studies, Tallinn University, Estonia
International Masters in Digital Library Learning (DILL)

Abstract: This paper discusses the data collection instrument and data analysis using phenomenography, a qualitative research approach used to investigate DILL students' conceptions of the use of Web 2.0 tools. The research was undertaken as researcher's master's thesis in the digital library learning programme at the Institute of Information Studies, Tallinn University. The iterative process of phenomenography research specialization and justification for its use for the current study are discussed.
Keywords: Web 2.0 tools, phenomenography, DILL students, semi-structured interview, categories of description, and outcome space

1. Introduction

In the past five years the use of Web 2.0 tools has permeated many human spheres including higher education sector. Its incorporation into higher education is a new phenomenon, though many higher education institutions have experimented with it. Consequently, evidence showed that its incorporation into higher education sector is not without challenges or problems (Franklin and Harmelen, 2007). The challenges of the incorporation of Web 2.0 tools into higher education, include, the students' preferences of the use of Web 2.0 tools and the required skills to use it. Therefore, the aim of the research was to acquire a deeper understanding of Digital Library Learning (DILL) students' conceptions of the use of Web 2.0 tools focusing on students' preferences and the required skills to use Web 2.0 tools. DILL programme is an international master in Digital Library Learning which runs among three European universities (Oslo University College, Norway, Tallinn University, Estonia and Parma University, Italy).

To achieve the aim of the research, the following research questions were framed.

Research Questions
1. How do DILL students experience Web 2.0 tools?
2. What are the DILL students' preferences of the use of Web 2.0 tools?
3. What are the required skills to use Web 2.0 tools?

Scope and Limitations
- The target sample for the study was DILL students (groups 2 and 3) from Africa and Asia, other DILL students were not considered.
- Only English language literature was reviewed for the study.

This paper examines phenomenography, a research approach used by the author for her master's thesis.

New Trends in Qualitative and Quantitative Methods in Libraries
A. Katsirikou and C. H. Skiadas (eds)
© *World Scientific Publishing Co (pp. 161-166)*

2. Methodology

The study is based on interpretivist paradigm and qualitative research design. Phenomenographic approach was used with semi-structured interviews. Data analysis was done phenomenographically which resulted in four categories of descriptions and an outcome space. This paper discusses the phenomenographic research approach from the data collection to results' stage.

Phenomenographic Research Approach

Phenomenography was etymologically derived from two Greek words '*phainemomenon*' which translates as appearance and '*graphein*' which means to describe in words or picture (Hasselgren and Beach, 1997, p.192). It originated from the Department of Education and Educational Research, Goteborg University in Sweden in the 1970s. It is a qualitative research approach which aims at understanding different ways a group of people conceptualize, perceive, understand, or experience a phenomenon, in order to bring out different variations in their experiences. Marton and Booth (1997, p.136) define phenomenography as a research approach that "aims to reveal the qualitatively different ways of experiencing various phenomena".

Ontological assumption of phenomenography is subjectivist, a non-dualist view and second order perspective. It is an empirical approach to study other people's perspective of the world around them and devise collective categories of description that describe the variation of these experiences (Marton and Booth, 1997, p.116). Orgill (2002) notes that the intent of phenomenographic research is to identify multiple conceptions or meanings that a particular group of people have for a particular phenomenon. In this study, the researcher investigated DILL students' experiences to identify multiple conceptions of Web 2.0 tools. In other words, the researcher looked into the use of Web 2.0 tools through the perspective of DILL students.

Research Sample

In phenomenographic study, the samples are traditionally small and purposive in order to cover variations of experience in population being covered. The population for the current research was DILL students set 2 and 3 from Africa and Asia. The sample size was two DILL students for pilot study and twelve DILL students for the main study. Six DILL students from each of the two continents comprising of three males and three females from each of the two continents.

Phenomenographic Data Collection Instrument

The study used an interview which is the main and richest data collection instrument in phenomenography (Marton, 1994; Akerlind, 2005). An interview is a descriptive qualitative and an in-depth data collection instrument (Pickard, 2007). In phenomenographic interview the motive is to elicit the meanings and variation in meanings of a phenomenon through the interviewee's experience of such phenomenon. The interviewee gives examples of how he or she have experienced the researched phenomenon (Akerlind, 2005). That is, the example is to show what the interviewee thinks about the phenomenon at the point of the interview to reveal the interviewee's awareness level of the phenomenon.

In this regards, how DILL students experienced the use of Web 2.0 tools revealed their level of awareness. The current study used the phenomenographic preferred method of data collection, a semi-structured interview, with open-ended questions which aim to persuade the interviewees to focus on describing their experience of the phenomenon. A semi-structured interview has a pre-determined interview guide where all the relevant areas of the topic have been listed in the questions but the interviewer is free to expand it. Apart from the interview guide the interviewer could ask other probing questions (Pickard, 2007).

The interview sessions were conducted using a natural conversational approach aiming to move from the general to the specific (Akerlind, 2005). Importantly, the interviewer bracketed her opinion on the phenomenon in order not to influence the interviewees and for validity of the data (Ashworth and Lucas, 2000). The main interview questions were (1) what do you think Web 2.0 tools are all about? How have you used them? Which of them do you use? Why do you use those Web 2.0 tools you mentioned? What skills do you think would be required to use these tools effectively in your opinion? How did you acquire these skills? What skills do you think you still need to enhance your usage of Web 2.0 tools? Also, other unstructured questions were asked to further probe the interviewees. The interview sessions were audio recorded for transcription purpose.

Phenomenographic Data Analysis

The data analysis in phenomenographic research aims at developing categories of descriptions which represent different ways of understanding a phenomenon, and an outcome space or 'giving' a map of the 'collective mind', (Marton, 1994), which are the phenomenography results. The analysis was iterative and in stages which included familiarization, condensation, comparison, grouping, articulating, labelling and contrasting to arrive at categories of description and outcome space (Bruce, 2003: Alsop and Tompsett, 2006).

The first phase is the transcription of an interview or "utterances of research subjects" (Hasselgren and Beach, 1997). In the current research, each interview session was transcribed verbatim immediately after each session, besides, the raw interview transcripts were used and manually analyzed. It was rigorous and iterative to get all the information transcribed verbatim. Having done the transcription, the researcher got familiarised with the transcripts, by reading through it several times, then condensed and compared the data.

The next stage was grouping of the data; the framework for this stage of the data analysis is based on referential components, the dimension of variation and structure of awareness (Marton and Booth, 1997). The referential aspect is the "what" of an experience or phenomenon, the core meaning given to a phenomenon or object of research by the respondent. For the current research, the core meaning that DILL students gave to the use of Web 2.0 tools.

The dimensions of variation are aspects or factors that are common to all the categories of description yet which are experienced differently in each category and it results in some expansion of awareness. These factors are presented as phenomenographic "dimensions of variation" (Boon, Johnston and Webber, 2007, p.214). In this study the dimensions of variation were the contextual focus, the preferential focus and the skills focus. The variation focuses on the context within which Web 2.0 tools were experienced by the DILL students; the students' preference among Web 2.0 tools; and the skills required and its acquisition to use Web 2.0 tools.

The structure of awareness is the "how" of an experience or phenomenon. It could be explained as what the subject is aware about an object at the time of the expression of the experience of that object. Marton and Pang (1999) note that structure of awareness in phenomenography analysis framework is a modern trend and it has been emphasized in the recent research. It consists of what Booth (1997) called 'theme', and Bruce (2003) referred to as 'internal horizon'. Internal horizon or theme is the central focus or initial theme (theme of awareness) that comes to the mind of subject/student when faced with an object/problem, The second element is 'thematic and margin' (Booth, 1997) or 'external horizon' (Bruce, 2003) which is the other associated both relevant and irrelevant themes present at the time of the awareness but recede at the background. For the current study, internal and external horizons were used for the structure of awareness.

At the initial stage of the grouping several themes were discovered. Afterwards, it was reduced to four articulated groups because the main aim of phenomenographic research is to identify small number of qualitatively distinct descriptive categories of the ways a group of people experience a phenomenon (Booth, 1997), in this context, Web 2.0 tools. Then the four categories of descriptions were labelled, the labels were taken from the interview transcripts.

Phenomenographic Results

As mentioned above, categories of description and outcome space are results of phenomenographic study. For the current research four distinct qualitative categories of descriptions were discovered: category 1: communication tools conception, category 2: educational tools conception, category 3: professional tools conception and category 4: multi-purpose tools conception. Subsequently, an outcome space was constructed. In phenomenography, outcome space is the articulation of a comprehensive expression of the researched phenomenon and it is often presented in a hierarchical way (Marton, 1994). The outcome space for this study is presented below in Fig. 1.

1: Communication tools conception

2: Educational tools conception

3: Professional tools conception

4: Multi-purpose tools conception

Fig.1: Outcome space showing the four categories of description of Web 2.0 tools of DILL students in hierarchical order.

3. Justification of Phenomenographic Approach for the Current Study

Phenomenographic approach was chosen for the current study because the research aimed to acquire a deeper understanding of the Digital Library Learning (DILL) students' conceptions of the use of Web 2.0 tools. To achieve this aim, phenomenography was found to be appropriate because it is a research approach that brought out the holistic variation in experience, with simplicity and elegant descriptions of the experience of the phenomenon. The focus of this study was on collective holistic variation of the experience of DILL students and the structural relationship between the different ways of experiencing Web 2.0 tools. Besides, the incorporation of Web 2.0 tools in higher education sector is a new phenomenon, thus, phenomenography is suitable to bring a detailed qualitative data.

4. Conclusions

A phenomenographic research approach was used to investigate students' conception of the use of Web 2.0 tools. Using phenomenographic research approach, four distinct categories of descriptions of the use of Web 2.0 tools were discovered and thereafter an outcome space was constructed. This research results brought out a detailed qualitative data on the use of Web 2.0 tools by the DILL students (sets 2 and 3) from Africa and Asia.

Importantly, the results of this research are limited to the group of DILL students studied. Therefore, there is a need for further research to study other groups of students if the results might be similar or different.

References

Åkerlind, G.S. (2005). Learning about phenomenography: Interviewing, data analysis and the qualitative research paradigm, Chapter 6 in J. Bowden and P. Green (Eds), Doing Developmental Phenomenography, RMIT Press: Melbourne Australia, pp. 63-73.

Alsop, G. & Tompsett, C. (2006). Making sense of 'pure' phenomenography, *Information and Communication Technology in Education',* ALT-J, *14*(3) 241- 259. Retrieved March 5, 2010 from Web site: http://dx.doi.org/10.1080/09687760600837058

Ashworth, P. & Lucas, U. (1998). What is the 'World' of Phenomenography?, *Scandinavian Journal of Educational Research*, 42(4), 415 - 431. Retrieved March 5, 2010 downloaded by Academic Library of Tallinn University, from Web site: http:////dx.doi.org/10.1080/0031383980420407

Boon, S., Johnston, B. & Webber, S. (2007). A phenomenographic study of English faculty's conceptions of information literacy. Journal of Documentation, 63(2), 204-228. January 31, 2010 from Elsevier Ltd, Web site: http://www.emeraldinsight.com/Insight/viewPDF.jsp?contentType=Article&Filename=html/Output/Published/EmeraldFullTextArticle/Pdf/2780630203.pdf

Booth, S. (1997). On phenomenography, learning and teaching, *Higher Education Research & Development,16*(2), *135 — 158* . . Retrieved March 5, 2010 downloaded by Academic Library of Tallinn University Database, from Web site: http://dx.doi.org/10.1080/0729436970160203

Bruce, C. S. (2003). Frameworks guiding the analysis: applied to or derived from the data? In Proceedings *EARLI Experience and Understanding SIG (SIG10) Meeting,* Australia National University, Canberra. Retrieved April 4, 2010 from QUT Digital Repository, Web site: http://eprints.qut.edu.au/

Franklin, T. & Van Harmelen, M. (2007). Web 2.0 for content for learning and teaching in higher education. (JISC Report) Retrieved January 15, 2010 from JISC Web site: http://www.jisc.ac.uk/publications/documents/web2andpolicyreport.aspx

Marton, F. (1994). Phenomenograhpy. In T. Husén & T. N. Postlethwaite (Eds.), The International Encyclopedia of Education 2nd Edn. 8, 4424 - 4429. Pergamon.

Marton, F., & Booth, S. (1997). Learning and Awareness. New Jersey: Lawerence Erlbaum Associates. Retrieved February 21, 2010 from http://books.google.com/ books?hl=en&lr=&id=S3pb1I6_R1kC&oi=fnd&pg=PR7&dq=marton+and+booth +1997&ots=_VlVzuNfjc&sig=LXF1-yE5Ni5dI7TByCzd-afUxJA#v=onepage&q =marton%20and%20booth%201997&f=false

Marton, F. & Pang, M.F. (1999). Two faces of variation. Paper presented at the 8th *European Conference for Learning and Instruction,* Goteborg, Sweden, August 24–28.

Pickard, A. J. (2007). Research methods in information. London: Facet Publishing.

Application of Preservation Metadata for Long-Term Accessibility of Digital Objects

Yibeltal Tafere Bayih

Tallinn University, Institute of Information Studies, Estonia

Abstract: This paper discusses the research methodology used to study the extent of implementing standard preservation metadata in the preservation practice at memory institutions. The research was undertaken as part of the researcher's master's thesis conducted at Tallinn University. This study adopts a qualitative method based upon a pragmatic approach and uses the case study strategy. Metadata experts/specialists in the selected memory institutions were interviewed using semi-structured interviews, accompanied by document analysis.
Keywords: Preservation metadata, digital objects, memory institutions, PREMIS, national library, national archives

1. Introduction

To ensure the long-term accessibility of digital objects, metadata is the key factor. Preservation requires special elements to track the roots of a digital object (where it came from and how it has changed over time), to detail its physical characteristics and to document its behavior in order to emulate it on future technologies. Literature revealed that valuable metadata is the best way of minimizing the risk of digital resources becoming inaccessible and to be most valuable for all and needs to be consistently maintained throughout the process (Alemneh, Hastings and Hartman, 2002; NISO, 2004).

Digital preservation is a relatively new phenomenon and the success of preservation metadata in supporting long-term preservation is largely untried; many specifications for preservation metadata have been published and significant progress has been made towards standardizing a core set of preservation metadata elements. However, "the movement from theory to practice in preservation metadata cannot be traced as a straight line" (Lavoie and Gartner, 2005, p.9).

In this regard a lot of efforts have been made to produce conceptual models and concrete metadata dictionaries for implementers of digital preservation services. For example, the set of core elements in the PREMIS data dictionary has now been widely accepted and plays a key role in creating coherence in the digital preservation metadata community. PREMIS provides a foundation to support interoperability across systems and organizations. However, literature revealed that there is a gap in its application into practice and this will have its own future challenge from the very aim of digital preservation like long-term accessibility of digital objects and others issues (Caplan, 2006). So, a number of case studies are expected to report on both implementation and use in carrying out preservation strategies (Caplan, 2006; Dappert and Farquhar, 2009).

New Trends in Qualitative and Quantitative Methods in Libraries
A. Katsirikou and C. H. Skiadas (eds)
© *World Scientific Publishing Co (pp. 167-173)*

Thus, the focus of this study is on practice of preservation metadata at memory institutions that aim to look the extent of implementing theoretical standard in to actual practice especially from the PREMIS standard perspective the *de facto* standard for preservation metadata.

Research Questions

The research questions of the study are:

1. How effective are preservation metadata theories into practice?
2. What tools, standards and strategies are adopted for metadata management in practice and why?
3. What is the level of granularity (e.g., representations, files, bitstreams) that preservation metadata is applied in the practice of memory institutions?
4. What type of risks can be anticipated when preservation metadata implemented only partially in practice?

Scope/ Limitations

The study was conducted within the following scope/limitations:

- The number of memory institutions used for the case studies was relatively small. This was mainly due to time and resource constraints of the MA thesis project.
- Due to geographic distance and potential inconvenience for the respondents, an interview at one of the memory institutions was conducted via email with follow-up questions.
- Only English language implementation documentation was used because of the language barrier.
- The literature review covers only publications in English.

2. Methodology

The study uses qualitative study methods based upon a pragmatic approach and the chosen research strategy is a case study. The study looks at three memory institutions and their use of metadata in their digital preservation practice. These institutions are the National Library of Estonia and the National Archives of Estonia and the National Library of Wales. Both interviews (face-to-face interview for the first two institutions and interview via email with follow-up for the third institution) and document analysis were used for the data collection exercise. The process of data analysis consists of coding the interviews and organizing codes and the data from documents into themes that correspond with the research objectives and research questions. This paper looks the qualitative method as research approach, case study as research strategy, interview and document analysis as data collection instrument and purposive sampling as sampling strategy as used in this research project.

Qualitative Approach: The choice of one method to employ over the other is dependent upon the nature of the research problem definition together with the kind of information that is needed. The study used a qualitative approach to study the extent of implementing standard preservation metadata into practice at memory institutions. The qualitative approach was the preferred solution for this study because the nature of the research questions required that the topic should be explored in detail for which descriptive and detailed data needed to be collected.

The study was interested to describe and explain on actions in local practices of preservation metadata. Thus, the philosophical stance for this study is a pragmatic approach which is used "to determine the meaning of words, concepts, statements, ideas and beliefs. It implies that we should consider what effects which might conceivably have practical bearings. Then our conception of these effects is the whole of our conception of the object" (Peirce (1878) as cited in Johnson and Onwuegbuzie, 2004, p.17). Hence, the pragmatic approach helps to practice contributions and active participation in testing and exploring new ways of working.

Thus, it was necessary to use the qualitative method for studying preservation metadata, which is rich in semantics and to make sure that all the meanings of elements get accounted for. It was also because of the research questions that were framed as open-ended questions that can support discovery of new information and the language barrier (the respondents were Estonian, study in English). Thus, it was better to approach them face-to-face for better understanding of the practice of preservation metadata and to explain the questions as needed to gain better ideas on the facts of the phenomenon and to get more in-depth qualitative information.

Case Study: A case study was employed as a research strategy for this study. Case study was suited for studying this research problem because no thorough analysis exists yet in the literature and I needed to collect my own data because the problem is very practical and need to conduct almost a "field study" to understand the issues involved in implementing the theoretical metadata standards. Principally, Anderson (1993) describes case studies as being concerned with how and why things happen, allowing the investigation of contextual realities and the differences between what was planned and what actually occurred. He also added that case study is chosen as a strategy because it is not intended as a study of the entire organization rather it is intended to focus on a particular issue, feature or unit of analysis in order to understand and examine the processes and activities in organizations.

Accordingly, the unit of analysis for this case study was "*preservation metadata*". In this case study, preservation metadata was assumed as a contemporary phenomenon that had been initiated and opened for discussion by and within digital preservation community especially in libraries and archives considering for long-term accessibility of digital collections. Therefore, case study, as a research strategy, was best suited to examine such interventions of memory institutions in implementing standard preservation metadata into practice in their digital preservation process considering their context, i.e., goals and settings. This was supported by Yin (2009, p.18) who defined the case study research strategy as "an empirical inquiry that investigates a contemporary phenomenon within its real-life context; especially when the boundaries between phenomenon and context are not clearly evident".

Data Collection Technique: The primary data for the analysis were collected through interviews. Secondary data were obtained through document analysis by gathering information from the institutions' websites, documentation about their preservation metadata and other relevant documents commended by the interviewees. Interviewing is one of the most common methods for collecting data in qualitative research. It allows participants to provide rich, contextual descriptions of events. Interview as a data collection technique is also one of the most significant sources of obtaining case study information (Yin, 2009). Glesne and Peshkin (1992) also state that data collection methods like interviews - are dominant in the naturalist paradigm. According to Gray (2004), if the objective of the research is largely exploratory, the aim of using interviews as a means of gathering in-depth information was to probe for more information and attain highly personalized data. This allowed the researcher to probe for more detailed responses where the respondent was asked to clarify what they had said.

A semi-structured interview technique was chosen to collect data from metadata experts/specialists about the implementation of standard preservation metadata in their respective institutions. Semi-structured interview as a data collection technique for this study was chosen because they are non-standardized and are often used in qualitative analysis (Griffee, 2005) and it also offered sufficient flexibility to approach different respondents differently while still covering the same areas of data collection (Noor, 2008). A semi-structured interview means that questions are predetermined, but the interviewer is free to ask for clarification, can change the order of the questions can give explanations or leave out questions that may appear redundant. So, the main job is to get the interviewee to talk freely and openly while making sure you get the in-depth information on what you are researching (Griffee, 2005).

Semi-structured interview is the most adequate tool to capture how a person thinks of a particular domain. Its combination of faith in what the subject says with the skepticism about what she/he is saying, about the underlying meaning, induces the interviewer to go on questioning the subject in order to confirm the hypothesis about his/her beliefs (Honey, 1987).

This research also used documentary evidence to supplement as well as to compensate for information gathered from interviews. Additionally, documents provide guidelines in assisting the researcher with his inquiry during interview.

The interview questions were compiled in such a way that the researcher identified different themes (for example, what preservation metadata standards, preservation strategies, metadata categories, tools used, about problems and challenges, etc) based on the research problem and questions while reviewing different literature for the study For the most part, the PREMIS data dictionary and works related to it was used. After the questions were designed, they were reviewed with the supervisor. Based on the inputs from the review the questions were redesigned.

Thus, the researcher conducted interviews (face-to-face interviews for the two institutions and an interview via email with follow-up for the third institution). These interviews were all recorded on Olympus Digital Voice Recorder and loaded to the computer for the sake of expediency for transcription. A written note was also taken to complement the recordings. In the case of the third institution because of geographic distance and time of inconvenience to the respondents, the interview was conducted via email with follow-up and the researcher was satisfied with the data collected with this technique too. However, a face-to-face interview was found much more informative than the e-mail, and that seeing metadata in action at the memory institution was an important aspect, not just reading what someone tells me they have in place.

Sampling Strategy: Understanding what purpose research will serve should be a decisive factor in selecting a qualitative sample. Qualitative researchers perform sampling with a purpose (Byrne, 2001) and qualitative research often works with small samples of people, cases or phenomena nested in particular contexts. Hence, samples tend to be more purposive than random (Gray, 2004). In practice, qualitative sampling usually requires a flexible and pragmatic approach since qualitative research is an iterative process, i.e., it is permissible to change the recruitment strategy, as long as the proper approvals are obtained (Marshall, 1996).

Purposeful sampling is the most common sampling technique that the researcher actively selects the most productive sample for qualitative study to answer the research question and it is used generally in case study research. This can involve developing a framework of the variables that might influence an individual's contribution and will be based on the researcher's practical knowledge of the research area, the available literature and evidence from the study itself (Marshall, 1996). Thus, purposive sampling is used in this research as a sampling strategy.

Therefore, institutions that practice digital preservation, the National Library of Estonia, the National Archives of Estonia and the National Library of Wales, were taken to see to what extent the theoretical metadata standards were implemented. There were several reasons for selecting these institutions into the sample. First, they already have digital collections and are practicing digital preservation; they also have a legal obligation to preserve digital materials. The experience of managing digital collections of the memory institution was taken into consideration. These institutions have practical experience with implementation of digital preservation and metadata management and therefore it is good to study the preservation metadata implementation with them. The study also applied to contrast the preservation metadata practice of the library vs archive and the selection was deliberate to study if any differences exist and what they might be. The third institution was just used for verification purposes and deliberately chosen from a different country to act as a comparison for the two from Estonia. The researcher also contacted several other institutions in the region without result, but it was the National Library of Wales that volunteered to cooperate with this study. Second, the choice for the first two institutions was influenced by the geographic proximity (the digital archive of the National Archives of Estonia is located in Tartu, the second biggest city in Estonia; the National Library of Estonia is located in Tallinn, the capital of Estonia).

The names of respondents were initially determined in each memory institution with their job responsibilities, position and involvement in the subject studied, i.e., preservation metadata. However, respondents were selected from each memory institution on the basis of the researcher's individual judgment, where permitted, and in consultation with the head of digital preservation unit of each memory institution. The selection was done on the ground that the respondents could provide the necessary information needed for the research (Noor, 2008). A total of six metadata experts/specialists were selected for the interviews: three from the National Archives of Estonia (the interview was held in a group), one from the National Library of Estonia and two from the National Library of Wales (the interview via email was done on both persons separately). The choice was based on the experts' job responsibility and position they have in the digital preservation unit and the availability of metadata experts/specialists in each memory institution. Among the kind of job and position they hold are the deputy director of the digital preservation unit, metadata expert/ specialist, software designer, project manager and database administrator. Based on this and other given information the researcher focused on the metadata experts/specialists and the deputy director of the digital preservation unit who has connection with the metadata management for the interview.

Credibility Strategy Employed in the Research: Establishing the credibility of research findings can be achieved through various strategies. Shenton (2004) stated that qualitative methodology applies iterative questioning, frequent debriefing sessions and tactics to help ensure honesty in informants as a means of establishing credibility on the result of research. In this study, iterative questioning had done in data collection dialogues and also frequent debriefing sessions had carried out between the researcher and superior (for example, the interview questions were discussed between the researcher and the supervisor frequently). Moreover, the researcher used ways to help ensure honesty in informants when they were contributing data (for example, participants encouraged to be frank). Therefore, adoption of these techniques along with the data sources (metadata experts with supplementary documents) was an option to ensure credibility.

3. Conclusion and Future Work

A qualitative study with a pragmatic approach is probably the appropriate way to answer the research questions of this study along with a case study research strategy by using semi-structured interview and document analysis as data collection instrument. The results of the study revealed that the implementation of theoretical standards to practice is imperfect. However, the study considers three memory institutions, two national libraries and one national archive. It would be interesting to conduct further research by taking and considering more memory institutions in number and variety like museums, cultural heritage institutions, educational institutions and all other kinds of institutions those practicing preservation of digital objects.

The study has been seen the use of PREMIS as information for the implementation of preservation metadata in the memory institutions from the general level focused mainly on the PREMIS entities with some semantic units. This study can be extended thorough consideration of all PREMIS data dictionary semantic units and constraints on them.

This study has focused on the application of PREMIS data dictionary preservation metadata standard. Research can be done to include the influence of other preservation metadata standards in the implementation of preservation metadata in memory institutions.

This study has discovered different tools adopted in the implementation of preservation metadata. It would be worthwhile to study to what extent these tools are automating the tasks of the preservation metadata processes and how they match to the preservation metadata standards and to what extent they satisfy the practical needs of memory institutions.

This study has discovered that some memory institutions are trying to come up with their own preservation metadata specifications. It would be interesting to study the cooperation level and its need between different memory institutions for the development of better specification that can cope up with the wide range of standards and formats.

This study has also shown that memory institutions have looked at different preservation metadata standards/schema to record metadata elements as well as developed their own metadata specifications. It would also be interesting to study the comparison and harmonization of various metadata specifications as well as the cooperation between the many metadata initiatives that have an interest in digital preservation.

References

Alemneh, D.G., Hastings, S.K. and Hartman, C.N. (2002). A metadata approach to preservation of digital resources: The University of North Texas Library's Experience. *First Monday*, 7(8). Retrieved on January 5, 2010 from http://firstmonday.org/issues/issue7_8/alemneh/index.html.

Anderson, G. (1993). Fundamentals of educational research. Falmer Press, London, pp:152-160.

Byrne, M. M. (2001). Sampling for qualitative research. *AORN Journal*, 73(2), 497-498.

Caplan, P. (2006). Preservation metadata: DCC Digital Curation Manual, S.Ross, M.Day (eds). Retrieved on January 12, 2010 from http://www.dcc.ac.uk/resource/curation-manual/chapters/preservation-metadata/preservation-metadata.pdf.

Dappert, A. and Farquhar, A. (2009). Implementing metadata that guides digital preservation services. Retrieved on January 13, 2010 from http://www.planets-project.eu/docs/papers/Dappert_MetadataAnd Preservation Services_iPres2009.pdf.

Glesne, C. and Peshkin, A. (1992). Becoming qualitative researchers: An introduction. White Plains, NY: Longman.

Gray, E.D. (2004). Doing research in the real world. Sage publication. London. Thousand Oaks. New Delhi.

Griffee, D. (2005). Research tips: interview data collection. *Journal of Developmental Education,* 28(3), 36-37. Retrieved on March 14, 2010 from http://www.eric.ed.gov/ERICDocs/data/ericdocs2sql/content_storage_01/000 0019b/80/2a/1c/bb.pdf.

Honey, M.A. (1987). The interview as text: Hermeneutics considered as a model for analyzing the clinically informed research interview. *Human Development,* 30, 69-82.

Johnson, R. B. and Onwuegbuzie, A. J. (2004). Mixed methods research: A research paradigm whose time has come. *Educational Researcher,* 33 (7), 14-26. Accessed on June 3, 2010 from http://www.aera.net/uploadedFiles/Journals_and_Publications/Journals/Educ ational_Researcher/Volume_33_No_7/03ERv33n7_Johnson.pdf.

Lavoie, B. and Gartner, R. (2005). Technology watch report: preservation metadata, Oxford University Library Services and Digital Preservation Coalition. Available at: http://www.dpconline.org/docs/reports/dpctw05-01.pdf.

Marshall, M.N. (1996). Sampling for qualitative research. *Family Practice,* 13: 522-525. Retrieved on January 10, 2010 from http://spa.hust.edu.cn/2008/uploadfile/2009-9/20090916221539453.pdf.

National Information Standards Organization. (2004). Understanding Metadata. Bethesda, MD: NISO Press. Available at http://www.niso.org/standards/resources/UnderstandingMetadata.pdf.

Noor, K. B. M. (2008). Case study: a strategic research methodology. *Am J Appl Sci,* 5: 1602–4. Retrieved on April 2, 2010 from http://www.scipub.org/fulltext/ajas/ajas5111602-1604.pdf.

Shenton, A. K. (2004). Strategies for ensuring trustworthiness in qualitative research projects. *Education for Information,* 22, 63-75. Accessed on June 5, 2010 from http://iospress.metapress.com/content/3ccttm2g59cklapx/

Yin, R.K. (2009). Case study research: design and methods. 4th ed. Thousand Oaks: Sage publication

Exploring Users' Information Behavior in Social Networks

Juan Daniel Machin Mastromatteo

Tallinn University, Institute of Information Studies, Estonia
International Master in Digital Library Learning

Abstract: This paper summarizes the methodology and conclusions used on a master thesis that had the research aim of exploring how Web 2.0 and social networks are having an effect on users' information behavior. The method used for the collection of data was a semi structured interview, containing questions constructed according to the issues of Web 2.0 and social networks identified on the literature, along with typical features or characteristics of social networks. Purposive sampling was used to select the interview participants. The method for analyzing data was discourse analysis and a framework of categories was created to present the data in a certain order. This study identified various trends and tendencies in users' information behavior and some future directions for research were proposed. Findings of this type of study provide insights to users' information behavior in information systems, they could contribute to a better understanding of the users and to the design of such systems; this is relevant when it is necessary to build information systems from the point of view of users needs and behaviors, that is, by taking a bottom-up approach.
Keywords: Information behavior, social networks, Web 2.0, students, academic staff

1. Introduction

Wilson defines information behavior as "the totality of human behavior in relation to sources and channels of information, including both active and passive information seeking, and information use." (Wilson, 2000, 1).

The review of the literature about information behavior, produced by some authors such as Wilson or Case leads us to confirm that information behavior is a well established research field in library and information science (LIS). For example, Case (2002) studies and reviews research made on information behavior, stating that it would be impossible to review the full body of literature on information behavior and he estimates that there's about 10.000 publications on this area and related topics (p. xv). Shultz-Jones (2009), states that a "movement in social network research towards attention to contextual variables mirrors a similar shift of information behavior research" (p. 611). Statements such as this one were source of inspiration and served also confirmation that this type of research was valid and pertinent. Information scientists are more often doing research around them. From an information science perspective, they are information systems and as such one of the relevant approaches we can use to study them is by analyzing their users' information behavior.

In the last decade, the term social networks is usually associated with web-based or Web 2.0 applications and services. Focus.com (2009) made an illustration of the

New Trends in Qualitative and Quantitative Methods in Libraries
A. Katsirikou and C. H. Skiadas (eds)
© *World Scientific Publishing Co (pp. 175-180)*

development of these social networks, showing that Classmates.com was the first one, created in 1995. But Kaplan and Haenlein (2010) set the genesis of these social networks earlier in time:

> By 1979, Tom Truscott and Jim Ellis from Duke University had created the Usenet (established in 1980), a worldwide discussion system that allowed Internet users to post public messages. Yet, the era of Social Media as we understand it today probably started about 20 years earlier, when Bruce and Susan Abelson founded Open Diary [in 1998] an early social networking site that brought together online diary writers into one community (p. 2).

Web 2.0 social networks inherit some of the issues that have characterized human interaction with other information structures and media throughout the history, like libraries, scientific literature and the Internet. The inventory of issues studied in this work was developed taking as a starting point and inspiration the article *The Dark Side of Information: Overload, Anxiety and Other Paradoxes and Pathologies* by Bawden and Robinson (2009), where they identify some of the "pathologies" in the information on the Web 2.0 and social networks. Further additions to their views resulted in the framework used to construct the interview questions and to analyze and present the data in the full work. This inventory is made up of the following issues: trust, decision making, users' satisfaction, information overload, quality control, loss of identity, permanence, repackaging, crowdsourcing, privacy and the clash with the real world. This inventory by no means pretends to include every issue or to be an extensive and final list. Most of them come from an information science perspective, some of them are also applied to the studies on information behavior for traditional or printed documents and some others are applied for the web, so they are not exclusive for social networks. As information systems and sources, social network applications also have these issues, the degree on which they affect and concern social networks studies may vary.

1.1. Research Questions

Research questions to this study were:

- What are the trends and tendencies of users' information behavior in social networks?
- How users confront Web 2.0 issues?

1.2. Limitations and Scope

Purposive sampling was used in this study, which together with the size of the sample represents a limitation of this study, as it can be considered small: 8 participants were interviewed and not so many differences were found on their answers. Another limitation is brought because of the broad definition of social networks adopted in this research. Some websites or Web 2.0 applications are named as social networks, even when their inclusion under this term could be argued. However, it was taken as a social network any platform that must allow for user interaction and user generated content. Finally, time was a limitation as well, and also because this thesis intends to be an exploratory study, the issues of Web 2.0 and social networks analyzed are not fully studied and the list of issues given is not a definitive one.

2. Methodology

The methodological approach for this research was qualitative, because the collection of in depth information about experiences and reactions was intended, as they are part of the social networks users behavior. Users' experiences in these social interactions were meaningful for the purposes of this thesis.

The method for the collection of data was a semi-structured interview, because it was assumed that the participants from the interview could bring up some topics that were not so explicitly asked for in the questions, or could make a really good contribution due to their own experiences. And this was true especially for the intended participants who were information professionals, colleagues and professors who used social networks to a high degree. This choice was also motivated for the possibility to make extra questions to the participants to further develop unexpected topics. The choice for a semi-structured interview was also justified broadly for the reason that this was an exploratory study. This approach was especially useful because it was more important to get qualitative data from the users using their own words as opposed to get data from methods such as log analysis or observation. These methods can give us information about what users do, but they do not report why users do things or what do they think about these things. They cannot tell us how users confront the issues of Web 2.0 and social networks either, and these issues were the focus of attention of this thesis.

2.1. The Sample

Purposive sampling has been used in this study because, as Pickard (2007) states, it is used for ensuring that participants can contribute different perspectives on the phenomena to study. The participants of the interview were chosen from the International Master in Digital Library Learning (DILL) program. They were four professors and four second year students of the Master program, including four male individuals and four females, two males and two females within each group. It was suspected that multiple perspectives would arise; similarities and differences between answers by students and professors were noted in the data analysis. However, there were no significant differences between the answers of interviewees of different sex. For that reason, sex was not connected with the findings. The motivations for the choice of participants were: firstly, by practical reasons as they were individuals whom the researcher knew in person and they were available and willing to participate in the study. Secondly, because of the previous point, their competence as social networks users could be assessed for their selection, so they should be individuals who have experience using social networks in order to get valuable data. The third motivation was because of their background, to know the information scientist's opinions on these topics and to be able to ask about concepts like user satisfaction and information needs, as they are information science concepts.

2.2. Interview Topics and Questions

The interview was intended to bring information to answer the research questions about trends and tendencies of users' information behavior in social networks and how are users confronting Web 2.0 issues. The scripted questions for the interview were constructed based on a series of issues of Web 2.0 and social networks. For grouping these questions, two main categories were created: general questions and issues of Web 2.0 and social networks. The general questions category contained questions related to important behavioral aspects of the participants on social networks, such as what roles they see social networks are fulfilling, which are their purposes of using them, why do they add friends or connections, which social networks do they use and why do they share information there and what kind of information do they share. The second category contained the following issues: trust, loss of identity & crowdsourcing; decision making & quality control; users satisfaction & information overload; permanence & repackaging; privacy and the clash with the real world.

2.3. Ethical Considerations

A privacy statement was handed over to the participants, although no personal information was needed for this research purposes, apart from the differences on the education level and sex. The privacy statement also asserts that, among other things, no information that could be used to identify these individuals was used in this work and that no personal information will be given to third parties. All interviews were recorded in audio format, following the consent of the participants and then transcribed for analyzing the raw data derived from them.

2.4. Methods for the Analysis of the Data

The method used for analyzing data was discourse analysis. Discourse analysis, as Pickard (2007) puts it, "is [used] to present an explanation of those shared meanings and assumptions." (p. 241). This refers to the shared meanings and assumptions of the participants. In the complete work, large parts from the interviews were cited in a narrative form, grouping tendencies; similar or different opinions and some keywords the participants used to define topics and issues. For this process, the interviews were transcribed from the digital audio files to text. The quotations used were not edited; they were presented in the language as used by the interviewees.

The interview questions and the first two interviews served to create an almost definitive framework of categories which were perfected when adding all the interviews to this framework. The raw data collected throughout the interviews was coded manually, using just word processor software. The categorization consisted of 16 topics. At early stages of the coding a spreadsheet was used primarily from the researcher's assumption that some quantitative data could be obtained from the interviews, but this idea was abandoned as there were more similarities than differences in the interviewees' answers, so it was not worth doing it. Table 1 illustrates the framework used to group and present the data on the complete thesis.

Table 1. Framework for data analysis and discussion.

Different Roles of Social Networks	Quality Control
The Friendship Factor	Information Needs and Overload
A Question of Purpose	Problem of Permanence and Volatility of Information
Sharing is Caring	Reblogging and Repackaging
Social Networks Used	On Privacy
Issue of Trust	Organizations and Social Networks
On the Negative Views	Communication vs. Alienation
The Wisdom of the Crowds	Negative Consequences

3. Conclusions

In this section, the conclusions of this study are provided, firstly, related directly the research questions, by stating the main trends and tendencies on users' behavior that emerged from this study and how the participants of this study confronted the issues of Web 2.0 social networks. Secondly, some concluding remarks were presented related to future research directions in this field.

3.1. Conclusions to the Research Questions

Research question #1: What are the trends and tendencies of users' information behavior in social networks?

The list of trends of participants' information behavior in social networks is the following:

- The academic staff and students use social networks for many purposes and fulfilling different roles: for communication, entertainment, academic and professional work. They share information, build and maintain friendships, see what friends do or share, keep in touch or track them, learn more about friends, and keep connections and track of news.
- Social networks' communication and connectivity capabilities that enable to share information in various sources with many people have become an everyday habit for academic staff and students and they can be used as compensation of being distanced from people.
- Academic staff and students do not use social networks as the main source of information but rather than complimentary sources of information.
- Usually academic staff and students are willing to share information in social networks, however, for privacy concerns they don't share information that is too personal or about their private lives or family.
- Usually academic staff and students add persons whom they know (either in person or by reference) to their network. However, adding someone they don't know in person, there should be a reason; for example, the person is the friend of friends or she/he has a relevant background.
- There are differences in the ways how academic staff and students select or use selected information; some respondents select information from the Internet and use social networks tools to disseminate that information among their contacts, others just follow the updates of friends with shared interests, instead of selecting the information themselves.
- There are two opposed trends regarding reblogging: some participants prefer to send private messages and others are happy to share with everyone in their network. The positive aspect they see about reblogging is that it serves to multiply information even when it means that it can contribute to information overload.
- The academic staff and students are aware that too much use or misuse of these technologies can lead to negative things, such as problems with the organizations they work in or alienation. They know they have to use social networks with caution, even restricting the time they put to them.
- The academic staff and students are aware that social networks can also be a source of negative consequences. Therefore they should be careful on the kind of information shared as it can damage one's personal image or compromise privacy.

Research question #2: How users confront Web 2.0 issues?

This second question resulted to be very connected to the first one. However, the first question deals with common behaviors found on the participants' answers. The answers to this question in change, reflects also common behaviors found but related on how the participants react to Web 2.0 issues. The issues present here are: trust, quality control, information needs and overload, permanence and privacy.

- The academic staff and students agree that the trust is on people; a piece of information is trustable when someone they know posts it, and they are sure that this person can be trustworthy.
- They use different criteria for validating trustworthiness of information; for example, checking the author, the profile of the source, the people who refer to this information, the way it's written - if its written in a rush or bad style - how many people shared the information could mean how many people believe in this, comments people make about it, own knowledge and judgment.

- The most common needs the social networks satisfy are about entertainment, people and organizations; because social networks are complimentary sources, the information needs they satisfy are not too complex in nature.
- The most common strategy to cope with information overload was to hide updates from certain friends and also restrict the time they spend in social networks. Any extra feature that allows filtering or clustering of friends or updates is welcomed by the participants.
- Privacy is very important for academic staff and students; they are careful about what information they share. If their privacy is compromised the first things they would do is contact the administrator of the network and change passwords. In an extreme case some of them would even consider to withdraw from the networks.
- Academic staff and students have different approaches to quality control. Quality control is good when it is used to keep the harmful content out of the networks, it can also improve reliability and access. The downside is if a producer controls the information, this can be detrimental to the networks.

3.2. Implications for Further Research

After this investigation, the same method proposed can be applied to a different sample of other professionals or more diverse user groups to see if the results are different. Most of the issues covered can be further studied. This study could be taken as a starting point for one more complex and ambitious with bigger and more heterogeneous samples of participants. It can be also interesting to find quantitative values to the issues discussed on this work. A future work can study if there are differences in participants' information behavior in social networks between locations, level of specialization, gender and profession. Also, it can analyze deeper uses of social networks, such as the information behavior in users who utilize the integration the different social networks allow, the participants of this study did not provide any insights into this. Some of the results of this study and similar ones can be taken into account for the design of a learning management system or digital library with the features of a social network.

References

- Bawden, D., & Robinson, L. (2009). The dark side of information: overload, anxiety and other paradoxes and pathologies. *Journal of Information Science*, 35(2), 180-191.
- Case, D. (2002). *Looking for information: a survey of research on information seeking, needs, and behavior.* Amsterdam: Academic Press.
- Focus (2009). The boom of social sites. Retrieved June 18, 2010 from http://www.focus.com/fyi/other/boom-social-sites/
- Kaplan, A. M., & Haenlein, M. (2010). Users of the world, unite!: The challenges and opportunities of social media. *Business Horizons, 53* (1), 59-68.
- Pickard, A. J. (2007). *Research methods in information.* London: Facet.
- Schultz-Jones, B. (2009). Examining information behavior through social networks. *Journal of Documentation*, 65(4), 592-631.
- Wilson, T. (2000). Human information behavior. *Informing Science*, 3(2), 49-55.

Using Qualitative Case Study Methodology to Assess Information Access Needs and Open Educational Resources (OER) Awareness among Faculty and Students of MOI University, Nairobi Campus – Kenya

Monica Wawira Gakindi

Tallinn University, Institute of Information Studies, Estonia
International Master in Digital Library Learning

Abstract: This paper discusses the methodology employed in a study conducted to find out the experiences of faculty and students of Moi University – Nairobi Campus, in accessing information resources for teaching, learning and research, and their awareness of OER. Background information of the study, statement of the problem and research questions are given, the methods and techniques used to collect data are also discussed.
Keywords: Open educational resources, Kenya, access to learning materials, higher education

1. Introduction
The rise of a global society has resulted in a global demand for education and a growing gap between demand and supply of education (Geith and Vignare, 2008). Kenya is not an exception in this demand for education and is experiencing an expansion of HEI's – universities and university colleges, in order to accommodate the growing numbers of students. Moi University, the second public university to be established in Kenya, has experienced phenomenal growth in the number of students, staff and academic programmes. From a single faculty of forestry and wildlife resources with less than 100 students at its inception, the university now boasts of fifteen schools and five directorates (as of 2009) (http://www.mu.ac.ke/about/home.html). Moreover, the university has expanded further in opening up satellite campus around the country. Since 2005, the university has established eight satellite campuses and two constituent colleges that are running semi autonomously. The Nairobi campus, one of its satellite campuses, has experienced the highest growth compared to other campuses.
This paper is based on a study carried out on the Nairobi Campus, as part of the author's master study requirement in the course Digital Library Learning (DILL). The study was carried out to find out the experiences of faculty and students on information access and to find out their awareness of OER and its adoption in the campus as a means to diversify their sources of information access and to facilitate collaboration among faculty with a goal to enhance teaching, learning and research

1.1 Statement of the Problem
Despite the expansion of universities with the setting up of satellite campuses, this expansion is not commensurate to expansion in access to facilities such as learning and research resources since the main campus hosts the equipped university libraries,

New Trends in Qualitative and Quantitative Methods in Libraries
A. Katsirikou and C. H. Skiadas (eds)
© *World Scientific Publishing Co (pp. 181-191)*

thereby rendering the students and faculty unable to access crucial library and learning resources for research. Though there are similar courses offered in the main and satellite campuses, and sometimes, taught by different teachers, there is no a formal forum/platform where faculty share courseware and other relevant resources for their courses, yet the students are expected to sit the same examinations. The response to the growing demand for university education by expansion is vital, but mere expansion alone is not enough. The big question is; does the expanding university fulfil/facilitate learning and research through enhancing access to relevant information resources and collaboration to enable it achieve the core function for which it was initiated? What more can the university do to facilitate access to information resources for teaching, learning and research? It is in quest for the answer to this question that the study was carried out.

1.2 Research Aim and Objectives

The aim of the research was to explore the potential of OER in enhancing university faculty collaborations and access to information resources for learning, teaching and research at the Moi university- Nairobi campus. The specific objectives were as follows:

(a) To find out the experiences of faculty and students on information access for teaching, learning and research at Moi University- Nairobi Campus.

(b) To explore the potential of OER in enhancing access to teaching, learning and research information resources and their potential to enhance faculty collaborations within Moi University campuses and beyond.

1.3 Research Questions

The following were the research questions asked for the study:

(a) How do faculty and students in Moi University – Nairobi campus access and share teaching, learning and research information resources?

(b) How can OER be adopted to enhance access to teaching, learning and research information resources at Moi University?

(c) How can faculty intra university collaboration be enhanced through OER adoption in Moi University?

1.4 Scope of the Study

The study focused on access to learning resources and OER. It highlighted the importance of education and particularly higher education in facilitating national and economic development in a global knowledge society. It further pointed out the importance of access to learning resources in facilitating a quality higher education where teaching, learning and research are carried out. Since it was a case study, experiences of faculty and students of the case being studied were sought. This involved how they access resources, internet and also the technology available to them to facilitate access, challenges they encounter while accessing information resources and opinions on how access to resources can be facilitated. The study however, did not go to the details of how teaching and learning are carried out. On OER, details relating to availability, accessibility, acceptability and adaptability, based on Tomasevski's (2001) 4A model of Human Rights to and in education were discussed. Since this is an idea that was not functional at the institution, only views were sought. Views from faculty, students and a librarian of the case institution were sought to ascertain their awareness of OER and their acceptability of such an engagement as a possible way to improve access to learning resources, and also views from an expert community from around the world to ascertain the viability of an OER engagement in such a situation.

2.0 Methodology

The study was guided by an interpretivist approach to research. According to Pickard (2007), "Interpretivists take the stance that any research activity will leave the subject of that research in an alerted state...interpretivism can offer understanding of the meanings behind the actions of individuals" (p. 12). The study aimed to propose OER to the institution being studied as a means to increase access to teaching, learning and research resources and to enhance collaboration among faculty staff within and without the institution. In this way, it hoped to leave the subject of the study alerted. The study sought to understand the experiences of the faculty staff and students of Moi University, Nairobi Campus, in accessing information resources and hence interpretation of findings was based on this particular context. Therefore, as Pickard (2007) notes, "Interpretivist tradition is concerned with individual contexts" (p. 13), transferability of the findings will depend on similar contexts. Furthermore, according to Weber (2004), "researchers who are labelled as positivists tend to use certain kinds of research methods in their work; experiments, surveys, and field studies. Interpretivists, on the other hand, tend to use other kinds of research methods in their work; case studies, ethnographic studies, phenomenographic studies, and ethnomethodological studies" (p. 10).

2.1 Research Method

The study employed case study method – single case with embedded unit of OER. The choice of a case study over other research methods was for four main reasons. To start with, the research questions being investigated were in the form of *why* and *how*. According to Yin, "why" and "how" questions are more explanatory and "deal with operational links needing to be traced over time, rather than mere frequencies or incidence" (Yin, 2009, p. 9). Secondly, no control of behavioural events was done as would be the case for experiments. Thirdly, the focus was of a contemporary nature, the experiences of information access as it is at present. Lastly, the multiple sources of evidence used lend a case study more suitable. As Yin (2009) states, "the case study's unique strength is its ability to deal with a full variety of evidence-documents.....beyond what might be available in a conventional historical study" (p.11).

2.2 Research Design

Yin (2009) defines a research design in the most elementary sense to be the logical sequence that connects the empirical data to a study's initial research questions and ultimately, to its conclusions. It is viewed as a "blueprint" for the research dealing with what questions to study, what data are relevant, what data to collect, and how to analyze the results (Schwab and Samsloss as cited in Yin, 2009). For a case study, he identifies five components that are important in a research design; a study's questions, its propositions – (if any), its unit(s) of analysis, the logic linking the data to the propositions and the criteria for interpreting the findings (p. 27).

The main unit of analysis in the study was Access. The embedded unit was OER. This was an exploratory case study and as Yin (2003) states, exploratory studies usually have no propositions and have rather a stated "purpose as well as the criteria by which an exploration will be judged successful" (p. 22).

2.3 Study Population

The study population encompassed students, librarians and faculty staff of the chosen case (Moi University – Nairobi Campus) and experts in the field of OER. The reason for this was because the study focused on experiences of access to information by students and faculty of the Nairobi Campus hence the need to collect data from them. Secondly, the library is vital in enabling access to information resources at the campus and hence the need to obtain data from the librarian about library services and use, and thirdly, the research aimed to propose OER as a way to increase opportunities for information access at the campus. Using OER experts to advice gave the research greater credibility since experts' advice was integrated with the resultant arguments, conclusions and recommendations of the study.

2.4 Sample

Purposive sampling was used for the selection of the case. "The logic of purposeful sampling lies in selecting information-rich cases for study in depth. Information-rich cases are those from which one can learn a great deal about issues of central importance to the purpose of the research" (Patton, as cited in Pickard, 2007, p.64). Further, Yin (2009) indicates that, the rationale for a representative case "is to capture the circumstances and conditions of an everyday or commonplace situation" (p. 48) In line with this, Moi University Nairobi Campus was chosen for the following reasons:

Out of the eight satellite campuses of Moi University, Nairobi campus has experienced the highest growth in terms of student admissions, faculty and number of courses offered. It has the most established faculty of information sciences, which is involved in training information professionals. It would be useful to gather their experiences and their proposals of how to better improve the situation of information access from their professional point of view.

Another vital reason for the choice of this campus was that the researcher is an alumni of the main campus and has created a rapport with the faculty community in the information science department of this campus (her former lecturers) who were vital in providing questionnaire data. Pickard (2007) supports this by her statement that "you must consider practical issues such as the time you have to conduct the field work, availability of the people you have sampled [...] always be aware that you must retain a rapport with the community".

The campus was easily accessible for the researcher since she had to carry out pre study observation by making several visits to the case to get a glimpse of the day to day activities of the campus and to gain consent of intent to carry out the research. It was also during that time that the researcher identified two contact persons to help in contacting questionnaire respondents to facilitate data collection.

For the faculty and student questionnaire, stratified random sampling was used. Since the campus has 6 schools and both undergraduate and post graduate students, this sampling proved to be the most representative. It is worth noting that, apart from providing quantitative data, the online questionnaires were used to obtain data that would help identify respondents who would be followed up for the interviews and hence a large sample was not necessary but rather a representative one was. Table 1 below indicates how the questionnaire respondents were chosen.

Table 1: Questionnaire Respondents for the Case Institution

SCHOOLS	UNDERGRAD UATE	POSTGRAD UATE	FACULTY
Information Sciences	2	2	2
Business and Economics	2	2	2
Human Resource Development	2	2	2
Public Health	2	2	2
Arts and Social Sciences	2	2	2
TOTALS	**10**	**10**	**10**

The team of four OER experts from Europe, Africa and North America were professionally recommended through the snowball sampling technique. The choice of Europe and North America is for the reason that the two were the first proponents of OER, and OER initiatives are developed in Europe and North America more than other continents. In addition, it was easy to identify experts from the two continents. An expert from Africa was contacted to present an African context and perspective since they are assumed to be aware of similar situations in the continent.

2.5 Techniques for Data Collection

To be able to answer the questions of the study, various techniques were employed and multiple sources of evidence were used. The techniques employed included interviews, online questionnaires and observation (done during the pre study site visits). Questionnaires were administered to students and faculty. Interviews were conducted with the librarian heading the Nairobi Campus, OER experts and follow-up interviews with faculty and students, carried out to enable further elaboration of what they had stated in the questionnaire. This would come in handy in improving the quality of the final report and also adding credibility to the study.

The steps and activities involved in this activity of data collection during the study are elaborated below.

2.5.1 Pre study site visits

The researcher took several visits to the Nairobi Campus in November 2009 till the end of January 2010. The aim of the visits was threefold. Firstly, to identify persons who would act as institutional contact persons and would support in identifying and collecting email addresses for administering online questionnaires, help to arrange the follow-up interviews with the identified persons and report of any eventualities since the researcher would be detached from the case for most of the research period. The second reason was to seek consent to carry out the study at the Nairobi Campus which was achieved. The last but not least, was to observe how the day to day activities of the campus were running and to visit the facilities that the institution provided; for example, the computer laboratory and the library.

2.5.2 Questionnaires

As stated earlier, both qualitative and quantitative data was collected for the purpose of this study. Quantitative data was collected to map the situation and issues at the Nairobi Campus and to facilitate selection of persons for the next stage to be interviewed. Thus, it was a part of the case study and as a preliminary stage for the interviews. Baxter and Jack (2008) support this idea of integrating quantitative survey data in a qualitative study in the following statements:

> Unique in comparison to other qualitative approaches, within case study research, investigators can collect and integrate quantitative survey data, which facilitates reaching a holistic understanding of the phenomenon being studied. In case study, data from these multiple sources are then converged in the analysis process rather than handled individually. Each data source is one piece of the "puzzle," with each piece contributing to the researcher's understanding of the whole phenomenon. This convergence adds strength to the findings as the various strands of data are braided together to promote a greater understanding of the case (p. 554).

The online questionnaires were used to derive necessary information about access to information resources for teaching, learning and research, collaboration and OER from faculty and students of the case. An online questionnaire was the instrument of choice for this research project because it was easy to administer while geographically distanced from the case. The setback with the online questionnaire is that some respondents were not in a position to respond to it immediately because of technological barriers such as unreliable Internet. In fact, at some point, when very low response was experienced, a printable version of the questionnaires was derived and was distributed by the contact persons in person to the respondents.

SurveyMonkey was the tool used to design and administer the questionnaire. It was chosen for the reason that, its capabilities enabled the researcher to cover every aspect she required. It allowed for all types of questions from open ended to closed questions and scales. On a paid upgraded version, as was the choice for the researcher, there was no limit to the number of questions asked. It was also possible to get more than one response from one IP address – which was a requirement since it was assumed that many respondents may not have personal computers and Internet but would rely on the campus computer laboratory or cyber cafes. In addition, the tool allowed for multiple downloads in different formats of the answered questionnaires.

The questionnaires were divided into four parts. The first part was a covering letter. It introduced the researcher and gave her contact details. It also indicated the purpose of the study and asked the respondents to participate assuring them that their data would be used for the sole purpose of the study. The second part was the default and longest with the main questions around access to information resources. The last question of this part asked if the respondents were familiar with the concept of OER. Logic was included in this question such that if the respondents said "yes", they would be prompted to the next session on OER, with more questions on the topic, after which they would be requested to provide their contact details and the most appropriate time they would prefer to be contacted for a follow-up interview by the researcher. If they responded "no", they would be automatically taken to the last session to finish the questionnaire, with a thank you note for participation. Details of the two online questionnaires are elaborated below.

2.5.2.1 Faculty questionnaire

The first set of questions in this questionnaire was about faculty teaching career; how many years they have taught at the university, in how many universities they have taught and if they are teaching elsewhere apart from the Nairobi Campus. Since the Nairobi Campus has most classes in the evenings and Saturday's, it was necessary to find out if faculty was engaged/taught elsewhere. If they did, an OER programme could even be more appropriate. The next questions asked about any works written during their profession, any hindrances for not writing and where they had published their works. This question was asked in order to understand if faculty have created the resources and find out some of the factors that hindered them from contributing or creating content. This understanding, according to the researcher, was important in the event that an OER project is to be initiated, issues like these would also need consideration. Other questions related to where they accessed information resources from the campus sources, facilities available to them to access these resources, alternative options that were available and internet access. The faculty was also asked to give their views on sharing of resources with fellow faculty who teach similar courses in other Moi Campuses or in other universities. In addition, they were asked to give their views on how access to information resources for teaching and research could be improved at their campus. Lastly but not least, they were asked about their familiarity with OER and if they had interacted with any OER's. Those who indicated to be familiar with OER were asked their views of adopting OER at their campus and barriers/ challenges of adopting such an initiative.

2.5.2.2 Student questionnaire

Most of the questions in this questionnaire were similar with the ones in the faculty questionnaire. The first set of questions was designed to collect information on student characteristics; for instance, if the students studied full time or they studied and worked, their level and their year of study.

The questions that followed were to enquire information about the sources from which they access information resources for learning and research; both from the campus and off-campus, since it was assumed that most of them do not spend full days at the campus if they took evening and Saturday classes. Further, they were asked about the formats of information resources they access and use, the challenges they encounter in terms of access to information resources and to learning in general. They were also asked to give their views on how access could be improved. Lastly, they were asked to indicate if they were familiar with the concept of OER and if they had interacted with any.

2.5.3 Interviews

Interviews are one way to obtain in-depth information in case study research. As Kvale (1996) states, "through conversations, we get to know other people, get to learn their experiences, feelings and hopes and the world they live in" (p. 5). In addition, Pickard (2007) states that, "interviews are appropriate when the purpose of the researcher is to gain individual views, beliefs and feelings about a subject" (p. 181). This was the specific purpose of this study – experiences of faculty and students in accessing information resources and views and opinions of experts on OER in the institution.

As stated earlier, interviews were conducted with the campus librarian, faculty and students and OER experts. Since the researcher did the interviews while still in Europe, the interviews had to be well planned for, in terms of technology and logistics. The researcher bought a digital recorder that was used to record all conversations. Two possibilities were expected during the interviews with participants at the institution under study - the interviewees may not have Internet connection and if they did, it may or may not be reliable for a Skype interview. In this case, the researcher would then use Voice over Internet Protocol (VOIP) to call at a fee, the interviewee's regular mobile or land line phone. The conversation would then be recorded using the digital recorder for later transcriptions. The service used in this case was InterVoip. As it later turned out, all participants of the case did not have reliable internet for free calls via Skype and so all the interviews were conducted by calling their regular mobile phones using InterVoip.

All the interviews took the form of "focused interviews". These, according to Yin (2009), are likely to be following a certain set of questions. They may be open ended and assume a conversational manner. According to Yin, a major purpose of such interviews "...might simply be to corroborate certain facts that you already think have been established" (p. 107). The reason for the focused interviews was because, faculty and students had already answered a questionnaire and a follow-up interview was to obtain more insights into the issues that they had already provided in the questionnaires. The interview with the campus librarian was arranged to gather information on the resources and services the library provides and to get details on the library usage. Some of these details had been noted by the researcher during the pre site visits at the case. Lastly, the interviews with the experts were arranged to obtain expert opinions about OER in the situation that was presented of the case.

Each interview was transcribed before conducting the next. This was done for two main reasons. First, to avoid a pile up of data that would cause much work and time doing it at a later stage. Secondly and more importantly, since the study was of a qualitative nature, each interview transcription allowed reflection of the questions under study and the researcher assessed if there was a need to change or add any questions to be asked in the next interview in order to obtain information that could help to answer best the research questions. In short, to allow each interview inform the next. Pickard (2007) supports this by the statement "...there is no reason to stick to a rigid set of questions if this will not achieve your research goals. You can learn from one interview before you move on to the next" (p. 178).

Pickard (2007) further notes that, "interviews can be used to confirm or refute data gathered from other tools such as observation, and diaries" (p. 181). This study used a variety of tools; observation, questionnaires and interviews. Data from these sources will be analysed for similarities and/or differences. Details of each interview are elaborated further below.

2.5.3.1 Interview with campus librarian

The Nairobi Campus has one librarian and three assistants who manage and run the day to day activities of the library. As an information professional, and a key figure in enabling access to information resources, the Nairobi Campus librarian was interviewed about the library use by staff and students, the library collection, services and subscriptions, collaboration with other libraries, institutional repository and also their views on how information resources can be enhanced to provide a wide variety for students and faculty at the campus. Lastly the librarian was asked her opinion on OER. The interview took the form of a telephone call and lasted for 50 minutes.

2.5.3.2 Follow-up interviews with faculty and students

Selected members of the faculty and student communities were interviewed after the submission of questionnaires. Selection was done on the basis of the knowledge of OER and the respondent's willingness to be contacted at a later time. This was derived at by a request to provide their contact details for a further discussion (in an interview) of the views they had indicated in the questionnaire on access and OER. Since this is a case study, such elaborations are necessary so as to get an in-depth view of the issues under discussion. These interviews took the form of telephone calls to regular mobile phones and lasted between 30 – 60 minutes. A total of three (3) students and one (1) faculty staff were interviewed.

2.5.3.3 Interviews with OER experts

A semi structured Interview guide was drafted and used for experts from the field of OER, to get their opinions on if OER was useful and applicable at the institution, and how OER could be implemented to enhance access to information resources for teaching, learning and research and to faculty collaboration. Prior to the interviews, the results of the faculty, students and librarian were given to them through email to give them insight into the situation at the Nairobi Campus.

Three in depth interviews were conducted via Skype with the experts from Canada (University of Toronto), United States (MIT) and United Kingdom (Open University). The fourth interview was conducted through asynchronous interviewing by email exchange since the OER expert from Africa (University of Western Cape) was busy and could not manage to schedule for an interview during the timeframe the researcher had for data collection. The data collected was transcribed and analysed for any concurring or differing opinions. All the Skype interviews took an average of 60 minutes.

2.5.4 Pilot study

Teinjlingen and Hundley (2001) indicate that:

> The term 'pilot studies' refers to mini versions of a full-scale study (also called 'feasibility' studies), as well as the specific pre-testing of a particular research instrument such as a questionnaire or interview schedule. Pilot

studies are a crucial element of a good study design. Conducting a pilot study does not guarantee success in the main study, but it does increase the likelihood (p. 1).

Pilot studies were carried out for the online questionnaires and also for faculty and student interviews. Details of these are elaborated in the section below.

2.5.4.1 Pilot for the questionnaires

The pilot study for questionnaires considered a 10% of the population undertaking the real study. Hence, based on the above table on the sample, the student questionnaire was piloted with two students and the faculty questionnaire with one faculty.

The aim of the pilot for questionnaires was twofold. First, to check for grammatical and language errors and secondly, to find out if the questions were understood/made sense and if they would elicit the answers the researcher anticipated from the main study. For this reason and for the student questionnaire, one student with English as a native language was used and one student from Africa who had studied in an African university and understood the situation at the universities were used. These were chosen among the researcher's course mates since they were easy to reach and follow-up.

The responses obtained from this pilot study went a long way in providing useful insights on the wording of the questionnaire and making it more understandable. Some things the researcher had ignored like "Please" proved to be very useful when used to give an instruction. One pilot participant complained that the questionnaire was too long and was tired by the time she finished filling it out. However, this was not changed since the researcher felt that all the data in the questionnaires was needed in the final analysis.

The faculty questionnaire was piloted with one staff member at Moi University who was not considered to take part in the main study. The respondent gave a crucial feedback that was used to improve the understandability of the questionnaire. For instance, he complained of technical phrases like – learning management system/platform and institutional portal which he said some faculty members may not understand unless further elaboration was provided. This change was effected by providing a short description of what the terms meant. Other comments were related to grammatical coherence, and rephrasing of questions that tended to cause confusion. For instance, a multi - choice question on Internet access that stated: "From what sources do you access internet", was rephrased to state "From where do you access Internet".

2.5.4.2 Pilot for the interviews

Interview pilots were carried out only for students and faculty. The same respondents used for the questionnaire pilots were used but only one student from among the two was used for the interview pilot. The reason for carrying out interview pilots was twofold. First, to practice the art of interviewing and to gather from the respondents if the questions posed to them were understandable. Secondly, to test the device – recorder that would be used to record the real interviews for further transcriptions.

A very important point was noted by the faculty pilot interviewee. He complained that during the interview, the researcher tended to "force" her idea to the participant and make them agree with her. This was noted and avoided during the real study. The researcher let the interviewees express themselves freely without influencing their opinions.

The device worked well – the voices were clear and no technical huddles were experienced. The network/Internet connection (for a Voip call) was good to facilitate the interview with the pilot interviewee in Kenya (a normal mobile phone call) and the voice too was clear when listened to later from the recorder.

2.5.5 Document review

Documents were reviewed to get an overview of the university and on issues relating to information access. In addition literature was reviewed to get an in-depth understanding of OER –availability, adaptability, licensing and sustainability. Various projects, both globally and in Africa were reviewed to have an in depth understanding in the subject.

2.6 Ethical Considerations

Mugenda and Mugenda (2003) affirm that the researcher has to be careful to avoid causing physical or psychological harm to respondents by asking embarrassing and irrelevant questions, threatening language or making respondents nervous. Similarly, Sommer and Sommer (1997) argue ethical considerations such as confidentiality, anonymity and avoidance of deception are very important issues in social research. For the purpose of the study, permission was sought from relevant authorities. Nevertheless, some participants such as the librarian of the campus could be easily recognized. They were alerted about it and agreed to take part all the same. The researcher explained the purpose of the research to the participants and assured them of confidentiality of their responses and identities. To ensure that this was adhered to, data analysis was done without mentioning of any names.

2.7 Credibility Strategy Employed in the Research

"We all want our findings to be believed and are responsible for ensuring that they can be believed" (Pickard, 2007, p. 18). Pickard further adds that qualitative methodology often applies triangulation as a means of establishing credibility since the use of multiple data collection techniques compensates for any limitations of individual techniques (p. 20). In the study, observations done during the pre study visits, the use of online questionnaires and interviews comprised of the multiple techniques that were employed to ensure triangulation. Furthermore, using a variety of data sources – students, faculty staff, a librarian and OER experts was an option to ensure greater credibility.

2.8 Delimitations of the Study

The sample for the online questionnaire was relatively small because it comprised of 20 students and 10 members of the faculty staff. Total responses were 10 from students and 8 from the faculty staff which was short of the expected number. This did affect the selection of interviewees for further interview follow-ups. If a larger sample had been selected and if all had responded, probably there would have been a greater chance of getting more respondents aware of OER and willing to participate in the interview.

There were only four interviews conducted at the case. Three with the students and one with the faculty member of the campus. Since interview follow-ups were conducted on the basis of OER awareness, most respondents indicated they were not aware of the concept. Those who did, not all agreed to be interviewed. In fact, the faculty staff interviewed indicated no awareness of OER but since the researcher needed the views of the faculty on other issues too, this criterion was ignored.

This is a qualitative case study and therefore, the findings are context specific; the arguments and recommendations in general can only apply in situations of shared or similar contexts and cannot be generalized.

3.0 Conclusions

The use of a questionnaire and interview data for this study was useful since a holistic understanding of the phenomenon being studied was reached. As Baxter and Jack (2008) state: "Each data source is one piece of the "puzzle," with each piece contributing to the researcher's understanding of the whole phenomenon. This convergence adds strength to the findings as the various strands of data are braided together to promote a greater understanding of the case" (p. 554). The study recommended more open practices to enhance teaching and research at the campus. Furthermore, more case study researches in OER, especially in Africa are needed since institutions differ in their practices, cultures, management and operations.

References

Sommer, B. and Sommer, R. (1997). A practical guide to behavioral research: tools and techniques (4th ed.), New York: Oxford University Press.

Mugenda, A. and Mugenda, O. (2003). *Readings in research methods: quantitative and qualitative Approaches.* Nairobi: African Centre for Technology Studies.

Tomasevki, K. (2001). *Human rights obligations: making education available, accessible, acceptable and adaptable.* Retrieved March 17, 2010 from http://www.right-to-education.org/sites/r2e.gn.apc.org/files/B6g%20Primer.pdf

Yin, K. R. (2009) *Case study research: design and methods* (4th ed) London: Sage.

Yin, R. K. (2003). *Case study research: design and methods* (3rd ed.). London: Sage.

Kvale, S. (1996). *Interviews: an introduction to qualitative interviewing.* London: Sage.

Geith, C. and Vignare, K. (2008). Access to education with online learning and open educational resources: Can they close the gap? *Journal of Asynchronous Learning* Networks, 12(1). Retrieved March 24, 2010 from http://www.sloan-c.org/publications/jaln/v12n1/pdf/v12n1_geith.pdf

Pickard, A. J. (2007) *Research methods in information.* London: Facet Publishing.

Baxter, P. and Jack, S. (2008). Qualitative case study methodology: study design and implementation for novice researchers. *The Qualitative Report, 13* (4), 544-559.

Weber, R. (ed.) (2004). The rhetoric of positivism versus interpretivism: a personal view. *MIS Quarterly, 28*(1), iii – xii.

A Mixed Model Study to Determine User Preferences for Delivery of Collection Content via Mobile Devices: Lessons for the Development of a Smartphone Application

Sara Grimm

Tallinn University, Institute of Information Studies, Estonia
International Master in Digital Library Learning

Abstract: This paper discusses the methodology and data collection technique used to gather data for the researcher's master thesis study on smartphone applications. The aims of the study were to describe current usage patterns of smartphone applications, to determine users' desired specifications for smartphone applications showcasing cultural heritage collections, and to carry out a user study of the Musée du Louvre iPhone application as a model for the development of a new cultural heritage application for smartphones. An online survey tool, QuestBack, was used to collect both quantitative and qualitative data. For the quantitative data, analysis was performed using tools offered by QuestBack, while for the qualitative data, the researcher performed the coding and analysis.
Keywords: Online survey, smartphones, mobile telephones, mobile applications, user studies, cultural heritage, iPhones

1. Introduction

The idea for this research project was born from the opportunity for libraries and memory institutions to enter the arena of mobile application development. Since libraries and digital libraries are only in the beginning stages of creating applications to showcase their collections, it is important to define the major factors these institutions must take into account in terms of planning and evaluation.

The ultimate purpose of the project was to develop a set of standards, as defined by the users, which would inform the creation of new smartphone applications displaying collections of cultural heritage objects, in particular one application that may be developed for UNESCO's Memory of the World program.

Research Questions

The major factors that should be taken into consideration when libraries and memory institutions begin planning for the development of a smartphone application can be summed up by the following three research questions:

1. What are users' current usage patterns of smartphone applications?
2. What are user expectations and preferences for applications with the aim of content delivery, particularly with regard to principles of information architecture and standards for design?
3. What examples can be taken from existing applications in this domain (in the case of this project, the application from the Musée du Louvre), when considering the requirements for the development of a new application?

In this work, my aim was to determine the necessary requirements for smartphone applications featuring collections of cultural heritage objects, as defined by the

New Trends in Qualitative and Quantitative Methods in Libraries
A. Katsirikou and C. H. Skiadas (eds)
© *World Scientific Publishing Co (pp. 193-198)*

potential users of these applications. Because the staff at UNESCO sees the Louvre application as the inspiration for the development of a Memory of the World application and would use the Louvre application as its model, it would be worthwhile to evaluate whether the existing Louvre application actually meets user needs prior to investing in the development of this new application. To accomplish this evaluation, I conducted an online survey of potential users regarding their use of smartphone applications and their perceptions of what makes an application easy to use, effective, and successful. To complement this information, I also asked these potential users to evaluate the Louvre application's effectiveness using criteria described in the literature. This survey was carried out using QuestBack, an online survey tool that offers features for both collecting and analyzing data.

The results of these surveys and evaluations can be instructive for memory institutions considering developing mobile applications to showcase their collections of cultural heritage items, including those who would ultimately be responsible for the development of a Memory of the World application, should it come to fruition.

<u>Limitations</u>

Certain limitations are inherent in the design and implementation of any study are. The survey method relies upon the answers participants provide to a set of questions. Participants' self-reported answers may not be truly accurate, whether this is intentional or unintentional deception on the part of the participants. Inaccuracies may also occur because of poor memory or misinterpretation of the questions. Additionally, the evaluation matrix and its use of a rating scale presents the potential drawback of not being able to precisely define what one person's assignation of a particular value means in comparison to another person's. I have attempted to mitigate this effect by providing participants with the ability to freely elaborate on their responses to these rating questions in their own words.

Additionally, the selection of a particular sample of people with certain characteristics intrinsically assumes limitations on the applicability of results. In this case, the choice was made to evaluate a sample of librarians or library school students who own an iPhone, compared against a baseline group of iPhone owners who do not have a library background The choice of the sample of iPhone users with a library background was made in order to obtain a sample of people who have some knowledge of principles of good information architecture, bearing in mind that this sample would be more likely to be able to provide constructive comments. Even so, the sample constitutes a special contingent of people and may or may not be truly representative of the future potential users of a smartphone application for the items on the Memory of the World Register.

Finally, the use of snowball sampling, starting with contact made with my personal acquaintances, who in turn provided references for additional iPhone users ("friends-of-friends"), has the potential to hinder the ability to generalize the results, since my circle of personal acquaintances and their acquaintances may constitute a set of people with specific characteristics. However, the inclusion of a baseline group of people (non-librarians) without a common background is intended to limit these effects, with the assumption that the group will be diverse enough to overcome that limitation since iPhone users from many different backgrounds and cultures were contacted to participate.

2. Methodology

I have elected to employ a methodology that is primarily qualitative in nature, but that also incorporates some quantitative elements. The choice of this type of mixed model approach to carry out the study appears to be the best way to address the issues involved. Tashakkori and Teddlie (as cited in Florida International University's Bridges Mixed Methods Network for Behavioral, Social, and Health Sciences glossary) have defined the mixed model approach as "a design in which mixing of qualitative and quantitative approaches occurs in all stages of the study (formulation of research questions, data collection procedures and research method, and interpretation of the results to make final inferences) or across stages of the study (e.g., qualitative questions, quantitative data)."

While it does make data analysis more complex, the incorporation of both approaches, qualitative and quantitative, has the best potential to respond to the three major research questions for this study. The quantitative elements are used to chronicle participants' self-reported smartphone usage patterns, to compute participants' ratings of particular aspects of the Louvre smartphone application, and finally, to provide backup for the narrative answers the participants were asked to provide in the open-ended qualitative questions that constitute the bulk of the remainder of the survey.

As noted, a qualitative methodology has been chosen as the primary methodology for the study. Open-ended questions have been used where appropriate in several sections of the survey in order to garner richer responses and a greater insight into the rationale behind the participants' answers than a purely quantitative design would permit. Accordingly, qualitative research methodology "assumes social constructions of reality." These constructions of reality are created both by those participants who are being studied and the researcher him or herself. (Gorman & Clayton, 2005, pp. 24-28) The researcher plays an active role in the data collection process, contributing his or her tacit knowledge to the investigation. This collaborative process "produc[es] meaning from data and us[es] that meaning to develop theory." (Gorman & Clayton, 2005, pp. 24-28)

For this study, I have included in the survey open-ended questions, which I have had to evaluate qualitatively according to both objective and subjective criteria. The creation of categories to classify the various types of participant responses to these open-ended questions is intended to provide an objective framework for categorizing the responses. However, the fact remains that any designation of categories and assignation to these categories is inherently the researcher's own subjective creation. Pickard (2007) argues that open-ended questions on surveys are "descriptive but rarely are they truly qualitative." (p. 195) However, many other commentators on the subject of research methodology, as well as guides on conducting research, do in fact place open-ended survey questions into the qualitative category. (Labuschagne, 2003; Patton, 2003; Trochim, 2006) It is my own view as a researcher that the addition of these types of open-ended, free-form questions to a survey lends a predominantly qualitative element to the research, mainly because of the data analysis process required to evaluate such responses.

Each Likert scale satisfaction rating item includes a space for the participants to explain in their own words why they have assigned a particular rating to each facet. These qualitative explanations are important since this type of rating scale has been described as having several potential drawbacks, namely: 1) Individual responses may bias the entire results. 2) The researcher may influence responses by forcing choices. 3) Without a space for the participant to elaborate on his or her choice, there is no indication of what a certain value means to that participant, for example, whether one participant's interpretation of one value is the same as another participant's interpretation of that same value. (Florida State University, n.d.) In this regard, Pickard (2007) notes that "The descriptive data that open-ended questions may produce can add detail to the closed questions and can often bring a totally new perspective to an issue [...]" (p. 195) She suggests using open-ended questions when:

"you need more extensive or more individual data; you have no way of knowing the range of possible answers; it is not a particularly sensitive subject area." (p. 195) This study fits those criteria. My intention in incorporating both types of methodologies, quantitative and qualitative, is to mitigate the drawbacks inherent in either method taken individually.

The approach for the qualitative portion of this study, the open-ended questions and comments section of the survey, was interpretivist, which presumes that "all knowledge we acquire is a product of the interaction between the known and the knower; the researcher and the subject are both 'changed' by the experience, and knowledge is a result of this interaction and is time and context bound." The realities experienced by different people, the potential users, whether they are the "expert" librarian users or "non-expert" non-librarian users, are "multiple, constructed, and holistic." (Pickard, 2007, p. 12) The information that is gathered is interpreted by the researcher, a process that inherently implies the introduction of bias on the part of the researcher due to his or her own personal characteristics and belief system. Truth and meaning emerge through the exchange of ideas between the researcher and the subject, and the researcher's subsequent interpretation of this dialogue. (Robert Wood Johnson Foundation, 2010) In this study, the dialogue is confined to the participants' free-form responses to the open-ended questions and the researcher's interpretation of and subsequent assignment of meaning to these answers.

Meanwhile, the quantitative portion of the study reflects two major requirements: first, the need to gather empirical data surrounding various aspects of user behavior as it relates to mobile application usage, and second, the need to compile numerical ratings assigned by users to different elements of the existing Louvre application in order to determine if there are any patterns in user satisfaction. These numerical ratings also act as a sort of confirmation of the participants' qualitative narrative answers, which the researcher has had to interpret. According to a glossary of research terminology compiled by Colorado State University (n.d.), the quantitative research methodology is "empirical research in which the researcher explores relationships using numerical data. Survey is generally considered a form of quantitative research. Results can often be generalized, though this is not always the case." In this case, the results cannot be broadly generalized due to the small sample size. However, to a limited degree they may be generalized as being representative of the two groups—expert and non-expert users—keeping in mind the potential limitations occasioned by the sampling method employed and the small number of participants. Nevertheless, since I have conceived this study to be primarily qualitative, the ability to generalize is not necessarily what is important; the instructive elements that will shed light on the research questions will be gleaned from the open-ended questions and participants' narrative responses to them.

The quantitative portion of the methodology for this thesis can be observed in two sections. Quantitative methodology is first used in Part 1, in which participants were required to answer multiple choice questions regarding their usage patterns of mobile devices and applications. Quantitative methodology is also used in Part 2, the evaluation matrix section of the survey. This section consists of a Likert-type satisfaction scale whereby participants were required to rate different aspects of the Louvre application based on how well it meets the user's needs and expectations. Instead of numbers, this scale used a total of five cartoon faces whose expressions range from extremely displeased to extremely pleased.

The Likert scale has been defined as "a rating scale designed to measure user attitudes or reactions by quantifying subjective information. Participants indicate where along a continuum their attitude or reaction resides." (Foviance) Further, Pickard defines the

Likert scale as: "a bipolar scaling technique [...] provid[ing] ordinal data [...] [I]t gauges intensity of attitude in relation to other respondents." (Pickard, 2007, p. 188) For purposes of analysis, these faces were automatically assigned numbers from one to five by QuestBack, the online survey tool used, with one indicating the lowest level of satisfaction and five the highest level.

3. Conclusions and Further Research

The choice of a mixed model approach was appropriate to answer the research questions, given the valuable set of quantitative and qualitative data provided by participants. This rich variety of data, while time-consuming and somewhat complex to analyze, is instructive for institutions interested in developing smartphone applications because of the unique personal insights provided by participants. The quantitative data from the survey made it possible to be more efficient in the process of data analysis than a purely qualitative study would have allowed. The data analysis tools offered as part of QuestBack were very useful in compiling and visualizing the quantitative data.

Future research might involve the evaluation of other applications for the delivery of cultural heritage content, as more and more applications of this type will continue to emerge in the near future. The results of such user-led evaluation efforts will better inform the development of standards for the most effective representation of this type of content in the medium of the smartphone application.

Research focusing on how people are using these applications, how well the applications meet the needs of different user groups, how to incorporate the latest developments in smartphone technology into highly interactive applications, and how best to market and deliver such services will be key to facilitating the success of such endeavors.

In the context of these lines of research, both quantitative and qualitative approaches should be considered, as each will offer its own advantages for best determining user preferences concerning different aspects of smartphone applications.

This area of research is still rapidly emerging and experiencing a great deal of growth, and doubtless there will be much research to be done in the near future on how to create applications that will effectively display items from cultural heritage collections.

References

Colorado State University. (n.d.) Glossary of key terms. Retrieved March 15, 2010 from http://writing.colostate.edu/guides/research/glossary/.

Florida State University. (n.d.) How do I collect and analyze student critique information? Retrieved May 11, 2010 from http://www.lpg.fsu.edu/charting/evaluation/ht-stucrit.asp.

Glossary. (n.d.) *Foviance*. Retrieved April 3, 2010 from http://www.foviance.com/glossary/.

Gorman, G. E. and Clayton, P. (2005). *Qualitative research for the information professional: a practical handbook*, 2nd ed., London: Facet Pub.

Labuschagne, Adri. (2003). Qualitative research: airy fairy or fundamental? *The Qualitative Report*, 8 (1). Retrieved May 13, 2010 from http://www.nova.edu/ssss/QR/QR8-1/labuschagne.html.

Patton, M. Q. (2003). Qualitative evaluation checklist. *The Evaluation Center: Western Michigan University*. Retrieved May 2, 2010 from http://www.wmich.edu/evalctr/checklists/qec/.

Pickard, A. J. (2007). *Research Methods in Information*. London: Facet Pub.

Robert Wood Johnson Foundation. (2010). *The Interpretivist paradigm: Qualitative Research Guidelines Project*. Retrieved March 21, 2010 from http://www.qualres.org/HomeInte-3516.html.

Tashakkori, A. & Teddlie, C. (2003). *Handbook of mixed methods in social and behavioral research*. Thousand Oaks, Calif.: Sage.

Trochim, W. M. K. (2006). The qualitative debate. *Research Methods Knowledge Base: Web Center for Social Research Methods*. Retrieved May 1, 2010 from http://www.socialresearchmethods.net/kb/qualdeb.php.

Data Collection Process and Technique to Determine the Image Characteristics of Photogrammetry in Cultural Heritage Domain

Mehrnoosh Vahdat

Institute of Information Studies, Tallinn University, Tallinn, Estonia
International Master in Digital Library Learning

Abstract: This paper discusses the data collection techniques, sampling and process of identifying the population in a study to determine the image quality, authenticity, and metadata characteristics of photogrammetric three-dimensional (3D) data in cultural heritage domain. The study was carried out as the researcher's master's thesis conducted at Tallinn University. This paper presents a brief overview of significant issues regarding methodology applied in this study and justifications for the decisions made. Details of sampling techniques and sources of the population are described along with the procedure of conducting semi-structured interviews. A discussion of advantages and disadvantages of applying text-based synchronous and asynchronous interviews as data collection technique are explored.
Keywords: Online synchronous interviews, online asynchronous interviews, chat, semi-structured interviews, sampling techniques, identifying the population, photogrammetry

1. Introduction

The objectives of my research are to introduce photogrammetry as a 3D digitization technique which can be effective in documentation and digitization of the cultural heritage objects and try to understand what the image characteristics are in data quality and authenticity and what role metadata plays in this technique. In a study of the foundation of 3D digital libraries, it is argued that the next major technological revolution will be affected by massive 3D data sets which will be produced with low-priced new technologies like 3D scanning and photogrammetry (Bustos et al., 2007). Production and dissemination of huge amounts of data without quality control and documentation policies can result in serious problems or damages for information management. Nowadays, 3D information is gaining more popularity among various kinds of users. For that reason, this study aims to provide a deeper understanding of some 3D data characteristics for information professionals by analyzing features leading to the high-quality, accurate and well-defined 3D data.

Photogrammetry is defined as a branch of remote sensing that is the process of gathering information about an object without any direct physical contact with the object. Seen this way, photogrammetry is a 3-dimensional coordinate measuring technique that performs the processes of recording, measuring, and interpreting photographic images as the fundamental medium for measurement ("Guidelines for procurement", 2008).

New Trends in Qualitative and Quantitative Methods in Libraries
A. Katsirikou and C. H. Skiadas (eds)
© *World Scientific Publishing Co (pp.199-204)*

2. Methodology

This study employs qualitative method since it offers a deeper, more subjective approach to produce descriptive data such as people's lives, their stories, and behavior rather than results that are not obtained by statistical procedures (Bouma & Atkinson, 1995). The philosophical stance for this study is an interpretive approach. Willis, Jost and Nilakanta (2007) state that context is an essential aspect of understanding your data in interpretivism approach. Furthermore, the objectives of interpretivism looks for understanding of a particular context which is critical to the interpretation of the data gathered in any form of research.

Seen this way, this study is going to interpret individual experiences in the context of photogrammetry. Each and every participant are professionals interacting with this area from different aspects since they were selected from various backgrounds and work areas and their perceptions are different toward the image characteristics and metadata features in the photogrammetry technique.

3. Sampling Strategy

The sampling of this study is purposive which has taken two approaches: "priori sampling, which establishes a sample framework before sampling begins; and snowball sampling, which takes an inductive approach to growing the sample as the research progresses" (Pickard, 2007, p. 64). The priori criteria was to find professionals and experienced people in the field, having in mind that the person is using photogrammetry along with the cultural heritage area. To reach this goal, sampling was done through searching various forums related to photogrammetry and 3D imaging, individual blogs, company websites and several social networks to find the most relevant people working in this area.

Alongside the purposive sampling, snowball sampling was applied as it was difficult to find the appropriate people in the field, so when a person was interviewed he could have a good understanding about who might be knowledgeable for this study among colleagues or community and might be interested in being interviewed.

As mentioned previously, the only criteria for sampling was having experience with photogrammetry. Age, gender and nationality were not major concerns in the process of sampling since these limitations would not add any related data to this study. Furthermore, finding people with appropriate background was very challenging. More than thirty emails, forum comments and messages within the communities were sent to skilled people. Initially, the level of skill and their work area were studied out of comments, profiles, blogs and website pages then samples were selected quite confidently after studying them. The interview invitations were sent to each and every email considering the ethical issues.

To be able to find appropriate people for this study, I tried to read about their viewpoints in the case of blog or companies websites, considering their works, exploring the 3D models they had there and trying to observe the models pictures and texture conditions. Carrying out the sampling in this way took a lot of time, although having such information about individuals was a help to seize the person interest since emails and messages were specifically oriented.

3.1 Identifying the population

Since in the interpretive approach participants influence the meaning and understanding developed by the research, using multiple sources of data are very important. Willis, Jost and Nilakanta (2007) argue that "different participants have different views of what really happened thus, writeups of qualitative research often present more than one perspective" (p. 203). To find the research population, various online sources were used as follows:

Forums

The forums have been used as sources of sampling are as follows:

    - Google Earth community:

This forum includes a lot of discussion rooms for the users of Google Earth around any subject related to the Google Earth ("Google Earth", n.d.). By searching the keyword "Photogrammetry", discussions and users interested in this topic could be obtained.

    - Photogrammetry forum:

Photogrammy.de is the website for PhotoModeler discussion forums which is a photogrammetry application, maintained by the PhotoModeler user community. The forums contain methods and tips for PhotoModeler and photogrammetry ("Photogrammy", n.d.).

    -The GIS forum:

The GIS Forum goal is to give GIS (geographic information systems) users a place to teach, learn, and explore the geospatial community in an interactive and social atmosphere ("The GIS Forum", n.d.).

In each of these forums by going through more related forum discussions and read the comments, looking at the commenter's profile if existed and observing the models they have shared in the community, I sent the interview invitation either by using the forum private messaging system or emails to individuals. Finally, by registering in the forum, an invitation was sent as a separate topic named "Photogrammetry research" asking for participation in this research.

Photogrammetry Blogs

Blogs are good sources of finding the population because usually people are active in blogs, show interest in learning and research, and they are more willing to participate and help. I tried to navigate through two groups of blogs, individuals' blogs which were retrieved by searching through Google blogs, Blogger or Blogspot and Wordpress; in addition to some applications and companies' blogs like Google Sketchup Blog which is a 3D modeling program.

Companies and Applications Websites

Companies which carry out photogrammetry projects or provide software and applications in this area are useful because they are familiar with up-to-date information. Also, people who are working are professionals dealing with the new technology in the area. The newest projects and researches can be found along with the employers and researchers names and contacts.

Social Networks

    -Flickr (www.flickr.com) is an online photo management and sharing application. By searching the word "photogrammetry" I could find some people having experiences in this area and sharing their photogrammetric experiences there.

    -Linkedin (www.linkedin.com) is a business-oriented social networking site; by searching the same keyword, I could find some professionals resume and see if they are experienced in the area. Finding their contact information was done through searching their names on Google and finding their profiles in other sites; since Linkedin does not provide any contact information or messaging system for free users.

    -The Google 3D Warehouse (http://sketchup.google.com/3dwarehouse) is a free, online repository where people can find, share, store, and collaborate on 3D models. This social network tool was a great help for the sampling since a lot of professionals share their 3D architectural models there. They can use either Sketchup or other applications to build the 3D model and if their models get accepted, will share on the website. There are a lot of 3D models of cultural heritage sites can be obtained through this application. Most of them contain information about the model and contact information of producers in addition to their profiles or blogs; thus, can be used as a good starting place to find skilled modelers and select them based on cultural heritage models with high quality pictures.

4. Method of Data Collection

Due to the time constraints of this study, 6-8 people were considered as a manageable number to do the interviews and analyze them. Among 7 number of respondents back from sent emails, three of them accepted to have chat interview and four did not have time for that but agreed to reply to the interview questions and continue the discussion via email. As the number of respondents was very limited, I took the opportunity to discuss around the topic by exchanging emails.

Several various ways of data collection were considered as possible ways to suit the study purposes and objectives. Initially, online semi-structured interview by using voice applications was selected; but after more investigation around the topic, semi-structured chat interviews with open ended questions seemed better and more appropriate for this study.

Denzin & Lincoln (2000) discuss about the advantages and drawbacks of 'virtual interviewing' in which internet connections are used synchronously or asynchronously to acquire information. "The advantages include low cost, as the result of no telephone or interviewer charges, and speed of return. Of course, face-to-face interaction is eliminated, as is the possibility, for both the interviewer and respondent, of reading nonverbal behavior or of curing from gender, race, age, class and other personal characteristics" (Denzin & Lincoln, 2000, p. 666). To name a critical reason for this data collection technique, the people I needed to interview are professionals and the field of study is very technical; having in mind that they name various frameworks, standards and guidelines, it could be very difficult to understand their statements from voice over IP (Internet protocol) interviews. In addition, since interviewees are from different countries with different accents and some names they might say, can be new and unfamiliar to me, chat interviews would match best for this kind of research because it can eliminate transcription error.

In addition to previously mentioned advantages of using online text-based interviews, there is no need to transcribe the interviews so it is an advantage for a study which has time constraint. However, the interviews take more time than voice over IP interviews. As mentioned before, as the answers contain lots of technical information, in a chat interview respondents could share websites, pictures and files to clarify their statements. Another fact is that geography and interviewee location are not limiting in this method and anyone around the world can attend the interview.

The difficulty of this method is the lack of visual and vocal cues. When a question is asked, the participant's reaction cannot be observed; for instance, if the person wants to take more time to answer the question with provision of more sentences, it was kind of challenging to be aware of it and wait for him rather than asking the next question. Another challenge is that, the interview itself takes more time than voice over IP interview. The whole interview was supposed to be done maximum half an hour, although the first one took almost an hour, but I tried to organize the rest in 30 minutes as it had been promised in the invitation. There was also a possibility of misunderstanding the text-based questions; to eliminate this problem, definitions and examples were provided in case the respondents ask for it. With all the drawbacks were mentioned while using this method, the advantages are critical since it would be obliging to gain thorough and accurate technical information during the interviews.

As mentioned before, some respondents were asked for doing the interview in a way that they can answer the questions by email and argue about different aspects by exchanging emails. Since the aim is to obtain in-depth qualitative data with a possibility of getting clarified information and asking follow-up questions if needed, email interviews was selected as a possible method. Additionally, due to the lack of time and contributors, this method was used to collect more data to this study. Regarding the email interviews, in addition to the previously mentioned issues, respondents have more time to think about their experiences and answer the questions thoroughly. The disadvantage is that the discussion takes longer because exchanging emails are more time consuming than instant messages.

5. Interview Procedure

Over thirty emails and messages were sent to the potential respondents to invite them for the interview. Every invitation was different from one another considering the individual interests, background and skills; however had ethical issues in common. Most of emails had statements and comments about their skills and models if observed on the internet to affect their feeling of contribution to the study. The invitation email had an explanation of study goal besides the aspects of photogrammetry that research aims to look for. In this procedure, pilot interview was not adopted since the number of responsive professionals was very limited and it was very hard to find a fair amount of interviewees, thus it preferred to use up all the potential interviews as the source of data for the study. For those who replied and were interested, an email to arrange the date and time of interview accompanying the ethical considerations of the research was sent back.

The interviews were carried out via Skype and Gtalk, for those who were willing to answer the questions via email, Gmail and forums private messaging system were used. In the chat interviews, open-ended questions were asked based on the participants replies and knowledge of specific photogrammetric aspects; in the email interviews after getting the replies, more questions were asked to clarify the fuzzy features and get more information about some remarkable views. After getting responses and interview ended, each participant was asked to pass any contact of people they know working in the same area and can be helpful in my study. In addition, they were informed about the possibility of receiving an electronic copy of the entire thesis if they were interested in greater detail.

6. Conclusions

This paper explains the data collection process and techniques were used in a study to present the role of photogrammetry in cultural heritage domain and explore the image quality, authenticity, and metadata issues related to this technique. Online text-based synchronous and asynchronous interviews were adopted as an appropriate data collection technique for the current study. Advantages and disadvantages of this technique have been discussed in this paper. In conclusion, it is appropriate to use this method when there is a need for an in-depth understanding of technical information and conducting face-to-face interviews is not possible in a tight research timeframe.

Identifying the population of this research was carried out by selection of a wide variety of sources. Since it was difficult to find professionals experienced both in photogrammetry technique and digitization of cultural heritage objects, it was necessary to have multiple sources to find the most appropriate samples of the study. Having various sources was useful to get respondents from various backgrounds and disciplines, thus the study could have a multidisciplinary approach toward photogrammetry. The whole process of identifying the population of this research has been explained in this paper.

References

Bouma, G. D., & Atkinson, G. B. (1997). *A Handbook of Social Science Research: A Comprehensive and Practical Guide for Students*. (2nd ed.). Oxford: Oxford University Press.

Bustos, B., Fellner, D. W., Havemann, S., Keim, D. A., Saupe, D., & Schreck, T. (2007, June 23). Foundations of 3D digital libraries: Current approaches and urgent research challenges. In *First international workshop on digital libraries foundations. In conjunction with ACM IEEE joint conference on digital libraries (JCDL 2007)*. Retrieved March 20, 2010, from http://www.inf.uni-konstanz.de/cgip/bib/fi les/ BuFeHa07.pdf

Denzin, N. K., & Lincoln, Y. S. (2000). *Handbook of qualitative research*. Thousand Oaks, Calif.: Sage Publications.

Google Earth. (n.d.). Retrieved March 15, 2010, from http://earth.google.com/

Guidelines for procurement of professional aerial imagery, photogrammetry, Lidar and related remote sensor-based geospatial mapping services. (2008). *Photogrammetric Engineering & Remote Sensing*, 1286-1295. Retrieved May 10, 2010, from http://www.asprs.org/publications/pers/2008journal/november/highlight1.pdf

Pickard, A. J. (2007). *Research methods in information*. London: Facet.

Photogrammy: User community site for PhotoModeler & photogrammetry. (n.d.). Retrieved March 13, 2010, from http://www.photogrammy.de/

The GIS forum beta. (n.d.). Retrieved March 13, 2010, from http://www.thegisforum.com/

Willis, J. W., Jost, M., & Nilakanta, R. (2007). *Foundations of qualitative research: Interpretive and critical approaches*. London: SAGE.

Chapter 4. Library and Information Science Post-Graduate Student Research

Documentation of Library Compliance in Regional Accreditation Standards: A Survey of Accreditation Liaisons and Librarians of Level-One Institutions of the Southern Association of Colleges and Schools

Donna S. Ballard

District Library Director, East Mississippi Community College, Campus Libraries in Scooba and Mayhew, Mississippi, USA

Abstract: A specific set of guidelines for academic library accreditation is difficult to determine, due to differences in levels of academic institutions. The purpose of studying the perceptions of accreditation liaisons and librarians of Level-One, Associate degree-granting institutions, was to examine their compliance with regional accreditation standards and utilize the results to help librarians better understand the process of preparing for accreditation. A suggestion for further research would include the interaction of multiple authors of varying skills such as survey writing, statistical analyses, and experiences in accreditation. Librarian inclusion on accreditation committees, training, and collaboration with overall institutional effectiveness could also be studied and encouraged. This paper was the Master's project of the author in May 2008, in the School of Library and Information Science, at the University of Southern Mississippi, Hattiesburg.

Keywords: Accreditation, library(s), standards, colleges, institution(s), compliance, academic(s), education, documentation

1. Introduction
General Background
The natural progression of democratic rights following the first century of America's formation as a nation was an impetus for the beginning of what are known as community colleges today. Following the Civil War, high schools became more prolific in numbers as local and state governments began funding education beyond primary schools. In addition, the federal government began to fund state universities through land grants. This benefited many, but not all students in the rural areas (Witt, Wattenbarger, Gollattscheck, and Suppiger, 1995, pp. 1-3). In order to provide further education for students unable to travel to cities or afford established private colleges and universities, a trend of six-year high schools began in rural areas. In a similar fashion, some private colleges removed the last two years of their courses, which became an early formation of two-year colleges. By the turn of the twentieth century, these schools became known as junior colleges (Witt et al., 1995, pp. 3-7).

The American Association of Junior Colleges was formed in the early 1920s and eventually became the American Association of Community and Junior Colleges by the late 1940s (Cohen, and Brawer 1996, pp. 4-13). The first state government to

New Trends in Qualitative and Quantitative Methods in Libraries
A. Katsirikou and C. H. Skiadas (eds)
© *World Scientific Publishing Co (pp. 205-208)*

establish a 'system of junior colleges' was Mississippi, on April 26, 1928. Regional accreditation became important to these institutions, in order for students to experience a more easy transference to four-year colleges and be at comparable levels of achievement with their peers (Young, and Ewing, 1978, p. 11).

Today, the regional entity responsible for guiding accreditation standards in eleven of the southeastern United States is the Commission on Colleges of the Southern Association of Colleges and Schools, also known as SACS, which was founded in 1895. The states in this association are: Alabama, Florida, Georgia, Kentucky, Louisiana, Mississippi, North Carolina, South Carolina, Tennessee, Texas, and Virginia (*Principles of Accreditation*, 2004, pp. 3-5).

2. Results

Data Analysis and Presentation

Applying the methodology discussed previously, 186 surveys were emailed to 93 Level-One, Associate degree-granting institutions (see Appendix C for plain-text survey instrument). Two surveys were sent via email to each college—one was for the accreditation liaison—the other was for the librarian. These numbers were close to within the sample size that was determined to be 139 and a sample response of 38. There were 37 total respondents to the survey within the time period of two weeks before the data were assembled. *Survey Monkey* online software was available to collect responses and apply filters, as needed. These filtered files were downloaded into Excel files and as text summaries. Four categories of files were printed for data analyses. These were summaries filtered according to "Liaisons", "Librarians", "Other", and "All".

R1. How many institutional libraries in this study had SACS accreditation findings or sanctions?

Of the 37 respondents, seven (18.9%) indicated that their institution's library had findings or sanctions due to unsuccessful demonstration of compliance in accreditation standards. The respondents were asked to specify the findings or sanctions, which are shown in Table 1. These comments were given by the respondents, were replicated within this text, and indicated that insufficient collections and staff accounted for the most findings or sanctions. Other reasons frequently mentioned, were the lack of evaluations in instructional services in the library.

Table 1

SACS Accreditation Findings or Sanctions for Libraries Surveyed (Refers to Survey Questions 3)

Answer Choices	Response Percent	Response Count
Unsure	0.0%	0
N/A	13.5%	5
NO, the library did NOT have findings or sanctions	67.6%	25
YES, the library did have findings or sanctions	18.9%	7

Note. Seven respondents indicated that the library did have findings or sanctions. Comments given about the findings included the following:

(1) In a substantive change visit for the opening of a new campus (2007), we were required to provide adequate and appropriately credentialed staff for the facility, and appropriately credentialed staff to do information literacy instruction. Both of these were under way at the new facility but had not been fully implemented.

(2) The collection was out dated, too small for a college of this size. I can't be absolutely positive what the sanctions actually were; however, I feel that much had to do with the lack of Administrative support both monetary and physical (people for staff as well.)

(3) The Off-Site Committee which evaluated our school in May 2007 marked "Non-Compliance" on Comprehensive Standard 3.8.2. The committee indicated that they did not find evidence of the evaluation of the instructional program of the Learning Resource Center.

(4) Insufficient collection to support math/science and technology, and follow-up charged library with not demonstrating improvement through adding new items in those areas. (I never understood that one.) Also, insufficient professional staff...there was only a director...myself, with an MLA. They told us we had to add another librarian. Even then, considering the (old) ACRL standards, a school our size in FTE should have 2.5 librarians, not counting the director. I expect another recommendation when SACS returns in 2009.

(5) Issues with collections

(6) In general, the finding was that the library did not have enough qualified staff

(7) This was either 2 or 3 accreditations ago, before I came on board. The library was faulted for not having general humanities materials...just items that supported the technical curriculum. The library budget was given large increases in materials money for 2 or 3 years to purchase philosophy, history, art, literature, etc. and the situation was corrected. We have had no recommendations or suggestions since then.

3. Conclusion

Concluding thoughts of this study relate to the discussion by John M. Budd (2007), in which he indicates that the U.S. Secretary of Education, Margaret Spelling's report on the future of higher education, should focus more on inputs. An example of the numbers of books in a library should change more toward measurement outcomes of how well students' understand the books. He suggests a shift to more outcomes assessment in relation to student learning experiences. Furthermore, he notes that community colleges traditionally spend more on student learning at lower tuition rates, than research universities, which tend to spend less on student learning at higher tuition rates. Due to the complicated differences in levels of institutions, it is apparently difficult to determine a narrow set of guidelines for accreditation.

Suggestions for further research on the documentation of library compliance in regional accreditation standards includes multiple collaborative authors, with varying skills such as survey writing, statistical analyses, and experiences in accreditation. In addition to SACS, other regional agencies could be the focus of similar research, which would help libraries understand accreditation procedures. The inclusion of librarians on accreditation committees and in training sessions, as well as collaboration with overall institutional effectiveness could be studied and encouraged.

References

Academic libraries survey (2003). In National Center for Education Statistics Handbook of Survey Methods (pp. 105-110). Retrieved September 14, 2007, from
http://nces.ed.gov/pubs2003/2003603.pdf.

Accreditation Liaison. (2007). Commission on Colleges Southern Association of Colleges and Schools. (pp. 1-2). Retrieved February 26, 2008, from
http://www.sacscoc.org/pdf/081705/accreditation%20liaison.pdf

Baker, R. L. (Jan-Mar 2002). Evaluating quality and effectiveness: regional accreditation principles and practices. *Journal of Academic Librarianship, 28*(1), 3-7. Retrieved July 22, 2007, from Academic Search Premier database.

Budd, J. M. (2007). The Spellings commission: challenges to higher education and academic libraries. *Libraries and the Academy, 7*(2), 137-146. Retrieved August 28, 2007, from Project Muse Scholarly Journals Online.

Bollag, B. (2006, November 24). Spellings wants to use accreditation as a cudgel. *Chronicle of Higher Learning, 53*(14). ERIC Document Reproduction Service No. EJ756915) Retrieved October 22, 2007, from ERIC database.

Cardell, C. (2008, February 22). Personal email communication.

Cohen, A. M. & Brawer, F. B. (1996). Background: evolving priorities and expectations of the community college. In *The American Community College* (pp.1-37). San Francisco: Joey-Bass Publishers.

Coleman, P., & Jarred, A. (1994, November). Regional association criteria and the Standards for College Libraries: the informal role of quantitative input measures for libraries in accreditation. *Journal of Academic Librarianship, 20*(5/6), 273-284. Retrieved July 22, 2007, from Academic Search Premier database.

Gratch-Lindauer, B. (2002, January-February). Comparing the regional accreditation standards: outcomes assessment and other trends. *Journal of Academic Librarianship, 28*(1), 14-25. Retrieved July 22, 2007, from Academic Search Premier database

Leach, R. G. (1992). Academic library change: the role of regional accreditation. *Journal of Library Management, 18*(5), 288-291. Retrieved September 24, 2007, from Library Literature & Information Full-Text database.

Library and Other Learning Center Resources. (2004). In SACS Handbook for Reaffirmation of Accreditation (p. 69). Decatur, GA: Commission on Colleges Southern Association of Colleges and Schools.

Member, candidate and applicant list. (2007, August). Commission on Colleges Southern Association of Colleges and Schools. Retrieved August 28, 2007, from http://www.sacscoc.org/

Principles of accreditation: foundations for quality enhancement. (2004). Decatur, GA: Commission on Colleges Southern Association of Colleges and Schools.

Sample Size Formulas. (2003). The Survey System. Retrieved February 22, 2008, from http://www.surveysystem.com/ssformu.htm.

Sample Size Terminology. (2003). The Survey System. (par. 1-4). Retrieved February 22, 2008, from http://www.surveysystem.com/sscalc.htm#terminology

Standards for College Libraries: 2000 Edition. (2006). American Library Association. Retrieved September 18, 2007, from http://www.ala.org/ACRLtemplate.cfm?Section=acrlstandards&Template=/ContentMana gement/HTMLDisplay.cfm&ContentDisplay.cfm&ContentID=8975

Standards for Libraries in Higher Education: 2004 Edition. (2006). American Library Association. Retrieved September 18, 2007, from http://www.ala.org/ala/acrl/acrlstandares/standardslibraries.cfm Document ID: 170127.

White, G. (1999). Managing the accreditation process: a survey of academic business librarians. *Library Management, 20*(8), 431-438. Retrieved September 24, 2007, from Library Literature & Information Full Text database.

Witt, A. A., Wattenbarger, J. L., Gollattscheck, J. F., & Suppiger, J. E. (1995). The evolution of an idea. In *America's Community Colleges: The First Century* (pp. 1-12). Washington, D. C.: American Association of Community Colleges.

Young, J. B. & Ewing, J. M. (1978). Section 1: The five decades. In *The Mississippi Public Junior College Story The First Fifty Years 1922-1972* (pp. 3-42). Jackson, Miss: University Press of Mississippi.

Publishing Patterns and Authorship in the Scholarly Literature of Digital Object Identifiers: A Bibliometric Analysis

Donna S. Ballard

District Library Director, East Mississippi Community College, Campus Libraries in Scooba and Mayhew, Mississippi, USA

A Digital Object Identifier (DOI) is an alpha-numeric standard for the use of identifying intellectual property within computer networks and is a recent trend in the field of the electronic publishing of scholarly articles. This study examines the publishing patterns in the scholarly literature of digital object identifiers. The research includes core journals, professional affiliations, gender, and geographic locations. Additionally, the primary disciplines represented in the authorship of the DOI literature are observed. This paper was submitted in the LIS651 course, Introduction to Library and Information Science, during April 2007, as a partial requirement for a Master's degree in the School of Library and Information Science, at the University of Southern Mississippi, Hattiesburg.
Keywords: Literature, information, Digital Object Identifier(s), DOI, articles, library, science, research, digital

1. Introduction
A Digital Object Identifier (DOI) is an alpha-numeric standard for the use of identifying intellectual property within computer networks and is a recent trend in the field of the electronic publishing of scholarly articles. According to Karen Coyle (2006), the general use of an identifier for intellectual property was not entirely modern. For instance, the Library of Congress Cataloging Number (LCCN) has been utilized for such identification for more than one-hundred years, as well as the International Standard Book Number (ISBN), and the International Standard Serial Number (ISSN), which were developed over thirty years ago. Various disciplines have also initiated their own schemes of identifiers, such as those used in music, audiovisuals, or medicine. The digital age of computers has opened a new cohort of identifiers in addition to digital object identifiers, including the Uniform Resource Identifier (URI), Uniform Resource Locator (URL), and the Uniform Resource Name (URN).
Carol Risher (1998), the first General Manager of the DOI Foundation, details the evolvement of DOI within an article in *Serials Review*. The article was co-authored by William Rosenblatt, who was also affiliated with the initial architecture of DOI. The use of digital object identifiers was portrayed as having emerged through the Association of American Publishers in 1997, and has experienced considerable global development since that time. DOI has enabled the action of a constant link through registries, which provide continuous updates in regard to intellectual property location. Through this technology, scholarly, peer-reviewed articles can be marked with unique and persistent DOI, and made available electronically with metadata for research and citation, before actually going to print.

New Trends in Qualitative and Quantitative Methods in Libraries
A. Katsirikou and C. H. Skiadas (eds)
© *World Scientific Publishing Co (pp. 209-212)*

Problem and Sub-Problems

This study examined the publishing patterns in the scholarly literature of digital object identifiers. The research included core journals, professional affiliations, gender, and geographic locations. Additionally, the primary disciplines represented in the authorship of the DOI literature were observed.

Research Questions

R1 What were the core journals in the field of digital object identifiers?

R2 What were the professional affiliations of authors who publish articles on DOI?

R3 What were the gender and geographic location of the authors who publish articles on DOI?

R4 What were the primary disciplines represented by DOI literature?

2. Results

Publication Patterns

Twenty full-text, scholarly and peer-reviewed articles were examined in a study of literature available on digital object identifiers. These articles ranged within publication dates from 1997 through 2006. The terms utilized as keywords in searching the databases for pertinent articles were "digital object identifier*".

The earliest date of a DOI found within this bibliometric study of literature was observed as occurring during 1997. This confirmed an earlier statement in the introduction of this paper, which indicated the emergence of the digital object identifier as a new technology in 1997. Among the literature examined, the frequency of publications on the subject increased in 2001. The results shown in Table 1: Frequency of Publication, by Year, indicated that *Publishing Research Quarterly* contained three of the twenty articles examined, followed by *DESIDOC Bulletin of Information Technology*, with two articles. One article was found in the *Journal of Electronic Publishing*. Thirteen articles were contained within individual library and information science publications, which were: 1) *College & Research Libraries*; 2) *Information Services and Use*; 3) *Internet & Higher Education*; 4) *Internet Reference Services Quarterly*; 5) *Journal of Academic Librarianship*; 6) *Journal of the American Society for Information Science and Technology*; 7) *Journal of Information Science*; 8) *Journal of Library Administration*; 9) *Law Library Journal*; 10) *Library Resources & Technical Services*; 11) *Serials Librarian*; 12) *Serials Review*; and 13) *Technical Services Quarterly*. In addition, one other journal, *Communications of the ACM* (Association for Computing Machinery) contained the remaining single article on DOI, among the twenty examined in this study.

3. Conclusions

Core journals in this study contained DOI articles that were found in the categories of publishing and a variety well-known library and information science titles. Moreover, tabulations indicated that greater than fifty percent of the twenty pertinent scholarly articles were also located within library and information science databases. These results were indicative of the type of results noted by Smith (1981) in the 'literature of' studies, in finding one or more specific journals useful in a particular study, as well as the potential for revealing publication patterns and subject areas.

Affiliations with academic libraries and publishers or other non-library and information science representatives of the DOI articles was nearly even in respect to authorship. This DOI study indicated more male than female authors. However, academic librarians were shown to be in the majority of authorship in DOI articles, and were also the nearest in equality of gender representation. Similar results were noticed in the study by Zemon and Bahr (1998), who found that college librarians were more evenly represented by gender in library and information science authorship. This outcome was also evident in the Joswick (1999) study, where actual female authorship was beginning to reach statistical numbers in representation of the discipline of librarianship.

A larger proportion of DOI authorship originated in the United States, followed by the United Kingdom, the Netherlands and India. In addition to the international scope of the subject, the interdisciplinary nature of DOI in this study corresponded to electronic publishing and the fields of library and information science, information technology and computer science. These findings were similar to those of Georgas and Cullars (2005), in which subject classification or discipline, and international scope were also observed in bibliometric studies.

This study indicated an increase in frequency of publication of DOI articles by year, beginning in 2001. In the literature review, authors Patra, Bhattacharya, and Verma (2006) commented that their studies revealed bibliometric growth patterns were highest in 1999 and most likely attributable to an increase in computer and information science technology during that time period. Articles were first published on the subject of digital object identifiers, although not during the same year, but within the same time period, probably for the same implied reasons.

Recommendation for Further Study

A more in-depth bibliometric examination of the literature of digital object identifiers, including citation analyses, could be constructive in further knowledge. The recognition of core journals, publishers, and authors of DOI literature could be improved with the utilization of comprehensive and detailed citation studies. This could have positive implications in areas such as: determining the most optimal databases for searches on the subject of DOI, and core journals and books for the purposes of collection evaluation and development in libraries. The implementation of digital object identifiers in areas such as digital libraries, academic libraries, special libraries, information science, computer science, government, and commercial enterprises could also benefit from supplementary bibliometric studies.

References

Coyle, K. (2006). Identifiers: unique, persistent, global. *The Journal of Academic Librarianship, 32*(4), 428-431. Retrieved March 9, 2007, from Library Literature & Information Full Text database.

Georgas, H., & Cullars, J. (2005). A citation study of the characteristics of the linguistics literature. *College & Research Libraries, 66*(6), 496-515. Retrieved March 12, 2007, from Library Literature & Information Full Text database.

Joswick, K. E. (1999). Article publication patterns of academic librarians: An Illinois case study, *College & Research Libraries,* 60(4), 340-349. Retrieved May 01, 2007, from Library Literature & Information Full Text database.

Patra, S., Bhattacharya, P., & Verma, N. (2006). Bibliometric study of literature on bibliometrics. *DESIDOC Bulletin of Information Technology, 26*(1), 27-32. Retrieved March 17, 2007, from Library Literature & Information Full Text database.

Reitz, J. (2004). *ODLIS: Online Dictionary for Library and Information Science.* [Electronic version]. Portsmouth, NH: Libraries Unlimited. Retrieved March 17, 2006, from http://lu.com/odlis/.

Risher, C., and Rosenblatt, W. (1998). The digital object identifier—an electronic publishing tool for the entire information community. *Serials Review, 24*(3/4), 12-21. Retrieved March 01, 2007, from the Academic Search Premier database.

Smith, L. (Summer 1981). Citation analysis. *Library Trends,* 83-106. Retrieved February 27, 2007, from University of Southern Mississippi Electronic Reserves 52779.

Zemon, M. and Bahr, A. H. (1998). An analysis of articles by college librarians. *College & Research Libraries, 59*(5), 422-432. Retrieved May 01, 2007, from Library Literature & Information Full Text database.

Characters of Color: A Content Analysis of Picture Books in a Virgin Islands Elementary School Library

Marilyn M. Brissett

Gladys A. Abraham Elementary School, Virgin Islands Department of Education, Virgin Islands

Abstract: The purpose of this qualitative content analysis is to determine if the picture book collection at the Gladys A. Abraham Elementary School Library accurately reflects and therefore serves the needs of the majority of its students. A disparity exists between the actual ethnicities represented by the school population and those depicted in the picture book collection. Less than ten percent of the books most frequently selected by kindergarten through 3rd grade students depict realistic stories and a disproportionate percentage (88%) of books have settings in the United States. This study can be used as a model to examine elementary school libraries on each of the three main islands (St. Croix, St. John, and St. Thomas) in order to identify how well their collections reflect the ethnicities of their students.
Keywords: Caribbean, collection development, content analysis, ethnic groups, picture books, school libraries, Virgin Islands

Introduction

The United States Virgin Islands lie between the Atlantic Ocean and the Caribbean Sea, just east of Puerto Rico. There are three main islands - St. Thomas, St. Croix, and St. John. Tourism drives the economy. The population hovers around 110,000. The majority of the population is black and West Indian, which reflect the colonial history of the islands. The United States purchased the islands from Denmark in 1917. The Virgin Islands current status is an unincorporated territory.

St. Thomas is the commercial center of the Virgin Islands. Unemployment rates are lower than St. Croix, but higher per capita than many large U.S. cities ("V.I. must grow jobs: our joblessness is serious", 2004). Immigration, both legal and illegal, from impoverished islands in the Caribbean has added to the heavy burden already being shouldered by the local government (Poinski, 2004).

Gladys A. Abraham Elementary School is located at 68-A Lindbergh Bay, an area just west of Charlotte Amalie, the only city on the island of St. Thomas. Three hundred ninety-six (396) students are enrolled from kindergarten to sixth grade (School Improvement Plan, 2008-2009). The families of the children who attend Gladys A. Abraham Elementary are ethnically diverse and vary in structure, socio-economic condition, and geographic origin.

Based on the April 1, 2008 enrollment statistics, sixty-four (64%) percent of the students are Black, thirty-three (33%) percent are Hispanic, and three (3%) percent are White. All written communication is sent out in both English and Spanish. A small, but growing, percentage of French Creole students are included in the Black

New Trends in Qualitative and Quantitative Methods in Libraries
A. Katsirikou and C. H. Skiadas (eds)
© *World Scientific Publishing Co (pp. 213-217)*

enrollment figures. A small number of Arab students are included in the White enrollment figures.

Purpose of the study

The purpose of this study is to determine if the picture book collection at the Gladys A. Abraham Elementary School Library accurately reflects and therefore serves the needs of the majority of its students.

Research Questions

R1. What percentage of the picture books has one or more main characters that represent people of color?

R2. What ethnicities do the main characters of color represent?

R3. What percentage of the picture books has one or more main characters of color and is set in the Caribbean?

R4. What percentage of the picture books has one or more main characters of color and is set in Africa?

Limitations

L1. The study does not include picture books located outside of the easy-to-read (primary) collection at Gladys A. Abraham Elementary School's library.

L2. The study does not include books about animals, fantasies, alphabets, counting or any other topic whose focus is not characters that could be encountered in real life situations.

L3. The findings of the study are limited to the picture book collection at Gladys A. Abraham Elementary School Library.

Methodology

Content analysis was used to identify the ethnicities of the main characters and the settings of the picture book collection at Gladys A. Abraham Elementary School Library. This type of research has been used to describe the content of children's books since Martin's landmark study of nationalism in 1934 (Bekkedal, (1973). It provides researchers with a method to objectively describe the content of books that have been systematically selected. It is also a useful method for collection development purposes because it allows books to be examined and evaluated for numerous constructs.

Coding Form

The research was conducted using a coding form to record the title of the book, the main character by ethnicity, the setting by geographic location, the author and illustrator by color (yes or no), and the publisher by name and location. The character that was the main focus of the text was identified as the main character. If uncertainties existed, the main character was determined by the number of times his/her picture appeared.

Ethnic Markers

The ethnicity of the main character was determined by using the Library of Congress Cataloging-in-Publication (CIP) Subject Data. If this information was not available, the book was examined for ethnic markers, using text and picture clues. Text clues included the introduction, book jacket, and actual text of the book. Picture clues included the book covers and the illustrations inside the book. Ethnic markers included, but were not limited to, reference to ancestors, race/physical characteristics, culture/customs, language, religion, and common values ("Ethnic Markers", 2007).

Results

R1. What percentage of the picture books has one or more main characters that represent people of color?

In order to determine how accurately the picture books in the easy-to-read collection at Gladys A. Abraham Elementary School Library reflect the children of color in the school population, the books that met the criteria were listed in the first column of an Excel spreadsheet. The second, third, and fourth columns addressed the ethnicity of the authors, illustrators, and main characters. The ethnicity of the main characters was determined by the ethnic markers described above. Forty-eight (48) picture books in the easy-to-read (primary collection) at Gladys A. Abraham Elementary School Library met the criteria outlined above. Twenty-six main characters (54%) represented people of color (see Table 1).

Table 1
Distribution of Main Characters by Ethnicity

Group	Frequency	Percentage
White	22	46
Black (not Hispanic)	21	44
Hispanic	2	4
Jewish	2	4
Asian	1	2

R2. What ethnicities do the main characters of color represent?

The ethnicities of the main characters are important because the picture book collection should reflect the diversity of the students in the school. They should not only see honest portrayals of themselves, but also other racial and ethnic groups in their school as well as society at large. A category of "Other", with space to write in the ethnicity, was included to ensure that no ethnic group would be excluded. As indicated in Table 1, twenty-two main characters (46%) were White, twenty-one main characters (44%) were Black (not Hispanic), two main characters (4%) were Hispanic, two main characters (4%) were Jewish, and one (2%) was Asian.

R3. What percentage of the picture books has one or more main characters of color and is set in the Caribbean?

It is important that students in the Caribbean have access to picture books that reflect their ethnic identity, which includes their geographic locale. Children need to see picture books whose geographic location is the same as theirs; so that they know that their region of the world, their place in the world, has value. The coding form identified major areas of the world, but also had an "Other" category to ensure that all regions would be included. As indicated in Table 2, forty-two books (88%) were set in the United States. Three books (6%) were set in Europe, two (4%) were set in the Caribbean, one (2%) was set in Africa, and one (2%) in Asia. The geographic location of one book was divided equally between the United States and Asia. Hence, the disparity in the "Frequency" and "Percentage" columns in Table 2.

Table 2
Distribution of Setting by Country

Country	Frequency	Percentage
United States	42	88
Europe	3	6
Caribbean	2	4
Africa	1	2
Asia	1	2

R4. What percentage of the picture books has one or more main characters of color and is set in Africa?

Children of color in the Caribbean should not only have access to picture books whose main characters reflect their ethnic identity and their setting, but books that honestly and accurately reflect their heritage. Since the majority of the students at Gladys A. Abraham Elementary School are the descendants of slaves, picture books depicting Africa should be available. As can be seen in Table 2, only one picture book (2%) had an African setting and a main character of color.

Conclusion

The Gladys A. Abraham Elementary School Library had 48 picture books in its easy-to-read (primary) collection that met the study's criteria. Since the collection numbers just over five hundred books, slightly less than ten percent of the books most frequently selected by kindergarten through 3rd grade students depict realistic stories. Of those, only fifty-four (54%) percent had main characters of color. Although forty-forty (44%) percent of the main characters were Black, only four (4%) percent were Hispanic. A disparity exists between the actual ethnicities represented by the school population and those depicted in the picture book collection. Forty-six (46%) percent of the books have main characters that are white, while just three (3%) percent of the student population is white. Although thirty-three (33%) percent of the school population is Hispanic, only four (4%) percent of the picture books have Hispanic main characters. The majority of students (64%), who are black, are only represented in forty-four (44%) percent of the picture books. Furthermore, there was only one book with a Haitian main character and none with an Arab main character; two small, but growing, minorities.

Unfortunately, there is also a disproportionate percentage (88%) of books that are set in the United States. Only four (4%) percent of the books had Caribbean locales and two (2%) percent African. It should be noted that there were only two (2) books set in the Caribbean; one in the Dominican Republic, the other Haiti. There were no picture books with Middle Eastern settings; the historic homeland and birthplace of some Arab students. If picture books have become the "genre of choice" (p.2) for teachers to read aloud and students to read independently as Mendoza and Reese (2001) assert, then it is important that the disparities mentioned above are addressed in a timely fashion. Picture books are powerful! They can not only influence a child's self-esteem, but also their view of others. Since only a small percentage of the books published each year represent minority cultures, it is often left up to school and public librarians to ensure that minorities are accurately represented in their picture book collections.

Instead of relying on traditional journals for book selection, that may or may not fairly represent minority cultures; librarians need to seek out journals that support and publicize authentic and accurate portrayals of minorities. Collections need to be developed that offer a broad range of quality picture books about numerous cultures, never relying on one book to depict a culture regardless of the accolades it has received. Librarians have a responsibility to make informed and objective judgments about the picture books they purchase. They are also responsible for what is already on their shelves.

Future Studies

Future studies may wish to examine several elementary school libraries on each of the three main islands (St. Croix, St. John, and St. Thomas) in order to identify how well their collections reflect the ethnicities of their students. Collectively, they may provide information that is representative of elementary school library picture book collections in the U.S. Virgin Islands, enhancing the collection development ability of not only individual librarians, but also territorial coordinators. It can be used to justify similar studies in other geographical locations.

Suggestions for Selection

Studies reporting the effects of picture books on children's self esteem, and their perception of other cultures, suggest that just as accurate and authentic portrayals can have positive lasting effects on their readers; inaccurate portrayals can negatively affect readers. If this statement is accepted at face value, the challenge then becomes to identify books that not only reflect the ethnicities of the students, but also offer accurate information from an insider's perspective when possible. Although school librarians' abilities to make informed judgments about picture books vary, those that accept the challenge and develop a selection criteria to root out bias and stereotyping, will develop collections that reflect the ethnicities of their students, build self esteem and accurately celebrate the people of the world.

References

Bekkedal, Tekla K. (1973). Content Analysis of Children's Books. *Library Trends*, October, 1973, 109-126.

Editorial. (2004, ay 24). V.I. must grow jobs: our joblessness is serious. *The Virgin Islands Daily News*. Available at:
http://www.virginislandsdailynews.com/index.pl/article_home?id=5532070

Ethnic Markers. (2007). Retrieved July 27, 2008, from IUPUI University Library Web site. Available at:
http://www.ulib.iupui.edu/kade/nameword/emarkers.html

Gladys A. Abraham Elementary School. (2008). *School Improvement Plan*.

Mendoza, Jean & Reese, Debbie (2001). Examining Multicultural Picture Books for the Early Childhood Classroom: Possibilities and Pitfalls. Early Childhood Research and Practice, 3(2), 1-17. Available at:
http://ecrp.uiuc.edu/v3n2/mendoza.html

Poinski, Megan. (2004, April 21). Federal and local authorities detain 20 illegal immigrants. *The Virgin Islands Daily News*, Retrieved July 3, 2004. Available at: http://www.virginislandsdailynews.com/index.pl/article_home?id=4894195

Anthropological Literature on Social Phobia: An Examination of Publishing and Indexing Patterns

Julie D. Shedd

Mississippi State University Libraries, USA

Abstract: Social phobia, or social anxiety disorder, afflicts 10 to 13 percent of Americans with anxiety that prevents them from entering performance situations and with physical symptoms of anxiety including nausea, sweating, and muscle aches. As a uniquely human ailment and possible culture-bound disorder, social phobia is a worthy topic to examine frequency of occurrence in anthropological literature. Word frequency analysis was applied to 36 years of anthropological journals with top ten impact factors as determined by *Journal Citation Reports* and words related to social phobia counted. Conclusions include implications for further study and proposed solutions to anthropology's endemic gray literature problem.
Keywords: Anthropology, bibliometrics, psychology, social phobia, shyness, word frequency analysis

Introduction

Social phobia, also known as social anxiety disorder, is a psychological condition which may affect ten to thirteen percent of the population of the United States (American Psychiatric Association, 2000). It has become the most prevalent anxiety disorder in the United States, and is one of the most prevalent mental illnesses overall, following only major depression and substance abuse. The disorder is made more serious by its high comorbidity with depression, substance abuse, and other anxiety or personality disorders (Beidel & Turner, 1998; Rapee, 1995). Shyness has existed whenever and wherever human social behavior has existed, but has not always been seen as problematic—in fact, shyness has often been considered a desirable trait, especially in women (McDaniel, 2003). It is only when a person feels a distinct fear of entering performance situations in which she perceives a danger of being negatively evaluated and humiliated by peers or by physical symptoms of anxiety, leading her to avoid such situations in a way that significantly inhibits her life or upsets her, that a diagnosis of social phobia can be made (APA, 2000).

In discussing speaking as performance, Duranti (1997, p.16) states that "speaking itself always implies an exposure to the judgment, reaction, and collaboration of an audience, which interprets, assesses, approves, sanctions, expands upon or minimizes what is being said…in addition to the dimension of accountability, there is also a dimension of risk or challenge." This is exactly what frightens socially phobic people—exposure to an audience who will, in the sufferer's mind, always disapprove. Therefore, they avoid other people, and so do not gain the experience they need to carry on successful social interactions. This presents an interesting anthropological problem: what does it mean for American culture if ten percent of its people are afraid to speak to one another? How can we learn more about socially phobic people and their impact on culture when the nature of their disorder prevents them from speaking to us? Has any anthropologist successfully studied socially phobic or shy people?

New Trends in Qualitative and Quantitative Methods in Libraries
A. Katsirikou and C. H. Skiadas (eds)
© *World Scientific Publishing Co (pp. 219-224)*

Literature Review

Despite the world of possibilities in an anthropological study of social phobia, preliminary searches of anthropological literature turned up little to no information about the disorder, and only marginally more about shy people. David Scruton's 1986 volume *Sociophobics: The Anthropology of Fear* seems to be the only anthropological book dealing strictly with social anxieties. Other types of fear and anxiety, including socially-related fears, and culture-bound syndromes which seem related to social phobia (such as the Japanese *taijin kyofu-sho*, a phobia of offending others, and *hikikomori*, "withdrawing" to one's room due to nervousness about communicating with others) are more often discussed.

As for methodology, anthropological studies which utilize bibliometric methods are rare. Preliminary searches for citation analyses, publication trends studies, or word frequency studies in anthropological journals yielded few results. Anthropological word frequency studies tend to be linguistic in nature, usually studies of the frequencies of color terms in languages or language families. One notable exception is Henry and Bankston's 2001 study of the self-image and stereotypes of Louisiana Cajuns' physical appearance. They organize descriptive terms into three overarching categories, and speculate that Cajuns' self-image is derived in large part from their stereotyping by outside sources.

Searching for "content analysis" is marginally more successful. One such search yielded David Altheide's article "Ethnographic Content Analysis," in which he suggests that "an ethnographic perspective can help delineate patterns of human action when document analysis is conceptualized as fieldwork" (1987, p.65). This article is especially relevant to the current study, which takes a body of documents as "the field" and the analysis of those documents as "the fieldwork."

Bibliometric methods, including word frequency studies, are, unsurprisingly, most often utilized in library and information science studies. One study with a similar methodology to this study is Susan Davis Herring's "Journal Literature on Digital Libraries: Publishing and Indexing Patterns, 1992-1997" (2000). Herring studied citations from studies of digital libraries, working to identify the core journals publishing articles on digital libraries, the best search terms, and the inconsistencies in indexing between journals.

Purpose of the Study

The purpose of this study is to examine publishing and indexing patterns in anthropological literature on social phobia and shyness from 1970 to 2006.

Limitations

This study is limited to the ten English-language cultural anthropology journals with the highest impact factors in 2006: *Africa, American Anthropologist, American Ethnologist, Annual Review of Anthropology, Anthropology & Education Quarterly, Cultural Anthropology, Current Anthropology, Ethos, Journal of the Royal Anthropological Institute*, and *Oceania*. Only the electronic versions of these journals, retrievable from the Academic Search Premier, AnthroSource, and JSTOR databases, are included. Front and back matter, including indexes, tables of contents, and covers, are excluded. Only issues published between January of 1970 and December of 2006 were examined.

Methodology

The journals for analysis were selected using ISI Web of Knowledge's *Journal Citation Reports*, Social Sciences Edition 2001, with journal impact factor being the major criterion for selection. Searches were performed in each journal for a selection of words related to shyness and social phobia:

- Anxiety, anxieties, anxious

- Phobia, phobias, phobic
- Shy, shyness
- Culture-bound, culture-bounded, culture-boundedness
- Disorder, disorders, disordered, disorderly, disorderliness.

The articles yielded by each search were collected into folders according to the search term that recovered them; the articles returned from a search for "anxiety" were collected in a folder named "anxiety," and so on. Most of the articles came formatted as .pdf (Portable Document Format) files.

Two distinct data-collection methods were performed. The more recent .pdf files were searched using Adobe Reader. Recently created .pdf files are usually digitally searchable; programs like Adobe Reader include search functions which examine the full text of documents. However, most .pdf files published before 1998 are only image files—snapshots of pages—displayed like a text document. The text in these files is not searchable. All of the articles archived in JSTOR—including articles from journals in the AnthroSource and Academic Search Premier databases, which often archive older material with JSTOR—were stored in such files.

For articles from *American Anthropologist*, the older .pdfs were carefully read for instances of the search terms. This soon proved to be not only tedious but fraught with error. The search terms tend to evade the eye after it has taken in several hundred instances, and on occasion the article's content itself draws in the researcher, so that the search terms are forgotten. To remedy this, a new workflow was developed for subsequent journals. Able2Doc Professional, an optical character recognition (OCR) software, was used to convert older .pdf files to Microsoft Word documents (.doc) while preserving the layout of the original document. Hermetic Word Frequency Counter software was used to provide automated word frequency counts. This software analyzed each Word document, counted the frequency of each word, and reported its findings in a plain-text document (.txt).

The results were entered into Microsoft Excel spreadsheets and compared. For each journal, the frequency of each search term was charted. Annotated bibliographies of articles that had some relation to shyness, social anxieties, social phobia, and related culture-bound syndromes were constructed as a resource for later research.

Analysis of Data

The total number of items in all the sampled journals for all thirty-six years was 33, 497. For some journals, indexes, tables of contents, conference advertisements, and even front and back covers had been digitized and archived in the databases. After this irrelevant matter was deleted, 31, 716 articles remained in the sample. Of these, 2858 articles were returned in searches for the specified search terms. (See Table 1)

Table 1. Frequencies of Each Search Term

Search Term	Frequency
Anxiety	2863
Disorder	1858
Disorders	879
Anxious	874
Anxieties	611
Shy	475
Culture-bound	328
Phobia	137
Shyness	124

Disorderly	113
Disordered	106
Phobic	70
Anxiously	43
Disordering	27
Phobias	24
Shyly	18
Disorderliness	11
Anxiousness	4
Culture-boundness	3
Phobically	2
Culture-boundedness	2
Shyer	1

Results

As expected, social phobia was not found to be a frequent topic of study in the journals selected. In fact, it was only mentioned in two articles—in the references. "Social anxiety" was also scarce; when mentioned at all, it was in the context of anxieties which are shared by a society, rather than as the name of a mental disorder.

Shyness and similar emotions were more frequently discussed, often as part of an anthropology-of-emotion approach. Shyness was usually mentioned as a matter of chance— "My informant asked me shyly", for instance—or as a desirable and expected personality trait for females all over the world, but the word "shy" was most often used as part of phrases like "shy away from" or "just shy of". The more sensitive database search mechanisms also returned it as part of words like "brushy". Interestingly, "shy" was often found as a descriptor in the obituaries of anthropologists and authors, including Lesley White and W. H. R. Rivers, and in interviews with and reminiscences about anthropologists including Sol Tax (who self-identifies as shy) and A. R. Radcliffe-Brown.

Anxiety was a very frequent topic of discussion, but rarely as something felt by an individual about social interaction. "Anxiety" could denote anything from grief to slight unease, felt by a single person or an entire nation. It was often present in a Freudian sense, as part of "Oedipal anxiety" or "castration anxiety". Few of the authors writing about shyness or related emotions mentioned anxiety, and authors writing about anxiety rarely mentioned shyness. In fact, if authors were writing about Freudian anxieties, they were usually discussing people as aggressive, not at all shy. Most often, the word and its variants were used as a synonym of "eager" (for instance, "I was anxious to tell him").

When the word "disorder" appeared, it was usually used to describe social unrest, crime, rioting, and the like. It was also used in psychological and medical anthropology papers to describe insanity or culture-bound syndromes, but never as part of "social anxiety disorder." It is intriguing that during the years (specifically the 1990s) in which there might have been a boom in research on social anxiety disorder, none was found, yet this study turned up many recent articles on attention deficit hyperactivity disorder.

Phobias were mentioned primarily as part of the word "xenophobia", but as time passed it also frequently appeared as part of "homophobia", and since 2001, "Islamophobia" has become a popular topic. The word was rarely found in the context of "social phobia," however.

"Culture-bound" is the only term that was most often found in the expected context: describing behaviors or beliefs that are uniquely held by a single culture. "Culture-bound syndromes" or "culture-bound disorders", however, were rarer. Often "culture-bound" served as a criticism of a researcher's work in article and book reviews, suggesting that the researcher could not overcome his own ethnocentrism enough to objectively study his chosen culture.

Discussion of Method

Three databases were searched in this study: Academic Search Premier, AnthroSource, and JSTOR. Each database has a distinct search engine and indexing system. Search results depend not only on how a search engine works but on how each document is indexed. Therefore, the accuracy of search results varies. JSTOR in particular seemed rather poorly indexed. Some articles returned in a particular search would have no instances of the term being searched for, but several instances of the other search terms. Accuracy would be increased, or at least more easily controlled, by searching only one database. In addition, hyphenated words, especially those split at the ends of lines, confused search engines and OCR software; for instance, "anxiety" was not often recognized as "anxiety". Short of simply reading through entire volumes of journals, there is no way to tell how many instances of the search words were ignored in this way.

The tools used to convert nonsearchable documents and count word frequencies also lent a significant margin of error. Able2Doc Professional, the OCR software, did not always convert items smoothly; distorted text, scans of dirty or stained paper, poor typesetting, poor scans, non-English text, diacritic marks, or simply running the software too many times in a row sometimes resulted in Word documents full of gibberish. Charts and images were also often rendered as garbled characters. These documents confused the word frequency counter and muddled the study results. OCR software is improving, but at the time of this study, it was simply not reliable. Hermetic Word Frequency Counter counted word fragments (such as words at the end of lines divided by hyphens) as two words, so frequent checking of articles was necessary. At the time of purchase, the software did not allow the isolation of specific words—only the recognition of words *not* to count. Therefore, each report had to be manually sifted for the search terms. Simply reading the articles was just as unreliable. The human eye is fallible, and the harder one looks for a specific word, the easier it is to overlook it. Articles had to be read and reread for the search terms. In a small sample, this would not be a problem; with over thirty thousand articles, it becomes impossible. This study should be redone on a single journal, or a single database, for no more than five years of journals, for a far more manageable sample.

Conclusions

Anthropology has paid some attention to shyness in passing. Notable informants who acted shy have been marked as such. Cultures such as the Malay which have a sort of shyness (for instance, *malu*) as an overarching social emotion have proven fascinating for Westerners, for whom shyness is often seen as pathological. Yet only a few anthropologists have researched social phobia. David Scruton's 1985 *Sociophobics: The Anthropology of Fear* brought together several researchers to examine social phobia from an anthropological standpoint. If those authors have published again on social phobia, they have not done so in the journals studied here.

Whether as a culture-bound disorder, a culturally universal condition, or a part of the American medicalization craze, the time is ripe for the anthropological study of social phobia. More people than ever are presenting with the condition; more people than ever are receiving treatment for it, both therapeutic and pharmacological. Still more may be quietly suffering. Is social phobia changing our culture? Is it preventing people from fully participating or contributing to culture? Only anthropological research can tell.

It was the intention of this study to lay a foundation for future anthropological study of social phobia, and it has given rise to many new questions. This study itself cannot answer many questions. It is too big and too inaccurate; the necessary technology has not yet caught up to demand, indexing is too inconsistent across journals, and database archival practices are just now catching up to the demands of the Information Age. A series of smaller word frequency studies might be more effective. What the study does show is that social phobia, along with shyness and other "social emotions", have been too long neglected in anthropology.

References

Altheide, D. L., 1987. Ethnographic content analysis. *Qualitative Sociology*, 10(1), pp.65-77.

American Psychiatric Association, 2000. *Diagnostic and statistical manual of mental disorders: Fourth edition, text revision (DSM-IV-TR)* 4th ed., Washington, D.C.: American Psychiatric Association.

Beidel, D. & Turner, S., 1998. *Shy children, phobic adults: Nature and treatment of social phobia*, Washington, D.C.: American Psychiatric Association.

Chapman, T., Mannuzza, S. & Fyer, A., 1995. Epidemiology and family studies of social phobia. In *Social phobia: Diagnosis, assessment, and treatment*. New York: The Guilford Press, pp.21-40.

Duranti, A., 1997. *Linguistic anthropology*, Cambridge: Cambridge University Press. Ettin, A., 1994. *Speaking silences: Stillness and voice in modern thought and Jewish tradition*, Charlottesville: University Press of Virginia.

Fonseca, A., Yule, W. & Erol, N., 1994. Cross-cultural issues. In T. Ollendick et al., ed. *International handbook of phobic and anxiety disorders in children and adolescents*. New York: Plenum Press, pp.67-84.

Henderson, L. & Zimbardo, P., 1999. Developmental outcomes and clinical perspectives. In L. Schmidt et al, ed. *Extreme fear, shyness, and social phobia: Origins, biological mechanisms, and clinical outcomes*. New York: Oxford University Press, pp.294-305.

Henry, J. M. & Bankston III, C. L., 2001. Ethnic self-identification and symbolic stereotyping: The portrayal of Louisiana Cajuns. *Ethnic & Racial Studies*, 24(6), pp.1020-1045.

Herring, Susan Davis, 2000. Journal literature on digital libraries: Publishing and indexing patterns, 1992-1997. *College & Research Libraries*, 61(1), pp.39-43.

JSTOR, 2006. JSTOR and accessibility. Available at: http://www.jstor.org/about/accessibility.html [Accessed November 2, 2006].

McDaniel, P.A., 2003. *Shrinking violets and Caspar Milquetoasts: Shyness, power, and intimacy in the United States, 1950-1995*, New York: New York University Press. Rapee, R., 1995. Descriptive psychopathology of social phobia. In R. Heimberg et al., ed. *Social phobia: Diagnosis, assessment, and treatment*. New York: The Guilford Press, pp.41-66.

Schneier, F., 1999. Extreme fear, shyness, and social phobia. In L. Schmidt et al, ed. *Extreme fear, shyness, and social phobia: Origins, biological mechanisms, and clinical outcomes*. New York: Oxford University Press, pp.273-293.

Scruton, D. ed., 1986. *Sociophobics: The anthropology of fear*, Boulder: Westview Press.

Educational Choices and Learning Careers of LIS Students as a Social Process: Theoretical and Methodological Considerations

Valentini Moniarou-Papaconstantinou and Anna Tsatsaroni

[1]Department of Library Science and Information Systems, TEI of Athens, Greece, valpap@teiath.gr
[2]Department of Social and Educational Policy, University of Peloponnese, Corinth, Greece

Abstract: This paper draws on a research study which explores the reasons behind young people' choice of Library and Information Science as a field of study, and traces their education careers within the existing higher education departments in Greece. In particular, it focuses on some data and findings in order to illustrate the thesis that subject choice is a complex social process, and to discuss theoretical and methodological implications. The problematic of the study has been developed with reference to the theories of Bourdieu and symbolic interactionism, and the core concept guiding the work, that of an *educational career*, provides the possibility for theorising in an integrated way students' LIS choice and their educational trajectories prior to and within the LIS institutions. Data was collected through a questionnaire and semi-structured interviews, and the analyses relied on quantitative and qualitative methods and techniques. The construction of specific analytical tools, namely the *Educational Career Index* and the *Divergence Index*, were used to identify internal differentiations in the sample of students, and to interpret their educational decisions. Developing ways for organising data and the constant interrogation of the data through the theoretical concepts, and vice versa, were used to elaborate the argument about the social character of students' educational choices and trajectories. One important finding of the study is the association observed between the different groups identified in the sample and the reasons attracting each of them to Library and Information Science. Another interesting finding relates to the students' transformations, and the trajectories they plan, which seem to be dependent on their possibilities to capitalise on the available resources, relative also to the institutional habitus of the department in which they study.
We shall discuss these two findings with reference to three interview cases, two of which are typical and conform to the quantitative part of the study, the other being recalcitrant vis-à-vis our main hypothesis. We shall thus have the opportunity to discuss, how the particular theoretical choices made in this study as well as the combination of quantitative and qualitative data analysis have helped in the illumination of the research problem.
Keywords: Educational choices, educational career, students' trajectories, cultural capital, quantitative and qualitative research

New Trends in Qualitative and Quantitative Methods in Libraries
A. Katsirikou and C. H. Skiadas (eds)
© *World Scientific Publishing Co (pp. 225-240)*

1. Introduction

This paper draws on a study that aimed to explore the ways in which young people conceptualise and act upon the structures of educational opportunities within which they are situated and to examine students' learning career and identity formation.

Currently, the transition of young people to institutions of H.E., and their trajectories within them is a key issue in educational research because of recent years policies and trends towards widening access and participation, and the expansion of the field of H.E. with the development of new subjects, conditions however which might cause new and more complex forms of educational inequalities. For the Information Sector, in particular, which is making huge efforts to recognise its position both in the field of H.E. and in the labour market, in an environment characterised by constant changes and fluidity, studying the choices of young people that enter Departments of LIS and exploring their learning trajectories within such departments is of the utmost importance.

Issues such as academic and social hierarchies in the H.E. sector, and the inequalities, indicated by research (e.g., Archer *et al.*, 2003; Reay *et al.*, 2005; Sianou, 2010) among young people from different socio-economic backgrounds, related to the availability of economic, cultural and symbolic forms of capital, consequently, also, their hypothesised differences in the ability to decode the contents of different subjects of study and to recognise the professional paths to which they may lead, have been the main reasons why we have attempted a sociological analysis and interpretation of students' choices of H.E. study.

We argue that decision-making on educational options, and choices made by young people involve complex social processes, formed in the course of time by social and cultural factors as well as the constant interaction of individuals with their social environment, and which tend to legitimise the existing, institutionalised social divisions within the H.E. sector. In this context, in studying the educational choices and educational careers of students, we have attempted to explore whether and how such choices relate to the basic socio-cultural features characteristic of the different social groups they belong to, and which may influence their horizons of action; the latter understood as the result of interactions between structural factors and the agency of the individuals who are involved in the process of decision making about subject study. We have also tried to trace the influences that the interactions between an individual and the wider social environment in which she functions may have on this process.

2. Theoretical framework

The main theoretical tools used to conceptualise the research process in the study of students' educational choices and their trajectories are Bourdieu's concepts of habitus, field, forms of capital and institutional habitus, together with the concept of learning career which draws, in addition, on theories of symbolic interactionism (Bloomer 1997; Bloomer and Hodkinson 2000a; 2000b; 1999; 1997). In particular, the concept of *educational career* is used here to capture the dynamic relationship between structure and agency in the field of education (Bloomer and Hodkinson 2000a; 2000b; Hodkinson and Bloomer 2001).

Habitus, in Bourdieu's words, is,

> "the strategy-generating principle enabling agents to cope with unforeseen and ever changing situations…a system of lasting and transposable dispositions which, integrating past experiences, functions at every moment as a matrix of perceptions, appreciations and actions and makes possible the achievement of infinitely diversified tasks" (Bourdieu, 1977, cited in Wacquant, 1992, p. 18).

Habitus, thus, provides us with the means for understanding young people's decisions, and the ways in which differences, of social, cultural and economic character, may influence the way they perceive the available opportunities and lead them to make the "right" or "appropriate" decisions with reference to H.E. subject choice and subsequent options.

Together with dispositions, young people bring to decision making processes varying forms and amounts of *economic, social, cultural and symbolic capital* (Bourdieu, 1990; 1997). *Cultural capital* is a cumulative result of educational and cultural effort, undertaken by the individual and her family. It consists of cultural beliefs, personal skills, knowledge, and dispositions, resources that enable one to be competent and successful in a given field of action. Cultural capital is always relative to a given field and to other forms of capital. Individuals who come from families rich in cultural capital, which has become part of their habitus, can be more competent players in using the rules required for participation in a "social game". They can understand the symbolic value of qualifications and titles within certain sectors when they are making decisions concerning different options, and, they have the socially acquired ability to opt for sectors with attractive future prospects (Bourdieu, 1984) as well as to develop behaviours and attitudes which enable them to be successful in their educational career, compared to individuals who have been socialised through different kinds of processes and conditions.

In the process of higher education choice the cultural capital interacts with *social capital*, a set of resources, actual or potential, which are possessed by an individual or a social group as a result of their participation in a durable network of relations of mutual recognition and respect. The amount of social capital available to individuals depends on the network of social relations that they can mobilise, and the volume of capital (economic, cultural or symbolic) available to the groups they are linked with (Bourdieu, 1997).

Relevant here is the concept of the *field*. In Bourdieu's theory, field, is a social space involving social actors, whose positions are defined by the interaction between the rules, specific to the field, an individual's habitus and the capital available (Bourdieu, 1984). Positions in the field differ among social groups, according to the distribution of power or capital, and the relations of power among the groups change in the course of time, as new agents manage to acquire dominant positions (Bourdieu, 1977). The H.E. field can, then, be seen as a social space in which young people enter with unequal resources, that is, with different forms of capital, possession of which might determine the positions as well as the strategies they develop, and which affect the rules of the game.

Thus habitus, field and capital interact in various ways, forming social practices in given fields of action. For a field to function there must be actors willing to participate in it, providing that they possess capital relevant to the field and the habitus that equips them with practical knowledge and acceptance of the rules of the game (Bourdieu,1993). The same habitus can activate various kinds of practices in any field, depending on the field and the kind of capital that determines the possibilities for action.

In addition, the concept of institutional habitus is important in the analysis of the dynamic interaction between the educational institutions and the student population. *Institutional habitus* refers to a complex "amalgam" of agency and structure, and is used to indicate the influence that cultural group membership or social class can exert on individuals' behaviour as this is mediated by an organisation, in this case an education institution (McDonough, 1997). The elements that are combined to form the habitus of institutions are the history of the formation of institutions, their educational status, their degrees of autonomy within the field of H.E., their programmes of study, their organisational structures and arrangements, their cultural features and their principles for regulating and controlling the actions and behaviours of individuals acting within a given field (Bernstein, 2000; Reay, *et al.*, 2001).

Of crucial significance for the study of students' trajectories, as already mentioned, is the notion of an educational career, formed by individual preferences, opinions and contingencies as well as by complex combinations of social and economic factors (Bloomer and Hodkinson, 2000b). In the educational career of an individual there are continuities but also noticeable changes in the perceptions, values, beliefs and dispositions of individuals towards their education and learning which often are transformed in irregular, unforeseeable and multiple ways. Transformations in educational careers are expressed in various ways and they are not predetermined, though they are influenced by the individual habitus, the forms of capital as well as the social environment(s) within which an individual has been brought up and functions. Transformations may result from young people's efforts to adapt to different cultural contexts, for instance the institutional habitus, as well as the "turning points" which might be linked to crucial and unforeseeable events in that particular phase in their lives (Bloomer and Hodkinson, 2000a; Hodkinson and Sparkes, 1997).

In this paper the notion of an educational career is understood in terms of an attempt to describe the ways in which attitudes, views and practices of students remain unchanged or are transformed as a result of their socialization into knowledge, their contact with the habitus of the educational institution they are studying in and the interactions with students from different social groups in the new environment in which they are situated. This concept has helped us to illuminate both issues around the initial educational decisions of participants in the study, and those related to processes of acceptance and/or negotiation of their positions within the field of H.E. and the particular departments within which they study, and ultimately their educational trajectories during their studies.

Drawing on the theoretical framework used in this research, we argue that individuals' decisions concerning the subject of their study are influenced to a great extent by their level of understanding of the field of H.E. and the hierarchies that structure this field; the latter also being affected by the habitus of the individuals and the forms of capital available to them. Furthermore, we argue that the educational career should not be seen as an individual action, which is based on the motives or the self-conception of individuals or even their objectively defined educational opportunities but it is subject to change, the causes and effects of which, in some occasions, are very difficult to predict.

3. Methodology

The study combined quantitative and qualitative research. Thus it was possible not only to enrich the data produced through the quantitative part of the study but also to be able to examine more thoroughly how the participants perceive the social processes and their position within them (Bryman, 1988; Cohen and Manion, 1994; Patton, 2002; Warren, 2002).

The study had been conducted in two stages, at crucial phases in participants' educational trajectory. During the first stage, the study focused on the turning point of their transition to higher education and the early period of their socialisation into the LIS departments. It employed self-completion questionnaires distributed to all first year students (N=177, F =138, M =39) who enrolled in the LIS schools (entry cohorts Academic year 2005-2006) at the first week of their studies; as well as semi-structured interviews with 41 students (F=34, M=7) from among those who expressed an interest to be further involved in this research, taken four to seven weeks after the students' enrolment in the LIS Departments. Although the participants volunteered, specific criteria were applied, such as gender, age, parental occupation and education as well as the institution in which the young people were studying.

The second stage was designed to be carried out two years and a half later, when the research participants were at the fifth semester of their studies, taking into account, among other things, Bernstein's (1971) insight that the inner mystery of a discipline, the dynamics influencing the production of knowledge that creates a new reality, is only revealed to individuals at the point of completion of their studies. This second stage employed semi-structured interviews with a purposeful sample of 15 students. Among the inclusion criteria were the students' participation in the interviews taken at the first stage of the research, information rich cases with respect to the research objectives, theoretical relevance of cases to the research study as well as their importance in relation to significant findings of the questionnaire data analysis.

The semi-structured interviews conducted at the first stage of the research included questions that young people's educational career before and after their admission to higher education, the role of social networks in higher education choice, students' perceptions of LIS, their plans and aspirations, etc. In the interviews during the second stage of the research, participants were asked to describe and assess their learning experiences, to refer to events and experiences they thought to be important to them, and to describe their interests, aspirations and future plans.

Semi-structured interviews were employed at both research stages because they permit a detailed and in depth examination of important issues related to structural characteristics of the research participants and their educational choices. Furthermore, they were useful in order to investigate participants' perceptions, experiences and the way they think, assess situations and formulate plans of action; thus taking into consideration the view that any attempt to comprehend social reality cannot ignore the experiences of the individuals themselves (Bryman, 1988).

Furthermore, analysis of interviews helped to illuminate aspects of the main findings of the quantitative part of the study, significantly the differentiation in the sample of students into distinctive groups, each associated with different reasons attracting them to Library and Information Science. In addition, the flexibility of the interviews and the fact that, in some cases, they developed into narratives, have helped to provide rich sets of data which allowed us to study the complex formation of young people's trajectories.

Among the analytical tools employed for questionnaire data organization, the *Educational Career Index* and the *Divergence Index* are worth mentioning. These were used to identify internal differentiations in the sample of students, and to interpret their educational decisions (see next section; Moniarou-Papaconstantinou *et al.*, in press). In addition, developing ways for organising interview data, and the constant interrogation of the data through the theoretical concepts, and vice versa, were the means through which we were helped to elaborate the argument about the social character of students' educational choices and trajectories. Specifically, for organising and coding interview data we found particularly useful the preparation of summaries for each of the interviews, emphasising the main topics, making a synopsis of the collected information, and identifying the silent, interesting or important issues (Evans, 2000; Miles and Huberman, 1994). The coding of information was based on thematic categories, emerging from constant and systematic examination of the overviews, readings of the complete set of interviews, and application of the theoretical concepts informing the study.

Each of the interviews lasted between one and one and half hours and was tape-recorded and transcribed. To ensure anonymity, the names of the participants were changed and LIS departments are referred to with the use of letters.

4. Results

An important finding of the study is the association observed between the different groups of students identified in the sample and the reasons attracting each of them to Library and Information Science (Moniarou-Papaconstantinou, 2009; Moniarou-Papaconstantinou, *et al.*, in press).

Specifically, analysis of the questionnaire with the use of elaborate statistical techniques (i.e. cluster analysis and MANOVA tests) revealed a clear differentiation of the research participants, with the identification of three groups, on the basis of distinctive social characteristics, namely parental education level, Educational Career index and Divergence index. It was found that the three groups of students are attracted to LIS by different factors. In particular, the first group which is characterized by middle parental education level, narrow range of educational experiences, as recorded in the Educational Career index (value: low), and substantial divergence between the marks they obtained in the higher education access examination and the place of LIS in their preferences (value: substantial) reasons about the LIS choice only in terms of the employment prospects, which are considered important also for the other two groups. To appreciate this finding, it should be associated with the social characteristics of this particular group, which indicate lack of familiarity with the cultural field and possibly difficulty with understanding the qualitative attributes of LIS.

In contrast, the second group, in which belong students with middle parental education level, wider range of educational experiences and substantial value in the Divergence index, appreciates more the intrinsic factors, namely the qualitative features of the profession, its social character and its worth as an academic field of study. This group seems to use these qualities to preserve the belief in an upwards moving and successful career (Moniarou-Papaconstantinou, *et al.*, in press).

The third group, which is characterized by high parental education level, good range of educational experiences, as recorded in the Educational Career index (value: high), and limited value in the Divergence index, like the second group, is attracted to LIS by intrinsic characteristics. However the differences between individuals in this group and those of the previous group regarding parental education level and respective values in the Divergence Index, help to identify them as "embedded choosers" (Ball *et al.*, 2002 p. 337). Specifically, this group makes informed choices and their decisions are made with more self-confidence. Obviously, these young people and their families are in a position to understand the hierarchies in the higher education field and to recognize the differences between different subject areas but also to discern specific qualities within a given field (Moniarou-Papaconstantinou, 2009; Moniarou-Papaconstantinou, *et al.*, in press).

The qualitative analysis has brought out the complexity and the social character of subject choice as a process in students' educational trajectories, reminding us that in order to avoid the untheorised assumption of a free agent, the term "choice" needs to be handled with great care (Ball et *al.*, 2002).

In particular, significant findings with reference to the qualitative analysis of our interview data relate to the students' transformations and the trajectories they plan, as a result of their socialization in the new environment, the influence of unplanned events upon them, and the interaction between institutional habitus and individual and family habitus. Specifically, it became apparent that the institutional habitus, negotiated through the interaction between teaching staff and students, interrelates with the students' habitus, forging perceptions and choices. Therefore, it exerts significant influence on their educational career, crucially with respect to their interest for their subject, their studies, their socialisation in the profession or in the academic field of information science and certainly in the careers they imagine and envisage. Moreover, it became clear that the institutions exert more influence upon the students' educational career in those cases, where the students are able to deal competently with educational issues requiring them to make choices, by utilising and capitalising on the resources available to them.

On the contrary, the institutions failed to help students facing difficulties associated with structural constraints, and they showed non-readiness in the need to support effectively their weak and unstable pedagogic identities.

Below, we analyse more intensively and more holistically three cases of participants in the study, coming from 2 out of 3 LIS schools, in order to discuss the aforementioned findings that was resulted from the cross-subject analyses of the two sets of interview data (see section on methodology).

Embedded and precarious identities: Analysis of three cases

The accounts we present of three students, participants in the study, are based, besides the interview data, on information drawn from the questionnaire administered at the first stage of this research. One of the students studies in the department of LIS which is located in the University sector of higher education, from which we must infer higher academic status. The other two students study in a department belonging to the technological sector of higher education, which was gradually upgraded through changes in its institutional context. It should be noted, that historically, in the consciousness of Greek society, the university sector, especially when compared to the technological, was considered superior. This stems from the deeply-seated views of the Greek public that university degrees ensure high prestige and considerable social status (Moniarou-Papaconstantinou and Tsatsaroni, 2008).

Fedra's both parents have finished only primary school. Her father is a driver, and her mother is a cleaner. She has two brothers, of whom one is also a driver, while the other one at the time had a temporary job. We infer that the family lacks economic, social and cultural capital. Regarding her educational trajectory, initially she attended the school in her village, which according to her report was poorly organised. She attended secondary education in a nearby town and finally she preferred to follow the Technical-vocational school and not the Integrated Lyceum. Also she is the first in her family to go to higher education, with the encouragement of her technical vocational high school teachers, who tried to guide her towards that direction, taking into consideration, as she said, her progress in her two final years in the school. Moreover, at the time of completing secondary education her family encouraged her strongly to continue her studies, and, as she describes it, her parents were very enthusiastic for her educational choices; though they would have preferred it if she had been admitted to an institution responsible for the training of military personnel. At the time, and still now, such a choice is seen to promise the prospect of immediate employment as well as a stable and fairly well paid job.

Fedra mentions that she had "no clue about the department", she heard friends, who had already been admitted talking about it, finally it was "her instinct that dictated her choice". From an early stage in her studies she realised that the subject of information studies is interesting, however she is not sure about seeking a job relevant to the field, since she believes that it is a difficult field of study. Furthermore, she thinks, that she has not, and - due to financial difficulties - she will not be able to acquire during her studies the additional qualifications (e.g., knowledge of foreign language at an advanced level) she thinks that are required for a job in the field.

Lina, the second of our cases, comes from a family with significant amounts of cultural and social capital and, as it was evident in her account in both rounds of the interviews, her parents, the father a primary school teacher and her mother a secondary school teacher, had done postgraduate studies themselves, and were very much involved in the formation of her educational choices. She had a wide range of educational experiences, and her initial aspirations were to be a psychologist; but her parents, being "strong framers" (Ball *et al.*, 2002, p.337.), had imposed their own choice. Her parents believed that LIS has a strong future, and had already started looking for postgraduate programs and even for potential links among LIS and a career in the Diplomatic Corps. Although initially Lina considered LIS to be "a low-level field of study", she did not relied solely on her parents opinions regarding LIS. Indeed, she sought further information through the relevant departments' websites. After her admission in the LIS department for a while she was rethinking whether she should stay or not. However, after a month, when she started adjusting to her new environment, her initial doubts were set aside, and she started finding the field of information studies "interesting, difficult and complex". She reached the conclusion that had the required information been available to her earlier in her educational career, "there would have been no need for her parents to impose their will upon her". Instead, she would have selected LIS herself without being influenced by her parents.

Emilia, the third of our cases, comes from a family with low education level. Her father works as a metallurgist and has finished low secondary education, while her mother has finished only primary school and is a housewife. Emilia so far had limited educational experiences as can be seen from the questionnaire data and what she described in her first interview. There seem to be huge fluctuations in the kinds of ambitions she had had for herself. While she was a student in secondary education she was dreaming of becoming a doctor, and then, something completely different, a policewoman. She managed to succeed in a public relations department of the technological sector of higher education but she decided to drop it because the institution was some distance from her residence. She discussed the choice of LIS as a field of study with her relatives, especially with her uncle, a bank executive, in a "a formal family occasion" where relatives were invited in order to discuss the possible choices. Emilia's decision to participate for a second time in the national examinations for higher education entry, after a three-year gap, indicates reflective processes at work and some degree of determination. Her account reveals that the main influence in her decision to leave her temporary job in a sports club as well as her ambitions around the subject of her studies at the first period in the LIS department, was her then boyfriend, himself a doctoral student. The desire to give a good impression to his family and social networks, had motivated her. In her own words, "I wanted to rise up to his level, they shouldn't say that she, who has a night job, is not good enough for our son, they shouldn't say a thing, the relatives, and his family and everybody else, shouldn't say a thing". These views of course are easily understandable, given that in Greece historically there has been a dominant view that linked social status and social mobility with acquiring a degree from higher education, preferably the university sector (Lambiri- Dimaki, 1983). Emilia initially intended to make career in the LIS sector, however she changed her orientations later, and attempted to exploit opportunities and to define the ways and the terms of her career and life prospects.

Fedra who studies the subject of LIS in one of the departments of the technological sector (Educational institution C), during the first stage of the research did not have any ambitions besides getting her degree and then immediate employment.

"I would like… just to get this degree… I want to finish, and if possible, work in a library."

Lina who studies the subject of LIS in the department of the university sector (Educational institution A), as a result of the available cultural and social capital and the impact of the institution, has already started realising the choices and opportunities available to her. The institutional habitus, which is being perceived differently by the students according to their characteristics, can support and influence their educational career (see also Reay, 1998).

" as time goes by I think that the information field is more suitable for me because when you are a person who wants to do something new constantly, who looks for something new, I believe this field is the best […]. You constantly deal with new things… any job if I have, in an office, to deal with research, with libraries, with archiving, whatever, it will be something that will not make me get bored …It involves communication, it is something more interesting"

A pattern which becomes apparent from the analysis of the interviews is that although the participants in the study expressed their views for their future plans as early as 4-7 weeks after starting their studies, students with significant amount of cultural capital had had already shaped ambitions, and were envisaging viable privileged trajectories. It appeared, that the family habitus had already helped to form these students' priorities and to define their personal choices. Lina, despite her initial unclear stance towards LIS as a field of study had developed high career aspirations from an early stage, (which to a great extent reflect those of her parents):

"I make lots of dreams and have many ambitions, now I don't know whether I will have the chance to achieve them. I asked recently whether an archivist could work in the diplomatic corps, or wherever there can be a link with archives, with information… I was told, that an archivist can work even in a ministry, if he likes his job, is good with his job, has lots of knowledge and many degrees. Now I don't know if I will be able after my twenty two years of age to have the same desire that I have now, to be able to get many degrees and lots of knowledge in order something so important to happen to me like a job in a ministry or in the diplomatic corps…. Still, yes… maybe I have great ambitions but I like the sound of it, the way I think about it, the way I imagine it, I would like this to happen."

Young people able to capitalise not only on their cultural and social capital accumulated during their lives but also their participation in social networks were in a position to deal effectively with educational choices. Those students also managed to comprehend the relation between higher education and employment as a process which evolves in a long time-span and is defined as a series of steps (see also Ball, 2003). They invested more time and effort in examining the possible alternatives, and were in a position to shape a realistic future professional route. It became apparent in the research that the family's cultural capital influences both the students' perception of reality, and their ability to shape their ambitions and actions in a world, in which they know how to be successful (see also Bowman, Colley and Hodkinson, 2004). In addition, the students' cultural capital contributed to their confidence and to their belief that their ambitions will be realised. The underpinnings of the ambitions regarding the career are often found inscribed in the individuals' imaginary, as an inextricable part of their socially defined personal biography (Ball *et al.,* 2002). In this context, in the following quotation, Lina, who was seen to be an embedded chooser at a critical point in her educational trajectory, is also clearly a typical case of an involved pedagogic subject. Indeed, she has shaped an identity for herself, based on both the process of re-socialisation due to her newly discovered faith in the information field and the activation of her forms of capital. In her case, the family habitus is in symmetry with the institution in which she studies. This institution shaped her academic habitus, by influencing her educational progress and helping her to expand her horizons, as a result of a policy of scientific collaborations and academic networking among the faculty members. Against this background, it can be seen from Lina's account of her career, that she can fully utilise accidental events or chances that are purposefully provided within and outside her education institution. Furthermore, she imagines herself as a researcher who would develop scientific activity across Europe and not only within her country. Her choices are not "short-term" and are not restricted to her acquiring the degree and a vague idea of finding a job. Instead, her choices are shaped in a manner which may lead to an interesting academic and professional career. To sum up, in this case the transformations in the student's dispositions, plans of action and ambitions were gradual and had as a result a strengthening of her dedication to the information field and to a promising career.

> "I was influenced by the head of archives ..., and the head of the public library... They were people... who knew the subject, who live it everyday practically, and not only theoretically, as I learn it from the lecturers and living with these people everyday, how they operated, how they worked... in this valuable archival material which surrounds them every day, they helped me a lot to understand better some things and think seriously of the future."

> "I am in love with their [lecturers] lectures, I am in love with their teaching method and of course I am influenced also by it, and I envy them, and I would very much like to do the same, in the future, to teach like they do, like they have managed to do [...] My ambition, now, has to do... with the subject I study... and may sound a bit immature, a bit crazy, because it is a dream, I would like very much to get a Master in the history of art ..., so I can become a lecturer [...]. In Italy, in Venice, in Florence... there are so many archives..., I would like very much [to work],... in an archive e.g. in Florence, in a museum, or in Venice and there to be a collaboration between the library – Archive –[place]– Florence, ... it is one of my ambitions ... to work in different countries on a common subject. I would have liked the academic career, but it is very difficult to make it, it needs lots of work, time, guts. Now, if you devote yourself in something, I believe everything can happen, I'll see [...]...I can't imagine myself working all day in a library... I would like an alternative career, I would like very much to go for the field of research..., very interesting for you and others who may learn through you, with the diffusion of the information. I would like to go for the subject of Information... I would be interested in teaching, it has lots of future, demands lots of time, many degrees, you have to get involved, to have lots of knowledge... to achieve it. I would like that."

On the contrary in Fedra's case who has a low social background, it appears that the structural constraints and the previous educational career were limiting the fulfillment of her aspirations which seem to be unstable and unclear so far. She is a contingent chooser, as we saw above, and is a typical case of a precarious pedagogic identity.

> "I would like to continue and get the degree. After the degree I haven't decided yet for a postgraduate degree but I don't think so, I don't think so [...]. Although, I think about it. It is just that, OK, I can't decide and know now for sure what I will do after [my degree] because I still have a year and a half ahead and depending on the situation. [...] After... when I 'm

finished from here, I 'll be in [place] where the university is, if I want to do something, I will be able to do it with a job, or something else. That is, I won't burden [the parents] in something."

Fedra's plans are constrained by her perception of her family's financial situation. Although she did not want to be a burden on them, she was trying to turn into advantage accidental events, perceived as opportunities, in order to materialise her dreams and desires. Her choices were defined by her restricted horizons of actions formulated, by the socially shaped perceptions she had for herself and her future identity, and her positioning. In the quotation that follows it seems that the main element that defines Fedra's choices, was the prospect of immediate employment in a stable working environment. This continuity is discernible in our analysis of both sets of the interview data concerning her case, and can best be explained by what Hodkinson and Bloomer (2001, p.136) write about young people's life trajectories: "young people carry with them their developing senses of identity, evolved from their life histories and grounded in their social and cultural context and experiences and indeed in their bodies". It seems that her choices are defined, to some extent, by her family's socio-economic position, values and expectations. Furthermore, it was found that in unstable learning identities, like Fedra's, the institution was not able or prepared to develop some kind of a compensatory mechanism, so as to limit structural determinants on students' actions and decisions and to help them be orientated towards, and more actively involved, with the subject of their study.

"... I want to sit for... the exams in the Coast Guard [...] and I am trying to study,... so I can pass. OK, that is something... I wanted to do, even before I joined the department, so I won't ... stop trying to achieve it, it is an opportunity, this advertising [for training for the Coast Guard], it doesn't happen often... I think it's difficult, but I'll try it, though this does not mean that I don't like the department I am in. It is just... what I wanted from the beginning. I prefer [the Coast Guard] because it has a more certain future. That is, you finish the [Coast Guard] academy, ... and then immediately,... you start working immediately... That is what interests me, yes, something more certain, in my life, professionally. [...] This moment, I could have dropped out of my studies for a semester, so I can manage to get in [the academy]. But I didn't do it, because it would have been very difficult for my parents, for financial reasons, if I tell them I 'll leave the department, it will sound too much..."

Emilia's educational career, the third of our cases, has many turns and twists. It is evident from her account that social class and gender interact in multiple ways, exerting great influence on her educational choices and aspirations. Her ambitions seem to be based more on "dreams and imaginings than on deeply held thought-through possibilities" (Bloomer and Hodkinson,1999, p.42).

"After finishing the semesters from now on, and when I get my degree from here, I would like to do a postgraduate degree, basically I would like to go abroad, to see how libraries operate abroad... And perhaps if I take some ideas from abroad... I 've heard about Finland.. the best words for their educational system... and I would like to go there and expand my knowledge and learn... and evolve and perhaps, if I can take the ideas from there, bring them here, in Greece."

However, these imagined contributions that she thought she was able to make to her field of study were soon replaced by other wishes and ambitions. Indeed, in her second interview, Emilia's values were redefined, her aspirations and perceptions for the academic knowledge and commitment to her studies had changed. The change was so significant, that although her family had invested emotionally on the successful completion of her studies, they were not able to change her disposition towards her educational career.

> "... like all parents, mine want to see me get a degree... To see me get the piece of paper [the degree]. That's their dream. And now that I am leaving this behind, they feel sad, and they say how many years we will be alive to see you graduate, and go on, continue it [studying] and leave the job... A reason I am not leaving the school, an important one, is my parents. To see me graduating. To frame my degree and look at it, to be proud. To put it above the fireplace and be proud. To say "here, our child got a degree". Only for this."

This dramatic staging of instances of social recognition on the basis of high educational qualifications and titles that make her parents proud is typical of her socio-economic position in the context of the Greek society (Mestheneos, and Ioannidi-Kapolou, 2002). However, it was noticeable that her socialisation in the working environment, which started in parallel with her studies, weakened her previous, on-going identity formation which was more academically oriented and contributed to the emergence of new elements as bases for identity formation. In this process, the embracing of new values, such as the importance of material goods and wealth influenced significantly her educational career. Accidental events and unexpected changes in her life made her to reassess her situation, to see it from a different perspective, and finally to change her plans and intentions by modifying the image of the future she desired for herself. Therefore, it can be said, that her educational career had turned according to the orientations of people she mixed with and to personal relationships she in the meantime developed. This transformation is a process in her search for an identity, and is dominated by traditional values recognised in her new environment. Although studying in higher education continues to be included in her plans, it is evident in her account that she was now moving to different directions, changing her dispositions towards her studies and forming aspirations that are linked to conditions and circumstances falling outside the institution. Her educational career in higher education, though seems to be valued in terms of its contribution to her personal growth, has not been proved significant: now a new person, "the working girl", is emerging. It is evident from her account that Emilia's educational career is influenced by external structures, her striving for her own agency, and unpredictable events. As already mentioned, her decision to participate in higher education was in important respects motivated by her boyfriend, and, as she states in the second interview, the break up of this relationship had affected dramatically her emotional stability. Then the support her uncle offered by facilitating for her in finding a job in a bank, and in fact guiding her to the job market, her socialisation with other persons, and a new relationship, all contributed significantly to how she perceives her educational career vis-à-vis her life plans. Emilia tends to shift from one condition where studies are considered to be important mainly in relation to social recognition, to another, where social recognition is immediate and can be achieved through the employment in socially acceptable jobs.

> "If it wasn't for some people [uncle] I would still be back in the department. Now... I have evolved and gone in another sector and I have other interests. Within my interests, still is the department, but now it has another role... perhaps secondary [...]. I decided that during this time I am more in need of experience, in need of work, I would like to go into this... because it motivates me, it gives me willpower, and some time, I 'll also finish my studies."

"My boyfriend says... to think again and pursue my studies, warmer, to get it [the degree] and perhaps I should study German a bit more intensely ... to also do postgraduate studies... and we will go to Germany.... [...] I wanted something different two years ago, ... it's different dreams I pursue today, two years ago, I wanted, and I was dreaming to be a career woman... and I would have liked to devote myself to a subject,... and I wanted to be the first name ... As time passes, I have changed 360 degrees and say now that I want to have a family. I don't know why, how this has changed like that. Its ok to work..., back in the day, I was saying I would even do work at home, I would do this and that. Now I am saying, my 8 hours of work, to come back home and see my family. I was also heavily influenced by my social environment, most of my friends have families, they have children, because my friends are older... and I am saying maybe I should slowly start pursuing a family ... my plans have changed a lot... And the only certain thing is that I am not a career woman, I am a family woman... My dream, the biggest dream of my life is to have a family, to have my children, my husband... Another goal is money, a dream besides family is to make a big fortune to leave to my children..."

The importance that social recognition has for Emilia does not necessarily limit us to a psychological explanation of her choices. This need for social recognition is heavily influenced by her gender and social positioning. The differences between her own background and the people she is socialising with seems to be played out constantly in her life trajectory. The latter didn't discourage her, on the contrary it seems that they supported her in her "struggle to be an actor" (McDonald, 1999, p. 11) in a field where she was situated at the time of the second interview, and in which she herself feels more confident about her abilities to exert control over her career. As she states, in her working environment her colleagues say: "Emilia is easily adapted to the situation, she is a "peoples' person", sociable, and receptive to others' ideas; she can influence other people, she is really good with banking, and she can persuade the customers." Despite her self-confidence it appears that she accepts traditional roles (such as the role of a *'family woman'*). Her case indicates that changes in young peoples' educational career might link to incidents and situations both inside and outside educational institutions (see also Bloomer and Hodkinson, 2000b).

On the contrary Fedra appeared to lack confidence in herself. Her pedagogic identity is unstable and it is her working class identity which is prevalent.

"... I am tired... and also being away, and ... at this point I have lost interest for my studies. Because I have started having difficulties, also for that. Because I am stuck, I have difficulties at a module... This module is a chain module [passing this module is a prerequisite to taking the next one in the chain], cataloguing. I haven't failed any of my modules to say that I am falling behind, and ... [...] I am interested in my studies, but this "failure", I feel I am doing nothing, that I am stuck. I don't want to stay here anymore, this has tired me, I want to rest".

In conclusion, our data analysis shows that educational choices involve complex social processes. Furthermore, analysis of the cases above shows that learning careers are not linear even when the transformations are slow and not easily discernible. That is, the exposures entailed in the pursuit of aspirations might lead young people into interesting careers such as research and academic jobs or into directions that may put at risk previously hard won positions with H.E. institutions.

5. Discussion and conclusions

The theoretical framework of the study, the design of the research in two stages and the construction of methodological tools such as the creation of an Educational Career and a Divergence index contributed decisively to the understanding of educational choices and the transformations in the values, beliefs and dispositions of young people towards their studies. These methodological decisions helped to facilitate the study of educational choices and trajectories in an integrated way and made possible the examination of structural issues together with agency, as important factors in decision making on subject choice and educational career development.

The cases presented here provide insights on important issues concerning the educational choices and students trajectories, and it should be noted that their "stories" reflect the accounts of many other participants in the study. It was clear from the interviews, that pursuing an educational career is not only a cognitive but also a social and cultural phenomenon. The students' dispositions towards their learning and education are linked to the wider social context and to the social conditions of their lives (see also Bloomer and Hodkinson, 2000b). Specifically, the cases illustrate three types of chooser who develop different learning careers:

The first is the type of the embedded choosers (Ball *et a.l.*,2002), those who are involved with their studies. Students coming from families with a significant amount of cultural capital respond to situations requiring from them to make decisions according to the dispositions of individual and family habitus, in interaction with the institutional habitus. They are also in a position to perceive differently the information field, to formulate aspirations and to think about educational and professional trajectories, which not only are "privileged" but seem also to be viable for people of their social position (Bourdieu, 1984; Power *et al.*, 2003).

The second is the type of the contingent choosers, those who have strong elements of lower social class as the basis of their identity. Individuals of this type did not have their aspirations changed significantly. Moreover, their horizons of actions remained constrained and their future plans were affected by values and expectations of their family environment. In those cases social structures dominated over students' possibilities of controlling their decisions. These students were not able to address effectively educational opportunities and important educational issues while the institutions failed to counter this socially shaped process.

Finally, individuals in the third type of choosers do not seem to have the ability to exert control over their social circumstances and are affected by happenstance or personal relations. These forces can help to open interesting options for them or on the contrary to lead them to completely different paths, which may endanger their prospects.

The research findings support partially the social reproduction theory of Bourdieu. More specifically, although the transformations in learning careers are influenced by the individual habitus, by the context whereby the habitus has been developed and by the person's positioning, the institutional habitus, personal relations, and finally accidental and unforeseen events also influenced the ways young people perceive and interact with the education field. But it must be stressed that the ways the latter are assessed and become part of students' lives are also strongly influenced both by their social backgrounds and their always socially shaped previous educational experiences.

Efforts made by young people to administer their position in the information field, and to formulate aspirations and construct new identities, is a continuing process, which is constantly under negotiation. Despite the fact that this process shows to be affected by structural factors, it was also altered as life experiences changed through the students' interactions with new persons, ideas and images encountered in the new environment in which they were being socialised.

References

Archer, L., Hutchings, M. and Ross, A., (2003). *Higher Education and Social Class: Issues of Exclusion and Inclusion,* Routledge Falmer, London.

Ball, S. J., (2003). *Class Strategies and the Education Market: the Middle Classes and Social Advantage,* Routledge Falmer, London.

Ball, S., Davies, J., David. M., and Reay, D., (2002). Classification and judgment': social class and the 'cognitive structures' of choice of higher Education, *British Journal of Sociology of Education,* Vol. *23,* No.1, 51-72.

Bernstein, B., (1971). On the classification and framing of educational knowledge. In M.F.D. Young (Ed.), *Knowledge and Control.* Collier-Macmillan, London.

Bernstein, B., (2000). *Pedagogy, Symbolic Control and Identity: Theory, Research, Critique,* Rowman & Littlefied, Boston.

Bloomer, M., (1997). *Curriculum Making in post-16 Education: The Social Conditions of Studentship,* Routledge, London.

Bloomer, M. and Hodkinson P., (1999). *College Life: the Voice of the Learner,* FEDA Publications, London.

Bloomer, M., and Hodkinson, P., (1997). *Moving into FE: The Voice of the Learner,* FEDA Publications, London.

Bloomer, M., and Hodkinson, P., (2000a). The complexity and unpredictability of young people's learning careers, *Education and Training,* Vol.,42, No.2, 68-74.

Bloomer, M., and Hodkinson, P., (2000b). Learning careers: continuity and change in young people's disposition to learning, *British Educational Research Journal,* Vol.26, No. 5, 583- 598.

Bourdieu, P., (1977). *Outline of a Theory of Practice,* Cambridge University Press, Cambridge.

Bourdieu, P., (1984). *Distinction: a Social Critique of the Judgement of Taste,* Harvard University Press, Cambridge.

Bourdieu, P., (1993). *Sociology in Question,* Sage, London.

Bourdieu, P., (1990). *The Logic of Practice,* Polity Press, Cambridge.

Bourdieu, P., (1997). The forms of capital. In A.H., Halsey, H. Lauder, P.Brown,. and A.S.Wells (Eds), *Education, Culture, Economy, Society* (pp. 46-58). Oxford University Press, Oxford.

Bowman, H., Colley, H.and Hodkinson, P., (2004). Employability and Career Progression for Full Time UK Resident Masters Students, Interim report for the higher education careers service unit.

Bryman, A., (1988). *Quantity and Quality in Social Research,* Unwin Hyman, London.

Cohen, L., and Manion, L., (1994). *Research Methods in Education* (4th ed.), Routledge, London.

Evans, J., (2000). *Adults' Mathematical Thinking and Emotions: A Study of Numerate Practices,* RoutledgeFalmer, London.

Hodkinson, P., and Bloomer, M., (2001). Dropping out of further education: complex causes and simplistic policy assumptions, *Research Papers in Education,* Vol.12, No.2, 117-140.

Hodkinson, P. and Sparkes, A., (1997). "Careership: a sociological theory of career decision making", *British Journal of Sociology of Education,* Vol. 18, No. 1, 29-44.

Lambiri-Dimaki, J. (Ed.), (1983). *Social Stratification in Greece, 1962-1982,* Sakkoulas, Athens. [in Greek]

McDonough, P., (1997). *Choosing Colleges: How Social Class and Schools Structure Opportunity,* State University of New York Press, New York.

Mestheneos, E., and Ioannidi-Kapolou, E. (2002). Gender and family in the development of Greek state and society. In P. Chamberlayne, M. Rustin and T. Wengraf (Eds.), *Biography and social exclusion in Europe, experiences and life journeys* (pp.175-192). Polity Press, Bristol.

Miles, M.B, and Huberman, A.M., (1994). *An Expanded Sourcebook: Qualitative Data Analysis (*2nd ed.), Sage Publications, London.

Moniarou-Papaconstantinou, V. and Tsatsaroni, A., (2008). Library and information science education in Greece: institutional changes and current issues, *Education for Information, Special Issue: Greek LIS Education,* Vol. 26, No. 2,. 85-100.

Moniarou-Papaconstantinou, V., (2009). Library and Information Science as a Field of Study: Socio-Cultural Influences on Students' Educational Choices and Trajectories, Phd thesis, University of Peloponnese, Department of Social and Educational Policy, Corinth.

Moniarou –Papaconstantinou, V., Tsatsaroni, A., Katsis, A., and Koulaidis V. LIS as a field of study: socio- cultural influences on students' decision making. (In press in Aslib Proceedings: New Information Perspectives).

Patton, M.Q., (2002)**.** Qualitative Research and Evaluation Methods 3rd ed., Sage Publications, Thousant Oaks, Ca.

Power, S., Edwards, T., Whitty, G., and Wingfall, V., (2003). *Education and the Middle Class,* Open University Press, Buckingham.

Reay, D., David, M., and Ball, S., (2001). Making a difference?: Institutional habituses and higher education choice, *Sociological Research Online,* Vol.5, No.4: http://socresonline.org.uk/5/4/ reay.html.

Reay, D., (1998). 'Always knowing' and 'never being sure': Familial and institutional habituses and higher education choice", *Journal of Education Policy,* Vol. 13, No. 4, 519-529.

Reay, D., David, M. and Ball, S., (2005). *Degrees of Choice: Class, Race, Gender and Higher Education,* Trentham Books, Stoke on Trent.

Sianou-Kyrgiou, E., (2010). Stratification in higher education, choice and social inequalities in Greece, Higher Education Quarterly, Vol.64, No.1, 22-40.

Wacquant, L.J.D., (1992). Towards a social praxeology: the structure and logic of Bourdieu's sociology. In P.Bourdieu and L.J.D Wacquant, *An Invitation to Reflexive Sociology* (pp.1-59). Polity Press in Association with Blackwell Publishers, Cambridge.

Warren, C.A., (2002). Qualitative interviewing. In J.F. Gubrium,. and J.A Holstein (Eds.), *Handbook of Interview Research* (pp.83-103)*.* Sage Publications, London.

Chapter 5. Users and Their Behaviours

Using Qualitative Approach for a Psychographic Segmentation of the Users of Library Services

Chiara Faggiolani

Scuola Speciale per Archivisti e Bibliotecari, Sapienza Università di Roma, Italy
Phd in Library and Information Science

Abstract: The paper reflects on the methods used to carry out user segmentation and the positioning of library services in comparison to other forms of cultural offers through the use of the qualitative approach. The reflection is based on the results of an in-progress investigation into the users of four libraries belonging to the City Library Network (one main library and three satellite public libraries) in Perugia, a city in the centre of Italy with 160,000 inhabitants. On an operational level, the investigation foresaw the use of questionnaires, face-to-face interviews and focus group interviews. Regarding user segmentation, specifically the possibility to simplify the market (in our case both real and potential) by dividing it into the most homogeneous segments of users possible and also the most different, we are encouraged to enquire if when examining libraries, like other forms of cultural consumption, the socio-demographic variables are still efficiently discriminating.
Demographic and socio-economic variables, such as age, gender, income and social class, widely used in analyses of library service users due to the fact they are easily accessed and inexpensive, nowadays risk being considered out-dated, as their treatment of user needs and desires is superficial and leaves a discrete margin of imprecision in dealing with the advantages and disadvantages of library services. Using qualitative survey techniques, our aim was to carry out a psychographic segmentation of the library user which would allow us to identify within the potential user basin homogeneous groups characterized by a shared image of what the library represents to them, sharing similar tastes, perceptions and habits, to whom the library can offer made-to-measure services through appropriate strategies in line with their preferences and expectations.
Keywords: Grounded theory, qualitative method, interview, focus group, psychographic segmentation, ATLAS.ti

1. Introduction

This contribution wishes to offer some considerations and make some suggestions for new hypotheses of development for the field of enquiry, which have recently attracted the interest of academics in the sphere of biblioteconomy which focuses on the management and organization of libraries, represented by the segmentation of the users of library services.

This research is in line with a new tendency within Italian biblioteconomy which, having understood the limitations of exclusively quantitative evaluation, based on performance indicators, seeking, by means of techniques of qualitative enquiry, to

New Trends in Qualitative and Quantitative Methods in Libraries
A. Katsirikou and C. H. Skiadas (eds)
© *World Scientific Publishing Co (pp. 241-248)*

examine the complex dynamics governing the subjective aspects of motivation, needs and the perception of what constitutes quality for users.

Acting on the supposition that traditional forms of the categorisation of libraries is inadequate (Galluzzi, 2009) it follows naturally to assume that the next step would be to question and test the concept of "institutional usage": the idea that every type of library (university, specialised, public library, etc.) has its own, very specific user-base to satisfy, based more on the basis of the institutional mission than verified needs, seems an over-simplification and impoverishment of a concept of usage which is a great deal more complex in terms of needs, requirements to satisfy, behavioural patterns and perceptions, therefore running the risk of labeling the contents in a reductive, over-simplistic way.

It is impossible to ignore how within library user-bases you can observe different needs and requirements which range from the wish to improve one's education, the desire to share and socialise, a need for peace and quiet in order to concentrate, but also for entertainment whatever professional branch a person is in, whatever his/her gender or age (as demonstrated by youthful life-styles led by older people).

Obviously, one must be aware of the risks of a generalised and generic ratio of library/user with which the library risks losing clarity of vision of its objectives and finalities. Naturally, one must remember that nowadays, thanks to the Internet, information service users are used to gathering information and data wherever they may find it, without worrying overtly about whether it is found in the "right place".

One can speak of users as socially complex subjects, characterised by transversal perceptions, motivations and needs which cannot be identified beforehand and which in order to be analysed require the implementation of two tools: first of all, the multi-discipline approach to the formulation of the questions and secondly, knowledge of "non-conventional" research instruments, not least of which, the interpretative capacity of the researcher.

The concept of "fluidity" (Bauman, 2007) of the individual can only point us to the need to evaluate the individual through a holistic approach is necessary also in the field of biblioteconomy, thus re-evaluating interpretation as a new research instrument, offering a means of obtaining a deeper understanding of the needs, motivations and perceptions of the user-base, although still aware that these are not linked to satisfaction and thus to the use of a library in an exclusively deterministic and causal relationship.

The equation which places the satisfied user making full use of a library and contrarily, the unsatisfied user avoiding using the library, ignores several factors, such as the quality of the individual's personal experience of libraries, the expectations that an individual may have regarding library use, the identity he or she perceives in such institutions and the ideal service which one might imagine, all of which could be seen to be potentially weakening factors to the net causal use/satisfaction or non-use/dissatisfaction of libraries, obfuscating or causing misinterpretation of the attitudes or behavioural patterns of the users.

These considerations stem from an empirical enquiry about the user-base of the City Library Network of Perugia, a central Italian city with 160,000 inhabitants, which, through the application of mixed techniques, aims not simply at photographing a single representative moment of library usage and at verifying, by means of questionnaires, whether he or she is satisfied, but one which attempts to dig much deeper, transforming the two-dimensional image into a three-dimensional one, complete with elements of psychology and subjectivity as the analysis reaches deeper into underlying meanings of language and communicative tools used by the library users (through qualitative interviews and focus groups).

The enquiry also aims at being a reflection on methodology, rooted in the thesis that sees the dicotomy "qualitative versus quantitative" as something belonging to the past, indicating complimentarity of the two approaches as the route to take (Campelli, 1999), which would require spending a little time in comparing the results obtained by using different research techniques.

The results of the comparison highlighted, above all, how the identification of typologies and clusters of users produced quite different results, as well as different types of data (*hard* vs *soft*). This generated the question which this enquiry aims to answer: are socio-demographic variables still to be considered discriminating when applied to libraries and cultural consumption in general?

This is the thesis we support and which we wish to demonstrate with this enquiry: "the demographic criterion and the study of personality cannot shed light on the attempts of individuals to unite with others in homogeneous groups. New variables able to segment, based on the conviction that cultural mentalities, styles and attitudes are better suited to identify diversity, can be perceived. The attempt was made to create segmentations using these types of variables as a starting point to identify consumer targets (segments) characterised by shared attitudes, values, interests and cultural outlooks which will contribute to creating a homogeneous cultural sub-group within the society all members belong to [...]. Thus, through a process of "differentiation" and of "change" of the consumer, we have reached a point of weakening and even of disappearance of differences which once distinguished categories of people defined on a basis of socio-demographic segmentation criteria" (Quadrelli, Riva, Siri, 2004).

Taken from other fields of discipline (management and marketing, for example), this type of experience is very much consolidated, and in this present contribution it will be used to describe the characteristics of a possible segmentation of the user-base of libraries which would allow for the identification within the potential clients of homogeneous groups characterized by a common representation of the library, to whom the institutions can offer, by means of appropriate strategies, services which satisfy the wishes and expectations expressed.

2. New variables: Sociality, curiosity and free-time

At the roots of the empirical investigation, the starting point for this reflection, is the awareness that for libraries, too, the capacity to interpret and know one's environment is a vital condition in order to be able to place oneself in a position of competitiveness within that reality.

It is indeed a "necessary condition" if a library can hope to satisfy the complexity of a demand characterised by two aspects: *variety* seen as a continual need for personalization of the service and *variability* seen as continual transformation of needs and requirements.

Interpreting and knowing the user also means bringing the relationship with the library within the context of social dynamics, in line with the context of the individual's life, his search for, and expression of, personal identity, "or rather better than the many identities which the new social actor interprets and shares. In post-modern society the concept of self is iridescent and fluid, polymorphic, multi-dimensional. Chameleonism, the many social masks – without attributing a judgmental dimension to these terms – which we wear, as we act our way through our daily lives, represent important poles for discussion for any sort of analysis" (Siri, 2004).

The value of libraries depends on the relationship users have with them and on the characteristics of the environment in which they are situated; it is the immaterial factor which very often has the greatest importance. It is the way in which each single individual experiences the library which allows us to identify critical issues we need to face: "satisfaction can arise from different causes but may not necessarily express satisfaction for the service itself but for a condition of the spirit" (Poulain, 2002). This is the "emerging" theory of data analysis carried out during numerous *focus group* sessions and in-depth interviews conducted according to Grounded Theory methodology: this theory, as the methodology foresees, is generated by an iterative process which requires a continual sample collection and constant analysis of quantitative data collected in concrete settings.

In this perspective, emerging theory means the development of a conceptualisation of the phenomenon being investigated which, as time goes on, distances itself from a simple description of data, whilst attempting to supply explanations able to shed light on underlying processes and relationships. (Strauss, Corbin, 1998).

The techniques used have allowed for the substitution of numbers and percentages with living experiences and perceptions recreated through a narrative of those experiences, the justifications supplied, the meanings given to them and the examples which the users themselves personify.

The *story line*, identified by means of data analysis carried out with the support of the text qualitative analysis software, ATLAS.ti, highlighted the high degree to which the perception of real users of the libraries being examined (*brand image*) was conditioned not only by their sense of satisfaction with the service on offer, but also by previous experiences with libraries, by the ability to transcend the stereotyped vision of libraries as cold, unfriendly institutions, detached from the users themselves and, lastly, by the ideal of the library as an integral part of the specific circumstances within which the user lives.

One could consider the concept of "situational" usage more relevant than institutional usage: "people are infinitely complex and flexible and can constantly change their minds regarding choices. In our postmodern society there are no sets of permanent values or needs and they are all subject to situational changes" (Locatelli, Perduca, 2004).

The choice of whether or not to use libraries and the choice of how to use them depend on various factors which contribute to creating those very specific circumstances which makes a person choose to use a library to satisfy specific needs which may or may not be linked to study and research. The same user in a different situation may opt for satisfying the same needs elsewhere.

Segmentation performed using socio-demographic variables appears extremely limiting, as does segmentation based on behavioural patterns or carried out by dividing the reference market into users and non-users and then again, into more or less frequent users, as such methods do not take into account the diversity of needs which might distinguish two equally regular users who make use of libraries with the same intensity but to satisfy quite different needs and objectives: one who goes there to study his own books in peace and quiet, another to carry out research and yet another as a way of spending his free-time.

Through the successive codifications (open, axial and selective), certain categories (*codes*) emerged, which, if read from the point of view of segmentation, can be considered as highly discriminating variables, and as such, are probably much more meaningful than socio-demographic ones.

The way in which users perceive their free time is also an important component in how they relate to using libraries. Free-time, which is greater in older, retired people who are thus free from work ties and in the young adult group of library users, in quantitative terms, when managed during the working life of a person, tends to be restricted and therefore used very carefully and rationally in an attempt to make the most of what is usually a limited resource.

Curiosity is another element which affects library use and it is tightly bound to the concept of exploration and adventure which a user may perceive in his approach to these institutions: the curious user will tend to use libraries whether or not he has a specific need for specific data, and will simply let himself go instinctively in a free and objective-free exploration.

Closely connected to this aspect is the variable degree of need for training, as users who are less open and curious will need greater stimuli from the library.

Add to these aspects, the other needs a library caters to: study, socialisation, interaction with the community and even simply as a meeting-place, as the conceptual network of the ideal library which emerged from the codification of the data demonstrates. (Figure 1).

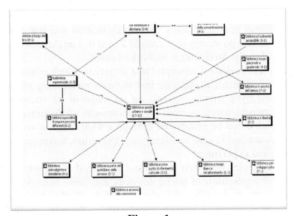

Figure 1

3. Towards psychographic segmentation

Psychographic enquiries focus on so-called life-styles, identified through variable factors which include habits, tastes, diet, use of mass media, health-consciousness and other social and psychological factors.

Regarding the concept of segmentation, understood as a simplified picture of the market, the sensation is that the use of socio-demographic variables is no longer able to provide a clear, precise image and actually impoverishes through banalisation the concept of simplification of the market: "whilst the socio-demographic approach takes into consideration behaviour and consumption (in our case, the type of reading performed, the books ordered or requested as reference material, sites visited, etc.), a variable dependant on demographics (for example age or academic titles), the physiographic segmentation works on a totally different basis since it considers the tastes and habits to be the starting point for categorizations in homogeneous groups to be analysed, even according to the classic demographic variables, considered complimentary" (Parise, 2008).

Having moved beyond the concept of socio-demographic variables, it must be remembered that library users cannot be fitted neatly into the notion of the individual as a purely economical subject who is also a psychological subject – that is to say, "no longer considered a rational machine built to calculate costs and benefits in consumer processes, but rather, a complex personality, characterized by ever-changing representations of self, able to elaborate environmental data whilst under the influence of emotional factors, processes of culturally influenced signification which are often sub-conscious" (Siri, 2006).

From the empirical enquiry, we can note how it was easier to describe the different user profiles by examining attitudes and wishes, rather than gender, age, academic titles, etc. Perhaps surprisingly, we find that both young students, who find libraries the ideal place to study, and young children, who feel reassured by the order and calm of these spaces, share the common concept of libraries as places of "tranquility" and "concentration".

Among those who see libraries as centres of socialization, there are both young adults and elderly people, to whom these spaces offer an almost unique opportunity for dialogue and interaction.

Furthermore, the use of transversal, multidisciplinary research does not belong solely to young academics, as one might imagine, but also to the eighty year old pensioner who, if asked, "What is a library for you?", might reply "Well, research, first of all, probably divided into branches, one's own specialisation and transversal links and anything which can add positively to it…while I'm at it, I might as well take a look at some other field of study. Study like a network of roads".

The above examples illustrate a concept: "in a society in which contamination is ever more frequent, it is difficult to imagine that the new positioning of public libraries could be instigated by a simple *reductio ad un unum* of its vocation, rather than following its pluralistic nature – both as a receptacle of documents and a social infrastructure which could be manifested through a wide range of services, making it appealing to everyone and in a personalized way"(Severino, Solimine, 2008).

4. A methodological experiment

Physiographical enquiries were first carried out at the end of the sixties and originate from the practical application of social sciences and from behavioural studies to market research: these describe the characteristics of the personalities of the user/consumer which may influence attitudes towards products, relative communication and also, in our field of interest, libraries. This attempt to verify a possible segmentation of library user-bases has been carried out by using the local context, the Italian social reality, as a reference point, taking a closer look at the origins and the evolution of psycho-graphical segmentation in the solely Italian context. In Italy, the main physiographer is Sinottica, part of Eurisko (http://www.gfk.com), the research institute, and it published its first edition in 1975. This is an integrated system of information relative to socio-cultural evolution and the behavioural patterns of Italians and which boasts both strategic and tactical instruments of analysis.

Sinottica is a single-source enquiry on the characteristics of the individual, his behavioural patterns, life-style and even his consumer habits and his relationship to communications. This is an annual enquiry and requires the once-yearly interviewing of 10,000 one-to-one interviews carried out at the homes of a sampling of adult (over 14) male and female members of the Italian population.

The physiographer produces the Great Map (Figure 2), an instrument with which one may focus on and interpret any phenomenon or characteristic of the population, whether it be structural or more specifically behavioural or attitudinal in nature. The map is by definition "unique", and a sit is a standard instrument, it can be applied to all sectors.

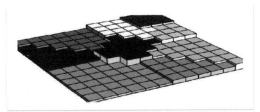

Figure 2

The Great Map originates at the meeting-point of two fundamental dimensions: the "masculine" dimension on the horizontal axis with the positive pole to the right and which includes individuals who are not necessarily males but who possess "hard features", that is to say, those interested in social confrontation, usually competitive, self-focusing in prioritizing achievements, projected towards discovery of the external world. The "feminine" dimension, on the other hand, on the vertical axis, includes individuals who, although not necessarily female, will exhibit "softer features": this is the dimension of moderation, containment and balance. The criterion which determine the exact positioning of each individual on the map depend on the degree of possession of hard and/or soft features.

In order to permit a deeper analysis, the map has been sub-divided into "cells" of approximately equal sizes, which are then used in all the analyses to identify and understand the greatest and least concentrations of analysed phenomena on the map. Every cell is then further sub-divided into 9 micro cells for a total of 144 micro cells.

Sinottica thus projects "Life-styles" onto the map, dividing the adult Italian population according to social behaviour and consumer patterns. The segmentation is based on a combination of 47 personal characteristics elaborated with a mixed technique of analyses of the highly varied groups and of algorhythms of conditioned classification. The result is a sub-division into profile types, which remain unvaried through time, with verified descriptive capacity within multiple research contexts (Figure 3).

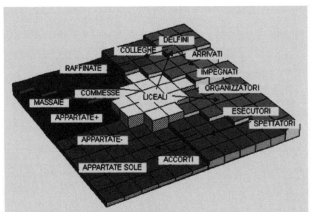

Figure 3

From the original 14 profiles we moved on to a more evoluted and precise segmentation which had already, several years ago, foreseen the categorising of some styles into sub-groups (for example, the *Loners* style into three sub-groups and more recently the sub-division of the *Arrived* style into two sub-categories, "Exuberant" and "Moderate").

Each life-style identifies a very specific way of living, thinking, working, consumer behavior and thus also the attitude towards libraries, although no direct reference to this is made in the descriptive profiles.

The methodological experiment consisted in comparing the characteristics of life-styles elaborated by Sinottica with the codes and conceptual categories relative to attitudes towards the libraries under examination which emerged from the codification of data obtained through Qualitative Interviews and Focus Groups.

Without becoming involved in the details of the results of the empirical research, in line with the aims of this contribution, perhaps it is more useful to draw more general conclusions applicable to all those attempts/researches carried out by libraries with the aim of segmenting their user-base.

The recurrent overlap in attitudes which are inherent to certain life-styles and certain codes can indicate which segments of the user-base represent the most frequent users of the library being examined and which benefit most from the features on offer, in as much as they are coherent with the users' own values, whilst also indicating which segments are "missing". This type of analysis could offer useful information for applying corrective measures and for designing ad hoc communication strategies to the library aiming at attracting specific absent segments by focusing on the "perceptive characteristics" which belong to that group.

References

- Bauman Z. (2007), *Homo consumens. Lo sciame inquieto dei consumatori e la miseria degli esclusi,* Edizioni Erickson, Trento.
- Campelli E., (1999). *Da un luogo comune. Elementi di metodologia delle scienze sociali*, Franco Angeli, Milano.
- Cicognani E. (2002), *Psicologia sociale e ricerca qualitativa*, Carocci, Roma.
- Dalton P., Elkin J., Hannaford A., (2006). *Joint Use Libraries as Successful Strategic Alliances* in Library Trends – Vol. 54, Number 4, Spring, pp. 535-548.
- Galluzzi A., (2009). *Biblioteche per la città. Nuove prospettive di un servizio pubblico*, Carocci, Roma.
- *La ricerca sul consumatore. Domande di marketing e prodotti classici*, (2006), a cura di Giovanni Siri, McGraw-Hill, Milano.
- Locatelli L. Perduca S., (2004). *Qualitativo e quantitativo*, in *Psicologia del consumatore. Consumi e costruzioni del significato*, a cura di Giovanni Siri, Mc Graw Hill, Milano.
- Parise S., (2008). *La formazione delle raccolte nelle biblioteche pubbliche*, Editrice Bibliografica, Milano.
- Poulain M. (2002), *La percezione della biblioteca: metodi e strumenti per l'analisi dei pubblici*, in Comunicare la biblioteca, Atti del convegno di Milano 15-16 marzo 2001, a cura di Ornella Foglieni, Editrice Bibliografica, Milano.
- Severino F., Solimine G. (2008), *Un nuovo modello di biblioteca civica. Il caso Idea Store di Londra*, in "Economia della cultura", 18 (2008), n. 2.
- Strauss A.L., Corbin J. (1998), *Grounded Theory Methodology: an overview*, in N. K. Denzin, Y.S. Lincoln, *Strategies of qualitative inquiry*, Sage, Thousand Oaks.

Do We Know Image Users?

Marija Petek

Department of Library and Information Science and Book Studies, Faculty of Arts, University of Ljubljana, Slovenia

Abstract: There are millions of digital images available and their use has been increasing. Image users are very diverse, from professional users to users searching for fun. An image can be seen and described in a different way by different users. What the user sees depends on his perception and cognitive processes. The purpose of this paper is to examine how users describe images. Students of the University of Ljubljana are surveyed on a random sample of images taken from Digital Library of Slovenia and Flickr in order to assign tags to each image. The tags are grouped into categories of image attributes such as objects, place, time, etc. and compared to tags assigned by Slovene library professionals and Flickr visitors. Finally, the obtained data are investigated to ascertain whether differences in tagging practices exist among students, library professionals and Flickr users.
Keywords: Digital images, image retrieval, describing images, visual perception, tagging, folksonomy, Flickr, Digital Library of Slovenia

1. Introduction

There are millions of digital images available and their use has been increasing, especially via the Internet. Image users are very diverse, from professional users such as art historians and designers to users searching for fun. An image can be seen and described in a different way by different users. What the user sees depends on his perception and cognitive processes as there is a difference between physical properties of the image and how it is perceived. So, discrepancies between users' and cataloguers' view of the image may exist.

The purpose of this paper is to examine image users' behavior and to find out what users see in the images and how they describe them. Students of the Department of Library and Information Science and Book Studies of the Faculty of Arts at the University of Ljubljana are surveyed on a random sample of images taken from Digital Library of Slovenia and Flickr in order to assign tags to each image. The tags are analysed and grouped into categories of attributes such as objects, place, time, etc. The tags assigned by students are compared to tags added by Slovene library professionals and Flickr visitors to investigate how well they match up. Finally, the obtained data are investigated to ascertain whether differences in tagging practices exist among students, librarians and Flickr users.

Digital Library of Slovenia (dLib.si, http://www.dlib.si) is a web portal providing free access to digitised knowledge and cultural treasures containing more than 300.000 documents published on the Web and on traditional media. Launched in November 2005 it offers access to various collections meaning that users are able to read, watch or listen to resources:

New Trends in Qualitative and Quantitative Methods in Libraries
A. Katsirikou and C. H. Skiadas (eds)
© *World Scientific Publishing Co (pp. 249-259)*

- text (scientific and scholarly articles, articles from old Slovene newspapers, books, education publications covering natural, social and library sciences)
- visual resources (photographs of Slovene poets and other famous persons - more than 10.50 items; posters such as advertising, promotional, film, war posters - more than 4.000 items; postcards; vedutas; caricatures; drawings; art library; manuscript; maps; sheet music)
- sound recordings (solo singers and ensembles)
- multimedia (virtual exibitions).

Users may search by bibliographic data such as author, title, publisher, publishing date, content, type of material. The content of items is indexed by library professionals using the Slovene controlled vocabulary. Users are also allowed to describe images and all other documents by assigning their own tags as well as removing inappropriate tags; however this feature has not been largely used so far.

2. Social tagging systems

Social tagging systems being characteristic of Web 2.0 allow Internet users to store, classify, share and search lists of bookmarked resources such as Web pages (Delicious, http://delicious.com/), blogs (Technorati, http://technorati.com/), academic references (CiteUlike, http://www.citeulike.org/), photographs, videos, etc. Tagging content is an act of organizing through labelling, a way of making sense of various items according to their meaning (Golder and Huberman, 2006). Tags are freely chosen keywords, a kind of metadata describing an item and allowing it to be found again; also considered as a tool to find similar items serving as a link to new items tagged the same way by others. They are usually added informally and personally by the item's creator or by its viewer, depending on the system. Popular tags in social tagging systems are referred as to folksonomy (Marlow, Naaman, Boyd and Davis, 2006). The term folksonomy is introduced by Vander Wal (2006) consisting of two words "folk" and "taxonomy" describing practice of tagging, the purpose of which is to add meaning to the particular piece of information or object. Vander Wal defines the folksonomy as a bottom-up social classification without hierarchy and without specified relationships among terms. The folksonomy is unlike formal taxonomies and classification schemes determining explicit relationships including broader, narrower or related terms. According to Vander Wal there are two types of folksonomies: broad and narrow. Broad folksonomies are those where many users tag the same item such as the same URL on Delicious. Narrow folksonomies are defined as those where users usually tag content for their own benefit like on Flickr. The folksonomy is also known as social tagging, collaborative tagging, tagsonomy, distributed classification, social classification, social indexing, ethnoclassification.

Flickr (http://www.flickr.com) developed in 2004 is a popular image and video hosting service. In October 2009 it hosted more than 4 billion of images indicating its phenomenal growth. Users are required to create an account and then they are able to upload, store and share digital images. Users are prompted to provide a title, a caption and a list of tags about each item. Tags being not obligatory can be added at the time of upload or later on. Users may describe each image by assigning up to 75 tags. Flickr is primarily used by individuals to manage their own photos and the majority of tags is created by themselves; users are also allowed to tag other users' photos. Images can be made private only for personal use, or made public if users want their images to be viewed by others. Besides, users can create networks of friends, join groups, send messages, comment on photos, choose their favorite photos, etc.

3. Literature review

In spite of fast expansion of social tagging systems, these systems have not been studied in detail yet and there has been only a few empirical data available. Marlow et al. (2006) propose a conceptual model for tagging systems consisting of three elements and relationships among them: resources, users and tags. Users assign tags to resources, users and resources are connected by tags, resources may be connected to each other and users may be associated, too. Literature review deals with related work being concentrated on what individuals see in images and how they describe them, on tagging motivations, kinds of tags used and dynamics of tags.

Describing images

Jörgensen (1998) surveyed library science students asking them to describe six randomly selected color images. Descriptions were grouped into three main classes of image attributes:

1. perceptual classes referring to physical content of the image (objects, people, color, visual elements, location, description)

2. interpretive classes being stimulated perceptually but requiring additional interpretive and intellectual processes (people-related atttributes, art historical information, abstract contents, content/story, external relation)

3. reactive classes (viewer's response).

Greisdorf and O'Connor (2002) agree that description and meaning of the image is open to individual interpretation being an integrated process of perception and cognition. In their research participants were asked to assign pre-determined terms to images as well as to supply their own terms. They identified three hierarchical levels of perception in image retrieval:

1. primitive features (content-based retrieval): colour, shape, texture

2. objects: person, thing, place/location, action

3. inductive interpretation (subjective belief): symbolic value, prototypical displacement (atmospehere - general feeling and emotional cue).

When looking at images, according to Panofsky's three levels of meaning in the work of art, the primary (pre-iconographic) level is based on recognition of objects and factual information; the secondary (iconographic) level on interpretation of objects requiring familiarity with cultural context of the image; and the third (iconological) level determines intrinsic meaning of the image context (Angus, Thelwall and Stuart, 2008). Panofsky's theory was reiterated by Shatford-Layne identifying four general attributes of images (Angus, Thelwall and Stuart, 2008): biographical attributes; subject attributes (images may be both of and about something: what an image is of is usually concrete and objective – pre-iconographic; what an image is about is usually abstract and subjective – iconographic); exemplified and relationship attributes.

Tagging motivations

Mathes (2004) speaks about individual and community motivations being not mutually exclusive; users organize resources in their own way using their own vocabulary on the basis of individual information needs, but at the same time they want to share their resources with others; similarly Hammond et al. (2005) deal with selfish and altruistic motivations. Golder and Huberman (2006) examining Delicious report that a significant amout of tagging is done for personal benefit. Marlow et al. (2006) define organizational and social motivations; the first one is an alternative to structured filing and the second one expresses communicative nature of tagging where users can express themselves and convey their oppinions; users are simultaneously influenced by a variety of motivations. Ames and Naaman (2007) surveyed users of camera-phone application ZoneTag to tag and upload photos to Flickr and developed a taxonomy for tagging motivations consisting of two categories: sociality and function being further divided into self-organization, self-communication, social-organization, social-communication.

Kinds of tags

In their research Golder and Huberman (2006) identify seven functions of tags: what or who the bookmarked page is about (topics); what it is (e. g. article, blog, book); who owns it (or who created the content); refining categories (e. g. numbers); qualities or characteristics (e. g. funny, stupid, etc.); self-reference (e. g. "my", "mystuff", etc.) and task organizing (e. g. "toread", "jobsearch", etc.).

The first four functions may be useful to the Delicious community, but all other functions are relevant only to the tagger reflecting differences among individuals.

Stvilia and Jörgensen (2009) found out that Flickr users used eight criteria to group photos into photosets: activity, place, thing, person, artistic/photographic technique, random, time and quality; the most important were activity and place.

Dynamics of tags

Mathes (2004) suggests that used tags follow a power law distribution: the most used tags are more likely to be used by other users as they are more likely to be seen. Guy and Tonkin (2006) tested this hypothesis on Flickr and Delicious and found out that tag usage actually followed the power law distribution.

Golder and Huberman (2006) studied dynamics of tags on Delicious: how tags are used by users over time and how tags for resources change over time.

4. Research design

The purpose of this research is to examine users' behaviour when viewing and describing images. The following research questions are addressed to:

1. How users describe images, what do they see and what do they notice about images? How many tags do they use describing images, what kind of attributes are represented by tags?

2. What are/or would be users' motivations for tagging?

3. How well do users' created tags match up with keywords assigned by Slovene library professionals in dLib.si and with tags assigned by Flickr visitors?

A survey of 80 students of the Department of Library and Information Science and Book Studies of the Faculty of Arts at the University of Ljubljana was conducted in March 2010. The students were asked to describe 10 images by assigning tags to each image; the number of tags was not limited, so students were free to put down as many tags as they wanted. The images for the research were selected randomly: 5 images from dLib.si and 5 from Flickr; the images are included in Appendix. The dLIb.si images were taken from various collections: photographs, posters, postcards and art paintings; images containing tags added by users were excluded from the sample. The Flickr images were chosen from the following categories: Places, Last 7 Days, This Month, Popular Tags, The Commons. Then, these images were printed out together with all textual data such as: author, title, publisher, year, annotation, the dLib.si keywords and the Flickr tags. The tags assigned by surveyed students were first translated into English. Finally, the surveyed data were collected and analysed, added tags were grouped into attributes and classes of attributes and compared to original sets of data from dLib.si and Flickr. The tags assigned to the dLib.si images were compared to the tags added by Slovene library professionals, and the tags assigned to the Flickr images were compared to the tags given by Flickr visitors. Finally, the obtained data were investigated to ascertain whether differences in tagging practices exist among library professionals, students and Flickrs users.

4.1 Findings

1. How users describe images, what do they see and what do they notice about images? How many tags do they use describing images, what kind of attributes are represented by tags?

The surveyed students assigned 577 tags to 10 selected images. The average number of tags per image is 57,7 ranging from 44 to 86 tags. The average number of tags per user 7,2, ranging from 0 to 18 tags. Each image in Appendix contain the most frequently used tag and its frequency.

To investigate tags assigned during the survey we partly followed Jörgensen (1998) and used her categorization of image descriptions (e. g. sweater) into attributes (e. g. clothing) and classes of attributes (e. g. objects). This categorization consists of three main classes referring to perception, interpretation and reaction of image viewers. The main classes are divided into twelve classes of attributes and forty-seven attributes. As seen in Figure 1 perceptual attributes present the largest part: 54,6% and there are only a few reactive attributes. The dominating perceptual attributes suggest that in describing images, naming of primary visual content is typical and logical. It is interesting that the portion of interpretative attributes is rather high referring to frequently used attributes of the content/story class such as activity, event, time, etc. as well as attributes of the abstract concepts class (Table 2).

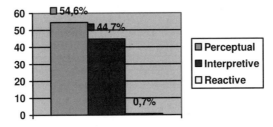

Figure 1: Main classes of image attributes

Table 1 shows frequency distributions of individual classes of attributes. The majority of tags 27,7% describe objects such as car, house, trees, giraffe, etc. It is followed by the content/story class with 20,5% consisting of attributes such as activity, event, time aspect, etc. The share of the abstract concepts class is 13,3%, etc. Our findings are similar to Jörgensen who also reports objects as the most frequently used class: 34,5%, followed by the color class with 9,2%, etc. Table 2 shows distribution of individual image attributes, the dominating ones are: objects 24,4%, abstract 11,4%, location-general 10,4% and people 9,4%; Jörgensen (1998) found out objects with 18,5% and people with 10,1% to be prevalent.

Comparing our findings to Stvilia and Jörgensen (2009) who claim that the most important criteria Flickr visitors use to group photos into photosets are activity 40,4%, place 24,6% and thing 11%, we may suggest that differences observed are due to different tasks and motivations of participants: the students being asked to describe imposed images on one side, and Flickr users organizing mostly their own photos on the other side.

Greisdorf and O'Connor (2002) conducted a research in which participants were asked to assign pre-determined query terms to images and their own terms. In the case of imposed terms categories such as color, shape and texture represented the largest share followed by affect/emotion. But in the case of user supplied terms the category affect/emotion represented the major part indicating the importance of the third level of perception, i. e. interpretation.

Table 1: Classes of image attributes

Classes	No. of tags	%
Objects	160	27,7
Content/story	118	20,5
Abstract concepts	77	13,3
Location	69	11,9
People	54	9,4
People-related	41	7,1
Art historical information	22	3,8
Colour	16	2,8
Visual elements	13	2,3
Personal response	4	0,7
Description	3	0,5
External relationship	0	0
TOTAL	577	100,0

Table 2: Individual attributes

Attributes	No. of tags	%
Objects	141	24,4
Abstract	66	11,4
Location-general	60	10,4
People	54	9,4
Activity	44	7,6
Time aspect	32	5,5
Emotion	27	4,7
Event	19	3,3
Color	16	2,8
Setting	14	2,4
Clothing	14	2,4
Atmosphere	11	1,9
Location-specific	9	1,6
Relationship	9	1,6
Body part	5	0,9
Perspective	5	0,9
Personal reaction	4	0,7
Other	47	8,1
TOTAL	577	100,0

According to semantic and cognitive aspects of tags we have observed some problems similar to the ones treated by Golder and Huberman (2006):
- synonymy (post – mail, postman – mailman)
- singulars and plurals (house – houses)
- generic and specific tags
    - trees, pine-trees, conifers
    - court, basketball court
    - grass, meadow
    - warm clothes, cap, gloves, trousers, scarf, sweater, shoes
- two/three-word-tags as opposed to two or three individual tags
    - mother and child; mother; child

- woman and daughter; woman; daughter
- different time aspects for the same image
    - summer, spring, autumn
    - morning, evening.

2. What are/or would be users' motivations for tagging?
The students in the survey were asked for motiviations to tag on Flickr but in case they did not use Flickr they were asked why they would tag. A majority of surveyed students 61,8% practice tagging on Flickr for personal benefit, 32,6% for community benefit and only a few for other reasons (Figure 2). Table 3 presents motivations in detail: 29,2% of students use Flickr to upload their own photos and 19,4% to tag their own photos, to tag for community benefit 7,6%. These findings are similar to Hammond et al. (2005) reporting that Flickr users mostly want to manage personal collections. As opposed to Hammond et al. (2005) Marlow et al. (2006) claim that Flickr users are primarily motivated by social incentives. Golder and Huberman (2006) report that a significant amout of tagging on Delicious is done for personal benefit. Ames and Naaman (2007) found social motivations to be the most common.

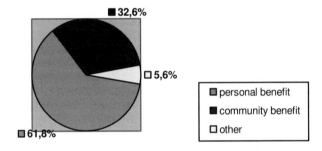

Figure 2: Tagging motivations

Table 3: Tagging motivations in detail

Motivations	No.	%
Uploading - personal	42	29,2
Tagging - personal	28	19,4
Sharing with friends, family	27	18,8
Organizing - personal	19	13,2
Tagging - community	11	7,6
Sharing with community	9	6,3
Looking for images	8	5,6
TOTAL	144	100,1

3. How well do users' created tags match up with keywords assigned by Slovene library professionals in dLib.si and with tags assigned by Flickr visitors?
The surveyed students assigned a much larger number of tags as compared to original data sets in dLib.si and Flickr. The students described the dLib.si images using 266 tags but these images had originally only 19 keywords. The Flickr images were assigned 311 tags and originally 92 tags. Comparing students' tags to original data sets it is observed that matching rate for all images is 41,4%; it is higher than expected. In Figure 3 it can be seen that matching is higher with the Flicker images i. e. 43,5%. However, we should be cautious as the number of keywords and the number of tags differs a lot. These results are only suggestive and more research is needed.

The tags assigned to the image no. 9 have got the best matching: 72,7%; the matched tags are Action – Attack - Chicago Wolves – Hockey – Ice - John Pohl – Rockfor – Sport. The tags Hockey and Ice were most frequently used by students; the former 44 times and the latter 34 times. The best matching among the dLib.si images has got the image no. 5 which has originally only 4 keywords, and 2 of them fit: House – Meadow. The tag Meadow was used 25 times, the most frequently tag used was Child (37 times). Table 4 presents data on matched tags in detail

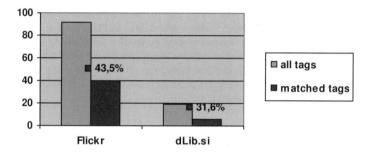

Figure 3: Matched tags on Flickr and dLib.si

Table 4: Matched tags with original data sets

Image no.	No. of tags (survey)	No. of tags (original set)	No.of matched tags	Matched tags %
1 - dLib.si	48	5	1	20
2 - Flickr	44	36	19	52,8
3 - dLib.si	49	4	1	25
4 - Flickr	71	7	3	42,9
5 - dLib.si	70	4	2	50
6 - Flickr	58	8	3	37,5
7 - Flickr	52	30	7	23,3
8 - dLib.si	51	3	1	33,3
9 - Flickr	86	11	8	72,7
10- dLib.si	48	3	1	33,3
	577	111	46	41,4

4. Conclusions

In this research we have observed tagging practices in describing selected images. It has been noticed that participants of our survey exhibit a great variety in tagging practice; some have got many tags and other have few; some tags are used by many participants, while other only by few. Tags vary in frequency of use and in what they describe. A majority of tags reflect perceptual attributes. Cognitive aspect of categorization has been evident, ranging from general to specific tags. Tagging is mostly done for personal benefit. The number of assigned tags differs greatly among participants, librarians and Flickr users; participants are heavy taggers while librarians assign only a few keywords. The matching of tags is better than expected especially with librarians but we should be cautious as the number of keywords is very small.

These results are only suggestive and more research is needed. To answer the question if we know image users, is not an easy task; we have provided some empirical data but we should go on examining processes of visual perception and cognition, so we have still to learn a lot. However, we want to better understand users' needs and to improve access to images.

Social tagging systems are extremely responsive to user needs and vocabularies. Creation of metadata is no longer performed only by library professionals and authors but also by users. Folksonomies represent a way of organizing infomation and the fact is that a lof of people use these systems. No special training or previous knowledge is needed to participate in such systems; participating is very easy also in terms of time, effort and cost. According to Mathes (2004) the folksonomies represent simultaneously some of the best and worst in organization of information; they are chaotic suffering from problems of imprecision and ambiguity as opposed to controlled vocabularies and name authority control

References

Ames, M. and Naaman, M. (2007). Why We Tag: Motivations for Annotation in Mobile and Online Media. *Proceedings of the SIGCHI conference on Human factors in computin systems 2007, San Jose, California, USA, April 28 - May 03, 2007.*

Angus, E., Thelwall, M. and Stuart, D. (2008). General Patterns of Tag Usage Among University Groups in Flickr. *Online Information Review*, Vol. 32, No. 1, 89-101.

Choi, Y. and Rasmussen, E. M. (2002). Users' Relevance Criteria in Image Retrieval in American History. *Information Processing and Management*, 38, 695-726.

dLib.si
http://www.dlib.si/v2/Default.aspx?&language=eng

Flickr.com
http://www.flickr.com/

Fukumoto, T. (2006). An Analysis of Image Retrieval Behavior for Metadata Type Image Database. *Information Processing and Management*, 42, 723-728.

Golder, S. A. and Huberman, B. A. (2006). The Structure of Collaborative Tagging Systems. *Journal of Information Science*, Vol. 32, No. 2, 198-208.

Greisdorf, H. and O'Connor, B. (2002). Modelling What Users See When They Look at Images: A Cognitive Viewpoint. *Journal of Documentation*, Vol. 58, No. 1, 6-29.

Guy, M. and Tonkin, E. (2006). Folksonomies: Tidying Up Tags?. *Dlib Magazine*, Vol. 12, No. 1. www.dlib.org/dlib/january06/guy/01guy.html

Hammond, T., Hannay T., Lund, B. and Scott, J. (2005). Social Bookimarking Tools (I): A General Review. *D-Lib Magazine*, Vol. 11, No. 4. http://www.dlib.org/dlib/april05/hammond/04hammond.html

Jansen, B. J. (2008). Searching for Digital Images on the Web. *Journal of Documentation*, Vol. 64, No. 1, 81-101.

Jörgensen, C. (1998). Attributes of Images in Describing Tasks. *Information Processing & Management*, Vol. 34, No. 2/3, 161-174.

Markkula, M. and Sormunen, E. (2000). End-User Searching Challenges Indexing Practices in the Digital Newspaper Photo Archive. *Information Retrieval*, 1, 259-285.

Marlow, C., Naaman, M., Boyd, D. and Davis, M. (2006). HT06, Tagging Paper, Taxonomy, Flickr, Academic Article, ToRead. http://www.danah.org/papers/Hypertext2006.pdf

Mathes, A. (2004). Folksonomies – Cooperative Classification and Communications Through Shared Metadata. *http://www.adammathes.com/academic/computer-mediated-communication/folksonomies.html*

Miller, A. D. and Edwards, W. K. (2007). Give and Take: A Study of Consumer Photo-Sharing Culture and Practice. *Proceedings of the SIGCHI Conference on Human Factors in Computing Systems 2007, San Jose, California, USA, April 28 - May 03, 2007.*

Rafferty, P. (2007). Flickr and Democratic Indexing: Dialogic Approaches to Indexing. *Aslib Proceedings,* Vol. 59, No. 4/5, 397-410.

Sethi, I. K. and Coman, I. (1999). Image Retrieval Using Hierarchical Self-Organizing Feature Maps. *Pattern Recognition Letters,* 20, 1337-1345.

Smith, G. (2004). Folksonomy: Social Classification. *Atomiq: A Weblog by Gene Smith.*
    http://atomiq.org/arhives/2004/08/folksonomy_social_classification.html

Stvilia, B. & Jörgensen, C. (2009). User-Generated Collection-Level Metadata in an Online Photo-Sharing System. *Library & Information Science Research,* 31, 54-65.

Vander Wal, T. (2006). Explaining and Showing Broad and Narrow Folksonomies. *Personal infoCloud.com.*
    http://personalinfocloud.com/2005/02/explaining_and_html

Appendix: Images

No. 1: Mountains (62x)

No. 3: Geometric elements (49x)

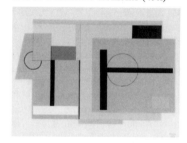

No. 2: Postman (74x)

No. 4: Giraffe (74x)

No. 5: Child (36x)

No. 8: Ljubljana (48x)

No. 6: Sunset (72x)

No. 9: Hockey (44x)

No. 7: Court (46x)

No. 10: Sled (55x)

Psychometric Properties of the Computer and Web Attitude Scale (CWAS): An Application to Greek Library Students

Aspasia Togia[1,2], Afrodite Malliari[1], Stella Korobili[1], Nikolaos Tsigilis[3]

[1]Department of Library Science and Information Systems, Technological Educational Institute of Thessaloniki, Greece, [2]aspatogi@libd.teithe.gr
[3]City College, An International Faculty of the University of Sheffield, UK

Abstract: The Computer and Web Attitude Scale (CWAS) is a self-reported instrument consisting of a Computer Attitude Scale and a Web Attitude Scale to discover individual attitudes towards computers and Internet technologies. The purpose of the present study was to examine the underlying structure of the CWAS in a Greek setting and to investigate the relationship between attitudes and selected background variables. A sample of 240 library science students completed a Greek version of the CWAS. Overall two separate exploratory factor analyses were conducted, for CAS and WAS respectively. Exploratory factor analysis of the CAS scores showed that three factors could adequately explain the 59.5% of the variance. In addition, the internal consistency of the factors as assessed by the Cronbach's α was satisfactory ($\alpha > .80$). Similar results were found for the WAS. In particular, three reliable factors were extracted, which accounted for the 62.3% of the variance. Again the internal consistency was satisfactory ($\alpha > .79$). Correlation analysis showed moderate positive associations among the six dimensions. Mean values of the CWAS dimensions suggested that participants had positive attitudes towards both the computers and the Web. Additionally, certain background characteristics were found to influence the levels of their attitudes. In conclusion, results showed that the Greek version of the CWAS is a valid and reliable instrument and can be safety used to assess attitudes towards Internet and computers in the Greek cultural context.
Keywords: Computer attitudes, Web attitudes, exploratory factor analysis, library science students, Greece

1. Introduction

Information and communication technologies have a considerable impact on modern education, and they are gradually transforming the teaching and learning process (Bonk & King, 1998). Educators have realized the potential of both computers and the World Wide Web (WWW) for enhancing the quality of teaching and learning. Recent developments in computer science, the proliferation of personal computers and the availability of a growing numbers of network resources have altered the environment of higher education. Students extensively use computers and the Internet for a variety of tasks: they study using educational software, they prepare course assignments, they communicate with peers and faculty, they keep up to date, they enjoy themselves, and they find information through a wide variety of electronic information resources, such as library catalogs, online databases and electronic journals (Sam, Othman & Nordin, 2005). For most individuals, computer literacy

New Trends in Qualitative and Quantitative Methods in Libraries
A. Katsirikou and C. H. Skiadas (eds)
© *World Scientific Publishing Co (pp. 261-270)*

skills are an essential part of college learning. In addition, these skills are considered necessary for anyone entering the workforce and indispensable for a successful career. The efficient and effective use of computers, the WWW and related Internet technologies may be even more critical for Library and Information Science students, since their future jobs will involve constant interaction with technology.

However, the effective utilization and incorporation of new tools into the curriculum are heavily dependent on perceptions of both teachers and students (Lawton & Gerschner, 1982). Many studies indicated that attitudes towards computers and Web technologies are significant predictors of the acceptance and actual use of computers and the Internet (Al-Khaldi & Al-Jabri, 1998; Anderson, 1996; Brock & Sulsky, 1994; Culpan, 1995; Daugherty & Funke, 1998; Johnson & Hignite, 2000; Moon & Kim, 2001; Pancer, George & Gebotys, 1992; Winter, Chudoba & Gutek, 1998). There is also evidence that attitudes affect learning outcomes and the effectiveness of training (Dweck, 1986; Noe, 1986; Noe & Schmitt, 1986).

2. Literature Review

The importance of attitudes emanates from theories shaped in the field of psychology, according to which attitudes are determinants of behavior (Igbaria & Chakrabati, 1990). Researchers have defined attitudes towards computers in many different ways (Liaw, 2002) and over the years a number of studies have been carried out to examine computer attitudes and to assess the relationship between attitudes and use and between attitudes and a variety of other variables, such as gender, computer experience, computer ownership, or computer self-efficacy.

Some studies found that males held more positive attitudes than females (Dambrot et al., 1985; Liaw, 2002; North & Noyes, 2002; Schumacher & Morahan-Martin, 2001), while other found that males and females did not differ significantly in their attitudes toward computers and the Internet (Kesici, Sahin & Akturk, 2009; Popovich et al., 2008; Sam, Othman & Nordin, 2005).

Researchers have also investigated the relationship between computer experience and computer attitudes, with inconclusive results. Al-Khaldi & Al-Jabri, (1998) found strong associations between computer use and all attitude components. According to Liaw (2002) and Sigurdsson (1991) experience with computers influences computer attitudes. On the other hand, Garland and Noyes (2004) argued that computer experience and use were rather poor predictors of computer attitudes, while Yushau (2006) found that experience did not have any impact on attitudes.

Ease of use and perceived usefulness have emerged as important predictors of attitudes towards computers and the actual use of both WWW and computers (Davis, 1993; Hsu, Wang & Chiu, 2009; Moon and Kim, 2001; Teo, Lee & Chai, 2007).

Scales of computer attitudes measure a wide range of constructs, including perceived ease of use, perceived usefulness, liking, negative feelings and beliefs, enjoyment and many others (Kay, 1993). Many studies have dealt with the question of computer attitudes dimensionality, providing evidence for a complex underlying structure of computer attitudes and suggesting several solutions (Brock & Sulsky, 1994; Gattiker & Hlavka, 1992; Koohang, 1989; Lee, 1970; Rafaeli, 1986; Sadik, 2006; Teo, 2008; Zoltan & Chapanis, 1982).

One of the most popular instruments is the Computer Attitude Scale (CAS) developed by Loyd and Loyd (1985). CAS consists of 40 items and measures four dimensions of computer attitudes: "(a) anxiety or fear of computers; (b) confidence in ability to use or learn about computers; (c) liking computers or enjoying working with computers; and (d) perceived usefulness of computers in present or future work" (Loyd & Loyd, 1985, p. 904).

While the majority of the instruments seem to lack a theoretical justification for the constructs they include, others are based on general attitude research (Kay, 1993). In general, theory suggests that attitudes consist of three components: the affective, the cognitive and the behavioral (Ajzen, 2005; Triandis, 1971). The affective component includes the feelings of individuals about certain things. The cognitive part refers to the beliefs an individual holds, and the behavioral component is what the individual actually does or intends to do. A fourth component, perceived control, added by Ajzen (2005), refers to people's perceptions of their ability to perform a particular behavior. Based on the attitude theory, Kay (1993) developed the Computer Attitude Measure (CAM), with considerably high internal reliability coefficients for the affective, the cognitive, the behavioral and the perceived control subscale.

Many studies on Internet attitudes have employed the Technology Acceptance Model (TAM) developed by Davis (1989; 1993), according to which use of technology can be predicted by attitudes, which in turn can be predicted by perceived ease of use and perceived usefulness (Lederer, et al, 2000; Moon & Kim, 2001; Tsai, Lin & Tsai, 2001). Within the framework set out by CAM, TAM and CAS, Liaw (2002) formulated the Computer and Web Attitude Scale (CWAS) "to discover individual affective, cognitive, and behavioral attitudes toward computer and Web technologies" (Liaw, 2002, p.20) and to assess the extent to which demographic variables and computer experiences can predict attitudes.

Although there are several scales measuring computer and Internet attitudes, the psychometric properties of any scale should be carefully considered before its use (Harrison & Rainer, 1992). Besides, there is always the need to assess the validity and reliability of the instruments in different cultural contexts (Hui & Triantis, 1985). Thus, the purpose of the present study was to examine the underlying structure of the CWAS in a Greek setting and to investigate the relationship between attitudes and selected background variables.

3. Method
3.1. Participants and procedure
The participants of the survey were students in the Library and Information Systems (LIS) Department of the Technological Educational Institute of Thessaloniki (TEI), Greece. The LIS student population is approximately 800 undergraduate students and the sampling method was the one-stage cluster sampling. With the help of the weekly schedule of the department, one class of each semester was randomly selected. The procedure resulted in distribution of the research questionnaire in seven classes and provided 240 usable questionnaires. Participation in the survey was voluntary and no extra credits were offered.

3.2. Instruments
The instrument of the survey was a structured questionnaire which included three major components: (1) demographic information, (2) computer and Internet experience, and (3) Computer and Web Attitude Scale (CWAS). Demographics included gender, semester, age and level of knowledge of foreign languages. The second part of the questionnaire assessed students' technological experience, computer education, computer ownership and access to the Internet. The respondents were asked to report the age at which they started using computer and the Internet, and the frequency of computer and Internet use for five different activities before and after their enrolment in the LIS Department. They were also asked to rate their perceived level of skills with regard to eight different activities on a scale wherein "1=novice" and "5=expert".

The final part of the instrument was the Computer and Web Attitude Scale (CWAS) which has been developed by Liaw (2002) and includes a Computer Attitude Scale (CAS) and a Web Attitude Scale (WAS), containing 16 items each. Each item is scored on a seven-point Likert scale (from "strongly disagree" to "strongly agree"), but for the purposes of the present study, responses were provided on a five-point Likert scale anchored by "1=strongly disagree to 5=strongly agree". The scales measure perceptions toward computer and Web self-efficacy, liking, usefulness, and intention to use and learn computers and the Web. The instrument has showed good internal consistency, as indicated by coefficients of Cronbach's α ranging from .91 for the CAS to .93 for the WAS (Liaw, 2002), but so far its factor structured has not been examined. The scales were translated to the Greek language by the authors and a bilingual scholar. Then, an independent backward translation of the Greek version into English was completed. Minor differences between the two versions were found.

4. Results

An exploratory factor analysis with oblique rotation was performed on the 16 items of the Computer Attitudes Scale, suggesting three interpretable factors, which accounted for 51.1% of the common variance explained (KMO = .902, Bartlett's test of sphericity = 1642.76, p < .01). Factor 1 contained four items measuring one's feelings when using a computer (e.g., "I like to use computers", or, "I enjoy talking with others about computers"). Factor 2 contained seven items assessing perceived usefulness of computers for the individual (e.g., "I believe using computers is worthwhile", or, "The use of computers in helpful for my studying"). Factor 3 contained 4 items dealing with perceived confidence in the ability to use and learn how to use a computer (e.g., "I feel confident using a personal computer", or, "I feel confident learning new computer skills"). The three factors were labeled "Affection", "Perceived usefulness" and "Perceived Confidence" respectively. Item 11 ("I use computers in multiple ways in my daily life") was excluded from the analysis because it had similar loadings on two factors. The internal consistency of the items representing the three subscales was assessed using Cronbach's α. As Table 1 shows, the α coefficients for all sub-scales were significantly high.

The same analysis was performed on the 16 items of Web Attitude Scale (WAS) and the factor structure was similar to that of CAS. Three factors emerged, which accounted for 53.7% of the common variance explained (KMO = .90, Bartlett's test of sphericity = 1955.15, p < .01). The first factor, named "Perceived usefulness" contained eight items measuring the extent to which individuals believe the WWW is helpful and has a potential as a learning tool (e.g. "I believe the Internet makes communication easier", "I believe that the Internet/WWW is able to offer online learning activities"). The second factor, named "Perceived confidence", contained four items referring to the perceived self-efficacy in using various Web technologies (e.g., "I feel confident using E-mail"). And the third factor consisted of four items dealing with the extent to which individuals find the Internet pleasurable or amusing (e.g., "I enjoy talking with others about the Internet", "I like to work with the Internet/WWW). This factor was named "Affection". Rotated factors loadings, Cronbach's α values, descriptive statistics and correlation matrix for the three factors (subscales) of the WAS are presented in Table 2.

Table 1: Rotated factors loadings, Cronbach's α values, descriptive statistics and correlation matrix for the three factors (subscales) of the CAS

CAS items	Affection (F1)	Perceived usefulness (F2)	Perceived confidence (F3)	h^2
1. I feel confident using a personal computer			.89	.80
2. I feel confident using different media to store my data files			.70	.63
3. I feel confident using word processors			.71	.51
4. I feel confident learning new computer skills			.55	.53
5. I like to use computers	.65			.65
6. I enjoy talking with others about computers	.51			.30
7. I like to have a computer in my home	.57			.60
8. I feel comfortable using computer in my day life	.81			.69
9. I believe using computer is necessary in my school life		.55		.42
10. I believe using computers is worthwhile		.51		.60
11. I use computers in multiple ways in my daily life				
12. An increased use of computers can enhance my academic performance		.62		.39
13. The use of computers is helpful for my studying		.61		.39
14. The use of computers can increase my job possibilities		.46		.19
15. I believe that computers can serve as tools for learning		.64		.42
16. I believe that knowing how to use computers is worthwhile		.42		.50
Eigenvalues	6.4	1.63	1.04	
Explained %	39.7	7.5	3.8	
Cronbach's α	.79	.81	.85	
Mean	3.8	4.1	4	
S.D.	.69	.55	.63	
F1	1.0	.60*	.64*	
F2		1.0	.51*	

An additional purpose of the present study was to examine the correlations between computer attitudes and a number of background characteristics. Pearson's correlation coefficients indicated significant relationships between age of first computer use and the three dimensions of both CAS and WAS, while age at which respondents had their first contact with the Internet correlated significantly with the Affection and Confidence subscales of CAS and WAS. Results also revealed that students who used computers more frequently scored higher in the three subscales of CAS and WAS, whereas those who perceived themselves more skilful in using computers for a variety of tasks scored higher in the three subscales of CAS and in the Affection and Confidence subscale of WAS. The zero-order correlations are presented in Table 3.

Table 2: Rotated factors loadings, Cronbach's α values, descriptive statistics and correlation matrix for the three factors (subscales) of the WAS

CAS items	Perceived usefulness (F1)	Perceived confidence (F2)	Affection (F3)	h^2
1. I feel confident using the Internet/WWW		.84		.71
2. I feel confident using e-mail		.60		.64
3. I feel confident using WWW browsers		.85		.78
4. I feel confident using search engines		.82		.77
5. I like to use e-mail to communicate with others			.76	.58
6. I enjoy talking with others the Internet			.65	.45
7. I like to work with the Internet/WWW			.70	.60
8. I like to use the Internet from home			.58	.56
9. I believe using the Internet/WWW is worthwhile	.40			.55
10. The Internet/WWW helps me to find information	.50			.47
11. I believe using the Internet makes communication easier	.39			.32
12. The multimedia environment of WWW is helpful to understand online information	.66			.54

13. I believe the Internet/WWW has potential as a learning tool	.76		.56
14. I believe that the Internet/WWW is able to offer online learning activities	.63		.42
15. I believe that learning how to use the Internet/WWW is worthwhile	.49		.33
16. Learning the Internet/WWW skills can enhance my academic performance	.57		.29
Eigenvalues	7.10	1.56	1.21
Explained %	41.76	6.99	5.0
Cronbach's α	.83	.90	.81
Mean	4.14	4.19	3.85
S.D.	.52	.65	.76
F1	1.0	.57*	.60*
F2		1.0	.60*

Table 3: Correlations with background characteristics

	CAS			WAS		
	Affection	Useful	Conf	Affection	Useful	Conf
Age-Computer use	-.29*	-.22*	-.20*	-.30*	-.25*	-.27*
Age-Internet use	-.18*	-.12	-.16*	-.21*	-.09	-.14*
Frequency of use	.31*	.29*	.27*	.32*	.21*	.27*
Perceived Skills	.38*	.25*	.49*	.30*	.09	.39*

5. Conclusions

Computer and Web Attitude Scale seems to be a valid and reliable instrument for the assessment of three computer and Internet attitude dimensions, namely Affection, Perceived Usefulness and Perceived Confidence. Positive moderate intercorrelations emerged between the two subscales, suggesting that increase in computer attitudes leads in increase in Web attitudes as well.

The high means of CAS and WAS subscales indicate that students enter the LIS Department with favorable computer and Internet attitudes. They enjoy using computers and the Internet, they believe that technology is useful and they feel capable of using it. Results of the present study showed that students who had access to computers and the Internet at younger ages and were more frequent computer users had more favorable attitudes towards technology, a finding consistent with similar research (Al-Khaldi & Al-Jabri, 1998; Liaw, 2002; Hong & Koh, 2002; Igbaria & Chakrabarti, 1990; Popovich et al, 2008; Teo, 2008). An additional factor, perceived computer skills, was found to influence attitudes as well. This finding is in line with Igbaria and Chakrabarti (1990) who argued that belief that one has acquired the skills necessary to use information technology influences computer attitudes. It was evident that students who became acquainted with computers at an early age, perceived themselves as skillful users and were extensively using information technology, had more positive attitudes toward computers and the Web. Educators in the LIS Department should try to enhance students' skills in using new technologies. They should also struggle to provide positive, successful and rewarding experiences that will increase students' confidence and improve their attitudes.

References

Ajzen, I. (2005). *Attitudes, Personality and Behavior.* Maidenhead: Open University Press.

Al-Khaldi, M. A., & Al-Jabri, I. M. (1998). The Relationship of Attitudes to Computer Utilization: New Evidence from a Developing Nation. *Computers in Human Behavior*, 14, 23–42.

Anderson, A. A. (1996). Predictors of Computer Anxiety and Performance in Information Systems. *Computers in Human Behavior*, 12, 61–77.

Bonk, C. J. And King, K. S. (1998). *Electronic Collaborators: Learner Centered Technologies for Literacy, Apprenticeship, and Discourse*, Mahwah: Lawrence Erlbaum.

Brock, D., & Sulsky, L. (1994). Attitudes Toward Computers: Construct Validation and Relations to Computer Use. *Journal of Organizational Behavior*, 15, 17–35.

Culpan, O. (1995). Attitudes of End-users Towards Information Technology in Manufacturing and Service Industries. *Information &Management*, 28, 167–17.

Dambrot, F.H., Watkins-Malek, M.A., Silling, S.M., Marshall, R.S., and Garver, J.A. (1985). Correlates of Sex Differences in Attitudes Toward and Involvement with Computers. *Journal of Vocational Behavior*, 27, 71-86.

Davis, F.D. (1989). Perceived Usefulness, Perceived Ease of Use, and User Acceptance of Information Technology. *MIS Quarterly*, 13, 319–339.

Davis, F.D. (1993). User Acceptance of Information Technology: System Characteristics, User Perceptions and Behavioral Impacts. *International Journal of Man-Machine Studies*, 38, 475-487.

Daugherty, M., & Funke, B. L. (1998). University Faculty and Student Perceptions of Web-based Instruction. *Journal of Distance Education*, 13, 21–39.

Dweck, C. S. (1986). Motivational Processes Affecting Learning. *American Psychologist*, 41, 1040-1048.

Garland, K. J. and Noyes, J. M. (2004). Computer Experience: A Poor Predictor of Computer Attitudes. *Computers in Human Behavior*, 20, 823–840.

Gattiker, U.E. & Hlavka, A. (1992). Computer Attitudes and Learning Performance: Issues for Management Education and Training. *Journal of Organizational Behavior*, 13, 89-101.

Harrison, A.W. & Rainer, R. K. (1992). An Examination of the Factor Structures and Concurrent Validities for the Computer Attitude Scale, the Computer Anxiety Rating Scale, and the Computer Self-Efficacy Scale. *Educational and Psychological Measurement*, 52, 735-745.

Hong, K. and Koh, C. (2002). Computer Anxiety and Attitudes Toward Computers Among Rural Secondary School Teachers: A Malaysian Perspective. *Journal of Research on Technology in Education*, 35, 27-48.

Hsu, M. K., Wang, S. W. and Chiu, K. K. (2009). Computer Attitude, Statistics Anxiety and Self-efficacy on Statistical Software Adoption Behavior: An Empirical Study of Online MBA Learners. *Computers in Human Behavior*, 25, 412–420.

Hui and Triandis (1985). Measurement in Cross-cultural Psychology: A Review and Comparison of Strategies. *Journal of Cross-Cultural Psychology*, 16, 131-152

Igbaria M. & Chakrabati, A. (1990). Computer Anxiety and Attitudes Towards Microcomputer Use. *Behaviour and Information Technology*, 9, 229-241.

Johnson, R. A., & Hignite, M. A. (2000). Student Usage of the World Wide Web: A comparative study. *Journal of Computer Information Systems*, 40, 93–97.

Kay, R. H. (1993). An Exploration of Theoretical and Practical Foundations for Assessing Attitudes Toward Computers: The Computer Attitude Measure (CAM) *Computers in Human Behavior*, 9, 371-386.

Kesici, S., Sahin, I. and Akturk, A. O. (2009). Analysis of Cognitive Learning Strategies and Computer Attitudes, According to College Students' Gender and Locus of Control. *Computers in Human Behavior*, 25, 529–534.

Koohang, A.A. (1989). A Study of Attitudes Toward Computers: Anxiety, Confidence, Liking, and Perception of Usefulness. *Journal of Research on Computing in Education*, 22, 137-50.

Lawton, J., & Gerschner, V. T. (1982). A Review of the Literature on Attitudes Towards Computers and Computerized Instruction. *Journal of Research and Development in Education*, 16, 50-55.

Lederer, A.L., Maupin, D.J., Sena, M.P. and Zhuang, Y. (2000). The Technology Acceptance Model and the World Wide Web. *Decision Support Systems*, 29, 269-282.

Lee, R. S. (1970). Social Attitudes and the Computer Revolution. *Public Opinion Quarterly*, 34, 53-59.

Liaw, S. (2002). An Internet Survey for Perceptions of Computers and the World Wide Web: Relationship, Prediction, and Difference. *Computers in human behavior*, 18, 17-35.

Loyd, B. H., & Loyd, D. E. (1985). The Reliability and Validity of Instruments for the Assessment of Computer Attitudes. *Educational and Psychological Measurement*, 45, 903-908.

Moon, J. W., & Kim, Y. G. (2001). Extending the TAM for a World-Wide-Web Context. *Information & Management*, 38, 217–230.

Noe, R. A. (I 986). Training Attributes and Attitudes: Neglected Influences on Training Effectiveness. *Academy* of *Management Review*, 11: 736749.

Noe, R. A. and Schmitt, N. (1986). The Influence of Trainer Attitudes on Training Effectiveness: Test of a Model. *Personnel Psychology*, 39: 497-523.

North, A. S. and Noyes, J. M. (2002). Gender Influences on Children's Computer Attitudes and Cognitions. *Computers in Human Behavior*, 18, 135-150.

Pancer, S. M., George, M, & Gebotys, R. J. (1992). Understanding and Predicting Attitudes Towards Computers. *Computers in Human Behavior*, 8, 211–222.

Popovich, P.M., Gullekson, N., Morris, S. and Morse B. (2008). Comparing Attitudes Towards Computer Usage by Undergraduates from 1986 to 2005. *Computers in Human Behavior*, 24, 986–992.

Rafaeli, A. (1986). Employee Attitudes Toward Working with Computers. *Journal of Occupational Behavior*, 7, 89-106.

Sadik, A. (2006). Factors Influencing Teachers' Attitudes Toward Personal Use and School Use of Computers: New evidence from a developing nation. *Evaluation Review*, 30, 86-113.

Sam, H. K., Othman, A. E. A. and Nordin, Z. S. (2005). Computer Self-Efficacy, Computer Anxiety, and Attitudes Toward the Internet: A Study Among Undergraduates in Unimas. *Educational Technology & Society*, 8, 205-219.

Schumacher, P. and Morahan-Martin, J. (2001). Gender, Internet and Computer Attitudes and Experiences. *Computers in Human Behavior*, 17, 95-100.

Sigurdsson, J.F. (1991). Computer Experience, Attitudes Toward Computers and Personality Characteristics in Psychology Undergraduates. *Personality and Individual Differences*, 12, 617-624.

Teo, T. (2008). Assessing the Computer Attitudes of Students: An Asian Perspective. *Computers in Human Behavior*, 24: 1634-1642.

Teo, T., Lee, C.B. and Chai, C.S. (2007). Understanding Pre-service Teachers' Computer Attitudes: Applying and Extending the Technology Acceptance Model. *Journal of Computer Assisted Learning*, 24, 128–143.

Triandis, H. C. (1971). *Attitude and Attitude Change*. New York: John Wiley.

Tsai, C.C., Lin, S.S.J. & Tsai, M.J. (2001). Developing an Internet Attitude Scale for High School Students. *Computers & Education*, 37, 41-51.

Winter, S. J., Chudoba, K. M., & Gutek, B. A. (1998). Attitudes Toward Computers: When do They Predict Computer Use? *Information & Management*, 34, 275–284.

Yushau, B. (2006). Computer Attitude, Use Experience, Software Familiarity and Perceived Pedagogical Usefulness: The Case of Mathematics Professors. *Eurasia Journal of Mathematics, Science and Technology Education*, 2, 1-17.

Zoltan, E. and Chapanis, A. (1982). Experience With and Attitudes Toward Computers: Accountants vs. Lawyers vs. Pharmacists vs. Physicians. *Behaviour and Information Technology*, 1, 55-68.

Generational Technology Expectations of Library Users: A Case Study

Rachel Williams[1] and Jennifer Cromer[2]

[1]University of Pittsburgh, USA
[2]San Jose State University, USA

Abstract: In order to more fully understand the cultural shifts in technology within and between generations, a sample survey of several public libraries in a rural university community will be analyzed. The following subjects will be addressed and compared on a generational level within this poster presentation: programming, technology—types and usage, and frequency and purpose of visits. A thorough analysis of the data in this case study will provide insight into the changing role of technology use among two distinct generations of library patrons.
Keywords: Web 2.0, technology, libraries, generation(s), librarians, patrons, user community, YouTube, Facebook, survey

1. Introduction

How do you define yourself? Perhaps you define yourself by your profession, your personal hobbies, your family, your age. Oftentimes when trying to define ourselves, we think about our generation. As Dempsey (2009) asserts, technology "represents a diffusion of communications and computational capacity into a growing part of our research, learning and social activities." This diffusion is signified through a constantly evolving culture of technology use within the library. No matter what generation we identify with, we are all faced with the need to spend a greater amount of time learning to understand and use technology on a regular basis.

Through a case study of two local public libraries within small university communities, this presentation addresses the implications of technology as a culture among several generations. Social networking and Web 2.0 has become nothing but mainstream within the technology culture in the library setting. Tweeting, updating statuses on Facebook, and emailing friends and colleagues YouTube videos all indicate that technology has taken hold of our communities. Snowball (2008) states "many libraries and authors of books have a profile on MySpace" (30). Libraries are environments which have embraced this cultural shift in technology use. With this growth of technology sharing, however, comes a decrease in expectations of privacy and personal identity—we are in fact becoming a culture of sharing. As Secker (2008) mentions, "facebook is a semi-public space where individuals should be careful about the type of information they share" (5). Ultimately, however, in acknowledging these diminishing expectations of privacy in constantly evolving technology, it is vital to examine the cultural impact of technology trends and the loss of personal identity inherent with this change.

This cultural shift, as well as changing expectations in privacy and personal identity is transparent, not just within the library user community, but among

New Trends in Qualitative and Quantitative Methods in Libraries
A. Katsirikou and C. H. Skiadas (eds)
© *World Scientific Publishing Co (pp. 271-277)*

librarians as well. The shared technologies librarians now utilize lend the workplace to one of collaboration and team projects, which enables librarians to be more open to changing technology. At times, however, librarians well-adapted to recent technology trends may be frustrated by those less flexible and open to an 'evolving environment.' In her article "A Neo-Modern Summary of the Futcha," Jane Scales (1999) questions our inherent assumptions about the role of libraries as 'evolving environments' when she asks, "If the library is changing as much as it seems to be, how can we be sure that the procedures, practices, and philosophies established twenty to thirty years ago are right for the evolving environment(25)?"

Scales acknowledges the changing needs of library users based on the changing structure of the library as an environment. She questions whether or not we are jaded by our own histories; are we in fact too rooted in the institutions set into motion thirty years ago to notice the changing technology culture within the library? A survey was performed in both Pullman, Washington and Moscow, Idaho to better examine how library users are reacting to the changing technologies available for use in the library environment. Both towns surveyed are unique in that they are agricultural as well as university communities and provided an interesting backdrop for this particular analysis. To get an adequate sample size, surveys were made available at Neill Public Library in Pullman and at all seven branches of the Latah County Library District. Surveying these two communities provided an opportunity to acquire a wide range of respondents. These communities are comprised of agriculturists, university professors and staff, students, and families.

Surveys were available for completion for three weeks at both Neill Public Library and at branches in the Latah County Library District. The surveys were also available in either a paper or online format, and respondents were encouraged to take the survey in the format most appealing to them. Though the surveys were available in both formats, every action was taken to ensure that the formats of the survey were very similar to elicit the most honest answers possible from survey respondents.

2. Results

A total of 130 respondents participated in the 15 question-survey, with 45 percent taking the survey in paper format. The 15 questions covered several subjects related to technology use, frequency of library visits, and purpose for visiting the library. Responses were divided into four generational categories according to the Municipal Research Services of Washington general definitions as outlined by Sweeney. Using these definitions, four generational categories were defined for the purposes of this survey: Millennials [born 1982-2000], Generation X [1961-1981], Baby Boomers [1944-1960] and the Silent Generation [1922-1943].

Generation and Number of Visits to the Library per Week

Age Range	Once	Twice	Three Times	Four Times	Five Times	Six Times	Seven Plus
Millennial	12	13	23	33	0	50	29
Generation X	40	26	23	17	29	0	0
Baby Boomer	31	45	23	17	57	0	14
Silent	17	16	32	33	14	50	57

Table 1. Number of visits to library per week, as shown in percentages of each generation's total responses.

Shown in Table 1 are four major generations and survey responses as to when users visit the library. The largest number of respondents who visit the library six or more times per week is either the Millennial generation or the Silent generation. Baby boomers visit the most either twice per week or five times per week compared to other generations. Generation X patrons, interestingly, seem to be more evenly distributed in their visits to the library, although they visit the most once per week compared to other generations.

Generation and Importance of Browsing Materials

Age Range	Most Important	Very Important	Important	Slightly Important	Not Important
Millennial	58	33	8	0	0
Generation X	48	28	21	3	0
Baby Boomer	57	7	29	0	7
Silent	63	13	13	0	13

Table 2. Importance of visiting the library to browse materials, as shown in percentages of each generation's total responses.

While respondents tend to visit the library a variable number of times per week based on their generational designation, there is less variance in *why* respondents visit the library. Table 2 above demonstrates that, no matter what the age group, respondents tend to visit the library to 1) browse materials, and 2) pick up materials. Combined totals indicate that 91 percent of Millennials, 76 percent of Generation X, 64 percent of Baby Boomers, and 76 percent of the Silent Generation felt it was at least 'Very Important' or 'Most Important' to them to visit the library to browse materials.

Generation and Importance of Picking up Library Materials

Age Range	Most Important	Very Important	Important	Slightly Important	Not Important
Millennial	23	38	15	15	9
Generation X	44	25	17	11	3
Baby Boomer	50	34	13	3	0
Silent	68	21	5	5	0

Table 3. Importance of visiting the library to pick up materials, as shown in percentages based on total responses for each generation.

Relative frequencies for Table 3 above indicate that picking up library materials is 'Most Important' or 'Very Important' to respondents. Whether Millennial or Generation X, library patrons feel it is important to look for and retrieve materials that interest them. The need for librarians to act as knowledge managers, both in a traditional sense and within the context of constantly evolving technological expectations, is clear from the survey respondents' answers to this query.

Generation and Importance of Internet Use

Age Range	Most Important	Very Important	Important	Slightly Important	Not Important
Millennial	33	17	17	6	28
Generation X	7	10	7	20	57
Baby Boomer	16	10	6	32	35
Silent	13	19	19	25	25

Table 4. Importance of internet use shown in percentages calculated by number of responses per category divided by number of total respondents within each generation.

Generation and Computer Use at the Library

Age Range	Internet	Catalog	Wireless
Millennial	91	30	70
Generation X	38	82	33
Baby Boomer	46	64	31
Silent	73	86	50

Table 5. Computer use shown in percentages calculated by number of responses per category divided by number of total respondents within each generation.

Interestingly, 91 percent of the millennial generation responded that they use internet computers while at the library (Table 5), but only 33 percent felt it was important to offer this service (Table 4). Additionally 28 percent felt that having internet computers was not important at all, although almost all respondents from this generation indicated that they use them. This could be the result of exposure to newer technologies; it would be understandable that an individual who has grown up in an environment filled with social networking technologies would make more use of it and yet feel it is not as important as other respondents.

A correspondence analysis using STATA was performed to derive a better understanding of the relationship between technology use and generation. The use of Web 2.0 technologies—specifically social networking sites such as Twitter, Facebook, MySpace, and YouTube—initially appeared to be evenly distributed. However, a correspondence analysis created fascinating results as shown below in Figure 1. The strongest correlations are between r1, or the Millennial generation, and technology use at the library, and between r2, or Generation X, and YouTube at the Library and Facebook at home.

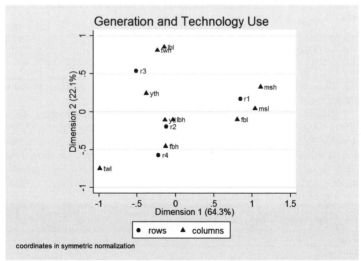

Figure 1. Correspondence Analysis illustrating technology use related to each generation. r1=Millennial, r2=Generation X, r3=Baby Boomer, r4=Silent. fbl=Facebook at the Library, fbh=Facebook at Home, ytl=YouTube at the Library, yth=YouTube at Home, msl=MySpace at the Library, msh=MySpace at Home,

twl=Twitter at the Library, twh=Twitter at Home, lbl=Library Blog at the Library, and lbh=Library Blog at Home. Figure (X) illustrates the correspondence between r1 and fbl, msl, and msh, as well as the relationship between r2 and ytl and fbh.

3. Discussion

This particular case study has facilitated exploration into some of the issues facing library users of various generations as they interact with a new technology culture. This case study provided insight into how often and why library patrons visit the library, how varying generations utilize Web 2.0 technology, and computer and internet use while at the library.

Library uses per week are dominated by the youngest and oldest generations, with variability in the number of visits per week by Generation X. Anecdotal experiences as well as statistics indicate that libraries are being frequented much more than they have been in the past. No matter when each generation visits, however, it is clear that it is 'Most Important' or 'Very Important' to all respondents to visit the library in order to browse and pick up library materials.

Computer use (internet, catalog, and wireless) provided insight into the habits of Generation X and Millennials. While Millennials use the internet computers and wireless service substantially more than other generations, they also do not feel that these are important services. The correlations between generations and Web 2.0 technology use as graphically demonstrated in Figure 1 suggest differing perspectives on privacy, as the Millennials appear to feel more comfortable using personal social networking sites at the library than other generations. While Generation X appears to be comfortable using Web 2.0 technologies such as YouTube at the library, they are more reserved in using personal social networking sites at home. R3, or the Baby Boomer generation, makes use of YouTube and Twitter at home. R4, the Silent Generation, appears to only be comfortable using Facebook at home and shows no correlation with other Web 2.0 technologies, whether at the library or at home. Deyrup (2010) asserts that "[r]adical trust forms the basis of community-building activities on the Web. Because the collective action of the many outweighs that of the few, user engagement is not only a positive, but a necessary thing—the force that makes these sites successful" (146). The idea of a collective community existing in lieu of an individual community lends itself to the use of social networking to continue to build that community. This shift in community also results in less privacy expectations on the part of the user. Figure 1 illustrates the generations which are more comfortable with this type of openness quite clearly.

Despite the fact that, overall, Americans have been atwitter with the idea of tweeting, the use of Twitter within the communities surveyed was minimal at best. This was a surprising result for two fairly large university communities. Even though the two library systems surveyed serve what could be perceived as very technologically savvy library user populations, it is clear that Twitter does not dominate in this instance. In fact, only 10 percent of respondents even acknowledged that they use Twitter. Of those respondents who said they do tweet, only 5 percent tweet on a regular basis, or at least 3-4 times per week.

Privacy was addressed subtly through the survey and through a specific question asking respondents whether they had experienced any problems with internet filtering. While only 3.3% of respondents stated that they had experienced a problem due to filtering, respondents who answered "yes" to this question were asked to explain further. These explanations indicated that in all but one case, filtering was not the problem—the problems were due to outdated computer hardware and software, tight network security, and user error. These statistics indicate that, for the most part, library users are satisfied with the minimal filtering common in many public libraries and that users understand the limitations inherent in utilizing computers in a public setting.

Beyond the survey statistics relating to privacy are the personal experiences of librarians in their interactions with library users. In May 2009, one library surveyed acquired six new internet terminals. This acquisition resulted in the necessary movement of computer terminals and new furniture to house the computers. The older furniture provided more space between computer terminals, as well as dividers to provide users with, at the very least, the perception of privacy. This change in furniture as well as the closer space and increased number of computer terminals resulted in library patrons attempting to haphazardly cover their computers or assert personal space in other ways. Patrons have covered up their computers with notebooks, books, papers, and even their hands in an effort to create a sense of privacy for themselves as they utilize computer stations.

Both librarians and patrons may find it difficult to accept a library technology culture that focuses on a social networking and Web 2.0 technologies. However, as Caudron (1997) points out, it is possible to train librarians of all generations to utilize new technology by employing several key techniques. In this case study, it is clear that what is really important is understanding that the culture of technology in the library environment is entirely fluid and constantly evolving. As we grow as librarians, both in understanding the technologies themselves and the needs of library users, we will be more effective knowledge managers in terms of assisting patrons to use new technologies that they may be unfamiliar or uncomfortable using at first.

4. Conclusions

As Saw and Todd (2007) assert, "[many] dimensions and properties of th[e] electronic frontier [are] unfamiliar and uncharted and our survival depends on how well we adapt our values and skills" (p. 10). Librarians are in a distinctive position to ride the waves of the changing culture of technology in order to contribute to the continued relevance of libraries. As a cartographer begins drawing a map, s/he does not simply put pencil to page and the map appears. Rather, the map takes shape slowly; similarly, as our understanding of social and Web 2.0 technologies grows, lines will appear on our technological map and we will be able to better understand the needs of our user communities. Young and Powell further state that "the need for a creative and constructively engaged library work force is imperative for the coming decades" (501). A creative, engaged librarian will be better equipped to handle generational differences as technology continues to evolve within the library environment. Remaining engaged and being adaptable as the landscape of technology changes will result in our being better equipped to handle the needs of library users.

Although the initial expectation was to see substantial gaps between generations, after examining the data, this simply is not the case. Despite the fact that there is some variation in expectations regarding technology use and services, library users of all generations had similar expectations regarding programming and what is of prevailing importance when they visit the library. Limitations to the survey include the fact that the survey size was fairly small and performed within an insulated community setting. Additionally, prior approval from the libraries surveyed was required, and the survey was censored more than the authors expected. As with any survey, due to the fact that the sample size was fairly small, there is the possibility that the survey is not fully representative of the population. However, overall, the survey provides an excellent snapshot into a typical library community.

Regardless of one's generational affiliation, collaboration on every possible level is the only way to secure the role of libraries as continuingly relevant institutions within the paradigm shifts occurring in the technological expectations of library users. As Pixey Anne Mosley states, "If librarians and administrators want to play an active role in the future, they must work to develop a shared vision of the paths they wish to follow and take an active role in creating their destiny" (170). How do librarians accomplish this? Mosley continues by admonishing librarians to "reach beyond the walls of the library" (170). Whether Millennial, Generation X, Baby Boomer, or a member of the Silent Generation, it is imperative that librarians take Mosley's advice. Reaching beyond the walls of the library and into the realm of technology will facilitate the library's continued relevance as a welcome environment for change.

References

Caudron, Shari. "Can generation Xers be trained?" *Training and Development,* 51.3 (1997). EBSCOhost Academic Search Premier. Web. 26 February 2010.

Dempsey, Lorcan. "Always On: Libraries in a Permanent World of Connectivity." *First Monday,* 41.5 (2009). Google Scholar. Web. 30 March 2010.

Deyrup, M. M. "Web 2.0 and the Library." *Technical Services Quarterly,* 27.2 (2010). EBSCOhost Academic Search premier. Web. 29 March 2010.

Kipnis, Daniel G. and Gary M. Childs. "Educating Generation X and Generation Y; Teaching Tips for Librarians." *Medical Reference Services Quarterly,* 23.4 (2004): 25-33.

Lancaster, Lynne C. "The Click and Clash of Generations." *Library Journal,* 128.17 (2003): 36-39. EBSCOhost Academic Search Premier. Web. 26 February 2010.

Mosley, Pixey Anne. "Shedding the Stereotypes: Librarians in the 21st Century." *The Reference Librarian* 37.78 (2002): 167-176. EBSCOhost Academic Search Premier. Web. 26 February 2010.

Saw, Grace & Todd, Heather. "Library 3.0: Where Art Our Skills?" *Conference Papers--World Library and Information Congress: 73rd IFLA General Conference and Council 2007*.19-23 August 2007. Web. 26 February 2010.

Scales, B. Jane. "A Neo-Modern Summary of the Futcha: An Explanation of the Generation X in Our Midst." *The Reference Librarian* 30.64 (1999): 21-30. EBSCOhost Academic Search Premier. Web. 26 February 2010.

Secker, Jane. "Case Study 5: Libraries and Facebook." *London School of Economics and Political Science,* January 2008. <http://clt.lse.ac.uk/Projects/Case_Study_Five_report.pdf> 29 March 2010.

Snowball, Clare. "Enticing Teenagers into the Library." *Library Review* 57.1 (2008): 25-35. EBSCOhost Academic Search Premier. Web. 26 February 2010.

Sweeney, Richard T. "Reinventing Library Buildings and Services for the Millennial Generation." *Library Administration and Management* 19.4 (2005): 165-175. EBSCOhost Academic Search Premier. Web. 26 February 2010.

Young, Arthur P., Hernon, Peter & Powell, Ronald R. "Attributes of Academic Library Leadership: An Exploratory Study of Some Gen-Xers." *The Journal of Academic Librarianship* 32.5 (2006): 489-502. EBSCOhost Academic Search Premier. Web. 26 February 2010.

User Preferences for Virtual Information Retrieval: A Qualitative Study

Alan MacLennan

Department of Information Management, Aberdeen Business School, Robert Gordon University, Aberdeen, Scotland

Abstract: This paper presents results of a piece of research conducted in order to determine user preferences as to the nature of virtual worlds to be used as an environment for information retrieval. A study was carried out amongst postgraduate students and staff at Robert Gordon University, using a Grounded Theory methodology. Over one hundred interviews were carried out, in three cycles of interviewing, analysis, and integration with literature. The findings revealed that user preferences were determined less by structural features than by affective factors, such as familiarity, organisation, assistance, and quality of information and presentation.
Keywords: Virtual worlds, information retrieval, grounded theory, user study, VRML

1. Introduction

The study arose from an interest in the novels Neuromancer, by William Gibson (1984) and Snow Crash, by Neal Stephenson (1992), both of which centre on virtual worlds. A review of literature on the topic, such as that by Card, Mackinlay and Robertson (1991) appeared to show little evidence of user input to the design of existing virtual worlds, and the question arose, if virtual worlds were to be designed for use as devices to facilitate information retrieval, what should they look like? There is an argument that designers, particularly those in highly technical fields, tend to create things which they perceive to be "cool", rather than focussing on what users actually want, and, given the fact that current increases in bandwidth and computing power make multi-user virtual worlds a real phenomenon, it appeared timely to seek out some user input before a "fait accompli" situation arose, where users were again constrained to adapt to an environment designed by people with priorities other than usability.

2. Aim and Objectives

The aim of the research was to discover user preferences for the design of a "virtual world" for accessing information, and the factors influencing those preferences.
The objectives of the research were:

- To conduct user interviews, using a "grounded theory" approach, to elicit user preferences for designs for 3-dimensional "virtual realities" for accessing information.
- To draw from these interviews conclusions as to common elements and recurrent designs.
- To construct "worlds", used to demonstrate different designs as vehicles to develop further depth of understanding of user requirements and preferences.

New Trends in Qualitative and Quantitative Methods in Libraries
A. Katsirikou and C. H. Skiadas (eds)
© *World Scientific Publishing Co (pp. 279-285)*

- To analyse user preferences with particular attention towards affective responses, which might be indicative of the influence of non-structural features of the "worlds".
- To draw conclusions as to possible factors influencing user preferences.

3. Methodology

A deliberate effort was made to avoid influencing user decisions by constraining their selection in any way, so it was decided that the worlds tested by the users, and on which their views were sought, should arise from the input of the users themselves. An earlier piece of work had sought user reactions to pre-constructed worlds, but was abandoned when it became evident that these worlds had been chosen arbitrarily by the researcher, and that the research methodology was in fact doing the very thing which it was now important to avoid.

The study was a type of naturalistic enquiry, a study of the reactions of a distinct group of people to a given set of circumstances. According to Linton, Joy and Shafer (1999 p.132), naturalistic enquiry "involves studying real-world situations as they unfold naturally in a non-manipulative, unobtrusive, and non-controlling manner, with openness to whatever emerges and a lack of predetermined constraints on outcomes. The point is to understand naturally occurring phenomena in their naturally occurring states".

It was decided that it would be appropriate to use a "grounded theory" methodology for data collection. This methodology takes as input data gathered directly from participants, and develops theory arising from that data. The process is iterative and recursive – as a theory develops, it is tested against the data, further data is gathered, the theory is refined and developed, and this cycle proceeds until such time as no further relevant data emerges , at which stage "saturation" has been reached. This methodology, developed by Glaser and Strauss (1967), and Strauss and Corbin (1990) appeared to be ideally suited to the collection and analysis of essentially qualitative data, and to the also cyclical nature of the experimental process.

First, interviewees were asked, with no constraints put upon their imagination, what their picture would be of an "ideal world" to use for information retrieval. These responses were analysed, and common factors were found. Next , four "worlds" were designed, based on these common factors. Another group of interviewees was asked to test these worlds, and to share their responses to them. The worlds were then redesigned in response to that input. Finally, another group of interviewees was asked to test the resultant worlds, and to discuss, based on this experience, what their ideal worlds would be like.

The process thus moved from unfettered imagination, through development and refinement of practical models, back to imagination, but this time based on experience.

Although the continuing availability of the same students over the course of the research would have been problematic if an extended quantitative study had been the methodology of choice, the grounded approach meant that there was no particular requirement to interview the same individuals several times - just to interview individuals, although sessions were therefore slightly longer, to allow for "scene-setting". As long as the necessary information was acquired, there was no necessity to repeat interviews. The development of the theory, and of the research instrument itself, takes place independently of any development in knowledge or skill on the part of the interviewee. For this reason, the methodology, like the literature review, was treated in a sectional, or sequential, manner. Grounded Theory allows, and indeed expects, that the theoretical structure will be developed through "rounds" of, in this case, interviews, and that each round will be both founded on previous rounds, and an attempt to reflectively develop a research instrument of greater precision than in the previous round. It is therefore considered more meaningful to show this development as the rounds progress, and the theory's development changes accordingly. As shown in fig. 1, the overall structure has a cyclical pattern, as older material is revisited and reviewed in the light of more recent material.

The fact that the study "evolved" into a series of "rounds", with a theory emerging and undergoing modification during the process, is in keeping with Grounded Theory practice, in that the theory "emerges" iteratively from the interviews, and is tested at each successive stage.

The interviews were transcribed, and analysed using Nvivo software, which allows significant words or phrases in documents to be marked up, and assigned identifiers. The identifiers can be the words or phrases themselves – this is "in vivo" coding, from which the software takes its name – or can be decided in advance by the user.

4. Findings

The first round of interviews, series A, produced a very wide range of ideas for virtual worlds, ranging from deep sea diving to space, with buildings, forests, car parks and a fun-fair also featuring. The first feature which became apparent was that there was a division between worlds which might be described as "realistic", and those which seemed more "imagined", or "fanciful". Even within realism, though, it seems that there are degrees – a "real" library seems firmly grounded in reality, especially when it has models of computers to access online resources. However, a mansion of branching rooms, laid out in a classification order, is concrete, but has a fantastic element.

A similar "fanciful" element seems to apply to the instances of a world of "bubbles", and the ones which relate to galaxies, planetary systems and "space" – these are real entities, but are used in an imaginative way, to serve an information access function which they would not normally have. It is true that planetary models have an internal "logic" – that of gravitational forces and the resultant orbiting behaviour – onto which an organisation of information might be mapped, but there appears to be an element of abstraction in these cases, where one order is being superimposed on another.

It seemed at this stage that the worlds could be categorised into four types, in a way which would also include the large number of more "idiosyncratic" worlds, by treating them as being split between realistic and non-realistic, and also between organised and un-organised.

The theory at this stage was that: All worlds could be classified into one of four groups, and that people would tend to prefer using a world typical of one of these groups. This allowed the next stages of the testing to be carried out using a practicable number of demonstration worlds.

The next stage was the development, then testing, of the representative models. The worlds were created in the Virtual Reality Modelling Language (VRML), initially using Microsoft Notepad, a text editor, and later using a specialised VRML editor called VrmlPad. The process is iterative, consisting of writing world files, testing them in by viewing with a web browser and VRML "plug-in" application – Cortona and BitManagement VRML clients were used – and then returning to the edit stage, to make corrections. Four worlds were created, with the intention of representing the major classes which had been found in the series A interviews, i.e. a) concrete and ordered, b) concrete and unordered, c) abstract and ordered d)abstract and unordered. Two worlds were "concrete" – a town, which was taken to be "unordered", in that there was no obvious rationale behind the placing of information, and a library, which was "ordered" in that the stock was arranged according to the Dewey Decimal Classification scheme. Two were "abstract", in that they were representations of real things, but of things which would not normally be considered as sources of information. The forest was unordered, in that the trees had no particular arrangement, whereas the space world was ordered by Dewey Decimal Classification.

The second series of interviews was carried out as the interviewees moved around in the four "worlds" which had been constructed to represent the most popular images from the first series. The worlds were accessed from an introductory web page, and it was necessary to close the world scene after each world had been tried out, and to return to the introductory page. The links to the worlds were labelled "Forest", "Library", "Space" and "Town". The worlds themselves were very simply constructed, and contained only sample resources.

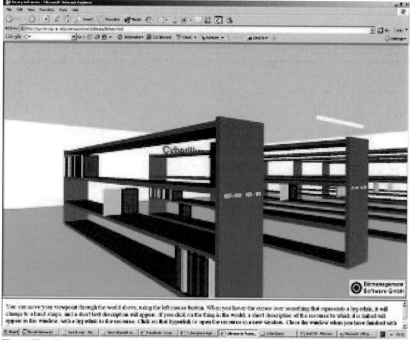

Fig. 1 The library

In this series, interviewees were not asked about ideal worlds, but the interviews were concerned with moving around in the worlds, and the interviewees were encouraged to comment on whether the worlds were more or less what they had expected, whether they found any features particularly easy or difficult to use, and whether they thought they might be able to use the worlds to access information.

The testing immediately showed up some basic flaws, suggested some "low cost" improvements, and helped shape the "interview technique". The plan at this stage was just to introduce each model – forest, town, space and library, and to let the subjects use each in turn, whilst observing and recording them. These interview tapes are long and there are long pauses, people do not say much, and tend to polarise into very enthusiastic or very unimpressed (mainly the former). There was also more criticism of minor features than was expected, perhaps due to a failure to communicate properly the prototypical nature of the worlds.

This material was interesting in view of a) it being the interviewees' first reaction to seeing this type of 3D information world, and b) their responses while moving around and interacting with the worlds. The worlds thus functioned as vehicles for the discovery of user preferences within a quite restricted set of options.

Part way through the series B interviews, modifications were made in response to feedback, which resulted in the worlds being positioned together, to allow for greater ease of navigation amongst them, an in having resources open in new windows, to remove the necessity to "restart" a world from the starting position each time. The resultant world is shown in Fig. 2. A memo at this stage notes the interviewer's negative reaction to criticism of the initial worlds, and successful adaptation in the light of that criticism. Two points of interest emerge here, Firstly, the approach of the methodology, with its cyclical nature, means that frequent examination of the data can provide insight to the interviewer's reactions, as well as to those of the interviewees. Secondly, the approach taken in the introduction to the interview can be adapted, as could the content of more structured interviews than those used in this study, to reflect changes in emphasis appropriate to different stages of the study.

Fig. 2 The amended world

The addition at this stage to the overall theory is that there is generally an enthusiasm for the idea and the potential of using 3D virtual worlds for accessing information, but that this is tempered by reservations as to the practicality of using them in this context.

For the third round of interviews, staff members of Aberdeen Business School were interviewed. The decision to use members of staff is, in grounded theory terms, an example of "theoretical sampling" – finding a sample who are the best to explore a particular aspect of the research question. What was required at this stage was a group who had the same common "universe of debate" as the first two, but who were more experienced in accessing information, and also more experienced as communicators, and who could add to the depth of description of their chosen worlds.

These interviewees were shown how to navigate in the world, given time to experiment, then asked, , "Now that you have seen examples of different worlds, if you were having a world designed for you to use for accessing information, what would it look like?". Interviewees typically first discussed their reactions to the models presented in the "amalgamated" world. They usually selected one or two of the "component" worlds – planets, town, forest and library – as their favourite, and justified this choice either by mentioning features they liked about that model, by mentioning features they did not like about other models, or both.

Not all interviewees discussed the models directly, or mentioned a favourite, but those who did not would sometimes use points about the demonstration models when discussing their ideal model.

Since these responses were not solicited on a user-by-user, world-by-world basis, their main value is impressionistic, in that they convey the stronger and more commonly held reactions to the demonstration worlds. This would be of value, should any of the demonstration models be developed further, but the principal use of the responses in this series of interviews is in revealing more about the interviewees' reasons for selecting their ideal worlds. It was not intended that the interviewees be asked to select their favourite model at this stage, rather that the models be used as a seed or an inspiration to give context to discussions of the desirable and less desirable features of virtual worlds.

It was during analysis of this series of interviews that an interviewee introduced the concept of "assistance" – that having a character to help would be useful in retrieving information. It then transpired that the idea had also appeared in other interviews, as a market trader, a librarian, a "cybrarian", and a shop assistant. The idea of assistance as an influential factor in assessing worlds led to the analysis looking more deeply for affective responses, whereas the focus had previously been on structural elements.

This change in focus, taking, as it were, a different slice through the data, started to produce persuasive results. It transpired that what influenced people in selecting or proposing a world was not structural factors so much as qualitative ones. People wanted worlds which had an element of familiarity, which had high quality presentation, in which they could get assistance when necessary, and which were recognisably ordered. This shift in perspective came about entirely because of "immersion in the data" – recommended in grounded theory as a means of increasing theoretical sensitivity.

Grounded theory is subject to criticism which appears to take three main forms. First, is that of interpretation, expressed by Bryman (1988 p.73) as "how is it feasible to perceive as others perceive?" Respondent validation, or "member checking" was carried out both at the level of establishing accuracy of transcription (with all groups of respondents) and at the final level of checking the validity of the researcher's interpretation for an academic audience, with respondents who were themselves also part of that audience.

The second question relates to whether research can be conducted in a theory-neutral way, and with specific regard to Grounded Theory, whether it actually provides theories, or simply generates categories. In this research, it would be true to say that the theory, substantive rather than formal, was arrived at during the transcription, rather than the collection phase, although the direction of the collection phase had been influenced by the development of the theory.

The third question is whether theory based on a study in a single setting, of a particular case, or of a particular group, can be generalised outside that setting. Rather than attempting to defend the questionable position that the (interpreted) experience of a specific group can be generalised to a larger population, as a quantitative survey might generalise quantifiable data about a rigorously sampled group of participants, grounded theory encourages the generation of formal hypotheses, which are open to testing against other contexts.

Grounded theory must be seen as flawed in some degree – it is doubtful whether it can really be theory-neutral, there is a question about interviewees' intentionality, there may be some constructivism, and there are also questions regarding the validity of interpretation. However, in this study, the use of grounded theory techniques has opened up an area of user experience which would have been very difficult to explore using a quantitative methodology, which in itself would have fundamentally changed the relationship between researcher and users. Grounded theory may not be able to live up to all the claims made by its supporters, but it remains the best tool for an investigation of this type.

5. Conclusions

This study approached the question of designing virtual worlds from a user-centred perspective, which appears to have been missing from other treatments of the subject. It found that it is possible to derive from interviews a set of properties which are distinct from, and complementary to, those considered in other publications. For example, it is widely acknowledged that "intelligibility" is a positive factor in the design of 3D worlds, but it does not appear to have been considered that "familiarity" of an environment might also play a significant part in the acceptance of the world as a "place" in which to work.

It was found that the properties of **familiarity, organisation or structure, mediation or assistance, and quality of presentation** were those deemed to be important by the participants in this study. It is felt probable that these properties, rather than the tendency to select a particular design, will be transferable across different groups of users, and that these findings can help to determine the course of further research and design work in the area of 3D worlds for information retrieval.

References

Bryman, A., 1988. *Quantity and quality in social research* Routledge, London.

Card, S.K., Mackinlay, J.D. and Robertson, G.G., (1991). The Information Visualizer: An Information Workspace. *ACM Conference on Human Factors in Computing Systems (CHI '91)*. 1991. ACM. 181-188

Gibson, W., (1986). *Neuromancer*. GraftonBooks, London.

Glaser, B.G. and Strauss, A.L., (1967).*The discovery of grounded theory : strategies for qualitative research*. Aldine de Gruyter, New York.

Linton, F., Joy, D. and Shafer, H., (1999). Building user and expert models by longterm observation of application usage. In: J. KAY, ed. *Proceedings of the 7th International Conference on User Modeling*. 20 - 24 June. Springer-Verlag, New York. 129-138

Strauss, A.L. and Corbin, J., (1990). *Basics of qualitative research : grounded theory procedures and techniques.*Sage, Newbury Park, CA.

Stephenson, N., (1992). *Snow crash*. Penguin, London.

Matching the Databases' User Interface with Ellis' Model of Information Seeking Behavior: A Qualitative Survey

Mohammad Azami[1] and Rahmattolah Fattahi[2]

[1]Ferdowsi University of Mashhad and Kerman University of Medical Sciences, Iran, mohammadaazami14@gmail.com
[2]Ferdowsi University of Mashhad, Mashhad, Iran, fattahirahmat@gmail.com

Abstract: Purpose – Considering a lack of database designers' attention to the features of user information seeking behavior in designating user-interfaces, the aim of this study is to investigate the extent to which user interface characteristics of some main databases (Ebsco, Emerald, Proquest and Science Direct) are in accordance with Ellis' model of information seeking behavior.

Design/Method/Approach – Using a heuristic evaluation method frequently used in human-computer interaction research, the necessary information was collected by direct observation of these databases' user interface against a checklist containing six features of Ellis' model.

Findings – Interface designers have rarely applied these features in the design and structure of the studied user interfaces. Some features of Ellis' model, i.e., starting, chaining and differentiating were relatively found in these interfaces. However, other three features of this model, namely browsing, monitoring and extracting were not supported by the interfaces. The degree of match between these user interfaces with Ellis' model is at average.

Originality/value – Taking information seeking behavior into account when designing user interfaces will improve them and help users in accessing more relevant information with ease and speed.

Keywords: User interface, human computer interaction, information seeking behavior, database interface, Ellis' model

1. Introduction

In our information age, databases are the most important online information sources available on the Web. One important instance of this space is the field of human-computer interaction (HCI). Human computer interaction deals with the interaction between users and computers in order to make computer systems more user-friendly (Hewtt and Card, 2004). As information databases are important scientific and research resources, the role of user interface as facilitator is undeniable. User interface design is of main subfield of human computer interaction which has attracted the research interests increasingly. Use of communication and information technologies in the production, storage, retrieval, organization and dissemination of information promotes the design of user interface (Belkin, Oddy, and Brooks, 1982a). User interface is the first and the starting point in user' information search process in databases. It makes a building bridge between the end-user and information databases. Then, achieving user satisfaction and effective and better access to provided information is of the main goals in user interface design. Regarding the variety of the existing databases and computer environments, users have serious problems in the satisfactory use of these databases. In addition, the role of skilled librarians, as

New Trends in Qualitative and Quantitative Methods in Libraries
A. Katsirikou and C. H. Skiadas (eds)
© *World Scientific Publishing Co (pp. 287- 296)*

intermediaries in guiding user in complex information environments has become weak due to some reasons such as using the databases out of libraries (.e.g. in work places) and personalization of information seeking process as a results of information technology development. User interface as an effective medium between users and information databases can be an appropriate replacement for human in the new environment. Optimal use of databases has not been achieved because of the emerging problems which stem from a lack of application of all necessary elements and characters for an appropriate user interface design. Some users can not use the system properly. Designers disregard all necessary conditions and characteristics of users when they design user interfaces (Hansen, 1998). Despite some development in the design of database's user interface, researchers confirmed the presence of problems such as ambiguous and unclear vocabulary, complexity of search operations, the lack of control means, no provision of well-timed and useful feedback in various user interfaces (Clark and Forest, 2003, Kengpeng, Ramiah and Foo, 2004, Luck, 1996, Mangiaracina and Marchitti, 1999). As a result, it can be concluded that the existing user interfaces can satisfy only some part of their users' expectations due to designer's focus on theoretical background of user interface design instead of focusing on user actual needs and requirements. As Saracevic (1996) points out, the greatest danger that threatens information science is the lack of attention to user aspect and human perspective in information system design and more attention to system aspect. He noted that linking user and system side aspects in information science research would lead to considerable success in our field.

Some databases are not understandable enough and their users have serious problems in interacting with them due to the lack of information system designers' attention to human factors in designing their user interfaces (Kennedy, 1999). The features needed in information seeking behavior have not been regarded in developing many user interfaces and instead, some absolute human factors have been taken into consideration (Beaulieu, 2000). Therefore, designers should consider the need of users and try to fulfil their expectations of information systems (Shniderman, 1998). Considering the multi-aspects of human information behavior and their various information needs, some databases are not matched with these needs. This resulted in inability to facilitate user information seeking process during search session from various databases. Then, the greatest challenge information specialists encounter these years is to design an effective user interface for databases containing and protecting the elements of user information seeking behavior. One solution for solving this problem is to consider the information seeking behavior when designing database interfaces. Since information seeking behavior is a reflection of user needs, it is necessary to apply its requirements in the design of user interfaces (Marchionini and Komlodi, 1998). These features help users control information system effectively and manage it easy for satisfying their information needs. So, studying the effects of these features of information seeking behavior on optimization and effectiveness of user interfaces is of great significance and value. Effective use of some basic features in interface design can improve the use of databases and accessing relevant information.

In this study, the quality of Ellis' information seeking features in user interface environment of some main databases, including Emerald, Ebsco, Proquest and ScienceDirect in relation to their accordance with these features is investigated and also some implications are discussed.

Information seeking behaviors in new environments

New environments (i.e. the Web, the Net, e-commerce and all e-entities of electronic age) have more potential capacities than traditional ones due to the effects of information technologies. New technologies have enabled all kinds of users to access and share information with one another. Many electronic resources are available in the library. The increase in information available on the Web has affected information seeking behavior. The study of user information seeking behavior in relation to users' interaction with these new environments has become of great interest of many researchers. As a purposeful process in which human beings attempt to enhance their knowledge status (Marchionini, 1995), information seeking behavior reflects user information needs. Identifying and understanding these "behaviors" has some implications for designing an appropriate user interface with which useful services to users can be provided. In addition, the possibilities of information seek and search via Net from home and workplace by all users in various levels necessitates the learning of information seeking skills by them. The influence of new technology on information seeking is also providing a new set of alternative models that describe more accurately the information seeking process as a dynamic activity. Illustrating the features of information seeking behavior based on a model or pattern is a common method used in library and information science for description and identification of information seeking behaviors. Some models of this type have been proposed by various researchers. They include Taylor (1962), Belkin (1982b), Ellis (1989), Kuhlthau (1991), Marchionini (1995) and Wilson (1999) among others. These models are user- centered and focused on users' needs and behavior rather than on technical aspects of information system.

Ellis' model was selected in this study for some reasons. It is applicable to all human knowledge fields and all user groups (Ellis, 1997). It has been designed especially for electronic environments and appropriate for hypertext environments, such as the Web (Wilson, 1999). This model has been affected research on information seeking behavior cited by related literature because of its empirical and experimental base. Studies by the Choo and colleagues (1998 and 2000) confirmed the applicability of Ellis' model in Web environment. Wilson (1999) proposed the combination of this model with other related ones. Meho and Tibbo (2003) set a study for revising the model in social science research. Makri and Blandford's study (2008) focused on information seeking behavior of lawyers based on this model.

Ellis in various studies (Ellis, 1989, Ellis, Cox and Hall, 1993, Ellis and Haugen, 1997) considered the information seeking behavior of different groups in academic communities in the UK. In his first study on a group of social science researchers (Ellis, 1989), Ellis proposed the model based on six features. He revised and developed this model in two later studies. As this model has been applied in many scientific fields, some changes and revisions have been made in these features. We considered the six features of information seeking behavior proposed in Ellis' first study (Ellis, 1989). These six features are starting, chaining, browsing, differentiating, monitoring and extracting. These features are briefly described here.

1. Starting refers to identify relevant sources on the Web. This feature is demonstrated as entrance to homepage or search page in electronic environments.

2. Chaining as the second feature indicates the process of tracing information resources. In this stage, user follows the citations, references, footnotes and hyperlinks for requested information. Chaining occurs when researchers notice information of interests, and then follow hypertext links to find more relevant information on those items.

3. Browsing as the third feature implicates the scanning of recently published issues of journals and tables of content of relevant books, browsing the online catalogs, titles, headings and persons and organization names, etc to know more about needed information.

4. Differentiating, is the fourth feature in which users try to distinguish and rank retrieved resources according to their quality, nature and relevance to their search topic(s).
5. Monitoring is the fifth feature and facilitates the up-to-datedness of retrieved resources regularly. This feature is characterized by activity of keeping abreast of developments in an area by regularly following particular sources.
6. Extracting is the six and last feature, includes the actions such as downloading, saving and printing demanded resources for using them by regular process inside the database.

Numerous studies have been done on user interface, but most of them have focused on general and common criteria (Fattahi and Parirokh, 2000; Nowkarizi, 2006; Zerehsaz, 2006; Entezariyan and Fattahi, 2008). Then, measuring the impact of information seeking behavior on improving database interface and determining their relations is very important. This research measures the compability of Ellis' information seeking behavior model to the user interface of four databases.

2. Methods

This study used a heuristic evaluation method. This is one of the methods basically used as usability testing in the study of human-computer interaction. According to this method, a few (3-5) evaluators are asked to mach graphical user interface with the usability principles (Nilsen, 1995). Heuristic approach aims to identify usability problems based on human factors in designing user interface (Entezaryan and Fattahi, 2008). In the heuristic evaluation, a checklist is used as a tool for examining user interface. Therefore, in this research, the features of Ellis' model are used as checklist to conduct the observation and comparison of the studied interfaces. In this research, three evaluators conducted their individual heuristic evaluations of the Ebsco, Emerald, Proquest and ScienceDirect interfaces. These databases are known as the most popular resources among the scientific community, especially in the field of library and information sciences. In this research, user interfaces of Emerald, Ebsco, Proquest and ScienceDirect were matched with the features of Ellis' model. The interfaces of four databases were observed by the researchers to determine to what extent each feature of the model corresponds the interfaces. The evaluators were asked to match the databases' interface with items in the check list. All evaluators' responses were reflected in a matrix. The evaluators' positive responses to checklist items were considered as the necessity of them to user interfaces features, and vice versa, their negative response to the items were considered as unnecessary of them to the use interface feature.

3. Results of the study

The evaluators identified a number of weakness and strengths in the studied databases. Results showed that each database applied these features in its interface differently. Some interfaces supported one or more features of the model relatively. As shown in Figure 1, all features of Ellis' model are supported to some extent by the user interface Emerald.

As mentioned earlier, the first feature of Ellis' model is called "starting". According to Ellis, starting includes those activities that form the initial search for information. Some of the studied databases support both keyword and browsing searches for novice and expert searchers who know their target and information needs who have little knowledge about their topic. The "search button" as a starting point is very common in all the databases. For example, Ebsco and ScienceDirect provide various key icons (advanced, basic, simple and smart search) in their interfaces to help users for starting of search of needed information. However, other databases, such as

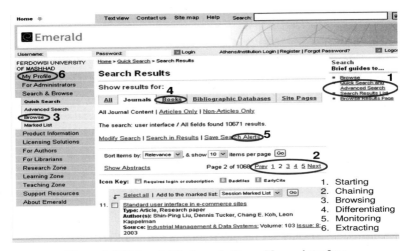

Figure 1: Ellis' model features in Emerald user interface

1. Starting
2. Chaining
3. Browsing
4. Differentiating
5. Monitoring
6. Extracting

Proquest, do not offer appropriate fields related to starting feature in their user interfaces. Ebsco's interface offers various facilities and icons related to the starting feature, such as: simple search, advanced search, expert search and etc. (Figure 2).

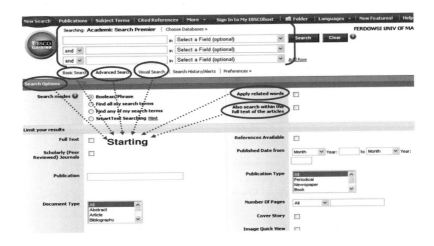

Figure 2: Starting feature in Ebsco

The second feature of the Ellis' model is known as "chaining". This feature is presented on the interfaces in different ways. ScienceDirect helps users to access "related articles" for retrieved documents (Figure 3). Proquest and Ebsco databases provide different links among all available sources. These databases also offer "smart search" in order to provide users with the ability to find more relevant documents. Other databases also interconnect a number of sources to each other through a variety of links.

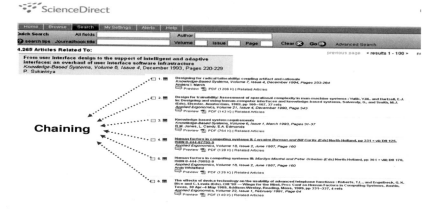

Figure 3: Chaining feature in ScienceDirect

The third feature of the Ellis' model is "browsing". While Proquest, ScienceDirect, and Emerald databases offer this feature on their interfaces, its task is not matched with the aims of "browsing" feature in Ellis' model and needs of the users. Ebsco database has ignored this feature. Figure 4 shows this feature in ScienceDirect.

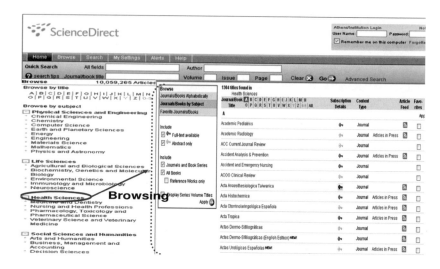

Figure 4: Browsing feature in ScienceDirect

The fourth key feature in Ellis' model is "differentiating". This feature is characterized as filtering and assessing sources for their usefulness. All studied databases provided possibility of distinguishing among different sources through items such as: language, books, papers, dissertation, abstract, full text, year and etc. This feature in Proquest is shown in Figure 5.

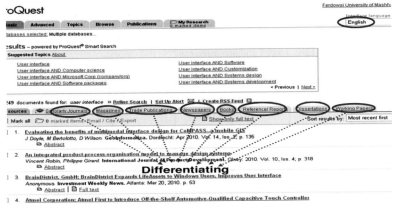

Figure 5: Differentiating feature in Proquest

The fifth feature of Ellis' model is called "monitoring". This behavior is the act of Keeping abreast of developments in a given subject area. Most databases offer appropriate sources along with relevant services in order to keep users up-to-date with new and relevant information. This demonstrates the monitoring feature. For example "push technology" is a kind of service which provides and sends relevant information to user profiles via the web.

The sixth key feature of Ellis' model is identified as "extracting". This features means systematically working through a given source for material of interest. Extracting behavior is the final use of information. All databases are capable to help their users to highlight sources they need through the "extracting" feature. There is also possibility of customizing, personalization for users in some of the databases. The monitoring and extracting feature in Proquest are shown in Figure 6.

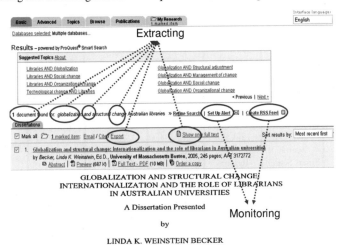

Figure 6: Monitoring and extracting features in Proquest

The Figure 6 summarized the features of Ellis' model in the studied user interfaces as matrix. The top row and the left column of the matrix represent the model's features and the studied databases respectively. It is notable that the structure and wording representing these features in each database are different from others and might be various even in the same database. In addition, these are not complete representatives of each feature of Ellis' model and are some relative indicators.

Table 1: Conceptual matrix of the features of Ellis' model in the studied user interfaces

Features / Databases	Starting	Chaining	Browsing	Differentia-ting	Monitoring	Extracting
Ebsco	Simple Search New Search Basic search Advanced Search Visual Search Smart Search	Journal Archive Authors Source		Publication Year Various sources Full text Information bibliographies Authors Title	Alert services	Save Categories Download Print
Emerald	Simple Search Quick search Advanced Search Search results Modify Search	Reference URL Article	Title Subject	Document type Publication year	Current awareness services	Save Categories Download Printing
Proquest	Basic Search Advance Search Modify Search	Web Site Author Journals Archive	Research Scientific reports	Topic Publication Year Full text Article types	Current awareness services	Categories Save Printing Download
Science Direct	Expert search Quick search Advanced Search Smart Search Help	Web Link Quick Links Link the database Related Resources	Title Headings Entry pages Site maps Journals Archive	Year Topic Sources Full text	Current awareness Services	bookmaking Save Downloading

4. Conclusions and implications

Considering the increasing use of databases, the design of very user interfaces with appropriate features and necessary facilities is very important for their easy use. Weak and insufficient design of user interfaces is a main obstacle in accessing database content. As main element is user communication with databases, user interfaces in databases have appropriates structure and user-friendly features in order to facilitate users tracing and searching process. As today's end-users have various social and educational backgrounds, taking their information seeking behavior besides other common elements into account is necessary. These features can improve the usability of databases, and increase their relative satisfaction of users.

Although the results of this study showed that some features of Ellis' model were somewhat applied in the user interface of these database, the studied databases do not match with Ellis' model. It seems that interface designers are not aware of the concepts and principals underlying information seeking behavior when designing the database interface. Designers should redesign database interfaces based on both user-oriented and system-oriented approaches (Saracevic, 1996). They must understand users' information seeking patterns to help them to have better interaction with the databases and as a result, better fulfillment of their various information needs. The findings of this study also confirmed that design of user interface should correspond to models of information seeking behavior and the contributions of librarian in their designation will improve their applicability and efficacy.

References

Beaulieu, M. (2000). Interaction in Information Searching and Retrieval. *Journal of Documentation*, 56(4): 431-439.

Belkin, N. J. , Oddy, R. N and Brooks, H. M. (1982a). ASK for information retrieval: Part 1 Background and theory. *Journal of Documentation*, Vol.38, No.2, 61-71.

Belkin, N. J., Oddy, R. N and Brooks, H. M. (1982b). ASK for Information Retrieval: Part 2 Results of Design Study. *Journal of Documentation,* Vol.38, No.3, 145-I 64.

Choo, C. W., Brian, D. and Don, T. (1998). A Behavioral Model of Information Seeking on the Web: Preliminary Results of a Study of How Managers and IT Specialists Use the Web. In: *Proceedings of 61st ASIS Annual Meeting held in Pittsburgh, Pa.*, edited by Cecilia M. Preston, 290-302, Information Today Inc.

Choo, C. W., Detlor, B and Turnbull. D. (2000). Information Seeking on the Web: An Integrated Model of Searching and Browsing. Retrieved 2009/12/19 from: http://firstmonday.org/issues/issue5_2/choo/index.html

Clark, N.; and Frost, D. (2003). User-centred Evaluation and Design: A Subject Gatway Perception, Retrieved 2009/12/19 from: http://www.vala.org.au/vala 2002pdf/38clafro.pdf

Ellis, D. (1989). A Behavioural Approach to Information Retrieval System Design. *Journal of Documentation,* Vol.45, No.3, 171-202.

Ellis, D. Cox, D and Hall, K., (1993). A Comparison of Information Seeking Patterns of Researchers in the Physical and Social Sciences. *Journal of Documentation*,49, 356-360.

Ellis, D. and M. Haugan., (1997). Modeling Information Seeking Patterns of Engineers and Research Scientists an industrial Environment. *Journal of Documentation,* Vol.53, No.4, 384-403.

Entzaryan, N. and Fattahi, R., (2008). Evaluating of user perception from databases user interface based on Nilsson Model. *Journal of* Library and information Science, Vol.47,No.3, 89-105.

Fattahi, R. and Parirokh, M., (2001). Studying quality of demonstrating information in Iranian Library OPAC and recommendation for how to improve it: In OPAC Seminar: application and development of Iranian libraries pp. 223-352, Ferdowsi University of Mashhad and Scientific and Information Center Ministry of Agriculture, Tehran, Iran.

Hansen, P., (1998). Evaluation of IR User Interface Implications for User Interface Design. Retrieved 2009/12/19 from: www.hb.se/bhs/ith/2-98/ph.htm

Hewtt, B., and Card. (2004). ACM SIGHI Curricula for Human-Computer Interaction. Retrieved 2009/12/19 from: http://sig.chi.org/cdg2.html

Kennedy, H. 1999. OPAC evaluation: patron power. Available online at: http//odin.instate.edu/forms.dir/opaceval.html

KenPeng, L., Ramaiah, C. K and Foo, S., (2004). Heuristic-based user interface evaluation at Nanyang Technological University in Singapor. Retrieved 2009/12/19 from:
http://www.emeraldinsight.com/insight/viewcontentservlet.jsessionid.

Kuhlthau, C., (1991). Developing a Model of the Library Search Process: Investigation of Cognitive and Affective Aspects. *Reference Quarterly*, 28, 232-242.

Luk, A.T., (1996). *Evaluting bibliographic displays from the user's point of view: a focus group study. Master of information studies Research project Report.* Toronto. Faculty of information studies, university of Toronto. Retrieved 2009/12/19 from:
http://www.fis.utoronto.ca/research/ programs/displays/annie2.htm

Mangiaracina, S.,and Marchetti, G. (1999). EINS-Web: User Interface Evaluation in Digital Libraries. Retrieved 2009/12/19 from:
http://www.ercim.org/publication/Ercim_News/enw36/marchetti.html

Makri, S., Blandford, A. and Cox, A. L. (2008). Investigating the Information-Seeking Behaviour of Academic Lawyers: From Ellis's Model to Design. *Information Processing and Management*, Vol.44, No.2, 613-634.

Marchionini, G. (1995). *Information seeking in electronic environments.* Cambridge, Uk: Cambridge University Press.

Marchionini, G., and Komlodi. A. (1998). Design of Interfaces for Information Seeking. In *Annual Review of Information Science and Technology*, 89-130. Medford, NJ: Information Today.

Meho, L. I. and Tibbo, R. H. (2003). Modeling the Information-Seeking Behavior of Social Scientists: Ellis's Study Revisited .*Journal of the American society for Information Science and Technology*, 54, 570-576.

Nielsen, J. (1995). Technology Transfer of Heuristic Evaluation and Usability Inspection. Retrieved 2009/12/19 from:
www.useit.com/papers/heuristic/learning_inspection.html.

Noowkarizi, M., (2006). Vocabulary analysis of user interfaces in Persian library Soft wares and determine the extent of student understanding to propose a conceptual model. *Doctoral thesis in library and information Sciences, Ferdowsi University of Mashhad, Mashhad, Iran.*

Sarasevic,T. (1996). Modeling Interaction in Information Retrieval (IR): a Review and Proposal. In *Proceedings of the American society for information science*, 33, 3-9, Proceedings of the 59th American Society for Information Science Annual Meeting, Baltimore, MD, USA 19-24 October

Shneiderman, B. (1998). *Designing the user interface:strategies for effective human – computer interaction.* Massachusetts: Addison Wesley Longman.

Taylor, R. S. (1968). Question-Negotiation and Information Seeking in Libraries. *College and Research Libraries*, 29, 178-194.

Wilson, T. D. (1999). Models in Information Behavior Research. *Journal of Documentation*, Vol.55, No.3, 249 – 270.

Zerehsaz, M. (2006) Investigation and analysis of elements and features discussed in the Simorgh user interface software and determine students' satisfaction from interacting with this user interface. *Master thesis of Library and Information Sciences in faculty of Education and Psychology, Ferdowsi University of Mashhad, Iran.*

Zerehsaz, M and Fattahi, R., (2009). Factors affecting the process of help users to use user interface in databases. *Journal of Library and Information Sciences,* Vol.43, No.3, 71-96.

Exploring the Research Knowledge Needs of Canadian Academic Librarians

Alvin M. Schrader

Director of Research, University of Alberta Libraries, and Professor Emeritus, University of Alberta, Edmonton, Alberta, Canada, alvin.schrader@ualberta.ca

Abstract: As academic librarians increasingly embrace the core value and challenge of engaging in research and scholarly work, and as senior library administrators continue to adopt evidence-based decision making, staff research knowledge and skills must be constantly and systematically developed and augmented. However, descriptive data on current competencies and competency gaps are not widely reported, nor are methodologies for capturing and articulating deeper insights into attitudes and perspectives. This paper describes the outcomes of a pilot project to shed light on the current levels of research knowledge, experience, interests, competencies, and learning needs of academic librarians employed by the University of Alberta Libraries, which serves faculty, staff, and students at one of the major research institutions in Canada. The longer-term goal is to build capacity, at both the institutional and the professional.

Keywords: Academic librarians, research librarians, academic libraries, research libraries, Canadian research libraries, academic librarianship, research, scholarly activity, Canadian Association of Research Libraries, CARL

1. Introduction: Research and Scholarship as a Core Value of Academic Librarians

An important mandate adopted by more and more librarians working in Canadian research libraries is to contribute actively to the knowledge base of their professional discipline, as well as to align themselves more centrally with the broader academic process of scholarly communication. Engagement with the scholarly communication process is increasingly recognized as a core value. Indeed, there is an increasing expectation in research libraries across Canada that librarians pursue active research and scholarship for purposes of tenure, promotion, and annual performance.

More recent is a nascent recognition of evidence-based management decision making to advance institutional service goals. Within the last decade or so, major research libraries in North America have begun participating in large-scale user assessment projects in order to enhance managerial decision-making; Lib-QUAL+, which is offered by the Association of Research Libraries (ARL) (2010), is the most prominent tool in this collective endeavour.

New Trends in Qualitative and Quantitative Methods in Libraries
A. Katsirikou and C. H. Skiadas (eds)
© *World Scientific Publishing Co (pp. 297-306)*

These parallel trends, professional participation in research and institutional interest in evidence-based management, are converging gradually to create heightened interest in an organizational and professional culture of research and assessment – not only within individual research libraries but within the broader community of library professionals and professional associations as well.

Nonetheless, as academic librarians take on the challenge of producing and disseminating both scholarly and applied research knowledge, and as administrators expect higher levels of research productivity and evidence-based decision making, it is important that staff research knowledge and skills be constantly and systematically developed and augmented. One of the little studied questions is the extent to which they have the requisite knowledge and skills to conduct high quality research and scholarship, and what further learning needs they have in order to maintain or even enhance their productivity.

Descriptive data on research competencies and competency gaps are not widely reported, nor are methodologies for capturing and articulating deeper insights into prevailing attitudes and perspectives regarding the research and scholarship enterprise. Two recent studies have addressed particular aspects of interest to the present study, Fennewald (2008) and Fox (2007a, 2007b). A sort of case study, Fennewald held face to face interviews with academic librarians at Penn State to shed light on their perceptions of research productivity and barriers. Fox conducted a web-based questionnaire survey of the motivations of Canadian academic librarians to engage in research and scholarly activities, the perceived importance of such activities as a criterion for tenure and promotion, and the availability of various types of support.

This paper describes one response to the dearth of knowledge in this area, a sort of selective case study snapshot of one institution, the University of Alberta Libraries (UAL). The paper describes the outcomes of a pilot project to shed light on the current levels of research knowledge, experience, interests, competencies, and learning needs of academic librarians at UAL, which serves faculty, staff, and students at one of the largest research-intensive universities in Canada. With a response rate of 68%, survey findings are strongly indicative, although the attitudes and opinions of non-respondents should not be forgotten.

2. Background: The University of Alberta Libraries

Over the years, in the gradual evolution and codification of collective agreements in Canadian research libraries, more and more consideration was given to librarians as scholar-researchers. Positioning itself as a learning institution, University of Alberta Libraries is a leader in fostering research and scholarly work by librarians on staff. Ongoing strategic priorities include support and enhancement of a "culture of assessment and research," both in the operations and services provided by the institution and among its librarian cohort. Several UAL policy traditions serve to promote this institutional and professional culture: UAL tenure and performance standards in the collective agreement; UAL strategic planning; UAL institutional supports; new librarian job expectations; librarian research competencies; and key functional initiatives, the assessment office and the director of research office.

Nonetheless, there still exists a great deal of variation among research libraries across Canada in tenure and performance requirements for research. Further, there are considerable differences in what is counted as research and scholarly work. UAL recognizes multiple approaches and types of scholarship, though there is a preference for applied research projects. Another Canadian academic library states that scholarship encompasses research, scholarly and/or artistic production in applied, subject, or theoretical/policy scholarship, with the quality and significance of scholarly work judged by the presence of a "programmatic approach."

Tenure standards in the UAL collective agreement refer to research in permissive terms as one component in a larger category of professional and scholarly contributions: "A staff member may participate in professional and scholarly research.... and may request that individual research projects be included in the specific responsibilities assigned" (University of Alberta 2007, article 7.03). Although permissively phrased, at the same time UAL tenure candidates must show evidence of "commitment to continuing professional growth as exemplified by formal or informal study" to ensure the continued growth and development of the Library, the University, and "future potential in the field of librarianship" (University of Alberta Libraries 2000). In some institutions, research engagement is a mandatory criterion for tenure, merit, and promotion.

In keeping with a more inclusive approach to research and scholarly endeavours, UAL acknowledges a diversity of vehicles for dissemination of findings. Research dissemination is broadly described in the Librarian Agreement to encompass publication in traditional formats, conference presentations, technology-based projects, online journal articles, and other digital and non-print publications, stipulating only that research should reach a wider audience than "the candidate's normal working environment" (University of Alberta Libraries 2000, sub D). In some institutions, peer-reviewed vehicles, with a preference for peer-reviewed journals, are the paramount criterion of research productivity.

Also reinforcing research engagement by University of Alberta librarians is the Library's strategic plan and ongoing strategic priorities, which include support and enhancement of a culture of assessment and research for both institutional and professional goals. The latest strategic plan refers to fostering "a spirit of innovation," supporting staff participation at conferences and meetings of professional organizations, and promoting "quality scholarly research and the exposure of that research by our librarians by way of publishing and academic presentations" (University of Alberta Learning Services 2006).

UAL institutional supports include the annual professional expense allowance, research travel support, and research funding support, although all of these are admittedly somewhat limited pools of money. In recent job ads, a greater emphasis on research credentials and research potential have been stipulated as an expectation of new librarians: "Successful candidates will also be interested in and seek opportunities for conducting research and the evaluation of services and collections" (University of Alberta Libraries, 2009). Recently, a research competencies statement has been incorporated into UAL librarian standards and core competencies. Under consideration as well is a high-level presence on the UAL website for a "Research and Assessment" page, which would list librarians' publications and presentations, internal resource links such as the site for research ethics applications, and research funding sources.

Two other important initiatives that advance UAL strategic priorities with respect to research are the creation several years ago of an assessment librarian office responsible for large-scale mission feedback research, and more recently the hiring of a director of research charged with coaching and advising librarians about their research activities. The Assessment Librarian position was created 8 or 9 years ago, first as a secondment for research and special projects involved in assessment work, and then as a newly-established permanent position in December 2003. While LibQUAL was an important factor, the overriding impetus was the more general move in ARL libraries towards more evidence-based management, that is, towards a state of continuously improving the institution on the basis of "data-based" decision-making that would be squarely focused on user-identified needs.

Another step by UAL was the creation of a Director of Research position in July 2009, responsible for working with librarians on staff to facilitate and encourage the development of a research culture. Specific activities are advising and encouraging librarians in all phases of the research process, and recommending strategies for enhancing research knowledge skills. Such strategies might include designing workshops, inviting speakers, identifying external expertise, planning colloquia and research fairs, assessing research competency needs, reviewing research ethics applications, advising on funding proposals. Also part of the mandate is contributing to a stronger foundation of evidence-based institutional decision-making.

3. Research Knowledge Learning Needs Study of University of Alberta Librarians

At the start, it is essential to acknowledge the already well established traditions and very high levels of research and scholarly contributions that characterize University of Alberta librarians. At the same time, with an increasing emphasis on research credentials and research productivity to bolster institutional reputations and to enhance evidence-based institutional decision-making, and in order to meet new challenges in research philosophy and methodology, staff research knowledge and research process skills must be continuously updated and expanded.

In recognition of this policy direction, a field-tested, web-based questionnaire survey was conducted in September 2009 to gain a better understanding of University of Alberta librarians' research and scholarly experience, research activity levels, research knowledge learning needs, the research topics on which further education and training would be helpful in support of continuing research activities, and preferences for how acquiring such knowledge could best be facilitated. It was hoped that this snapshot of a particular institution at a particular time would shed light on strategies for fostering and enhancing the quality of research produced by University of Alberta librarians.

The immediate motivation was preparation for an all-day introductory research methods workshop in October 2009, sponsored by the Council of Prairie and Pacific University Libraries (COPPUL) and conducted by Joan Giesecke and Nancy Busch (Dean of Libraries and Associate Dean for Administration, respectively, University of Nebraska Lincoln Libraries); they have conducted workshops for the ARL leadership and career development program as well as for other university libraries throughout North America. Research ethics approval was obtained so that survey findings could be shared with colleagues beyond University of Alberta Libraries. A total of 76 librarians were asked to complete the survey, resulting in 52 usable responses, for a very positive participation rate of 68% that suggests survey findings can be considered strongly indicative of the majority of the UAL cohort. At the same time, the attitudes and opinions of non-respondents should not be forgotten or ignored.

4. Study Findings – Executive Summary

The survey shows that University of Alberta librarians are active researchers, authors, and presenters. In the last two years, almost 80% of responding librarians reported making a presentation at a conference or workshop or on a panel, and more than 40% have engaged in other dissemination activities such as publishing a journal article (digital or paper); reviewing a book; and making a poster presentation. Other research activities have included publishing a paper in conference proceedings, acting as a journal editor or referee, organizing a conference, publishing in digital form such as a wiki, database, or website, publishing a book chapter, acting as a book editor, conducting an environmental scan, and offering a webinar.

Survey participants said they plan to be just as active in the next couple of years. Some 8 out of 10 respondents intend to present a paper or poster or otherwise share research results. As well, more than half are interested in advice, coaching, or other assistance, principally in the areas of poster presentations, oral presentations, and research methods.

In terms of research engagement within the next year or two, 75% of responding librarians are currently involved in research activity at various stages, from "the thinking stage" and general exploration to collaboration and article writing. They are investigating a wide variety of research topics and areas, ranging from a study of catalogue use and development of organizational assessment schema to information literacy, search filtering, and mental health literature bibliometric analysis. They plan to publish the results of their research in a variety of communication formats including paper and online journals, book chapters, conference proceedings, and conference presentations. Two-thirds of them are interested in advice, coaching or other assistance with their research projects, notably with writing for publication and publishing choices, various aspects and types of methodology, and proposal development.

Half of the responding librarians are "quite confident" of their own knowledge of research and the research process, while others feel a bit uncertain or need a refresher on a wide variety of particular aspects. Several mentioned the need for time for thinking, researching, and writing. More than half of them thought it was important to increase their knowledge in each of the following areas:

- analyzing data/results
- choosing an appropriate methodology for research
- sources of and applying for research support/funding
- writing a research proposal
- ethics approval
- publishing your findings
- writing a journal article
- peer reviewing/refereeing conference proposals, journal article submissions, etc.

By far the preferred delivery mode for acquiring more knowledge in these areas was workshops, variously described as instruction, collaborative sessions, active discussions, seminars, presentations, classroom sessions, lectures, and focused meetings; one librarian suggested "a format that would allow seasoned researchers to present their experiences, what worked for them, etc."

Other delivery mode preferences mentioned several times by responding librarians were:

- one-on-one coaching and consultation – "someone to consult with about any of these areas would be better as the research project unfolds"; "access to colleagues with a lot of knowledge in this area"
- peer group discussion, informal support of colleagues
- resource lists, tip sheets, help documents
- online workshops, refreshers

- self-study and reading.

In response to another survey question about collaboration, more than 90% of the responding librarians indicated an interest in collaborative research arrangements, suggesting many ways in which the Libraries could support such collaboration. The most frequently mentioned ideas were:

- research or release time, even short research leaves such as one week would help promote a culture of research because it would formalize research as an activity
- research ideas seminars or forums for brainstorming, inspiration, making connections, and potential collaboration – especially between units, as one librarian noted, "because we often work on projects within our own units or with close colleagues, and we need to get out more to shake things up a little"
- website, database, or "knowledge-base" listing current projects, research interests, finding collaborators
- formal recognition and evaluation of collaboration.

Some 70% of them were also interested in participating in a mentoring program for research activity, again providing helpful suggestions for program planning. Ideas were: having a forum or allowing time for meetings so people could get together for peer mentoring, developing a resource list of possible mentors with qualifications and research interests, and suggested criteria for mentors, such as people with an extensive research background, people with similar research interests, or only if the mentor is a co-author or co-investigator. Two respondents offered to act as mentors.

5. Study Conclusions
While there has long been a subjective, impressionistic sense that University of Alberta librarians were professionally active in research and scholarship, this survey provides strong evidence of their engagement at very high levels. The survey also helps to shed light on their educational needs for more research knowledge in key areas: applying for research funding support; formulating researchable questions and developing research proposals; obtaining research ethics approvals; matching quantitative and qualitative methodologies to research questions; analyzing data; writing for publication; and engaging in peer review. University of Alberta librarians said they preferred knowledge acquisition in these areas through the following modes of delivery: interactive workshops, both in person and online; one-on-one coaching; peer group sharing, discussion, and brainstorming; collaborative research arrangements; resource lists and tip sheets; and peer mentoring.

Concluding remarks by several respondents in both the original and post-workshop surveys echoed earlier concerns about the crucial need for release time for research. Another concern addressed academic freedom, and asked for clear guidelines from the library system on how much freedom and how much research support one should expect to have in the UA Libraries context. Others commented, variously, that they looked forward to being supported in their research; appreciated the opportunity to respond to the survey questions; appreciated the Library's emphasis on research and all that is being done; thought the library is really trying to help them along this path; and believed this to be an important area for development in the system. And finally, one respondent noted, "This is an exciting initiative!"

This snapshot sheds light on current levels of research experiences, research interests, attitudes to research, research competencies, and research knowledge learning needs of academic librarians at the University of Alberta. It also provides a framework for designing educational opportunities for ongoing research knowledge acquisition.

6. Fostering a Research and Scholarly Culture among Academic Librarians: Towards Best Practices

This study has stimulated broader institutional policy questions. How is a climate of research and scholarship achieved? What are the essential elements of a strong research culture? How can this culture be fostered, and by whom? What are the barriers to research and research productivity? Some implications for identifying best practices come out of the UAL needs assessment in part, but corroborated and expanded through experience, the literature, and colleagues. One goal might be to draft a template of best practices for fostering a research culture at individual institutions.

Some key factors can be identified in enhancing an organizational culture of research and scholarship. They pertain broadly to policies, strategies, and practices for research and scholarship. One place to start in thinking about these issues is to identify the multiple stakeholders and constituencies involved, among whom are:

- university administration
- library administration
- librarian cohort and peers in other institutions
- user communities
- faculty as collaborators and resource persons
- university research grants and research ethics offices
- institutional, professional, and related associations
- professional journals and other professional publishing venues.

In Canada, the key institution-based association is the Canadian Association of Research Libraries (CARL), which has produced a "competencies" statement and offers small research grants to promote knowledge production (Canadian Association of Research Libraries 2008), and in its 2010-2012 strategic plan, CARL (2009) identifies the development of research skills in research libraries and the promotion of evidence-based librarianship as strategic components. In addition, CARL provides research and development grants. There is also the membership-based Canadian Association of College and University Libraries, a division of the Canadian Library Association (CLA), which promotes research activity through a small research support grant program, a program of peer-review of CLA conference proposals for two sessions per year, and hosts the Canadian Academic Libraries Network (2010); CLA itself supports and promotes research through an annual research grants competition. The Education Institute is a program of short audio programs on many topics, including research and scholarship, sponsored by The Partnership, a consortium of provincial, territorial, and regional library associations in Canada. A related national agency is the Canadian Association of Universities and Colleges (CAUT), which has an active Librarians' Committee, a standing committee of CAUT, and which has adopted policies endorsing academic status and academic freedom for Canadian university librarians; participation in academic governance through library councils; guidelines for the appointment and review of chief librarians; and librarians' involvement in scholarly communication (Canadian Association of Universities and

Colleges 2010). Of particular note is CAUT's (2003) statement, "A Model Clause on the Scholarly Activities of Academic Librarians."

At the broader level are a multitude of stakeholders who are among the most important leaders in fostering and promoting a research culture in the profession: ARL; the American Library Association (ALA); the Association of College and Research Libraries, a division of ALA; the Medical Library Association; the Special Libraries Association; OCLC; and the International Federation of Library Associations and Institutions. As well, at the national level in Canada, there are research granting agencies, most notably the Social Sciences and Humanities Research Council (SSHRC). Finally, there are university workshops and programs for research knowledge development.

Commitment to a culture and climate of research is two-pronged, applying to both research library administrators and to academic librarians. Among the chief factors in this challenge is the level of commitment by senior library leadership, both moral and operational, to evidence-based management. Research for evidence-based decision making must permeate institutional policies, strategic plans, decision processes, budgetary priorities, human resources and staff development, supervision, academic standards, travel support, research funding, and institutional projects.

At the professional level, and in the old tradition of the scholar-librarian but now redefined as new modes of evidence-based work, there needs to be institutional support for individual librarians as producers and disseminators of research and scholarly work. At the broadest level, tenure, promotion, and performance standards in collective agreements should address research and scholarship. It is also suggested that an inclusive approach be adopted in conceptualizing the scope of research and scholarly activity, as well as in endorsing multiple channels of dissemination. Research and scholarly activity should be built into annual job expectations, rewarded, acknowledged, and celebrated; all organizational levels should be included. Time for a variety of focused efforts should be supported in the form of research leave, study leave, continuing professional development events such as workshops and conference attendance, as well as dedicated work days or weeks. It should also be remembered that new graduates also require ongoing research training – we cannot simply rely on their newly-completed professional education; research competency means lifelong learning. Lifelong learning involves individual librarian recognition of the need for continuous self-assessment of learning needs to ensure and maintain lifelong competency to conduct quality research. Also important is the development of a research community, a network of like-minded colleagues both local and at other institutions as resource persons, potential collaborators, supporters, reviewers or critics, and mentors; active support of peers is an especially critical factor. Celebration and public recognition of research achievements, awards, and so on, by and with this network is part of the pleasure of research and scholarly engagement. Last but not least, there must be passion!

In the long term, it is hoped that the quality and quantity of research produced by University of Alberta librarians will grow in quality and diversity, thereby enabling them to become recognized players in the scholarly communication process, nationally and internationally. It is also hoped that the strategic directions of UAL will be informed and strengthened by more systematic foundations of evidence-based policy and decision making. Both trends will help to build capacity.

It is also anticipated that the present study will serve as a research prototype and pilot for a multi-institutional, nationwide project along similar lines to capture a national snapshot of research productivity and competency found among Canadian academic librarians. Recognizing that engagement with the scholarly communication process is a core value of academic librarians across Canada, it is anticipated that the University of Alberta pilot study represents a solid springboard to the national level.

Acknowledgments and Disclaimer

I wish to acknowledge conference travel support by E Ingles, Vice-Provost and Chief Librarian, University of Alberta Libraries. I also wish to acknowledge the collaboration of my colleagues at University of Alberta Libraries, K De Long (Associate University Librarian), D Clark, (Staff Development and Training Librarian), and A Sivak, (Assessment Librarian), in the development of the survey instruments and for reading an early draft of the study findings.

Please note that the opinions expressed in this article are the personal views of the author and do not necessarily reflect official policy of University of Alberta Libraries.

References

Association of Research Libraries. 2010. What is LibQUAL+? At http://www.libqual.org/home

Canadian Academic Libraries Network. 2010. At http://caculnetwork.ning.com/.

Canadian Association of Research Libraries. 2008. *Library Education Working Group: Final Report to the CARL Board of Directors.* At http://www.carl-abrc.ca/about/working_groups/library_education_mandate-e.html. Also includes:
- National Research Priorities Survey
- Research Competencies for CARL Librarians
- Librarians as Researchers and Writers: Research Priorities for Canada's Research Libraries
- Resources for librarians and LIS students interested in research

Canadian Association of Research Libraries. 2009. CARL Strategic Directions 2010-2012. At http://www.carl-abrc.ca/about/strategic_plan_2010-2012e-html.

Canadian Association of Universities and Colleges. 2003. Model Clause on the Scholarly Activities of Academic Librarians. At http://www.caut.ca/pages.asp?page=412&lang=1.

Canadian Association of Universities and Colleges. 2010. Librarians and Libraries. At http://www.caut.ca/pages.asp?page=219.

Fennewald, Joseph. 2008. Research Productivity among Librarians: Factors Leading to Publications at Penn State." *College and Research Libraries*, 71, 104 - 116.

Fox, David. 2007a. Finding Time for Scholarship: A Survey of Canadian Research University Librarians. *portal: Libraries and the Academy*, 7.4, 451 - 462.

Fox, David. 2007b. The Scholarship of Canadian Research University Librarians. *Partnership: The Canadian Journal of Library and Information Practice and Research*, 2.2, 1 - 24.

Schrader, Alvin M. 2010. Fostering a Research Culture in Canadian Academic Libraries. *Resources from Super Conference 2010, Ontario Library Association.* At http://www.accessola.com/superconference2010/sessions.php#t.

University of Alberta. 2007. *Librarian Agreement.*

University of Alberta Learning Services. 2006. *Learning Services: Submission to the University of Alberta Academic Plan 2007-2011 (Final) "From Good to Great."* University of Alberta, Edmonton, June 2006.

University of Alberta Libraries. 2000. Tenure Appointments for Librarians. Endorsed by Library Council, University of Alberta Libraries, June 6, 2000.

University of Alberta Libraries. 2009. Recruitment to Public Service Position [Advertisement for new positions], University of Alberta Libraries, June 24, 2009.

Chapter 6. Academic Libraries

UCSC Nexus Project: Fostering Networking between Academic Scholars and Library Staff: Qualitative Methods for Assessing Perceived Value of Library Services

Liliana Gregori, Luca Losito and Paolo Sirito

Milan Campus Library, Catholic University of Sacred Heart, Italy

Abstract: Looking for excellence in library services and fostering closer and better relationships between academic scholars and library staff is a major ongoing trend. According to that, the library of the Catholic University in Milan is promoting a pilot project – codename Nexus – aimed to:
- designing, implementing and delivering a "one stop information shop" for internal researchers, bundling together homogeneous resources and tools,
- carefully selecting and optimizing available services, with a clear understanding of users' behaviour and with a project perspective (e.g: helping scholars in producing high quality educational material).

In order to do so, we are in the process of developing suitable qualitative methods, enabling us to assess the perceived value of library services, through a close relationship with a selected panel of scholars, giving a structured feedback about:
- "dos and don'ts" when introducing new services in an academic library context
- scope and scale economies gained in releasing a defined range of "research deliverables" (e.g.: educational materials, bibliographies, papers)
- cost/benefit analysis of new services, in terms of effective usage.

Expected major benefits for the library will include:
- deeper understanding of effective users' needs and qualitative evidences about perceived value of new services (including spending rationalisation)
- improved partnership between administrative staff and the internal research community, leading to a better academic climate
- increased support to library innovation initiatives, including necessary resources (mostly in the human resources and technology areas).

Keywords: Innovation, partnership, perceived value, qualitative methods, rationalisation

1. Introduction

The issue of cooperation of libraries within their institutions has been widely discussed in the past, for example by Miller and Pellen (2005) and we strongly agree with their vision that rarely libraries exist in a vacuum.

According to that, the Central Library of the Catholic University of Sacred Heart in Milan is strongly tied with the internal structure of the Milan Campus, as well as with the whole University structure, whose other campuses are spread across Italy: Piacenza, Brescia, Rome and Campobasso.

New Trends in Qualitative and Quantitative Methods in Libraries
A. Katsirikou and C. H. Skiadas (eds)
© World Scientific Publishing Co (pp. 307-313)

In such a context, looking for excellence in library services and fostering closer and better relationships between academic scholars and library staff is a major ongoing trend.

Obviously, turning these concepts into practice is not a simple task and requires - at least - three key elements:

- shared values
- concrete projects
- clear methodology.

We envision that mutual information sharing, library liaison programs and support to researchers may be considered a roadmap to innovation and a noteworthy provision to library branding.

In a nutshell, we have embraced the vision of Biddiscombe (2002), referring to subject librarians as learning support professionals and we strive for turning it into practice.

Project Description

Designing and implementing a work environment where academic staff can consider librarians as trusted partners is part of the mission of central library of the Catholic University of Sacred Heart in Milan.

The Nexus Project is part of a structural effort, aimed to innovate the overall service model of the library, by focusing on the value concept. A cross functional team of liaison, reference and cataloguing librarians has been devoted to investigating the concept of value for academic patrons, with a particular focus on what they need – and what they could find suitable – for preparing and delivering their research and learning material.

In our experience, the main issues of the relationship between teaching faculties and teaching librarians are the very same stated by Kraat (2005):

- "assigning grades,
- the teaching and learning environment,
- course growth and maintenance,
- time,
- understanding the student,
- respecting each other: collegiality".

2. Project Details

Project Scope

According to that, the main aims of the pilot project have been:

- designing, implementing and delivering a "one stop information shop" for internal researchers, bundling together homogeneous resources and tools
- carefully selecting and optimizing available services, as well as proposing brand new ones, with a clear understanding of users' behaviour and with a project perspective (e.g: helping scholars in producing high quality educational material)
- measuring, by appropriate qualitative means, the level of interest, acceptance and commitment of a selected panel of scholars, in order to deliver highly focused services to the academic community.

Expectations

By developing suitable qualitative methods, enabling us to assess the perceived value of library services, we expected to get a structured feedback about:

- "dos and don'ts" when introducing new services in an academic library context
- scope and scale economies gained in releasing a defined range of "research deliverables" (e.g.: educational materials, bibliographies, papers, training)
- cost/benefit analysis of new services, in terms of effective usage.

Project Plan
A structured project management methodology has been used, with a clear mission and well defined responsibilities.
Below are described the overall project phases and the main activities related to each step:

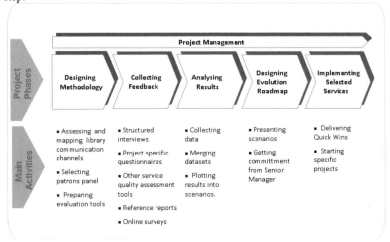

3. Methodological Approach
Library Communication Channels
According to our experience and with regard to the current organizational structure of the library, the main institutional actors in charge of communicating with the research community are:
- Liaison Librarians
- Reference Librarians
- Cataloguing Librarians.

The pilot project team (3 people) has been therefore build up from these areas, even if some data – as well as technological support – have been provided by our system librarians.
Panel Structure
A small, but representative, group (20 people) of library patrons has been carefully selected, covering all major categories of academic users. They were treated as a focus group and their feedback, collected through dedicated tools, like:
- structured interviews
- project specific questionnaires.

In addition to that – and in order to cross-verify collected data – upcoming results have been matched with other datasets previously collected from different internal sources:
- OPAC usage statistics
- standard service quality questionnaires
- reference reports.

Service Catalogue
Currently available services, as well as potential ones, have been segmented into discrete "chunks" and mapped into a Service Catalogue, whose details have been included into the patrons' questionnaires.

Selected categories of library services:
- editing services
- research services
- customer care
- learning services.

By doing this, we took into due consideration what suggested by Harrington (2009): "Librarians who are considering developing a program of instruction and support for undergraduate thesis writers or expanding their work thesis students might explore the following broad issues, which recur in the literature: preparing program groundwork, options for program format and content, marketing and outreach, collaboration, assessment, and the unique elements of the undergraduate thesis."

Levels of Analysis

Three evaluation levels have been implemented:
- strategic: which (new) services should the library make available to internal patrons and to the overall research community
- tactical: priority ranking, roadmap and timescale for delivering such services (quick wins and structured innovation projects)
- operational: how such services should be delivered (directly supported by people and/or made available in a self-service manner)

Scenario Planning

After that, results have been matched with different possible evolution scenarios of library services.

Such scenarios are to be meant for exemplification purposes only and have been built upon two axis:
- managing existing knowledge vs. creating new knowledge
- internally oriented services vs. externally oriented services

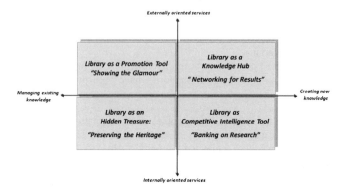

4. Results

Main findings refer to the evaluation levels previously mentioned:
- strategic:
  - support to academic research and teaching activities got the highest value rankings among new services. Publishing seems to be an emerging issue, with a special focus to the open access model
  - selecting, purchasing and preserving library resources (both paper-based and electronic ones) are still perceived as core activities

- tactical:
  - o improving communication between patrons and library staff has emerged as the main priority. Several activities have been suggested, falling into both implementation categories (quick wins and structured projects)
  - o the academic landscape is becoming more competitive (also for Humanities) and the interest for new research evaluation tools is raising
- operational:
  - o professional staff is perceived as the medium "par excellence" for getting high quality library services. Technology is seen as an enabler (as well as structured processes), but human factors still make the difference,

Finally, one recurring definition about reference librarians is that they are becoming "Teaching Assistants". Such vision is really close to what Lupton (2002) stated: "in order to facilitate students' 'getting of wisdom', librarians who design and deliver information literacy programs should see themselves as teachers rather than trainers".

Evolution Roadmap

According to the collected data/feedback, a possible evolution roadmap have been plotted, connecting – as a "fil rouge" – different scenarios.

The image below is depicting such emerging trend:

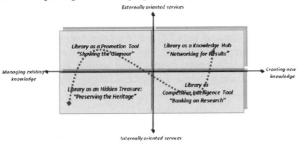

Collected evidences show infact that:

- at present time, different visions of the library live together, even if the services ranked as most valuable for the future mainly lie into the "knowledge hub" quadrant
- no direct relation have been still found between specific aspects (e.g.: age of patrons or subject areas) and the visions themselves. This could mean that request for innovation in library services is becoming pervasive across faculties and the research community, but more evidences / analysis are needed.

In practical terms and with regard to the changing role of library staff, the subject librarian new roles, are really close to those ones listed by Pinfield (2001): "The old job ... plus

1. More emphasis on liaison with users
2. Advocacy of the collections
3. New roles
4. Enquiries – the new way
5. Working with technical staff
6. Selection of e-resources
7. More information skills training
8. Organising the information landscape
9. Involvement in educational technology and learning environments
10. Team working
11. Project working ",

In a broader sense, and with regard to the creation of new knowledge – especially within the framework of Open Access – we feel close to the position of Vitiello (2009): "After the open access revolution libraries acquire, process and disseminate publications created within the organization they belong. Their fundamental paradigm has therefore shifted. They have reached the tipping point after which they become knowledge incubators in scientific dissemination and a new medium in the world of communication."

Lesson Learned

Some evidences have been raised:

- patrons in the Humanities (e.g.: Philosophy, Literature) may be as innovative as Economists and Social Scientists, but they look at technology only as a tool: this means that they tend not to be early adopters of new IT based services. On the other hand, researchers in Economics and Political Science asked for new services, even if they could be still in the pipeline and proposed themselves as beta testers
- this could lead to a "double speed model" for innovation, to be applied for emerging issues, just like mobile services. It sounds appealing, but it requires a structured product management approach and a careful preliminary analysis of the (internal) market potential
- a common field for nurturing innovative services could be the semantic web and – in particular – ontology development: the large majority of researchers felt that full text searching is definitely not an answer for coping with resources proliferation and information overflow and see librarians as best positioned for designing and implementing a new generation of easy to use knowledge based services (e.g.: semantic engines).

Next Steps

The project team is currently engaged in submitting to Senior Management a selected listing of activities, splitted into two main categories:

- Quick Wins
    - o scheduling "Library Days" and easy-to-implement promotion initiatives, to be included into existing University initiatives
    - o promoting new (electronic) resources through short seminars to be held with selected reserchers
- Structured Projects
    - o reinforcing the liason librarians team, focusing on single faculties
    - o showing to patrons real-life examples of editorial cooperation (e.g: re-designing the researcher's web pages on University site)
    - o promoting the development of semantics based services (e.g.: experimenting open source tools for designing ontologies).

References

Janet H. Parsch, M. Sue Baughman (2010), Towards healthy organizations: the use of organization development in Academic Libraries, "The Journal of Academic Librarianship", 36.1, pp.3-19.

Steiner, Heidi M. and Holley, Robert P.(2009), The Past, Present, and Possibilities of Commons in the Academic Library, "The Reference Librarian", 50: 4, 309 — 332

S.Adelle Berg, K. Hoffmann and Diane Dawson (2009), Integrating research into LIS field. Experiences in Academic libraries, "The Journal of Academic Librarianship", 35.6, pp. 591-598

Harrington, Sara(2009), Librarians and Undergraduate Thesis Support: An Annotated Bibliography, "The Reference Librarian", 50: 4, p. 397 – 412.

Vitiello, Giuseppe (2009), Seven years after the Open Access revolution:(research) libraries as media and knowledge management centres, "BollettinoAIB", 2 p. 171-179.

W. Miller, R. Pellen (2005), Libraries within their institutions: creative collaborations, Binghamton, NY, Haworth Information Press.

Kraat, Susan (2005), Relationships between teaching faculty and teaching librarians, Binghamton, NY, Haworth Information Press.

Biddiscombe, Richard (2002), Learning support professionals: the changing role of subject specialists in UK academic libraries, "Program. Electronic Library and Information Systems", 36, 4, p. 228-235.

Lupton, Mandy (2002), The getting of wisdom: reflections of a teaching librarian, "Australian Academic & Research Libraries", 33, 2.

Pinfield, Stephen (2001), The changing role of subject librarians in academic libraries, "Journal of Librarianship and Information Science", 33, 1, p. 32-38.

Research Library Statistics: For Whom and for What Purpose? The Statistics Users' Views and Wishes

Cecilia Bodelsson[1], Catarina Jacobsson[1] and Tore Torngren[2]

[1] Project Librarians, Lund University Libraries, Head Office, Lund, Sweden
[2] Assistant Director of Libraries, Lund University Libraries, Head Office, Lund, Sweden; Chairman, National Library of Sweden's Expert Group on Library Statistics Sweden

Abstract: The paper reports a project conducted within the framework of the National Library of Sweden's Expert Group on Library Statistics. The project is financed by the National Library of Sweden, and it aims to capture how library managements make use of the current library statistics (based on the ISO-standard) in the decision-making process. Questions are also asked about the quality and usefulness of the existing statistical data, whether data covers all relevant aspects of library activity, and what additional data is required in order to enhance the validity of collected statistics.

The primary method used is semi-structured group interviews (focus groups). Four such interviews were held with the participation of 15 library directors from academic and other research or special libraries from different parts of Sweden. The results show that there is considerable ambivalence among the informants concerning the usefulness of current statistics. On the one hand there is severe criticism of what today is reported on a national level (too much and too little), on the other hand statistical data is used locally to underpin arguments supporting library activities.

Stakeholders representing university or institutional management were not available for group interviews. With the support of the interviewed library directors a group of 12 vice-chancellors or other senior managers were identified and approached with a mail survey. Questions were asked about what kind of documentation of library activities they use or prefer, be they quantitative, qualitative or of other kind.

Keywords: Sweden library statistics, use of statistics, group interviews, focus groups, survey, library management, academic management, decision-making process

1. Introduction

The Swedish Arts Council is the government agency responsible for Sweden's national library statistics. There are currently 77 libraries included in the statistics, made up of national libraries (1), university and university college libraries (39) and special libraries (37). All of these are accessible to the public and either wholly or partly financed through public funds. The National Library of Sweden (KB) is responsible for the content, definitions and analyses of the statistics. The statistics are based on the ISO standard and include information about staff, finances, stocks, loans and activities. KB has also defined the aims of the national research library statistics, which are to:

- Report on the activities of the research libraries from a national perspective
- Provide an overview of the activities of the individual libraries

New Trends in Qualitative and Quantitative Methods in Libraries
A. Katsirikou and C. H. Skiadas (eds)
© *World Scientific Publishing Co (pp. 315-322)*

- Form a basis for planning, budgeting and grant applications
- Serve as an instrument for comparisons between libraries

In 2008 an expert group for library statistics was appointed at KB, with representatives of different types of library. The expert group's task is to draw up proposals for improvements to the collection, analysis and communication of the national library statistics. This study is now conducted as a step in the process. The aim of the study is to gather the views of the research library managers on the value and usefulness of the national statistics that are produced today and in what respects these can be improved. A further aspect of the task is to provide an insight into what the senior management of the libraries' parent organisations would like in terms of information to form a basis for management and development of the libraries' activities. The aim of the survey is to contribute the views of the users on the national statistics and form a basis for the development of the statistics.

2. Method and execution

The study builds on interviews with 15 library managers, of whom 12 come from university or university college libraries and three from special libraries, and survey responses from 10 senior managers from parent organisations of the research libraries.

Interviews

The interview method used can be described as semi-structured group interviews, or 'focus group interviews'. A semi-structured interview method means that the interviewer only partly directs the interaction in the group in order to obtain answers to a small number of specific questions; otherwise the interviewees discuss freely with one another.

Invitations to interview were sent to 36 library managers. Of these, 15 participated in four interviews in three locations. The selection of library managers was partly directed by logistics and partly by which individuals were able to participate. The library managers were divided into four groups of between three and five participants per interview. In order to give the interviewees the opportunity to prepare ahead of the interviews, information was sent out together with a number of questions on which to reflect. The first interview was intended as a pilot interview, with the possibility to adjust the information material, questions, interview guide, etc. afterwards. However, it was found to be advantageous to make small adjustments before each interview, on the basis of the loose ends that were identified in the previous interview.

All the interviews were recorded and transcribed in their entirety, and this provides a wealth of data and the possibility for various types of analysis. Two project managers were present at all the interviews and discussed the interview outcomes together before the analysis work that followed. The study is to be regarded as qualitative. The word *focus* indicates that the discussion will address a pre-decided topic and the moderators' role in the discussion is to ensure the discussion content is in agreement with and focuses on the established objective of the study. After four focus group interviews, lasting on average 90 minutes, clear information saturation could be seen. The responses tend to be so similar that more interviews would probably not produce more comprehensive results, and this is wholly in line with the focus group methodology.

Surveys

The study was complemented with a survey aimed at senior managers from the libraries' parent organisations. The survey comprised an explanatory text followed by three open questions. The original idea was for the senior managers and library managers to both be part of the focus groups. For a number of reasons it was decided that a survey was preferable. There are advantages and disadvantages of both homogeneous and heterogeneous focus groups. However, a basic supposition is that people with shared experiences and areas of interest feel more comfortable sharing their opinions with one another. In addition, it became clear early on that it was difficult to arrange interviews with the senior managers within the timeframe that had been decided.

The survey was sent to 12 senior managers at universities, university colleges and special libraries, of which 9 responded. Among the respondents were four pro vice-chancellors, one vice-chancellor, one vice-chancellor's council, one archive council, one head of division and one controller.

The details of the library managers and senior managers who participated are kept confidential.

3. Results of interviews with library managers

A common perception among the library managers is that the national statistics reflect a different reality with a more traditional focus to activities and not the reality of the libraries' activities today. The library managers interviewed are in agreement that there is value in having national statistics, but wonder for whom the statistics are primarily collected. Since the aim of the statistics is that they should be useful on a local, national and international level, the managers wonder who the real 'end user' is at national and international level.

To begin with, it appears that the national statistics are not used at all. However, all the interviewees say that they use different types of statistics in their work, but that the statistics they view as most interesting and useful are from other sources or those they gather themselves. During the course of the interviews, however, a more balanced picture emerges of the interviewees' use of statistics and it becomes clear that the majority do find the statistics interesting to some extent – or at least feel that they could be of interest – and possibly also useful on a local level.

The national statistics are primarily used to make comparisons. With regard to the university and university college libraries, the majority tend to compare themselves with libraries at higher education institutions of the *same size*, and some with libraries of which the parent organisation has a *similar organisational structure*. Three interviewees consider that *international comparisons* with similar universities are most important. The library managers from the three special libraries say that they are mostly interested in making comparisons with themselves.

The notion that high and increasing figures are good figures, while low and falling figures are poor figures appears to be firmly rooted. In all the interviews, the same phenomenon is seen on a variety of topics. Even if the library managers themselves consider that there is not necessarily any connection at all, they still work on the presumption that others, including colleagues and senior managers, see it as so. Today many libraries work actively to reduce the amount of printed media, which means that lower stock levels and fewer visits indicate a positive change, because the results are in line with the goal. Yet falling figures generally still have to be explained to a much greater extent than rising figures.

In all interviews, statistics and rhetoric are discussed. It is clearly the case that those who have the right of interpretation choose what is interesting to present and how it is presented to best serve a purpose.

The national statistics are seen to fulfil the role of indicating potentially interesting information. The library managers consider that it is necessary to delve deeper into the statistics and to assess the plausibility of other libraries' statistics. These must often be checked, processed and placed in relation to something else. Furthermore, information must be gathered from a number of other sources, e.g. the Swedish National Agency for Higher Education and the libraries' websites and annual reports.

It emerges in all the interviews that the managers would consider using the national statistics more if they were more reliable. The five main weaknesses are felt to be:

- Many uninteresting statistics
- Low reliability – many errors occur in the statistics and a number of these are well known
- Large amounts of missing data – all the libraries have left out some information, the most common is virtual visits
- No defined aims – difficult to know with whom it is best to compare oneself when an underlying strategy is lacking
- Unwieldy format – too much, unwieldy material and format too static to work with.

Missing data and in particular incorrect figures were discussed at length in the interviews. Errors are sometimes entered unconsciously, but some of the errors appear to be known to both the one submitting the information and colleagues at other libraries. From the four interviews, five main reasons for missing data and incorrect figures are put forward:

- Irrelevance – if information is not seen as relevant, this can lead to figures being estimated
- Unclear definitions – uncertainty as to what information is being requested leads to different interpretations
- Errors by tradition – errors inherited from former employees are time-consuming to correct and require explanations
- Poor routines – the time it takes to complete the statistics questionnaire correctly is not always taken into account in planning
- Lack of technical equipment – not all libraries are able to measure online activities and OPAC searches.

All the library managers interviewed would like the national statistics to be improved in order to be more useful. The wishes expressed – both large and small – can be summarised as follows:

- A clearer aim to raise interest and ambition
- Clear and simple definitions
- A technical platform for national library statistics
- Expanded information on electronic publishing
- Measurement of interactive activity on the Internet
- Measurement of bibliometric activity
- Information about the number of presumptive users at individual libraries
- Information about costs of the libraries in relation to the parent organisations
- Fixed recurring data and temporary 'hot' statistics
- An in-depth focus on issues of particular importance.

Library statistics on a local level

In the discussions on the usefulness of the national statistics on a local level it emerged that the library managers do not consider the statistics particularly useful. The national statistics may be useful in making comparisons, but otherwise the libraries use their own statistics. When the issue of own statistics is raised in the interviews, the discussions often drift into integration, reporting and methods and conditions for creating useful statistics.

The research libraries come under parent organisations that can differ significantly from one another. The integration of the library into its parent organisation is discussed a number of times. Although no-one in the group goes into a definition of what integration means in this context, the impression is that the libraries are very independent and have extensive freedom to operate in relation to their parent organisations. Some libraries are organised as completely separate service functions, while others can be regarded as more or less integrated into the activities of their respective parent organisations. There is a desire to see the library more as an integrated part of the parent organisation and to be able to describe its work on the basis of the activities of the higher education institution rather than 'internal library activities'. The importance of not seeing oneself as an isolated actor but as a partner is stressed.

It is seen as difficult to get leaders within the organisation to pay interest to library statistics. Library activities are often discussed in qualitative terms because senior managers in large organisations are not in a position to look at the detail. The library managers interviewed often choose to talk about the activities in broader terms. They emphasise the importance of presenting the statistics in combination with an analysis in activity reports and suchlike. All the library managers feel that the management trusts them to do their job and in the main they receive a brief and a pot of money and are trusted to operate their activities in the best way possible. There is sometimes a desire for more feedback from management.

The discussions address whether useful local statistics could be included in the national statistics, but the conclusions are that they are too locally grounded and vary from year to year, and that it is therefore not possible. Emphasis is placed on the process; everyone must begin with the question, i.e. the library's brief, and not be misled into measuring something simply because it can be measured, or gathering statistics that exist but that do not really provide anything significant. In general it is considered self-evident that there must be links between the parent organisation's overall objectives and that the ideal is to be able to break these down. It is often claimed that statistics gathered at the individual libraries are more useful than the national statistics. However, when practical examples are mentioned they are strikingly similar to the data that can be found in the national statistics, sometimes in relation to something else.

One interviewee considers it to be a major problem that, at the same time as the library has developed from merely being a library to becoming part of education and research, it is still so difficult to account for links between the library's work and the students' information skills. This is seen as a particularly important strategic issue.

4. Results of survey of senior managers

The aim of the survey is to obtain a picture of what the senior managers consider to be relevant and interesting information on which to base decisions concerning the libraries. By senior managers we mean those who have the ultimate responsibility or part of the responsibility for the parent organisation as a whole and thus also for the libraries, and to whom the library managers report. The results are based on 9 survey responses.

The survey comprises the following three questions:

1. What types of information do you find interesting/relevant/useful as a basis for decisions about the library's activities and development?

2. What role does quantitative data play as a basis for decisions about the library's activities and development?

3. What types of information for decisions on the library's activities and development do you feel are lacking today?

A number of senior managers begin by explaining that it is the goals set for the library that decide what types of information are relevant for follow-up and governance and that what is most interesting is to see how the activities are developing in relation to the brief. In addition, as the libraries' role changes and new opportunities open up, it is important that the libraries are given a clear brief and that a planning discussion is held based on the library as a strategic resource.

Useful information as a basis for decisions

Financial data is key. The budget result and cost developments, e.g. for staff, premises and procurement, are highly relevant information, as are user statistics and borrowing statistics, which reflect the use of the library. Also various types of user survey, including analyses that map needs and wishes. There is an interest in seeing the library's role in the organisation as a whole. There is also an interest in reports of teaching activities undertaken, cooperation between librarians and teaching staff, and specific initiatives that are of importance for the institution. Along with activity reports, the senior managers also want to see comparative figures for benchmarking. There is an awareness that the role of the library is changing, and for this reason there is a demand for business intelligence with regard to technological developments and new system solutions.

Quantitative data as a basis for decisions

Quantitative data is of most importance for budget discussions and other financial follow-up. For planning and allocation of resources such as staff, media etc. and for monitoring trends over several years, user statistics are considered useful. Activities are principally reported and discussed in qualitative terms. A number of senior managers state that quantitative data is only interesting as a basis for decisions if goals have been established that are measured or followed up with quantitative data.

Information for decisions that is currently lacking

A number of senior managers would like to see comparative data on other higher education institution libraries, with regard to both finances and use, for *benchmarking*. Libraries are increasingly expected to produce various types of *bibliometric information* that forms the basis for strategic decisions on how the university should focus its research investments. One senior manager states that there will be a need for information to follow up how the library responds to this and to describe how the university's need for these analyses changes. The role of the libraries in making available full-text material from the universities' researchers is expanding. One senior manager considers that the discussion on 'open access' places additional focus on this and that therefore the library, in dialogue with the institution, has to try to forecast how the volume of work in this area will increase, in order that investments in equipment and training can be made at a sufficient rate. One senior manager states that the planning of the library's activities is, to a certain extent, dependent on political decisions and that information is required at times of cabinet reshuffles and sudden decisions to shut down or reorganise government agencies.

5. Reflections and conclusion

It is very clear that the library managers interviewed find the national statistics much too traditional. They are not seen to describe the activities of the libraries today; the reality is far beyond the traditional statistical data that makes up the national statistics. The libraries' brief, ways of working, stock and accessibility have changed. Not least, the library habits and needs of the user have changed. The perception is that these changes are not reflected in the statistics.

However, this should not necessarily be interpreted to mean that the existing statistics in themselves are poor, rather that they are insufficient. The traditional statistics describe the traditional activities and in fact do so fairly well. The libraries still have staff, collections and loans and therefore costs and workflows that must be measured. On the whole, the same types of statistics are used in the libraries' various presentations on websites, in activity reports and also in reporting, to the extent that quantitative data is reported to senior management. The data in the national statistics and in the libraries' own statistics is for the most part the same.

The research libraries that are included in the national statistics have very varied briefs. The university and university college libraries, for example, call for certain methods for measuring their activities in relation to education and research. On the other hand, the special libraries have quite different briefs. The national statistics cannot be expected to fulfil all these specific data needs for the follow-up of work at the different libraries, based on their local needs and objectives. Neither can this be the purpose of the national statistics.

When all the shortcomings of the national statistics have been voiced and discussed, the library managers interviewed are in principle agreed that they are to be taken for what they are; a starting point with a number of useful basic statistics from which to work. This does not mean that the national statistics cannot or should not be improved. It is important to give an accurate picture of the libraries' work and therefore it is of utmost importance that the whole of their activities are included in the statistics gathered.

The suggestions made in the interviews could largely improve the statistics. There is demand for a technical platform for the national statistics. Such a platform already exists in a number of other countries. There is a desire to be able to select appropriate comparison institutions and relevant data and possibly also incorporate interesting local data in order to create useful specific profiles for the individual library's needs. This would make the national statistics more user-friendly. A good start.

It is essential that ways of measuring the virtual activities are developed – to balance against loans and visits. There is a desire to see the expansion of the data on e-publishing. This is only of interest if theses, articles and papers are counted separately. The importance of the bibliometric analysis methods increases in connection with research evaluations. New activities require new statistical data so that the libraries are seen as partners within their parent organisations. This is important. Libraries may increasingly be required to account for usefulness in the future. The survey responses from the senior managers show that there is a consensus with regard to the need to develop new statistics and new types of information that reflect the libraries' new activities. The survey responses also show that there is an interest in comparative library statistics.

One clear purpose of the national statistics that emerges in this study is thus that they should form good material for comparisons. The question is whether they are good enough for this use. It is clear in the discussions among the library managers that the statistics suffer from apparent quality problems. The negative cycle must be broken. If there are clear areas where the national statistics can be of use then this increases the motivation in the libraries to deliver the statistics. With improved quality, the use of the statistics increases and so it goes on. User-friendliness is one watchword. Usefulness is another. These must constantly be kept in mind when decisions are made to proceed with changes.

References

Johansson, Annette (2009). *Dikt eller verklighet?: En introduktion till bibliteksstatistik i Sverige och i andra länder* [electronic resource] Svensk Biblioteksförening.

Kungl. biblioteket/Statistiska centralbyrån (2009). *Forskningsbiblioteksstatistiken 2008.*

LibQUAL. http://www.libqual.org/

Research Library Statistics Database (Finland)

https://yhteistilasto.lib.helsinki.fi/language.do?action=change&choose_language=2
URANK. http://www.urank.se/
Wibeck, Victoria (2000). *Fokusgrupper: om fokuserade gruppintervjuer som undersökningsmetod.* Lund: Studentlitteratur.

Performance Appraisal of Library Staff Working in Universities

Leyla Kanik

Director of Library and Documentation Centre, Abant Izzet Baysal University, Bolu, Turkey, kanik_l@ibu.edu.tr

Abstract: Staff appraisal is one of the controversial and significant topics of staff management. Staff appraisal is an important component of a well organized staff management. It influences areas such as employment criteria, task planning, waging policy, promotion, professional development, motivation, career development and training etc.

The issue of performance appraisal has become widespread in libraries since 1980s. Today, rapid development in the world affects libraries like any other institutions. It is vital for libraries providing service in a competitive environment to improve the quality of their service and efficiency. For this reason, libraries should benefit from staff appraisal methods in each phase of their services.

The research aims to reveal how and by whom staff appraisal efforts are carried out in university libraries in Turkey and how library staff perceive and consider staff appraisal. In the research, the applications in public and private sector libraries were compared; the points to be considered in a modern staff appraisal model applicable throughout the country were presented while the troubles observed as a result of the evaluation and the expectations on performance appraisal criteria were pointed out.

In the research, which uses the descriptive method, the data were collected by use of such techniques as literature survey, questionnaire and interview. The questionnaire was applied to all staff working in university central libraries in public and private sector in Ankara.

The hypothesis that advocates "the current performance appraisal methods applied in university libraries adversely affect the attitude of the library staff" has been proved at the end of the research.

As a result, it is established that the opinions of the university library directors and staff about the efficiency of the performance appraisal method used are negative. Other findings of the research reveal that there is a significant difference in the attitude of the staff working in university libraries towards the performance appraisal method applied depending on the status of the library and their position as a director or staff.

Keywords: Performance appraisal, performance management, staff management, university libraries

1. Introduction

The change in management phenomenon as old as human history has increased the importance of being effective and efficient in management. In time, there have been changes in the qualifications of staff and job. All these changes have made organizations more dynamic. The changes, especially in the understanding of quality, have generated a rapidly growing competition. The competition innately has effects

New Trends in Qualitative and Quantitative Methods in Libraries
A. Katsirikou and C. H. Skiadas (eds)
© *World Scientific Publishing Co (pp. 323-330)*

on service sector, too. While there are efforts to use the existing physical resources most effectively and efficiently, the human resources in institutions are also tried to be utilized most effectively and efficiently.

Robbins (1996), who points out that the success of an institution requires audit of staff behaviors with an effective audit function, also suggests that the most open ways for directors to audit staff behaviours are direct audit, performance appraisal and discipline. Directors achieve the goals of the institution together with the staff they work with. For this reason, audit of behaviours is directly related to the efficiency and motivation of staff.

2. Performance Appraisal and Its Importance

Performance appraisal means evaluating the professional success of staff. Through performance appraisal, the skills of staff are defined and the decision on progress, promotion, and discharge is made (De Cenzo, 1996).

To define more broadly, performance appraisal is an interactive management process that supports objectives such as employment, rewarding-punishing, waging, promotion or replacement by ensuring an open institutional communication in an appropriate working setting where staff can use and develop his/her qualifications and skills in line with the objectives of the institution and thus continuously improve his performance (Kanık, 2008). In order to achieve these objectives, it is imperative to define open objectives, measurable standards, job descriptions and job requirements.

It is aimed to compare the previous and current performance of employees with the performance standards in this process, which supports the objectives of an institution and ensures staff performance (Dessler 2005).

When the historical process of performance appraisal is examined, it is observed that some resources mention appraisals during III century in China. These appraisals, which are subjective, can be considered the first examples of performance appraisal (Goodson, 1997).

With respect to libraries, performance management, of which first examples were introduced in 1960s, has become a process considered more important by library directors in 1970s and has been used more commonly in libraries since 1980s (Aslan, 1993; Çakmak, 2005).

There are scientists who suggest that having a perfectly working performance appraisal system is difficult, even impossible. General difficulties faced in finding solutions to problems, whose subject is human, needs a different performance appraisal model for each profession group, each different culture and each different organizational structure since people are different from each other; the problem is complicated and multi-sided and differences in standards of judgement do not allow an objective approach (Palmer, 1997; de Cenzo, 1996) and thus there are various methods in performance appraisal.

Appraisal allows directors to make decisions on rewarding, punishing and taking corrective and developmental precautions. Directors make some decisions as required by the situation by getting informed about whether the institution has reached the objectives, what and how staff does at work (Goodson, 1997).

Policy implementers on staff management do not discuss whether performance appraisal is necessary or not but the issues about when and how to conduct performance appraisal. According to Palmer (1993), what makes performance appraisal indispensable is, as a criterion whether everything runs smoothly in an institution, that staff in the institution focuses on job performance. Staff firstly would want to have the provisions of their work. That is why; they expect a difference between the ones working and not working; the successful and the unsuccessful. On the other hand, the one with knowledge of his level of success also finds the opportunity to correct and improve himself.

Performance appraisal provides various data for a new effort as well as giving information to the staff about performance. It is helpful in staff planning and encourages staff. van House summarizes the advantages of performance appraisal in terms of library and staff as follows:

"- control of data flow about procedures,
- ensure daily performance,
- control of the quality of library services,
- improve the efficiency of library,
- ensure a better and more effective planning,
- improve staff motivation,
- make comparisons in and outside library about services,
- make comparisons with other libraries in similar conditions" (van House, 1990).

Performance appraisal should not be considered only as a tool which corrects or improves the performance of librarians (Cevallos, 1992). Performance criteria also serve as a guide to libraries to take decisions, improve planning, effectiveness and efficiency. It is possible to consider performance appraisal important for libraries in that it helps develop individual perfromance, discover potential performance of staff, understand future human power resource of libraries, achieve the objectives of libraries and create a competitive superiority (Gedeon, 1991; Martey,2002).

Many libraries in the world have similarities in some aspects despite the fact that they are different in terms of cultural and institutional characteristics. One of these similarities is that libraries have limited resources with respect to human and physical resources. The economic conditions in the world enforce libraries, like all other institutions and people, to limit their financial resources. Therefore, libraries must decide their priorities in their services (Evans, 1982). In this context, libraries which make effective planning and take efficiency as a basis will be more successful.

3. Research Phases

3.1. The objective of the research

The objectives of the research can be given under two main topics:

1. to learn how and by whom the performance appraisal efforts are carried out in university libraries in Turkey and understand the perception and opinions of library staff about the appraisal,
2. to reveal the expectations about the performance appraisal criteria and the troubles observed as a result of the evaluation and finally suggest the characteristics necessary in a modern appraisal model for the related arrangements that might be done in Turkey.

3.2. The research problem

The basic research problem can be defined as follows:

What is the attitude of the staff towards the performance appraisal methods implemented in university libraries?

The sub-problems of the research are:

1. Sub-problem 1. Is there a significant difference in the attitude of the staff in university libraries towards the performance appraisal implemented in the library in terms of the status of the library?
2. Sub-problem 2. Is there a significant difference in the attitude of the managerial and non-managerial staff in university libraries towards the performance appraisal methods implemented?

3.3. The research hypothesis

The hypothesis of the research is "The performance appraisal methods implemented in university libraries adversely affect the attitude of the library staff."

The sub-hypotheses of the research are;

Sub-hypothesis 1. That the university library is a state or foundation library affects the attitude of the library staff towards the performance appraisal methods.

Sub-hypothesis 2. The position of the staff in university libraries affects his/her attitude towards the performance appraisal methods.

3.4. Method of the study

The descriptive method was used in the research. The questionnaire and interview techniques were based on the descriptive method.

As a result of the literature survey and field study, 34 items were defined for individual performance appraisal methods. These items composed based on an expert opinion were grouped under the dimensions given below.

The dimensions used in the questionnaire

  A. Knowing the Aim and Objectives of the Library
  B. Appraisal Method and Appraisal Criteria
  C. Areas of Use of Appraisal Results
  D. Who Makes Appraisal
  E. Appraisal Time

The questionnaires were prepared in the same context for three different groups, namely university library directors, librarians and other staff.

3.5. The area and scope of the study

The study was carried out in university libraries of public and private sectors in Turkey. As applying the research to all university libraries in Turkey would not be possible, the study was carried out in state and foundation university libraries in Ankara.

3.6. The universe and sample

The universe of the research is the staff working in university libraries of public and private sector in Turkey. The sample of the research is all the staff working in university libraries of public and private sector in Ankara. In sample selection, the fact that the university has a central library was taken into consideration.

3.7. Pilot implementation

The pilot implementation and preliminary work of the research were carried out on 30 people working in Beytepe Campus Library at Hacettepe University. The group was asked to answer the questions in the questionnaire prepared beforehand. At the end, the opinions and suggestions, if any, were obtained as well as the answers to each question and to the questionnaire as a whole. The questions in the questionnaire were asked to the same group twice at intervals of 15 days for the purposes of validity and reliability test. The values of the validity and reliability test were found to be at variable values ranging from .87 and .97 . Some questions were asked in a different style as control questions. An expert was consulted for preparation, validity and reliability of the questionnaire.

3.8. Data collection

The questionnaires were applied to 305 staff working in Atılım, Başkent, Bilkent, Çankaya, Gazi, Hacettepe, METU, TOBB-ETU and Ufuk University Libraries in Ankara. 248 completed questionnaires were received back. The rate of receiving back is 81.3%.

3.9. Data analysis

The data obtained by questionnaires were assessed on computer by use of "SPSS" for Windows 15.0 (Statistical Package for the Social Sciences) package programme.

In data analysis and interpretation, the percentages and frequencies of all answers were taken and formulated tabulations were interpreted. In analysis of sub-problems, Pearson Q-Square simple correlation technique was used.

In interpretation of the answers revealing the opinions of directors and staff in university libraries in Ankara towards the performance appraisal method, 5 "Likert" type scale was used.

4. Results (Results on Individual Data)

Distribution of the participants by sex:

Table1. Sex Distribution of the Participants (248 participants; 64.1% female, 35, 9% male)

Sex	Frequency	%	Valid %	Total %
Male	89	35,9	35,9	35,9
Female	159	64,1	64,1	100,0
Total	248	100,0	100,0	

Distribution of the participants by status of library:

Table 2. Distribution of the Participants by Status of Library (54% of the participant staff work in state university libraries while 46% work in foundation university libraries)

Status of Library	Frequency	%	Valid %	Total %
State	134	54,0	54,0	54,0
Foundation	114	46,0	46,0	100,0
Total	248	100,0	100,0	

Distribution of the participants by working period:

Table 3. Distribution of the Participants by Working Period (It is observed that 25.4% of the participants have been working for 0-5 years, 24.6% for 6-10 years, 23.0% for 16-20 years and 6.5% for 21 years and more.)

Working Period	Frequency	%	Valid %	Total %
0-5 years	63	25,4	25,4	25,4
6-10 years	61	24,6	24,6	50,0
11-15 years	57	23,0	23,0	73,0
16-20 years	51	20,6	20,6	93,5
21 years and more	16	6,5	6,5	100,0
Total	248	100,0	100,0	

Distribution of the participants by education level:

Table 4. Distribution of the Participants by Education Level (19.4% of the participants completed secondary education, 14.1% completed a two-years programme, 49.2% completed an undergraduate and 17.3% completed a master programme.)

Education Level	Frequency	%	Valid %	Total %
Secondary education	48	19,4	19,4	19,4
Two-years programme	35	14,1	14,1	33,5
Undergraduate	122	49,2	49,2	82,7
Master	43	17,3	17,3	100,0
Total	248	100,0	100,0	

Distribution of the participants by their position:

Table 5. Distribution of the participants by their position (6.0% of the participants work as a director, 16.1% as a unit leader/chief, 27.8% as a librarian, 50% as an officer/other positions.)

Titles	Frequency	%	Valid frequency	Total frequency
Director	15	6,0	6,0	6,0
Unit Leader/ Chief	40	16,1	16,1	22,2
Librarian	69	27,8	27,8	50,0
Officer/Other	124	50,0	50,0	100,0
Total	248	100	100,0	

Results concerning the problem

The results obtained in the research are assessed under two subparts as the problem and the sub-problems.

Result concerning the basic problem

The attitude of the staff towards the performance appraisal methods applied in university libraries was found to be negative.

Results concerning the sub-problems

-Results concerning the sub-problem 1

A significant difference was found in the attitude of the staff working in university libraries towards the performance appraisal method in terms of the status of the library in the dimensions of appraisal method and criterion, areas of use of the appraisal results and appraisal time.

Besides, similarities were found in the attitude of the staff in items in the dimensions of knowing the aim and objective of the library and by whom the appraisal is made.

-Results concerning the sub-problem 2

A significant difference was found in the attitude of the staff working in university libraries towards the performance appraisal method with respect to the managerial or non-managerial position of the staff in the dimensions of appraisal method and criteria and by whom the appraisal is made.

Besides, similarities were found in the attitude of the staff in items in the dimensions of knowing the aim and objectives of the library, areas of use of appraisal results and appraisal time.

For the opinions of directors and staff about the criteria needed to be included in a modern appraisal model, criterias aiming to evaluate job performance were preferred in the first places. Criteria such as personalities, clothing and appearance were preferred at the end places.

As a result, directors and staff prefer a performance appraisal system that focuses on and orients to the job.

5. Recommendations

The features which must be taken into consideration in building a modern appraisal model that can be implemented in university libraries in Turkey are as follows:

A. Knowing the aim and objectives of the library: The library management should make the arrangements necessary to ensure the staff precisely knows the aim and objectives of the library. Knowing the aim and objectives of the library precisely will ensure elimination of uncertainties about the future efforts and services of the library.

In establishing an individual performance appraisal system, the system should be built and implemented in line with the aims and objectives of the library.

B. Appraisal method and appraisal criteria: The library management should organize training programmes where not only unit responsible and other directors making the appraisal but also the staff can get the necessary information on performance appraisal method.

Legal arrangements for a new and effective performance appraisal system should be made since the Confidential Personal Record used especially in public institutions do not bear modern characteristics. The parts related to waging based on performance appraisal and performance in the Employee Law, which still remains as a draft, should be prepared considering the modern approaches.

The library management should establish a modern appraisal method the most suitable for the existing circumstances and its resources by using the existing standards and guidance.

The performance criteria to be used in appraisal should be open and clear and be precisely known by the library staff.

In libraries where job analysis has not been made yet, job analysis and job flow schemes should be prepared.

Job descriptions should be prepared in line with the areas of expertise and skills of the staff.

Each library should receive full support from the senior management in the process of establishing and implementing the new performance appraisal system to be established.

The performance appraisal system should be fair and objective.

The performance appraisal system should have features to ensure participation of the staff in appraisal and the areas of expertise and skills of the staff should be considered.

The performance appraisal system should be prepared as an alterative to the official appraisal system currently applied in libraries and contribute to the results of the official appraisals.

C. Areas of use of appraisal results: Performance appraisal system should be an open and interactive system.

The library staff should be informed about the results and reasons of the performance appraisal and the necessary arrangements should be made for the points missing and requiring correction.

Promotion or advancement in position should be made according to the professional success of staff and rewarding of the successful staff should be made taking into consideration the results of performance appraisal.

The library management should take into consideration the results of performance appraisal in staff planning, career development or change in position of the staff.

Training programmes appropriate to the professional development of the library staff should be organized in line with their areas of expertise and skills and staff should continuously be encouraged to this end.

Decision on increasing the existing performance of library staff should be made according to the results of performance appraisal.

Feedback should continuously be provided for the points where performance is low.

Directors and staff should come together at intervals to discuss whether the performance level and objectives are achieved.

Performance appraisal results should guide to increase the quality and efficiency of services already provided and planned to be provided in the future.

Training needs of staff should be determined according to the results of performance appraisal. Training activities should start after deciding which staff will be trained on which subjects.

D. Who makes appraisal: Performance appraisal should be made by the nearest senior and then the library top management should be asked for opinion and approval for appraisal.

Directors making performance appraisal should have the sufficient knowledge and education on performance appraisal method.

E. Appraisal time: Library top management should decide on which periods individual performance appraisal will be made and staff should be informed in advance.

Directors should make review meetings (quarterly, semi-annually/annually) with staff before performance appraisal.

Other points to be taken into consideration about performance appraisal system: Library top management should elegantly organize training and adjustment activities related to the system.

The opinions of library users should also be taken into consideration in deciding performance appraisal model.

Library orientation and user training programmes should be organized to support performance appraisal system.

Performance appraisal system should be dynamic and adaptable to new approaches.

Performance appraisal system should always be kept updated in line with the requirements.

References

Aslan, S. (1993) "Başarıyı Kanıtlamanın Bir Aracı: Performans Ölçmesi".*1. Symposium on Public Librarianship. Ankara: 29 November – 1 December. 47-50.*

Cevallos, E.E. (1996), A Study of Participant's Perceptions of the Effectiveness of Performance Appraisals for Librarians in Colleges and Universities (Academic Libraries).Columbia University.DLS.Library Science.

Çakmak, N., (2005), Kütüphanelerde Performans Değerlendirmesi ve Yönetime Etkisi. Published Master thesis. Ankara. Ankara University, Institute of Social Sciences.

Dessler, Garry. (2005), *Human Resource Management*, Harlow, UK: Pearson Education, 10.th.ed.

De Cenzo, D. (1996), *Human Resource Management*, New York: John Wiley & Sons, 5th.ed.,

Evans, G.E., and Benedict Rugaas. (1982), Another Look at Performance Appraisal in Libraries. In *Performance Evaluation:A Management Basic for Libraries,*ed.by Jonathan A.Lindsey,Phoneix,Arizona:The Oryx Press.

Goodson, C. F., (1997), *The Complete Guide to Performance Standards for Library Personnel.* N,Y,Neal-Schuman Publishers.

Kanık, L., (2008), Türk Üniversitelerinde Kütüphane Çalışanlarının Performans Değerlendirmeleri. Published Doctoral thesis. Ankara, Hacettepe University, Institute of Social Sciences.

Gedeon, J. A., (1999), "Attribution Theory and Academic Library Performance Evaluation". *The Journal of Academic Librarianship.*25(1):18-25 .

Martey, A.K., (2002) "Appraising the Performance of Library Staff in Ghanaian Academic Library"., 2006 [available at: http://www.blackwell-synergy.com/doi/full]

Palmer, M. J., (1993), *How to Plan and Conduct Productive Performance Appraisals / Performans Değerlendirmeleri.* (translated by Doğan Şahiner), İstanbul:Rota.

Robbins, S.P., (1996), *Management.* N.J: Prentice Hall. 5th.ed

Van House, N., (1990), *Measuring Academic Library Performance: A Practical Guide,*Chicago,ALA.

Automated Metadata Harvesting Among Greek Repositories in the Framework of EuropeanaLocal: Dealing with Interoperability

Alexandros Koulouris[1,4] Emmanouel Garoufallou[2,4] and Evangelos Banos[3,4]

[1]Department of Librarianship and Information Systems, Technological Educational Institute (T.E.I.) of Athens, Agiou Spyridonos Str., 12210 Egaleo, Athens, Greece, koulouris.a@gmail.com, akoul@teiath.gr
[2]Department of Library Science and Information Systems, Technological Educational Institution (T.E.I.) of Thessaloniki, P.O. BOX 141, 57400 Thessaloniki, Greece, garoufallou@yahoo.co.uk, mgarou@libd.teithe.gr
[3]Evangelos Banos, Openarchives.gr, Greece, vbanos@gmail.com
[4]Veria Central Public Library, 8, Ellis Str., P.O. BOX 236, 59100 Veria, Greece

Abstract: EuropeanaLocal is a best practice network project, which will help Europeana to enhance its content and service by applying automated metadata harvesting among distributed repositories. Greek content providers and its metadata aggregator, the Veria Central Public Library (VCPL), are in a testing metadata harvesting period, in the framework of EuropeanaLocal. This paper analyzes the practices that the Greek Institutional Repositories follow in order to transform their metadata schemas to European Semantic Elements (ESE) profile and to export this profile through OAI-PMH to the VCPL aggregator. In addition, it describes the way in which the VCPL aggregates the ESE exported metadata output. Finally, it emphasizes on the transformation and aggregation tools that have been launched on a local level, before Europeana disseminates its official ones.
Keywords: Europeana, EuropeanaLocal, public libraries, cultural content, digital projects, interoperability, repositories, harvesting, metadata, European Semantic Elements

1. Introduction

Europeana is an evolving service, which will constitute an umbrella of European metadata from distributed cultural organizations. The European Digital Library "Europeana" is enhanced in this effort by various European projects. One of the most representatives is EuropeanaLocal, which will feed Europeana with metadata of local cultural content. Europeana will collect these metadata in an automated metadata harvesting procedure. Greece is participating in EuropeanaLocal with six Greek content providers, a meta-search engine of Greek repositories (openarchives.gr) and a metadata aggregator, the Veria Central Public Library (VCPL). These organizations are in a testing metadata harvesting period, in the framework of EuropeanaLocal. The practices that the Greek repositories follow in order to transform their metadata schemas to European Semantic Elements (ESE) profile and to export this profile through OAI-PMH to the VCPL aggregator are analyzed. Emphasis is given on the transformation and aggregation tools that have been launched on a local level, by

New Trends in Qualitative and Quantitative Methods in Libraries
A. Katsirikou and C. H. Skiadas (eds)
© *World Scientific Publishing Co (pp. 331-337)*

VCPL. Finally, results from the test harvesting that have been conducted until the time of papers' writing are presented.

2. Europeana and EuropeanaLocal: Brief Analysis

Europeana currently gives access to 5.9 million items representing all Member States including film material, photos, paintings, sounds, maps, manuscripts, books, newspapers and archival papers, rising to a target of 10 million by 2010 (Davies, 2008; Annual Report, 2010). The Europeana service (Koninklijke Bibliotheek, 2009) is designed to increase access to digital content across Europe's cultural organizations (i.e. libraries, museums, archives and audio/visual archives). This process will bring together and link up heterogeneously sourced content, which is complementary in terms of themes, location and time. By February 2010, Europeana's active partner network consists of 180 organizations.

In order to achieve these goals European Union launched in June 2008 the EuropeanaLocal project in the framework of eContentPlus program. Up to 2011, the EuropeanaLocal partners aim to make available to Europeana more than 20 million items, held across 27 countries. At the same time, they are committed to exploring and developing efficient and sustainable processes and governance procedures so that the growing numbers of regional and local institutions can easily make their content available to Europeana into the future by adopting and promoting the use of its infrastructure, tools and standards (McHenry, 2008).

Key challenges, like metadata, system and semantic interoperability, the harvesting protocol compatibility, the data format diversity, arise. EuropeanaLocal will ensure that the approaches, standards and tools developed by Europeana are widely adopted, thereby supporting the interoperability of content. In brief, this will involve the establishment of a harvestable network of OAI-PMH compliant metadata repositories, which will aggregate local content and which will complement the developing Europeana network. In addition, tools such as Europeana's metadata 'installer' and automated metadata conversion tools, will be made available for EuropeanaLocal partners to use (McHenry, 2008).

The cultural heritage management prototype that Europeana and EuropeanaLocal will implement is the project's innovation. This distributed and automated metadata harvesting model based on OAI-PMH, is represented in Figure 1, which describes the Europeana services structure.

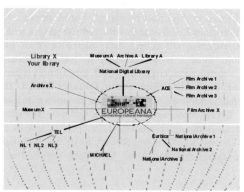

Figure 1. Possible Europeana structure.

3. EuropeanaLocal in Greece: Current Status and Results

Until March 2010, seven Greek cultural organizations, participate in EuropeanaLocal and they will made their metadata available through Europena service. These organizations are:

- Veria Central Public Library (VCPL) (aggregator)
- American Farm School (AFS)
- Music Library "Lilian Voudouri"
- National Documentation Centre of Greece (NDC)
- National Technical University of Athens (NTUA)
- openarchives.gr (Greek digital repositories meta-search engine)
- Technical Chamber of Greece – Regional Department of Corfu

Among these repositories, VCPL is the national aggregator in the framework of EuropeanaLocal until the finalization of the project, in June 2011. Openarchives.gr is an established meta-search engine of Greek digital repositories which provides consulting and technical support whereas the other organizations are content providers.

In order to analyze the "landscape" in Greek cultural organizations, a metadata, content and technical survey was conducted. This survey was part of the main one that was conducted through EuropeanaLocal partners, from November 2008 till January 2009. The results of the survey are accessible, only for partners, via EuropeanaLocal's website.

The main conclusion derived from the survey, is that some Greek organization that was at the initial plan for participating at the first phase of the project, will not be able to participate at this stage. Some of the reasons are:

- They are hesitant to provide their digital content widely available though the World Wide Web
- The project's innovation and the lack of previous experience
- The lack of interoperability standards (e.g. OAI-PMH) that has been adopted by Europeana
- The low level of digitization
- Non-established repositories

In addition, existing fears on intellectual property rights prevent local repositories in participating in EuropeanaLocal. However, this problem has been solved, because the content does not migrate in Europeana, and its provider (repository) is responsible for the content and controls the access.

However, from the organizations that already participate in the project useful remarks were extracted. Most of them use open-source software to provide their digital content. The majority uses DSpace, which is interoperable in metadata schemes; Dublin Core is usually the scheme that the DSpace implements. They strictly follow Dublin Core v1.1 qualified or their application profiles are compatible with this version. In addition, OAI-PMH has been already implemented, and in cases where is not in use, it is already been embedded into the system. That means that it can be implemented any time. Finally, the content varies in formats, from PDF files to AVI. However, all types of forms are compatible with Europeana data format standard (Koulouris and Garoufallou, 2009).

The EuropeanaLocal (2008) helps the Greek cultural organizations to gain new knowledge, to improve their content, metadata, interoperability, and to provide new services. These are some of the reasons that the EuropeanaLocal Greek team encourages the institutions to participate in the future phases of the project (Trohopoulos, Koulouris, Garoufallou and Siatri, 2009).

4. Harvesting Procedures among Greek Repositories

Greek content providers and its metadata aggregator, the Veria Central Public Library (VCPL), are in a testing metadata harvesting period, in the framework of EuropeanaLocal. This section analyzes the practices that the Greek Institutional Repositories follow in order to transform their metadata schemas to European Semantic Elements profile (2009) – that has been developed by Europeana – and to export this profile through OAI-PMH to the VCPL aggregator. In addition, it describes the way in which the VCPL aggregates the ESE exported metadata output. Finally, it emphasizes on the transformation and aggregation tools that have been launched on a local level, before Europeana disseminates its official ones.

It is worth noted that in this process only the metadata are harvested and copyright agreements, firstly between the local content providers and the national aggregator for each country, and secondly between each national aggregators and Europeana should be signed. For example, in Greece, and for the duration of the project EuropeanaLocal (June 2008 – June 2011), each content provider will sign bilateral agreement with VCPL. Then, VCPL will sign an agreement with Europeana. As a result, each Greek content provider has the obligation to export the ESE metadata using OAI-PMH to VCPL, and on the other hand VCPL has the obligation to collect and harvest automatically the ESE metadata from the content providers and to disseminate them to Europeana. Specifically, Europeana will apply automated harvesting to VCPL and to all national aggregators. More on the harvesting procedure and the progress on ESE transformation and aggregation that have been implemented by the Greek EuropeanaLocal partners and the support team are analyzed below.

4.1 Europeana Semantic Elements Compliance

One of the most important aspects in the process of creating a Europeana Compliant digital repository is the support for ESE, which is virtually a new Dublin Core Profile, developed by Europeana in order to fulfill its operational requirements. Existing digital repository software in general does not support ESE by default as it is the case with Dublin Core. Nevertheless, the nature of the formats makes it feasible to alter existing software and data in order to add support for ESE. Specific information about the process can be found at the DSpace plugin for Europeana Semantic Elements webpage (Banos, 2010).

The first step in the process is to use the Europeana XML Namespace http://europeana.eu/schemas/ese/ and augment existing systems' configuration in order to support the additional ESE elements. Figures 2 and 3 illustrate a sample metadata set for a specific record from the VCPL digital repository using Dublin Core and ESE formats.

Figure 2. Sample Dublin Core Record

```
- <record>
  - <header>
      <identifier>oai:medusa.libver.gr:123/903</identifier>
      <datestamp>2010-04-15T08:01:52Z</datestamp>
      <setSpec>hdl_123_902</setSpec>
    </header>
  - <metadata>
    - <oai_dc:dc xsi:schemaLocation="http://www.openarchives.org/OAI/2.0/oai_dc/ http://www.openarchives.org/OAI/2.0/oai_dc.xsd">
        <dc:contributor>Καλλιβωκάς, Αντώνης Δ., 1855-1910</dc:contributor>
        <dc:contributor>Ποταμιάνος, Δημήτριος</dc:contributor>
        <dc:date>2009-10-14T20:26:31Z</dc:date>
        <dc:date>2009-10-14T20:26:31Z</dc:date>
        <dc:date>1899</dc:date>
        <dc:date>1899</dc:date>
        <dc:identifier>http://medusa.libver.gr/handle/123/903</dc:identifier>
        <dc:format>784</dc:format>
      - <dc:publisher>
          Εν Αθήναις, Εκ του βιβλιοεκδοτικού καταστήματος Αναστασίου Δ. Φέξη, 1899
        </dc:publisher>
        <dc:subject>Ιατροδικαστική</dc:subject>
      - <dc:title>
          Ιατροδικαστική : μεθ' ερμηνείας των σχετικών νόμων, διατάξεων κτλ : προς χρήσιν των ιατρών και νομικών/ Α.Καλλιβωκάς, Δ. Ποταμιανού
        </dc:title>
        <dc:type>Βιβλίο</dc:type>
      </oai_dc:dc>
    </metadata>
  </record>
```

4.2. Batch import of the ESE elements

After implementing ESE support, the repository has to be populated with the appropriate metadata values. This task can be either performed manually through the appropriate interface of each digital library or automatically using special software tools developed for this purpose. It must be noted that due to the wide usage of the DSpace software among almost all digital repositories, the focus has been the implementation of tools for this specific platform. National Documentation Center has developed a DSpace plugin written in Java, capable of the addition of the Europeana schema in any DSpace repository and the automated completion of the metadata fields. Thorough instructions have also been published in English and in Greek in order to allow anyone to utilize this software (Banos, 2010). Alternative, a simpler PHP Metadata Updater script has been implemented in order to allow the batch insertion of ESE metadata in existing DC records. (Banos, 2010)

Figure 3. Sample Europeana Semantic Elements Record

```
<record>
 - <header>
     <identifier>oai:medusa.libver.gr:123/903</identifier>
     <datestamp>2010-04-15T08:01:52Z</datestamp>
     <setSpec>hdl_123_902</setSpec>
   </header>
 - <metadata>
   - <europeana:record>
       <dc:contributor>Καλλιβωκάς, Αντώνης Δ., 1855-1910</dc:contributor>
       <dc:contributor>Ποταμιάνος, Δημήτριος</dc:contributor>
       <dc:date>2009-10-14T20:26:31Z</dc:date>
       <dc:date>2009-10-14T20:26:31Z</dc:date>
       <dc:date>1899</dc:date>
       <dc:date>1899</dc:date>
       <dc:identifier>http://medusa.libver.gr/handle/123/903</dc:identifier>
       <dc:format>784</dc:format>
     - <dc:publisher>
         Εν Αθήναις, Εκ του βιβλιοεκδοτικού καταστήματος Αναστασίου Δ. Φέξη, 1899
       </dc:publisher>
       <dc:subject>Ιατροδικαστική</dc:subject>
     - <dc:title>
         Ιατροδικαστική : μεθ' ερμηνείας των σχετικών νόμων, διατάξεων κτλ. : προς χρήσιν των ιατρών και νομικών/ Α.Καλλιβωκάς, Δ. Ποταμιανού
       </dc:title>
       <dc:type>Βιβλίο</dc:type>
     - <europeana:object>
         http://medusa.libver.gr/retrieve/7070/GRVER_000000000000000022.jpg.jpg
       </europeana:object>
       <europeana:provider>Veria Central Public Library</europeana:provider>
       <europeana:type>TEXT</europeana:type>
       <europeana:isShownAt>http://medusa.libver.gr/handle/123/903</europeana:isShownAt>
     </europeana:record>
   </metadata>
 </record>
```

4.3 DSpace OAI-PMH support for ESE

The final step in the process of achieving the ESE compliance of a DSpace digital repository is the modification of the OAI-PMH interface in order to export not only DC but also ESE metadata. This is achieved through a new DSpace Crosswalks Plugin which implements these features. To illustrate the results of this plugin a simple example is listed below. Currently, the VCPL DSpace installation exports DC metadata through the following URL: http://medusa.libver.gr/oai/request?verb=ListRecords&metadataPrefix=oai_dc

Using the DSpace ESE Plugin, it is now possible to retrieve ESE metadata through the following: http://medusa.libver.gr/oai/request?verb= ListRecords&metadataPrefix=ese

Last but not least, source code and instructions for installation are available at the DSpace plugin for Europeana Semantic Elements webpage (Banos, 2010).

4.4 Support for legacy digital libraries

Except from DSpace and other modern digital libraries software, there are also numerous digital libraries built with older or closed source technologies which do not support OAI-PMH or any other form of automatic metadata exchange. In these cases, special techniques should be applied in order to extract metadata through plain HTTP requests.

DEiXTo (or ΔEiXTo) (Donas, 2010) is a powerful web data extraction tool that is based on the W3C Document Object Model (DOM). It allows users to create highly accurate "extraction rules" (wrappers) that describe what pieces of data to scrape from a web page. When used appropriately, DEiXTo can extract meaningful metadata from digital libraries and generate DC and ESE metadata records according to the standards. These records can be utilized by any standards compliant metadata harvester in order to insert the specified repository in Europeana.

DEiXTo is currently used to import Music Library "Lilian Voudouri" in Europeana and gives the possibility to extract metadata from virtually any web site willing to participate in Europeana, regardless of its current technology.

4.5 Aggregation

In order to optimize the process of aggregating the metadata of all European digital repositories, Europeana suggests that aggregators should be implemented on national or regional scale. VCPL has implemented an aggregator (Veria Central Public Library, 2010) which ingests ESE metadata from current Europeana participants in Greece and after performing some rudimentary checks, exports this metadata to Europeana. All new participants willing to participate in Europeana Local from Greece must be checked and ingested from the VCPL Aggregator which in turn propagates their metadata to Europeana (see Figure 4).

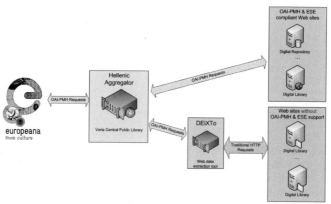

Figure 4. VCPL Aggregator

4.6 Current status

As of March 2010, all content providers except Music Library "Lilian Voudouri" use the DSpace software for their digital libraries and have followed closely the aforementioned instructions, thus implementing full support for ESE. Sample metadata records from these libraries have been tested successfully with the Europeana Content Checker, a special tool provided by Europeana in order to check metadata compliance with the standards. Additionally, all these libraries have been harvested successfully by the VCPL Aggregator.

5. Conclusions

It is evident that in a couple of years Europeana, the European Digital Library, will be one of its kind worldwide since it will compile a variety of media from across Europe, all house under one umbrella. These collections and cultural heritage resources of immense importance will change the 'digital library map' in Europe. It is therefore our obligation as Greek harvesting point to assist, drive and enrich the quality of metadata, build tools that will assist small and medium libraries, archives and museums in order to be part of this effort that the European Community undergoes. This vision for the future is a common vision for every European country and Greek content providers need to be part of this. We hope that in the following months the Greek section of EuropeanaLocal to be first in the agenda of Greek Library, Museum and Archive community.

Acknowledgement

We thank the Greek EuropeanaLocal team and the content providers for their support that make this paper possible.

References

Annual Report. Grant Agreement Number: 558001 Europeana v1.0. 1 February 2009 -31 January (2010). http://version1.europeana.eu/c/document_library/get_file?uuid=df49b382-aa16-497f-8405-948b532dc0d7&groupId=10602 [accessed: 31/03/2010].

Banos, E. (2010). DSpace plugin for Europeana Semantic Elements (ESE), http://vbanos.gr?p=189 [accessed 25/3/2010]

Davies, R. (2008). Europeana: an Infrastructure for Adding Local Content. *Ariadne*, 57, http://www.ariadne.ac.uk/issue57/davies/ [accessed: 28/03/2010].

Donas. K. (2010). DEiXTo, http://www.deixto.com [accessed 25/3/2010] European Commission (2008). *eContentplus*, http://ec.europa.eu/information_society/activities/econtentplus/index_en.htm [accessed: 15/8/2009].

Europeana Semantic Elements specifications. Version 3.2.1, 06/11/2009. Europeana v1.0 (2009). http://www.europeanfilmgateway.eu/downloads/Europeana_Semantic_Elements_Spe cifications_v3_2_1_2009-11-06-1.pdf [accessed: 31/03/2010].

EuropeanaLocal (2008). *EuropeanaLocal: connecting cultural heritage*, http://www.europeanlocal.eu [accessed: 28/03/2010].

Koninklijke Bibliotheek (2009). *Europeana*, http://www.europeana.eu [accessed: 28/03/2010].

Koulouris, A. and Garoufallou, E. (2009). Managing cultural heritage content in the context of Europeana. *Proceedings of the International Conference of Marketing and Management Sciences (ICMMS 2009)*, Kos Island, Greece, September 11-14, 2009 (to appear).

Lagoze, C., et al. (2008). *The Open Archives Initiative Protocol for Metadata Harvesting*, http://www.openarchives.org/OAI/openarchivesprotocol.html [accessed: 15/8/2009].

McHenry, O. (2008). EuropeanaLocal – its role in improving access to Europe's cultural heritage through the European Digital Library. *11th Annual International Conference «EVA 2008 Moscow»*, Moscow. http://conf.cpic.ru/upload/eva2008/reports/dokladEn_1509.pdf[accessed: 28/03/2010].

Trohopoulos, I., Koulouris, A., Garoufallou, E. and Siatri, R. (2009). Harvesting metadata of Greek institutional repositories in the context of EuropeanaLocal. *Workshop on harvesting metadata: practices and challenges, 13th European Conference on Digital Libraries (ECDL 2009)*, Corfu, Greece, September 29 - October 2, 2009.

Veria Central Public Library (2010). Europeana Local Aggregator http://aggregator.libver.gr [accessed 25/3/2010]

The Benefits of a Quality Management System: The Case of the Merger of Two Universities and Their Libraries

Jarmo Saarti[1] and Arja Juntunen

University of Eastern Finland Library, Finland, [1]Jarmo.Saarti@uef.fi

Abstract: At the turn of this century, it was decided to renovate higher education in Finland, and as a result three new universities were created by merging existing units. One of these new Universities is the University of Eastern Finland which was formed from the Universities of Joensuu and Kuopio. The merger started in the year 2007 and in 2008 and 2009 there was a reorganisation of the two previous libraries' management and service provision to create a single new Library. The quality management system that the Library has been building was used in this process. The paper describes how the strategy was defined; the organization developed as well as the working order and a quality manual for the new merged library was created. The benefits of a participant management style as well as retaining the best practices from the old libraries into the new unit are emphasised.

Keywords: Quality management, evidence based management, mergers, university libraries, Finland

1. Introduction

Recently the higher education legislation and structures were reorganized in Finland. A new University Act was passed in the summer of 2009 (see Ministry of Education 2009). The new act means that the formerly state-owned Universities have become more autonomous; in addition the number of Universities in Finland is being reduced by merging some of the existing units into newer, larger versions. One of these new institutions is the University of Eastern Finland (UEF) was created out of the Universities of Joensuu and Kuopio. The new University will have three different campuses, about 130 kilometres apart in the eastern part of Finland (see Fig. 1).

Fig. 1. Three campuses of the UEF

New Trends in Qualitative and Quantitative Methods in Libraries
A. Katsirikou and C. H. Skiadas (eds)
© *World Scientific Publishing Co (pp. 339-344)*

The development of the university education in the eastern part of Finland only started in the 1960's with legislation that founded three universities - Universities in Joensuu, Kuopio and Lappeenranta. That decision also meant that the eastern part of Finland was endowed with three universities that each had their own specific profile. Joensuu's profile was mainly the humanities and social sciences, Kuopio's was health sciences whereas Lappeenranta specialized technology.

After the EU's decision in the 1990's to create a European Higher Education Area via the so-called Bologna-process (see more from: http://www.ond.vlaanderen.be/ogeronderwijs/bologna/) also the Finnish government devised new goals for restructuring its higher education system. In reality, this meant two things: to increase the quality of Finnish higher education in order to meet the requirements of the international competition and at the same time to increase the effectiveness, especially in financial terms, of the universities.

One result of this decision was that several of the higher education units decided to merge; and as mentioned earlier one of those was the merger of Joensuu and Kuopio Universities. Both Universities were active in this process and viewed it as a competitive advantage in order to gain a better status both nationally and internationally. The Libraries were incorporated into the merger process from its very start.

The merging process started in the year 2007. The years 2008 and 2009 meant the reorganisation of the two previous libraries' management and provision of services so that it became one new Library. The existing quality management system in the Library was used as a tool. The paper describes the work involved in defining the strategy, organization, working order and quality manual for the new merged library. It was also decided to adopt a participant management style as well as disseminating the best practices of the old university libraries.

2. Preparing for the merger

The active creation of the new University of Eastern Finland started in the year 2007 when a working group led by Professor Reijo Vihko submitted its report on how to intensify the cooperation between the Universities of Joensuu and Kuopio. It was significant for the library that it was incorporated into this process from the very onset. The library made a proposal on how it could contribute to the merger and what projects it would need to initiate. In the fall of the year 2007, the former Universities started to discuss a total merge.

The year 2008 was a busy planning year. The organisational structure and strategy of the University of Eastern Finland were completed. The library obtained funding for two of its projects: the aim of the first one was to merge the collection databases into one – this task was completed in the summer of 2009. The aim of the second project was to develop a joint policy of information literacy and tutoring. Here the emphasis was put on building distant learning courses.

These two projects represented the first concrete steps for the joint library. A joint collection database was also a clear signal to the library staff and customers that the library had to act as a single unit. During the preparatory phase, the two former University libraries' management started to work in parallel.

A decision was also made about the library's management structure: library director, deputy director as well as the six heads of services were appointed to their positions. This meant that people responsible for the change were physically present and had the power to act and make decisions.

3. Making tools for the new library's management

From the beginning of the 1990's, different types of quality management (QM) and evaluation systems have become integrated into higher education institutes in Finland.

Such that today the higher education institutions have the responsibility for quality control on their campuses. The auditing is carried out by the Finnish Higher Education Evaluation Council (FINHEEC) (see FINHEEC, 2004). Kuopio University had already passed this auditing and the development of its quality management system had reached quite an advanced level (e.g. Saarti & Juntunen 2007 and Saarti & Juntunen & Taskinen 2009).

The most remarkable change in the creation of the UEF has been that the new University is larger in size and that it has campuses widely separated from each other. In addition both of the former Universities have their own rather distinct and different histories and cultures. This has meant new challenges for the library's management. The two main tasks have been a) to integrate and unify the service provision processes and b) to give birth to a new organizational culture. Of course these go hand in hand in routine tasks.

The development of the new management culture for the library started with the clarification of the new strategy and working order. In this process, the entire staff was involved which meant that at the same time when the new guidelines were created as the foundation for the management system, the staff of the previous libraries' met for first time together and discussed the values, mission, resources and basic tasks of the library. This process also highlighted the size and diversity of the new university and its library.

This discussion then led to the initial innovation in the management culture shown in the illustration (Fig. 2). Here the physical "library wall" thinking that was attached to the libraries of the former Universities came to an end and the library started to discuss about their core services and how they should be jointly provided in the different campuses.

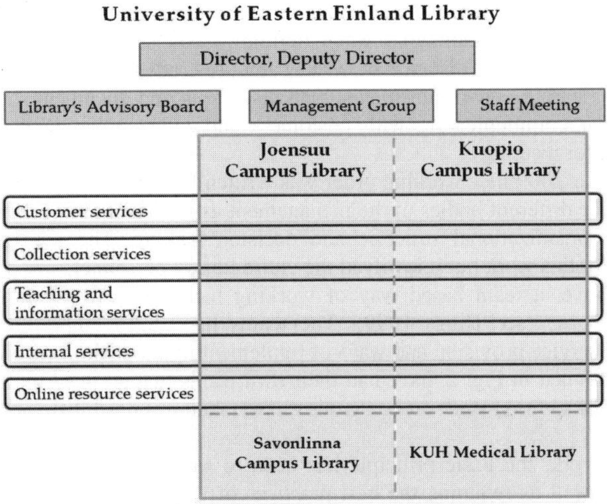

University of Eastern Finland Library

Fig. 2. The organization of the UEF Library

The next step was delegated to the heads of the services. Their mission was to unify the service production, rethink resource allocation as well re-evaluating job descriptions of each staff member. Here the tools used were the quality documentation and the process based ideology implemented within the system. The first results of this work were achieved when the integration of the e-services started in the summer 2009.

The documentation process started with the design and the creation of the new web-pages for the library; they were launched from the beginning of the year 2010. This meant also much executive work for the management: customers' rights and obligations were re-thought, the new price list was harmonized with the requirements of the new University Act, all e-resource subscriptions were renewed etc. Within a mere two years, a totally new library grew out of the structures of the two previous institutes. This created considerable stress and challenges to the staff and thus a major priority during the transitory phase was to have an effective human resources management protocol (see Ogilvie & Stork 2002).

4. Managing humans and cultures in the merge

When merging two organizations that have their own strong organizational cultures, one must emphasise the building of the new unit and at the same time as providing time for "bereavement" for those who have strong connections with the dying organizations. Databases can be combined overnight but cultural transition may take a lifetime.

King (2003, 259 - 260) states that an effective knowledge organization has the following knowledge-related components:

- enhancing the knowledge of the individuals via different types of learning;
- using teamwork in learning to create social capital;
- incorporating an intellectual property management component;
- ensuring an innovative component that uses creative thinking processes;
- Managing and disseminating effectively documented knowledge via an information/communication system infrastructure.

In building a common culture, the Library used methods for promoting social integrity which involved arranging joint seminars where the whole staff worked together, a team building process where staff members from the different campuses worked together towards a common goal when defining basic services and their process optimization. Due to the distance between campuses, advantage was taken of new technologies: learning environments enabled discussion and document sharing, blogs were used for communicating with customers and videoconferencing became an ordinary tool for meetings.

During the year 2009 new working order was written for the new library that defined the roles of the different bodies of the management as well as those of the staff which clarified the organizational structure and decision making. The management was responsible for this work but it involved the entire library personnel.

As stated above, a team based way of working has been utilized throughout the preparatory phase (see Higgs 1999). The teams have been empowered to make decisions on service provision and ways of implementing the main tasks. All the main services mentioned in Fig. 2. have had their own teams that are lead by the heads of the services. In addition some ad hoc groups have taken responsibility for project type cases.

In the team work, the basic principle has been to satisfy the needs of the campus customers as well as retaining the best practices of the old institutes. This involved many meetings, every year about 200. Although most of these have been arranged via videoconferencing, it has taken time. This resource allocation on the other hand increased commitment to the work being done by the library.

At the same time while building the new modes of action for the library, all these activities have been documented by the library's quality system. It can be said that documenting the activities has almost been like taking an outsider's point of view when planning the new library, and furthermore it has increased the library's quality documentation which were tested in internal audits carried out by the university during the fall 2009.

Perhaps the greatest challenge has been the communication both inside the library and to the world outside. All the decisions cannot please everyone during such a radical change, this has meant being alert when informing the customers of the sometimes rapid changes in services and rules and thus the collection of feedback from the users has been carefully monitored.

Communication within the library has needed new tools, as already mentioned. Without the modern communication technologies the management of a UEF type of university with three campuses situated about 100 kilometres apart from each other would be impossible. A period of change is a stressful time for the staff when fears and rumours can quickly spread. Thus the library management has tried to be as open as possible and here the modern intranet technologies have been most useful.

One challenge in communication has been the information overflow. After an organization reaches a certain point in their size, it becomes impossible for all the staff members to be aware of everything. Thus the management must also be able to compose brief but accurate notices of the main points that everyone must know.

5. Conclusions

Table 1. shows the most important decisions that were made at the State, University and Library level during the merger process.

	management system	human management	service provision	resource allocation
state level	-new University act -decision about the auditing of the new University in the year 2010	-from civil servants to workers	-centralized services	-from being a part of the State budget to allowance based funding
university level	-University's strategy and rules and regulations -University's quality management system	-University's human resources management	-University's strategic choices and service priorities	-new model for resource allocation, towards a more profit responsible organization
library level	-Library's strategy and working order -Library's quality management system	-Library's human resources management	-service provision and tailoring for the new University	-resource allocation with fewer input and with a need for more output

Table 1. Decisions at different levels that merging needed at the UEF

For the university and its library the greatest challenges were the timelines that did not exactly coincide with these procedures. The new University Act, for instance, became effective from the beginning of the year 2010, but the University had to function almost as a single unit from the fall 2009. The same was true about the library: e.g. the final budget for the year 2010 was completed only in late March 2010.

These timeline discrepancies created major headaches for the management and the need for rapid decision making and modern tools for communicating with the staff and customers. Recently the concept of *chaordic enterprise* has been introduced when one attempts to utilize the chaos theory when analysing complex organizational cultures and environments, see Eijnatten & Putnik 2004.

The quality management system thinking has clearly been a good tool during the implementation of this transition. It has set schedules and been issued with clear tasks from the university's side as the university will be audited in the fall 2010. Documentation of the library's core services and processes has helped in creating the new environment and provided a more objective basis for negotiations.

One clear challenge has been ensuring the well-being and motivation of the staff. In this respect, a purely bureaucratic process will not suffice. One must provide time for the personnel to adapt to the new situation and to give space for activities which can be likened to rituals and symbolic activities. This translates into a commitment for the management to discuss and to be willing to sit down with the staff.

Documentation has also proven to be important. Since it has helped library's management to be able to define the roles and liabilities of each individual. The involvement of the staff in the making of the documentation has been a good tool in committing the personnel to the new university, its library and to the radically changed environment.

Acknowledgements:
The authors are grateful to Dr Ewen MacDonald for revising the English.

References
Eijnatten Frans M. van & Putnik, Goran D. (2004). Chaos, complexity, learning, and the learning organization: towards a chaordic enterprise. *The Learning Organization* 11(6):418 – 429.

FINHEEC (2004). *Plan for Action 2004-2007*. Helsinki, FINHEEC. [Last visited 1st February, 2010.] Available from: http://www.kka.fi/files/189/KKA_0104Venglanti.pdf

Higgs, M. (1999). Teams and team working: What do we know? Henley Management College Report, No. HWP 9911.

King, William R. (2003). The effective knowledge organization. Business *Process Management Journal* 9(3): 259 – 260.

Ministry of Education (2009). Proposal for the new Universities Act in brief. Helsinki, Ministry of Education. [Last visited 24th March, 2010.] Available from: http://www.minedu.fi/export/sites/default/OPM/Koulutus/koulutuspolitiikka/Ha nkkeet/Yliopistolaitoksen_uudistaminen/liitteet/HE_yolaki_eng_20.2.2009.pdf.

Ogilvie, John R. & Stork, Diana (2002). Starting the HR and change: conversation with history. *Journal of Organizational change* 16(3):254 – 271.

Saarti, Jarmo and Juntunen, Arja, (2007). From the Rhetoric of Quality Management to Managing Self-Organizing Processes: A Case Study on an Expert Organization.
In: *Advances in Library Administration and Organization*, editor James M. Nyce, 25, 97-112.

Saarti, Jarmo & Juntunen, Arja & Taskinen, Aino (2009). Multi-Faceted Measuring of the Quality as a Tool for Quality Improvement in the Kuopio University Library, Finland. In: *Proceedings, Qualitative and Quantitative Methods in Libraries QQML 2009, International Conference, Chania, Crete, Greece: 26-29 of May 2009*. Proceedings edited by: Anthi Katsirikou & John Dimotikalis.

Chapter 7. Digital Libraries

Paving the Way for Interoperability in Digital Libraries: The DL.org Project

Katerina El Raheb[2], George Athanasopoulos[2], Leonardo Candela[1], Donatella Castelli[1], Perla Innocenti[3], Yannis Ioannidis[2], Akrivi Katifori[2], Anna Nika[2], Stephanie Parker[4], Seamus Ross[5], Costantino Thanos[1], Eleni Toli[2] and Giuseppina Vullo[3]

[1] Istituto di Scienza e Tecnologie dell'Informazione "A. Faedo", Consiglio Nazionale delle Ricerche, Italy
[2] Dept. of Informatics and Telecommunications, University of Athens, Greece
[3] Humanities Advanced Technology and Information Institute, University of Glasgow
[4] Trust-IT Services Ltd, UK
[5] Faculty of Information, University of Toronto, Canada

Abstract: While Digital Libraries (DLs) are moving towards universally accessible collections of human knowledge, considerable advances are needed in DL methodologies and technologies to make this happen. Interoperability between DLs is a crucial requirement to achieve this goal. The European project, DL.org, is focused on advancing the state of the art in this area by proposing solutions, fostering best practices and shared standards, drawing on the knowledge acquired during the DELOS Network of Excellence, and harnessing the expertise of DL domain stakeholder communities. By serving this goal, DL.org is paving the way for the embedding of new research achievements into real-world systems, opening up new cross-domain research perspectives and supporting the advancement of the European Information Space for the knowledge-based economy.
Keywords: Digital Libraries (DLs), interoperability, DELOS digital library reference model, content, user, functionality, quality, policy, architecture.

1. Introduction

While many DL initiatives exist worldwide, they act in isolation and adopt ad-hoc solutions and methodologies resulting in duplication of effort and slow progress. Interoperability, which is key to efficient and effective DL systems advancing cross-domain research through universal access to a broad spectrum of resources, is a complex and multi-faceted concept encompassing technological, legal and policy aspects requiring a co-ordinated approach.

This paper describes the results of DL.org, a two-year Coordination Action project starting December 2008 funded by the European Commission under the 7th Framework Programme ICT Thematic Area "Digital Libraries and Technology-Enhanced Learning".

DL.org, which stems from the DELOS Network of Excellence (www.delos.info), a major output of which is the *DELOS Digital Library Reference Model*, is aimed at

New Trends in Qualitative and Quantitative Methods in Libraries
A. Katsirikou and C. H. Skiadas (eds)
© *World Scientific Publishing Co (pp. 345-352)*

identifying effective methods for achieving interoperability among Digital Library (DL) systems, pinpointing and promoting best practices and successful technological approaches on key aspects of DL systems, and forging strong alliances with DL stakeholders and research communities. DL.org addresses two important and closely related DL issues: (a) strengthening the modelling foundations in the field by consolidating and enhancing the *DELOS Digital Library Reference Model* (b) identifying requirements, solutions and future challenges for achieving DL interoperability.

To pursue its goals, DL.org harnesses the global expertise that exists through a network of experts comprising distinguished European, as well as North American researchers, who have acquired relevant experience through DL related projects, such as DRIVER (http://www.driver-repository.eu), 5S Framework for DL (http://www.dlib.vt.edu/projects/5S-Model), Europeana (http://europeana.eu), Papyrus (http://www.ict-papyrus.eu) and Shaman (http://shaman-ip.eu), among others.), while also offering an open forum where researchers from a broad spectrum of DL-related disciplines can engage in discussions on cutting-edge technologies in DL modelling, design, and development.

Current outputs of DL.org comprise an expanded and enhanced version of the *Digital Library Reference Model* (Candela et al., 2008) and a *State-of-the-Art Survey*, which contains new facets for the revised Model with on-going activities towards a *Digital Library Technology and Methodology Cookbook* on best practices and solutions to common problems faced regarding large-scale interoperable DL systems.

Section 2 of this paper describes the methodology and approach of DL.org with regard to its Working Groups, write-up contributions and the support activities. Section 3 details the outcomes of each WG (content, user, functionality, policy, quality, and architecture), the State of the Art Survey and the first enhanced version of the *Reference Model*. Section 4 outlines future work plans of the DL.org team, while the conclusion (Section 5) summarizes the main outcomes of the project to date.

2. Methodology and Approach

The *DELOS Model* has defined the main concepts characterizing DL and DL systems, that is, content, functionality, user, policy, quality and architecture. Given the widely distributed nature of future DLs, heterogeneity is expected to be the norm with regard to these aspects. Therefore, techniques for interoperability are crucial in reconciling different approaches in such systems. DL.org is undertaking a comprehensive analysis of interoperability in the domains of all six concepts mentioned above through a critical and thorough review of the current situation and of emerging trends. The goal is to identify techniques, methods and approaches for DL interoperability based on the requirements of existing systems. To this end, DL.org co-ordinates six Thematic Working Groups (one for each domain) bringing together experts and practitioners (cf. Section 2.1), to deliver key project outputs based on their findings (cf. Section 2.2), while ensuring these findings and primers on interoperability filter down to the wider stakeholder community through targeted support activities (cf. Sec. 2.3).

2.1 Thematic working groups on interoperability

The DELOS Model provides the conceptual foundation with regard to the domains characterizing the DL universe (Content, User, Functionality, Policy, Quality, and Architecture). Each WG comprises between six to nine high-profile experts recruited to investigate domain-specific interoperability issues and propose the best applicable solutions. The WGs operate in a peer-to-peer way to identify and evaluate interoperability concerns in a qualitative rather than quantitative approach as this is a rather cumbersome task (Carney et al., 2005).

2.2 Write up contributions

WG members have carried out a critical and exhaustive study of the state-of-the-art and the solutions implemented by WG participating projects. *The State of the Art Survey* reflects the results of this study, laying the foundations for a deeper understanding of the current status in DL technology and research. The consolidated and enhanced version of the *Digital Library Reference Model* provides a widely-accepted reference framework governing future DL development towards improved interoperability across DLs, and a common language for a systematic approach to interoperability. The *DL Technology and Methodology Cookbook* will comprise a comprehensive collection of best practices and approaches (*patterns*) for common issues in developing interoperable DLs.

2.3 Support activities

Research outcomes of the WGs are published in international journals, presented at conferences and workshops, and incorporated into the educational material of the DL.org training programme, which comprises both eLearning courses and a Summer School. Moreover, DL.org fosters a broader understanding of the benefits and importance of interoperability through interviews and primers and a constructive exchange of ideas on interoperability in DLs at its international workshops bringing together participants from Europe, North America, Asia, the South Pacific and South Africa and hosted within the European Conference on Digital Libraries (ECDL) series.

DL.org also plays an educational role through its Training Programme (eTraining and Summer School). The eTraining is a suite of eCourses on DL concepts and domains captured by the DELOS Model, designed to enable a shared understanding on DL interoperability and develop related competences among DL students, researchers, developers, designers and end-users. The eTraining is built on Moodle environment and hosted on the project's website (http://etraining.dlorg.eu/).

The *Summer School*, 6-10 June 2010 in Tirrenia (Pisa), Italy will assist attendees in understanding how to address interoperability challenges within the context of DLs and DRs, along the lines of process and function, while offering participants the opportunity to explore core aspects of the *Reference Model* and network with other international researchers, experts, and professionals across disciplinary boundaries.

3. Project Results

The findings and outcomes of DL.org can be summarized as: (*i*) the artefacts produced by the WGs during their co-ordinated activities, (*ii*) the extensive survey on DL technologies and approaches focusing on interoperability and (*iii*) the enhanced version of the Reference Model.

3.1 The WG outcomes

Each of the six Working Groups co-ordinated by DL.org have actively pursued interoperability issues, evaluated the current landscape in terms of possible solutions and pinpointed priorities to address future research challenges in their respective domains, i.e. Content, User, Functionality, Policy, Quality and Architecture characterizing the DL universe.

The ***Content Working Group*** is chartered with one of the most studied interoperability domains in the DL world, viz. content interoperability. Since their conception, DLs have been associated with content-centric systems the main role of which is to make human knowledge available, generating a proliferation of diverse knowledge sources that have to be integrated into a coherent whole. Despite the strong background in this area, Working Group members recognized early on that – in its entirety – the content interoperability problem is far from being fully modelled and solved. In essence, DL content is the set of *information objects* forming it, thus content interoperability is achieved when the provider and the consumer systems are interoperable with regard to the objects they are interested in. The team decided to analyze interoperability issues and approaches from the perspective of object *identifiers, structure, metadata* in general, *provenance* and *context*. Moreover, an interoperability framework (Candela et al. 2010) has been defined to systematize the identification and description of the diverse facets bound up with interoperability issues and consequently related solutions. With regard to interoperability solutions, the WG members recognize that, irrespective of the specifics connected with individual approaches adopted, these approaches are invariably based on (*a*) *model agreements*, e.g. the adoption of Dublin Core metadata schema; (*b*) *meta-model agreement*, e.g. the usage of a lingua franca like the DOLCE ontology; and (*c*) *reconciliation*, e.g. mappings, cross-walks and transformations based approaches.

The *User Working Group* is investigating the most important interoperability issues that prevent heterogeneous DL systems from working together with regard to User perspective, with the aim of proposing approaches that effectively resolve key issues. The User WG has drawn a distinction between and subsequently defined two categories of user-level issues for DL interoperability, i.e. interoperability concerning what is captured within each DL about a user as well as interoperability between users through their use of the DL. User-level interoperability arises with regard to issues such as user modelling, user profiling, user context, and user management whereas user-to-user interoperability is chiefly concerned with issues of collaboration and participation in the context of the DL as well as the preservation of user's privacy. The User WG has identified existing approaches that resolve the aforementioned issues. Particularly, available proposals that manage the semantic and syntactic heterogeneity of user models and profiles include the shared format approach with the General User Model Ontology (Heckmann et al., 2005) and the conversion approach with the Generic User model Component (Sluijs et al., 2005). Additionally, the Semantic Web infrastructure, which enables the dynamic composition of disparate and autonomous DLs while preserving user's privacy, can be considered as a solution to the privacy issue (Rezgui et al., 2004). The User WG is planning to further analyse these issues and approaches in order to create a portfolio of best practices and pattern solutions to be included in the Cookbook.

The *Functionality Working Group* follows a function oriented perspective on the identification of interoperability issues and solutions which could be applied to overcome them. Achieving function interoperability can significantly attain objectives such as providing users of one DL access to the content and functionality of other DLs; harmonizing the user experience provided by different DLs so that the user who has learned to use one DL can easily use other DLs, thus avoiding effort needed to create new DLs or adding functionality to an existing DL by reusing existing software components.

An early milestone achieved by the WG was to establish a common understanding with regard to the notions of *"function"* and *"function interoperability"*. According to the WG, *"a function is an action a DL component or a DL user performs"* and likewise *"a digital library (DL A) is interoperable with another digital library (DL B) on a function (F) if and only if either DL A or DL B can invoke F and/or combine F with other functions, with or without the use of brokers"*.

A thorough investigation of contemporary literature and DLs has yielded a set of functional interoperability concerns that include interface (e.g. Application Programming Interface (API) incompatibilities), behaviour, pre/post condition, taxonomy (or ontology) and composition concerns. Due to their generic nature all these concerns have also been addressed in other domains, e.g. Service Oriented

Computing. Approaches that have been applied can be classified into static ones such as RosettaNet and the e-Framework or dynamic ones including the automated creation of appropriated adapters or mediators (Dumas et al., 2008; Benatallah et al., 2005; Yellin and Storm, 1997; Noy, 2004).

In addition to the aforementioned issues, the focus of the WG has brought to light an additional concern, which is particularly important when dealing with the interoperation of DL functions. An appropriate function specification and discovery mechanism needs to be in place, i.e. a function registry. As a preliminary step towards the specification of such a mechanism, the group has provided a preliminary specification of such a function description framework. This framework along with the solutions identified will inform the Cookbook.

The *Policy Working Group* – in the first year of the project – contributed to the DL.org State-of-the-Art Survey, reviewing scientific literature, analyzing potential policy representation methods and providing original research on policy interoperability issues. One of the outcomes of this activity is the proposal to reposition the Policy domain within the DELOS Model. This stemmed from the reflection that underpinning every digital library, there is an organization governed by an organizational policy framework that makes the DL viable. The policy domain is a meta-domain, situated both outside the DL and any technologies used to deliver it, and within the DL itself. Policy permeates the DL from conceptualisation through to operation and so needs to be represented at these diverse levels: at high (organizational) level, then instantiated at process level - whether those processes are being handled by humans or machine. Policy Interoperability has therefore been defined by the WG as Business Level Interoperability making it possible to compare and trust values and purposes of each organization. This type of interoperability is concerned with peer-to-peer interoperability, but also third-party service providers' interoperable policies (i.e. data archives and the policy exchange with cloud providers).

To ground its research into a real-life context, the Policy WG has embarked upon a two-fold strategy. The Policy team has both produced user scenarios on the policy interoperability issues identified, and elaborated a survey on the interoperability of policies, targeting a number of current international DLs and Digital Repositories (DRs).

The research outcomes of the Policy Working Group are being presented and published jointly with the Quality Working Group in several forthcoming international journals and conferences.

The *Quality Working Group* – in addition to the enhancement of the DELOS DL Reference Model – has agreed to elaborate a simplified quality pattern grounded on the Quality Concept Map of the DELOS DL Reference Model, which is viewed to be the most characteristic for DLs and should help them to interoperate. This pattern has been called the "Quality Core Model" and its completion will be the main Quality WG outcome. The Quality Core Model includes a selection of quality parameters which have been analyzed by the Quality team with regard to interoperability.

The Quality WG has contributed to the DL.org Interoperability State-of-the-Art Survey, with particular attention to data quality, quality parameters and DL evaluation issues, generating research questions and user scenarios which formed the basis for the DELOS Reference Model v1.0. The interoperability issues identified were developed during the first phase of activities with preliminary outcomes that were well very received at the 1st DL.org Workshop (1st October 2009) in Corfu within ECDL 2009.

To achieve its overall objectives, the Quality WG is currently conducting a survey for targeted DLs on quality interoperability, which will test the feasibility of the Quality Core Model. The Quality team also continues to investigate and deliberate quality interoperability issues within and outside the WG, to provide feedback and recommendations to enhance the DELOS DL Reference Model and the DL.org Cookbook. As this will also involve interaction with external experts, it will further expand the DL.org stakeholder network.

The **Architecture Working Group** mission is to identify and analyze the main barriers preventing different DL software systems from working together with regard to the architectural perspective, proposing approaches and technologies dealing with these issues. In recent years, a considerable number of such software systems have been implemented, ranging from *Repository Systems* to different types of *Digital Library [Management] Systems,* developed independently from each other with very limited effort spent on the design of facilitating technologies that promote the reuse and sharing of system assets from other systems. The team has identified two important issues for analysis in Components Profiling (a characterization of the distinguishing feature of a system component) and Application Framework (a characterization of roles, component-to-component interaction patterns, and prescribed interfaces and protocols to which components should conform in order to interact). The approaches adopted to solve these issues are widespread and can be divided into (*a*) approaches based on the adoption of different kinds of standards, e.g. messaging-oriented (SOAP), description and discovery (WSDL), application-oriented (OAI-PMH, OAI-ORE, SRU) and (*b*) approaches based on the development of Architectural Components specifically conceived to host the interoperability machinery needed to reconcile the provider and the consumer to some extent, e.g. *mediators* (Wiederhold 1992). The WG is currently focusing on is the definition of a Reference Architecture for Digital Library Management Systems (DLMS) stemming from experience gained while developing large-scale systems with a significant set of interoperability problems (e.g. Europeana, D4Science (http://www.d4science.eu) and DRIVER).

3.2 The State of the Art survey

The State of the Art survey provides a clear understanding of the current status of DL technology and research with regard to approaches for specific interoperability issues that belong to the six DL domains. This survey serves as groundwork for several other DL.org activities. The State-of-the-Art Survey begins with an overview of the DELOS Digital Library Reference Model, the core instrument used by DL.org to address interoperability issues. This is followed by some basic definitions of DL interoperability (but also interoperability in general), as well as the definitions of ten levels of interoperability that have been identified.

Six of the main chapters of the Survey are dedicated to the detailing interoperability issues in each of the respective domains. This section is the outcome of deliberations between the WG experts on the one hand and an evaluation of issues explored in pertinent scientific literature on the other. Solutions to the issues identified are also presented. These have already been implemented by projects or the result of a new approach, proposed by WG experts for issues investigated for the first time. Each domain section ends with a summary description of the issues discussed and concluding remarks in what is a first attempt to evaluate the different approaches against criteria set by the WGs. The conclusion wraps up the main findings of the survey and suggests approaches that can be adopted in the enhanced version of the DELOS Model.

3.3 The revised Digital Library Reference Model

The enhanced *Digital Library Reference Model v1.0* (Candela et Al., 2008; Athanasopoulos et al., 2010) draws on the collective understanding of DLs acquired by European research groups active in the DL field for many years, aggregated under the DELOS Network of Excellence umbrella in the past and now under the DL.org umbrella, as well as by the international research and scientific communities operating in this domain.

The Model comprises three parts each forming a self-contained artefact. The *Digital Library Manifesto* declares the intentions, motives, overall plans, and views of a long term initiative leading to the creation of a foundational theory for DLs, and introduces the main notions characterizing the whole DL domain. The *Digital Library Reference Model in a Nutshell* briefly provides the overall picture underlying a comprehensive model conceived to capture the essence of DLs in terms of the main domains characterizing them, the principal concepts existing in each domain and the main relationships connecting such concepts.

The *Digital Library Reference Model Concepts and Relations* detail the main concepts, axioms and relationships characterizing the DL domain independently from specific standards, technologies, implementations, or other concrete details. For each concept and relation included in the model, the document provides a detailed characterization comprising a definition, the set of connections with other concepts, the rationale explaining its existence and a set of examples of concrete instances of the specific entity.

While the Reference Model sets out to contribute to DL foundations, its value is not merely theoretical as it also provides a core instrument for a wide variety of different concrete usages, perfectly illustrated by feedback received since the very first draft was issued. The Manifesto, for example, has proved a valuable asset to demonstrate to stakeholders the complexity of the DL universe and the value of DL 'systems' in the content production and management workflow. Among the different concrete usages, Reference Model concepts and relations can be used to assess and improve DL services across the board in the large and thus drive and systematize the design and implementation of qualitative and quantitative analyses.

4. Future Work

The State of the Art Survey has laid the foundations for the expanded and enhanced *Reference Model* and *DL Technology and Methodology Cookbook*. Additionally, attempts to evaluate and validate the interoperability frameworks in real scenarios have also been the focus of our activities. Maximizing the impact of co-operation is part of a strategic process and DL.org is committed to extending synergies with similar or complementary initiatives (e.g. OpenAIRE (http://www.openaire.eu), related initiatives from the Europeana group of projects and DC-NET (http://www.dc-net.org/)). Outreach and educationally-focused activities also form an important part of the future work plan: In addition to the Summer School in June 2010, the project's 2nd workshop, held during ECDL2010, 9-10 September 2010 in Glasgow, Scotland, UK, will examine current approaches and new research directions for addressing the DL interoperability challenge from a six-faceted approach.

5. Conclusion

DL interoperability is a highly complex notion along a multi-dimensional spectrum ranging from organizational to technological aspects and conceivable at multiple levels. Our findings have shown that a well-grounded reference model is key to addressing interoperability. Efforts to formulate conceptual interoperability frameworks, either general or domain specific, thus mark a significant step forward. Drawing on the outcomes of the DELOS Network of Excellence, DL.org is successfully carrying forward these activities, adapting qualitative methods, proposing shared standards, opening up new research perspectives and engaging with a network of major stakeholders driven by a common vision for interoperable DL systems that enable advanced cross-domain research.

Acknowledgements
The work reported has been partially supported by the DL.org Coordination and Support Action, within FP7 of the European Commission, ICT-2007.4.3, Contract No. 231551). Acknowledgements to all DL.org and WG members.

References
Athanasopoulos G., Candela L., Castelli D., Innocenti P., Ioannidis Y, Katifori V, Nika A., Vullo G., Ross S. (2010) *The Digital Library Reference Model. D3.2a.* DL.org Project Deliverable.
Benatallah B., Casati F., Grigori D., Nezhad R., Toumani F. (2005) Developing Adapters for Web Services Integration. In The 17th Conference on Advanced Information Systems Engineering (CAiSE 2005), Porto, Portugal.
Candela L.; Castelli D.; Ioannidis Y.; Koutrika G.; Pagano P.; Ross S.; Schek H.-J., Schuldt H. (2006) *The Digital Library Manifesto.* DELOS. ISBN 2-912335-24-8.
Candela L., Castelli D., Ferro N., Ioannidis Y., Koutrika G., Meghini C., Pagano P., Ross S., Soergel D., Agosti M., Dobreva M., Katifori V., Schuldt H. (2008) *The DELOS Digital Library Reference Model - Foundations for Digital Libraries.* DELOS: a Network of Excellence on Digital Libraries.
Candela L.; Castelli D.; Thanos C. (2010) *Making Digital Library Content Interoperable.* Sixth Italian Research Conference on Digital Libraries (IRCDL 2010).
Carney J. D., Fisher D., Morris J. E., Place R. P. (2005) Some Current Approaches to Interoperability, Technical Note, Software Engineering Institute, Carnegie Mellon University, CMU/SEI-2005-TN-033, August 2005
Dumas M., Benatallah B., Nezhad M. (2008) Web Service Protocols: Compatibility and Adaptation. IEEE Data Eng. Bull. 33(3), 40-44.
Heiler S. (1995) Semantic interoperability. *ACM Comput. Surv.*, 27(2):271–273.
Heckmann, D., Brandherm B., Schmitz M., Schwartz T., Von Wilamowitz-Moellendorf B. M. (2005) *GUMO - the general user model ontology.* In Proceedings of the 10th International Conference on User Modelling, Edinburgh, Scotland.
Lagoze C. and Van de Sompel H. (2001) The open archives initiative: building a low-barrier interoperability framework. In *Proceedings of the first ACM/IEEE-CS Joint Conference on Digital Libraries*, pages 54–62. ACM Press.
Noy N. (2004) Semantic Integration: a Survey of Ontology-based Approaches. ACM SIGMOD Record 33(4), 65-70.
Paepcke A., Chang C.-C. K., Winograd T., and García-Molina H. (1998) Interoperability for Digital Libraries Worldwide. *Communications of the ACM*, 41(4):33–42.
Rezgui A., Bouguettaya A., Eltoweissy M. (2004) *SemWebDL: A privacy-preserving Semantic Web infrastructure for digital libraries*, Int.J. of Digital Libraries, 4, pp. 171-184.
Sluijs K., Houben G.J. (2005) *Towards a generic user model component*, in: Proceedings of the Workshop on Decentralized, Agent Based and Special Approaches to User Modelling. International Conference on User Modelling, Edinburgh, Scotland, pp. 43-52.
Wegner P. (1996) Interoperability. ACM Comput. Surv., 28(1):285–287.
Wiederhold G. (1992) Mediators in the Architecture of Future Information Systems. Computer, 25(3):38–49.
Yellin M., Strom E. (1997) Protocol Specifications and Component Adaptors. ACM Transactions on Programming Languages and Systems (TOPLAS) 19(2), 292–333.

Squaring the Circle: A Comparative Perspective on Digital Library Evaluation Models

Giuseppina Vullo

Humanities Advanced Technology and Information Institute (HATII), University of Glasgow, UK

Abstract: This paper describes the key research advances on digital library evaluation models. Digital library evaluation has a vital role to play in building digital libraries, and in understanding their role in society. The paper covers the theoretical approach, providing a comparison of the existing models, the current research questions and an integrated evaluation framework.
Keywords: Digital libraries, digital library evaluation, digital library evaluation models, quality

1. Introduction

Digital library evaluation is a growing interdisciplinary area. Research and professional communities have specific viewpoints of what digital libraries are, and they use different approaches to evaluate them. Each evaluation approach corresponds to a digital library model, although there is no common agreement its definition.

Despite that, more and more efforts have been made to evaluate digital libraries and to build global evaluation models, even if an accepted methodology that encompasses all the approaches does not yet exist.

Investigating digital libraries' quality is a challenging activity, as digital libraries are complex, dynamic and synchronic entities which need flexible approaches. Nevertheless, real-world digital libraries and ongoing research have reached a level of maturity such that - in order to allow and encourage comparisons and communication between research and professional communities - a comprehensive approach to digital library evaluation is needed.

Since 1999, when Christine Borgman described the gap between the perspectives of digital library researchers and professionals (Borgman, 1999), several initiatives have been undertaken to establish a framework for exchange between the two communities. The reference definitions of "digital library" in this work are:

1. "Digital libraries are organizations that provide the resources, including the specialized staff, to select, structure, offer intellectual access to, interpret, distribute, preserve the integrity of, and ensure the persistence over time of collections of digital works so that they are readily and economically available for use by a defined community or set of communities" (Waters, 1998), which has been adopted by the Digital Libraries Federation in 2002

2. "A possibly virtual organization that comprehensively collects, manages, and preserves for the long term rich digital content, and offers to its user communities specialized functionality on that content, of measurable quality and according to codified policies", formulated within the DELOS project (Candela et al., 2008)

New Trends in Qualitative and Quantitative Methods in Libraries
A. Katsirikou and C. H. Skiadas (eds)
© *World Scientific Publishing Co (pp. 353-358)*

We will also keep a background library science approach taking into account Ranganathan's five laws (Ranganathan, 1931), considering them as powerful as in the traditional library world:

1. Books are for use.

2. Every reader his [or her] book.

3. Every book its reader.

4. Save the time of the Reader.

5. The library is a growing organism.

2. State-of-the-art

Digital library (subsequently DL) evaluation has been investigated since the end of the nineties, when Saracevic and Kantor (Saracevic & Kantor, 1997) reviewed the traditional libraries' evaluation criteria identified by Lancaster (Lancaster, 1993) and Saracevic (Saracevic, 2000) systematized the issue within a continuative approach, highlighting the need to focus on the DL mission and objectives.

According to Saracevic, considering evaluation as the appraisal of the performance or functioning of a system, or part thereof, in relation to some objective(s), the performance can be evaluated as to:

– Effectiveness (how well does a system do what it was designed for?)

– Efficiency (at what cost, in terms of money or time?)

– A combination of these two (i.e. cost- effectiveness) (Saracevic, 2000, p. 359).

Saracevic also indicated two evaluation levels, which is challenging to integrate:

– user-centered level (which can be social, institutional, individual or focused on the interface)

– system-centered level (which can be focused on engineering, processing or content). (Saracevic, 2000, p. 363-364).

In the same year, Marchionini (Marchionini, 2000) proposed the application of the same techniques and indicators used for traditional libraries, such as circulation, creation and growth of collections, user data, user satisfaction, and financial stability indicators. According to Marchionini, a DL evaluation can have different aims, from the understanding of basic phenomena (e.g. the users' behavior towards IR tools) to the effective evaluation of a specific object. He presented the results of a longitudinal analysis of the Perseus DL, which lasted more than ten years (Marchionini, 2000). Among the evaluation corollaries of that study, he stated that successful DLs should have:

- clear missions

- strong leadership and a strong talent pool

- good technical vision and decisions

- quality content and data management

- giving users multiple access alternatives

- ongoing evaluation effort. (Marchionini, 2000).

Successively, some guidelines to evaluate DLs were proposed (Reeves, Apedoe & Woo, 2003), focusing on the decision process that is behind any evaluation and the need to focus on the "global" impact that a DL has on its users and on society was highlighted (Chowdhury & Chowdhury, 2003), by integrating LIS, IR and HCI criteria.

Through the analysis of eighty DL case studies, Saracevic observed the small quantity of "real data" in comparison to the explosion of meta-literature (Saracevic, 2004), concluding that there is no "best" methodology: different aims can lead to heterogeneous methods. He also stated that DLs are still too difficult for the general public to use, although they can have a far-reaching impact on education, on scholarly research publishing and on society.

The development of an evaluation model has been carried forward by the DELOS project (http://www.delos.info/); its evaluation schema initially had three dimensions:
- data/collection
- system/technology
- users /uses. (Fuhr et al., 2001).

This schema was then integrated into Saracevic's four evaluation categories (Saracevic, 2004; Fuhr et al., 2007).

A quality model for digital libraries was elaborated in 2007 within the 5S (Streams, Structures, Spaces, Scenarios, and Societies) theoretical framework (Gonçalves et al., 2004; Gonçalves et al., 2007): the model was addressed to digital library managers, designers and system developers, and defined a number of dimensions and metrics which were illustrated with real case studies.

Within the DELOS Digital Library Reference Model (Candela et al., 2008), quality facets and parameters have been investigated to model the Quality domain. Quality is defined as "the parameters that can be used to characterize and evaluate the content and behavior of a DL. Some of these parameters are objective in nature and can be measured automatically, whereas others are inherently subjective and can only be measured through user evaluation (e.g. in focus groups (Candela et al., 2008, p. 20).

The ongoing EU-funded project DL.org (http://www.dlorg.eu/) is currently investigating and identifying solutions for interoperability, according to the six domains of the DELOS Reference Model (Architecture, Content, Functionality, Policy, Quality and Users) (Candela et al., 2008), and its Quality Working Group (https://workinggroups.wiki.dlorg.eu/index.php/Quality_Working_Group) aims to continuing the research on quality parameters and dimensions developed within DELOS.

Research advances on digital library evaluation and quality are especially needed considering the amount of national and international collaborative projects aiming the interoperation between diverse DLs, and their connection with individuals, groups, institutions, and societies; they can also have a crucial role within DL projects political and social acceptance.

3. Digital library evaluation models

Concepts and models for evaluating digital libraries come mainly from three research areas: library and information science (LIS) studies, computer science studies, and human–computer interaction (HCI) studies.

They can adopt the following types of approach:
- content-based approach (DLs as collections of data and metadata)
- technical-based approach (DLs as software systems)
- service-based approach (DLs as organizations providing a set of intangible goods, i.e. benefits)
- user-based approach (DLs as personal and social environments)

Considering the dynamic nature of digital libraries, and the spread of projects dedicated to them, the research on comprehensive evaluation models is quite limited.

In this study we present a selection of models that not always come from the DL field: however, they are considered relevant for building global DL evaluation frameworks.

The first comprehensive and multidimensional model comes from information systems research. It is known as the D&M IS success model (DeLone & McLean, 1992) and was updated in 2003 (DeLone & McLean, 2003), when the authors decided to revise it considering the advent and explosive growth of eCommerce. The updates concerned the adding of a "service quality" measure as a new dimension, and the grouping all the "impact" measures into a single impact or benefit category called "net benefit" (in the original model, there were "individual impact" and "organizational impact").

The D&M IS success model (DeLone & McLean, 2003) identifies the interrelationships between six variable categories involved in the "success" of information systems: "information quality", "system quality", "service quality", "intention to use/use", "user satisfaction", "net benefits".

The three types of quality (which – in the DL world – correspond to content quality, DL system quality and DL services quality) concur to the quantitative and qualitative interactions with the information system, respectively "intention to use/use" and "user satisfaction". The final entity of the model is "net benefits", which within the DL world could become "social benefits", either to the individuals than to groups and communities. This model doesn't offer any specific quality parameter or metrics: on the contrary, it aims to be simple and as general and applicable as possible.

The second model comes for the Library Science field and was created in 2004 for the holistic evaluation of traditional libraries services (Nicholson, 2004). The model is a pyramid describing the evaluation workflow; it adopts an operational approach, and identifies core steps and actors involved in the evaluation process. Nicholson's model is relevant not only because it is the first one that aims to consider library's evaluation holistically, but mostly because it takes into account the role of the administrators – who are also the decision-makers – at the head of the evaluation pyramid.

At the basis of Nicholson's pyramid there is the measurement matrix, i.e. the measurements from different topics and perspectives; the upper level is constituted by the evaluation criteria; the highest level corresponds to the evaluation viewpoints which are classified hierarchically (from the lowest to the highest) as evaluations by "users", by "library personnel", and by "decision-makers". Once the decisions have been made, the evaluation cycle moves fro the pyramid's top to its bottom, with the "changes implemented by the library personnel". "users impacted by changes", "evaluation criteria selected to measure impact on system" and, at the basis the pyramid again, the "measurements from different topics and perspectives selected", where the cycle starts again (Nicholson, 2004). Nicholson's focus is the organisational context of evaluation, and doesn't explain how the different viewpoints and measurements can be combined or integrated, nor the quality parameter and metrics involved.

The third model – known as "a generalised schema for a digital library" - is the result of a research developed within the EU-funded DELOS project. It constitutes the first holistic model specifically created for the DL evaluation from the research community (Fuhr et al., 2001). The model describes the DL domain and its three core entities – "system/technology", "data/collection", and "users" – all directing to a fourth entity called "usage". The DL domain is over-arched by a larger circle called "research domain". The research domain identifies the research areas involved in the four entities of the DL domain as follows:

System/technology: system and technology researchers
Data/collection: Librarians, LIS Researchers
Users: Publishers, Sociology of Science, Communication Researchers
Usage: HCI, Librarians, Systems researchers
(Fuhr et al., 2001).

This model effectively illustrates the heterogeneity of research fields involved in DLs. However – excluding policy makers, managers, senior librarians and administrators - doesn't take into account the organisational context of the DL.

The fourth and most recent one, grounded on Saracevic's evaluation dimensions, identifies the most important evaluation criteria according to the different digital libraries stakeholders, within a holistic perspective ("Holistic DL evaluation model", Zhang, 2010).

4. A LIS oriented framework for digital libraries evaluation

While conducting a comparative study on digital library evaluation models, I developed a LIS oriented framework, as illustrated in Fig. 1. The model includes both the user and system perspective. The arrows indicate the routes corresponding to the two perspectives, i.e. the DL core directions, respectively "use" and "mission".

The core entities of the DL are organisation, content, services and users. According to these four entities the evaluation can focus on organisational aspects (such as management and policies), content aspects (quality of data, metadata, digital collections and even digital libraries), service aspects (quality of technological tools or quality of design), or users aspects (quality of interactions between users and the DL).

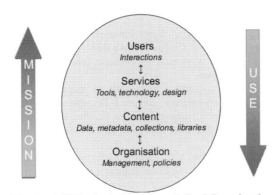

Fig. 1 – A LIS oriented framework for DL evaluation

5. Conclusions

In this paper we indicated interdisciplinary routes towards a global approach to DL evaluation, describing the state-of-the art, proposing models from different research field and presenting a LIS oriented framework.

There is no common agreement on how to evaluate DLs and evaluation activities are still low-prioritized issues within the DL field. However, several assessment methodologies have been built, and the interdisciplinary research is growing, while a broadly accepted model is still lacking. It would help DLs to communicate and to exchange their evaluation experiences.

References

Borgman, C.L., (1999). What are digital libraries? Competing visions, *Information Processing and Management,* Vol. 35, No. 3, 227 – 243.

Candela, L. et al., (2007). Setting the foundation of digital libraries, *D-Lib Magazine,* 13, 2007, <http://www.dlib.org/dlib/march07/castelli/03castelli.html>.

Candela, L. et al., (2008). *The DELOS Digital Library Reference Model. Foundations for Digital Libraries*, Version 0.98, Project no. 507618, DELOS, <http://www.delos.info/files/pdf/ReferenceModel/DELOS_DLReferenceModel _0.98.pdf>.

Chowdhury, G.G., Chowdhury, S., (2003). *Introduction to Digital Libraries*. Facet Publishing, London.

DeLone, W.H., McLean, E.R., (2003). The DeLone and McLean model of information systems success: a ten-year update. *J. Management Information Systems*, Vol. 19, No. 4, 9 – 30.

Fuhr, N. et al., (2001). Digital libraries: a generic classification and evaluation scheme. Proceedings of *ECDL 2001*. LNCS, Vol. 2163, 187 – 199. Springer, Heidelberg.

Fuhr, N. et al., (2007). Evaluation of digital libraries. *Int. J. Digital Libraries*, Vol. 8, No. 1, 21 – 38.

Gonçalves, M.A. et al., (2004). Streams, Structures, Spaces, Scenarios, Societies (5s): A formal model for digital libraries. *ACM Trans. Inf. Syst.*, Vol. 22, No. 2, 270 – 312.

Gonçalves, M. A. et al., (2007). "What is a good digital library?" A quality model for digital libraries. *Information Processing and Management*, Vol. 43, No. 5, 1416 – 1437.

Marchionini, G., (2000). Evaluating digital libraries: a longitudinal and multifaceted view. *Library Trends*, Vol. 49, No. 2, 304 – 333.

Lancaster, F.W., (1993). *If you want to evaluate your library*, 2nd ed. Morgan Kaufman, San Francisco.

Nicholson, S., (2004). A conceptual framework for the holistic measurement and cumulative evaluation of library services. J. Documentation, Vol. 60, No. 2, 164 – 182, <http://www.bibliomining.com/nicholson/holisticfinal.html>.

Ranganathan, S., (1931). *The Five Laws of Library Science*. Edward Goldston, London.

Reeves, T.C., Apedoe, X., Woo, Y.H., (2003). *Evaluating Digital Libraries: A User-Friendly Guide*. National Science Digital Library, University of Georgia, Athens, GA.

Saracevic, T., Kantor, P.B., (1997). Studying the value of library and information services. Part II. Methodology and taxonomy. *J. American Society for Information Science*, Vol. 48, No. 6, 543 – 563.

Saracevic, T., (2000). Digital library evaluation: toward an evolution of concepts. *Library Trends*, Vol. 49, No. 3, 350 – 369.

Saracevic, T., (2004). *Evaluation of digital libraries: an overview*. Paper presented at the DELOS Workshop on the Evaluation of Digital Libraries, <http://dlib.ionio.gr/wp7/WS2004_Saracevic.pdf>.

Su, L.T., (1992). Evaluation measures for interactive information retrieval. *Information Processing and Management*, Vol. 28, No. 4, 503 – 516.

Waters, D.J., (1998). What are digital libraries?, *CLIR Issues*, 4, 1998, <http://www.clir.org/pubs/issues/issues04.html#dlf>

Zhang, Y., (2010). Developing a holistic model for digital library evaluation. *J. American Society for Information Science*, Vol. 61, No. 1, 88 – 110.

Digital Libraries and the Digital Working Environment: What is Their Effect on Library Staff for Sharing Their Knowledge?

Garoufallou Emmanouel[1,3] and Asderi Stella[2,3]

[1]Lecturer, Department of Library Science and Information Systems, Alexander Technological Educational Institution of Thessaloniki, Greece, mgarou@libd.teithe.gr, Garoufallou@yahoo.co.uk
[2]American College of Thessaloniki, Library, Greece, sasderi@act.edu
[3]Deltos Research Group

Abstract: The development of digital libraries, the mass digitization of cultural heritage resources and the increasing use of electronic information resources both by library staff and users have changed the library environment and played a critical role in managing and disseminating knowledge. This new working environment has transformed the way in which employees share their knowledge. This research project aims to investigate the intrinsic and extrinsic factors that motivate librarians to share knowledge in their workplace. A data gathering tool applied in four European countries (Greece, Czech Republic, Portugal and Slovenia) in order to find out what factors motivate library staff to share their knowledge and manage its flow assists in its dissemination. The Results indicate that library staff acknowledges that the new digital working environment affects the way in which they share knowledge and recognize the importance of the role of intrinsic motivation in knowledge sharing and that team-based culture can benefit the success of knowledge sharing initiatives within libraries. Cross reference of data show similarities and differences from different countries. Finally, a set of Spearman's correlations were used in order to check any connection between the values under research.
Keywords: Digital libraries, knowledge management, sharing knowledge, knowledge flow, motivational factors, motivation, librarians, library staff, digitization

1. Introduction

There have been several years since the term "century of information" was first initiated for describing the increased quantity of information and knowledge as well as the various ways with which that knowledge is disseminated in the 21st century. Internet and web 2.0 technologies have played undoubtedly a key role to this change. Their contribution is so essential and dramatic that we could easily refer to the 21st century as the "century of digital information".

Since nowadays information is so rich, there is an intensive need of managing knowledge within organizations. "Knowledge Management is an organisational practice that manages to balance the human and technological aspects of current organisations into a new management philosophy that values knowledge as an important capital for organisations" (Garoufallou et al., 2009). Furthermore, according to Paroutis and Saleh (2009) each organization has to clarify what motivates employees to share their knowledge in order to implement practices for creating such behavior; this can lead the organization to the practice of a knowledge management system. This system can be used for enhancing productivity, innovation and organizational competitiveness.

Technology implementation is vital for creating knowledge management systems. Mirghani et al. (2006) indicated that IT can significantly contribute to the eight metrics that Levett and Guenov (2000) had proposed for KM analysis (motivation, knowledge capture, stored knowledge, personal training, knowledge transfer, creative thinking, knowledge identification, and knowledge access), and they also presented technology as a pillar of knowledge management systems.

Additionally, Web 2.0 applications are easily and commonly used because of their interactive features that facilitate information sharing, creativity and collaboration. In their study Paroutis and Saleh (2009) determined the benefits that motivated employees to use Web 2.0 applications, which included communicating effectively, managing personal knowledge, generating discussion about new concepts and ideas, finding answers to particular problems, staying informed about the latest news and activities of fellow colleagues, and receiving desired help and feedback.

In digital libraries, (digital) objects and their descriptive data are collected, organized and uploaded via appropriate software (e.g. DSpace, Fedora, DLibra) in a way that this information is disseminated to and retrievable from the worldwide end users. Alternatively, a digital library is also referred as a repository, often institutional because of the type of the organization that establishes this digital library.

The question that rises is "can a digital library be or represent a knowledge management system?" Shuhun (2002) mentioned that a "digital library is an ideal digital environment... (but) ...it would not be so efficient without effective knowledge management." Anyhow, since a digital library includes metadata and indexes this makes it a priori a knowledge management system. Otherwise we would talk about digital collections and not libraries. At the same study Shuhun presented five factors that could influence the effectiveness of a knowledge management system within a digital library. The factors are understanding user needs, better knowledge of subject, metadata, and strategic planning. These factors were also used for the purposes of this study. Although theoretically this issue has started being under discussion, no actual research has been conducted yet examining people or librarians' perceptions on digital libraries and their role as knowledge management systems.

2. Aim and objectives

This research paper is consisted of two surveys. The first one was more focused on knowledge sharing attitudes. The aim of that study was to examine knowledge sharing attitudes among librarians of different countries. The objectives of this study included the assessment of the intrinsic or extrinsic factors that motivated this attitude. The second research was investigating whether digital libraries, are considered as knowledge management systems and if so, what were the factors that influenced their effectiveness.

3. Methodology

This paper presents two studies conducted in 2010 that gathered data from four countries: Greece, Slovenia, Portugal and Czech Republic. The first study on knowledge sharing attitudes used a questionnaire instrument developed by Harder (2008) and adapted by Garoufallou et al. (2008). The total number of the respondents from all four countries was 162. The questionnaire includes three sections, one for collecting demographic data, one for researching knowledge sharing attitudes and one for examining the intrinsic or extrinsic factors that may influence knowledge sharing attitudes. The questions followed a seven point semantic referential scale. The sample was selected by using a set of two non-probability sampling techniques; specifically judgmental and snowball sampling techniques were performed for both reaching and expanding respondents. The questionnaire was spread to the sample via e-mail for time and cost efficiency. The data collected was analyzed through SPSS. The tests that were performed included descriptive statistics, such as frequencies for qualitative variables and comparison of mean values for the quantitative data. Furthermore, a set of Spearman's tests was used for examining any correlations between knowledge sharing attitudes and the intrinsic - extrinsic factors that motivated these attitudes.

The second study focused on selecting data regarding digital libraries and knowledge management systems. The questionnaire instrument includes two sections, one on librarians' perceptions about digital libraries as knowledge management systems, and the other on the elements that influence the effectiveness of a knowledge management system within a digital library. All questions were built in a seven point semantic referential scale. The sample was also purposefully selected and contacted via e-mail. The respondents, whose total number was 109, came from the same four countries as the research mentioned above. The analysis of the data followed the same procedure as the aforementioned study. A comparison of mean values and a set of Spearman's correlations were performed in SPSS.

4. Results

The total number of people that participated in the first study (examining the way people share their knowledge) was 162. Seventeen respondents were Slovenian, nineteen Portuguese, seven came from Czech Republic and the majority of the participants (119) came from Greece. Most of the people were female (n=130) and thirty were male. From the total number of participants only 58 responded to the type of library which they were working. The results revealed that the majority was working in academic libraries (n=34), 9 in college libraries, 3 in school libraries, 2 in special and 2 in children libraries, and 1 in public library. There were also 7 people who were either unemployed or working as faculty. Regarding the position, most of the participants (n=32) mentioned that they were librarians without however indicating a specific department. Thirteen were library directors, twelve working at the automation department, ten at the reference/circulation department, two were catalogers, one was archivist, one working at the journals department and 5 were library assistants. Also 55 people were still students of library school and one mentioned being project manager. As for the years of experience, most of the respondents had been working for less than 10 years (n=53), twenty three had been working between 10-14 years, eleven respondents between 15-19 years, and thirteen for more than twenty years.

The product of the analysis is the following table, which shows each country's mean values to all of the questions. At the scale of 1-7 is really interesting to see that the mean values in most of the questions are high. This shows that librarians tented to value more intrinsic rather than the extrinsic motivation factors in sharing knowledge. Furthermore, comparing the mean values of each country we can see that Portugal gathered the higher mean values in most of the intrinsic motivation factors and Czech Republic in all of the extrinsic. Also, from the mean values of all of the four countries it is clear that the participants tended to share their knowledge especially when they were asked to (6.62). The intrinsic factor that motivated them more was that "sharing knowledge was important value for them" (6.39). On the other hand, the extrinsic factor that mostly motivated librarians to share their knowledge was "the evaluation of their job performance" (4.82).

Table 1. Attitudes towards knowledge sharing

Knowledge sharing attitudes	Mean Values				
	GR	PO	SL	CZ	Total
When I have knowledge that might be relevant for others in the library, I do what I can to make it available to them.	5.97	6.95	6.24	6.57	6.14
When a colleague asks me for help or assistance, I share what knowledge I may have on the subject	6.58	6.89	6.88	6.00	6.62
I stay updated by exploring the information I can find on the different knowledge systems and databases	5.59	6.26	6.06	5.71	5.73
When I encounter a work related problem, I seek knowledge and help from my colleagues	6.08	6.63	5.94	5.43	6.10
Factors of intrinsic motivation					
I share knowledge because is an important value for me	6.29	6.79	6.53	6.57	6.39
I share knowledge because I want to find out whether my ideas are relevant	5.15	5.79	5.71	6.14	5.33
I share knowledge because I think it is an important part of my job	6.07	6.47	6.41	6.29	6.16
I share knowledge because I enjoy doing so	5.49	6.63	5.94	5.86	5.69
I share knowledge because it fulfils my personality	5.41	6.58	6.13	5.86	5.70
I share knowledge because the senior management does so	3.96	3.44	3.44	5.17	3.89
I share knowledge because I trust my colleagues	5.01	5.12	5.56	5.43	5.10
I share knowledge because I am working as a team with other colleagues	5.85	6.33	6.19	6.14	5.96
I share knowledge because sharing is safe and confidential	4.85	4.19	4.81	5.67	4.80
I share knowledge for the pleasure of discovering new insights	6.00	5.75	6.25	6.33	6.01
I share knowledge because I can use knowledge from others which is provided to me just in time	5.90	6.22	5.07	5.67	5.85
I share knowledge because I can use knowledge of value from other colleagues	5.83	5.89	5.00	6.00	5.76
I share knowledge because it is easy to do so	4.23	5.22	4.31	4.67	4.37

Factors of extrinsic motivation					
I share knowledge because It may help me get promoted	3.20	3.06	3.81	5.29	3.34
I share knowledge because I want my manager to praise me	3.05	2.67	3.37	5.00	3.13
I share knowledge because I want my colleagues to praise me	3.15	2.78	3.37	4.83	3.20
I share knowledge because it may help me get a salary increase	3.28	2.50	2.87	3.71	3.17
I share knowledge because it is important for the evaluation of my job performance	4.91	5.11	3.63	5.29	4.82

Spearman's correlations were performed in order to check any relationships between the knowledge sharing attitudes and the motivational factors. The purpose of selecting this test was based on the fact that the data was not normally distributed. From the results it can be assumed that the participants tended to share their knowledge ("When I have knowledge that might be relevant for others in the library, I do what I can to make it available to them") because "sharing knowledge was important value" for them (r_s=0.505, N=162, p<0.01, two-tailed), and also because "they enjoyed doing so" (r_s=0.452, N=159, p<0.01, two-tailed). Also librarians tended to share knowledge ("When a colleague asks me for help or assistance, I share what knowledge I may have on the subject") because "it was an important part of their job" (r_s=0.409, N=162, p<0.01, two-tailed), and also because it used to strengthen their perception of "working as a team with their colleagues" (r_s=0.446, N=156, p<0.01, two-tailed). What was also interesting was the fact that librarians tended to stay updated ("I stay updated by exploring the information I can find on the different knowledge systems and databases") because "it fulfilled their personalities" (r_s=0.413, N=124, p<0.01, two-tailed). The last attitude "When I encounter a work related problem, I seek knowledge and help from my colleagues" was positively correlated with the intrinsic factors "I trust my colleagues" (r_s=0.407, N=156, p<0.01, two-tailed) and "I work as a team with other colleagues" (r_s=0.523, N=156, p<0.01, two-tailed). Conclusively, we could arrive to the assumption that a team-based spirit, servicing colleagues' information needs and staying informed of latest changes on the profession are some of the existing attitudes among librarians.

Some of the comments that verify this practice are the following: "It is important to network with one's colleagues; in this way we all learn and advance together"; "I like my colleagues and enjoy working as part of a team"; "With unity, there is strength"; "Keeping things to oneself has a negative effect and I prefer to be positive in my work and life" (Archivist, Professor, Greece). Another participant mentioned that "using other colleagues' knowledge makes my job and life easier" (Library assistant, Greece).

The second survey was conducted in order to check the latest trends in knowledge management and knowledge sharing. Digital libraries are tools being used from the academic libraries and other institutions for managing and organizing knowledge in digital format, and simultaneously making it available to the whole world. A total number of one hundred and nine (109) people participated in this survey, all coming from the same countries as the previous survey; Greece (48), Slovenia (23), Portugal (20) and Czech Republic (18).

The table below shows the mean values of each country and totally in all of the questions. The numbers show that the participants from Greece were more positive in using digital libraries as knowledge management systems. Even though the participants from Czech Republic collected the highest mean value at the perception of digital libraries having affected the way people share their knowledge in the workplace, Greek participants scored highly in believing that the design of a digital library affects the way knowledge is shared. Furthermore, comparing the total mean values of the elements that should be considered in creating an effective KM system within a digital library, it is clear that "technology support" (6.10) and "rich metadata description" (5.76) are perceived as more vital.

Table 2. Digital libraries as Knowledge Management Systems

Digital libraries as KM Systems	Mean Values				
	GR	PO	SL	CZ	Total
Do you think that digital libraries can be used as Knowledge Management Systems?	5.62	5.45	5.00	5.39	5.42
Do you think that digital libraries have affected the way people share their knowledge on workplace?	4.19	4.05	3.87	4.39	4.13
Do you think that the designing of a digital library affects the way knowledge is shared?	5.06	4.65	4.70	4.78	4.86
What elements should be considered in creating an effective KM system within a digital library? **Understanding User needs**	5.75	5.70	5.65	5.78	5.72
What elements should be considered in creating an effective KM system within a digital library? **Good knowledge of subject**	4.92	5.90	5.87	6.00	5.48
What elements should be considered in creating an effective KM system within a digital library? **Rich metadata description**	6.06	5.55	5.48	5.56	5.76
What elements should be considered in creating an effective KM system within a digital library? **Strategic plan establishment**	3.96	4.89	4.73	5.06	4.46
What elements should be considered in creating an effective KM system within a digital library? **Technology support**	6.21	5.89	6.00	6.17	6.10

A set of Spearman's tests were also performed in order to examine possible correlations between the variables. The purpose of selecting Spearman's correlations was due to the fact that the data was not normally distributed. The effect of the design of a digital library in the way people share their knowledge was positively correlated with two elements that should be considered in creating an effective KM system within a digital library. These were "understanding user needs" (r_s=0.611, N=109,

$p<0.01$, two-tailed) and "rich metadata description" ($r_s=0.699$, $N=109$, $p<0.01$, two-tailed). Also, "good knowledge of subject" was positively correlated with "strategic plan establishment" ($r_s=0.712$, $N=106$, $p<0.01$, two-tailed) and "understanding user needs" ($r_s=0.516$, $N=109$, $p<0.01$, two-tailed).

Some interesting comments regarding the design and digital libraries in general are also presented: "Interface design plays a key role in making knowledge available faster and easier" (Greece), "It demands good strategic planning and perfect knowledge of technology. The progress in digital libraries era is ascending and the first results already show how vital their existence is" (Greece). In contradiction, there was one participant from Slovenia who had a completely different opinion regarding digital libraries: "Digital libraries can't be KM systems, they are not intelligent systems that can analyse and disseminate knowledge".

Overall, the survey results and the participants' comments can lead to the assumption that digital libraries are developing systems adopting technological innovations. A good strategic plan, good knowledge of subject as well as rich metadata descriptions from librarians can "affect the way people share their knowledge in the workplace while making access to information easier and direct" (comment from Greece).

5. Conclusions

Due to the fact that the two studies were carried out in four European countries, it was difficult, not feasible and practical to use probabilistic or random sampling methods. However, the overall well-designed of the research instruments provided the grounds to extract useful conclusions concerning the library population in these four European countries.

It is evident that library staff in all countries value more intrinsic (*I share knowledge because is an important value for me* (6.39)) rather than extrinsic (*I share knowledge because it is important for the evaluation of my job performance* (4.82)) motivation factors in sharing knowledge. Thus, it is apparent that all library staff from the four countries have a tendency to share knowledge that they hold, when a colleague asked for ((*When a colleague asks me for help or assistance, I share what knowledge I may have on the subject* (6.62)).

As far as digital libraries concerned as knowledge management systems the survey showed that in Greece (5.62) the library staff were more positive about the subject than in Portugal (5.45), Czech Republic (5.39) and Slovenia (5.00). Furthermore, we believe that libraries in all countries suffered, up to a point, from "*technology support*" given that all library staff considered this a very important element in creating an effective KM system within a DL. In contrast, it comes as a surprise to value less elements like the "*good knowledge of subject*" and to "*understand user needs*".

In overall, the two surveys showed that library staff had a tendency to share their knowledge in their working environment and considered digital libraries as knowledge management systems, yet they have a long way to go.

References

Ardichvili, A,. Page, V and Wentling, T. (2003). Motivation and barriers to participation in virtual knowledge-sharing communities of practice. *Journal of knowledge management*, **7**, 1, 64-77.

Ardichvili, Alexandre, Martin Maurer, Wei Li, Tim Wentling, and Reed Stuedermann (2006). Cultural influences on knowledge sharing through online communities of practice. *Journal of Knowledge Management* 10, 1, 94-107. [accessed 19.3.2010]

Balatsoukas, P., (2005). *From information to knowledge management.* In Proceedings of the 14th Hellenic Conference of Academic Libraries, Athens: TEIA, 63-71. http://eprints.rclis.org/archive/00011871/01/14psab014.pdf, [accessed 8.3.2010].

Garoufallou, Emmanouel, Panos, Balatsoukas, Stella, Asderi, Panagiota, Ekizoglou and Rania, Siatri (2008). *What factors motivate librarians to share knowledge in their workplace?* International Conference of Marketing & Management Systems (ICMMS) 23-25 May 2008, Athens, Greece. http://www.icmms.org/ [accessed 8.3.2010]

Garoufallou, Emmanouel, Siatri, Rania, Asderi, Stella and Balatsoukas, Panos (2009). *Sharing knowledge on workplace: what factors motivate librarians to share their knowledge?* In: proceedings of the International Conference on QQML (Qualitative and Quantitative Methods in Libraries): theory and applications, Katsirikou, Anthi and Skiadas, Christos H. eds., Chania, Crete, Greece, 26-29 May 2009. World Scientific 2010. ISBN: 978-981-4299-69-5, 981-4299-69-3.

Dixon, N. M., (2000). *Common Knowledge: how companies thrive by sharing what they know.* Boston, Mass. Harvard Business school press.

Grace, Tay Pei Lyn (2009). Wikis as a knowledge management tool. *Journal of Knowledge Management* 13, 4, 64-74. [accessed 19.3. 2010]

Harder, M. (2008). *How do rewards and management styles influence the motivation to share knowledge.* Social Science research network http://papers.ssrn.com/sol3/papers.cfm?abstract_id=1098881, [accessed 2.3.2010]

Huseman, R. C. and Goodman, J. P., (1999). *Leading with knowledge: the nature of competition in the 21st century.* Thousand Oaks: Sage publications.

Jashapara, A., (2004). *Knowledge management: an integrated approach.* London: Prentice hall.

Kwok, James S.H., and S. Gao (2004). Knowledge sharing community in P2P network: a study of motivational perspective. *Journal of Knowledge Management* 8, 1, 94-102. [accessed 17.1.2010]

Nonaka, I. and Takeuchi, H., (1995). *The knowledge creating company: how Japanese companies create the dynamics of innovation.* New York: Oxford University press.

Mirghani, Mohamed, Michael Stankosky, and Arthur Murray, (2006). Knowledge management and information technology: can they work in perfect harmony? *Journal of Knowledge Management* 10, 3, 103-16. [accessed 17.1.2010]

Paroutis, Sotirios, and Alya Al Saleh (2009). Determinants of knowledge sharing using web 2.0 technologies. *Journal of Knowledge Management* 13, 4, 52-63. [accessed 20.1.2010]

Robertson, Scott (2002). A tale of two knowledge-sharing systems. *Journal of Knowledge Management* 6, 3, 292-308. [accessed 3.2.2010]

So, Johnny C.F., and Narasimha Bolloju (2005). Explaining the intentions to share and reuse knowledge in the context of IT service operations. *Journal of Knowledge Management* 9, 6, 30-41. [accessed 5.2.2010]

Case Study Method for Research on Digital Library, Information Policies, and Bibliographic Organization

Georgina Araceli Torres-Vargas[1], Ariel Alejandro Rodríguez-García[2] and Egbert John Sánchez-Vanderkast[3]

Centro Universitario de Investigaciones Bibliotecológicas, Universidad Nacional, Autónoma de México, Torre II de Humanidades, piso 12, Ciudad Universitaria, D. F. 04510, Mexico, [1]gatv@servidor.unam.mx, [1]arageo@yahoo.com, [2]rgarciaa@servidor.unam.mx, [3]egbert@servidor.unam.mx

Abstract: Case study method has been used to develop investigation mostly of descriptive treatment. Poor exploitation of this method is observed as a means to gain knowledge of general problems or to establish a more refined theory. From this point of view, the present document is arguing for the use of the mentioned method in an instrumental way. Examples are presented related of investigation in the area of digital libraries, information policies and bibliographic organization.

Keywords: Case study method, digital libraries, bibliographic organization, information policies, library and information science

1. Introduction

The ignorance of case study method poses the risk to develop sample of cases, case study and case analysis imprecisely or reject it as a valid research methodology. However, the case study method is a valuable tool, it has been an essential method in Social Sciences and Humanities in subjects such as education, technological development, and investigations on social issues. We have to consider that case study has different conceptions. Gundermann-Kroll (2001) mentions two general conceptions:

1. it is not the set of methodological procedures, but the specificity of a study object what defines a case study. In this conception, case study is not a methodological choice of a research strategy, but the election of an object to be studied (Gundermann-Kroll calls it *intrinsic purpose*).

2. emphasizes research through cases as a means not as a study object. In this context, the study of a particular entity is undertaken to achieve an enhanced understanding of a general issue or to define a more structured theory. Seen in this light, the case assumes a secondary significance (Gundermann-Kroll calls it *instrumental purpose*).

A marked trend towards the intrinsic purpose is reflected on case study in Library and Information Science, where the case helps to learn from a particular situation (of a library, learning center, and information system, among others) not contributing to a generalization, but in the best of the scenarios to a solution of such case problems. Indeed, theoretical aspects supporting the study of a particular situation should be addressed first; however, the study is not embarking from a more or less finished theory that contributes to generalization, but from a reference setting serving as introduction to the intrinsic purpose.

From the point of view of instrumental purpose, inference is possible, only if it is grounded on a theoretical-conceptual analysis. Before using case study methodology,

New Trends in Qualitative and Quantitative Methods in Libraries
A. Katsirikou and C. H. Skiadas (eds)
© *World Scientific Publishing Co (pp. 367-376)*

a theory or explanatory model on the study object is required. The model or theory serves as a conceptual mold or net against which the empirical results of the case are compared.

Eckstein (1975) and Yin (2003) points out that case study may include one or multiple cases, which can be analyzed from different perspectives or areas. This delimitation is important when considering investigations where the case is helpful to scrutinize theories established from different lines of research or areas of knowledge.

2. Case Study Method as an Alternative to Bond Research and Practice in Library Science

Nowadays, posing investigations that, through case study method, pursue an instrumental purpose is required. It is expected the case would be helpful to scrutinize a previously developed theoretical model.

On that account, case study could be seen useful from two aspects:

1.   As an opportunity to establish a relationship between investigation and empirical aspects.

2.   As a bridge so people in the professional practice sphere may get closer to research results in a way these can be useful for them.

In the first aspect, it should be mentioned that theories describe patterns, but they are not absolute rules or laws and may be the product of a particular cultural or historical situation, requiring verifications in various situations.

The latter contradicts the work done in the area since, as was already mentioned, the case is usually considered as a resource to analyze a given current situation. However, this use allows generalizations. Description and explanation of certain domains of reality require diverse conceptual systems (theories), sometimes opposed, and even grounded in non-classical logic.

Currently, Library and Information Science require investigations that provide more than examples of what is being done and problems affecting professional practice. Surely, it is not possible to completely detach research from practice; it is not possible to deny it and provide solutions that do not agree with the reality of problems. It should be kept in mind that any law or theory has only an approximate value depending on verifications, theoretical constructs, and observation instruments, among others, to corroborate the studied object.

From this perspective, the researcher requires to be an individual capable to get rid of his/her subjectivity to study the object or social reality from an external setting, where the case study can provide the interpretation required to develop a deeper research. According to Orozco-Gómez (1996), this means to "verify what exists regardless of the relationship with that existing, or to understand that existing and somehow get involved in that being known".

In this sense, case study is an alternative to establish an adequate bond which may provide a continuous feedback between investigation and practice in Library and Information Science. The approach of the suitable case study is where it is manifested as a means, not as a purpose itself. For example, information services in a given academic library can be analyzed not for knowing how services are developed, but to have a comparison parameter with a previously delimited service model for the academic library, from a theoretical research.

According to Gundermann-Kroll (2001) generalizations performed from case studies can be done through any of the following:

- By saturation.

Here, an interpretative model is developed, then refined and extended through the aggregation of new cases, until the incorporation of another not enriching nor modifying the conceptual network, and the interpretation model is achieved.

- By replication.

Cases are compared among them according to one or more theories previously established which are empirically contrasted and thus, enriched or rejected in some important issue. The diversification of the analyzed cases will allow the knowledge of a wide range of factors and conditions producing different results. In that way, the formulation of a diversified theory on the phenomenon or phenomena subject to study may be achieved.

Regarding the second aspect, a demand of the professional practice community can be identified. They ask for feasible and useful research in the solution of specific problems and special circumstances. This is clearly evident in the literature on Evidence-Based Librarianship (EBL).

This idea arises from Medicine, since Evidence-Based Medicine (EBM) had a great impulse in Medicine from 1992. According to the number of references in MEDLINE, Sánchez-Mendiola (2001) indicates that only two references on the subject were found in 1992, but for 1999 the number increased to more than 1300.

The same author mentions that other areas adopted some of the key concepts of EBM under evidence-based practice. EBM is, according to Sackett and colleagues (2000), *"... the integration of the best research evidence with clinical expertise and patient's values ..."*

The process of EBM practice is structured in five stages or consecutive steps:

1. The elaboration of a relevant, well structured clinical question, originated from an actual clinical problem, is perhaps the most important and valuable step proposed by EBM. The main axis determining this step is the intellectual interest encouraged by a reflexive attitude, which is alert to detect gaps in knowledge during professional practice. It is the search for information, for the patient's benefit and the professional personal development.

2. Search of the best scientific evidence currently available (search of research results related to the problem).

3. Critical analysis of located information.

4. Use of the information with a critical assessment in the solution of the crucial problem, in the patient who originated the question (Sanchez-Mendiola, 2001).

In library science several authors try to define this term. Eldredge (2006) considers it as the process integrating scientifically generated production with decision-making. EBL combines the use of evidence investigation with the pragmatic perspective developed from work experiences in library science.

For the authors, suitable *evidence investigation* will be the one arising from the case study, considered as a means allowing generalizations. This way, the professional practitioner will have a more or less closer parameter to his/her situation, letting him/her to make decisions for problem solving.

Turner (2002) states that nowadays many investigations are not consulted because there is a discrepancy between them and the reality concerning practice. She also considers practitioners frequently accuse investigations to show practice future, more than current situations.

In a study published in 1992, Powell (2002) tried to answer questions such as "How many professionals read research articles? Can practitioners apply investigation results in their work?"

Additionally, Koufogiannakis (2006) states that the practitioner does not have the findings, time, experience, or support required to carry out research; therefore, EBL is an excellent alternative for those in professional practice to solve different situations supported by rigorous investigations.

This is why case study method may be useful to bond research with practice and vice versa. Thus, three research situations which case study may enrich are described below.

3. Case study use in Three Investigations on Library and Information Science
In the following research areas, the usefulness of the case study in Library and Information Science shall be described.

Studies that help to exemplify are currently developed at the Centro Universitario de Investigaciones Bibliotecológicas (University Center of Library Science Research) of the Universidad Nacional Autónoma de México (National Autonomous University of Mexico) (UNAM).

Digital libraries.
During the nineties, the study of digital libraries began to arise according to key authors like William Arms; Borgman (2007); Brophy(2005); Gary Marcionini and Saracevic and Dalbello(2003). This theme being approached from practice was not for nothing. The development of library duties had a growing stronger interference of Information and Communication Technologies (ICT's), resulting on questions about how to lead every aspect formerly more or less controlled in the printing setting, but modified with digital media appearance.

Like so, alternatives began to take place from practice. The big international projects to create digital libraries are an example. Their promise was to transform the information world, scan everything on print, as well as to offer faster and distance services.

Afterwards, the need originated to clarify what that library was, which characteristics it had, and towards where would it lead us. This means theoretical study was subsequent, but grew rapidly. Up to date, the theme has been widely discussed with regard to several angles and focuses. While debate has not ended, since multiple questions still exist, an intersection between research and practice in digital library has not been shown.

In the matter, Saracevic and Dalbello (2003) mentions that the current study of digital libraries has the following characteristics:

- Research and practice on digital libraries are conducted independently with a scarce or null connection.
- The agenda for digital library (DL) practice is established by the involved institutions and organizations, thus DL projects are ruled by their interests not by investigation needs.
- In many cases, research projects about digital libraries are carried out in institutions that have a great practical project of DL; however, no visible relations exist between theoretical investigation and the DL institutional project, much less feedback among both.

This situation has prevented the delimitation of a general frame reflecting the elements which intervene in the establishment of digital libraries and their interrelations. Such a frame could release the problems of digital libraries and offer solution alternatives. These alternatives will come forth only from proposals determined by a systemic analysis of digital libraries and, above all, from a study that pays attention to the conditions of the society in which DL are immersed.

Case study method is a fine choice to establish relations between research and the empirical component. Beginning with the study of several situations, there is a need to confront the theories emerged through research on digital libraries.

Concerning the specific case of the Centro Universitario de Investigaciones Bibliotecológicas of the UNAM, the investigation developed *El acceso universal a los documentos: su relación con la biblioteca virtual* (Universal access to documents: its relation with the virtual library) highlights the delimitation of a digital library model (Torres-Vargas, 2008).

What could this model represent except a hypothetical situation? It should be contrasted with what is actually happening. In that sense investigation is not finished, referents should be the starting point. In this case, local referents are the most viable, i.e. digital libraries in Mexico. So another investigation that would first determine which may be considered digital libraries in Mexico was resumed. Afterwards, one more phase of the broad study on the subject may be continued.

Up to date, approximations have been made, but they require a clearer concretion in the professional practice surroundings. For example, which are the practices in digital collections development, and mainly if such development is present in Mexican digital libraries are questions that need to be answered. It is also essential to approach the practices on organization, information access, and use of digital contents.

Summarizing, each variable from the above-mentioned model requires verification as well as an approach to its current situation in a determined context.

The case study could bring forth valuable data for those librarians who, from experience, wonder how to solve several problems. In this sense, the use of the case study method is an excellent alternative to establish the required bond and consequently be able to advance in digital library investigation.

Information policies.

During the seventies, the subject of information policies began to have a strong impulse in the scope of Library Science.

UNESCO has delivered multiple documents about national information policies, and the analysis of particular situations in Mexico and Venezuela in the eighties made clear that investigation work has been slow in this matter.

In the region of Spanish America, the theme was managed as *national information policies*, at a macro level. This distinction between micro and macro was proposed by Lancaster and Burger (1990), who from an analysis of microsociology and macrosociology according to Collins, suggest an analogy about micro and macro levels on Information Sciences.

Therefore, it should be noticed that at first glance national information policies are closely bonded with public information policies or government information policies.

At micro level, research has demonstrated it considers particular aspects that may lead us to a better view about the work in specific countries. Micro level studies have been the most representative of reality to establish information policies of different kind.

Examples of such studies are those carried on by Páez-Urdaneta (1990) narrating two experiences, one in Egypt and another in Venezuela. On his part, Worlock (1996) deeply analyzed the development of information policies focused on the commercialization of government information in the United Kingdom.

Hitchens (1997) discussed two specific instances about environmental information from international organisms, one from the European Union, the second, a project financed by the World Bank and the Environmental Program of the United Nations.

The previous examples allow the understanding that every change occurring on any emergent theme causes the evaluation of existing information policies, and the design of more relevant ones. That is, on transforming some surrounding elements a problem is unleashed, and it has to be defined so possible solutions or answers may be identified. The need to evaluate the options would lead us to choose the best policies to execute.

Visualizing policies establishment as a process is usually helpful to comprehend the organizational and social factors that influence on the stages of policies design, implementation, and evaluation.

The idea to follow the model by stages was discussed and criticized by several authors, while Parsons (2007) considers this model should be kept for the procedures that take us along in the holistic analysis.

Nevertheless, authors as Sabatier and Jenkins-Smith sustain that *"the notion of the cycle of [public] policies disowns the real world of policies formulation, which implies multiple government levels and cycles of interaction"* (Parsons, 2007).

On this circumstance, the case study as a methodological instrument would be very helpful to approach the real world, a better understanding of the problematic originated, and propose the most appropriate options.

Bibliographic organization.

Case studies have provided bibliographic organization with the necessary elements for planning the development of several information systems such as the library catalogue. However, as Ivey (2009) points out, on the last ten years a considerable part of the discussion has been oriented towards the analysis of the future of Anglo-American Cataloguing Rules. Furthermore, between 2006 and 2007, a dramatic increase in publications was observed, basically on subjects related with the cataloguer role and cataloguing future in specialized libraries.

Since the sixties, bibliographic description should be normalized and unified for a better information exchange, so cataloguing regulations, guidelines, and rules are originated with an international point of view. Evidence of this integration are the International Cataloguing Regulations (1961), Guidelines for Bibliographic Description (1967), and the Anglo-American Cataloguing Rules (1967).

This meant every library had to create its catalogues systematically according to such guidelines, achieving then a common design that allowed the procurement of optimum results, in regard to the objectives Cutter indicated about the catalogue. In some sense, the catalogue is the "ideal" representation of the cataloguing process. This is why it is considered as the central activity for bibliographic control, with no presumption of being copied or imitated literally, but adapted to the needs and problems shaping a real situation in each country or region.

In the following three decades, catalogues changed gradually from being elaborated in 3x5 inches cards to microfiches, CD-ROM, and lately to modern on-line access catalogues.

Bibliographic organization has established that, generally, case studies have been documented and contextualized as *system analysis* or *system thinking*. Each research has contributed in the revision of productivity standards, cost reduction, and has observed what an automated system of bibliographic information means for any type of library. That is, understanding users' needs to provide them required information in determined timings and specific aims.

Case study presents itself in diverse manners in bibliographic organization, depending on the purpose wanting to be resolved. The conceptions of a librarian and an administrator are completely opposite. The librarian administers, organizes, and coordinates the cataloguing process, being the protagonist who centers his/her attention on the use and management of bibliographic information. Moreover, his/her information sources are books, maps, discs, tapes, videotapes, among other documents. The administrator becomes an element who only interacts with economic and financial resources to achieve general and specific goals of the library. A few case studies within the bibliographic organization setting are described below.

Palmer (1972) performs a bibliographic review of the studies about migration from the card catalogue to the automated catalogue. From this review, he designs a methodology to investigate the needs of university users for employing a catalogue.

Gough and Srikantaiah (1978) explain the problem of *copied cataloguing* in terms of the process and cost that cataloguing implies, physically preparing a book to place in the shelf and producing the card set for a divided catalogue.

During the eighties and nineties, case studies were oriented towards two situations. First, the analysis of how budget cutback of libraries affected the cataloguing process, second, the identification of the four directives that caused a significant change in the working nature of the cataloguer. These indicators were 1) libraries experienced a continuous decay in the number of physical bibliographic objects to be catalogued; 2) libraries had to face budget cutbacks against *outsourcing* operations, specially those related with cataloguing (Lopez-Rodriguez, 2006); 3) libraries rather adjusted their budgets noticing a lower cost for traditional cataloguing, due to the competition in the information market and increase of on-line information consumers (electronic books or data bases); 4) the increase of new digital information resources provoked that cataloguers require new abilities to accomplish their work (Rodriguez-Garcia, 2006).

Most of the investigations performed on that period are not clearly showing an indicative methodology about how case study was used, the only conclusion is it was employed as a strategy to trace change establishment in bibliographic organization.

On the other hand, an analysis of case studies completed on the first decade of the century indicates that all coincide in three characteristic elements mentioned by Eckstein (1975), a) are basically descriptive, b) interpret patterns, and c) constitute studies aimed at the development of interpretational schemes.

Regarding *descriptive case studies*, a series of contributions have been found. Such contributions related with the use of the conceptual model named Functional Requirements for Bibliographic Records (FRBR) created by IFLA in 1997, and with modifications to the Anglo-American Cataloguing Rules, revised second edition (Catalogacion: tendencias y aplicacion, 2006; Tillet, 2008)

Pattern-interpretation case studies include those investigations relative to the explanation, use, and adaptation of the conceptual model FRBR to several guidelines of bibliographic description, such as the International Cataloguing Regulations and cataloguing codes, as well as authorities control and adaptation of bibliographic databases in the setting of the cooperative cataloguing program (Tillet,2007; Rodriguez-Garcia, 2006; Cristan, 2007).

Finally, *interpretational schemes case studies* show investigations which point out how the conceptual model FRBR affects retrieval systems, such as on-line catalogs. This research also indicates the new abilities the user must develop, both the creator of databases and the final user, in the retrieval, access, and use of information (Martinez-Arellano, 2009;Shandle, 2009).

This added sample of case studies elaborated in bibliographic organization could determine, at a given time, up to what extent the cataloguer has reached the objectives in the cataloguing process. It could also evaluate costs and time, among other issues.

Therefore, from our point of view, case studies are currently used to interpret schemes which have an impact in the normalization of information description, access, retrieval, and use. As much as the cataloguer systematically follows the method, it may be called to a generalization and theorization in information studies.

4. Conclusions

Two basic case study types are observed:

1. Where emphasis is given to the particular case. In this perspective, the method is used in the initial phases of research and it is conceived as the study object.
2. Where the case study is taken as a means not as the study object; it is used to fully understand a problem, or to enrich and/or modify a theory. The case becomes secondary.

Case studies in the area of library science and information studies have been more common in the first perspective, that is, they are useful to describe particular situations (a library, an information system, etc). This does not contribute to a generalization, but, in the best scenario, to a case representation; leading us to confirm that many works which imply to be case studies, actually are not.

This is why we consider the need to encourage the use of case study method in the area of library science and information studies, as Gundermann-Kroll mentions, at the *instrumental purpose* point where the case is taken as a means not as study object. For this to happen, research must be conformed from explanatory and partial models from each study area. The intention is to perfect these and develop general models of each study object in particular. This may also contribute to develop cross-disciplinary work.

From this point of view, case studies would also be useful from two aspects:

1. Establish a relation between research and empirical aspects.
2. Approach research results so people may find them useful in the professional practice setting. In this sense, evidence could be originated from case studies. Such evidence may transform into reality what is called *Evidence-Based Librarianship*, offering the professional *evidence research*. Through generalizations this research could provide him/her a guide for specific situations.

Considering the above-mentioned and the instrumental purpose of case studies, we determine the following benefits of its utilization in the areas of Digital Library, Information Policies, and Bibliographic Organization:

Digital Library. Up to date, approximations have been made, but they require a clearer concretion in the professional practice surroundings. Which are the practices in this library multiple areas is unknown, from collections development to service provision.

Information Policies. Micro level research on information policies offers a better view about the work in specific countries. Case study is shown as an adequate method for performing micro studies that represent social (relations, structures, positions, and roles), cultural (categories or symbolic forms by which a program, an event, a person, a process, an institution, or group represent the social world, producing, reproducing, and transmitting it) and psychological reality (processes which allow individuals to order the world and take actions upon it), and for establishing information policies of different kind.

Bibliographic Organization. Case studies performed in the area of bibliographic organization during the first decade of the 20th century are basically descriptive, interpret patterns, and constitute studies aimed at interpretational schemes development. Case study method is required for generalization and theorization in this area, so achievements may go further than simple description. This method could even help to determine up to what extent the cataloguer has reached the objectives in the cataloguing process, including cost and time analysis, and make the cataloguing process effective and efficient. Therefore, we believe that if case study methodology is completely applied to research in the area of library science and information studies, great contributions will enrich this discipline.

References

Arms, W. Y., (2000). *Digital libraries.* MIT press, Cambridge, Massachusetts.

Borgman, C., (2007). *Scholarship in the digital age: information, infrastructure and the internet.* MIT press, Cambridge, Massachusetts.

Brophy, P., (2005). *The Academic library.* 2nd ed. Facets London.

Catalogación: tendencias y aplicación, (2006): *Memorias de Nuevas Tendencias en la Normalización y Sistematización de la Información: ponencias y conclusiones.* Biblioteca Nacional del Perú, Fondo Editorial, Lima, 27-122.

Cristan, A. L. (2006): Los programas de cooperación en catalogación de la Library of Congress de EUA (LC) en el ámbito internacional- ¿éxitos o fracasos?. *Memoria del Segundo Encuentro Internacional de Catalogación: Tendencias en la teoría y práctica de la catalogación bibliográfica, 12 al 14 de septiembre de 2006.* Centro Universitario de Investigaciones Bibliotecológicas, Instituto de Investigaciones Bibliográficas, Library Outsourcing Services, México, 43-54.

Denzin, N.and Lincoln Y., (1994). 2nd ed. *Handbook of qualitative research.* Sage, Thousand Oaks.

Díaz, J. L. (2005): Modelos científicos : conceptos y usos. *El modelo en la ciencia y la cultura.* Siglo XXI, UNAM, México, 11-28.

Eckstein, H. (1975): Case study and theory in political science. *Strategies of inquiry.* Adisson-Wesley, London.

Eldredge, J., (2006). Evidence-based librarianship : the EBL process. *Library Hi Tech*, Vol.24, 341-354.

Espina-Prieto, M. P. (2007). Complejidad, transdisciplina y metodología de la investigación social. *Utopía y Praxis Latinoamericana,* Vol.12, 29-43.

Gough, C. & Srikantaiah, T., (1978). *Systems analysis in libraries: a questions and answer approach.* Linnet Books, Hamden.

Gundermann-Kroll, H. (2001): El método de los estudios de caso. *Observar, escuchar y comprender : sobre la tradición cualitativa en la investigación social.* Facultad Latinoamericana de Ciencias Sociales, México, 251- 288.

Hitchens, A., (1997). A call for IGO Policies on Public Access to Information. *Government Information Quarterly,* Vol.14, 143-154.

Ivey, R. T., (2009). Perception of the future of Cataloging: is the sky really falling? *Cataloging & Classification,* Vol.47, 464-482.

Koufogiannakis, D., (2006). Research in librarianship : issues to consider. *Library Hi Tech,* Vol.24, 324-340.

Lancaster, F. W. & Burger, R. H. (1990): Macroinformatics Microinformatics and Information Policy. *The Information Environment: a World View. Studies in Honour of Professor A. I. Mikhailov.* FID, Hague, 152-155.

López-Rodríguez, R. (2006): Los outsourcing en la catalogación: experiencia de la Biblioteca Luis Ángel Arango. *Memorias de Nuevas tendencias en la normalización y sistematización de la información: ponencias y conclusiones.* Biblioteca Nacional del Perú, Fondo Editorial, Lima, 247-261.

Marcionini. G., (2000). Evaluating digital libraries: a longitudinal and multifaceted view. *Library Trends,* Vol.49, 304-333.

Martínez-Arellano, F. F. (2009): Características, implicaciones y retos del nuevo código de catalogación, RDA (Resources Description and Access). *Memoria del Tercer Encuentro de Catalogación y Metadatos, 29-31 octubre de 2008.* UNAM, Centro Universitario de Investigaciones Bibliotecológicas, Instituto de Investigaciones Bibliograficas. México, 3-16.

Morin, E., (1999). *Los siete saberes necesarios para la educación del futuro.* UNESCO, Paris.

Páez-Urdaneta, I. (1990). *Información para el progreso de América Latina.* Universidad Simón Bolívar, Congreso de la República, Caracas.

Palmer, R. P. (1972). *Computerizing the card catalog in the university library.* Libraries Unlimited, Littleton, Colorado.

Parsons, W., (2007). *Políticas públicas: una introducción a la teoría y la práctica del análisis de políticas públicas.* FLACSO, México.

Powell, R. R., (2002). Library and Information Science Practitioners and Research. *Library & Information Science Research,* Vol.24, 49-72.

Rodríguez-García, A. A., (2006). La unificación en la descripción: el modelo FRBR y las RCAA2R. *Investigación Bibliotecológica,* Vol. 20, 43-54.

Sánchez-Mediola, M., (2001). La medicina basada en evidencias en México: lujo o necesidad? *Anales Médico de la Asociación Médica del Hospital ABC,* Vol. 46, 97-103.

Saracevic, T. & Dalbello, M., (2003). *Digital Library Research and Digital Library Practice: How Do they Inform Each Other?* [unpublished study]. Last retrieved, February 16, 2010, from:
http://www.scils.rutgers.edu/~tefko/Saracevic_Dalbello_DLib_02.doc.

Shandle, S. C. (2009): WorldCat Local @ University of Washington libraries: local discovery and delivery at the network level. *Memoria del Tercer Encuentro de Catalogación y Metadatos, 29-31 octubre de 2008.* Centro Universitario de Investigaciones Bibliotecológicas, Instituto de Investigaciones Bibliograficas, México, 17-40.

Tillett, B. B. (2007): RDA y la influencia del FRBR y otras iniciativas de IFLA. *Memoria del Segundo Encuentro Internacional de Catalogación: Tendencias en la teoría y práctica de la catalogación bibliográfica, 12 al 14 de septiembre de 2006.* UNAM, Centro Universitario de Investigaciones Bibliotecológicas, Instituto de Investigaciones Bibliográficas, Library Outsourcing Service, México, 3-26.

Tillett, B. B. (2008): RDA (Resource Description and Access) status report the new cataloging code= Informe sobre el nuevo código de catalogación. *Los umbrales del Nuevo código de catalogación: Memoria del Segundo Encuentro de Catalogación y Metadatos, 24-26 octubre de 2007.* UNAM, Centro Universitario de Investigaciones Bibliotecológicas, México, 3-34.

Torres-Vargas, G. A., (2008). *Un modelo integral de biblioteca digital.* Centro Universitario de Investigaciones Bibliotecológicas, México.

Turner, K. (2002): Do Information Professionals Use Research Published in LIS Journals?. *IFLA Council and General Conference (2002:Glasgow, Scotland).* Last retrieved February 16, 2010, from:
http://www.eric.ed.gov/ERICDocs/data/ericdocs2sql/content_storage_01/0000019b/80/1a/c0/0d.pdf.

Worlock, D. (1996): Real policy or 'virtual policy'? a case study or tradeable information policy. In I. Rowlands (Eds.), *Understanding Information Policy: proceedings of a workshop held at Cumberland Lodge.,* NJ: Bowker – Saur, New Providence, New Jersey.

Yin, R. K., (2003). *Case study research : design and methods.* 3rd ed. Sage, Thousand Oaks.

Experimental Workflow Development in Digitisation

Mustafa Dogan[1], Clemens Neudecker[2], Sven Schlarb[3] and Gerd Zechmeister[4]

[1]Goettingen State and University Library, Platz der Goettinger Sieben 1, 37073 Goettingen, Germany, Tel.: +49 551 39 52 12, dogan@sub.uni-goettingen.de
[2]Koninklijke Bibliotheek, Prins Willem-Alexanderhof 5, 2595 BE Den Haag, The Netherlands, Tel. +31 70 3140781, clemens.neudecker@kb.nl
[3]Austrian National Library; Josefsplatz 1, A-1015 Vienna, Austria, Tel.: +43-1-53410-491, sven.schlarb@onb.ac.at
[4]Austrian National Library; Josefsplatz 1, A-1015 Vienna, Austria, Tel.: +43-1-53410-506, gerd.zechmeister@onb.ac.at

Abstract: Digitisation projects require well-rehearsed workflows to save time and costs while generating high value for both content-providers and end-users. But cultural heritage institutions such as museums, libraries and archives (MLA) often lack advanced knowledge and experience in this field and tend to contract service providers to carry out digitisation services. This paper outlines an innovative approach that will enable the MLA community to develop their own workflows and share the knowledge gained with others. The core concept is to collaboratively create, share, modify and manage workflows without in-depth technical and procedural knowledge. This paper introduces the applied framework model and its underlying architectural principles. Its main focus lies on the perspective of the content-providing libraries.
Keywords: Digitisation, digital library, OCR, text recognition, workflow

1. Introduction
Library collections are largely composed of assets containing text, such as books, newspapers or manuscripts. While OCR technologies can achieve very high accuracy on most modern documents, they do not deliver satisfying results when applied to documents published before 1900. The reasons are manifold: Beside the large variation of typefaces and fonts, complex layouts, and historical spelling variations, the physical layout of the original pages introduces challenges such as bleed-through letters or inconsistent paper textures. In addition distortions can be found in the text caused by the item's storage conditions (warping, discolouration, mould, shrinkage, fading etc.) and usage (folds, tears, annotations, stains, repairs, holes etc.). Some of these issues may not be obvious to the human eye and only become apparent once the scanning process has been completed. In order to identify such issues and deal with such complicated documents, the experience in the IMPACT project indicates that in principle the use of high resolution (300 ppi) and colour depth (8 Bit greyscale or even 24 Bit colour) in the capture approach tends to yield better chances in obtaining usable results from the text recognition process.

New Trends in Qualitative and Quantitative Methods in Libraries
A. Katsirikou and C. H. Skiadas (eds)
© *World Scientific Publishing Co (pp. 377-384)*

Faced with the complexities of producing full-text digital representations of historical printed material, many cultural heritage institutions contract third-party suppliers to provide OCR and/or rekeying services. Outsourcing the creation of full-featured electronic text of historical documents can thus become prohibitively expensive. Specific know-how is not retained in many institutions which causes a momentous lack of information (Balk and Ploeger 2009). Such expertise is vital in adapting existing digitisation workflows for OCR processing or defining the expectations and feasibility of a new project. There is thus an obvious need for a system which "manages the whole process of digitisation with its phases" to "execute elementary activities within a digitisation phase such as image processing and OCR" (Yakout et al. 2006).

The objective of this paper is to introduce a concept for collaboratively developing workflows in mass digitisation projects, which is independent from the underlying software platform. The term workflow in this paper refers to a software-based execution of a sequence with the goal to "reduce both human and computation costs and accelerate the speed of turning large amounts of bits and bytes into knowledge and discovery" (Lu 2009). Collaboration is defined as the "ability to have broader interactions through the sharing of data, experimental approaches and both intermediate and final results in systems that will maintain a history of the data, processes, outcomes and conversations" (Wright et al. 2007). Traditionally, digitisation processes tend to be very time-consuming, especially on complex historical material: any failures of individual processes on the one hand must not halt the entire iteration of a workflow (Hagen 2000) and on the other must be clearly documented on an item level, as outlined in digitisation principles by the University of Exeter (Abu-Zayed 2009). Therefore, the setting up of a workflow for full text conversion is a complex exercise that includes the coordination of a large number of specific processes and requires considerable hard- and software resources as well as experienced personnel in each domain.

Workflow development is presented here as a community-driven activity using an experimental workflow development platform. The framework implementation and the development and improvement of the software components (comprising pre- and post-processing tasks from image enhancement down to language correction) are being carried out in the EU-funded research project IMPACT (IMProving ACcess to Text). This project brings together twenty-six national and regional libraries, research institutions and commercial suppliers to work on lowering the barriers for cultural heritage institutions to conduct mass digitisation projects in standardised, efficient and reliable ways. A main project objective is to show the usability, quality, effectiveness and scalability of the protoypes of software tools developed in the project and their contribution towards overcoming the challenges of OCR processing of printed historical text material. The experimental framework and its software components will be accompanied by strategic and operational guidelines as well as training events supporting the uptake of full- text conversion of historical printed material in the MLA community.

In the following sections, we describe the general framework architecture and the underlying principles, and present the community-driven experimental workflow development for digitisation as a promising approach to address the challenges of digitisation for content holding institutions.

2. Architectural principles and framework architecture

The concept is aimed towards the implementation of a technical framework and the integration of the software components within that framework. The requirements outlined below follow architectures proposed for scientific workflows (Lu 2009,

Warner et al. 2007). Interoperability of all tools as a main principle is achieved by two abstraction layers: individual software tools wrapped as web services, which are then wrapped in a so-called "basic" workflow. A dedicated software will support building and management of comprehensive workflows. The output and results are evaluated in order to determine optimal workflows in relation to the kind of material processed.

The technical realisation and provision of workflow fragments is carried out by technicians and is focused on the integration of software tools developed within the project (or of any other relevant software tools) with the purpose of making them available within the technical framework, exposing relevant features of the software tools in the form of ready-to-use basic workflows. Based on these well-documented basic workflows, the conceptual work of workflow development and evaluation is carried out by people with knowledge of the characteristics of the material being processed.

From the IMPACT point of view, the framework architecture for experimental workflow development presented in this paper has beneficial characteristics in various aspects:

Modularity: Individual modules can be combined in a vast number of combinations, thereby enabling the user to identify the most suitable processing chain for the material being processed and guaranteeing the reusability of the components. In this respect, the service-oriented-architecture (SOA) is the guiding architectural design principle; more specifically the principle of loose coupling of reusable processing units, minimising interdependencies between them.

Transparency: Each individual processing step can be tested and evaluated separately, so that it is obvious to the user whether a unit produces expected results and contributes to the overall quality of the digitisation workflow and what the cost is in terms of processing time.

Flexibility: Due to the framework being platform-independent and capable of integrating different types of software tools, automated workflows can be composed and rearranged whereas new workflows can be created and adapted from existing ones, and the performance of these can be compared easily.

Extensibility: Third party components can be installed with very small extra effort. Therefore experimenting with and evaluating workflows is not restricted only to software tools developed during the IMPACT project.

Open standards based: The framework is using well-documented and widely supported open source software, mostly projects of the Apache Software Foundation. Data exchange between software components is based on widely used XML standards such as METS/ALTO for encoding of structural information and of the OCR-recognised text, and SOAP as the message exchange protocol.

Accessibility: The technical framework can be accessed via different types of interfaces. There is a user-friendly, graphical workflow design and execution interface, a web client generator which allows seamless integration into web sites, and a machine interface (API).

Scalability: The web service components, as the basic layer of the framework, will be deployed in the IT infrastructure of different partner organisations in Europe. This will create a distributed network with cloned services available in a redundant way, which allows distributing the workload and adding additional computing capacity when needed.

Collaboration: The community-wide applicability and optimisation of workflows strongly depends on users actively working with them. IMPACT will make workflows accessible by various channels (including Web 2.0 features) to the stakeholders. In order to encourage people to actively participate, it is necessary to create easy-to-use workflows which are comprehensively described and documented. It must be pointed out that the focus of the framework lies on *experimental* workflow development, keeping in mind that transferring large amounts of data over the internet is a time-consuming process: Operations will be carried out by retrieving preselected data sets from an online repository and processing them by using distributed computing capacity to show the benefits of sharing, reproducing and adapting workflows. Productive mass digitisation by using the framework - although generally possible - is not the intended use due to the massive online data transfer it would entail.

Nevertheless, if software tools and services are deployed locally, high volume of data processing can be envisaged, and the slight lack of performance due to the use of web services is easily compensated by workload distribution and process parallelisation. Considering these architectural principles, a community-driven approach for experimental workflow development and execution with a clear focus on OCR processing of historical material has been created and is outlined in the next section.

3. Community-driven experimental workflow development

In IMPACT, the community participating in the experimental workflow development is defined as a group of cultural heritage institutions already undertaking mass digitisation projects. The participants share the objectives to establish technical and operational expertise and experience in the field of OCR processing. They all have large digital collections of printed historical material, each of them with specific characteristics and challenges due to the corresponding historical period and storage conditions. The knowledge gained from using the *experimental workflow development platform* will lead to sustainable improvements and expertise that can be shared with other institutions which are planning or undertaking mass digitisation and OCR projects.

Five content providing libraries, the national libraries of Austria, France, the Netherlands and the United Kingdom, and the Bavarian State Library along with the Goettingen State and University Library as technical partner are currently the core participants of this community. The community can generally be extended but is restricted to project partners during the course of IMPACT. However, it is planned to grant access to interested cultural heritage institutions by establishing a centre of competence where the project outcomes will be sustained.

The main advantages of performing experiments as a community activity is the ability to share, comment on, rate, organise, maintain and manage workflows together: The community participants build their workflows by combining ready-to-use software components requiring only basic technical knowledge. Sharing workflows in a central place - the *workflow registry* - allows the community participants to test, review, modify and adapt workflows. Figure 1 provides an overview of the platform's general architecture and the community.

Workflow development comprises the three phases "Design", "Execute", and "Evaluate", which are preceded by the "Select" phase, as shown in Figure 2.

Predefined material from digital collections is stored in an online data repository. In the **"Select" phase** the community participants compile data sets from this material, according to specific criteria, such as descriptive meta data (e.g. document type, publication year) or the presence of certain characteristics like page skew/warping, bleed/shine through, etc. A data set determines the basis and general focus of an experiment. For example, one institution is planning a book digitisation project and is interested in the overall results of a workflow using different software components.

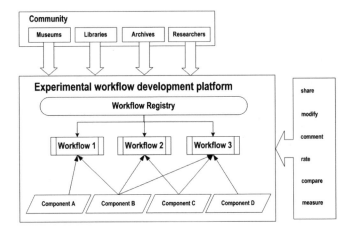

Figure 1: The community and the experimental workflow development platform

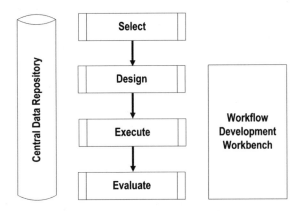

Figure 2: Phases of experimental workflow development

Therefore she/he selects a representative set of scanned images of book pages making sure that all known characteristics and challenges in the total collection are represented. Another institution, by contrast, is planning a newspaper digitisation project, and is focusing on challenges related to the bad paper quality of old printed newspapers. Therefore she/he selects different data sets to evaluate in different workflows tailored to the specific types of challenges.

In the **"Design" phase** participants can either select one of the existing workflows and adapt them to their needs, or design a new workflow from scratch. Because complex workflows can be built from basic components, in-depth technical knowledge is not required. However, we advise that teams using this approach should consist of both technical and conceptual staff. Web 2.0 features will allow them to actively participate in and benefit from other participants' reviews or comments:

existing workflows will provide an overview of available software components, show application scenarios (input data set and workflow), and explain the functionality and use of components in application contexts.

In the **"Execute" phase** a workflow is executed using a defined data set as input. During the workflow run, successful execution can be monitored and intermediate as well as final results can be analysed continuously. Furthermore, a workflow run can be re-executed or applied to other data sets.

The **"Evaluate" phase** refers to the assessment of the workflow performance and the quality of the OCR text output to show the benefits of the concept and its results for the community participants. The following section describes criteria more detail.

4. Evaluation criteria

Main criterion is to see significant improvements in the **quality of OCR** in terms of accurate results. Evaluating OCR accuracy on the basis of OCR results, however, is a difficult and very time-consuming task, which usually requires iterative human intervention and quality control to ensure highest accuracy (Tanner 2009). In order to receive reliable results it is necessary to produce *Ground Truth Data* (Van Beusekom et al. 2008) to assess the OCR output. In the context of OCR, Ground Truth is defined as the 100% correct transcription of the text visible on a document page. The quality is measured in accuracy levels, expressed in percentage of correctly recognised characters and/or words among the total number of characters and/or words recognised. The results will be categorised by defining expected, acceptable and unacceptable accuracy level. The determination of these thresholds takes into account the complexity of the relevant material and the intended type of use. Full text requires higher levels than a search index (Feng and Manmatha 2006).

A set of pre-OCR processing software components will enhance the machine readability of images by removing digital noise such as borders and dewarp and deskew images to increase the OCR accuracy. Further benefits are the creation of e-Books and other digital surrogates. This pre-OCR processing also encompasses a layered **segmentation** of the physical layout of the page elements . The focus of evaluation from library's standpoint lies in the correct segmentation of images into text and graphical regions. Identifying the regions is especially relevant for complex layouts but can also be used for a general layout analysis to detect page numbers, marginalia etc. Ground Truth Data here refers to the coordinates of regions, according to the detection level (blocks, paragraphs, lines, words or characters). The ideal evaluation result in this case is the complete matching of ground-truthed and software-detected coordinates for those regions (Bridson and Antonacopoulos 2008). Defining thresholds requires more testing on the performance: Deviations between coordinate values of Ground Truth and Production Data not necessarily mean bad results. Main requirement is to preserve the correct reading order in the segmentation of different regions.

In the workflow design phase it is recommended to build several workflows to tackle the same type of material, and compare the output of each. The **evaluation of workflows** against each other is one of the major benefits of this approach. By comparing outputs, the community participants can then identify best-fitting workflows. Using image enhancement tools prior to OCR processing, for example, is supposed to deliver higher accuracy, given that the selected material exposes challenges to these tools.

The inclusion of **statistical data** provided by the workflow development platform (e.g. execution times per workflow, per web service or per image) and descriptive data about data sets (e.g. document type, time period, language, exposed characteristics) offer even more possibilities to evaluate the results and view the output from various angles and perspectives. This allows the community participants to report on trends and constraints, strong and the weak points of each workflow and the software components it includes.

5. Conclusions

Digitisation workflows are most often developed locally in single organisations, and the labour and cost-intensive evaluation of existing software components for creating automated software-based workflows is undertaken at the start-up phase of each successive project. This paper presents a concept of experimental collaborative workflow development with the aim of overcoming these barriers to the success of digitisation project planning, describing the general architecture and approach. Making use of a platform where knowledge and experiences can be exchanged, workflow development as a collaborative activity shows clear benefits for all community participants.

Acknowledgements

The IMPACT Research and Development work presented here is partially supported by European Community under the Information Society Technologies Programme (IST-1-4.1 Digital libraries and technology-enhanced learning) of the 7th framework programme - Project FP 7-ICT-2007-1.

References

Al-Zayed, A. (2009): Digitisation Workflow and Guidelines. Digitisation Processes. Accessed at http://projects.exeter.ac.uk/charter/documents/DigitisationWorkflowGuidev5.pdf

Balk, H. and Ploeger, L. (2009): IMPACT. working together to address the challenges involving mass digitization of historical printed text. *OCLC Systems & Services: International digital library Perspectives* 25(4), 233-248

Bridson, D. and Antonacopoulos, A. (2008): A geometric approach for accurate and efficient performance evaluation of layout analysis methods. *19th International Conference on Pattern Recognition* 1-4. Accessed at http://figment.cse.usf.edu/~sfefilat/data/papers/TuBCT10.21.pdf

Feng, S. and Manmatha, R. (2006): A Hierarchical, HMMbased Automatic Evaluation of OCR Accuracy for a Digital Library of Books. *Proceedings of the 6th ACM/IEEE-CS joint conference on Digital libraries* 109-118. Accessed at http://ciir.cs.umass.edu/pubfiles/mm-489.pdf

Hagen, C. and Alonso, G. (2000): Exception Handling in Workflow Management Systems. *IEEE Transactions on Software Engineering*, 26(10), 943-958. Accessed at http://www.iks.inf.ethz.ch/publications/publications/files/ha00.pdf

IMPACT Project (2008-2011): Improving Access to Text. http://www.impact-project.eu

Lu, S. et al. (2009): A Reference Architecture for Scientific Workflow Management Systems and the VIEW SOA Solution. IEEE Transactions on services computing. 2 (1). Accessed at http://www.cs.wayne.edu/~shiyong/papers/tsc09.pdfTanner, S. et al. (2009): Measuring Mass Text Digitization Quality and Usefulness. Lessons Learned from Assessing the OCR Accuracy of the British Library's 19th Century Online Newspaper Archive. *D-Lib Magazine* 15(7/8). Accessed at http://www.dlib.org/dlib/july09/munoz/07munoz.html

Van Beusekom, J. et al. (2008): Automated OCR Ground Truth Generation, *8th IAPR International Workshop on Document Analysis Systems* 111-117.

Warner, S. et al. (2007): Pathways. Augmenting interoperability across scholarly repositories. *International Journal on Digital Libraries* 6(4), 363

Wright, M. et al. (2007): Connecting Digital Libraries to Escience. The Future of Scientific Scholarship. *International Journal on Digital Libraries* 7(1/2), 1-4

Yakout, M. et al. (2006): Digitization Workflow Management System for Massive Digitization Projects. *Proceedings of the 2nd International Conference on Universal Digital Library (ICUDL 2006).* Accessed at http://www.bibalex.org/isis/UploadedFiles/Publications/Massive_Digit_Workfl ow_Mgmt_Sys.pdf

Chapter 8. Library Applications and Methodologies

Co-Word Analysis of Doctoral Dissertations in Information Science in the Republic of Croatia from 1978 to 2007: Contribution to Research of Development of Information Science

Miroslav Tuđman[1] and Đilda Pečarić[2]

The University of Zagreb, Faculty of Humanities and Social Sciences, Department of Information Sciences, Ivana Lučića 3, 10000 Zagreb, Croatia, [1]mtudman@ffzg.hr, [2]dpecaric@ffzg.hr

Abstract: For the analysis of doctoral dissertations in information science in the Republic of Croatia (from 1978 to 2007), keywords are used in order to get an insight into the development of information science. By the method of co-word analysis of keywords with which doctoral dissertations are indexed, a network of clusters that match following scientific disciplines is obtained: archival and documentation science, librarianship, communicology, museology, information science, information systems and lexicography. By cluster and data visualization and the overview of keywords frequency, the development of subjects and the correlation of clusters in information science, during the period of thirty years in which doctoral dissertation are made, is shown. The results of the co-word analysis about the development of information science in the Republic of Croatia are shown according to time periods, but also according to affiliation to certain disciplines inside the information science.
Keywords: Co-word analysis, cluster, data visualization, information science, keywords analysis, doctoral dissertations

1. Introduction

The framework for theoretical and practical development of information science in Croatia was founded by Prof. Dr. Božo Težak in early 1960s (1969, 1971). B. Težak also established the first postgraduate studies of information science in 1961, with the curriculum based on the idea that different information-documentation disciplines belong to the same field. At the beginning of 1960s he was convinced that all "traditional information and documentation activities which differ among themselves according to the nature of the objects they are dealing with (archive documents, publications, museum exhibits, etc.)" can develop as scientific disciplines if they share the information science as a common theory (Tudjman, M. 2007). That is why the domain of Information science in Croatia is composed of following disciplines: archivistics and documentation, librarianship, communicology, museology, information science, information systems and lexicography. Doctoral dissertations in these disciplines can be done (in Croatia) on Faculties in Zagreb, Varaždin and Zadar.

New Trends in Qualitative and Quantitative Methods in Libraries
A. Katsirikou and C. H. Skiadas (eds)
© *World Scientific Publishing Co (pp. 385-392)*

First doctoral dissertation in information science was made in 1978. First doctoral dissertation in communicology was made in 1979, then in 1980 in information systems and librarianship. First doctoral dissertation in museology was made in 1988, and in archivistics and documentation in 1991.

Since Težak's time until today, one theoretical and pragmatic question has remained: are all of the above mentioned disciplines a part of information science or are they sciences that jointly make information sciences? This duality, in theory and practice, can be noticed in the usage of both terms (information science and information sciences) in course titles that are studied at the Department of Information Sciences at Faculty of Humanities and Social Sciences in Zagreb (Program studija Odsjeka za informacijske znanosti, 2005.).

Our hypothesis is that the verification of division and understanding of field of information sciences can be empirically researched with co-word analysis of doctoral dissertations. This quantitative method can be used for mapping the structure of information science. We want to explore "knowledge map", i.e. structure of research topics and their correlation inside broadly defined field of information science without making a priori commitment to any definitions of information sciences. In this way, we want empirical confirmation, not only about the structure and dynamics of the development of information sciences, but also about correlation of disciplines in information sciences.

2. Methodology

The co-word analysis technique was first proposed to map the dynamics of science. Based on the co-occurrence of pairs of words, co-word analysis seeks to extract the themes of science and detect the linkages among these themes directly from the subject content of texts (Qin He, 1999). Our research of information science field is done on the corpus of 134 doctoral dissertations in information science at Croatian Universities from 1978 to 2007. The distribution of doctoral dissertations according to disciplines is: librarianship 20, information science 21, information systems 53, communicology 22, museology 9, archivistics and documentation 8, lexicography 1. The majority of doctoral dissertations were made at the Faculty of Organization and Informatics in Varaždin (FOI) – 69, followed by the Faculty of Humanities and Social Sciences in Zagreb – 49 doctoral dissertations. According to the periods of production: 21 doctoral dissertations were made until 1989; 62 doctoral dissertations from 1990 to 1999; 51 doctoral dissertations from 2000 to 2007.

We used co-word method to analyze key words that are retrieved from doctoral dissertations' abstracts and indexes (average number of key words per doctoral dissertation is 8). The total number of key words is 1053. From that number 430 key words occur only once (41% of all occurrences); 70 key words occur twice (14 %); 22 key words occur 3 times (6%); 13 and 11 key words occur 4 and 5 times respectively (10%). 18 key words occur 6 to 10 times (13%). 5 key words occur 11 to 19 times (7%), and only 4 key words occur with 20 to 28 times, and they hold 9,6% of overall frequency of all key words.

Pairs are made from key words that have frequency bigger then 1. The total number of pairs is 1524, from which 887 pairs occur only once (58% pairs), 214 pairs occur twice (28%), 29 pairs occur 3 times (6%), 13 pairs occur 4 times (3%), and remaining 10 pairs occur 5 to 10 times (5%).

Software Bibexcel is used for the analysis of key words, and software Pajek for the visualization of data.

3. Mapping the Structure and Dynamics of Information Science Development in Croatia

A co-occurrence matrix of keyword was organized and analyzed according to several criteria. Our goal was to extract central themes in the domain of information science, in order to detect the linkages among these themes. In order to follow the dynamics of information science development, density of certain clusters and their linkages, interaction and transformation of centrality, we mapped key words from doctoral dissertations according to time periods, disciplines and faculties on which dissertations were done.

With such methodological approach, we obtained series of maps that allow us more precise interpretation of empirical domain and the dynamic of information science development in Croatia.

Structure of Information Science Domain. Table 1 shows the structure of main topics and domains in information science based on the key words according to which analyzed texts are indexed. Dominant cluster has several central nodes, whose hierarchy and linkages can be determined by frequencies of words, pairs of words, and amount of linkages. Central nodes according to the frequency of pairs of words are:

Information	Communication	10
Information system	System	10
Information	Information system	9
Information	System	8
Information	Model	6
Information system	Model	6
Model	System	6

In this case linkage density of these words inside the cluster is more than obvious and that is the indicator of internal strength of the cluster. Likewise, this is the indicator of the existing subject areas inside but also among the clusters. Thus, from map in Table 1, sub-clusters inside dominant clusters can also be discerned: *e-learning, museums, archives, methodology, factor analysis*. These sub-clusters are linked with *mediators' words* with dominant clusters and also between themselves.

Central poles of the main cluster are: *information, information system, system, model, communication*. Clusters that occur on the periphery of the central cluster are: *factor analysis, media, museums, bibliometrics, thesaurus, university*. First two clusters *(factor analysis* and *media)* belong to the subject area of communicology: through nodes *communication* and *media,* they are mutually linked with other clusters and belong to information science domain. Cluster *museums* is linked with mediators words *information technology* and *web* to the central cluster, and that makes the subject area of *museums* a mutual subject area of the information science research. Clusters *bibliometrics* and *thesaurus* are on Table 1 recognized as isolated clusters, that is, as isolated subject areas. However, they are also linked via mediator words to two sub-clusters or subnets: *e-learning* and *libraries.* Algorithm that is used to generate the maps of science, recognized *e-learning* as a sub-cluster. It is easy to notice that the cluster *libraries* is also a substructure with rather large density of mutually linked key words. So, based on the empirical data, four recognizable thematic topics *libraries, e-learning, bibliometrics* and *thesaurus* are divided between two different disciplines, librarianship and knowledge organization.

Dynamics of Information Science Development. Information science occurred in 1960s and the dynamic of its development can be followed with the development of thematic topics and growth of knowledge production. Only when we show cumulative knowledge map, shown in Table 1, in temporal series of production of analyzed documents (i.e. according to the publication of doctoral dissertation), we can get the insight into the occurrence and transformation of clusters, and thus also the internal dynamics of the development of thematic topics in Information Science. Since doctoral dissertations have been made in the range of 30 years, we

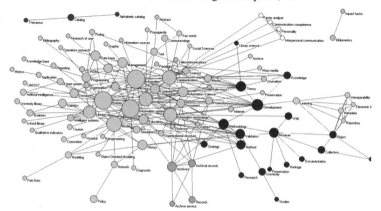

Table 1. Representation of the Structure of Information Science in Croatia
(1978-2007)

observed the development of clusters in ten-year-time periods. Being unable to show maps for each period, only "knowledge" map in third time period (2000 - 2007) is shown in Table 2.

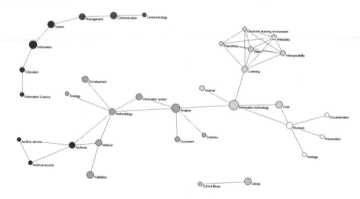

Table 2. Dynamics of Information Science Development (3rd Period 2000- 2007)

During the period of 30 years in which analyzed documents were made, key word map shows constant change of central poles and dominant nodes in the clusters. In the first decade (1978-1989) following pairs have dominant nodes and central position in the cluster: *information - communication, information – information systems*; dominant nodes are: *system, information science, information, computer, data base, and programming.*

In the first period only two clusters are distinguished: dominant cluster with 4-5 central topics: *information, communication, model, computer, information science.* The second cluster is: *data base* which is determined by topics *programming* and programming language *Prolog.*

In the second period (1990-1999) central pairs of clusters shift: *information system – system, decision – system, information system – model.* However, central nodes with close linkages still remain: *information, information system, expert system, information technology, archive* and *library.* Inside the dominant cluster several *substructures* formed by nodes with large number of linkages (as indicated in the brackets) can be recognized: *information system* (15), *systems* (11), *information* (10), *model* (8), *decision* (7), *library* (6). The density of these linkages refers to the content of information science field in that period. Isolated clusters in the same period are: *library science, applications* and *document processing.*

In the third period (2000-2007) several clusters can be followed (Table 2.): *information technology, IS methodology, archives, e-learning, general theory* and *libraries.* The most frequent key words in this period are: *information technology, analysis, information, libraries, communication, system, validation, web.* In this example we can see that the frequency of certain words alone is not crucial in forming the cluster, but if it co-occurs with other frequent words it determines thematic area and overall knowledge map.

With cluster comparison in Tables 1 and 2, large differences in number and content of the cluster can be noticed. Although these knowledge maps are done on the same corpus of data, their time sequence warns us that knowledge corpus constantly changes, transforms and re-structures.

Universities and mapping the Information Science. Following tables (Tables 3-5) show maps of information science as they been created at the University, more precisely Faculty of Humanities and Social Sciences (FHSS) and Faculty of Organization and Informatics in Varaždin (FOI). Namely, most doctoral dissertations were done on these two faculties.

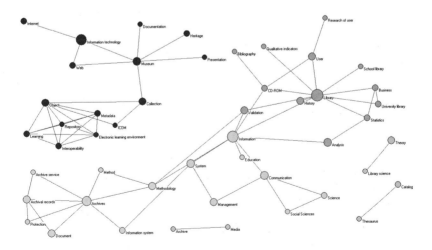

Table 3. Faculty of Humanities and Social Sciences: Information Science Structure according co-word clusters

Table 3 shows knowledge map, the "structure" of information sciences as it has been "produced" at the Faculty of Humanities and Social Sciences at the University of Zagreb by the doctoral dissertations analysis. Clusters are obtained from empirical data, i.e. based on the co-occurrence of pairs of words, extracted subject areas and their linkages. Several clusters can be recognized: dominant cluster with three subclusters: *libraries, archives and information systems,* and isolated clusters: *museums, e-learning, library science, thesaurus, archiving.*

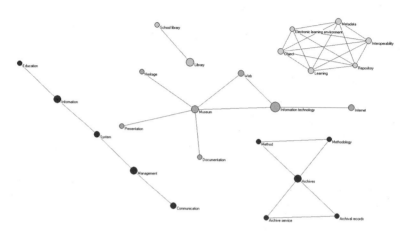

Table 4. The dynamics of Information Science Development (Faculty of Humanities and Social Sciences: Period 2000-2007)

These clusters or more precisely subject areas that are bound by those clusters, greatly correspond with organizational scheme of the Department of Information Sciences. The department constitutes the following chairs: archival and documentation science, librarianship, social-humanistic informatics, museology, knowledge management and lexicography. Apropos, these subject areas greatly match the curricula offered by the Department of Information Sciences: archival science study, library science study, museum study and informatology study.

Table 4 shows another evidence that, in the last observed period (2000-2007) at the Faculty of Humanities and Social Sciences, the same subject areas are repeated: *archives, museums, information technology, e-learning, general theory* and *libraries.* Apparently, according to the number of links and density of clusters, subject area *e-learning* is "the most coherent". Also, clusters *library* and *general theory* are not disperse, so it is hard to predict in what direction these subject areas will continue to develop.

Table 5 shows subject areas that are embedded in the map of information sciences by the Faculty of Organization and Informatics. Apart from two subjects area marked with two "undeveloped" clusters *applications* and *university study*, central subject area is *information systems.* Information systems are, at the same time, scientific and teaching areas at the Faculty of Organization and Informatics.

The most frequent pairs of words and, at the same time, central nodes of clusters are: *information system, system, information model, decision, analysis.* Those nodes are the center of subnetworks inside the large area of *information system* that belongs to information science.

According to cluster density and subject area correlations inside this cluster, it can be concluded that the cluster *information system* is a homogenous area. More detailed analysis, by ranking subject areas in terms of their internal coherence, would give us additional insight into subject areas hierarchy and their correlations.

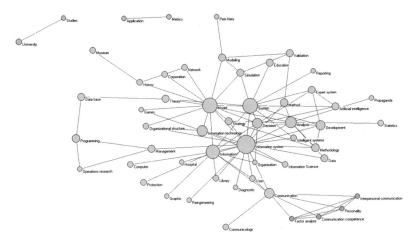

Table 5. Faculty of Organization and Informatics: Information Science Structure according co-word clusters

For our research it is important to notice the interpolation of this cluster, that is the subject area which it shows, in the overall corpus of information sciences' knowledge map. Or in other words: information science structure shown in Table 1, is the result of integration and linkages of topics and subject areas of information sciences shown in Table 3 and Table 5.

Discussion or instead of conclusion

The goal of this paper was to show how co-word analysis and techniques can be used to study development and interactions among information science disciplines. Co-word method enabled systematic content analysis of doctoral dissertations in information sciences made at Universities in Croatia in a period of thirty years. The results are the maps of dominant subject areas which were of interest for the information scientist in the analyzed period. We believe that we also succeeded to describe the dynamics of development of those subject areas and their transformation during longer time period, as well as interaction among information science disciplines.

The analysis of "knowledge map", i.e. thematic topics and their dynamics on the Faculty of Organization and Informatics and on the Faculty of Humanities and Social Sciences indicates the existence of two different areas of research interest and research topics. But, our analysis also indicates the existence of the cooperation and correlations between those two Faculties inside broadly defined area of Information sciences.

We did not get the answer on whether we are dealing with information science or with information sciences. It is still not clear is information science a sum of several disciplines, or information sciences are a common name for several sciences? However, we came to the empirical confirmation that the analyzed subject areas share mutual structure and the dynamic of development, and we offer confirmation about those correlations. This points us to the conclusion that differences in the definition of information sciences are derived from the differences in the comprehension of information as a basic subject (Saracevic, 1999). But those differences disappear when all subject areas become a part of matrix and maps of the information research area. At the same time those differences are the driving force of the dynamics and development of new subjects and thematic topics in broadly comprehended area of information science.

References

Bibexcel free-ware for academic non-profit use program. URL:http://www8.umu.se/inforsk/Bibexcel (1.03.2010.)

He, Qin (1999). Knowledge Discovery Through Co-Word Analysis. Library Trends, Vol. 48, No. 1. Summer 1999, pp. 133-159.

Pajek - open source program for visualization and clustering; freely available for academic use at http://vlado.fmf. Program studija Odsjeka za informacijske znanosti uni-lj.si/pub/networks/pajek/ (1.03.2010.)

. Odsjek za informacijske znanosti Filozofskog fakulteta Sveučilišta u Zagrebu. Zagreb, 2005. URL: http://www.ffzg.hr/programi/preddiplomski.html (16.03.2010.)

Saracevic, Tefko (1999). Information Science. Journal of the American Society for Information Science. Vol. 50 No. (12):1051–1063,

Težak, Božo (1969). Informacione znanosti i službe: njihova struktura, odnosi i politika – Information sciences and Services: Components, Relationships and Politics. // Informatologia Yugoslavica. Vol. 1, No. 1/4 , str. 13-31.

Težak, Božo (1971). Informatika – ime za zbunjujući ili razjašnjavajući koncept – Informatics – the Name of Confusing or Clearing Concept. // Infomratologia Yugoslavica. Vol. 3, No. 1/4, str. 1-13.

Tuđman, Miroslav (2007). Profesor dr. Božo Težak i razvoj informacijske znanosti. // Profesor Božo Težak, lučonoša znanosti / uredila Đurđica Težak i sur. Zagreb: Hrvatska sveučilišna naklada, str. 257-271.

Satisfaction and Relevance of Libraries and Technology in Ukraine and Romania

Svetlana Kolesnik and Katie Sheketoff

International Research & Exchanges Board (IREX), USA

Abstract: This presentation will address the results of national public opinion surveys conducted in Ukraine and Romania by the Global Libraries programs, implemented by IREX. The surveys assess national library visitation rates across demographic groups, satisfaction with the library and librarians, information search and information literacy patterns, and ICT familiarity and skills. The results of these surveys form a key basis for national and local advocacy and outreach efforts on behalf of libraries, and the surveys will be repeated in 2011 and 2013 to assess changes. The Global Libraries programs in Ukraine and Romania, funded by the Bill & Melinda Gates Foundation, aim to help libraries better serve their communities through training and technology.
Keywords: Ukraine, Romania, impact assessment, national survey, library satisfaction, technology

1. Introduction

Access to information is an essential component of development in today's globalized society. In Romania and Ukraine, more than 70% of the population lack access to the internet. While these countries have made rapid economic advances over the last two decades, libraries have been largely left behind and, as a result, millions are left without critical access to information. With the right kind of investment and attention, however, public libraries can be the link that connects people from all backgrounds with the information they need.

Through the Global Libraries programs in Romania and Ukraine, public libraries are becoming a common space where citizens can come together, inform their lives, and contribute to community discourse. The programs, funded by the Bill & Melinda Gates Foundation and implemented by the International Research & Exchanges Board (IREX), aim to improve people's lives by dramatically increasing public access to information—equipping public libraries with computers, training librarians, and strengthening the voice of the library sector.

In November 2009 – February 2010, IREX, in cooperation with the Kyiv International Institute of Sociology (KIIS) in Ukraine and the Center for Urban and Regional Sociology (CURS) in Romania, conducted two national public opinion surveys of citizens. The surveys assess national library visitation rates across demographic groups, satisfaction with the library and librarians, information search and information literacy patterns, and ICT familiarity and skills. The results of these surveys form a key basis for national and local advocacy and outreach efforts on behalf of libraries, and the surveys will be repeated in 2011 and 2013 to assess changes.

New Trends in Qualitative and Quantitative Methods in Libraries
A. Katsirikou and C. H. Skiadas (eds)
© *World Scientific Publishing Co (pp. 393-398)*

2. Methodology
In each country, IREX developed a survey tool to measure citizen's perceptions of the library and their community, use of information and information literacy patterns, and usage and familiarity with computers and the internet. The surveys were developed in cooperation with KIIS (Ukraine), CURS (Romania), and several international library impact professionals. The surveys were pretested with representative communities, and subsequently adjusted for miscommunication, unclear phrasing, and cultural miscommunication.

Survey Tool
The surveys in both countries differed slightly based on cultural contexts, but covered the same issues and asked many similar questions. In Ukraine, the survey consisted of 23 substantive questions and 8 demographical questions, several of which were multi-part questions. The Romanian survey consisted of 24 substantive questions and 11 demographical questions. The final versions of the survey tool can be found at http://www.irex.org/programs/gl/library.asp.

Sampling
In Ukraine, the survey targeted people 14 years of age and older. The sample was stratified by administrative units of Ukraine: 24 oblasts, Autonomous Republic of Crimea (ARC), and Kyiv city. Each stratum was divided into substrata on the basis of type of settlement – urban or rural.

In Romania, the survey targeted people 15 years of age and older, and was split into two parts: one 800-person national sample, and a 400-person sample of only library visitors. The 800-person sample was stratified by the eight development regions and milieu of residence (urban/rural areas), and was representative for major social demographic characteristics, such as gender and age. The 400-person sample of library visitors was similarly stratified.

Survey Implementation
In person interviews were held with 2530 respondents residing in rural and urban areas of Ukraine, and 1200 in person interviews were held in Romania.

Results were checked and tested by both survey companies, and confirmed by IREX staff. In Romania, the sample error margin is +/- 3.5% with a 95% level of trust. In Ukraine, the theoretical sample error (without design effect) does not exceed 2% with a level of trust of 95%.

3. Ukraine Results
23.6% of Ukrainian visit libraries to satisfy their information needs at least once a year. The most frequently used services are checking out books (18.7%), and reading reference materials in the library reading hall (8.7%). The least used services are checking out multi-media (video, DVD, audio CDs), using the internet, and working on PC (1.2%). However, only 4% of the Ukrainian public libraries currently offer access to Internet as a library service (Бібліотечна Україна в цифрах, 2007–2008).

87.6% of library users are generally satisfied with their public library and the unsatisfied patrons constitute only 1.5% of all library users. User satisfaction is considerably higher in urban areas than in rural areas.

There are two major groups of library visitors: "students" and the "mature book readers". A typical "student" is a 14-26 year old Internet user, with some higher education and a higher informational literacy score. A typical "mature book reader" is a 45-59 year old woman with vocational school level of education, lower informational literacy score and lower income. The mature book reader checks out books more often than any other services.

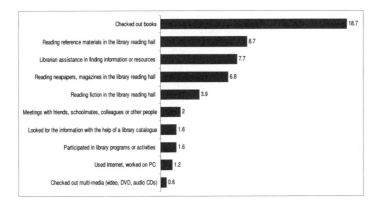

The national survey failed to provide a clear answer to a question "why people do not visit libraries". Although the public libraries are the least used source of information in Ukraine, the main causes for non-visiting libraries are lack of time, absence of such necessity and an inconvenient library location.

32.3% of respondents admitted that they never visited a public library. Most frequent non-users of public libraries are people who are over 60 years old, respondents with lowest levels of education, and the unemployed.

26.7% of the Ukrainian population believes that public library should be a place where one can find new and interesting books to read which shows somewhat conservative vision of population of the role of libraries. Only 6.1% of the Ukrainian population believes that public libraries should be a place where people may access the internet for free.

59.9% of the Ukrainian population has never used the internet. Younger people, men, urban citizens, students and working specialists, as well as people with higher levels of education are more likely to be internet users than older people, women, villagers, unemployed (or employed with low qualification job) and people with lower levels of education.

Most frequently Ukrainians use the internet at home (24.9% - at their own home; 12.2% at home of their friends and/or relatives) and at work (11.9%).

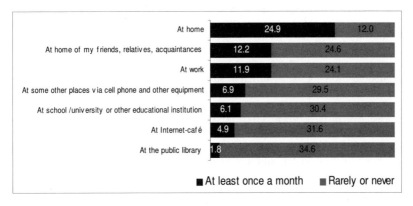

According the survey results, the younger respondents more often use the internet for recreation, while people aged 30-44 more often use the internet for public activity and business as well as for making purchases.

The internet is used mostly by urban population (43% of urban residents are internet users) compared with the rural population (27.7%), and largely by people who have higher education (36%). 51.1% of internet users are 14-29 years old, 32.1% are 30-44 years old, and 13.1% of internet users are 45-59 years old. Only 3.7% of users are 60+ years old. Overall level of internet penetration in Ukraine is 36.5%. Additionally, 16.2% of the population have access to Internet via their friends and relatives. Internet penetration increases with the increase of income. Penetration among the higher income group (Hrv 6000+) is 83.5%.

For 80.7% of users the internet is important (very important or rather important) in their everyday life. 76.3% maintained that if they would fully lose access to the internet it would be a problem for them. The most frequently gained benefits are communication, fulfillment of tasks connected with work and learning news.

Only 1.8% of respondents use the internet in libraries at least once a month. 73.8% of them are people who live in urban areas and 26.2% live in rural areas. The majority of those who use the internet in libraries reside in Western regions of Ukraine (47%) and the minority of public library internet users comes from the Eastern regions of Ukraine (5.4%). This correlates with the numbers of library attendance – people in Western regions of Ukraine visit libraries more often than people residing in the East of Ukraine.

People who use the internet in libraries tend not to use it elsewhere. The same observation was made about the people who use the internet at work.

The data analysis has shown that younger people are more willing to attend free computer and internet course in public libraries (61.5% of respondents who are 14-29 years old). 50.3% of respondents aged 40-44, 34% of respondents aged 45-59, and only 13.2% of respondents who are 60+ years old said they would attend free computer and internet courses in libraries.

4. Romania Results. 16% of Romanian citizens have visited a library within the last year. Level of education correlates strongly with library visitation. 36.7% of library users, compared to 30.5% in the national sample, have graduated from high school, and 23.1% users, compared to 18.9% nationally, are university graduates.

Similar to Ukraine, internet usage is a strong indicator for library visitation. The use of the internet is much more frequent in the families of library users than nationally (70% compared to 58%). Additionally, going to the library is learned in the family: 61% of library users have family members that have also visited libraries, compared to 34% at the national level.

Informational literacy—defined in this study as overreliance on one source of data and double-checking data—differed strongly along social and economic lines. "Patient" searchers, who searched through multiple sources of data, were usually ages 25-34, among those who: have university education; use the internet; public library services; live in large towns (100-200,000); in the North-East region, North-West regions, or Bucharest; and are part of the highest income quintile. Those who give up easy are mainly male, with elementary education, living in rural areas. Library users were more likely to check information reported in newspapers and on the internet (58% of library users compared to the average of 39% in the national sample).

Women, those with higher education, internet users, and library users are more likely to ask for help if they are unable to find information. Inhabitants of large towns (over 200,000 inhabitants) are the most reluctant to ask for help.

The main services provided by the public library are: checking out books (30-31%), help from the librarians, use of the reading hall.

The mostly requested activities in public libraries refer to methods to find information about high schools and universities, where to find appropriate medical advice, information about the labour market, about banking services and cultural activities. These activities reflect the concrete needs of the communities where the public library conducts its activity.

Additionally, the main services requested were the internet and computers. Except for printing services within the library, other requests focus on infrastructure developments, including construction or reconstruction of the reading hall, heating, proper furniture, equipment of exhibition rooms, video rooms, clubs, and places where one can drink coffee or tea. Special attention should also be given to the children, including those with disabilities, who come to the library.

	(cumulated) agreement in the national sample	(cumulated) agreement in the users sample
Public libraries should be a place where people may meet and share their experience and information with the others.	63.1%	60.5%
Public libraries should be a place where I can find new and interesting books to read.	94.1%	99.2%
Public libraries should be a place where I can find information about a hobby, skill or other personal interest.	77.8%	86.3%
Public libraries should be a place where I can learn about a legal, social or political issue, such as voting, taxes, laws, government forms, and others.	50.5%	56.2%
Public libraries should be a place where one may access Internet for free	73.8%	85.3%
Public libraries should be a place to go when I need help finding a job.	35.9%	45.2%

The main reasons called upon by the subjects who had not been to the library for at least one year is lack of time (24.8%). Not being interested in reading is called upon by 20.1% of the respondents of the national survey.

58% of Romanians have used internet in the last month, while 38% have never used the internet. However, 85% of Romanian library users have used the internet in the last month, and only 12% have never used the internet.

5. Conclusions

Visitation rates in both countries are extremely low. In contrast, 68% of Americans have a library card, and 76% have visited their library in the past year (ALA 2008). Countries in similar situations also have low rates, but not to the same extent as Ukraine and Romania: in Latvia, 36% of the population visited libraries in 2007 (Marketing and public opinion research centre 2007), 29% of the Polish population visited libraries in 2008 (MillwardBrown 2008), and 41% of Finnish citizens borrowed books or multimedia materials in 2008 (Finnish Public Library Statistics 2008).

Despite the low visitation rates, satisfaction with libraries is very high; in Ukraine, 95% of library users are satisfied. To the contrary, in the US, 68% of those with library cards are satisfied with their library (ALA 2008). However, this statistic is likely misleading: so many library users are satisfied with their libraries because their expectations of what a library can provide are low.

For those who do not visit libraries, neither the Ukraine nor the Romania survey were able to identify concrete responses. A response of "I do not have time" or "I am not interested in reading" shows that libraries have not sufficiently created public demand for their services nor demonstrated their relevance. In order to increase visitation rates, Ukrainian and Romanian libraries must both develop relevant services for their communities and advertise those services so that nonusers understand the new services in the library.

In both countries, internet users were significantly more likely to also be library users. Younger citizens are also more likely to be library users, as well as those in school and with higher levels of education. Library users in both country scored higher on information literacy tests. The challenge for libraries in these countries, then will be to draw in those who do not fit the typical user profile.

Surprisingly, many respondents in both countries responded that they would not attend a free computer course in their library, or would not use computers for free in their library. This group will be the most difficult to bring in: generally older, this population is likely apprehensive about the potential of computers—they were also the most likely to respond that there was nothing useful on the internet for them.

Romania and Ukraine face a challenging road ahead to increase relevance and modernity of public libraries, but the there remain many positive indicators for change. In Ukraine, most library users both check out books and use other services— a sign that adding new services, such as computers, would not be unreasonable. In Romania, 74% of the population believes that public libraries should be a place where one can access the internet for free.

In both countries, librarians are willing and ready to make the necessary changes to bring their libraries into the twenty-first century, and Biblionet and Bibliomist aim to guide these librarians towards this goal.

References

Бібліотечна Україна в цифрах (2007–2008).
    http://profy.nplu.org/articles.php?lng=uk&pg=1213.
ALA Library Fact Sheet 6.
    http://ala.org/ala/professionalresources/libfactsheets/alalibraryfactsheet06.cfm.
    Accessed 21 March 2010.
Marketing and public opinion research centre (2007). "Attitude towards Libraries: Survey of Latvia's Population." SKDS: Latvia.
MillwardBrown (2008). "Public libraries – opinion, use, needs: Rural population and library users survey." Information Society Development Foundation: Warsaw, Poland.
Finnish Public Library Statistics (2008). "Basic Statistics."
    http://tilastot.kirjastot.fi/en-gb/basicstatistics.aspx?AreaKey=Y2008T1N1.
    Accessed 21 March 2010.

Library Performance Management in Rio de Janeiro, Brazil: Applying DEA to a Sample of University Libraries in 2006-2007

Frederico A. de Carvalho[1], Marcelino José Jorge[2], Marina Filgueiras Jorge[3], Mariza Russo[4] and Nysia Oliveira de Sá[5]

[1]UFRJ – FACC, Portugal, [2]IPEC- FIOCRUZ, Portugal, [3]IPEC- FIOCRUZ, Portugal, [4]UFRJ – FACC, Portugal, [5]UFRJ – FACC, Portugal

Abstract: The paper assesses the performance of a sample of 37 libraries pertaining to a federal university in Rio de Janeiro, Brazil. Referring to the years 2006-2007, the assessment is based upon the estimation of a DEA model that generates both efficiency scores and optimal changes in current allocations for each year. Markovian analysis indicates that the percent of efficient libraries will likely decrease in the long run. One can assert that efficiency analysis enhances the assessment of library performance by providing both relative positions and potential improvements along time. The present case served only as an empirical excuse and no special difficulty is to be expected when trying to replicate it in other library systems.

Keywords: Library management, performance assessment, efficiency analysis, data envelopment analysis.

1. Introduction

When one considers the characteristics of the decision-making process in the so-called managerial public administration model, it can be concluded that (a) in terms of managing by results, the extent to which efficacy varies may be taken as an indicator of organizational adaptation to change and (b) this adaptation can be measured in terms of the evolution of both social efficacy and efficiency scores along time. Therefore, systematic performance assessment, through monitoring and evaluation, contributes to improve management since it produces the information needed to understand the reasons for success and failure.

In this paper, efficiency scores for the years 2006 and 2007 are firstly calculated and compared for a sample of 37 academic libraries pertaining to a public university in Rio de Janeiro. In order to reach the research objective one more step is accomplished in order to determine which quantitative actions might be proposed to managers so that a library eventually classified as "inefficient" could be displaced towards the group of efficient units.

The text is organized in five sections. In the second section the elements composing the analytical framework on which the research is grounded are presented, followed by the methodology adopted, in the third section. Results are presented in the fourth section, whereas some conclusive comments are gathered in the last section.

2. Background

2.1 Performance management in public organizations

The definition and maintenance of a system of efficiency and efficacy indicators for public organizations present challenges and difficulties associated to three traits that

New Trends in Qualitative and Quantitative Methods in Libraries
A. Katsirikou and C. H. Skiadas (eds)
© *World Scientific Publishing Co (pp. 399-407)*

characterize such organizations and that, at the same time, illustrate the complexity of their study, namely:

a) Public organizations use multiple inputs and work under budget constraints, so that it makes full sense to evaluate the use of resources that are both diversified and limited;

b) Public organizations provide services for which seldom exist "market prices" that would signal "optimal" allocations of resources, and

c) Public organizations are multi-purpose and multi-product endeavors, so that there are not only difficulties for result measurement, but also for tackling the issue of suboptimization due to coordination gaps.

In the day- by- day of public administration, all those complexities often converge as to intimidate managers to the extent that their belief on the possibility of a satisfactory analytic approach to support performance assessment for public organizations becomes doubtful. Accordingly, those managers end up resorting to the seduction of macro arguments, then forgetting their own managerial needs in meso or micro terms (Vakkuri, 2003).

2.2 Performance management in public libraries

Public libraries – including general, university and school libraries across government levels - present the same three traits previously highlighted:

a) they use multiple inputs - such as employees, collections of printed or audiovisual material, and a physical area - and operate under budget constraint;

b) in general, "market prices" don't exist for some of the multiple products and services provided, in spite of the enormous development experienced for some years now by sectors producing "informational services "; and

c) they are multi-purpose organizations, their mission including themes of high social meaning, beside typical micro-organizational questions.

Successive reforms on educational systems have never prioritized reading nor libraries. Hence, in spite of the full social meaning of libraries, it is evident that not even its prominent role was enough to justify an appropriate allocation of resources. Until the time he wrote, Suaiden (2000) argued, there were not indicators proving the efficiency of public libraries in Brazil. As far as efficacy is concerned, he points out (Id., p. 56) that it was only in the 1970s that user research gained momentum. Stressing on the idea that proximity was the basic requirement for library use in many countries, one of the answers to non-use took shape in the slogan - "in each municipality a library ". What should be done in the case of demographic and territorial characteristics such as those prevailing in Brazil?

In technical jargon, services, products and collections have quite specific characteristics in the case of public academic libraries. Due to these specific characteristics and spatial scope, much simpler should be the management of public academic libraries, object of this paper. In Brazil, the recognition of academic libraries' importance is not new and today it is practically unanimous, even in institutional terms (see e. g. Lemos, 2001, p. 1). However, in spite of their much more specific attributes, public academic libraries are also confronted with the aforementioned three analytical issues. In fact, there persist both micro- and macro-organizational questions. Even though these managerial challenges are much more restricted in scope, they are far from trivial, even for academic libraries in developed countries. For example, Cullen and Nagata (2008, p. 163) state that, in Japan, notwithstanding being well-equipped and recognized as an important support to national research capability, academic libraries still reflect, in several ways, the strongly bureaucratic culture of that country.

Following international trends (see, e. g. , Balagué, 2007), focus on efficacy is also much more common in Brazil, both in what refers to user studies (see e. g. Cullen, 2001; Aabo, 2005), as well as to quality research (Amboni, 2002; Rebello, 2004; Valls and Vergueiro, 2006).

According to Favret (2000, p. 341), in the United Kingdom there exists a long tradition of efficiency measurement and assessment in public libraries, especially in terms of the so-called *benchmarking approach*, presented and discussed by the Favret himself and by Laeven and Smit (2003). In Brazil, in contrast to international trends, research on efficiency assessment in public libraries is scant. The *benchmarking approach*, although previously reviewed by Suaiden and Araújo Jr. (2001), only later has come to be effectively applied (Maciel Filho *et al.*, 2004). In addition to *benchmarking*, the international literature includes other alternatives for organizational performance analysis (Aabo, 2005; Holt, 2007; Maciel Filho *et al.*, 2007).

As long as the public manager is concerned, those approaches mostly suffer from an extremely perverse limitation: due to their focus on each organizational unit separately, they hinder systemic comparison among organizational units.

Stemming from a long (see Emrouznejad; Parker; Tavares, 2008) but much more ignored analytical tradition, the pioneer Mary Susan Easun (1992; 1994) and later Chen (1997a, 1997b), and Vitaliano (1998) can be considered the precursors in the application of DEA to library assessment. Ever since the international literature keeps growing, especially in the case of academic libraries (Reichmann and Sommersguter-Reichmann, 2006; Stancheva and Angelova, 2004). In the Brazilian case, only a single application of DEA to library assessment has been identified, due to Pereira and Bueno (2005).

2.3 Efficiency as an organizing principle

In association to the efficiency principle there corresponds an approach to organizational analysis whose basic feature refers to "optimally using resources to produce goods or services". In this simple framework it is equally accepted as virtuous any productive process allowing to *produce more output with the same resources* or to *produce the same output with less resources*. This is the basic principle of efficiency, undeniably attractive for any organization having to employ limited resources, particularly for public organizations.

3. Method

3.1. Data envelopment analysis

The efficiency of productive units can be calculated by means of a deterministic production frontier whose construction process is implemented by formulating and solving a linear programming problem (Coelli, Rao and Battese, 1998). This procedure, known as Data Envelopment Analysis (DEA), was initially introduced in the literature by Charnes, Cooper and Rhodes (1978, 1981) and later modified by Banker, Charnes and Cooper (1984). The most important difference between those two models is the possibility of treating scale economies. The Banker, Charnes and Cooper model (BCC model), used in the present paper, allows to calculate a deterministic production frontier with variable returns to scale, whereas Charnes, Cooper and Rhodes model (CCR model) assumes constant returns to scale.

DEA may be applied under varied forms, but it is always used to assess productive efficiency of individual Decision Making Units (DMUs) that use multiple inputs to obtain multiple outputs. Therefore it has been particularly used to evaluate several types of public organizations, such as schools, hospitals and military units or systems, each unit being properly understood as examples of " complex organizations" (Emrouznejad, Parker and Tavares, 2008). This flexibility in the use of DEA comes from the fact that no previous definition of a functional form for the production function is needed, in contrast to parametric approaches to library assessment (Vitaliano, 1997).

Among DEA features that are of interest of the DEA for the assessment of public organizations operating under budget constraints one may highlight the flexibility of the method. It is worth pointing out that the direct use of flexibly measured inputs and outputs discards the need to define or redefine "performance indicators" such as those frequently found in the literature.

The computed efficiency values are not absolute, as they take into account the relative positions among several DMUs. By so doing DMUs located in the frontier will be "relatively more efficient" and the extent to which an inefficient unit deviates with respect to that empirically observed frontier would in turn be its inefficiency measure. In this paper version 2.1 of DEAP® - *Data Envelopment Analysis (Computer) Program* was used to calculate the production frontier by means of DEA. The computed models also provide production targets – to be called operation plans - to be reached by inefficient productive units in order to become efficient (Marinho, 2001).

Since two years of observations were available, it was possible to investigate the temporary evolution of the evolutionary process that separates the efficient units from the inefficient ones. Assuming the Markovian hypothesis (Kemeny and Snell, 1972), expressed as the transition matrix between "efficient" and "inefficient" states along the two years, and using the concept of equilibrium distribution, the long term percent distribution of the units between these two states can be determined (Id., p. 131).

3.2. Data collection

The population is formed by the group of units composing an integrated system of libraries in a public university in Rio de Janeiro. Access and time issues associated to data collection led to consider a sample of 37 libraries, representing some 90% of the universe.

Data were collected from the managerial database created and maintained in the university as an integrated system with the purpose of monitoring performance. Following Pereira and Bueno (2005) and considering available data, two years were chosen - 2006 and 2007 – for data collection. For each year, three inputs - namely, *Number of employees*, *Area* (in square meters) and *Volumes* - and four outputs - *Consultations*, *Loans*, *Enrollments*, and *User Traffic* - were considered. Furthermore, some demographic data were collected (for instance, library's age in years or geographical location).

4. Results

4.1. Library classification according to efficiency

The main result of the paper, empirically supporting all the others, appear in Table 1: the efficiency scores, for each library and each year, computed from a product-oriented, variable returns to scale DEA model. Since by definition the efficient scores are all equal to 1, the table shows only the inefficient scores in some of the two years, decreasingly ordered for 2006. According to the theoretical model, scores equal to 1 represent (relatively) efficient units. The (relatively) inefficient units receive scores below 1. Table 1 also displays the time change in efficiency, indicating, on the one hand, that there were both efficient (16) and inefficient (14) units that stayed in the same state along the two years. On the other hand, there were changes from one condition to another between 2006 and 2007: 4 efficient units in 2006 turned into inefficient in 2007, whereas 3 units went the opposite way in the same period.

If one considers "efficient" and "inefficient" as two possible states for any library and then makes use of the data in Table 1, the matrix P of (yearly) transition probabilities between states can be written. Adopting the Markovian hypothesis that, over time, the transition probabilities between states depend only on the previous state, we can compute the long run percent distribution of the libraries in each of the two states (Kemeny and Snell, 1972, p. 131). The long run distribution is the line vector π whose elements add to 1 and satisfying the matrix equation $\pi P = \pi$, so that: π_E (percent of Efficient) = 46.9%; π_{NE} (percent of Inefficient) = 53.1%.

Table 1: Scores and efficiency *ranking* – 2006 and 2007

UNIT	SCORES 2006	RANK 2006	SCORES 2007	RANK 2007
18	0.807	23	1.000	1
22	0.680	25	1.000	1
34	0.626	27	1.000	1
13	1.000	1	0.945	20
31	1.000	1	0.921	21
11	0.384	33	0.863	22
20	1.000	1	0.820	23
5	1.000	1	0.679	24
32	0.548	28	0.650	25
24	0.847	21	0.646	26
25	0.466	31	0.624	27
30	0.775	24	0.574	28
35	0.543	29	0.560	29
6	0.640	26	0.506	30
4	0.401	32	0.381	31
15	0.328	34	0.370	32
28	0.319	35	0.320	33
7	0.496	30	0.241	34
19	0.842	22	0.121	35
2	0.145	36	0.115	36
26	0.010	37	0.017	37

4.2. Efficient operation plans

The yearly allocative changes that allow moving each inefficient unit to an efficient position are shown in Table 2 for the year 2006; the case for 2007 is identical.

It is worth pointing out that there are many indications of change in the amounts of inputs that suggest the optimality of reducing them while increasing efficiency; this kind of conclusion would hardly be reached in the absence of a DEA model. Staff reductions prevail in the table; in the public service this may simply mean that it is sufficient to relocate employees and increase output all the same. In order to get rid of public managers' eventual discomforts in such situations, it is worth reminding that this relocation can be internal, given that not all internal activities are related to the production of the four services here adopted as *outputs*. Another outstanding feature of the tables is that there is a lot of ways whereby output increase is possible.

Indications of volume decrease, technically called disposal, deserve attention because disposals are not a simple matter of numerical decrease since there are collections that just cannot be broken or interrupted, as well as there are volumes and titles that must be maintained for some specific reason. Anyway, the findings point to the fact that managers need be alert and perhaps more proactive in their disposal initiatives.

The comparison with actual data for 2007 shows that the adoption of input changes consistent with the signaling from computed operation plans was practically inexistent. Actually there were many cases of a significant increase between the two years, very likely thwarting the search for efficiency.

Table 2: Operation plans – 2006

UNIT	ENROLLM T _2006	LOANS _2006	CONSUL T _2006	TRAFFI C _2006	EMPLO Y _2006	AREA _2006	VOLUME S _2006
2	1156	3470	7334	57638	-1	0	0
4	2027	21821	16189	79024	0	-1996	-11160
6	1440	8752	9687	54047	0	-19	-48235
7	1265	2866	5346	29325	0	0	-55046
11	1584	4200	6263	55316	-3	0	0
15	504	2979	7247	14416	-1	-98	0
18	108	264	551	14868	0	0	-1705
19	322	918	2043	4498	0	0	-7740
22	855	2910	4907	23276	-6	0	0
24	386	1297	9298	16247	0	0	-12400
25	905	3817	12086	66410	0	0	-10612
26	1408	4135	24122	49026	0	0	-22759
28	1228	4661	12370	74643	0	-21	0
30	369	2589	2869	18800	-6	0	0
32	879	2544	5889	87109	-3	-134	0
34	620	1039	2684	51074	-2	-458	0
35	609	1447	5548	41238	0	-523	-5012

5. Conclusions

Firstly, note that computed scores may be deemed as relatively "benevolent", since there are so many efficient units (20 and 19, in 2006 and 2007) as inefficient ones (17 and 18, in 2006 and 2007). This conclusion might have been made sharper if more contextual information had been gathered or introduced. For instance, if the sample includes some very singular units- e. g., a research library that doesn't make loans – then it is very likely that any other library providing loans would be ranked as efficient relative to the singular one. Anyway, although the exclusion of units from a sample of DMUs could improve the consistence of the exercise, it surely should not happen without the consent of the involved manager. In addition, to the extent that singular and nonsingular might be competing for the same budget, then the mix should be kept.

Upon adopting the Markovian hypothesis and computing the long-term percent distribution of libraries in each of two efficiency states, it can be concluded that there is a slight movement towards the increase of systemic inefficiency, if no initiative is taken in managerial terms.

Data and results reveal a high potential of overall increase in output. As argued by Pereira and Bueno (2005), the appropriateness of changes prescribed in optimal operation plans is guaranteed as they have been computed from actual data relating to observed performance of sampled units, as opposed to being based on either external data or proposals of intended action.

The allocative indications contained in the efficient operation plans were practically ignored in the sampled units. In comparison to observed data, there were no changes in inputs that might be considered similar to the signaling from computed plans. On the contrary, there were many cases of significant increases between the two years. Those results show that managers need to be alert against such perverse results.

The existence as well as the seemingly persistence of technical inefficiency among sampled libraries indicates the need for more studies tackling the issues of volume disposal and replacement, of developing and renewing collections and, especially, of human resource management both at the unit and the system levels. The use of Data Envelopment Analysis revealed a potentially useful instrument to support managers in the ranking and classification of libraries according to their performance while, at the same time, to supply quantitative targets for performance improvement in each unit pertaining to the system of public libraries in the selected university. Admittedly the present case served only as an empirical excuse so that no special difficulty is to be expected in terms of hindering its replication in other organizational systems in the public sector.

In terms of Brazilian literature and of national practices prevailing in the library sector, the present study confirmed the conclusion of Pereira and Bueno (2005) who stated that academic references to and practical evidences of modern performance management models are still lacking in public libraries, in contrast to actions and intentions of an essentially bureaucratic nature. In other words, it is likely that Brazilian public libraries remain linked to the paradigm of bureaucratic management, while still awaiting the implementation of genuinely managerial mechanisms and procedures.

References

Aabo, S., (2005). Valuing the benefits of public libraries. *Information Economics and Policy*, Vol. 17, No. 1, 175-198.

Amboni, N. F., (2002). *Qualidade em serviços*: dimensões para orientação e avaliação das bibliotecas universitárias federais brasileiras. Tese (Doutorado). Programa de Pós-graduação em Engenharia de Produção – UFSC. Florianópolis, SC, Brasil.

Balagué, N., (2007). Consolidando la calidad en las bibliotecas universitarias: evaluaciones, sellos, diplomas y certificaciones. *El Profesional de la Información*, Vol. 16, No. 4, 338-342.

Banker, R.; Charnes, A.; Cooper, W. W., (1984). Some models for estimating technical and scale inefficiencies in Data Envelopment Analysis. *Management Science*, 30, 1078-1092.

Charnes, A.; Cooper, W.; Rhodes, E., (1978). Measuring the efficiency of decision making units. *European Journal of Operational Research*, Vol. 2, No. 3, 429-444.

Chen, T., (1997a). A measurement of the resource utilization efficiency of university libraries. *International Journal of Production Economics*, Vol. 53, No. 1, 71-80.

_____, (1997b). An evaluation of the relative performance of university libraries in Taipei. *Library Review*, Vol. 46, No. 3, 190-201.

Coelli, T.; Rao, D. S. P.; Battese, G. E., (1998). *An introduction to efficiency and productivity analysis*. Kluwer, Boston, Mass.

Cullen, R., (2001). Perspectives on user satisfaction surveys. *Library Trends*, Vol. 49, No. 4, 662-682.

_____; Nagata, H., (2008). Academic libraries in Japan. *The Journal of Academic Librarianship*, Vol. 34, No. 2, 163-167.

Easun, M. S., (1992). Identifying efficiencies in resource management: an application of data envelopment analysis to selected school libraries in California. Ph.D. Thesis. School of Information, University of California – Berkeley, Berkeley, CA.

_____, (1994). Beginner's guide to efficiency measurement: an application of data envelopment analysis to selected school libraries in California. *School Library Media Quarterly*, Vol. 22, No. 2, 103-106.

Emrouznejad, A.; Parker, B.; Tavares, G., (2008). Evaluation of research in efficiency and productivity: a survey and analysis of the first 30 years of scholarly literature in DEA, *Socio-Economic Planning Sciences*, Vol. 42, No. 3, 151-157.

Favret, L., (2000). Benchmarking, annual library plans and best value: the implications for public libraries. *Library Management*, Vol. 21, No. 7, 340-348.

Holt, G. E., (2007). Communicating the value of your libraries. *The Bottom Line*, Vol. 20, No. 3, 119-124.

Kemeny, J. G.; Snell, J. L., (1972). *Mathematical Models in the Social Sciences*. The MIT Press, Cambridge, Mass.

Laeven, H.; Smit, A., (2003). A project to benchmark university libraries in The Netherlands. *Library Management*, Vol. 24, No. 6/7, 291-304.

Lemos, L. A. P., (2001). Biblioteca acadêmica: cliente ou usuário. *Biblos*, 13, 171-184.

Maciel Filho, A. R.; Aquino, M. C.; Soares, A. P.; Lyra, C. S., (2004). As melhores práticas administrativas: uma investigação empírica do Sistema das Bibliotecas Públicas Municipais do Estado de Pernambuco, *Informação e Sociedade: Estudos*, Vol. 14, No. 1, 129-144.

_____; _____; Farias, E. R.; Candido, P. M.; Moraes, A. P., (2007). Avaliação de bibliotecas: uma discussão de experiências empíricas recentes. *Informação e Sociedade: Estudos*, Vol. 17, No. 1, 53-62.

Marinho, A., (2001). *Estudo de eficiência em alguns hospitais públicos e privados com a geração de rankings*. Texto para Discussão, n. 794, IPEA, Rio de Janeiro, RJ. ()

Pereira, M.; Bueno, R., (2005). Estudo da eficiência produtiva das bibliotecas públicas de São Paulo no ano de 2002. *In*: Asamblea Anual del CLADEA, 38, 2005, *Anales*. CLADEA y Universidad de Chile, Santiago de Chile, CD-ROM.

Rebello, M. A. F. R., (2004). Avaliação da qualidade dos produtos/serviços de informação: uma experiência da biblioteca do Hospital Universitário da Universidade de São Paulo. *Revista Digital de Biblioteconomia e Ciência da Informação*, Vol. 2, No. 1, 80-100.

Reichmann, G.; Sommersguter-Reichmann, M., (2006). University library benchmarking: an international comparison using DEA. *International Journal of Production Economics*, Vol. 100, No. 1, 131-147.

Stancheva, N.; Angelova, V., (2004). Measuring the efficiency of university libraries using Data Envelopment Analysis. *In* INFORUM 2004 – Conference on Professional Information Resources, 10, *Proceedings*, Prague.

Suaiden, E. J., (2000) A biblioteca pública no contexto da sociedade de informação. *Ciência da Informação*, Vol. 20, No. 2, 52-60.

_____; Araújo Jr., R. H. A., (2001). Biblioteca pública e a excelência nos produtos e serviços: a técnica do benchmarking. *Informação e Sociedade: Estudos*, Vol. 11, No. 1, 15-34.

Valls, V. M.; Vergueiro, W. C. S., (2006) A gestão da qualidade em serviços de informação no Brasil: uma nova revisão de literatura, de 1997 a 2006, *Perspectivas em Ciência da Informação*, Vol. 11, No. 1, 118-137.

Vakkuri, J., (2003). Research techniques and their use in managing non-profit organizations: an illustration of DEA analysis in NPO environments. *Financial Accountability and Management*, Vol. 19, No. 3, 243-263.

Vitaliano, D. F., (1997). X-inefficiency in the public sector: the case of libraries. *Public Finance Review*, Vol. 25, No. 6, 629-643.

_____, (1998). Assessing public library efficiency using Data Envelopment Analysis. *Annals of Public and Cooperative Economics*, Vol. 9, No. 1, 107-122.

A Grounded Analysis of the Use of Public Libraries in Appalachia by Non-Residents

Sheri Ross

Master of Library and Information Science Program, Department of Information Management, Saint Catherine University, 2004 Randolph Ave., St Paul, MN 55105, USA

Abstract: Because of municipal, state, and federal budget constraints, public libraries increasingly need to demonstrate their value to their communities. They often provide evidence of the demand for and use of services by their tax-paying residents. This project explores the use of public libraries by non-residents and how public library directors perceive the value of non-resident use for their libraries and communities. In-depth interviews were conducted with eighteen library directors throughout the Appalachian region of the eastern United States. A grounded analysis of these interviews using NVivo 8 software reveals a variety of non-resident user types and policies and approaches to offering services to non-resident users. Potential directions for future research into the relationship between non-residents, public libraries and the community business sector are suggested.
Keywords: Public libraries, rural libraries, non-resident user

1. Context

Public sector services have experienced pressure to prove their worth through measurable impacts on the community. Libraries are often perceived by decision-makers to be non-essential public services and, as a result, are the first to experience budget cuts (Aabo, 2005). Using the contingent valuation approach to assess the value enjoyed by citizens, the British Library showed that it generates value around 4.4 times the level of its public funding (British Libraries, 2004). Florida Public Libraries conducted a return on investment study and determined that libraries play an important role in the overall economic development of the state with a total direct economic impact on the state economy of $6 billion a year (Missingham, 2005). While these studies are valuable, they look primarily to the direct value of their libraries' services to the resident community, neglecting the indirect economic benefits, such as the potential commerce generated by non-residents who are attracted to the community to use library services.

Each year, approximately 2,000 people attempt to thru-hike the Appalachian Trail. In 2007, I was one of these. I have many memories of the experience, but as a librarian, the memories that stand out most are those of the libraries that served the hikers. When a hiker arrives in a trail town, they are dirty, hungry, and anxious for information about their friends, family, and the civilized world. They immediately seek out a shower, a grocery store and a library; though, not necessarily in that order. Often, the decision about whether to stop and visit a trail town is determined by the facilities available there. If a hiker knows that the library will be closed on a given day, or that the library doesn't have public internet access, he or she may decide to continue on to the next town. Appropriate library services to this non-resident

New Trends in Qualitative and Quantitative Methods in Libraries
A. Katsirikou and C. H. Skiadas (eds)
© *World Scientific Publishing Co (pp. 409-416)*

population attract consumers to the community. To investigate whether these libraries recognized the importance of their services to non-resident users, I invited library directors to participate in interviews and conducted a grounded analysis of their responses.

The libraries in the sample are largely located in small towns or cities surrounded by rural areas. According to most of the respondents, the communities are economically sustained by tourism and retail commerce. Visitors to the communities demonstrate heterogeneous characteristics and use the libraries for a variety of purposes. Library personnel in these trail towns recognize the special needs of their various non-resident users and have developed policies over time that reflect the unique contexts in which they engage with this segment of their customer base. Characteristics of non-resident users, such as the duration of their visit and proximity of their permanent residence to the library determine policies that inform services, such as the use of circulating collections and to a lesser degree, the use of the internet.

While it was evident that these library directors had given a great deal of consideration to the needs of their non-resident users, most had not considered assessing non-resident use and the potential positive impacts that it has on their primary resident community. In a few cases, the resident community explicitly acknowledged the value that the library provides through supporting tourism and providing a hospitable environment. Other communities recognized that the library, along with other service establishments, was a "magnet," drawing residents from nearby municipalities. In one instance, however, non-residents were required to pay a high fee equivalent to the estimated tax paid by each resident, suggesting that the resident community did not regard library services to non-residents to be a means of promoting local commerce.

2. Process

Motivated to better understand the library services available to non-residents, whether these services attracted visitors to the community, and how these services to visitors were perceived by the community, I began the study. Using the *Appalachian Trail Thru-Hiker's Companion*, I identified a purposive sample of 25 libraries located in communities close to or directly on the Appalachian Trail (Appalachian Long Distance Hikers Association, 2010). In a purposive sample, the informants have a range of characteristics relevant to the study (Gorman & Clayton, 1997). I contacted the directors of these libraries and invited them to participate in a telephone interview regarding their services to non-residents. Eighteen responded affirmatively and interviews were conducted over the next several months. Respondents were asked to comment on their legal, organizational, and funding structures; their services to non-residents and the policies that support them; and the perceptions of non-residents by library staff, residents and local businesses. Interviews were transcribed and imported into NVivo 8.

To round out my understanding of these libraries and the communities they serve, I consulted the U.S. Department of Education's (2005) National Center for Educational Statistics (NCES) data for public libraries, and the U.S. Census Bureau's (2007) North American Industry Classification System (NAICS) data. As there are no NAICS categories that specifically address tourism, the sectors that were considered were Arts, Entertainment and Recreation; Accommodation and Food Services; Forestry, Fishing, Agriculture, and Hunting; and Retail Trade. This data was added to the project in NVivo 8, which has the capacity to create cases with attribute variables that can then be queried along with the qualitative data.

One of the first things I discovered is that "non-resident" is a much broader category than initially imagined. While the study began as an investigation into services for and perceptions of long-distance hikers, it soon encompassed services to a spectrum of non-resident library users from forest service interns to visiting grandchildren to commuting workers to genealogists. Additionally, data to support my original interest in the communities' perceptions of the libraries' services to non-residents was not forthcoming. In most cases, the respondents had never considered this aspect of non-resident service; it had never been an issue for their governing board, funding authorities or their resident users. They were more interested in relating their experiences with non-resident users and the services and policies in place to accommodate them. This, then, became the data that primarily informed the grounded analysis.

In order to generate initial categories, coding began with microanalysis of the transcripts. After creating more than 75 free nodes, patterns began to emerge and I was able to group concepts together into tree nodes. After trying out several arrangements under multiple labels, I settled on two broad categories: Non-resident Users, subcategorized by Purpose of Visit to the Community, and Library Services for Non-resident Users, subcategorized by Type of Service. As open coding proceeded, a number of properties for each category stood out as being important to the respondents. These properties did not always lend themselves to being understood along a dimensional range, however. For instance, for the category of Library Services, while the property of Policy might nicely be described along the dimension of Equity (same as residence service…different from resident service), the property of Service Philosophy did not present a dimension so cleanly structured.

Inductive theorizing proceeds by intuiting concepts and formulating them into explanatory schemes (Strauss and Corbin, 1998). Using NVivo's query tool, I began to explore potential relationships. Through the process of theoretical sampling, certain Non-resident Users properties, such as Duration of Visit to the Community revealed alignment with certain Library Services properties, such as Cost. Linking these categories at the level of properties and dimensions is known as axial coding; though, in NVivo, there is no need for additional coding as such, as matrix queries can be run to determine references with common coding. After the determination of a number of axial relationships, I then began selective coding of the transcripts, to ensure that all of the potential references to the identified properties and dimensions would be included in the analysis. Of course, the research was not so neatly sequenced; grounded analysis is an iterative process and the importance or strength of certain categories, properties, dimensions and relationships evolve as the researcher becomes more tuned to the data.

3. Analysis

As mentioned previously, the first category that surfaced was type of Non-resident Users. This occurred during the interviewing phase before any analysis had begun. It was apparent during the first interview that my conception of non-resident was far too narrow, that not all non-residents were just "passing-through folks," and that I needed to take care not to lead my respondents to focus on one particular non-resident segment. Conversely, if respondents themselves tended to focus on one particular group, I probed them to broaden their responses. Six distinct types of non-resident users were identified during the first interview alone. During the initial briefing of subsequent interviews, I requested that all types of non-residents be considered when responding.

All references to a distinct type of non-resident user were identified during the open coding process. As I reviewed and considered these references, sub-categories of non-resident users according to their purpose for visiting the community emerged as shown in Figure 1. Potential properties and dimensions were also identified, many of which were not ultimately used in this analysis. The interview responses indicated that Library Services varied according to three primary non-resident characteristics: Distance of the Non-resident's Residence from the Library (within community... non-contiguous state), Duration of the Non-resident Visit (less than one day...more than two months), and Frequency of the Non-resident Visits to the Community (daily...one-time visit). These properties and dimensions were considered further after examining the services offered to non-residents.

Figure 1. Subcategories of Non-resident Library User According to Their Purpose for Visiting the Community

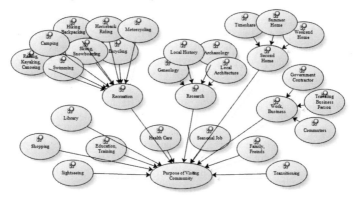

The libraries in this study offered a variety of services to non-residents, including the use of circulating and non-circulating collections, access to electronic subscriptions, computing and telecommunications, programs, meeting rooms, and a warm, dry, friendly environment in which to relax. Policies regarding Library Services were examined through the properties of Accessibility (no barriers...many barriers), Cost (free...expensive), and Equity (different from resident service...identical to resident service), among others. As was found in a survey of academic libraries regarding their services to unaffiliated users by Courtney (2003), "borrowing privileges are considerably more restricted than building access" and the onsite use of resources (p. 4).

Many of the respondents acknowledged that the primary reason that non-residents visit their libraries is to use the internet. In most instances, the policies in place regarding internet use (as well as other computing and telecommunication services) applied to all users, regardless of resident status. This was not always the case, however. For instance, one library had a multi-step process for permitting non-residents to use the internet, which entailed finding the reference desk, requesting the use of a computer, providing photo identification, reading the internet use policy, signing an acknowledgment that they understood the policy, being assigned a guest username and password, finding an open terminal, and logging in. A resident with a library card could simply sit down at an open terminal and log in with their library card number.

Library-as-place was the second most acknowledged reason that non-residents visited the libraries in the study, and again, the policies in place regarding the use of the library space applied to all users, regardless of resident status. Respondents were overwhelmingly proud of the welcoming environment they create for non-resident library users; personnel in these libraries interact with non-residents several times a day and recognize the importance of their role to provide visitors to their community with a positive experience. The following exchange exemplifies the kind of environment these libraries seek to provide.

Librarian: We did harbor some dogs that were with thru-hikers during the cold portion. And I'm a dog lover and I saw them shivering outside my office window.

Me: Oh!

Librarian: We invited them inside (since the library was closed to the public) and the dogs spent the day, basically in my office and in this area. We do allow dogs in the library.

Me: You do! That's wonderful!

Librarian: Yep - as long as they're well behaved. So, the hikers, we'll let them - I mean, they bring the dog in and as long - I mean, most of the dogs that are hiking are well behaved.

Me: Right.

Librarian: So they can come in and just hang out and we do have biscuits and a water dish. And, you know, we're pretty accommodating. We just ask that they leave their packs in sort of this vestibule area that we have because we're a little tight for space in the computer area. And, you know, just so people aren't tripping over packs.

Other phrases offered by respondents that characterize library-as-place include: comfortable seating – nice bathrooms – not trapped in (motel) room – big welcome sign – convenient – give mini-tour – restful area – hear their tales – grand piano – paperback exchange – friendly atmosphere – feel more like they are a part of our town – trail stories – a great way to spend a rainy day – develops community spirit – great big topographical maps – free box – air conditioning – trail angels – where are you from – provide transportation – washing facilities – fireplace. The personnel in these libraries were focused on creating an inviting environment for the visitors to their communities. Robertson (2006) noted that tourists often find refuge in public libraries where they can sit comfortably in the quiet, away from their hectic schedules. Librarians were particularly proud of the beauty and history of their library buildings, many of which lived such previous lives as a train station, a federal court room, a Universalist Church, a bank, and a department store. The newer libraries have been strategically situated near tourist services, such as public restrooms, ranger stations, and visitor centers. One library has even received a grant to design and build a facility that combines the library with the town's visitor center. The collocation of libraries with local government services, such as tourism facilities, can be a boon to a small library. This trend has been described as a rising phenomenon in Australia and has the impact of increasing library hours, staff and overall use (Monley, 2006).

While some policies for library services for non-residents were identical or similar to those for residents, other policies were not, particularly those regarding the use of the circulating collection and remote access to electronic subscriptions; in all but one case, the use of these required a library card of some sort. Obtaining a temporary or guest library card was possible for non-residents in most cases if they met certain criteria; the policies differed according to variations in non-resident characteristics. Through axial coding, I identified relationships between the properties and dimensions of the Non-resident Users category to those of the Library Services category. Generally, for non-residents who lived close by, visited often, or stayed in the community for an extended period of time, library policies for obtaining a temporary library card cost less, presented fewer barriers to access, and provided for an experience more similar to that of a resident.

There were anomalies in these trends, however. In the analysis of the distance of the non-resident's residence from the library and the temporary card policies, the group of non-residents geographically closest to the community, that is living within it, revealed that they enjoyed fewer services, incurred more barriers to access, and had a less similar experience to residents than non-residents who live in an adjacent county. It may seem unusual that someone living within a community would be classified as a non-resident. This classification, however, was made by the respondents themselves in several instances. Non-residents living within a community were classified in three subcategories: homeless and people living in their automobile (Transitioning), students in job corps programs (Education, Training), and patients in psychiatric hospitals (Health Care).

Another deviation from the general pattern described above was a bimodal distribution of data. Library policies for obtaining a temporary library card cost less, presented fewer barriers to access, and provided for an experience more similar to that of a resident if the duration of a non-resident's visit to the community was greater than two months; this was equally so for non-residents on the opposite end of the spectrum whose visits lasted less than one day. These non-residents typically lived in nearby communities and visited for the purposes of shopping, working, or specifically to use the library. Non-residents visiting for less than one day tended to have a permanent address relatively close to the library. Proximity seems to give the librarians more confidence that their materials will be returned. In only one library was there no proximity distinction; they used the same collection agency for the retrieval of fines and materials, regardless of the permanent residence of the customer.

To better understand the communities' perception of the non-resident users of their libraries, I made an effort to the delineate properties of the Community; this category never fully developed due to gaps in the data. The respondents were not inclined to speak about the communities' perception of non-residents or the relationship between the libraries' services to non-residents and the business sector, even when directly asked. It was evident in a few cases that the community was extremely accommodating to visitors. For instance, a couple of communities allowed visitors to stay for free, camping in the town park or bunking in the basement of the police station. Also, several respondents referred to the trail angels in their communities; these are locals who do good deeds for weary hikers, such as leave food and water at trail heads or provide transportation to and from town.

Those respondents who did remark on the relationship between non-resident library services and local business usually referred to the offering of library services to the non-resident employees of the local businesses, such as seasonal workers or interns. Often, special policies were in place to accommodate these employees. In one case, the library director shared collection development tools with the owner of the local bookstore. Interviewees were asked if they felt their library services competed with services offered by the business sector. The responses were consistent across the board; they felt that library services complemented the services offered by local businesses, and vice versa. Examples of potentially redundant services include wireless internet access at coffee shops, movie rental stores and Chambers of Commerce. One respondent claimed that "the Chamber of Commerce sends people down here all the time. We have a good relationship with the Chamber."

In many instances, respondents acknowledged that tourism was a driving economic force in their community. One small-town library director commented that "we have very few opportunities for employment here. There's a furniture factory and a couple of – mostly it's tourists and that's where the future of this county is going to be." Another noted that their town is "basically built on tourism, I mean, that's the economy here." I sought relationships between tourism as a percentage of total industry and various properties of Community, including Level of Visitor Accommodation and Degree of Appreciation for Visitors. However, only a few of the interviews provided these insights; library personnel, in general, did not presume to know the affect of their community toward visitors. However, one did remark that "anything to encourage tourism and invite people back and continue to come back, I think, would be viewed favorably in our county."

It was difficult for me to restrain from leading the interviewees to comment directly on what I perceived to be the positive impact of non-resident library users on the local economy. There were a couple of unsolicited responses, however: "the hikers add a lot of, you know, they eat – we have a couple of restaurants, we have a grocery store in town – they buy things" and "I think it's just a big boost to the local economy to have these (library) services." At present, I have been unable to uncover enough relevant data in the interviews to support an assertion of relationships between properties of Community and those of Library Services. There was also an attempt to link case variables such as Level of Local Funding and Expenditure per Capita with dimensions of policy in the Library Services category; however, no clear relationships surfaced. Relating these variables to other policy dimensions such as Origin (In-house...Professional Guidelines) might prove more fruitful.

4. Discussion

While these transcripts are rich with information and reveal interesting and unexpected facets of non-resident library services and users, which I intend explore further, to address my initial research questions, additional data should be obtained. As library directors can only speak from their own experiences and most do not collect data from or about their non-residents, it would be extremely useful to have first-hand responses from non-resident users regarding their experiences in the community in general and the library in particular. Additional properties of Non-resident Users that might prove useful for future analysis are their primary purpose for visiting the community, their primary purpose for visiting the library, their mode of transportation, the amount of money they spend per day, their level of satisfaction with community services, their level of satisfaction with library services, their likelihood of returning to the community, and their likelihood of returning to the library. This might be accomplished through a short survey.

Likewise, characteristics of the community should be examined from the perspective of the residents of the community rather than trying to infer their perspectives from the responses of library personnel. That said, the responses received in this study did uncover potential *intangible* benefits to the community resulting from the provision of library services to non-resident users that I had not previously considered; these deserve further attention. For instance, one respondent remarked that "I think that it's important to learn about people from different areas. I just think that they add a flavor to the town that's just necessary." Another suggested that non-residents "help to bring a... newness or rejuvenation...it may make them (residents) look at things a little differently." Yet another recognized that "they bring in a diverse intellectual perspective."

Courtney (2001) discussed the history of services to unaffiliated users in academic libraries and describes the dilemma of "librarians who find themselves caught between a professional instinct to provide access to all and the realities of budget, space, and the needs of their own clientele" (p. 473). For the personnel employed by the public libraries in this study, the professional instinct to provide access to all was a prevailing theme, even though many did consider the potential consequences of non-resident services on the resident community, as exemplified by this comment, "they both should have access to information. That's why I got into public library work, personally. And that's sort of an idealistic view, since it takes money to run public libraries." The service philosophy of librarians who serve a large non-resident customer base deserves further investigation.

The respondents who were most passionate about providing library-services-to-all relayed personal anecdotes of their experiences when traveling and using libraries as non-residents themselves. Describing non-resident users, one respondent noted that "they're no different; they just live somewhere else. I've been one of those people, as you have." Some had negative experiences and wanted to ensure that visitors in their libraries would never be treated badly. The relationship between librarians' experience as a non-resident user and the quality of the library services they provide to non-residents is worth further exploration. It was mentioned by two respondents that the library expresses the character of a community. Others noted that it was a central hub from which all community services and resources might be accessed; "Especially as transient as we are and as mobile as our society is, there has to be a community touch-point whenever you travel. And I think that the library is the perfect place for that."

References

Aabo, S. (2005). The value of public libraries. *Proceedings of the 71st IFLA Council and General Conference*, Oslo, Norway. Retrieved on April, 1, 2009 from http://www.ifla.org/IV/ifla71/papers/119e-Aabo.pdf.

Appalachian Long Distance Hikers Association. (2010). *Appalachian Trail Thru-Hiker's Companion.* Harpers Ferry: Appalachian Trail Conservancy. Retrieved on March 29, 2010 from http://www.aldha.org/comp_pdf.htm.

Courtney, N. (2001). Barbarians at the gates: a half-century of unaffiliated users in academic libraries. *The Journal of Academic Librarianship, 27(6)*, 473-80.

Courtney, N. (2003). Unaffiliated users' access to academic libraries: a survey. *The Journal of Academic Librarianship, 29(1),* 3-7.

Gorman, G. E. & Clayton, P. (1997). *Qualitative Research for the Information Professional: A Practical Handbook.* London: Library Association Publishing.

Missingham, R. 2005. *Libraries and economic value: a review of recent studies.* Sydney: National Library of Australia. Retrieved on April 1, 2009 from http://www.nla.gov.au/nla/staffpaper/2005/missingham8.html.

Monley B. (2006). Colocated rural public libraries partnerships for progress. *Australasian Public Libraries and Information Services, 19*(2), 70-5.

Robertson, G. (2006). Abroad in your library: what tourists want, what they get. *Feliciter, 52(4),* 176-9.

Strauss, A., & Corbin, J. (1998). *Basics of Qualitative Research: Techniques and Procedures for Developing Grounded Theory, 2nd ed.* Thousand Oaks, CA: Sage.

U.S. Census Bureau. (2007). 2007 Zip Code Business Patterns. Retrieved on March 29, 2010 from http://www.census.gov/econ/cbp/index.html.

U.S. Department of Education. (2005). National Center for Education Statistics. Library Statistics Database. Retrieved on March 29, 2010 from http://nces.ed.gov/surveys/libraries/librarysearch/.

Supporting PDF Accessibility Evaluation: Early Results from the FixRep Project

Andrew Hewson[1] and Emma Tonkin[2]

UKOLN, University of Bath, UK, [1]a.hewson@ukoln.ac.uk, [2]e.tonkin@ukoln.ac.uk

Abstract: The aim of this paper is to present results from a pilot study exploring automated formal metadata extraction in accessibility evaluation. Information about some types of accessibility may make up part of the formal metadata for a document. As the importance of document accessibility has become more widely accepted and relevant legislation has been identified and characterised, the possibility of storing information about document accessibility as part of the formal metadata held by the system has become more attractive. This is useful in order to provide a starting-point for an accessibility assessment. This study reviews accessibility issues linked to the PDF format in use. We demonstrate a prototype created during the FixRep project, that aims to support capture, storage and reuse of accessibility information where available, and to approach the problem of reconstructing required data from available sources. Finally, we discuss practical use cases for a service based around this prototype.
Keywords: Automated metadata extraction, accessibility, text analysis

1. Introduction

The aim of this paper is to present results from a pilot study run within the FixRep project, which aims to examine and enhance existing techniques and implementations for automated formal metadata extraction. Formal metadata, such as filetype, title, author and image captions (by comparison to subject metadata, which usually draws on information extrinsic to the document itself) is mostly intrinsic to the document and its citation. Some formal metadata is collected by almost all repositories. Information about some types of accessibility may make up part of the formal metadata for a document.

In this study, we began with exploration of the PDF format, widely used across a large number of contexts of use in the digital library environment. Web-based uses of relevance to digital libraries for example include: forms; printable versions of resources, particularly those (such as PowerPoint documents) for which there is no free viewer available; and pre-prints of papers and articles. It is not always widely recognised that two different encodings for a given PDF may have entirely different properties as regards accessibility. A well-formed document with extensive annotation may be quite usable via a screen reader. Another may be entirely unreadable with accessibility software. When printed or viewed on screen, the two may appear identical.

A variety of software packages and services exist that aim to support the accessibility assessment of PDF documents. In general, what is meant by 'accessible' PDF files is 'tagged', or 'structured' PDFs. These are a structured, textual representation of the

New Trends in Qualitative and Quantitative Methods in Libraries
A. Katsirikou and C. H. Skiadas (eds)
© *World Scientific Publishing Co (pp. 417-424)*

PDF, which are intended for use by screen readers. These represent additional information, so the creation of a tagged PDF usually requires additional work. It is often simpler from an accessibility viewpoint to represent documents as HTML (Clark, 2005). However, where PDFs exist, it is possible to assess just how usable or accessible those documents are. We introduce a prototype written during the FixRep project, that aims to support the capture, storage and reuse of accessibility information where it is available, and to reconstruct required data from available sources where it is not. Finally, we discuss possible use cases for this prototype in a practical repository context, exploring how and where automated evaluation methods such as these can be usefully applied.

Document accessibility in self-deposit repositories

In repositories that are centrally managed, it is often possible to put reasonably strict requirements in place, and enforce them with a reasonable degree of success. However, this is rapidly complicated by widening the eligibility and encouraging a greater degree of self-deposit activity; in effect, a greater breadth of document types and content implies a wider variety in the resulting document set. The well-ordered, carefully managed repository lies at one extreme; at the opposite extreme is a chaotically organised file-store. In most cases, the reality lies somewhere between these extremes.

As a result of these practical limitations, it is perhaps inevitable that details such as complete and appropriate representative metadata or the use of appropriate mechanisms to ensure that accessibility requirements are met should be approached opportunistically – that is, 'nice to have if they're available'. But there are considerable legal and practical considerations that should represent an encouragement to users and repository managers alike to look upon accessibility as a concern, as well as a realistically achievable goal.

The legal aspects of accessibility are well-known and documented, at least from a UK perspective. Bailin (2007) notes that in 2002, the European Parliament "*set the minimum level of accessibility for all public sector websites3 at Level Double-A. However, a... survey of public sector services showed that 70% of websites in the European Union failed to conform to Level-A of the W3C guidelines.*" As the importance of document accessibility has become more widely accepted and relevant legislation, such as the Disability Discrimination Act (1995) in the UK, has been identified, the possibility of storing information about document accessibility as part of the formal metadata held by the system has become more attractive. This is useful for various purposes, primarily in order to provide a starting-point for an accessibility assessment, leading into a triage process.

The practical considerations mentioned are to do with the availability of the document for reuse. A badly formed or non-machine-readable document placed online is of marginal practical use. Obviously, it is better to place it online than to fail to publish it at all. However, if there were a review mechanism enabling users to be aware of the usability issues, then they would be in a better position to review their documents at an early stage, and to decide for themselves whether they prefer to accept the limitations of the current expression of the document, or to recreate an alternative or additional document to place onto the repository, to replace or supplement the original file. What is suggested here is not strict validation, but support for user-level review and triage.

What's in a repository?

Our research questions are the following: at present, what span of content appears in a document repository that enables user deposit? Does this variation in document format imply a reduction in accessibility, what sort of reduction, to whom, and to what extent? Is it possible for us to automatically identify issues that may be of particular concern, or for us to identify good practice where it is used?

As is often the case, it is important to separate that which is simply non-optimal from 'show-stopper' issues. The former are of some concern, most specifically in terms of potential impact on preservation and longer-term accessibility, whilst the latter may be of immediate concern or, at least, pose a significant enough difficulty to request the user to review the issue as a matter of some urgency. An unreadable or corrupt document, for example, is a 'show-stopper'. A PDF that is missing fonts or has certain issues that impair formatting or reduce readability is problematic, but it is likely to be possible to work with it for at least some users. A PDF that is simply a collection of images is relatively unproblematic for sighted users, but poses significant difficulties for the non-sighted.

In this paper, we characterise the problems that are detectable using our prototype software, and compare this approach to a more formal mechanism of accessibility-checking. We characterise the papers stored within one institutional repository, and discuss the potential impact of institutional repository policies such as the placement of a cover page onto the head of each PDF.

2. Methodology

As part of the FixRep project, a prototype has been developed for analysis of PDFs. This extracts information about the document in a number of ways:

- **Header and formatting analysis**: information about the PDF can be extracted from the document headers, such as:
  - o The version of the PDF standard in use
  - o Whether certain features, such as PDF tagging, are declared to be in use
  - o The software used to create the PDF
  - o The publisher of the PDF
  - o The date of creation and last modification
- **Information from the body of the document**: information about the content of the document, such as:
  - o Whether images or text could be successfully extracted from the document and, if they could, information about those data objects.
  - o If any text could be extracted from the object, further information such as the language in which it appeared to be written and the number of words in the text
- **Information from the originating filesystem**: metadata from the originating filesystem such as document path, size, creation date, etc.

This, then, is a much simplified form of metadata extraction that places little emphasis on complex content analysis, but more emphasis on the different object types stored within the document and the format of the document.

The prototype has been developed in Perl using a number of well-known tools: *pdfinfo, pdftotext,* and *pdfimages*. It also uses a number of CPAN modules in order to identify language, tokenise, and return relevant metadata about images. The service API is designed along the lines of a REST service, which is to say a simple HTTP-based service that makes use of simple, standard web protocols to surface relevant functionality. It makes use of syntax calls such as the following:

Document submission:

http://fixrep.ukoln.ac.uk/pdfAssay/=/link/http://example.com/a.pdf

Retrieval of a single component content:

http://fixrep.ukoln.ac.uk/pdfAssay/=/retrieve/unique-id-of-component

This prototype has been written primarily for the purpose of supporting rapid development of applications depending on access to components or content of PDF files, such as graphics, content, and format metadata. It is a sister service to formal metadata extraction systems.

We chose to explore the OPUS repository, managed by the University of Bath, UK. In order to enable this, we began by spidering the site in order to identify all the PDFs available on the site. These were then cached offline, and, via a batch processing job, were passed to the service prototype for analysis. The responses were added into a mySQL database in order to enable the results to be analysed. The data analysis process was, as this is the first pilot study, completed largely by hand – that is, through a handcrafted series of SQL queries. We envisage that in future it will be possible to largely automate this process.

3. Results

A proportion of the documents (approximately 20%) were not successfully processed during the first sweep for a variety of reasons. The rest of the statistics given here relate to those files that completed at least partial processing (Fig. 1). More detailed statistics are given in the following figure (Fig. 2) which pulls out each category of metadata collected and reviews the proportion of the documents for which the terms could be extracted.

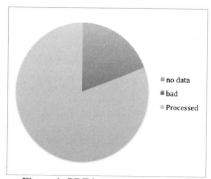

Figure 1: PDF harvested from Opus

Some of these terms are extracted directly via the software packages previously mentioned, such as 'Creator', 'PDF-version', and 'Author'. Others are generated by the software prototype, such as the guessed language and the number of words in the document. It is important to realise that in the context of PDF metadata, terms such as 'Creator' do not have the meaning that would be ascribed to them in the Dublin Core standard, for example – or if they do, it is a coincidence. In PDF, for example, the 'Author' keyterm exists to describe the individual who authored the document; 'Creator' refers to the software used to create the content (the editor, such as Microsoft Word), whilst 'Producer' is the software used to generate the PDF – such as a printer driver or a PDF creation/format transformation program.

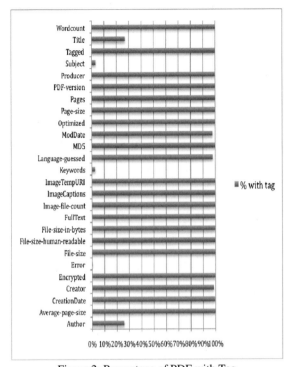

Figure 2: Percentage of PDF with Tag

It is important to note that the 'traditional' metadata (author, title and keywords, for example) are sparsely populated in this dataset. This speaks for the importance of an external metadata record containing this information.

While 'traditional' values might be missing, overall the average number of metadata tags utilised and the statistical mode of their use correspond closely (at approximately 21 per document), so that we can infer somewhat consistent usage of metadata tags within PDFs; this is not surprising as many of these are defined as required within the PDF standard. A few of these are also generated by our software to enhance our understanding of the content, such as 'Language-guessed', and these will be present in the vast majority of cases.

Fig. 3 & Fig. 4 below, show the distribution of PDF versions in use, and for those where the 'Tagged' metadata was provided (the vast majority), the proportion of (structured) PDFs was 9.35%. This means that only 10% of all PDFs processed have any likelihood of conforming to accessibility guidelines, and even then we would require further content level analysis to evaluate the extent to which they do indeed conform.

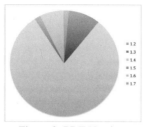

Figure 3: PDF Versions.   Figure 4: Structured PDF Proportion

Fig. 5 shows the distribution of 'Producer' applications. These are essentially alternative format-to-PDF conversion applications. This statistic offers us our first clear hint that something is influencing the distribution of conversion applications; as can be seen in the pie chart superimposed, there is one utility used by around two-thirds of file creation processes! As with Fig. 6, it has not been represented in the main bar chart as it is disproportionately large and damages visibility of the main distribution. This does not appear to fit the distribution that we would expect; inspection of these files shows that each one has been recreated with a prepended cover sheet. It seems that the producer in these instances has been 'reset' or overwritten by this prepending process. The same is true of the PDF creation tools (see Fig. 6), which show a similar distribution, although with a different application. It appears that the 'pdftk' tool is used to concatenate a cover-sheet that was itself generated using the 'itext-paulo' library.

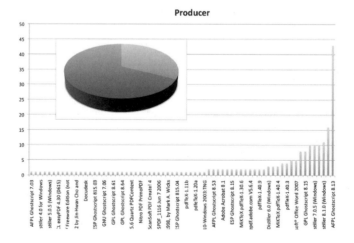

Figure 5: Utilities used in production of PDFs. Insert chart demonstrates relative popularity of utilities named in graph, and most popular utility (itext-paulo)

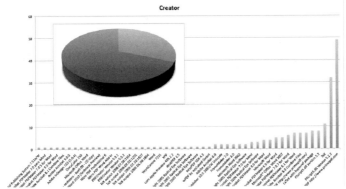

Figure 6: Utilities used to create PDFs. Insert chart demonstrates relative popularity of PDF creator utilities named in graph, versus the most popular utility (pdftk 1.12)

PDF files that generated errors

The following table shows the types of errors encountered in working with this content and the number of files involved, and whether they are recoverable for use in the context of the project.

Error type	Count	Recoverable
Copying intentionally disabled	13	No
Structural errors relating to fonts	5	Yes
Damaged / corrupt file	1	No
Structural damage	2	Yes

The damaged files in total only represent about 3% of all files that could be processed. The surprising outcome of this is that the largest single cause of rendering files unusable for the purposes of machine processing is the use of copy protection to limit content extraction and reuse.

Exploring the full text extracted from each document by means of inspecting the first lines of each document demonstrates another of these unexpected distributions seen earlier (i.e. the 'Creator' and 'Producer') and again this is related to the addition of cover sheets to the PDFs: inspection shows that two-thirds of documents ostensibly begin with the title *"University of Bath Opus Online Publications Store"*. A human reader will recognise this page as a cover sheet, and thus skip forward to the main content of the document. However it is arguable that the same cannot be said of automated processes without prior knowledge of this phenomenon.

The impact of cover pages on document indexing services

Many repositories, including but by no means limited to the University of Bath repository, have developed or identified a means of adding a cover sheet to each document within the repository. This has potential for positive impact, for example, as a means of clearly indicating the provenance of an item (Puplett, 2008). As can be seen in Fig. 7, Google Scholar does not necessarily recognise the cover sheet for what it is, and this has negative implications for effective indexing and retrieval.

[PDF] University of Bath Opus Online Publications Store http://opus.bath ...
File Format: PDF/Adobe Acrobat - Quick View
by J Davenport - 2009 - Cited by 1 - Related articles
University of Bath Opus. Online Publications Store http://opus.bath.ac.uk/. COVER PAGE.
This version is made available in accordance with publisher policies ...
opus.bath.ac.uk/12505/.../UnivOfBathDavenport_et_al_Final_Full_Paper.pdf

[PDF] University of Bath Opus Online Publications Store http://opus.bath ...
File Format: PDF/Adobe Acrobat - Quick View
by P McCombie - 2009 - Related articles
1 May 2009 ... University of Bath Opus. Online Publications Store http://opus.bath.ac.uk/.
COVER PAGE. This version is made available in accordance with ...
opus.bath.ac.uk/14633/1/McCombie.pdf

[PDF] University of Bath Opus Online Publications Store http://opus.bath ...
File Format: PDF/Adobe Acrobat - Quick View
by T Crick - 2004 - Related articles
University of Bath Opus. Online Publications Store http://opus.bath.ac.uk/. COVER PAGE.
This version is made available in accordance with publisher policies ...
opus.bath.ac.uk/16850/1/CSBU-2004-06.pdf

[PDF] University of Bath Opus Online Publications Store http://opus.bath ...
File Format: PDF/Adobe Acrobat - Quick View
by J Millar - 2003 - Cited by 12 - Related articles
University of Bath Opus. Online Publications Store http://opus.bath.ac.uk/. COVER PAGE.
This version is made available in accordance with publisher policies ...
opus.bath.ac.uk/1253/1/Millar_SPS_2_3_2003.pdf

Figure 7: Indexing on documents with cover pages

4. Conclusions

We find that 10% of documents implement tagging; this indicates that there may well be a number of authors who are potentially able to develop well-structured PDFs. This is a higher proportion than was expected and is certainly a cause for optimism for human accessibility. However, the addition of a cover sheet has caused a number of issues beyond those that are usually encountered with the PDF format (ie. font problems, file corruption, etc). This limits the ability for automated processes to make use of this information, and could therefore be said on the level of automated indexing and other software access (such as conversion) to be a retrograde step. If this becomes common practice it may be necessary to review both the assumptions under which automated systems are developed, and perhaps the rationale that lead us to make use of cover sheets in this context.

References

Adobe (2010). Acrobat built-in accessibility checker. Retrieved April 20, 2010, from http://www.adobe.com/accessibility/products/acrobat/faq.html
Bailin, A (2007). Delivering inclusive websites: user-centred accessibility. Retrieved April 20, 2010, from http://www.cabinetoffice.gov.uk/media/cabinetoffice/corp/assets/publications/government_it/consultations/pdf/delivering_inclusive_websites1.pdf
Clark, J. (2005). Facts and Opinions about PDF Accessibility. A List Apart. ISSN:1534-0295
Coonin, B. (2002), "Establishing accessibility for e-journals: a suggested approach", Library Hi Tech, Vol. 20 No.2, pp.207-13.
Poppler (2010). A PDF rendering library. http://poppler.freedesktop.org/
Puplett, D. (2008). Version Identification: A Growing Problem. *Ariadne* 1(54), January 2008. ISSN 1361-3200
Richardson, L.; Ruby, S. (2007), *RESTful Web Services*, O'Reilly (published (May 8, 2007)), ISBN 0596529260
Web Content Accessibility Guidelines (WCAG) 2.0 - W3C Recommendation 11 December 2008. Retrieved April 20, 2010 from http://www.w3.org/TR/2008/REC-WCAG20-20081211

Heuristics for the Evaluation of Library Online Catalogues

Thomas Weinhold[1], Sonja Oettl[2] and Bernard Bekavac[3]

Swiss Institute for Information Research, University of Applied Sciences (HTW) Chur, Switzerland, [1]thomas.weinhold, [2]sonja.oettl, [3]bernard.bekavac@htwchur.ch

Abstract: A widely used instrument to assess the quality of web interfaces is the so called heuristic evaluation. However, the evaluation criteria mentioned in commonly used heuristics, like for example the 10 heuristics of Nielsen (1994) are too generic for an in-detail analysis of certain website components and so extensive knowledge in the field of user interface design is needed, in order to be able to use these guidelines in a purposeful manner. To simplify this process, within the project "E-lib.ch – Swiss Electronic Library" a modular list of criteria was elaborated, which allows considering the specific aspects of library websites and in particular of their online catalogues. Therefore, this criteria list is suited to be used for self-evaluations by the library staff.
Keywords: Library online catalogue, usability evaluation, quality assurance

1. Introduction

Nowadays, websites are as common for libraries as books are. They provide a vast amount of information and offer additional service to the customers regardless of opening hours. An attractive website can be a show-stopper, but also the opposite is true. If the visitors lose themselves in ambiguous structures and therefore are not able to quickly satisfy their information needs, they will seek this information somewhere else. In the worst case, such visitors will not only rate the website as not very helpful, but rather the library as a whole will get a negative image. Therefore, libraries are challenged with the responsibility of developing a website that provides a vast amount of information in a non-cluttered, easy-to-use way (Norlin, 2002).

Since over the last 20 years Online Public Access Catalogues (OPAC) have become the most important retrieval tool in libraries, they play a key role for the development of user-centred library websites. While the introduction of web-based OPACs had improved accessibility for remote users immediately, the usability of these tools was sacrificed for quite a long time. On the one hand, the search forms were not designed from an end-user perspective but rather from a librarian view. On the other hand, the interaction possibilities with the catalogue were quite restricted. With the availability of new technologies such as AJAX, it became possible to build richer and more dynamic user interfaces. Among other enhancements, modules for spelling correction, subject based query expansion and known item detection have been integrated into online catalogues in order to assist the users in their search operations (Gozali&Kan, 2007). But up to now there is a lack of empirical evidence which of these new components really deliver an added value for the users and especially it is not entirely clear how these elements should be designed and integrated into library websites. Therefore, these concepts impose not only new challenges for the implementation of

New Trends in Qualitative and Quantitative Methods in Libraries
A. Katsirikou and C. H. Skiadas (eds)
© *World Scientific Publishing Co (pp. 425-432)*

library websites but also for usability evaluations of these resources.

2. Aspects of user-centred library websites

From a user's perspective three aspects are essential for the quality of a library website. The first aspect deals with the functionality a website offers. It is not necessary to integrate all conceivable fancy items into a website; rather the focus should lie on which elements are really needed by the users in order to fulfill their tasks. In order of doing so, profound knowledge about the users and their information needs is necessary. Clearly defined priorities in terms of the "who" and "what" provide the base to implement systems that offer an ideal task support (Battleson et al., 2001).

Aside from supporting the user in his tasks, it is crucial that a website is usable in a sense, that makes it possible to use it intuitively, efficiently and with a low error rate. When users rate a system as not usable, this might lead to the fact they will try to avoid using it in the future (Yushiana&Rani, 2007). Therefore, usability is a key factor for designing high-quality websites. Usability related aspects are crucially important for web applications, where a differentiation to competitors cannot be achieved by the offered functionalities.

The third aspect deals with the usefulness of a website. In the HCI community these two aspects are integrated into a holistic approach, where usability is interpreted as a part of usefulness, but in the context of libraries this factor has a slightly different meaning and is particularly related to the ability of providing users with the relevant literature according to their information needs. To secure the optimal support for the users varying information needs the library website should provide different possibilities for accessing literature, such as specific search options as well as browsing options for users with vague information needs. In this sense, usefulness has got a strong relationship with the ranking of search objects and respectively with the relevance of these documents in the context of a search. But because of the fact that the relevance of a document is a quite subjective criterion it is hard to evaluate the usefulness of search results in a reliable manner. Therefore, aspects concerning the relevance or the ranking of documents are not further investigated in this work. Instead the focus of this paper lies on functional aspects and the usability of these components. Whereas, functionality assesses whether a website provides the users with the wanted components and actually works in the manner as it is intended by them, usability assesses how users interact with the software. In doing so, personal impressions such as satisfaction, helpfulness, benefits, frustration and self-efficacy play an important role (Bertot et al., 2006).

3. Evaluation methods

There exist many different methods, which can be used for usability evaluations. These methods can mainly be categorized according to two different criteria: the moment on which the evaluation takes place as well as which type of evaluator is involved in the analysis. In relation to the date of the assessment, a differentiation can be made between formative and summative evaluations. The formative evaluation will already take place during the development process. Such evaluations focus on finding concrete improvement opportunities for optimizing a website, whereas in particular qualitative data such as verbal protocols plays an important role. In contrast, summative evaluations are used for assessing a finished product, whereas the focus lies on the overall quality of this product (Nielsen, 1993). According to which type of evaluators is involved in the assessment, it can be distinguished between user-oriented respectively empirical methods and expert-oriented respectively analytical methods. A well known example for an empirical evaluation method is formative usability testing. As part of such a formative usability test, real users are observed using a prototype or a finished product, while performing realistic tasks in order to achieve a set of defined goals (Dumas&Redish, 1999). The best known analytical method is the so called heuristic evaluation. Heuristic evaluation investigates the conformity of interface elements to established usability principles (Nielsen, 1994). Based on these guidelines one or more reviewer examine a user interface for potential usability problems. As it is easy for a reviewer to overlook a problem, the best results are achieved when several evaluators inspect the website independently (George, 2008).

Since usability testing is time consuming and therefore cost expensive, heuristics are an economical possibility to identify the usability deficits of a website. A further advantage of heuristics is the fact, that they can be applied during the whole development process (George, 2008). Among other, the results of heuristic evaluations allow identifying problems with terminology, consistency issues and the visibility of links. Also the need for help documentation may be uncovered (McMullen, 2001). Therefore, heuristics are a widely used instrument for the evaluation of websites in general and also in the context of library websites and digital libraries. Manzari and Trinidad-Christensen (2006) present a study in which a combination of heuristic evaluation and formative usability testing was used for an iterative redesign of the library website at the C.W. Post campus of Long Island University. Aitta et al. (2007) used the classical list of heuristics from Nielsen (1994) to assess 15 public library websites. Yushiana and Rani (2007) applied the same heuristics to evaluate the usability of a web-based OPAC from an academic library.

However, the evaluation criteria mentioned in commonly used heuristics, like for example the ones from Nielsen (1994) are too generic for an in-detail analysis of certain website components and so extensive knowledge in the field of user interface design is needed, in order to be able to use these guidelines in a purposeful manner. Thus heuristics, which are especially tailored to the specific context of libraries would be of great use and could give a good impression on which aspects should be considered for a website redesign even to persons without an in-depth experience in the field of usability evaluations.

4. Heuristics for the evaluation of library websites

The development of our library specific heuristics was based on three different sources. In an early stage we accomplished a literature review about usability evaluations in libraries, which aim was to identify suitable criteria for the assessment of such websites. Additionally, we conducted a best-practice-analysis of library websites, in order to gain more insight about the current state-of-the-art as well as the dissemination and the design of certain website components. Based on these findings, an initial version of heuristics has been generated. Subsequently this draft was discussed in the context of a focus group, attended by eight experts from the fields of library, web design and usability engineering, and was then further refined.

As a result we developed a modular useable, hierarchical structured list of evaluation criteria. In this context, modular means that with regard to the functionalities of a website, we made a differentiation between which parts are indispensable for the user and which parts are rather of an optional character (classified as "must" and "optional"). This modularization aims at maximizing the applicability of the heuristics for libraries of different size and type. Whereas small institutions with little resources for evaluating their websites get the chance to focus on the most relevant features, larger institutions can use the criteria list for performing a comprehensive and detailed analysis of their entire website.

Regarding the structure of our heuristics, we decided to use a two-folded hierarchy, whereas the level of detail increases continuously from top to bottom. On the top level we identified four main aspects ("sections") which are essential for the quality of any library website: information & communication, personalization, user participation and most important the online catalogue. The section "catalogue" includes all functionalities related to searching, browsing and accessing the library collection. "Information & communication" covers all aspects of information distribution and user support. For instance, this includes information about the opening times of a library or other resources like a newsletter or a live chat service. The section "personalization" incorporates all features, which allow the user to adjust the settings of the website to his individual preferences. "User participation" is related to the term web 2.0, and encompasses all functions that enable users to participate in the processes of creating, exchanging and sharing information (Linh, 2008). For all these four sections we provide some common questions, to ensure their general applicability. These questions have a strong affinity to classical heuristics for user interface design (e.g. consistency issues and the compliance with common standards). On the next level, criteria for the assessment of the different components of these sections are provided. The assignment of a component to a certain top-level section was conducted with respect to their overall intention. Most of the time the assignment of the components was rather obvious, but there are some components for which a unique classification was not possible. For instance, depending on the content and the intention of a wiki or a blog, both can either be used only for information and communication purposes, as well as they can be interpreted as an instrument of user participation. In this case the classification of these components depends on organizational characteristics (e.g. can only the library staff create new articles or is this right granted to any user). As already mentioned above, in addition to the functional classification we also carried out a distinction between mandatory and optional components. This segregation was based on our estimations of the components' relevance for the users as well as the commonness of these features. For instance, regarding the section "information & communication", the availability of a site providing information about opening times and contact persons was rated as a "must", while features like social networks (e.g. Facebook or MySpace) or microblogging services (e.g. Twitter) were classified as "optional".

For all these components we provide detailed questions, which allow the assessment of the individual features of a component, whereas again a distinction is made between mandatory and optional criteria. Concerning the online catalogue an example for such a question is, if the fields of the advanced search form support a multiple selection of items where this reasonable in the context of a search.

Rating	Description
0	not applicable
1	no usability problem
2	minor usability problem
3	moderate usability problem
4	severe usability problem
5	not implemented though required

Table 1: Severity rating of usability problems (adapted from Nielsen, 1994)

To determine the impact of the identified problems, a severity rating should be carried out. Such a categorization can be used for the resource allocation, in order to be able to eliminate the most serious shortcomings first (Nielsen, 1994). For this purpose we propose the scale presented in table 1.

5. Use case

For the further illustration of our concept, the following use case shall give an impression about how our heuristics can be applied for concrete evaluations. As an example we have chosen Swissbib (http://www.swissbib.ch), a new meta-catalogue of the Swiss university libraries, currently developed in the context of the project E-lib.ch (http://www.e-lib.ch). Since Swissbib is only available as a beta version at the moment, it is an ideal example to illustrate how our heuristics can be used for the further optimization of a library website. Due to the fact that it is not possible to present all sections of our heuristics within this paper, the use case is focused solely on features concerning the search possibilities of Swissbib. In this context, initially the "simple search" (figure 1) is used as an example in order to give a concrete impression about the questions we defined for the assessment of individual components. Later on some further results concerning the "advanced search" and other related features (e.g. the use of operators, search help, search history, etc.) will be provided. In doing so, we want to demonstrate, that our heuristics do not only allow the identification of a website's general shortcomings, but are also suited for detailed evaluations of certain components.

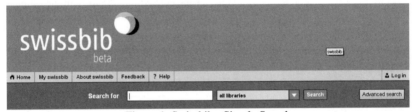

Figure 1: Swissbib - Simple Search

In figure 1 a screenshot of the "simple search" of Swissbib is shown, which is rated as a mandatory component. Using the "simple search" a user can perform a full-text search, either in all catalogues of the Swiss university libraries or only in a particular library. For the evaluation of this component we defined five questions, which are presented in table 2.

Question	Comment	Category	Severity Rating
Can the search either be started by pressing a dedicated button or by pressing enter?	both must be possible	must	1
Does the search engine allow for queries with a different amount of search terms?		must	1
Is the search field wide enough to display all items simultaneously if several search terms are inserted?	At least the combination of three search terms including operators should be visible without scrolling.	must	3

Is it transparent for the user, how multiple search terms are connected (which operator is used per default)?	Are the search terms connected with OR or AND if the user doesn't enter any operators when formulating a query with several terms?	must	1
Is it possible to switch directly to the advanced search without the loss of an already entered query?		must	3

Table 2: Evaluation criteria for the "simple search"

Summarizing the above results, the "simple search" of Swissbib works quite well, apart from two aspects. On the one hand, the input field should be widened by about 50% to allow for better feedback when several search terms are used. On the other hand, the interaction between "simple" and "advanced search" should be improved, in order to allow that search terms, which have been entered into the form of the "simple search", are passed correctly to the corresponding input field when a user changes to the "advanced search".

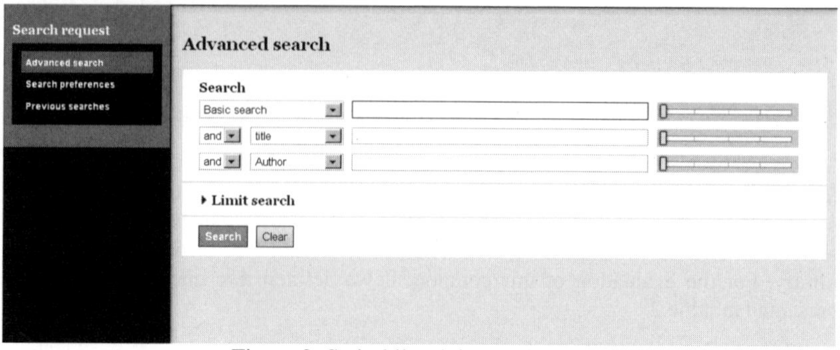

Figure 2: Swissbib - Advanced Search

In the course of the further evaluation of Swissbib, by using our heuristics we identified some more problems. Concerning the "advanced search" (figure 2), we found some issues related to the design of that search form. As shown above some elements are not labelled, so that the functionality of the sliders on the right side is not apparent to the user. Moreover, the order of some items in the drop-down-lists is not intuitive, because it seems they are neither ordered alphabetically nor by relevance. Regarding the users' information needs, some of these options like the filtering by media type ("format") should allow for multiple selections of several items.

Furthermore, we could identify some problems related to the use of operators. Although the Boolean Operators AND, OR and NOT usually work quite well, nevertheless a problem occurs if they are inserted into the search field in lower case. By doing so, the operators are interpreted as additional search terms. Moreover, the precedence of these operators is not clear if a user does not use parentheses for more complex queries. Since such information is of great relevance in the context of a search, a help function should be provided to clarify such issues. In general, the help function should be located clearly visible nearby the input fields and offer information about all input options and search functionalities. Thereby each topic should be explained in simple sentences and further illustrated by examples. Unfortunately, Swissbib does not provide any explanations about the available search options, other than some rough information in case a search did not match any documents.

Apart from the search help, which we rated as a mandatory component, all other features which assist the user in performing a search were rated as optional. Nevertheless, if such features are provided, they have to fulfill some criteria to be intuitively useable. Regarding Swissbib, an example for such a feature is the provided search history, which allows the repetition of previous queries. However, in the present implementation, the former queries are transferred into a non-editable drop-down-menu which is provided as part of the "advanced search". Since this does not allow for an adjustment of certain parameters from the former search, the benefits from this feature are limited. Another helpful feature, in order to assist the user in formulating his search queries is an auto-complete function, which provides the user with adequate search terms according to his already entered characters. Swissbib provides such an "on-key-filtering", but since the generation of these recommendations is not always transparent for the user (e.g. sometimes the input of four characters delivers more suggestions than the use of three characters), this feature should be further improved with respect to a stable release of the website.

Another shortcoming of Swissbib is that the site does not offer any browsing possibilities independent from specific search results. With respect to vague information needs, features like the possibility to browse the index or keyword lists, could further enhance the quality of the meta-catalogue. However, it has to be noted that implementing such browsing components is challenging for meta-catalogues, since it is time consuming and cost expensive to consolidate the different vocabularies used by the individual libraries.

Summarizing those results it can be stated that our heuristics do not only allow the identification of usability problems and therefore the further improvement of a website, but can also be used in order to deliver some hints, which components are missing for an ideal task support. Since all provided questions are easy to check, we believe we build an efficient tool to ensure the quality of library websites.

6. Conclusions and further work

A frequently mentioned point of criticism in relation to the heuristic evaluation is the fact, that this method cannot be applied effectively without further knowledge in the field of user interface design and in the specific domain of investigation (Blandford et al., 2007; Warren, 2001). Conversely, it is difficult for evaluators who are familiar with the terminology of a domain, to remember how non-specialist users would interpret certain terms or objects (Blandford et al., 2007). As we tried to focus on an end-user perspective, we believe that the presented approach can make an important contribution in order to overcome these issues. There is no doubt, that with regard to comprehensive evaluations the knowledge of usability experts is crucial, nevertheless using our heuristics a large amount of potential usability issues on library websites should be traceable by the library staff itself. Even though the use of heuristics, is rather suitable for the identification of problems on a micro level (such as poor wording, poor grouping of information, etc.) which entails the risk of losing the "big picture" (Blandford et al., 2007), nevertheless libraries can benefit from their utilization. Due to the fact, that every usability problem that is discovered by users during their work lowers the websites claim to quality and diminishes the users trust into the product, such self evaluations are an effective instrument for a continuous improvement process. Although it has to be stated, that in case of sufficient resources always a combination of different methods should be applied in order to enhance the validity of the evaluation results.

As a next step we plan the further refinement of our criteria catalogue by applying it for the assessment of some more (digital) library websites in direct comparison with other traditional evaluation methods. At the same time we want to implement an electronic version of our concept with extended interaction possibilities. In this context we are aiming at developing a web-based tool, which will allow interested institutions to select which criteria of the overall list are relevant for their specific needs in order to generate an individual criteria catalogue tailored to their particular situation. Thus, the applicability of the heuristics will be further simplified. Based on the concept presented in this paper, we are also working at developing a modified questionnaire, which can be used for user surveys, in order to complete the results of the heuristic evaluations.

Acknowledgement

Part of this work has been developed in the context of a student project at the bachelor programme in information science of the HTW Chur. The authors would like to thank all involved members of the class IW07vz for their contributions to the concept presented in this paper.

References

Aitta, M. R., Kaleva, S. and Kortelainen, T. (2007): Heuristic evaluation applied to library web services. *New Library World*, Vol. 109, No. 1/2, 25-45.

Battleson, B., Booth, A. and Weintrop, J. (2001). Usability Testing of an Academic Library Web Site: A Case Study. *The Journal of Academic Librarianship*, Vol. 27, No. 3, 188-198.

Bertot, J. C., Snead, J. T., Jaeger, P. T. and McClure, C. R. (2006). Functionality, usability and accessibility: Iterative user-centered evaluation strategies for digital libraries. *Performance Measurement and Metrics*, Vol. 7, No. 1, 17-28.

Blandford, A., Keith, S., Connell, I. and Edwards, H. (2007). Analytical Usability Evoluation for Digital Libraries: A Case Study. *Proceedings of the 7th ACM/IEEE-CS joint conference on Digital libraries (JCDL'07)*, 27-36.

Dumas, J. S. and Redish, J. C. (1999). *A practical guide to usability testing.* Exeter: Intellect.

E-lib.ch – Swiss Electronic Library (http://www.e-lib.ch/index_e.html).

George, C. A. (2008). *User-Centred Library Websites: Usability evaluation methods.* Oxford: Chandos Publishing.

Gozali, J. P. and Kan, M. Y. (2007). A Rich OPAC User Interface with AJAX. *Proceedings of the 7th ACM/IEEE-CS joint conference on Digital libraries (JCDL'07)*, 329-330.

Linh, N. C. (2008). A survey of the application of Web 2.0 in Australasian university libraries. *Library High Tech*, Vol. 26, No. 4, 630-653.

Manzari, L. and Trinidad-Christensen, J. (2006). User-centered design of a Web site for library and information science students: Heuristic evaluation and usability testing. *Information technology and libraries*, Vol. 25, No. 3, 163-169.

McMullen, S. (2001). Usability testing in a library Web site redesign project. *Reference Services Review*, Vol. 29, No. 1, 7-22.

Nielsen, J. (1993). *Usability Engineering.* San Diego: Academic Press.

Nielsen, J. (1994). Heuristic Evaluation. In: Nielsen, J. and Mack, R. L. (Eds.), *Usability Inspection Methods*, 25-62. New York: Wiley.

Norlin, E. (2002). *Usability Testing for Library Web Sites: A Hands-On Guide.* Chicago: American Library Association.

Warren, P. R. (2001). Why they still cannot use their library catalogues. *Proceedings of Informing Science Conference*, 542-546.

Yushiana, M. and Rani, W. A. (2007). Heuristic evaluation of interface usability for a web-based OPAC. *Library Hi Tech*, Vol. 25, No. 4, 538-549

The Next Generation of OPACs: What do Experts Consider as Musts and Don'ts?

René Schneider

Haute Ecole de Gestion, 7, rte de Drize, CH-1227 Carouge, Switzerland
rene.schneider@hesge.ch

Abstract: In this paper we present the results of two focus groups that were realised within the E-lib.ch initiative, a project to establish a Swiss digital library.
The Swissbib project will provide the future Swiss meta-catalogue which integrates most of the regional or other local catalogues in one application whereas the project ACCEPT provides user-friendliness and assures that the important aspects of usability are implemented. Both focus groups lead to very interesting results that did not only influence the design of Swissbib, but are worth to be considered in the general context of digital libraries.
Keywords: OPACs, meta catalogue, evaluation, focus groups, prototyping

1. Introduction

Since the prevalence of the WorldWideWeb and the growing use of the directly available digital information found on websites after being delivered by search engines, OPACs still struggle with the equivalent response to this evolution. Two developments seem to be posssible: OPACs will either be absorbed by search engines or they will maintain their inner locus of control by building themselves a new generation of online catalogues that contain fast and flexible search engines combined with user friendly browsing and information managing functionalities, inviting the user to become part of the cataloguing process.

Swissbib (www.swissbib.ch), the new swiss meta-catalogue – being part of the E-lib.ch project (www.e-lib.ch) – gives an example for one of these initiatives making use of new technologies. During its development process, Swissbib is accompanied by the usability-oriented research Project ACCEPT (an acronym for French **A**nalyse du **C**omportement des **C**lients – **E**valuation des **P**restations de **T**éléchargement), serving as a regulatory dispositive to assure that the expert and user needs are respected and become an integrative part of the new tool.

As a part of this cooperation, two focus groups were arranged at an early development stage, with experts from public & academic libraries, library and information science and the usability community to transfer the expert's view to the Swissbib technical group. Every focus group put emphasis to different aspects and combined distinct qualitative methods for the evaluation of software. The methodology of these two evaluations and their major results are presented in the following chapters.

2. Methodology

Focus groups – despite the fact that the validity of their results are sometimes disputed and discussed (Krug 2000) – are a very helpful evaluation method before the development of information systems starts or at an early stage of the development

New Trends in Qualitative and Quantitative Methods in Libraries
A. Katsirikou and C. H. Skiadas (eds)
© World Scientific Publishing Co (pp. 433-438)

cycle. While user acceptance tests may be indispensable to assure the learnability of a system, esp. shortly before deployment, focus groups – from the author's point of view - remain the method of first choice whenever the development has started and the system is fully open for adjustments: this is definitely the case, when experts for the system to be developed form the member of a focus group, since their profound knowledge of the matter being evaluated overcomes some methodological lacks of focus groups. Although they are generally considered as a user based evaluation method (Schweibenz 2003), they might also be used to find out the experts meaning before the following user evaluations.

2.1. Background

In the study presented in this paper, two successive focus groups were organized: a first one in May 2009, shortly before the first prototype of Swissbib was about to be finished, and a second one five months later, in October 2009, in a development phase, where the prototype – after major changes in the user interface design – reached a pre-deployment degree of maturity. The first focus group consisted of nine members, the second had seven members (in both cases the two organizers not counted) with three participants of the second focus group not having participated at the first one.

The participants were in most cases prospective users of Swissbib, originating from different backgrounds having a strong relationship to libraries. On the other hand, some of them were professionals that – to a later point of time – would form or consult users interacting with Swissbib.

In detail, the participants of the first focus group represented an academic library (1 participant), the Swiss national library (1), public libraries (2), library (1) and information science (1) with one more member focusing on usability issues. For the second focus group, the focal point was slightly scrolled towards usability issues, hence the group was formed by participants from public libraries (2), library science (2) and four participants from information science working daily within the field of evaluation. Some of the participants were rather double experts since their work was related to two of the fields mentioned above.

2.2 Hybridization of evaluation methods

The fact that a) the focus groups where organized in close cooperation with the project managers during two different stages of the development cycle, and b) that all participants were users and experts at the same time, gave place to some methodological experiments: beside the rather traditional approach of simply giving an oral stimulus to initiate the discussion; this approach was mixed with two different evaluation methods.

For the sake of comprehensibility we will repeat that the first focus group took place during the development of the first prototype that had not reached full maturity yet. Therefore it seemed appropriate to the organizers to give the participants the opportunity to discover the development status via some paperbound screenshots of the prototype. These were handed out after finishing the first discussion round (see 3.1) to make the focus group become a kind of collaborate *rapid prototyping* session.

During the second meeting, the group members had full insight to the system via a projection of the online system. The participants could instruct the moderator and compare the system's status to the one evaluated before. But they were also invited to spontaneously click through the system and give comment on its functionalities and to have a more dedicated look on some features, simulating the user interaction, like in a *cognitive walkthrough*. According to this denomination, this activities were announced and entitled to the participants as *spontaneous* and *dedicated walkthrough*.

From the author's point of view, this hybridization of evaluation methods, gave a dynamic input to both sessions, preventing monotony or stagnation, allowing thus a longer and in-depth discussion of usability problems. This experimental approach lead to interesting results that gave a direct feedback to the developers of Swissbib, but are also worth to be considered in the general context of digital libraries, esp. issues concerning the general design, faceted browsing, advanced search interfaces, the presentation of search results, as well as functionalities allowing the user to personalize the website and to contribute his own knowledge.

The complete results als well as the written records (documented in German) of both sessions can be downloaded, see (Birri and Schneider 2009a / Birri and Schneider 2009b). These documents reflect in detail all questions and features discussed. Since their simple quantity would extend considerably the limits of a paper, we will only point out to the most interesting results.

3. Results
3.1 First focus group
One week prior to the first focus group, the participants were invited to reflect about the announcement of a "new Swiss meta-catalogue including Web 2.0 elements". What were the musts and don'ts of such a catalogue for them? Which functionalities should be in such a catalogue, what experience of the past should be avoided? And what about the so called Web 2.0 features? The focus group started with the repetition of these three essential question as a stimulus for the following discussion. We will resume in brief the major points:

- All participants agreed that the meta-catalogue should be "as open as possible", i.e. open for any type of libraries, any local catalogue, open towards the web and open towards any type of media, i.e. it should allow the integration of web resources as well as meta data of all type of media.
- The integration of a local catalogue should not mean that the data would be completely absorbed without any later local identification being possible, i.e. the data needed for localisation of the medium should be kept as an added value in order to allow the advanced user a search that only filters the libraries of his interest.
- User should not have any prior knowledge about meta-data and understand its meaning intuitively, even in the context of an advanced search: the system should always speak the language of the non-initiated user. Besides that the meta data should be visible as early as possible.
- Special attention should be given to the fact that Switzerland is a tri-lingual country, the user interface should therefore be available in German, French and Italian, and – if possible – in English.. The multilingualism should also consider the meta data.
- The catalogue should be indexed by a fast and flexible search engine that ranks the results and allows search refinement from any point of the research process. This issue led to an increasing discussion: if relevance-ranking should be allowed, what should be the criteria for determining this relevance? Participants having a critical eye on relevance-ranking underlined that relevance is always based on a subjective issue making objective ranking impossible. Even in a scientific context, where objectivity gains importance, relevance differs from the academic background (student, assistant, professor, scientist) and is prone to manipulation. Therefore, the parameters defining research should always be visible, understandable and reconstructable for the user. At the end of this discussion, some participants suggested that maybe the principles of user-friendliness and relevance ranking would contradict each other.

- Special attention was also given to the fact of enriched and digitized data as well as other integrative elements. Should they be part of the catalogue and/or accessible to the user? In this context, licensing and billing of data plays an important role. Most of the participants agreed that the user itself should not be molested with these questions and all licensing questions resolved before respectively after the log-in procedure.
- A longer discussion aroused after mentioning the so called 2.0 elements. In this context, the following features where announced as desiderata: first and foremost the Long Tail (without explicit mentioning of this term), similar to that of online book vendors in combination with Tagging & Rating, Mashing & RSS-enabled search feeds. Users should in any case be able to leave their opinions or comments to the books or movies. On the other hand, similar documents they might have interest in should be presented to them as a result of inference algorithms in the search engine. The catalogue should on the other hand be open for the integration of recensions left elsewhere and should not simply build up another opaque data silo.

The second part of the focus group was spent discussing the paperbound screenshots after a small pause. Since this prototype never went online in this form, it will not be discussed further in this context. Importance will only be given to the fact that this discussion was the fundament for the succeeding second focus group where the new Swissbib prototype was presented online to the participants.

3.2 Second focus group

In addition to the first focus group, the second meeting lead to videos and screenshots that illustrated the most important usability problems discovered. These videos originated in the recorded screen activities as conducted by the participants and communicated to the organizer who accomplished them following the participants' instructions. The recording of all online activities stimulated the discussion and allowed a better analysis of the results as well as their later presentation to the Swissbib project managers.

As described above in section 2.1, this focus group was – similar to the prior one – divided into two parts: a first part named spontaneous walkthrough, during which the participants could freely discuss the issues that arouse while regarding the start page and using its functionalities, a second part named dedicated walkthrough where issues not treated or not sufficiently treated during the first part where discussed again. In both cases, the participants where asked to simulate the later user. As for that, several user activities (e.g. log-in, searching, browsing) where executed in collaboration, it is thus primarily interesting to know, which topics were treated spontaneously and which topics found a dedicated and repeated interest.

For the sake of conciseness, we will focus on theses issues instead of giving a detailed list of the usability problems described in this context. (Their detailed description can be found in the verbose focus group reports, see the download address in the bibliography (Birri / Schneider 2009b)).

The most important elements discussed spontaneously in the first part of this focus group covered first and foremost the main page and its central elements, such as

- the mission statement: the participants indicated the strong desire for a clear mission statement. From the beginning, it should be clear for every type of user what the site is about and what can be done. This should be inferable from the icon or a headline-like textual information.

- the general page design with a special emphasis on icons, colors and textual information: As often, the opinions concerning the general design, diverged considerably and resulted in different aesthetical points of view.
- the search box with its central drop down menu leading to the sub-catalogues: the search functionality was compared to that of other search engines, mainly Google, and – to a certain extend, Bing and Wolfram Alpha. It should therefore be clear for any catalogue search engine that users will expect any other search functionality to lead to the same results as the "big players".
- the missing "Help" information. Here again, the participants compared the system to with other existing search engines and their "Help" function, esp. WolframAlpha.
- and finally the log-in procedure, which was tested in depth.

The diversity of these topics does not only show the importance for a consistent home page design, but also the vastness of information bundled on these pages, be it static information, be it links, be it functionalities that lead to the underlying information, in this case the catalogues or advanced search functionalities. Since the participants had the opportunity to simply test the system on-line, it is interesting to see, which of the functionalities were tested. In our case, the major interest was first in the login-procedure and the watch list, that users could assemble whilst searching, the MySwissbib favourites and finally the hit lists after doing a search.

During the following dedicated walkthrough, the participants showed a special interest for a) the faceted browsing facility, b) the advanced search, c) the full title representation, d) the document functions, such as printing, saving, forwarding (which were unfortunately not implemented at this point of time), e) web 2.0 functionalities, f) other functions such as scrolling from page to page, and finally g) other remarks concerning accessibility, and the general look & feel.

Amongst all these parts, most of the time was spent discussing the faceted browsing and the advanced search functionality. Faceted browsing found more interest, since it is a rather new feature gaining more and more interest. All participants welcomed this feature but had a variety of propositions to change the facets and their representation. They also agreed that it would be best to test both, the faceted browsing and the advanced search with user acceptance tests.

As for the latter, the discussion went around the pros and contras of a Boolean or a fuzzy search, respectively their combination. No agreement could be found concerning this issue, since it left too much space open to assumptions and the short tests done in this focus group did not lead to satisfactory results. Anyway, the walkthrough showed that even a "simple" Boolean search becomes a tedious work, if the user does not clearly know if the search operators (AND, OR, NOT etc.) have to be written in English and/or in upper case. If this is not clear to the user, the already low percentage of searches done using the advanced search will decrease even more and probably no longer justify the development efforts behind.

During this second part of the focus group, the participants did also come back to some points discussed earlier, esp. the main page and the desired "Help" function, before finishing the focus group with some general remarks concerning the manifestable advance done with an implementation of an indexed search engine.

4. Conclusions

Two major methodological conclusions can be drawn from the study described in this paper: firstly, expert-driven focus groups are an effective and helpful method to find out what users need and how their needs matches with the developers point of view.

Secondly, the expert knowledge allows the integration of other evaluation procedures such as rapid prototyping and cognitive walkthroughs.

Nevertheless, the results of a focus group with experts from different related domains shows that experts never forget their personal user preferences and still express their own subjective preferences. As often, unanimous opinions are difficult to yield, which makes generalisations a difficult matter.

In any case, the results of expert-based focus groups build an excellent basis for the following user acceptance tests. They do not only help to find out the topics of major interest, but do also allow the comparison of an expert's and the user's point of view.

References

Birri, R., Schneider, R., (2009a). *Fokusgruppe 1: Swissbib: Abschlussbericht*, Genf, Haute école de gestion HEG, Juli 2009.
[http://campus.hesge.ch/id_bilingue/projekte_partner/projekte/accept/doc/fg1_a bschlussbericht.pdf]

Birri, R., Schneider, R., (2009b). *Fokusgruppe 2: Swissbib: Abschlussbericht*, Genf, Haute école de gestion HEG, Juli 2009.
[http://campus.hesge.ch/id_bilingue/projekte_partner/projekte/accept/doc/fg2_a bschlussbericht.pdf]

Hegner, M. (2003). *Methoden zur Evaluation von Software*. IZ-Arbeitsbericht nr. 23.
[http://www.gesis.org/fileadmin/upload/forschung/publikationen/gesis_reihen/iz _arbeitsberichte/ab_29.pdf]

Krug, St., (2000). *Don't Make Me Think! A Common Sense Approach to Web Usability*. Que Publisher.

Nielsen, J, (1994). *Usability Engineering*. Morgan Kaufmann.

Schweibenz, W., Thissen, F. (2003). *Qualität im Web. Benutzerfreundliche Webseiten durch Usability Evaluation*. Springer.

Chapter 9. Information and Learning

Books Circulation and Teaching Support: A Case Study in a Nutrition-Dietetics Department Library

Maria Kampouraki, Nikos Thalassinos and Georgios A. Fragkiadakis

Technological Education Institute (T.E.I) of Crete, Department of Nutrition and Dietetics Library, Trypitos area, 723 00 Siteia, Crete, Greece

Abstract: The support offered to tertiary education by the general books collection for circulation of a department's library is very significant, especially at the undergraduate level. In this research, we monitored the book loans in a department of Nutrition-Dietetics, in Greece, for the year 2009. The book titles loaned for a year were classified by subjects and the data were compared with the undergraduate syllabus of the department, to conclude on the teaching support these books offered. The results indicated that most of the books circulated in the library concerned tables of food composition, dietetics handbooks, and biochemistry-physiology books. On the other hand, the number of book titles loaned to students within 2009 was limited compared with those offered for loan. Our results show the need for close cooperation between librarians and tertiary education teachers in library management as well as the need for constant monitoring of the students changing needs.
Keywords: Circulation, books collection, tertiary education, syllabus

1. Introduction

The support offered to tertiary education by the general books collection for circulation of a department's library is very significant, especially at the undergraduate level. Nutrition and Dietetics study prepare graduates that use food and diets to help sustain or recover human health, at the individual and community level. During training Nutritionist-Dieticians, it's necessary to integrate and apply principles derived from the science of nutrition, biochemistry, physiology, human metabolism, applied dietetics, food science, exercise science, and behavioral and social sciences. Relevant material is provided through print sources (such as books, periodicals) or electronic sources (such as databases) that can be accessed via computer stations (Smith 1999).

The Department of Nutrition and Dietetics of the Technological Education Institute (T.E.I) of Crete, Greece, is a new academic institution, sited in the area of Trypitos at Siteia, Lasithi, and serving approximately 700 active students, enrolled in undergraduate programs. Courses are offered in a broad array of subject areas. Concerning print sources, the Departments Library offers 820 monographs, initially selected mainly on a title-by-title basis by the Department's academic teachers, and purchased in a rate of 50-200 titles per year. The titles were classified utilizing the complete Library of Congress classification list. Eight years after the Departments foundation a more specialized book selection plan, taking in mind how the students utilize the offered monographs, is necessary. In addition, as the syllabus content

New Trends in Qualitative and Quantitative Methods in Libraries
A. Katsirikou and C. H. Skiadas (eds)
© *World Scientific Publishing Co (pp. 439-442)*

evolves, new emphasis must be given to new monographs across relevant disciplines of science and technology as well as humanities and social sciences.

2. Monographs Circulation Evaluation for the Year 2009

In order to evaluate the coverage of the students needs, we determined whether or not the books offered in the library were being actually used. All the monographs had been tagged with an identifier based on bar code, so that the circulation information for these books could be recorded and analyzed electronically. We focused on subject areas of high use, as well as on the groups that were making use of these books. The circulation statistics for the titles offered, concerning the year 2009, are presented in Table 1.

Table 1. Circulation statistics for the year 2009

No	Borrower status	Book loans
1	Academic teachers	156
2	Undergraduate students	1,059
3	Students preparing diploma thesis	91
4	Department clerks	13
4		Total: 1,319

The primary borrowers of the books are undergraduate students, of the 1st to 7th semester, accounting for 80.3% of checkouts. The books are also being used by students preparing their diploma thesis, faculty and staff members, but no other members of the local community. However, from the 820 titles offered by the Departments Library only 143 circulated through loaning. The subjects of the loaned books relate mainly to the following: Greek food caloric content, food composition, diet therapy, clinical nutrition, nutrition evaluation, nutrition research, nutrition handbooks, biochemistry and physiology.

When comparing the titles loaned with the Departments syllabus (data not shown) to conclude on the teaching support these books offered, we found that were mainly helpful for courses as: "Diet composition for healthy individuals", "Clinical nutrition and diet composition for patients", "Nutrition for athletes", "Nutrition for pregnant women and for children", "Introductory medicine", "Energy balance and weight management", "Nutrition and metabolism", "Biochemistry of metabolism etc. In Table 2, we present the characteristics of the 10 more frequently loaned categories of books.

Among these 143 books, only 15 were in the English language, the rest 128 were either book of Greek authors or of foreign authors but translated in Greek. The Department does offers three courses on English language and emphasizes the use of international literature, however the students tend to borrow monographs in Greek; an obviously understandable tension that saves work but gives them fewer chances to improve terminology expertise, therefore, a tension that must be counterbalanced through training within the Department.

The major question that appeared, in view of the above data was: what are the characteristics of the books that were not loaned? The topics covered by the non-loaned books were mainly peripheral to Dietetics applications, as: mathematics, statistics, physics, general chemistry, certain topics of food science as food analysis techniques, vitamins, food irradiation, food additives, food microbiology; human pathology, cell culture, computer program manuals concerning software released within the 1997-2007 period, dictionaries, as well as the few offered tittles of literature and poetry.

Table 2. Characterization of the 10 more frequently borrowed categories of books, within 2009

a/a	Monographs Content	Number of Loans	Taxonomy
1	Food--Caloric content / Home economics--Nutrition. Foods and food supply--Examination and analysis. Composition. Adulteration--Dietary studies, food values, experiments, tests, etc.	253	TX 551.T7519
2	Diet therapy / Therapeutics. Pharmacology--Diet therapy. Clinical nutrition.	235	RM217.P37
3	Biochemistry / Physiology--Animal biochemistry.	140	QP514.566
4	Exercise—Physiology, Exercise--Physiological aspects / Physiology--Musculoskeletal system. Movements.	130	QP301.M111
5	Diet therapy--Handbooks, manuals, etc, Nutrition--Handbooks, manuals, etc. / Therapeutics. Pharmacology--Diet therapy. Clinical nutrition.	92	RM217.2.M6616
6	Diet therapy / Therapeutics. Pharmacology-Diet therapy. Clinical nutrition--Outlines, syllabi, etc.	91	RM217.5.Z3
7	Nutrition—Evaluation / Physiology--Nutrition--Study and teaching. Research--Research techniques--Special, A-Z--Anthropometric assessment	72	QP143.5.A58 M35
8	Dairying /Animal culture--Cattle--Dairying--Machinery, tools, etc. Dairy engineering	68	SF247.M31
9	Nutrition / Physiology--Nutrition	65	QP141.G7616
10	Diet therapy; Dietetics Therapeutics. Pharmacology--Diet therapy. Clinical nutrition.	62	RM216. T73816

3. Discussion

A library development must provide all the obvious material need for a discipline (Eldredge 1996). However, undertaking any new library project always involves balancing risks and benefits. The risks concern the potential for cost overruns, receipt of unwanted materials, receipt of duplicate materials, inability to evaluate the use of the offered material etc. The results of our evaluation indicated that most of the books circulated in the library concerned tables of food composition, dietetics handbooks, and biochemistry-physiology books, that is material either necessary for composing diets in practice or acquiring basic information on how the human body works. On the other hand, the number of book titles loaned to students within 2009 was very limited compared with those offered for loan and concerned mainly books in Greek.

The utilization of the print library sources by students is a complex phenomenon influenced by the teacher's tactics, the exams tactics, the students attitudes, the local culture etc. Focused interventions are required, to "involve" the library more with the syllabus and the curriculum of the Department. Furthermore, our results indicate the need for more close cooperation between librarians and tertiary education teachers in library management, as well as the need for constant monitoring of the students changing needs. Some choices maybe obviously not correct, as the purchasing of books concerning software that soon becomes out of date. The opinion of collection development committees (Koufogiannakis, Campbell and Ziegler 2007), based on circulation statistics and having in mind the changing syllabus, may lead to better assess and meet the needs of the library users.

References

Smith, A. M., (1999). Mapping the literature of dietetics. *Bulletin of the Medical Librarians Association*, 87, 292 - 297

Koufogiannakis, D., Campbell, S. and Ziegler, F., (2007). Building an Undergraduate Book Approval Plan for a Large Academic Library. *Partnership: the Canadian Journal of Library and Information Practice and Research*, 2, 1 – 9.

Eldredge, M., (1996). Major Issues in Approval Plans: The Case for Active Management. *Acquisitions Librarian*, 16, 51 - 59.

Electronic Scholarly Communication, Availability, Utilization and its Imperatives to Academic Libraries in Nigeria

Scholoastica A. C. Ukwoma[1], Victoria N. Okafor[2] and Ifeoma Udeh[3]

University of Nigeria, Enugu State, Nigeria, [1]stica2004@yahoo.com, [2]vickaforn@yahoo.com, [3]nwifo@yahoo.com

Abstract: The paper identified the databases that constitute the electronic scholarly communication of academic libraries in Nigeria. The study employed survey method and online questionnaire was sent to serials and ICT librarians. The major findings were that most libraries in Nigeria depend on open access for information. Problems of access to information were identified as follows: Epileptic power supply, lack of awareness of available journal, Lack of internet connectivity and subscription rate.
Keywords: Electronic scholarly communication, availability, academic libraries, nigeria.

Introduction

Technological advancement has created deep impact in different spheres of human activities throughout the globe, as Bette (2003) pointed out that science has provided the swiftest communication between individuals, recorded ideas that enable man to manipulate and make extras from such records to ensure knowledge evolution and sustainability throughout the life of a race rather than of an individual. The internet, a complex communication system has made significant change in information communication and exchange. It expedites the process of knowledge transfer to a wider community, in the form of electronic scholarly communication which is characterized by many advantages over the conventional scholarly communication. Electronic scholarly communication (ESC) is the circulation of research results/ findings of academics to the public through electronic medium. These finding may be in books, conference proceedings and journals. The main focus of this work is on electronic journals (E-journals) which have proved to be the panacea for all disciplines.

It is not yet clear whether libraries in Nigeria are fully involved in acquiring electronic journals through subscription to databases. Because it is through these databases that libraries could acquire journals that academics could access online, for their research works. These databases could be open or closed access. Due to economic crisis, information explosion and specialized courses, libraries could not acquire the printed journals on regular basis. Electronic scholarly communication is the only alternative that can help in scholarly communication. However, there are some obstacles that can hinder electronic scholarly communication like fund and infrastructure. Prior to the 17th C traditional scholarly communication has been the medium for communicating ideas, such informal communication medium include conferences, circulation of drafts and preprints and conversation among colleagues.

New Trends in Qualitative and Quantitative Methods in Libraries
A. Katsirikou and C. H. Skiadas (eds)
© *World Scientific Publishing Co (pp. 443-449)*

Objectives

The study will achieve the following objectives

1   To identify the databases that constitutes the electronic scholarly communication of Academics libraries in Nigeria
2   To ascertain how these databases are accessed by users in Academic libraries in Nigeria
3   To examine the contribution of electronic scholarly communication to Academic libraries in Nigeria.
4   To identify the constraints that hinder utilization of electronic scholarly communication in Academic libraries in Nigeria.

Data for this paper was collected from serials librarian and those in Information and Communication Technology unit, this is because, these librarians assist users with information on online resources available in their libraries. They are the centre of scholarly communication in Nigerian libraries which means they are in a better position to access the rate of availability, access and use of these electronic scholarly communications. To investigate this, questionnaire was sent to this group of librarians online. It is quite unfortunate that most university libraries do not have access to online resources in their institution and some could not respond and return the questionnaire. The analysis was based on seven institutions that indicated access to ESC. Out of these seven we have three federal universities namely University of Nigeria Nsukka, University of Lagos, and Nnamdi Azikiwe University, Awka; Two Universities of Technology which include Federal University of Technology Owerri, and Federal University of Technology Minna; Ekpoma State University which is a state University and American University Yola which is private University.

Accessibility and Availability of Electronic Scholarly Communication

Digitization of information has speed up availability while saving the printing and shipping costs, and offers the convenience of not having to visit the library every time an item is needed (Wills cited in Mason 2010), This explains the convenience and easy accessibility of ESC over the conventional printing. ESC publishing has tried to overcome the shortcomings and challenges of access, subscription, submission of papers for publication. History have shown that Electronic scholarly communication is mostly cited because much emphasis of citing ESC is that they are peer reviewed and can be relied upon for integrity of the information. Some analyst hoped that electronic journals would enable review process to be fairer and clearer with rapid communication, broader access to scholarly literature, new and documentary form (Kling and Callahan, 2002). In addition, ESC aid to minimize subscription rate, as it is believed that publication cost of electronic journals is much lower than the cost of paper publications. Late 1980s witnessed economic crisis in scholarly publishing due to the cost of scientific journals rising faster than both inflation and the growth of library budget (Miller 2000: Kirkpatrick, 2001; cited in Kling and Callahan 2002). As long as most of us can remember, journal price increase has far out paced the growth of library budgets. As a result, libraries cannot afford access to the broad range of information needed by researchers, (Johnson, 2004). Rising journal prices have forced libraries to forgo the purchase of books, this affect the growth of library collection within that period. The introduction of electronic scholarly communication made an improvement to library collection and usage as most libraries recorded a considerable growth rate in collection use. As was recorded by Odlyzko (2001) in his analysis of rapid evolution of scholarly communication, he discovered that the growth rate of usage in online resources stands at about 100% per year for four years 1995-1998 which is most auspicious. Most libraries in Nigeria have also witnessed a tremendous increase in their collection, as their users can have access to a variety of resources irrespective of their location.

Accessibility could be seen as being subject to availability because if these resources are available, users can have access to them. (Lawrence cited in Odlyzko, 2001) opined that recent studies show that papers in computer science which are freely available online are cited more frequently than others, which implies that accessibility is dependent on availability. There is indeed evidence that there is growing demand for high quality scholarly information which can be easily accessed on the web Odlyzko (2001). In recent times much emphasis have been placed on electronic publication and web visibility of academics which is one of the criteria for web ranking of Universities, as was highlighted in the July (2009) edition of webmetric ranking

> We intend to motivate both institutions and scholars to have web presence that reflect accurately their activities. If the web performance of an institution is below the expected position according to their academic excellence, university authorities should reconsider their web policy, promoting substantial increases of volume and quality of their electronic publications. We intend to motivate both institutions and scholars to have a web presence that reflect accurately their activities.

This implies that electronic publishing of academics is very important. Electronic communication has the advantage of being faster, easy transfer of documents, direct communication between author and reader. It has the ability to manipulate objects like moving pictures, three dimensional objects and hypertext to allow links to other related works in different format Bette (2003).

The analysis of the respondents on accessibility of these e-journals are as follows, six out of the seven universities have access representing (85.7%), while one does not have access showing a (14.3%). This means that a greater percentage have access to e-journals. The institution that does not have access is as a result of no internet connectivity.

The bar chart in figure 1 shows the databases these university libraries subscribe to and the rate of access by these institutions. Ebscohost and Agora ranked highest with (85.9%) each meaning that all the institutions access them, science direct and OARE has (71.4%) respectively while Jstor has (42.9%) they also access HINARY.

Figure 1: A bar chart showing the databases that constitute their e-journal collection.

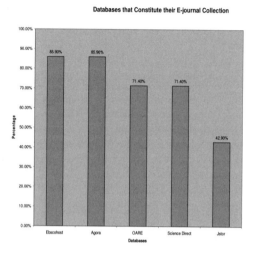

Fig 2: A pie chart showing the sources of internet access these databases are accessed.

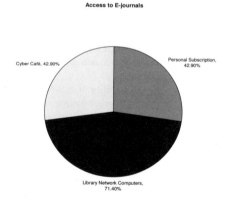

The chart shows that users can access from more than one source, many of the institutions studied has networked systems where their users access these databases, this is encouraging as librarians will also give them the necessary service they need, it makes it easier and more comfortable for users to access the online resources. Unlike what obtains in commercial cyber café where such assistance is not rendered.

Open Access Initiative
Open access is enormous to library development in Nigeria, most of this ESC is in open access which makes many institutions access them without subscription. They have contributed a lot to their collection development. Writing on open access, (Bailey 2006) highlighted that scholars, students and other users do not need to seek permission to utilize open access works as they want nor do they make payments to do so. This is a radical departure from conventional publishing, where the right to use are constrained by hard- to- determine fair-use copyright provisions, restrictive publisher license agreements, and permissions fee. The internet, the web and related digital publishing developments have made open access possible. IFLA theme for the past years have centered on providing access to knowledge, it is not an issue of stocking the library with collections. Bailey (2005) recommended two complementary strategies to achieve open access to scholarly literature-Self-Archiving (making "e-prints" available on the web) and open access journals (e-journals that are freely available). Suber (2003) states that providing free access removes price barriers. Open access has contributed a lot to library development in Nigeria this implies that many libraries can boost of access to a large volume of journal titles. From the responses gathered from serial librarians the following databases were identified as being in open access. DOAJ, African Index medicus, ABC chemistry, Development and gender, Digital Book Index, Electronic Journal of Biotechnology, Electronic Medical Resources, High wire, INASP, Aloka, African South of the sahara, African Study Centre, Bioline International, Open Journal Systems, Pubmed, Los Alamos national Library and the Nigerian students. These open access sites are quite encouraging and most auspicious.

Features of electronic scholarly communication
Electronic publications contain attributes that are not provided in print medium, which makes it more flexible and interactive, such as video and sound ability to link from main work to cited articles or other related works (Napoli, 2005). These features place Electronic publication in class of its own, unlike in conventional print publication that does not have these attributes. Documents are reviewed, modified, and uploaded back to the internet for readers to access with ease. Research indicates relatively low levels of enthusiasm for enhanced features (Swan and Brown cited Napoli, 2005). These features could be the results of why researchers prefer electronic publishing of scholarly communication. Bell (2002) highlighted that the evolution of scholarly communication towards an electronic format is driven by two main factors; Potential cost saving, and attractive new features.

Extent of satisfaction of users
From the responses of the Librarians the users are very much satisfied with the information they get from these databases, this makes their research work well enriched and also contribute a lot to their collection development. With online resources, majority of them have access to current materials. Also from the rating of how these faculties in these institutions makes use of e-journals, it was discovered that Arts/Humanities, Biological Sciences, Engineering, and Environmental Sciences were rated highest in extent of use followed by Physical Sciences, Social Sciences, Education and Agriculture. Majority of the open access resources are available for the highly rated faculties than for the later ones. This call for more open access to other databases, to enable researchers gains the works of other academics.

Challenges to effective utilization of e-journal

The following challenges were identified by the respondents according to their ratings, Epileptic power supply and lack of awareness of available journal were rated 85.7% respectively followed by Lack of internet connectivity having 57.1% and subscription rate 42.9%. This means that power supply and lack of awareness of available journal title are the most critical problems facing access to e-journals in Nigeria.

Imperative of ESC to academic library

Though there are many challenges to access e-journals in Nigeria, but for the institutions that have been able to access it, they have benefited to a lot from e-journals. From the responses of the respondents, it shows that the library collection has been on the increase since the introduction of e-journals in libraries, the increase as recorded from the past four years are from 1000-3000 increase. This is encouraging with this rate, most of the libraries in the next five years will have enough resources in their collection. The interesting aspect of it is that these materials are current. Effort have also been made by both the national and state bodies of the Nigerian Library Association (NLA) to sensitize librarians and create awareness on the relevance and access to e-journals, workshops have been organized severally, in March 2008 a workshop was organized on Use of Internet by LIS professionals 110 professionals attended. Later part of this year, December 2008 another national workshop on access to free resource was held, over 78 professionals attended. The sectionals groups of NLA also organized workshops regularly based on their mission to sensitize their members on the relevance of these e-resources. Anunobi and Ukwoma (2009) identified several measures taken by the sectional groups as The Informational Technology (IT) Sections has annual workshops series termed **Library and Information Technology Today (LITT).** Aimed at identifying areas of ICT skill needs of the professionals in Nigeria and address it in its annual workshops. In 2007, the LITT2007 theme was 'the Automation that Works' attended by 35 participants while LITT 2008 revolved around 'Web Development and Web Publishing' attended by 45 professionals.

Conclusion and Recommendations

The study has shown that academics valued e-resources highly because they are peered reviewed. It is therefore necessary that all the universities in Nigeria should embrace e-resources in their libraries. The following strategies have been outlined as a forward in improving access and utilization of E-journals they are:

- Continuous and constant training for librarians on E-journal use, access and importance this will give librarians an insight on how to navigate the search engines to retrieve the necessary information.
- Consortium should be informed to reduce cost. This is a very important way to overcome the high subscription rate of some of these important journals.
- Search skills must be improved as some of the available titles lack the search criteria.
- Internet cost must be reduced and power improved for us to make positive impact on the use of online resources. Most libraries have not been able to have internet access as a result of cost of internet connectivity.
- There should be awareness on the introduction of new issues. This could be done through sending alerts to different subscribers or pop up messages.

- International support: There should be encouragement organizations and donor agencies to assist the developing countries, in access to online resources.

This could be in form of conversing for more open access sources or reduction in the subscription rate of some of these e-journals.

References

Anunobi, .C. V. and Ukwoma S.C (2009) Strategies for re-skilling the library information profession in Nigeria in Strategies for regenerating the library and information Professions. Ed. Jana Varlejs and Graham Walton. IFLA, The Hague, Netherlands. Pp245-259.

Bailey, C.W (2005). Open Access and Libraries.
http://www.digital-scholarship.com/cwb/OALibraries2.pdf. Retrieved 10/2/2010.

Bailey, C.W (2006). Open Access and Libraries.
http://www.digital-scholarship.org/cwb/OALibraries2.pdf. Retrieved 10/2/2010.

Bell, A. (2002). Electronic Publishing: Issues and trends. Report on USTLG meeting, John Rylands library, University of Manchester, 28th November.

Bette, A. (2003). Issues and Impacts of the Changing nature of Scientific Communication. Optometry and Vision Science 80(6) 403-410

Kling R. and Callahan E. (2002). Electronic Journals, the internet, and scholarly communication. CSI working paper. 01-04.Mason, M.K (2010). Academic Scholarly Publishing and the Serials Crisis. *www.moyak.com/papers/journals-crisis.html*

Napoli, P. (2005). The Impact of Electronic Publishing On Scholarly Communication. *aaupnet.org/resources/mellon/electronic.pdf.*

New July edition of the Web Metrics Ranking. http://www.webometrics.info/ accessed on 1st December 2009.

Odlyzko, A. (2001). The Rapid Evolution of Scholarly Communication
www.dtc.umn.edu/~odlyzko/doc/**rapid**.**evolution**.pdf.

Suber P. (2003). How should we define open access? SPARC Open Access Newsletter, no64. http://www.earlham.edu/~peters/fos/newsletter/08-04-03.htm . Retrieved 10/2/2010

Author Index

Title Index